A WORLD DICTIONARY
OF LIVESTOCK BREEDS
TYPES AND VARIETIES

A WORLD DICTIONARY OF LIVESTOCK BREEDS TYPES AND VARIETIES

by I. L. MASON

lately Animal Production and Health Division,
Food and Agriculture Organization of the United Nations,
Rome, Italy

formerly Agricultural Research Council Unit of Animal Genetics,
Institute of Animal Genetics,
Edinburgh, Scotland

C·A·B INTERNATIONAL

First published in 1951
Reissued with Supplement 1957
Second (Revised) Edition 1969
Third (Revised) Edition 1988

Published by
C·A·B International
Wallingford
Oxon OX10 8DE
UK

Tel: Wallingford (0491) 32111
Telex: 847964 (COMAGG G)
Telecom Gold/Dialcom: 84: CAU 001
Fax: (0491) 33508

British Library Cataloguing in Publication Data

Mason, I. L. (Ian Lauder) *1914–*
   A world dictionary of livestock breeds,
   types and varieties. — 3rd ed.
   1. Livestock
   I. Title
   636

   ISBN 0–85198–617–X

Printed in the UK by The Cambrian News Ltd, Aberystwyth

ACKNOWLEDGMENTS

As Fowler says in the Concise Oxford Dictionary, "A dictionary-maker, unless he is a monster of omniscience, must write of a great number of matters of which he has no firsthand knowledge". This dictionary would have been impossible without immense help from breeders and scientists, and from government and breed society officials, all over the world. I want to thank publically all those who have helped me, whether by information or advice, in person or in correspondence.

At the risk of being invidious I would like to thank specially the following who have helped me recently, not only with single breeds but with all (or most) of the breeds (or all the breeds of a single species) in the countries concerned:

Australia: Prof. J. S. F. Barker, Dr. H. N. Turner, state departments of agriculture, breed societies. *Austria*: Prof. F. Pirchner. *Belgium*: Dr. R. Hanset. *Bolivia*: Mr. J. V. Wilkins. *Brazil*: Dr. F. E. Madalena. *Bulgaria*: Dr. S. Alexieva, Prof. Ts. Hinkovski. *China*: Prof. Cheng Peilieu, Mr. Huang Haigen, Prof. Zhang Zhongge. *Czechoslovakia*: [Dr. R. Šiler], Dr. J. Vachal. *Ethiopia*: Dr. M. Alberro. *France*: Mr. J. J. Lauvergne. *Germany*: Dr. D. Altmann, Prof. P. Glodek, Prof. H. H. Sambraus, Prof. D. Simon. *Great Britain*: Mr. G. L. H. Alderson, Ms. E. Henson, breed societies. *Greece*: Prof. N. P. Zervas. *Hungary*: Prof. I. Bodó. *India*: Dr. R. M. Acharya. *Iran*: Mr. M. Moném. *Ireland*: Dr. J. P. Hanrahan. *Italy*: Prof. G. Rognoni. *Japan*: Dr. Y. Yamada. *Mongolia*: Mr. P. Millar. *New Zealand*: Prof. A. L. Rae. *Norway*: Prof. M. Braend. *Pakistan*: Dr. H. U. Hasnain. *Poland*: Prof. Z. Reklewski, Dr. M. Stolzman. *Portugal*: Dr. C. A. M. de Andrade Fontes, Prof. J. Lima Pereira. *Spain*: Dr. A. Sanchez Belda. *Sweden*: Prof. J. Rendel. *Switzerland*: Mr. L. Avon. *Turkey*: Dr. B. C. Yalçin. *USA*: Ms. E. Henson, Prof. R. E. McDowell, Prof. W. E. Rempell. *USSR*: Prof. N. G. Dmitriev, Mr. I. A. Paronyan, Dr. E. M. Pern, Dr. S. I. Semyonov, Mr. G. E. Shtakelberg. *Yemen, North*: Dr. H. U. Hasnain. *Zimbabwe*: Dr. H. P. R. Tawonezvi. *Goats*: Prof. C. Gall.

To the staff of the Commonwealth Bureau of Animal Breeding and Genetics in Edinburgh, and, particularly to Helen Doran and Paul Millar, I am greatly indebted for the tracking down and translating of essential literature.

Finally my thanks to my son for putting this very tricky material into a word processor and to my wife for help with the checking of the typescript and for bearing up so long as a "breed dictionary widow".

Edinburgh, April 1988   I. L. Mason

CONTENTS

FOREWORD

Only a few species of domestic livestock are used by man for food, fibre and work, but there are many breeds within each species which are adapted to a wide variety of environments. Known by local names which often exist in several forms, some breeds have achieved international value and are household words everywhere. Others are being replaced by or crossed with exotic breeds better suited to present economic conditions, and are in need of preservation before they disappear. Yet others, especially in developing countries, are still used locally. As a result, the names of breeds which earlier were of only local concern are now of widespread interest. An orderly classification of world breeds is therefore an increasingly valuable resource.

This is the only dictionary of breeds of domestic animals covering the main livestock species in all countries of the world. It is the authoritative work. The author, Ian Mason, foresaw the value of such a dictionary many decades ago, and he is specially equipped to produce it. He has the unique blend of human gifts needed to bring the venture into being. They include a commitment to animals, a lifelong interest in livestock classification, and an academic detachment from those who promote special interests, combined with an earthy contact with rural livestock people. Needed above all is a patient, diligent and systematic plan to capture the essential information from any and all sources whenever and wherever it occurs. The sifting, analysing, checking and classifying can be carried out later in the study. Accurate and comprehensive information, however, cannot be collected quickly nor from an armchair.

The author's interests extend into the whole system of animal production and the environments in which animals are kept. For many decades, he has travelled extensively throughout the world, often on missions when he was a staff member of the Food and Agriculture Organization of the United Nations (FAO) at headquarters in Rome and later as an FAO consultant. He has also made many private journeys connected with his other wide interests. Always, whatever the prime purpose of the travel, he has carefully sought for and sometimes even inadvertently stumbled across valuable new information on local breeds, and has carefully gleaned and garnered it for this dictionary. During these travels, he has established professional contacts from whom he continues to receive further information. Other sources are the increasing numbers of FAO publications on national, regional or special types of livestock.

This is the third edition of the dictionary, the first having been published in 1951 and the second in 1969. Additional information

expands the contents by more than a third and consists mainly of new
entries, while also adding to existing entries. The style of the breed
names has been changed a little in this edition. The most familiar
name is used rather than insistence upon an arbitrary system which
would make the dictionary less valuable to most users. The provision
of synonyms and known relationships between breeds have always
been attractive features of the dictionary.

These are days of growing interest and concern about animal
genetic resources at local, national and international levels. There
are many new activities. They include national improvement projects,
the development programmes of international agencies, global trade
in animals and germplasm, the creation of cryogenic gene banks and
livestock farms for preserving endangered breeds, data banks, new
synthetic breeds, molecular genetics and biotechnology, all of which
will increasingly affect animal genetic resources in decades to come.
The book is an invaluable source of information in this changing
world. Many will be grateful that the author has undertaken a third
edition which is a fitting successor to his earlier works.

John Hodges
Senior Officer
(Animal Breeding & Genetic Resources)
FAO, Rome, Italy

INTRODUCTION

IN order to understand the aim of this dictionary, to explain its form, and to excuse its omissions, it is necessary to consider how the idea of compiling it arose and what has been its development.

Quite early in the history of *Animal Breeding Abstracts* (*A.B.A.*) it became clear that consistency in terminology was desirable if the abstracts were to have their full value. The names of breeds of livestock formed one of the most important categories in which uniformity was essential. In preparing abstracts from many languages the problem arose of how to render foreign breed names into English. At the same time even English names were liable to have several different spellings or alternative forms. A standard list was necessary to show the English forms and spellings recommended for use in *A.B.A.*

The next development was an attempt to avoid the confusion which can arise by the same breed having entirely different names in different parts of the world. The most notable examples of this are Shorthorn ≡ Durham and Large White ≡ Yorkshire. In order to decide which names were synonymous it was necessary to consider the characteristics and distribution of the breeds listed. To save space, and because comparable information about all breeds is hard to obtain, the description has been restricted to "breed characters" such as colour and horns— those traits, in fact, which are least affected by the environment. No attempt has been made to compile an encyclopaedia containing a complete account of each breed. The work has remained at the stage of a dictionary.

In brief, then, the aim of this dictionary is to list the livestock names which may be encountered in the literature (*i.e.* names which have been applied to groups of horses, cattle, sheep, pigs, goats, buffaloes and asses on the basis of common origin, similarity of appearance, or geographical proximity), to indicate which names are synonymous, and to recommend one form for English use. For these "breeds", "types", or "varieties", whichever they may be, a brief indication is given of their place of origin or present distribution, their economic use, their relationships to other "breeds", a description of their breed characters, and the origin of the name.

Spelling of Names

Many breeds are named after geographical features. For these I use the spellings in the *Times Atlas of the World* (1980). An exception has been made in the case of Russian names for which I employ the simpler system of "anglicisation" used by the National Geographic Society of America. (*see* p. xx).

Where possible, foreign descriptive names have been translated (*e.g.* "*Schwarzbuntes Niederungsvieh*" becomes "Black Pied Lowland") but sometimes translation is impossible (*e.g.* Préalpes du Sud).

Type used for Names

1. Heavy type (*e.g.* **Shorthorn**) is used for breeds which are important numerically or historically, but the term is relative and may mean slightly different things in different countries. Thus a variety may be in heavy type if it has a separate breed society, or if it is bred under a different name in a different country from the main breed (*e.g.* **Finnish Ayrshire**).

2. Ordinary (roman) type is used for:
   a. Minor, new, or disappearing breeds even though they have breed societies (*e.g.* Luing)
   b. Extinct breeds; these are placed in square brackets, *e.g.* [Galloway Pony]. No attempt has been made to include all extinct breeds. Those listed are here because their extinction was recent or because they are important in the origin of other breeds.
   c. Varieties—whether geographical or genetic *e.g.* Poll Friesian.
   d. Non-uniform populations or geographical terms meaning "cattle of such and such a place" or even "breeds of such and such a place".
   e. Names used for crossbreds (*e.g.* Greyface) or other types which are not true-breeding.
   f. Wild species. These are included if they are commonly referred to as "wild cattle", "wild sheep", etc. They may be recognised by the absence of an initial capital letter and by being followed immediately by their scientific name (*e.g.* mouflon = *Ovis musimon*).

3. Small capitals (*e.g.* ENGLISH LONGWOOL) are used for breed groups or "types".

4. Italics (*e.g.Durham*) are employed for names not recommended for use in English. These may be synonyms, alternative forms or spellings, obsolete names, mis-spellings, or foreign forms.

Place of Breeding

The geographical name in round brackets refers primarily to the place of origin of the breed, *e.g.* **Shorthorn** (N.E. England). For improved breeds, which may now have a world-wide distribution, this is clear enough. Their further distribution is indicated by the countries in which they have herdbooks, breed societies, varieties, or derivatives. For native breeds, however, it has often been possible to give only the present distribution, whilst assuming that the place of origin was in the same area. In either case only the country, province or county may be given; the more exact place of origin is shown by the name of the breed itself or by its synonyms or origins, *e.g.* "**Shorthorn** (N.E. England) . . . orig. from Holderness + Teeswater; syn. *Durham*".

In the case of synonyms the name in round brackets refers to the place in which this particular synonym is used. Likewise for varieties it refers to the place where this variety is bred.

Uses of Breeds

The letters immediately after the round brackets enclosing the country name indicate the functions of the breed ("aptitudes") or the products obtained from it. For example, "d" means only that the breed is used for milk. It does not necessarily indicate a breed of dairy type but is used equally to describe a low-yielding unimproved native breed.

Horses are classified as heavy (h), light (l), or pony (py). In addition to recognised ponies, "py" is also used to describe any small horse, *i.e.* one which is, on the average, less than 14 hands or 140 cm. high at the withers. Their use is given as riding (ri), pack (pa), or draft (dr). Pigs are classified as lard (ld) or meat (m). Cattle, buffaloes, sheep and goats are described as producers of work (dr), milk (d), meat (m), wool (w), mohair (mo), or cashmere (ca). In the case of dual- or triple-purpose breeds the products are listed, as far as possible, in order of importance.

Wool sheep are divided into Merino type (fw), carpet wool type (cw), and intermediates. Where possible the latter have been subdivided into longwools (lw), shortwools (sw), and the crossbred (Merino × longwool) type (mw). When information is insufficient to permit sub-classification in this way the description is simply "w".

Products in square brackets are past history, *e.g.* [dr]—a former draft breed.

Relationship to Other Breeds

This includes origin (if known) and derivatives or varieties. If two dates are given for the origin of a breed, the first is the year when selection or crossbreeding began, and the second the year when the new type was fixed or the name recognised officially. When only a single date is given it usually refers to the latter event.

When a new breed has been developed by crossing two others the founder breed names are joined in the usual way by the multiplication sign and the male parental breed is put first, *e.g.* "**Oxford Down** . . . orig. about 1830 from Cotswold × Hampshire Down". The formation of a new breed by treating two existing breeds or varieties as one is indicated by the addition sign, *e.g.* "**Swedish Red-and-White** . . . orig. from Swedish Ayrshire + Red Pied Swedish". Contrary to the usual mathematical convention, "and" should be taken before " × " in such a case as "orig. from Swiss Brown and Simmental × Ukranian Grey".

The breed groups or "types" unite breeds which have a common origin or are more similar to each other than to the other breeds of a particular country. The largest group is that of the humped cattle or zebu (z). When there are only two breeds in such a group they are connected by "similar to" (sim. to). This is used in a purely relative sense and means only that the two breeds are more similar to each other than to neighbouring breeds. (N.B. "Breed group" in Russian means a breed in formation).

When two breeds appear to have something in common (in name, characteristics, or distribution) but I have not been able to find out the true relationship, the breed names are cross-referenced by "compare" (*cf.*). For example I do not know whether the Pyrenean cattle bred in Spain is the same as the Pyrenean Blond in France or whether merely have the same name, so I have written "Pyrenean (Spain) . . . *cf.* Pyrenean Blond (France)" and *vice versa*.

Breed Characters

As stated above, descriptions are confined to clear-cut morphological characters. No attempt has been made to give a measure of size. This would undoubtedly be very desirable, but size is so much influenced by age, sex, feeding, and management that many figures would have to be given before it would be possible to compare different breeds. Dwarf breeds (and ponies) are noted, however. Descriptions implicit in the breed name (*e.g.* Red Poll) are not always repeated. Descriptions of varieties of a breed or breeds of a breed group are confined to differences from the parent type.

If no *colour* is given it means, in the case of sheep and pigs, that the breed colour is white, in the case of buffaloes that it is black, or at least dark, and in the case of other species that there is no characteristic breed colour. The colour given is the typical colour but there are few breeds in which off-types do not occur. The description refers to the adult female; the young may be different from the adult and bulls are often darker than cows. Patterns are not always described in detail. For instance, I have not specified that grey or grey-white cattle are darker on the shoulders than on the rest of the body.

Cattle and goat breeds are *horned* unless they are described specifically as polled (pd). Differences in horn size between the sexes are not mentioned but it can be assumed that the cow and the castrate male have longer horns than the bull. The reverse holds in goats and sheep. Owing to the wide variation among sheep, the presence or absence of horns in each sex is noted wherever the information is available.

The *coat* is described only if it is exceptional in some way, *e.g.* absent, very long, curly, or hair instead of wool (sheep only). Likewise only abnormal ears are mentioned.

Sheep *tails* are classified as long (lt), *i.e.* down to the ground, short (st), *i.e.* less than half way to the hocks, or fat (ft). If the tail is not mentioned it may be assumed that it is of the thin, medium-length type so common among European breeds. No distinction is made between the docked and undocked breeds having this type of tail.

Breed Societies

If there is a society, association or club devoted to the promotion of the breed, this is indicated by the abbreviation BS; the date following indicates the year of its formation. If there is no special society but the breed is recognised by the government and a breed standard has been established, the sign is BSd. If pedigrees are published in a stud-, flock- or herdbook, this is indicated by HB, followed by the date of publication of the first volume. Sometimes early pedigrees were published in a herdbook covering several breeds, so the date given may be earlier than the first volume of the breed society herdbook. Confusion may have arisen here because of the use in some foreign languages of the English word "herdbook" to mean breed society.

Synonyms

The synonyms are usually preceded by the official name of the breed in the language of its country of origin. This applies in the case of the common European languages and when the recommended English name is different from the official vernacular name.

In the interest of simplicity all Cyrillic names (Russian, Bulgarian, or Serbian) are transliterated, (*see* p. xx), as well as Arabic, Chinese and other oriental languages.

Proscribed Names

The names following the "not" at the end of an entry are in quite a different category from the synonyms. They are not alternative names used in different times or places, but wrong forms—mis-spellings or definite misnomers which really refer to quite different breeds. For instance, the German Red cattle should not be called "Red German", since that name was used (until World War II) for the Russian breed of German origin which is now called Red Steppe.

Etymology

In the majority of cases breeds are named from the geographical region in which they originated, from the tribe which bred them, by some descriptive feature (*e.g.* Shorthorn, Red Poll), or by a combination of two of these categories (*e.g.* Exmoor Horn, Red Bororo). It is assumed that such derivations are self-explanatory and no etymology is given. At the same time it must be borne in mind that the descriptions implied in a name may be inaccurate, *e.g.* the Blackhead Persian did not come from Persia, nor the Holstein-Friesian from Holstein.

In all other cases the origin of the name is given, if it is known. The explanation may appear in the description of the origin of the breed or among the synonyms; otherwise it is given in square brackets at the end of the entry, *e.g.* "Criollo . . . [= native]".

ABBREVIATIONS

A.B.A. = *Animal Breeding Abstracts*
adj. = adjective
Afrik. = Afrikaans
Agric. = Agricultural, Agriculture
Alb. = Albanian
approx. = approximate(ly)
ASSR = Autonomous Soviet Socialist Republic
BS = breed society (or societies)
BSd = breed standard
Bulg. = Bulgarian (transliterated)
C. = central
c. = century
c. = *circa* (about)
ca. = cashmere
cf. = compare
Ch. = Chinese (romanised according to the Pinyin system)
Cro. = Croatian
cw. = coarsewooled (*i.e.* mattress, mixed, or carpet)
Cz. = Czech
d. = dairy (milk)
Dan. = Danish
dist. = district
dr. = draft
Du. = Dutch
E. = east
e.g. = for example
esp. = especially
et al. = and others
etc. = *et cetera*

etym. = etymology
Exp. = Experiment(al)
fem. = feminine
Finn. = Finnish
Fr. = French
fr. = fat-rumped
ft. = fat-tailed (broad or S-shaped)
fw. = finewooled (*i.e.* Merino type)
GB = Great Britain (*i.e.* England, Wales and Scotland)
geog. = geographical
Ger. = German
Gr. = Greek (transliterated)
h. = heavy (horse)
HB = herd-, flock- or studbook
hd = horned
hr. = long hair
Hung. = Hungarian
hy = short hair, woolless
I. = Island
i.e. = that is
inc. = includes, included, including, inclusive
Is = Islands
It. = Italian
Jap. = Japanese (romanised)
L. = Lake
l. = light (horse)
lat. = latitude
ld = lard
lft. = long fat tail
Lith. = Lithuanian
lt. = long thin tail

lw.	= longwooled (medium fine)	Serbo-cro.	= Serbo-Croatian
m.	= meat	sft.	= short fat tail
mo.	= mohair	sim.	= similar
mt.	= mountain	sing.	= singular
mts	= mountains	Sl.	= Slovak
mw.	= medium wool (*i.e.* intermediate between cw. and fw.)	Sp.	= Spanish
		sp.	= species
N.	= north	spp.	= species (pl.)
Nor.	= Norwegian	*s.s.*	= *sensu stricto*
nr	= near	SSR	= Soviet Socialist Republic
NSW	= New South Wales	St·	= Saint
obs.	= obsolete	Sta.	= Station
occ.	= occasionally	sw.	= shortwooled (medium fine)
orig.	= origin, original(ly), originated		
		Swe.	= Swedish
pa.	= pack	syn.	= synonym(s)
pd	= polled, hornless	Turk.	= Turkish
Pers.	= Persian	UK	= United Kingdom of Great Britain and Northern Ireland
pl.	= plural		
Pol.	= Polish		
Port.	= Portuguese	Univ.	= University
prim.	= primitive (*i.e.* native unimproved type)	usu.	= usually
		var.	= variety or sub-breed
Prov.	= Province	vars	= varieties
py	= pony	Vet.	= Veterinary
q.v.	= which see	*viz.*	= namely
R.	= River	W.	= west
recog.	= recognised (as a breed)	w.	= wooled (but not cw. or fw.)
reorg.	= reorganised		
ri.	= riding	W.G.	= Chinese romanised according to Wade-Giles system
Rom.	= Romanian		
Russ.	= Russian (transliterated)		
S.	= south	z.	= zebu

PRONUNCIATION EQUIVALENTS

English	sh	ch	ts	j	zh	y	kh
French	ch	tch	ts	dj	j	y	—
Spanish	—	ch	ts	—	—	y	j or x
Turkish	ş	ç	—	c	j	y	—
Romanian	ş	c(i)	ţ	g(i)	j	i	h
Italian	sc(i)	c(i)	z	g(i)	—	i	—
German	sch	tsch	z	dj or dsch	sh	j	ch
Hungarian	s	cs	c or cz	—	zs	j	—
Polish	sz	cz	c	dż	ż	j	ch
Czech	š	č	c	dž	ž	j	ch
Croatian	š	č	c	đ	ž	j	h
Russian (transliterated)	sh	ch	ts	dzh	zh	y	kh

TRANSLITERATION OF RUSSIAN

А	a
Б	b
В	v
Г	g
Д	d
ДЖ	dzh[1]
Е	e[2]
Ж	zh
З	z
И	i
Й	ĭ[3]
К	k
Л	l
М	m
Н	n
О	o
П	p
Р	r
С	s
Т	t
У	u
Ф	f
Х	kh
Ц	ts
Ч	ch
Ш	sh
Щ	shch (Bulg. sht)
Ъ	''[4]
Ы	y
Ь	'[5]
Э	ė[6]
Ю	yu
Я	ya

For geographical and breed names:
(1) j
(2) ye initially
(3) omit after И or Ы elsewhere i

(4) omit in Russ., u in Bulgarian
(5) omit.
(6) e

xx

ASS

Abkhasian; var. of Georgian; Russ. *Abkhazskaya*
Abyssinian (Ethiopia); usu. slate-grey, occ. chestnut-brown; sim. to
　Sudanese Pack
achdari: see Syrian wild ass
African wild ass (formerly N. Africa and possibly Arabia) = *Equus
　africanus* Fitzinger; vars: [Nubian wild ass] and Somali wild ass
akhdari: see Syrian wild ass
Albanian (Albania)
Algerian (Algeria); dr.m; chestnut or grey
American: see Mammoth Jack Stock, Standard, Large Standard, Spotted,
　Miniature and burro
Amiatina (Mt Amiata, Grosseto, Italy); agouti with shoulder cross;
　nearly extinct
Anatolian (Turkey); black and grey vars.
Andalusian (S. Spain); grey; syn. *Campiñesa, Córdoba*; HB; Sp. *Andaluza*;
　nearly extinct
Apulian: see Martina Franca
Armenian (Armenia, USSR); Caucasian type; Russ. *Armyanskaya*
Asian wild ass: see kiang and onager; syn. *Asiatic wild ass*
Asinara (Asinara I, Sardinia, Italy); white; almost extinct
Atbai: see Etbai
Ausetan: see Catalan
Azerbaijan (USSR); Caucasian type; Russ. *Azerbaĭdzhanskaya*

Baladi (Lower Egypt); var. of Egyptian
Baluchi wild ass: see Indian wild ass
Benderi (S. Iran); orig. from onager × Iranian
Berga; former var. of Catalan
Bokhara: see Bukhara
Brazilian (São Paulo, Brazil); syn. *Paulista*; see also Northeastern and
　Pêga
Bukhara: see Uzbek; not *Bokhara*
burro (USA); feral

Campiñesa: see Andalusian
Canary Island (Spain); local type of Common Spanish sim. to Andalusian

1

Canindé (Ceará, Brazil); rarer var. of Northeastern; black with pale belly
Cardão (Ceará, Brazil); commoner var. of Northeastern; yellow or bay
[Cariovilli] (Aquila, Abruzzo, Italy)
Cassala: see Kassala
Castelmorone (Caserta, Campania, Italy); nearly extinct
Castilian (Spain) = Common Spanish in Castille; Sp. *Castellana*
Catalan (Catalonia, Spain); black, dark grey or brown with pale
    underparts; HB 1880; Sp. *Catalana*; syn. *Ausetan, Catalonian, Vich*;
    former var: Berga; nearly extinct
Caucasian (Transcaucasia, USSR); small native type; inc. Armenian,
    Azerbaijan, Dagestan, Georgian; Russ. *Kavkazskaya*; syn. *Transcau-*
    casian (Russ. *Zakavkazskaya*)
Central Asian (USSR); small native types; inc. Kara-Kalpak, Kazakh,
    Kirgiz, Tajik, Turkmen, Uzbek; Russ. *Sredneaziatskaya*
chigetai (Mongolia and E. Kazakhstan, USSR) = *Equus hemionus*
    hemionus Pallas and *E.h. luteus* (Matschie); vars. of onager; syn.
    kulan (Kirgiz), *Mongolian wild ass*; not *chiggetai, djigitai, dzeggetai,*
    dzhiggetai, dziggetai; rare. [Mongolian *tchikhitei* = long-eared, from
    tchikhi = ear]
Chinese (China); inc. large (Guanzhong, Jinnan, Shandong, and Siumi),
    intermediate (N. and N.E. China), and small types
Common Spanish (Spain); unimproved native type; inc. Moruna and
    local Canary Island, Castilian and Majorcan; Sp. *Común*
Córdoba: see Andalusian
Cyprus; orig. from African and Asian with Catalan blood; not *Cypriot*

Dagestan (USSR); Caucasian type; Russ. *Dagestanskaya*
Damascus; larger var. of Syrian; usu. brown to black, also white
djigitai: see chigetai
dzeggetai, dzhiggetai, dziggetai: see chigetai

Egyptian (Egypt); vars: Baladi (Lower Egypt), Hassawi (saddle), Saidi
    (Upper Egypt)
Etbai (N.W. Sudan); smaller var. of Sudanese Riding; not *Atbai*

French: see Poitou

Gascon, Gascony: see Pyrenean
Georgian (Georgia, USSR); Caucasian type; Russ. *Gruzinskaya*; vars:
    Abkhasian, Kakhetian, and Meskhet-Javakhet
ghor-khar: see Iranian onager, Indian wild ass

Guanzhong (Wei R, C. Shaanxi, China); dr; large type of Chinese; usu. black with paler muzzle and underparts, also dark grey with shoulder bar; W.G. *Kuan-chung*, Russ. *Guanchzhun*; formerly *Kwanchung*

half-ass: see onager
Hamadan (Iran; also Turkmenistan, USSR); sim. to Mary; usu. white; var: Kashan; not *Hamodan, Khamodan*
Hassawi; white, ri. var. of Egyptian
hemione: see onager

Indian (India); light grey to white
Indian wild ass (Rann of Cutch, India, formerly also Baluchistan) = *Equus hemionus khur* Lesson; var. of onager; syn. *Baluchi wild ass, ghor khar, Indian onager, khur*; rare
Iranian (Iran); small native type; syn. *Persian*; orig. of Benderi; see also Hamadan
Iranian onager (C. Iran) = *Equus hemionus onager* Boddaert; var. of onager; syn. *ghor-khar, Persian onager, Persian wild ass*; rare
Irpinia (Benevento and Avellino, Campania, Italy)
Italian: see Amiatina, Irpinia, Martina Franca, Pantelleria, Ragusan, Sardinian Dwarf

Jinnan (Yuncheng basin, S. Shanxi, China); black often with white on nose, around eyes and on belly

Kakhetian; var. of Georgian; Russ. *Kakhetinskaya*
Kara-Kalpak (Uzbekistan, USSR); Central Asian type; Russ. *Kara-Kalpakskaya*
Kashan (Iran); var. of Hamadan; not *Koshan*
Kassala: see Sudanese Riding; not *Cassala*
Kazakh (Kazakhstan, USSR); Central Asian type; Russ. *Kazakhskaya*
Khamodan: see Hamadan
khur: see Indian wild ass
kiang (Tibet, Sikkim, Ladakh) = *Equus kiang* Moorcroft; dark red-brown with white underparts and patch behind shoulder; not *kyang*. [Tibetan]
Kirgiz (Kirgizia, USSR); Central Asian type; Russ. *Kirgizskaya*
Kuan-chung: see Guanzhong
kulan (Turkmenistan, USSR) = *Equus hemionus kulan* (Groves and Mazák); var. of onager; syn. *Transcaspian onager*; not *koulan, kulon*; see also chigetai. [Kirgiz]

Kwanchung: see Guanzhong
kyang: see kiang

Large Standard (USA); see also Standard
León-Zamora, Leonés-Zamorana: see Zamorano-Leonesa
Libyan (Libya); smaller (usu. bay with pale belly), and larger (ri; dark bay or grey) vars.

Majorcan (Balearic Is, Spain); local type of Common Spanish; Sp.
   Mallorquina; not *Mallorcan*
Mallorcan, Mallorquin: see Majorcan
Mammoth Jack Stock (USA); orig. from Andalusian, Catalan, Majorcan, Maltese and Poitou; BS 1888, HB 1891; syn. *American Jack*
Martina Franca (Apulia, Italy); nearly black with light underparts; HB 1943, BS 1948; syn. *Apulian* (It. *Pugliese*), *Martinese*
Mary (Turkmenistan, USSR); usu. white; sim. to Hamadan; Russ. *Maryĭskaya*; syn. *Merv*
Masai (Kenya and Tanzania); usu. brown
Mediterranean (USA): see Miniature
Merv: see Mary
Meskhet-Javakhet; var. of Georgian; Russ. *Meskhet-Dzhavakhetskaya*
Mesopotamian onager: see Syrian wild ass
Miniature (USA); BS; syn. *Mediterranean*
Mongolian wild ass: see chigetai
Moroccan (Morocco)
Moruna (Spain); small black type of Common Spanish. [= black]
Muscat (Tanzania); larger and paler than Masai; ? orig. from Egyptian or Arabian

Northeastern (N.E. Brazil); grey, agouti, or purple-brown; Port. *Nordestina*; vars. Canindé, Cardão
[Nubian wild ass] (Sudan-Eritrea border) = *Equus africanus africanus* Fitzinger; var. of African wild ass; grey with pale underparts and legs, and dark mane, dorsal stripe, tail tuft and shoulder cross-stripe; orig. of domestic ass, *Equus 'asinus'* Linnaeus; extinct in 1960s

onager = *Equus hemionus* Pallas; pale yellowish-brown with paler underparts and darker mane and back-stripe; vars: chigetai (Mongolia) = *E.h. hemionus* and *E.h. luteus*; Indian wild ass = *E.h. khur*; Iranian onager = *E.h. onager*; kulan = *E.h. kulan*; and [Syrian wild ass] = *E.h. hemippus*; syn. *Asian wild ass, half-ass, hemione*; rare. [Latin, from Greek = wild ass]

Pantelleria (Italy); dark brown with pale belly; syn. *Pantesca*; not *Pantellaria*; almost extinct

Pantesca: see Pantelleria

Paulista: see Brazilian

Pêga (Minas Gerais, Brazil); roan or dark grey; ? It. and Egyptian orig. in 19th c, 1810 on; HB and BS 1949; syn. *Lagoa Dourada*. [= manacles, the brand of the original breeder, J. de Resende of Lagoa Dourada]

Persian: see Iranian

Persian wild ass: see Iranian onager

Poitou (W. France); black or dark brown; long hair; HB; Fr. *baudet de Poitou, Poitevin*; syn. *French*; nearly extinct

Pugliese: see Martina Franca

Pyrenean (France); local population; Fr. *Pyrénéen*; syn. *Gascon, Gascony*

Qaramani (N. Yemen); small local type

Ragusan (Sicily, Italy); nearly black with pale muzzle and belly, sometimes grey; orig. from Martina Franca and Catalan × native and Pantelleria; HB 1953; It. *Ragusana*; syn. *Sicilian*; nearly extinct

[Romagnola] (Romagna, Emilia, Italy)

Saidi (Upper Egypt); var. of Egyptian

[Sant' Alberto] (Ravenna and Forli, Emilia, Italy)

Sardinian Dwarf (Italy); grey or agouti; It. *Sarda*; nearly extinct

Sennar (Ethiopia): see Sudanese Riding; not *Senaar, Sennaar, Sinnari*

Shandong; large type of Chinese; W.G. *Shan-tung*

Shantung: see Shandong

Sicilian: see Ragusan

Siumi (N. and S. Shaanxi, China); pa; large type of Chinese; usu. dark with paler muzzle and underparts; syn. *Four-eyebrows, Swallow-coat*

Somali (Somalia, Ogaden and N. Kenya); sim. to Toposa of S.E. Sudan; grey

Somali wild ass (N. Somalia and S.E. Eritrea) = *Equus africanus somaliensis* Noack; var. of African wild ass; reddish-grey with dark mane; dorsal stripe and shoulder cross-stripe rare; nearly extinct

Spanish breeds: see Andalusian, Catalan, Zamorano-Leonesa; see also Common Spanish

Spotted (USA); BS; syn. *American Spotted*

Standard (USA); BS; see also Large Standard

Subyani (N. Yemen); Sudanese orig.

Sudanese Pack (N. Sudan); grey; sim. to Abyssinian
Sudanese Riding (N. Sudan); dark brown or reddish-grey, sometimes
    pale grey or white; larger than Sudanese Pack; syn. *Kassala* (N.W.
    Eritrea), *Sennar* (Ethiopia); var. Etbai (N.E. Sudan)
Syrian (Syria and Israel); grey, brown or black; larger var: Damascus
Syrian onager: see Syrian wild ass
[Syrian wild ass] (Syrian and Iraq deserts) = *Equus hemionus hemippus*
    I. Geoffroy; var. of onager; Fr. *hémippe de Syrie*; syn. *achdari, akhdari,
    Mesopotamian onager, Syrian onager*; extinct in early 20th c.

Tajik (Tajikistan, USSR); Central Asian type; Russ. *Tadzhikskaya*
Tibetan (Tibet and Nepal); dark brown, occ. dark grey or dun; small
Toposa (S.E. Sudan); sim. to Somali
Transcaucasian: see Caucasian
Tunisian (Tunisia)
Turkmen (Turkmenistan, USSR); Central Asian type; see also Mary;
    Russ. *Turkmenskaya*

Uzbek (Uzbekistan, USSR); Central Asian type; Russ. *Uzbekskaya*; syn.
    Bukhara (Russ. *Bukharskaya)*

Vich: see Catalan
[Viterbo Grey] (Viterbo, Latium, Italy); It. *Grigio viterbese*

wild: see African wild, Asian wild

Zamorano-Leonesa (Zamòra and León, Spain); black with paler muzzle
    and underparts; long hair; HB 1941; syn. *Leonés-Zamorana*; rare
Zebronkey (USA); name for zebra × donkey hybrid; syn. *Zeedonk*

BUFFALO

African buffalo (Africa S. of Sahara) = *Syncerus caffer* Sparrman; vars:
  Cape (black) = *S.c. caffer*, Congo (red) = *S.c. nanus*, and *S.c.
  aequinoctialis* (Ethiopia to Niger) (red-brown to black)
Albanian; var. of European
American bison = *Bison bison* (Linnaeus); not *buffalo*
Anatolian (N.W. Turkey); d.dr; dark grey to black; often white on head
  and tail; sickle or crescentic horns; syn. *Turkish*
anoa (Sulawesi, Indonesia) = *Bubalus (Anoa) depressicornis* Smith;
  brown to black with white marks on head and feet; syn. *dwarf, pigmy,*
  or *chamois buffalo*
arni (N.E. India) = *Bubalus arnee* (Kerr); dark grey to black; ♂ arna,
  ♀ arni; syn. *Indian wild buffalo*; orig. of domestic buffalo (*B. 'bubalis'*
  Linnaeus); not *arno*. [Hindi]
Assam (N.E. India); Swamp type
Azerbaijan: see Caucasian

Badavan, Badavari: see Bhadawari
Baladi (Egypt); subvar. or syn. of Beheri; not *Baledi*
Bangar (N. Bangladesh); local var.
Bangladesh; Swamp and River types; local vars inc. Bangar, Kachhar,
  Mahish, Manipuri
Beheri (Lower Egypt); d; var. of Egyptian; slate-grey; subvars (or syn.):
  Minufi and Baladi; not *Beheiri*. [= towards the sea]
Berari: see Nagpuri
Bhadawari (Agra, Uttar Pradesh, India); d.dr; copper-coloured with pale
  legs; syn. *Etawah*; not *Badavan, Badavari*
Bhavanagri: see Jafarabadi
Białowieza bison: see Polish bison
Binhu (S. Hunan, China); var. of Chinese; called Jianghan in Hubei. [=
  nr the lake (Dongting)]
bison: see American, European; and Indian (under Cattle)
Bombay: see Surti
Borneo buffalo (N. Sarawak); feral; not *Bubalus arnee hosei* (Lydekker)
Buffalypso (Trinidad); m; reddish-brown or black; orig 1950-70 from
  Murrah, Surti, Jafarabadi, Nili and Bhadawari imported 1900-49
Bulgarian (Bulgaria); d.m.(dr); var. of European
Burmese (Burma); Swamp type

7

Cambodian (plains of Kampuchea); Swamp type; shorthorned; Fr. *Cambodgienne*; syn. *krabey leu*; see also Moi

Cape buffalo (E. and S. Africa) = *Syncerus caffer caffer* (Sparrman); var. of African buffalo; black

carabao (Philippines): see Philippine carabao. [= buffalo]

Caucasian (North Caucasus and Transcaucasia, USSR); d.m.dr; dark grey to black, occ. brown, often white on head and tail; breed selected 1935-70 (recog.) in Azerbaijan from native type; syn. *Azerbaijan, Dagestan, Georgian, Improved Caucasian, Russian, Transcaucasian*

[Caucasian bison] = *Bison bonasus caucasicus* Grevé; var. of European bison extinct before 1927; syn. *mountain bison*

Ceylon: see Lanka

chamois buffalo: see anoa

Charotar: see Surti

Chinese (S.E. China); Swamp type; Ch. *shui niu* (= *water cattle*); recog. geog. vars: large - Haizi and Shanghai, medium - Binhu, Dechang and Dehong, small - Wenzhou, Xinglong and Xilin; other named vars: Jianghan, Yuandong

Congo buffalo (W. Africa and Congo basin) = *Syncerus caffer nanus* (Boddaert); var. of African buffalo; red; syn. *bush cow*

Dagestan: see Caucasian

Dangyang (Hubei, China); inc. in Jianghan; W.G. *Tang-yang*, Ger. *Dang-jiang*

Deccani: see Surti

Dechang (Sichuan, China); var. of Chinese

Dehong (Yunnan, China); var. of Chinese

Delhi: see Murrah

desi (India and Pakistan) =. native, indigenous, and hence nondescript, breedless, unimproved; not *deshi*

Dharwari: see Pandharpuri

Durna-Thali: see Nagpuri

dwarf buffalo: see anoa

Egyptian (Egypt); d.dr; grey-black; short curved horns; vars: Beheri (Lower Egypt), Saidi (Upper Egypt)

Ellichpuri: see Nagpuri

Etawah: see Bhadawari

European (S.E. Europe); d.m.(dr); dark grey to black, often white on head, tail and feet; vars: Albanian, Bulgarian, Greek, Italian, Macedonian, Romanian, Transylvanian

European bison = *Bison bonasus* (Linnaeus); brown; HB 1932; semi-wild or in captivity; Ger. *wisent*, Pol. and Russ. *zubr*; Polish and [Caucasian] vars; not *aurochs*. [Latin, from Teutonic *wisand*]

Ganjam: see Manda
Gaulani, Gauli: see Nagpuri
Georgian: see Caucasian
Gir: see Jafarabadi
Gowdoo: see Sambalpur
Greek (N. Greece); var. of European
Gujarati, Gujerati: see Surti

Haizi (N. Jiangsu, China); var. of Chinese; W.G. *Haitzü*, Russ. *Haĭtszy*; not *Haidzi*. [= son of the sea]
Hechu (Hubei, China); inc. in Jianghan; W.G. *Wuchü*
Hungarian: see Transylvanian

INDIAN (India, except Assam, and Pakistan): River type; inc. 7 recog. breeds in India (Bhadawari, Jafarabadi, Mehsana, Murrah, Nagpuri, Nili-Ravi, Surti), 2 in Pakistan (Kundi and Nili-Ravi), and many local types (*e.g.* Jerangi, Kalahandi, Manda, Sambalpur, Tarai); see also desi
Indian wild buffalo: see arni
Indo-Chinese: see Cambodian and Moi, Laotian, Vietnamese
Indonesian (Indonesia); Swamp type; Indon. *kerbau* (= *buffalo*), also spelt *karbo, karbou, karbouw*; syn. *Javanese*
Iranian (Iran): *cf.* Iraqi (in Khuzestan) and Caucasian (in Azarbaijan and Gilan); syn. *Persian*
Iraqi (S.E. Iraq); d; black or dark grey, often with white on head, feet and tail, occ. pied; sickle horns
Italian (Caserta and Salerno, S. Italy); d.(m); var. of European

Jafarabadi (Kathiawar, Gujarat, India); d; usu. black; large drooping horns; syn. *Bhavanagri, Gir, Jaffri*; not *Jaffarabadi, Jaffarbadi, Jafferabadi, Jaffrabarri, Jafrabadi*; HB in Brazil
Javanese: see Indonesian
Jerangi (Orissa-Andhra Pradesh border, India); dr; black; syn. *Zerangi*
Jianghan (Hubei, China); var. of Chinese; inc. Hechu and Dangyang (and Binhu in Hubei)
Jiangsu Round-Barrel; W.G. *Chiang-su*; formerly *Kiang-su*; ? = Shanghai

Kachhar (N. Bangladesh); local var; ? Kachkar
Kalahandi (Orissa, India); d.dr; grey, usu. with white tail; syn. *Peddak-imedi* (Andhra Pradesh)
Kanara, Kanarese: see South Kanara
karbo, karbou, karbouw (Indonesia) = buffalo
kerabou, kerbau, kerbou (Malaysia) = buffalo
kerbau-banteng (Sumatra): see Murrah
kerbau-sapi (Malaysia): see River buffalo (i.e. Indian - Murrah or Surti). [= cattle buffalo]
kerbau-sawah (Malaysia): see Malaysian. [= swamp buffalo]
kerbau-sungei (Malaysia): see River buffalo (i.e. Indian / Murrah or Surti)
Kiangsu: see Jiangsu
Kimedi: see Sambalpur
krabey (Indo-China) = buffalo
krabey-beng: see Moi
krabey-leu: see Cambodian
Kundi (N. Sind, Pakistan); d; Murrah type; usu. black, occ. brown, often with white on head, tail and feet; syn. *Sindhi Murrah*; not *Kundhi*. [= fish-hook (horns)]
kwai (Thailand) = buffalo
Kwangtung: see Xinglong

Lanka (Sri Lanka); Swamp type; fawn to black; syn. *Ceylon, Sri Lankan*; former vars: Mannar, Tamankaduwa
Laotian (Laos); Swamp type
Lithuanian bison: see Polish bison
lowland bison: see Polish bison

Macedonian (S. Serbia and Macedonia, Yugoslavia); var. of European
Mahish (Bangladesh); local var.
Mahratta, Mahratwada: see *Marathwada*
Malabar: see South Kanara
Malaysian (W. Malaysia); Swamp type; syn. *kerbau-sawah* (= swamp buffalo); obs. syn. *Malayan*
Manda (Orissa-Andhra Pradesh border, India); d. dr; brown or grey; syn. *Ganjam, Paralakhemundi, Parlakimedi*. [= herd]
Manipuri (Sylhet, Bangladesh); local var; large horns; not *Manpuri*
Mannar; larger, reddish var. of Lanka buffalo; not *Manaar, Manar*
Marathwada: see Nagpuri; not *Mahratta, Mahratwada*
Mediterranean: see Anatolian, Egyptian, European, Syrian
Mediterranean (Brazil); d; orig. from Italian; HB

Mehsana (N. Gujarat, India); d; black, occ. brown or grey; orig. from Murrah with Surti blood; not *Mehasana*

Menoufi, Menufi: see Minufi

Mestizo (Philippines); Indian × carabao

Middle Eastern: see Anatolian, Caucasian, Egyptian, Iraqi, Syrian

Mindoro: see tamarao

Minufi (S. Delta, Egypt); syn. or subvar. of Beheri; not *Menoufi, Menufi*

Moi (plateau of Kampuchea); Swamp type; longhorned; syn. *krabey-beng*

mountain bison: see Caucasian bison

Muntenesc: see Romanian

MURRAH GROUP (N.W. India and Pakistan); d; black; short coiled horns; syn. *Delhi, kerbau-banteng* (Sumatra), *kerbau-sungei* or *kerbau-sapi* (Malaysia); inc. Murrah (*s.s*), Nili-Ravi, Kundi; not *Mura, Murra*

Murrah (Haryana and Delhi, India); HB 1940; HB also in Brazil; see above

Nadiad, Nadiadi: see Surti

Nagpuri (N.E. Maharashtra, India); dr.d; usu. black, sometimes white on face, legs and tail; long horns; syn. *Berari, Durna-Thali, Ellichpuri* (Berar), *Gaulani, Gauli, Marathwada, Varadi*; var: Pandharpuri (S.E. Maharashtra)

Nepalese (Nepal); d.m; River or Swamp type; regional vars: Nepalese Hill, Nepalese Mountain, Tarai

Nepalese Hill (C. Nepal); ? Swamp type; light grey; long horns

Nepalese Mountain (N. Nepal); ? Swamp type; light grey or blond; medium horns; hairy; syn. *Himalayan Mountain*

Netherlands Indies: see Indonesian

Nili (Sutlej R. valley, Pakistan and India); local var. of Nili-Ravi; not *Nelli*. [= blue (waters of R. Sutlej)]

Nili-Ravi (Punjab, Pakistan and India); d; Murrah type; usu. black, occ. brown, often with wall eyes and white marks on head, legs and tail; vars: Nili, Ravi

Nelli: see Nili

Palestinian: see Syrian

Pandharpuri; var. of Nagpuri in S.E. Maharashtra; syn. *Dharwari* (Karnataka)

Paralakhemundi: see Manda

Parlakimedi : see Manda

Peddakimedi: see Kalahandi

Persian: see Iranian

Philippine carabao (Philippines); Swamp type. [*carabao* = buffalo; ♀ is *caraballa*]

pigmy buffalo: see anoa

Polish bison = *Bison bonasus bonasus* (Linnaeus); var. of European bison (*q.v.*); syn. *Białowieza bison, Lithuanian bison, lowland bison*

Ravi (Ravi and Chenab R. valleys, Pakistan); local var. of Nili-Ravi; syn. *Sandal Bar*

RIVER BUFFALO (Asia W. of Assam, Egypt, S.E. Europe); d.m.dr; black, occ. brown; short coiled or sickle horns; orig. from Swamp buffalo (or directly from wild arni) by selection for colour, horns and milk yield; syn. *kerbau-sungei* (Malaysia); inc. Indian, Middle Eastern, European

Romanian (Danube valley, S. Romania); d; var. of European; black; Rom. *Muntenesc* (= Muntenian *i.e.* Walachian)

Rosilho (Brazil, esp. Marajo I.); m.dr; Swamp type; grey skin and cream hair. [= roan]

Russian: see Caucasian

Saidi (Upper Egypt); dr; var. of Egyptian; black

Sambalpur (Bilaspur, Madhya Pradesh, India); d.dr; usu. black, occ. brown or grey; syn. *Gowdoo, Kimedi* (Andhra Pradesh)

Sandal Bar: see Ravi

sapi (Malaysia): see *kerbau-sapi, sapi-utan*. [= cattle]

Shanghai (China); var. of Chinese

Siamese: see Thai

Sindhi Murrah: see Kundi

South Kanara (S.W. Karnataka, India); dr. racing; syn. *Kanara, Kanarese, Malabar*

Sri Lankan: see Lanka

Surat, Surati: see Surti

Surti (N. Gujarat, India); d; black or brown, usu. with two white collars; syn. *Charotar, Deccani, Gujarati, Nadiadi, Surati, Talabda*. [from Surat]

SWAMP BUFFALO (S.E. Asia); dr; dark grey, occ. white; crescentic horns; orig. from, and sim. to, arni, *Bubalus arnee*; inc. Assam, Burmese, Cambodian, Chinese, Indonesian, Lanka, Laotian, Malaysian, Nepalese, Philippine, Thai, Vietnamese; ? orig. of River buffalo

Syrian (Syria and Israel); d.dr; black; obs. syn. *Palestinian*; extinct in Israel, rare in Syria

Taiwan; var. of Chinese

Talabda: see Surti; not *Talbada*

Tamankaduwa; d; largest var. of Lanka buffalo; not *Tamamkaduwa*

tamarao (Mindoro, Philippines) = *Bubalus mindorensis* Heude; greyish-black to brown; syn. *Mindoro buffalo*; not *tamarau, tamaraw, tamaron, timarau*; rare

Tangyang: see Dangyang

Tarai (N. Uttar Pradesh, India and S. Nepal); d.m.dr; black (occ. brown) with white tail; ? Murrah blood; not *Terai*

Terai: see Tarai

Thai (Thailand); Swamp type; often white in N; syn. *Kwai* (= buffalo), *Siamese*

timarau: see tamarao

Toda (Nilgiris, N.W. Tamil Nadu, India); d; ? Swamp or River type; numbers declining

Transcaucasian: see Caucasian

Transylvanian (C. Romania, esp. Cluj and Făgăraş); var. of European; grey-black; Rom. *Transilvăniană*; obs. syn. *Hungarian*

Turkish: see Anatolian

Varadi: see Nagpuri

Vietnamese (Vietnam); Swamp type

Wenzhou (Zhejiang, China); var. of Chinese

wisent: see European bison

Wuchü, Wu-tchü, Wu-tshü: see Hechu

Xilin (W. Guangxi, China); var. of Chinese

Xinglong (Guangdong, China); var. of Chinese; syn. *Kwangtung*

Yuandong (Fujian, China); var. of Chinese; W.G. *Yuan-tung*

Zerangi: see Jerangi

zubr: see European bison

zubro-bison = European × American bison

CATTLE

Aalstreep: see Witrik

Aberdeen-Angus (N.E. Scotland); m; black; pd; orig. from Angus Doddie + Buchan Humlie in late 18th c; recog. 1835, named 1909; Polled HB (with Galloway) 1862, BS 1879; syn. *Angus, Northern Scotch Polled, Polled Angus*; var: Red Angus; BS also in Argentina 1927 (HB 1879), Canada 1906 (HB 1885), S. Africa 1917 (HB 1906), New Zealand 1918, Australia (Angus) 1926, Uruguay, Zimbabwe, Ireland 1967, Greece 1970, Denmark 1973, Japan, Finland, Norway, Sweden, Mexico, Paraguay 1980, HB also in Brazil 1906, USSR; orig. of American Angus, German Angus

Aberdeenshire Shorthorn: see Beef Shorthorn

Abgal: see Gasara

Abigar (Akebo, Gambela, Ilubabor, S.W. Ethiopia); var. of Nilotic; syn. *Anuak*

Abondance (Haute Savoie, France); d.m.[dr]; French Red Pied group; smaller, darker, white confined to underside and extremities, and usu. with spectacles; HB and BS 1894; Fr. *Race d'Abondance*; syn. *Chablaisien* (from Chablais), *Pie rouge française de Montagne*. [La Chapelle d'Abondance]

Abori: see Red Bororo

[Abruzzese] (Abruzzi, Italy); former var. of Apulian Podolian; It. *Podolica abruzzese di montagna*

Abyssinian Highland Zebu (mts of Bale, Ethiopia); various colours and horn shapes

Abyssinian Shorthorned Zebu (Harer plateau, N. Sidamo and Shewa, Ethiopia); dr.m.d; often grey, fawn, reddish, also black, bay, roan, pied; horns variable, occ. pd; ? orig. of Arsi

Abyssinian Zebus (C. Highlands, Ethiopia); m.d.dr; East African Shorthorned Zebu type; small; inc. (Abyssinian) Highland Zebu, (Abyssinian) Shorthorned Zebu, Jem-Jem Zebu, Jijjiga Zebu; *cf.* Ingessana and Murle; orig. of Arsi

Acchai: see Lohani

A.C.D.C.: see Australian Commercial Dairy Cow

Aceh (N. Sumatra, Indonesia); z; local var; not *Acheen, Acheh, Achin, Achinese*

Acheen, Acheh: see Aceh

Achham (W. Nepal); z; dwarf; light brown; ♂ hd, ♀ hd or pd; syn.

14

Sanogai. [= small cow]
Achin, Achinese: see Aceh
Acreno: see Carreña
Adal, Adali: see Danakil
Adamawa (N. Cameroon and N.E. Nigeria); m.d.dr; West African Zebu
type; usu. red or pied; syn. *Adamawa Fulani, Adamawa Gudali.*
Cameroons Fulani, Cameroons Gudali; vars: Banyo (with Red Bororo
blood), N'Gaoundéré (typical) and [Yola] (with Muturu blood); not
Adamaoua
Adar: see Azaouak
Aden (S. Red Sea coast); d.m; z; usu. chestnut, also pied; syn. (Eritrea)
Arab, Bahari, Berbera; *cf.* North Somali
Adige: see Grey Adige
Afghan (Afghanistan); z; syn. *Kabuli*; vars: Kandahari, Konari, Shakhan-
surri
[African aurochs] (N. Africa) = *Bos primigenius opisthonomus* Pomel;
var. of aurochs; syn. *B.p. hahni* Hilzheimer, *African urus*; ? orig. of
Hamitic Longhorn
Africander (S. Africa); m.dr; Sanga type; usu. red; long lateral horns;
orig. from Hottentot in 18th and 19th c; HB 1907, BS 1912;
Afrik. *Afrikaner*; orig. of Bonsmara (with Shorthorn and Hereford),
Drakensberger (with Friesian); not *Africaner, Afrikander*; BS also in
Australia 1969.
Africangus (Jeanerette, Louisiana, USA); m; orig. 1953-63 from
Africander (30%) × Aberdeen-Angus (70%)
African Zebu: see East African Zebu, Sanga, West African Zebu
AFS: see Australian Friesian Sahiwal
Agerolese (Agerola, nr. Sorrento, Campania, Italy); d; local var. orig.
in 19th c. from Italian Brown, Jersey, Friesian, Podolian, *et al.*;
chestnut to almost black, with pale dorsal stripe; rare, by crossing
earlier with Italian Brown and later with Friesian
ago: see galiba
ah gohr: see galiba
A.I.S.: see Illawarra
Akamba: see Kamba
Akele-Guzai: see Aradó
Akou: see White Fulani
Akshi (Syria): see Baladi
Alambadi (W. and N.W. Tamil Nadu, India); dr; z; Mysore type; grey;
syn. *Bestal, Cauvery, Kaveri, Lambadi* (Hyderabad), *Mahadeswarabetta, Malai-madu, Salem*; not *Alambady, Alambudi, Alumbadi*
Ala-Tau (S.E. Kazakhstan and N.E. Kirgizia, USSR); d.m; usu. brown;
orig. 1929-40, esp. at stud farm Alamedin, from Swiss Brown and

Kostroma, × Kirgiz (also some Friesian, Simmental and Aulie-Ata blood), recog. 1950; HB; Russ. *Alatauskaya*

[Alb] (Württemberg, Germany); absorbed by German Simmental

Albanian (Albania); dr.d; Iberian (*i.e. brachyceros*) type; sim. to Buša (Yugoslavia) and Greek Shorthorn; yellow to reddish-black; syn. *Illyrian* (inc. Buša); vars. inc. Albanian Dwarf and Shkodra Red

Albanian Dwarf; var. of Albanian; syn. *Illyrian Dwarf*

Alberes (Alberes mts, E. Pyrenees, France/Spain); semi-feral; Fr. *Massanaise* (R. Massane); rare

Albese (Alba, Cuneo); double-muscled var. of Piedmont

Alderney: see Channel Island

Alentejana (Alentejo, Portugal); m.dr; sim. to Retinta (Spain); golden red; long horns; HB 1973; syn. *Transtagana*; var: [Algarvia]; ? orig. of Southern Crioulo (Brazil) and of Mértolenga; not *Alemtejo*. [= S. of Tagus]

Aleppo: see Damascus

[Algarvia] (Algarve, S. Portugal); var. of Alentejana; extinct 1970s by crossing with Limousin

Algerian: see Guelma type and Oran var. of Brown Atlas

Aliab Dinka (S.E. of S. Sudan); local var. of Nilotic

Alistana-Sanabresa (Aliste and Sanabria, N.W. Zamora, Spain); m.dr; Morenas del Noroeste group; chestnut; var: Berciana (León)

Allgäu, Allgäuer: see German Brown; not *Algau*

[Almanzoreña] (R. Almanzora, Almeria); former var. of Murcian

Alpenfleckvieh: see Bergscheck, Simmental

Alpine: see Austrian Yellow, Brown Mountain, Grey Mountain, Pinzgauer, Simmental

[Alsatian Simmental] (Alsace, France); d.m.dr; orig. from Swiss Simmental; HB fused with Pie rouge de l'Est 1945; Fr. *Simmenthal d'Alsace*

[Altai]; m. or m.d; var. of Siberian; Russ. *Altaĭskaya*; syn. *South Siberian*

Alumbadi: see Alambadi

Alur (W. of L. Mobutu, N.E. Zaïre); Sanga-Zebu intermediate; usu. red, also red pied or black; orig. from Bahima × Lugware; syn. *Blukwa* (name of a chief), *Nioka*

Amabowe: see Mangwato

Amanjanja: see Mashona

Ambo: sing. of Ovambo

American Angus (USA); var. of Aberdeen-Angus first imported 1873; BS 1883, HB 1886; var: Red Angus (BS 1954)

American Beef Friesian (Colorado, USA); d.m; var. of Friesian; orig. from British Friesian imported from Ireland; BS 1972

American Brahman: see Brahman

American Breed (New Mexico, USA); m; orig. 1948-74 by Art Jones,

Cactus Road, Portales; $\frac{1}{2}$ Brahman, $\frac{1}{4}$ Charolais, $\frac{1}{8}$ bison, $\frac{1}{16}$ Hereford, $\frac{1}{16}$ Shorthorn

American Brown Swiss (USA); d.(m); orig from *c.* 155 Swiss Brown imported 1869-1906; BS 1880, HB 1889; syn. *Brown Swiss*; BS also in Canada 1914, UK

American Dairy Cattle (USA); d; BS 1936 to register dairy cattle with performance criteria only

American Friesian: see Holstein

American Lineback (USA); colour type; HB; vars: 1. American "G": dark mahogany to black with white back-line, tail and belly, ? Glamorgan or Gloucester blood; 2. coloursided, red or black with speckled face and white back-line, belly and lower legs, ? Witrik or Longhorn blood; BS 1985; rare

American White Park (USA); m; white with black points (occ. red); pd (occ. hd); orig from British White imported 1941 and 1976-84, ? with some White Park blood; BS 1975, replaced 1988 by British White and White Park BSs; rare

Amritmahal (Karnataka, India); dr; z; Mysore type; grey with lighter markings on face and dewlap; orig. in 17th c. from Hallikar; former vars: (up to 1860) Chitaldrug, Hagalvadi, Hallikar; not *Amrat Mahal, Amrit mahal, Amrit-mahal.* [= nectar department, *i.e.* government dairy]

AMZ: see Australian Milking Zebu

Anatolian (Syria): see Baladi

Anatolian Black (C. Anatolia, Turkey); d.dr.m; *brachyceros* type; usu. black; Turk. *Anadolu Yerli Kara* (= *Anatolian Native Black*)

Anatolian native (Turkey): see Anatolian Black, East Anatolian Red, South Anatolian Red

Ancient Cattle of Wales (Wales); inc. coloured vars of Welsh Black *viz.* Belted, White, Linebacked, Blue, Red and Smoky/Mouse-coloured; BS 1981; Welsh *Gwartheg Hynafol Cymru*; syn. *Coloured Cattle of Wales*; rare

Ancient Egyptian: see Hamitic Longhorn

Andalusian: see Andalusian Black, Andalusian Blond, Andalusian Grey, Berrendas, Retinta; ? orig. of Criollo (S. America) and Texas Longhorn (USA)

Andalusian Black (W. Andalucía, Spain); m.(dr); sim. to Black Iberian; black or black-brown; Sp. *Negra andaluza*; syn. *Negra campiñesa, Negra de las Campiñas andaluzas*

Andalusian Blond (Huelva, S.W. Spain); m.(dr); yellow to corn-coloured; Sp. *Rubia andaluza*; syn. *Blond Extremadura* (Sp. *Extremeña rubia*); now var. of and being absorbed by Retinta; *cf.* Alentejana (Portugal)

Andalusian Grey (Córdoba and Huelva, Spain); m; colour var. of

Andalusian; Sp. *Cárdena andaluza*; rare

Andalusian Red: see Retinta

Andaluz (Colombia): see Costeño con Cuernos

Angeln (E. Schleswig, Germany); d; Baltic Red type, sim. to Danish Red; linked to German Red since 1942; BS 1879, HB 1885; Ger. *Angler*; syn. *Red Angeln (Angler Rotvieh)*; HB also in USSR

Anglesea, Anglesey: see North Wales Black

Angola: see Barotse, Barra do Cuanzo, Humbi, Ovambo, Porto Amboim

[Angola] (Sertão, N.E. Brazil); ? orig. from (African ?) zebu × Curraleiro in 19th c; coloursided, dark red, brown or black

Angoni (W. and S. of L. Malawi, S.E. Africa); m.d.dr; East African Shorthorned Zebu type; many colours; syn. *Ngoni*; vars: Malawi Zebu, Mozambique Angoni, Zambia Angoni; not *Angone*

Angus: see Aberdeen-Angus, American Angus

[Angus Doddie, N.E. Scotland]; orig. (+ Buchan Humlie) of Aberdeen-Angus. [doddie = pd]

Anjou: see Maine-Anjou

Ankole (L. Mobutu to L. Tanganyika, E. Africa); Sanga type; often red, also fawn, black or pied; syn. *Ankole Longhorn*; vars: Bahima, Bashi, Kigezi, Watusi; not *Ancholi, Ankoli*

Annamese, Annamite: see Vietnamese

[Ansbach-Triesdorfer] (Middle Franconia, Bavaria, Germany); d.m.dr; orig. from East Friesian and Simmental × local; extinct *c.* 1940

Antakli, Antakya: see Lebanese

Antioqueña, Antioquia: see Blanco Orejinegro

Anuak: see Abigar

Aosta (N.W. Italy); d.(m); BSd 1937, HB 1958; syn. *Val d'Aosta*; see Black Pied, Chestnut, Oropa, Red Pied

Aosta Black Pied; var. of Aosta; It. *Valdostana pezzata nera*, Fr. *Valdotaine pie-noire*; declining by spread of Aosta Chestnut

Aosta Chestnut; var. of Aosta; ? orig. from Hérens × Aosta Black Pied; HB 1983; It. *Valdostana castana*, Fr. *Valdotaine chataignée*

Aosta Red Pied; chief var. of Aosta; white and red or yellowish-red, with white head; It. *Valdostana pezzata rossa*, Fr. *Valdotaine pie-rouge*

Apulian Podolian (Apulia, Basilicata and Calabria, Italy); m.[dr]; Podolian type; grey; BS and HB 1931; It. *Podolica* or *Podolica pugliese*; former vars: Abruzzese, Calabrian, Lucanian, Murgese, Venetian

Aquitaine Blond: see Blonde d'Aquitaine

Arab (Israel): see Baladi

Arab (S. Red Sea coast): see Aden

Arab (Sudan): see North Sudan Zebu

Arab (W. Africa): see Azaouak (Niger), Maure (Mauritania) or Shuwa (Chad)

Arabi (Iran): see Nejdi

Arabian (Egypt): see Maryuti

Aracena (Ribatejo, Portugal); m; black with white back, tail and belly; rare

Aradó (highlands of Eritrea, Ethiopia); dr.m; Sanga-Zebu intermediate; usu. shades of red, often red pied or black pied, occ. black, brown, grey or white; small muscular hump; local names: *Akele Guzai, Asaorta* (It. *Assaortina*), *Bileri* (Keren), *Tigray* or *Tigré* (N. Ethiopia)

Archangel: see Kholmogory

Ardebili: see Sarabi

Argentine Criollo (N. Argentina); m.dr; sim. to Southern Crioulo (Brazil); lyre horns; BS; vars: large *Chaqueño* (Chaco), medium *serrano* (S.E. Salta) and small *fronterizo* (5 N. provinces)

Argentine Friesian (Argentina); d.(m); Sp. *Holando-Argentino*; syn. *Dutch Argentine*

Aria: see Gasara

Armorican (N. Brittany, France); d.m; sim. to Maine-Anjou but smaller; usu. red, also red-and-white or roan; orig. from Shorthorn (imported 1840-1914 and 1951-53) × local Breton; HB 1919-66, named 1923; Fr. *Armoricain*; combined with Maine-Anjou 1962-70 under name Rouge de l'Ouest; crossed (1966 on) with Meuse-Rhine-Yssel and German Red Pied to form (together with the 3 pure breeds) the Pie Rouge des Plaines (1970); purebred nearly extinct

Arouquesa (Arouca, N. Beira, Portugal); m.dr.(d); light to dark chestnut; ? orig. from Barrosã, Mirandesa, Minhota *et al.*; not *Aroucesa*

Arsi (C. Ethiopia); z; developed from Abyssinian Shorthorned Zebu; usu. red, also white or light grey, with black spots on side; syn. *Arusi, Arussi*; not *Arssi*

Artón del Valle: see Hartón

Arusi, Arussi: see Arsi

Arvi: see Gaolao

Asaorta: see Aradó

Asiago: see Burlina

Astrakhan; see Kalmyk

Asturian (Oviedo, N. Spain); m.(dr.d); North Spanish type; shades of red with paler extremities; HB 1933; Sp. *Asturiana*; larger Carreña (lowland) and smaller Casina (mountain) vars.

Atacora, Atakora: see Somba

Atlas: see Brown Atlas

Atpadi Mahal; var. of Khillari; syn. *Hanam* (= *south*)

Aubrac (Aveyron-Lozère, France); m.[dr.d]; fawn to brown; BS and HB 1914; syn. *Laguiole*

Aulie-Ata (S. Kazakhstan and N. Kirgizia, USSR); d; usu. black with white markings on underside, occ. grey; orig. (1885-1912 and 1926 on) from Friesian × Kazakh; HB 1935; recog. 1950; Russ. *Auliéatinskaya* or *Auliatinskaya*

Aure et Saint-Girons (S. Haute Garonne, S. France); chestnut; syn. *Aurois, Casta, Central Pyrenean* (Fr. *Race des Pyrénées centrales*), *Race de St Girons et d'Aure*; almost extinct

[aurochs] = *Bos (Bos) primigenius* Bojanus; dark brown to black; forward lyre horns; Ger. *Ur*, Latin *urus*, Hebrew *reem, rimu*; syn. *wild ox*; vars: *B.p. primigenius* (Europe), *B.p. opisthonomus* (N. Africa), *B.p. namadicus* (Asia); orig. of domestic cattle; extinct 1627 (Poland); not *European bison*. [Ger.]

Australian Braford (N. Queensland, Australia); m; white face; hd or pd; orig. 1946-52 from Brahman ($\frac{1}{2}$) × Hereford ($\frac{1}{2}$); HB 1956, BS 1962; *cf.* Braford (USA)

Australian Brangus (Queensland, Australia); m; black; pd; orig. 1950-60 from Brahman ($\frac{3}{8}$) × Aberdeen-Angus ($\frac{5}{8}$); HB 1956, BS 1961; *cf.* Brangus (USA)

Australian Charbray (N. Australia); m; white to light red; orig. 1970s from Charolais ($\frac{1}{4}-\frac{3}{4}$) × Brahman ($\frac{3}{4}-\frac{1}{4}$): BS 1977; *cf.* Charbray (USA)

Australian Commercial Dairy Cow (Australia); d; BS (? 1985) breeding from superior animals regardless of breed; syn. *A.C.D.C.*

Australian Friesian Sahiwal (N. Queensland, Australia); d; black to red or pied, sometimes brindle; orig. 1961 on by selection for tick resistance, milk let-down and milk yield from F_2 and F_3 of Sahiwal × Friesian cross at Ayr and Kairi Research Stas; HB 1983, BS 1987; syn. *AFS*

Australian Grey (Australia); BS 1979 to register both pedigree and off-type Murray Grey and Tasmanian Grey

Australian Illawarra Shorthorn: see Illawarra

Australian Milking Zebu (N. of NSW, Australia): d; Jersey colours; orig. since mid 1950s from Sahiwal and Red Sindhi × Jersey; F_3 selected for milk yield, heat tolerance and tick resistance; recog. 1973; BS; syn. *AMZ*

Australian Sahiwal (Queensland, Australia); d; orig. from 10 Sahiwals imported 1954 used to grade Shorthorn, Devon and Jersey to at least $\frac{7}{8}$ Sahiwal; BS 1975

Australian Shorthorn (N. Territory and N.W. Australia); m; var. of Beef Shorthorn which has become naturally adapted to tropical N; syn. *Kimberley Shorthorn, North Australian Shorthorn, Northern Territory Shorthorn*

Australian White (Australia); m; pd; orig. from 3 British White heifers imported 1958 in calf to White Galloway, and purebreds imported 1984; BS 1983

[Austrian Blond] (Carinthia and Styria, Austria); d.m.dr; nearly white; Ger. *Blondvieh*; syn. *Carinthian Blond* (Ger. *Kärntner Blondvieh*), *Lavanttal* (Carinthia), *Mariahof* (Styria), *Mariahofer-Lavanttaler*, *Plava* (Yugoslavia), *Styrian Blond* (Ger. *Steierisches Blondvieh*); inc. in Austrian Yellow *c*. 1960; see also Slovenian White

Austrian Brown (W. Austria); d.m.[dr]; Brown Mountain type; BS and HB; Ger. *Österreichisches Braunvieh*; former vars: Montafon (Vorarlberg), Styrian Brown, and Tyrol Brown

Austrian Simmental (Austria); d.m.[dr]; orig. (1830 on) from (Swiss) Simmental and German Simmental × local (*e.g.* Bergscheck); BS and HB; Ger. *Österreichisches Fleckvieh* (= *Austrian Spotted cattle*); former vars: Danube, East Styrian Spotted, Innviertel, and Tyrol Spotted; see also Bergscheck

Austrian Yellow (C. Austria); d.m; white or yellow; orig. *c*. 1960 from Austrian Blond + Murboden + Waldviertel; [BS and HB]; Ger. Österreichisches Gelbvieh; syn. *Light* (or *Pale*) *Alpine* (Ger. *Lichtes Alpenvieh*), *Light Mountain* (Ger. *Lichtes Höhenvieh*), *Pale Highland*; nearly extinct

Avai: see Ethiopian Boran

Avétonou (Togo); orig. at Avétonou Research Centre; 50% N'Dama, 25% "local", 25% Yellow Franconian

Avileña (Avila, C. Spain); dr.m; black; BS 1974; syn. *Barco-Piedrahita, Barqueña* (from Barco), *Black Carpetana, Piedrahitense* (from Piedrahita); joined with Black Iberian (1980) to form Avileña-Black Iberian

Avileña-Black Iberian (C. Spain); m.[dr]; black; orig. 1980 by union of Avileña and Black Iberian; BS; Sp. *Avileña-Negra Iberica*

Awankari: see Dhanni

Aweil Dinka (N.W. of S. Sudan); local var. of Nilotic

Ayrshire (S.W. Scotland); d; red-brown and white; lyre horns; orig. in late 18th and early 19th c. from Teeswater *et al.* × local, Highland blood in 19th c; recog. 1814, BS 1877, HB 1878; obs. syn. *Cunningham, Dunlop*; orig. of Finnish Ayrshire and Swedish Ayrshire; part orig. of Red Trondheim and Norwegian Red-and-White; BS also in USA 1863 (HB1875), Canada 1870, Australia (HB 1892), S. Africa 1916 (HB 1906), New Zealand 1909, Kenya, Zimbabwe, Brazil, Czechoslovakia, Colombia, HB also in USSR; not *Ayr*

Azaouak (E. Mali, W.C. Niger and N.W. Nigeria); pa.d; West African (shorthorned) Zebu, sim. to Shuwa; variable; Hausa *Shanun Adar*, Fulani *Azawa, Azawal* (pl. *Azawaje*); syn. *Arab, Damerghou* or *Tagama* (Niger), *Tuareg*; not *Azawak*

Azawa, Azawaje, Azawak, Azawal: see Azaouak

Azebuado (Brazil); intermediates between zebu and European cattle; syn. *Indu-Europeu, Zeburano*; inc. [Angola], Brazilian Dairy Hybrid,

Canchim, [China], Dairy Indo-European, [Guademar], Ibagé, [Javanês], Lavinia, [Malabar], Mantiqueira, [Nilo], Pitangueiras, Riopardense, Santa Gabriela, [Tatu]

Azerbaijan Brown: see Caucasian Brown

[Azerbaijan Red]; subvar. of Lesser Caucasus var. of Caucasian; Russ. *Krasnaya Azerbaĭdzhanskaya*; crossed with Swiss Brown to form Caucasian Brown

Azerbaijan Zebu (S.E. Azerbaijan, USSR); z; usu. red, black or pied; Russ. *Azerbaĭdzhanskiĭ zebu*; syn. *Caucasian Zebu, Talysh* (Russ. *Talyshinskiĭ*); *cf.* Talishi (Iran)

Azores (Portugal); m.d; orig from Mirandesa and Minhota with exotic blood; Port. *Açoreana*

[Babaev] (Kostroma, USSR); orig. from Allgäu (German Brown) × local; orig. (with Miskov and crossed with Swiss Brown) of Kostroma

Bachaur (N. Bihar, India); dr; z; grey-white shorthorned type; sim. to Hariana; syn. *Sitamarhi*; not *Bachchaur, Bachhaur, Bachur*

Baden Spotted: see Messkircher

Baggara (Darfur and Kordofan, Sudan); pa.d.m; North Sudan Zebu group; often white with red (or black) markings, also grey, red, black, yellow or dun; influenced by Fulani cattle in W. and by Nilotic in S. [*baggar* = cattle]

Baggerbont (Netherlands); colour var. - red or black pied with spotted legs; rare. [= mud-pied]

Bahari (S. Red Sea coast): see Aden

Baharié (W. Africa): see Kuri. [Arabic *bahar* = sea]

Bahima (Kibali-Ituri, N.E. Zaïre and S.W. Uganda); var. of Ankole; syn. *Banyoro* (incorrect), *Nsagalla* (Uganda); not *Bahema, Wahima, Wakuma*

Bahu: see Lugware

Baila (Kafue flood plain, Zambia); var. of Barotse; orig. from Tonga by crossing with Barotse in 20th c. (hence earlier a syn. of Tonga); sing. *Ila*; syn. *Bashukulumpo, Mashuk, Mashukulumbwe*

Bakosi (Bangemo, S.W. Cameroon); var. of West African Savanna Shorthorn; black, brown or pied; syn. *Kosi*; not *Bakossi*; disappearing

Bakwiri (foot of Mt Cameroon, S.W. Cameroon); var. of West African Dwarf Shorthorn; syn. *Muturu*; nearly extinct

Baladi (Lower Egypt); dr; var. of Egyptian; syn. *Beheri*; subvar: Menufi; not *Balladi, Beladi*. [= native]

Baladi (Syria, Lebanon, Israel and Jordan); dr; *brachyceros* type; Jaulan is sim. but larger; brown to black, or pied; 30% pd; small; syn. *Akshi, Anatolian* (Hama), *Arab* (Israel), *Bedouin, Djebeli, Kleiti* (Homs), *Oksh*

(Israel)

Bali cattle (Bali, also in Lombok, Timor, S. Sulawesi, E. Java and S.E. Kalimantan, Indonesia); m.dr; ♂ red turning black, ♀ red; orig. from banteng; syn. *Balinese*; orig. of Cobourg Peninsula cattle (Australia)

Balkan: see Illyrian

[Ballum] (S.W. Jutland, Denmark); red; part orig. of Danish Red; syn. *Slesvig Marsh* (Ger. *Schleswigsche Marschrasse*)

Baltic Black Pied (Baltic States, USSR); d; var. of Russian Black Pied; orig. (1830 on) from East Friesian × local; inc. Estonian and Lithuanian Black Pied; Russ. *Pribaltiĭskaya chernopestraya*

BALTIC RED: see Angeln, Danish Red, Estonian Red, Latvian Brown, [North Slesvig Red]; orig. from *brachyceros* type; orig. of Bulgarian Red, Red Steppe, Romanian Red

Bamangwato: see Mangwato

Bambara (S.W. Mali); m; yellow-brown to red; orig. from N'Dama × zebu (Sudanese Fulani); syn. *Mandé, Méré* (= small, not zebu)

Bambawa (Eritrea-Sudan border); strain of Red Desert cattle sim. to Butana; It. *Bambaua*

Bambey (Senegal); stabilized crossbred ($\frac{13}{16}$ N'Dama $\frac{3}{16}$ Gobra zebu) of Djakoré type bred at Bambey Research Centre since 1921

Bamenda: see N'Gaoundéré

bami (Bhutan): see mithun

Bami (Kerman province, Iran); m; z; yellow to brown, occ. black

[Bamiléké] (S.W. Cameroon); var. of West African Savanna Shorthorn

Bangladeshi: see Bengali

Banioro: see Nyoro

Bannai: see Kankrej

banteng (S.E. Asia) = *Bos (Bibos) javanicus* (d'Alton); brown (♀) or black (adult ♂) with white stockings and rump patch; syn. *B. banteng* Wagner, *B. sondaicus* Schlegel and Müller; vars: tsine (Burma) = *B.j. birmanicus*, Malay banteng (*B.j. butleri*), Borneo banteng (*B.j. lowi*); orig. of Bali cattle; not *bantin, banting*; rare

Bantu: see Sanga

Banyo (Cameroon); var. of Adamawa with Red Bororo blood; red or red pied, often white face and belly

Banyoro (Uganda): see Nyoro; used incorrectly in Zaïre to mean Bahima

Baoulé (Ivory Coast); m; var. of West African Savanna Shorthorn; usu. black pied

Bapedi (Sekhukhuneland, E. Transvaal, S. Africa); var. of Nguni; usu. black with white belly; syn. *Pedi*

Baraka, Barca: see Barka

Barco: see Avileña

[Bardigiana] (Bardi, Parma, W. Emilia, Italy); dr.d.m; var. of Pontremolese; red; subvars: Cornigliese and Valtarese

Bare: see Kuri

Bargur (W. Coimbatore, Tamil Nadu, India); dr; z; Mysore type; usu. red-and-white spotted; not *Barghur, Burgaur, Burghoor, Burgoor, Burgur*

Bari (S. Sudan): see Mongalla

Baria (Cochin-China, S. Vietnam); var. of Vietnamese

Baria (N.W. Madagascar); small hump; ? orig. from zebu × humpless; rare

Barka (W. Eritrea, Ethiopia); d.m; North Sudan Zebu group; usu. white with black spots or splashes, occ. red or coloursided; occ. pd; syn. *Begait*; not *Baraka, Barca*

Barotse (W. Zambia and E. Angola); Sanga type, sim. to Tswana; usu. brown, black, dark red, or fawn; syn. *Lozi, Rowzi, Rozi*; vars: Baila (Kafue flood plain) with Tonga blood, Porto Amboim (Angola); not *Barotsi*

Barqueña: see Avileña

Barra do Cuanzo (W. Angola); m; improved Sanga var; light tan to red

Barrosã (Terra de Barroso, N. Portugal); dr.m; reddish-brown with black legs; wide lyre horns; syn. *Maiana* (from Maia); not *Barroza*

Barroso (Guatemala); m.d; Criollo type; rare and declining. [= dun]

Barzona (C. Arizona, USA); m; usu. red; occ. pd; orig. 1945-68 at Bard-Kirkland Ranch from [American Angus × (Africander × Hereford)] × [Santa Gertrudis × (Africander × Hereford)]; BS 1968. [*Bard Arizona*]

Basco-Béarnais: see Béarnais

Bashi (S. Kivu, E. Zaïre); d.m; var. of Ankole; smaller and with shorter horns; sim. to Kigezi

Bashukulumpo: see Baila

Basque: see Pyrenean Blond (France), Pyrenean (Spain)

Bassanese: see Burlina

Basta: see Canary Island

Basuto (Lesotho); Sanga type; usu. black; often with European blood

Batanes Black (Batan Is, Philippines); small-humped var. of Philippine Native

Batangas (Luzon, Philippines); improved humpless var. of Philippine Native; red, yellow or black; not *Batanges*

Batawana (Ngamiland, N.W. Botswana); var. of Tswana with (formerly) very long horns; syn. *Ndawana, Ngami, Tawana*; not *Batawama, Batwane*

Batusi, Batutsi: see Watusi

[Bavarian Red] (Fichtelgebirge, N. Bavaria, Germany); var. of German

Red; Ger. *Bayerisches Rotvieh*; syn. *Sechsämter*; displaced by German Simmental; extinct *c.* 1940. (Red cattle in Bavaria since 1954 are Danish Red and Angeln)

Bavarian Spotted: see Miesbacher

Bavenda (Sibasa, N.E. Transvaal, S. Africa); Sanga type; sim. to Mashona and Nguni; usu. black or black-and-white, but also many other colours and patterns; sometimes pd; syn. *Sibasa*

Bayaro: see Diali

Bazadais (Gironde-Landes, France); m.[dr]; grey to grey-brown with pink mucosae; HB. [from Bazas]

Béarnais (Béarn, S.W. France); d.m; remnant of Pyrenean Blond not absorbed by Blonde d'Aquitaine; syn. *Basco-Béarnais*; nearly extinct

Bechuana: see Tswana

Bedouin (Syria): see Baladi

Beefalo (California, USA); m; orig. 1960s from $\frac{3}{8}$ bison $\frac{3}{8}$ Charolais $\frac{1}{4}$ Hereford by D.C. Basolo, Tracy; BS; *cf.* cattalo

Beef Devon: see Devon

Beef Friesian: see American Beef Friesian

Beefmaker (Nebraska, USA); m; orig. 1960s by G.A. Boucher from Charolais (*c.* 50%) × Hereford, Angus and Shorthorn, with Brown Swiss and some Brahman blood

Beefmaker ('Wallamumbi', Armidale, NSW, Australia); m; white face; orig. 1973 on from (Simmental × Hereford) × Hereford

Beefmaster (USA); m; often dun, red-brown or pied; hd or pd; orig. (1930 on) at Lasater Ranch (S.W. Texas to 1954, now Colorado) from Hereford ($c.\frac{1}{4}$) Shorthorn ($c.\frac{1}{4}$) and Brahman ($c.\frac{1}{2}$); BS 1961

Beef Shorthorn (N.E. Scotland); m; breed of Shorthorn developed in mid-19th c; HB (Beef section) 1959; syn. *Shorthorn* (overseas), *Scotch* or *Scottish Shorthorn*; obs. syn. *Aberdeenshire Shorthorn*; var: Australian Shorthorn; USA HB 1846, BS 1882, New Zealand HB 1866, BS 1914, Canada HB 1867, BS 1886, Australia HB 1873, BS 1920, Argentina HB 1889, BS 1921, Uruguay, S. Africa BS 1912, HB 1919, USSR HB; rare in GB

Beef Synthetic (Alberta Univ., Canada); m; 37% Aberdeen-Angus, 34% Charolais, 21% Galloway, 5% American Brown Swiss, 3% other breeds

[Beevbilde] (England); b; red; pd; developed in 1960s by E. Pentecost (Notts.) with 65% Lincoln Red, 30% Beef Shorthorn and 5% Aberdeen-Angus

Begait: see Barka

Beheri (Egypt): see Baladi

Beijing Black Pied; var. of Chinese Black and White; orig. from Holstein-Friesian and Japanese Friesian × Pinzhou; syn. *Peking Black-and-White*

Beiroa (Beira, N. Portugal); dr.m.(d); var. of Mirandesa

Beirut: see Lebanese

Beja (N.E. Sudan); ? var. of North Sudan Zebu; grey

Beladi, Bélédie: see Baladi

Belgian Black Pied (Belgium); d; orig. 1966 from Hervé Black Pied + Polders Black Pied; Fr. *Pie-noire de Belgique*, Flem. *Zwartbont ras van België*

Belgian Blue (C. and S. Belgium); m.(d); white, blue pied, or blue; orig. from Shorthorn (1850-90) and Dutch Black Pied (1840-90) × local red or red pied; HB 1919; Fr. *Blanc-bleu belge*, Flem. *Witblauw ras van België* (= *Belgian White-Blue*); syn. (to 1971) *Central and Upper Belgian* (Fr. *Race de la Moyenne et Haute Belgique*, Flem. *Ras van Midden- en Hoog-België*); syn. *Belgian Blue-White, Belgian White and Blue Pied, Blue, Blue Belgian, Central and Upland, Mid-Belgian, White Meuse and Schelde*; cf. Bleu du Nord (France); orig. of Danish Blue-and-White; BS in GB 1983

Belgian Red (W. Flanders, Belgium); d.m; sim. to Flemish (France); Shorthorn blood; HB 1919; Flem. *Rood ras van België*, Fr. *Rouge de Belgique*; syn. *Red Flemish, West Flemish Red* (Flem. *Rood ras van West-Vlaanderen* or *West Vlaamse*, Fr. *Rouge de la Flandre occidentale*)

Belgian Red Pied (N.E. Belgium); d.m; orig. 1838 on and esp. 1878-88 from Meuse-Rhine-Yssel × local, with some Shorthorn blood 1844-51; HB 1919; Fr. *Pie-rouge de Belgique*, Flem. *Roodbont ras van België*; syn. (to 1971) *Campine Red Pied* or *Red and White Campine* (Flem. *Roodbont Kempisch* or *Kempen*, Fr. *Rouge-pie Campinoise* or *Pie-rouge de Campine*); inc. Eastern Red Pied (*Pie rouge de l'Est* or *Pie rouge Ardennes-Liège*)

Belgian White-and-Red (E. Flanders, Belgium); d.m; orig. in 2nd half of 19th c. from Shorthorn and Dutch × local; HB 1900; Flem. *Witrood ras van België*, Fr. *Blanc-rouge de Belgique*; syn. *East Flemish Red Pied* (Flem. *Roodbont ras van Oost-Vlaanderen* or *Oost Vlaamse*, Fr. *Pie-rouge de la Flandre orientale*), *Red and White East Flemish, Red Pied Flemish*

Belgian White and Blue Pied, Belgian White-Blue: see Belgian Blue

Belmont Red (Queensland, Australia); m; orig. 1953-68 at National Cattle Breeding Sta., 'Belmont', Rockhampton from (Africander × Hereford) × (Africander × Shorthorn) selected for fertility, weight gain and tick resistance; BS

belted: see Belted Galloway, belted Swiss Brown, Belted Welsh, [Broadlands], Dutch Belted, Lakenvelder and [Sheeted Somerset]; syn. *beltie, sheeted, white-middled*; belt due to single dominant gene

Belted Galloway (S.W. Scotland and N. England); var. of Galloway; black or dun with dominant white belt; BS 1921 (with Dun Galloway till 1951) HB 1922; syn. *Beltie, Sheeted* or *White-middled Galloway*; HB also registers Red, Red Belted and White (but not Dun) Galloway; BS also in New Zealand 1948, USA 1951, Australia 1975, W. Germany

Belted Welsh (N. Wales); var. of Ancient Cattle of Wales; Welsh *Bolian Gwynion*; syn. *Belted Welsh Black*; rare

Bengali (Bangladesh and Bengal, India); z; small to dwarf; local vars: (Bangladesh) Chittagong Red, Dacca-Faridpur, Kamdhino, Madaripur, Munshigunj, North Bangladesh Grey, Pabna

Berbera: see Aden

Berciana (El Bierzo, N.W. León, Spain); var. of Alistana-Sanabresa; rare

[Bergscheck] (Styria, Austria); d.m.dr; red with white head, forequarters, belly and legs; local breed improved since 1900 by Pinzgauer and Simmental and finally absorbed by Austrian Simmental c. 1950; grade was termed *Alpenfleckvieh*; syn. *Enns, Ennstaler Bergscheck, Ennstaler Schecken, Helmete* (= *(white) helmet*), *Kampete* (= collared, from Ger. *Kummet* = collar, *i.e.* white head), *Mountain Spotted*

Berlin cattle (Berlin zoo, Germany); orig. (1920s) from Corsican, Camargue and Spanish Fighting cattle by Lutz Heck, so-called 'bredback aurochs'; *cf.* Munich cattle

[Bernese] (Switzerland); orig. of Simmental; syn. *Bernese Oberland*

Bernese-Hanna, Berno-Hana: see Moravian Red Pied

Bernsko-český: see Bohemian Red Pied

Bernskohanacký: see Moravian Red Pied

Berrendas (W. Andalucía, Spain); m.dr; used for herding fighting bulls; syn. *Berrenda andaluza, Berrendas españolas*; red-and-white (Berrenda en colorado) and black-and-white (Berrenda en negro) vars; orig. of Guadiana Spotted (Portugal). [= pied]

Berrenda en colorado; white with red head and forequarters; red area occ. roan (*Salinera*); syn. *Berrenda roja andaluza, Capirote* (= hooded). [= red pied]

Berrenda en negro; coloursided with black head and legs (Pinzgauer pattern); syn. *Berrenda negra andaluza.* [= black pied]

[Bessarabian Red]; name used for Red Steppe in Bessarabia 1918-45 when it was part of Romania

Bestal: see Alambadi

Bestuzhev (Kuibyshev, USSR); m.d; red, often with white marks on head, belly and feet; orig. (by S.P. Bestuzhev 1810 on) from Friesian, Simmental, and Shorthorn, × local, with Kholmogory and Oldenburg blood in early 20th c; HB 1928; Russ. *Bestuzhevskaya*

Betizuak (Goizueta, N. Navarre, Spain); feral; dwarf; blond; syn. *Betisoak* (sing. *Bétiso*) (France); nearly extinct. [Basque = wild cattle]
Bettola, Bettolese: see Pontremolese
Beyrouth: see Lebanese
Bhagnari (Kalat, Baluchistan and N. Sind, Pakistan); dr.d; z; grey-white shorthorned type; usu. grey; syn. *Kachhi, Nari*; larger type in Baluchistan and smaller in Sind; var: Dajjal (Punjab); not *Bhag Nari*. [Bhag village and Nari R.]
Białogrzbiety: see Polish Whitebacked
Bianca padana: see Modenese
Bierzo: see Berciana
Bileri: see Aradó
Bimal (Somalia); small var. of Garre; *cf.* Gasara
Binda: see Burlina
[Binga] (N.W. Zimbabwe); dwarf; humpless; long horns
Bionda tortonese: see Montana
Bisre: see Jaulan
[Biu] (Bornu, Nigeria); orig. from Muturu (Shorthorn) × White Fulani zebu; absorbed by zebu
Blaarkop: see Groningen Whiteheaded
Black Africander: see Drakensberger
Black Anatolian: see Anatolian Black
Black-and-White Friesland, Black-and-White Holland: see Dutch Black Pied
Black-and-White Swedish: see Swedish Friesian
black baldy = Hereford × Aberdeen-Angus cross
Black Carpetana: see Avileña
Black-eared White (Colombia): see Blanco Orejinegro
Black Forest (Germany); d.m.[dr]; Ger. *Wäldervieh* (= *forest cattle*); syn. *Gelbscheck* (= *yellow pied*), *Scheckig* (= *pied*), *Small Spotted Hill*; inc. Hinterwald and Vorderwald
Black Highland (Ethiopia): see Abyssinian Shorthorned Zebu
Black Hill Zebu (Nepal): see Nepalese Hill
Black Iberian (mts of C. Spain); dr.m; Sp. *Negra iberica*; syn. *Serrana* (= *mountain*); improved by Avileña and joined with it 1980 to form Avileña-Black Iberian
Black Pied: see Friesian
Black Pied Aosta: see Aosta Black Pied
Black Pied Breton: see Breton Black Pied
Black Pied Danish: see Danish Black Pied
Black Pied Dutch: see Dutch Black Pied
Black Pied East Belgian: see Hervé Black Pied
Black Pied Hervé: see Hervé Black Pied

Black Pied Jutland: see Jutland Black Pied
Black Pied Lowland: see Friesian and esp. German Black Pied
Black Pied Podolian: see Podolian Black Pied
Black Pied Polders: see Polders Black Pied
Black Pied Valdostana: see Aosta Black Pied
Blacksided Trondheim and Nordland (N. Norway); d; sim. to Swedish
  Mountain and North Finnish; white with black (occ. red) side or spots
  on side; pd; HB 1943 (on union of Blacksided Trondheim with
  Nordland breed); Nor. *Sidet trønderfe og nordlandsfe*; syn. *Black
  Trondheim, Coloursided Trondheim and Northland, Nordland, Røros*;
  rare
Black Spotted (Switzerland): see Swiss Black Pied
Black Trondheim: see Blacksided Trondheim and Nordland
Black Welsh: see Welsh Black
Black-White: see Black Pied
Black Zebu (Ethiopia): see Jem-Jem Zebu
Blanca cacereña, Blanca guadianese: see White Cáceres
Blanco Orejinegro (Andes, Colombia); m.d; Criollo type; white with
  black points; BS; syn. *Antioquia* (Sp. *Antioqueño*), *Bon* or *BON*; vars:
  red-eared (Sp. *Blanco orejimono* or *BOM*), blue roan and pied (Sp.
  Azul y Pintado). [= black-eared white]
Blauw and Blauwbont (Netherlands); colour vars—blue roan or blue
  roan and white; rare
Blazed: see White-marked
Bleu du Nord (Canton of Bavai, Nord Département, N. France); d.m;
  blue, blue pied or white; BS 1986; syn. *Blue*; cf. Belgian Blue
Blond: see European Blond and Yellow
Blonde d'Aquitaine (S.W. France); m.[dr]; yellow or yellow-brown; orig.
  1961 from Garonnais + Quercy and then absorbed Pyrenean Blond;
  HB; syn. *Aquitaine Blond*; BS also in Canada, GB 1971, Denmark,
  Australia and New Zealand, USA 1973, Ireland, Belgium
Blonde du Cap Bon: see Cape Bon Blond
Blonde du Sud-Ouest (S.W. France); suggested, but unused, name for
  Blonde d'Aquitaine + Limousin. [= southwestern blond]
Blond Moroccan: see Oulmès Blond
Blond Tortona: see Montana
Blond Zaërs: see Oulmès Blond
Blue (Belgium): see Belgian Blue
Blue (France): see Bleu du Nord
Blue (Netherlands): see Blauw and Blauwbont
[Blue Albion] (N. Derbyshire, England); d.m; blue roan or blue roan
  and white; orig. from white Shorthorn × Welsh Black and possibly
  Friesian; HB 1920-40, BS 1920-66; syn. *Blue English*; current 'Blue

Albions' probably crosses
Blue Grey (Great Britain); Whitebred Shorthorn or white Beef Shorthorn
 × Galloway, 1st cross
Blue Macedonian: see Macedonian Blue
Blue Nile: see Kenana
Blukwa: see Alur
Boccarda: see Burlina
Bodadi: see Red Bororo
Boenca: see N'Dama
[Bohemian Red] (Czechoslovakia); d.m.dr; Central European Red type;
   Cz. *České červinky*; larger var: Cheb (Cz. *Chebský*, Ger. *Egerländer*)
[Bohemian Red Pied]; former var. of Czech Pied; Cz. *Česky červenostrak-
   atý*; syn. *Bohemian Berne* (Cz. *Bernsko-Český*), *Bohemian-Simmental,
   Bohemian Red Spotted*
Bokoloji: see Sokoto Gudali
Bolivian Criollo (Bolivia); m.dr.(d); selected for milk at 2 herds in E.
   lowlands; see also Chaqueño, Chusco, Yacumeño
[Bolowana] (Transkei, Cape Prov., S. Africa); Sanga type; sacred herd
   of Chief Ngubezulu in Bomvanaland; syn. *Izankayi*; now graded to
   Africander; *cf.* Ondongolo
BOM: see red-eared var. (*Blanco orejimono*) of Blanco Orejinegro
BON or *Bon*: see Blanco Orejinegro
Bonsmara (Transvaal, S. Africa); m; red; orig. 1936-55 at *Mara* Cattle
   Res. Sta. by J.C. *Bonsma* from Africander ($\frac{5}{8}$), Shorthorn ($\frac{3}{16}$) and
   Hereford ($\frac{3}{16}$); BS 1964
[Bonyhádi] (County Tolna, Hungary); d; former var. of Hungarian Pied;
   not *Bonyhád*
Boran (N. Kenya, S. Ethiopia, S.W. Somalia); m; East African Shorthorn-
   ed Zebu type; usu. white or grey, also red or pied; vars: Ethiopian
   (orig.) and Kenya (improved); not *Borana, Boram, Borena*
[Bordelais] (S.W. France); d; Dutch and Breton blood; black, with white-
   speckled body; extinct in late 1960s, replaced by Friesian. [from
   Bordeaux]
Borgou (N. Benin); usu. white, often with black points, sometimes with
   black spots or black-and-white or coloursided; orig. from humpless
   (Somba or Muturu) × zebu (White Fulani); syn. *Borgawa, Borgu*; =
   Keteku (Nigeria)
Borneo banteng (Sabah and Kalimantan) = *Bos (bibos) javanicus lowi*
   (Lydekker); var of banteng
Borneo Zebu (Kalimantan, Indonesia); vars: Kabota, Kaningan
Boro, Bororodji: see Red Bororo
Bororo, Red: see Red Bororo
Bororo, White: see White Fulani

Borrié: see Kuri
Borroro: see Red Bororo
Bosnian: see Buša
Botswana beef synthetic; m; orig. from Tswana, Tuli, Brahman, Bonsmara and Simmental; 48% Sanga, 23% zebu, 29% European
Boudouma: see Kuri
Boyenca: see N'Dama
Boz Step: see Turkish Grey Steppe
BRACHYCEROS (Europe); *i.e.* derivative of *Bos tauros brachyceros* (Adametz); usu. red, brown, or black; short horns, deep forehead, small; syn. *Celtic Red*; inc. Central European Red, Iberian, *et al.*
Braford (southern USA); m; white face; Brahman × Hereford, F_1 or later; BS 1969; syn. *Herebu* (Argentina); not *Bradford*; see also Australian Braford
Bragado do Sorraia (Ribatejo, Portugal); dr.m; var. of Mértolenga; red with spots inside legs (= *bragado*); ? orig. from Fighting bull × Alentejana; syn. *Charnequeira* (from *charneca* = heath)
Bragança (N.E. Portugal); dr.m; var. of Mirandesa
Brahaza: see Red Bororo
Brahman (S. of USA); z; usu. silver grey; orig. from Ongole, Krankrej, Gir, and Krishna Valley breeds imported from India 1854-1906, and from Brazil 1924-25 and 1946, possibly with some European blood; BS 1924; syn. American Brahman; not *Brama*; BS also Australia, S. Africa 1958 (HB 1967), Argentina 1954; see also Jamaica Brahman
Brahmental: see Simbrah
Brahmin (India); z; sacred free-roaming bull; syn. *Sandhe* (Nepal)
Brahorn (Texas and Louisiana, USA); m; Brahman × Shorthorn, 1st cross
Brandrood IJsselvee (Netherlands); dark red var. of Meuse-Rhine-Yssel; syn. *Brandrod*; rare
Brangus (Texas and Oklahoma, USA); m; black; pd; orig. from Brahman ($c.\frac{3}{8}$) × Aberdeen-Angus ($c.\frac{5}{8}$); crossing started Jeanerette, Louisiana in 1932; BS 1949; var: Red Brangus; see also Australian Brangus; BS also in New Zealand
Bra-Swiss (Texas, USA); m; Brahman × Brown Swiss cross
Braunesgebirgsvieh, Braunvieh: see Brown Mountain
bravo (Spain): see Fighting bull
Bravon (Florida, USA); m; Brahman × Devon cross
Brazilian Dairy Hybrid (Minas Gerais, São Paulo and Rio de Janeiro, Brazil); d; open population, orig. from European (mainly Holstein but also Brown Swiss, Caracú, Danish Red) × zebu (mainly Guzerá and Gir) based on National Dairy Cattle Research Centre, Coronel Pacheco, Minas Gerais; Port. *Mestiço leiteiro brasileiro*

Brazilian Gir (Brazil); m.d; z; red, white or spotted; orig. from Gir
imported from India 1918-62; HB 1936; vars: Dairy Gir, Polled Gir;
not *Gyr*

Brazilian Polled (Goiás, Brazil); m; red; ? orig. from Southern Crioulo;
recog. 1911; HB and BS 1939; Port. *Mocha nacional*; nearly extinct

Brazilian Zebu: see Dairy Zebu, Brazilian Gir, Guzerá, Indo-Brazilian,
Nelore, Polled Zebu; BS

bree: see yak ♀

[Breitenburger]; orig. var. of Red Pied Schleswig-Holstein

[Bressane] (Ain, E. France); yellow; absorbed in Pie rouge de l'Est in
early 20th c; not *Bressanne*. [from Brèsse]

Breton Black Pied (S. Brittany, France); d; BS, HB 1919; Fr. *Breton pie-
noir*; syn. *Breton, Brittany Black and White, Morbihan* (Fr. *Morbihannais*); rare

bri: see yak ♀

British-Canadian Holstein-Friesian: see British Holstein

British Dane (England); d; red; hd or pd; orig. from Danish Red imported
1961 and used to grade Red Poll; named 1967; BS; not *British Red*

British Friesian (Great Britain); d.m; orig. from imports (chiefly Dutch)
1860-92 and 1914-50; BS 1909, HB 1912; vars: Poll Friesian, Red and
White Friesian; orig. of American Beef Friesian

British Holstein (England); d; BS 1946 to register Holstein cattle first
imported from Canada 1944-48; obs. syn. *British-Canadian Holstein-
Friesian*

British Polled Hereford (England); pd var. of Hereford from Galloway
cross; BS 1949

British White (Great Britain); m.d; white with black (occ. red) points;
pd only (since 1946); ? orig. from White Park; some white Shorthorn
and white Galloway blood in 1930s; Swedish Mountain blood 1949;
BS 1918; syn. *Park* (1918-46), *White Polled*; orig. of American White
Park, Australian White; rare

Brittany Black and White: see Breton Black Pied

[Broadlands] (England); belted; imported from the Netherlands to Moor
Park, Sheen, Richmond, by Sir William Temple; extinct 1934

BROWN (MOUNTAIN) (Alps); d.m.(dr); grey-brown; BS 1963 (Association
of Breeders of Brown Mountain Cattle); Ger. *Braunvieh* (= *Brown
cattle*), Fr. *Brune des Alpes*, It. *Bruna alpina* (= *Brown Alpine*); syn.
Brown Swiss, Grey-Brown Mountain (Ger. *Graubraunes Höhenvieh*);
inc. Swiss Brown, Austrian Brown, German Brown and their derivatives, *viz.* American Brown Swiss, Bulgarian Brown, French Brown,
Hungarian Brown, Italian Brown, Romanian Brown, Russian Brown,
Sardinian Brown, Slovenian Brown, South African Brown Swiss,
Spanish Brown, Turkish Brown; BS also in Brazil 1938, New Zealand

Brown Alpine: see French Brown, Italian Brown

Brown Atlas (Maghreb, North Africa); dr.d.m; Iberian type, sim. to Libyan; Fr. *Brune de l'Atlas*; formerly divided into Guelma and Moroccan, each with vars; pure only in mountains

Brown Finnish: see West Finnish

Brown Karacabey: see Karacabey Brown

Brown Moroccan: see Moroccan Brown

Brownsind (Allahabad, India); d; $\frac{3}{8}$ - $\frac{5}{8}$ Brown Swiss; orig. at Allahabad Agric. Institute 1960s from American Brown Swiss × Red Sindhi; not *Brown Sind*

Brown Swiss (USA): see American Brown Swiss

Bruna alpina, Brune des Alpes: see Brown Mountain, esp. Italian Brown and French Brown

Bruno-sarda: see Sardinian Brown

Bruxo: see Southern Crioulo

[Buchan Humlie] (N.E. Scotland); orig. (+ Angus Doddie) of Aberdeen-Angus; syn. *Polled Aberdeenshire*. [humlie = pd]

[Bucşan] (E. Romania]; former var. of Romanian Steppe, sim. to Moldavian but darker and smaller; Ger. *Bukschaner*; not *Boucsan, Bukshan*

Budduma: see Kuri

Budějovice, Budějovický: see Šumava

Buduma, Budumu: see Kuri

Budweiser: see Šumava

Bukedi: see Nkedi

Bukschaner, Bukshan: see Bucşan

Bulgarian Brown (S.W. Bulgaria); d.m; orig. from native graded to Montafon (first imported 1894), recog. 1951; Bulg. *B"lgarska kafyava*; syn. *Sofia Brown* (to 1963) (Bulg. *Sofiĭska kafyava*, Ger. *Sofioter Braunvieh*)

Bulgarian Grey: see Iskar

Bulgarian Red (N.E. and S. Bulgaria); d.m; orig. 1950-60 from Swiss Brown, Bulgarian Brown and Bulgarian Simmental, × Iskar, Red Sadovo and Red Steppe, with Latvian Brown, Red Sadovo and esp. Danish Red bulls since 1954; Bulg. *B"lgarsko cherveno govedo*, Ger. *Bulgarisches Rotvieh*

Bulgarian Simmental (N.W. Bulgaria); d.m.[dr]; usu. cream and white; orig. 1948 on from Simmental (first imported 1894) × Iskar; Bulg. *B"lgarska simentalska*; syn. (to 1969) *Kula* (Bulg. *Kulska*, Ger. *Kulaer*)

Bulgarian Steppe: see Iskar

Bunaji: see White Fulani

Bunyoro (Uganda): see Nyoro

Burgaur, Burghur, Burgoor, Burgur: see Bargur

Burlina (Mt Grappa, Treviso-Vicenza, Venetia, Italy); d.(m); black pied; syn. *Asiago, Bassanese, Binda, Boccarda, Pezzata degli altipiani* (= *Pied Highland*); rare, by crossing with Friesian

Burmese (Burma); dr; z; usu. red (*nwar shwemi*) or yellow (*nwar shwewar*); crossbreds with Hariana and Tharparkar are *nwar pyiase* (usu. white)

Burmese banteng: see tsine

Burmese bison: see Burmese gaur

Burmese gaur (Assam, Burma, Thailand, Laos, Kampuchea and Vietnam) = *Bos (Bibos) gaurus readei* (Lydekker); var. of gaur; Burmese *pyaung, pyun*; syn. *Burmese bison*

Burundi: see Watusi var. of Ankole; not *Barundi*

Burwash (Burwash Industrial Farm, N. Ontario, Canada); m; orig. 1957 on from Charolais × Hereford and other breeds; one group is $\frac{1}{2}$ Charolais $\frac{1}{4}$ Hereford $\frac{1}{4}$ Shorthorn

Buša (S. of R. Sava, Yugoslavia); Iberian type; sim. to Albanian, Greek Shorthorn and Rodopi (Bulgaria); red, black, grey or brown; syn. *Bosnian, Illyrian* (inc. Albanian); vars: Croatian Red, Lim, Macedonian Blue, Metohija Red, Pešter; orig. (with Yugoslav Steppe) of Kolubara and Spreča, and (with Tyrol Grey) of Gacko; not *Busa, Buscha, Busha*

Bushuev (Uzbekistan, USSR); d.m; white with black points; small hump in ♂; orig. from Friesian and Swiss Brown, × local zebu (1907-23) with further Swiss Brown blood (1923-31), and Simmental and East Friesian blood (1932-48) by M.M. Bushuev; recog. 1967; Russ. *Bushuevskaya*; syn. *Tashkent* (Russ. *Pritashkentskaya*)

Butana (between R. Atbara and Nile, Sudan); d.dr; North Sudan Zebu group; usu. dark red, also light red; related strains of Red Desert cattle are Bambawa, Dongola, and Shendi; syn. *Red Butana*; not *Butane, Butanne*

Byelorussian Red (USSR); d; Central European Red type; improved by Angeln and German Red (late 19th and early 20th c.), Polish Red and Danish Red (1920s and 30s), Estonian Red and Latvian Brown (1950s), and Danish Red (1980s); HB 1967; Russ. *Krasnaya belorusskaya* or *Krasnobelorusskaya*; syn. *Red White-Russian, White-Russian Red*

Cabannina (Cabanne, Genoa, Italy); d.(m); brown with pale dorsal stripe; rare, by crossing with Italian Brown

Cabella, Cabellota: see Montana

Cáceres: see White Cáceres

Cachena (Entrino, S. Orense, Galicia, Spain); semi-wild; sim. to Barrosã; dwarf; light blond; long horns; rare. [= very small]

Caiuá (Matto Grosso, Brazil) = Chianina × Nelore cross at Caiuá farm of Liquifarm

Calabrian; former var. of Apulian Podolian; It. *Calabrese*; syn. *Cotrone, Crotone* (It. *Crotonese*)

[Calasparreña] (Calasparra, N.E. Murcia, Spain); former var. of Murcian

Caldeano (S. Minas Gerais, Brazil); d; var. of Caracú; light red; selected (1895 on) by Dias family at Fazenda 'Recreio', Poços de Caldas (Minas Gerais); HB and BS 1960; syn. *Caracú caldeano*

Caldelana (Castro Caldelas, N. Orense, Spain); m.dr; Morenas del Noroeste group; black

Calvana (Calvana mts, Florence, Italy); small var. of Chianina; nearly extinct

[Camandona] (Piedmont, Italy); local var. absorbed by Italian Brown

Camargue (Rhône delta, France); half wild, used for bull fights; black or brown; rare and local

Cambodian (Kampuchea); small hump; Fr. *Cambodgien*

Cambodian wild ox: see kou-prey

Cameroon Fulani, Cameroon Gudali: see Adamawa

Campine Red Pied: see Belgian Red Pied

[Campurriana] (Campóo, W. Santander, Spain); larger, valley var. of Santander; absorbed by Swiss Brown and Tudanca in 1940s

Canadian (Quebec, Canada); d; usu. black to dark brown (born brown); orig. from 16th and 17th c. imports from Normandy and Brittany; Brown Swiss blood (up to $\frac{1}{8}$) in 1980s; BS 1895, HB 1896; Fr. *Canadien*; syn. *Black Jersey, Black Canadian, French Canadian* (till 1930), *Quebec Jersey*

Canadian Friesian: see Holstein

Canary Island (Gran Canaria, Spain); m.d.dr; reddish; ? orig. from Galician Blond; Sp. *Canaria*; syn. *Basta, Criolla, de la Tierra*

Canchim (São Paulo, Brazil); m; $\frac{5}{8}$ Charolais $\frac{3}{8}$ zebu (Indo-Brazilian); orig. (1940 on) at Government Breeding Farm at São Carlos (formerly Canchim farm); cream or white; small hump in $\male$; BS and HB 1971; not *Canchin*

Cape (Sri Lanka): see Hatton

Cape Bon Blond (Tunisia); Fr. *Blonde du Cap Bon*

Capirote: see Berrenda en colorado

Caracú (R. Pardo valley, Minas Gerais and São Paulo, Brazil); m.d.dr; usu. yellow; long horns; orig. from Southern Crioulo; recog. 1909, BS and HB 1916; var: Caldeano. [? from Tulpian *Acarahu, cf.* R. Acaracu]

Carazebú (Brazil) = Caracú (polled var.) × zebu cross

Cárdena (Salamanca, Spain); grey var. of Morucha

Cárdena andaluza: see Andalusian Grey

Carinthian Blond: see Austrian Blond

Carnation (USA); strain of Holstein with great influence on Italian Friesian

[Carniella] (Carnia, Friuli, Italy); red; absorbed by Italian Brown in early 20th c.

Carora, Caroreña: see Tipo Carora

Carpathian Brown (Trans-Carpathian Ukraine, USSR); d.m; dark brown to light grey; orig. from local graded to Brown Mountain since 1879; recog. 1972; American Brown Swiss and Jersey blood 1980s; Russ. *Buraya karpatskaya*; *cf.* Hungarian Brown

Carpetana: see Avileña

Carpi, Carpigiana: see Modenese

Carreña (S.W. Oviedo, N. Spain); larger, lowland var. of Asturian; red to mahogany; syn. *Asturiana de los valles*; being crossed with Brown Swiss and Friesian; not *Acreno*

Casanareño (R. Casanare valley, N.E. Colombia); Criollo type; tan or spotted; syn. *Llanero* (also W. Venezuela)

Casina (S.E. Oviedo, N. Spain); dr.d.m; smaller, mountain var. of Asturian; light to dark red; syn. *Asturiana de las montañas*. [from Caso]

Casta: see Aure et Saint-Girons

Castana: see Aosta Chestnut

Castille-León (Duero valley, Spain); former grouping to inc. Avileña, Black Andalusian, Morucha and Sayaguesa; Sp. *Castellano-Leonesa*

[Castle Martin]; var. of South Wales Black

Castro Caldelas: see Caldelana

[cattalo] (Canada); m; orig. from domestic bull × American bison (10-50%); project abandoned 1964 because of infertility; not *catalo*; *cf.* Beefalo

Cauca: see Hartón

Caucasian (USSR); d; Russ. *Kavkazskaya*; syn. *Transcaucasian*; inc. smaller, usu. black, var. in Greater Caucasus (inc. Dagestan and Georgian Mountain) and larger, usu. red, var. in Lesser Caucasus (Mingrelian Red) and in Transcaucasian lowlands (inc. Azerbaijan)

Caucasian Brown (Azerbaijan, USSR); d.m; brown with dark markings; orig. *c.* 1930-60 from Lesser Caucasus graded to Swiss Brown for 3 generations; also Kostroma and Lebedin blood; recog. 1960; Russ. *Kavkazskaya buraya*; syn. *Azerbaijan Brown, Caucasus Brown*; not *Caucasian Red*; inc. Dagestan Brown and Loriĭ

Caucasian Zebu: see Azerbaijan Zebu

Cauvery: see Alambadi

CCC: see Costeño con Cuernos

cebú: see zebu

Cecina, Cecinese: see Chianino-Maremmana

Celtic Red: see *brachyceros*

Central American Dairy Criollo (Costa Rica); var. of Tropical Dairy

Criollo; orig. at Turrialba in 1959 chiefly with animals from Rivas, Nicaragua, also from Honduras and local; syn. *Costa Rican Dairy Criollo, Reyna* (Nicaragua)

Central and Upland, Central and Upper Belgian: see Belgian Blue

Central Asian: see Turano-Mongolian

Central Asian Zebu (Turkmenia, Tajikistan and Uzbekistan, USSR); z; Russ. *Sredneaziatskiĭ zebu*; syn. *Turkestan Zebu* (Russ. *Turkestanskiĭ zebu*); vars: Fergana, Khurasani, Kuramin, Turkmen; usu. with European blood (= zeboid, Russ. *zebuvidnyĭ skot*)

CENTRAL CHINESE (China); dr.m; usu. cervico-thoracic hump; ? orig. from Mongolian and South China Zebu; inc. 4 recog. breeds: Jinnan, Luxi, Nanyang, Qinchuan, and other local vars: Dabieshan, Zaobei; syn. *cervico-thoracic-humped 'yellow' cattle of Central China*; *cf.* also Dengchuan, Guanling, Wenshan

CENTRAL EUROPEAN RED; *brachyceros* type; inc. [Bohemian Red], Byelorussian Red, German Red, [Lišna Red] (Moravia), Lithuanian Red, Polish Red

Central Pyrenean: see Aure et Saint-Girons

Central Russian Black Pied (C. Provinces of European Russia); d; var. of Russian Black Pied; orig. in 1920s from East Friesian × crossbreds by Yaroslavl, Kholmogory, Schwyz, and Simmental bulls out of local cows; HB 1940; Russ. *Srednerusskaya* (or *Tsentralnaya*) *chernopestraya*

Ceylon: see Sinhala

Chablais, Chablaisien: see Abondance

Chad: see Kuri

Chagga (Kilimanjaro, Tanzania); dwarf var. of Tanzanian Zebu; syn. *Wachagga*

Chaissi: see Chesi

Chan-Doc; var. of Vietnamese

Channel Island: see Jersey, Guernsey; French orig; obs. syn. *Alderney*

Chaouia (Constantine, Algeria); former subvar. of Guelma var. of Brown Atlas

Charbray (Texas and Louisiana, USA); m; creamy white; orig. since 1936 from Charolais ($\frac{5}{8}$-$\frac{7}{8}$) × Brahman; BS 1949-67, HB 1949 on; not *Charbra*; see also Australian Charbray

Charford (N. Arizona, USA); m; in formation (1952) at Ash Fork Ranch; $\frac{1}{2}$ Charolais, $\frac{3}{8}$ Hereford, $\frac{1}{8}$ Brahman

Charnequeiro: see Bragado do Sorraia

Charolais (C. France); m.[dr.d]; white (or cream) with pink mucosae; Shorthorn blood 1850-80; BS 1864, HB 1887; not *Charollais*; BS also in USA 1951, S. Africa 1955, Canada 1960, GB 1962, Denmark 1963, Argentina, Brazil, Germany, Japan, Mexico and Uruguay (all by 1964), Ireland 1966, Sweden 1968, Australia, Netherlands, Norway and Spain (all 1969), New Zealand 1972, Belgium and Paraguay 1975, Zimbabwe 1983, Finland 1986, HB also in Hungary 1981, Portugal, USSR. [from Charolles district]

Charollandais (France); d.m; cross (1960s) of *Charol*ais × Friesian from Hol*land*

Char-Swiss (Nebraska, USA); m; orig. by G.A. Boucher, Ravenna; $\frac{3}{4}$ Charolais $\frac{1}{4}$ American Brown Swiss

Charwiss (California, USA); m; Charolais × American Brown Swiss, 1st cross

chauri (Nepal) = ♀ offspring of yak × cattle inc. reciprocal crosses and backcrosses to yak; Nepali *cāuri* from *cāvar* = tail; syn. *chaunri, chowri, churi, tsauri*; see dzo

[Cheb] (Czechoslovakia); larger var. of Bohemian Red; Cz. *Chebský*, Ger. *Egerländer*

Cheju (Cheju I, Korea); var. of Korean Native; syn. *Jeju* or *Jeju native, Korean Black*

Chernigov (N.W. Ukraine, USSR); m; orig. 1961-79 from Charolais ($\frac{3}{4}$), Russian Simmental ($\frac{1}{8}$) and Ukrainian Grey ($\frac{1}{8}$); recog. 1979; Russ. *Chernigovskiǐ tip*; not *Chernigorsk*

Chesi (Syria); d; Damascus × Baladi; syn. *Chaissi*; not *Chezi*

Cheurfa (Constantine, Algeria); light grey; former subvar. of Guelma var. of Brown Atlas

Chezi: see Chesi

Chianina (Chiana valley, Tuscany, Italy); m.[dr]; white with black points and mucosae; ? orig. from Podolian × local in early 19th c; HB 1956; former vars: Calvana, Perugina, Valdarno, Val di Chiana; orig. (with Podolian) of Marchigiana (improved) and Pasturina; BS in Brazil 1969, Canada 1971, USA 1973, GB 1973, Australia

[Chianino-Maremmana] (Tuscany, Italy); m.dr; grey-white; orig. from Chianina × Maremmana; syn. *Cecinese* (from Cecina), *Improved Maremmana*

[Chilean Criollo] (C. Chile); m; pure Criollo extinct, name used for nondescripts of Criollo orig. with Shorthorn and some Friesian and Normande blood; Sp. *Criollo chileno*; syn. *Chilean*

Chillingham (Northumberland, England); semi-feral herd of pure White Park cattle, closed since 17th c. (and possibly since 13th); red ears and points; BS 1939; reserve herd in N. Scotland

[China] (Rio de Janeiro, Brazil); orig. from Southern Crioulo with Indian Zebu blood imported by Baron de Bom Ritiro in 1855

Chinampo (Lower California, Mexico); Criollo type; usu. white with black or red markings; declining by crossing with zebu

Chinchuan, Chinchwan: see Qinchuan

Chinese: see Central Chinese, Mongolian, South China Zebu, Yanbian;

syn. *Chinese Yellow*
Chinese Black-and-White (China); d.m; orig. from Holstein, Dutch Black
Pied, and other Friesians (esp. German and Japanese), × local Chinese;
BS; syn. *Chinese Black Pied*; var: Beijing Black Pied
Chino Santandereano (Lebrija valley, Santander, Colombia); local Cri-
ollo var. with zebu blood; sim. to Costeño con Cuernos but more
milk. [*chino* = hairless]
[Chitaldrug]; former var. of Amritmahal now merged in Hallikar; not
Chitraldrag, Chittaldroog
Chittagong Red (Bangladesh); z; local var.
Choa: see Shuwa; not *Choas*
Choletais: see Parthenais
Cholistani (Cholistan desert, Pakistan); d; z
Cholmogor: see Kholmogory
Cholung: see Tibetan ♂
Chosen: see Korean Native
Chou-pei, Chowpei: see Zaobei
Chowri, chowrie: see chauri
churi: see chauri
Çifteler Brown: see Turkish Brown
Çildir; var. of East Anatolian Red; not *Cildi*
Cinisara (Cinisi, N.W. Palermo, Sicily, Italy); d; Podolian type but black,
occ. white tail and belly; sim. to Modicana
Coastal Horned (Colombia): see Costeño con Cuernos
Coastal Polled (Colombia): see Romosinuano
Cobourg Peninsula (Northern Territory, Australia); feral; orig. from
Bali cattle imported 1827
Cobra: see Gobra
Colombian Criollo: see Blanco Orejinegro, Costeño con Cuernos, Romo-
sinuano and Sanmartinero breeds, and Casanareño, Chino Santander-
eano and Hartón vars
Coloniã (Brazil): see Southern Crioulo
Colonist: see Ukrainian Whiteheaded
Colorada (Spain): see Retinta
Coloured Cattle of Wales: see Ancient Cattle of Wales
coloursided; syn. *finchbacked, finched, inkone* (Zulu), *rigget, Rücken-
scheckig* (= back pied) (Ger.), *Sidet* (Nor.);
   1. White tail, back-stripe and belly; coloured head and legs; see
   Aracena, Gloucester, Pinzgauer, Tux (white less extensive)
   2. White tail, back and underside; white or parti-coloured head and
   legs; see Black Forest (often), Blacksided Trondheim and Nordland,
   East Finnish, Istoben (often), Kravařsko, Kłodzka, Longhorn,
   Polish Whitebacked, Sudeten Spotted (often), Telemark, Ukrainian

Whitebacked, Vosges
3. White with coloured points (muzzle, inside ears, etc); colour on
   sides reduced to a few spots only, or absent; see Blacksided
   Trondheim and Nordland (often), Blanco Orejinegro (Colombia),
   Boran (often), British White, Mauritius Creole (often), North
   Finnish, Polish Marsh, Swedish Mountain, White Fulani (often),
   White Park

Coloursided Trondheim: see Blacksided Trondheim and Nordland
Colubara: see Kolubara
Comtois: see Tourache
Coopelso 93 (S.W. France); m; strain of Blonde d'Aquitaine selected by
   *Coop*érative d'*El*evage du *S*ud-*O*uest
Cornigera de la costa: see Costeño con Cuernos
Cornigliese; small greyish-red var. of Bardigiana. [from Corniglio]
Correi: see Magal
Corsican (Corsica); m; Iberian type; prim.; colour various; Fr. *Corse*; *cf.*
   Sardinian; rare
Costa Rican Dairy Criollo: see Central American Dairy Criollo
Costeño con Cuernos (Sinú valley, N. Colombia); m.d; Criollo type;
   usu. red or orange, also chestnut; lyre horns; syn. *Andaluz, CCC,
   Cornígero de la costa, Sinuano de cuernos* (= *horned Sinú*); orig. of
   Romosinuano; rare. [= coastal horned]
Cotrone: see Calabrian
Costino: see Chilean Criollo
Creole (Mauritius): see Mauritius Creole
Creole (West Indies): see Criollo
Cretan Lowland (Crete); former var. of Greek Shorthorn; syn. *Messara*
Cretan Mountain (Crete); former var. of Greek Shorthorn
Crimean Red: see Red Steppe
Criolla (Spain): see Canary Island
CRIOLLO (Spanish America); Sp. orig; syn. *Creole* (Guyana and anglo-
   phone West Indies); inc. Argentine Criollo, Barroso (Guatemala),
   Bolivian Criollo, Colombian Criollo, Cuban Criollo, Ecuador Criollo,
   Tropical Dairy Criollo, Venezuelan Criollo; *cf.* Crioulo (Brazil) and
   Texas Longhorn (USA). [= native]
Crioulo (Brazil); inc. Curraleiro (Northeastern Crioulo), Pantaneiro and
   Caracú (Southern Crioulo)
Croatian Red (Yugoslavia); var. of Buša; usu. red; Serbo-cro. *Hrvatska
   buša*
Croatian Simmental: see Yugoslav Pied
Crotone, Crotonese: see Calabrian
Cuanzo: see Barra do Cuanzo
Cuban Criollo (E. Cuba); m.d; tan; Criollo type with some zebu blood;

var: Tinima
Cubante: see Marchigiana
Cuban Zebu (Cuba); m; orig. from Colombian, Venezuelan and Puerto
   Rican imports in early 1900s
Cuiabano: see Pantaneiro
Çukurova (S. Turkey); var. of South Anatolian Red; orig. from Anatolian
   Black × Aleppo (= Damascus); not *Cukurova*
Cumberland White: see Whitebred Shorthorn
Cuprem Hybrid (Nebraska, USA); m; orig. 1960-76 by A. Mulford,
   Kenesaw; ♀ is 50% Red Angus, 25% Santa Gertrudis, 25% Limousin;
   ♂ is 50% Shorthorn, 25% Charolais, 25% Chianina; BS
Curraleiro (N.E. Brazil); m.d.dr; sim. to Tropical Dairy Criollo; red,
   fawn or dun with pale belly and escutcheon, and darker head, shoulder
   and legs; short horns; syn. *Crioulo nordestino* (= *Northeastern Crioulo*),
   Goias, Pé duro (= *hard foot*), *Sertanejo* (= *inland*); var: [Irecé];
   purebreds rare. [= penned]
Cutchi (Cutch, N.W. Gujarat, India); local type with Tharparkar and
   Gir influence; syn. *Kachhi*
Cyprus; dr.m; zebu × humpless orig; sim. to Damascus, Egyptian and
   Lebanese; fawn to black; vars: Messaoria (plains), Paphos (hills)
Czech Pied (Bohemia and Moravia, Czechoslovakia); d.m.[dr]; orig.
   from Bernese and Simmental imported 1850-1911 × Bohemian and
   Moravian Reds; HB; Cz. *Česky strakatý*; syn. (to 1969) *Czechoslovak-
   ian Red Pied* (Cz. *Československý červenostrakatý*), *Czech* (or *Czecho-
   slovak*) *Red and White, Czech Red Spotted, Czech Simmental, Czech
   Spotted*; (former) vars inc. Bohemian Red Pied, Hřbínecký, Kravařský,
   Moravian Red Pied
Czerwona Polska: see Polish Red

Dabieshan (E. Hubei and S.W. Anhui, China); dr; Central Chinese type;
   shades of yellow; inc. Huangpi
Dacca-Faridpur (Bangladesh); z; local var.
[Dagestan Brown] (Dagestan, USSR); d.m; orig. from Swiss Brown ×
   Dagestan Mountain with Carpathian Brown blood; Russ. *Dagestan-
   skaya buraya*; absorbed by Caucasian Brown
Dagestan Mountain (USSR); dwarf subvar. of Greater Caucasus var. of
   Caucasian; not *Daghestan, Dhagestan*; rare
Dahomey: see Lagune
Dairy Criollo: see Tropical Dairy Criollo; also Barroso (Guatemala),
   Blanco Orejinegro and Costeño con Cuernos (Colombia), Bolivian
   Criollo, Caldeano (Brazil), Cuban Criollo
Dairy Gir (Brazil); d. var. of Brazilian Gir; BS 1967; Port. *Gir leiteiro*;

cf. Dairy Zebu of Uberaba

[Dairy Hungarian Brown] (Hungary); d.(m); orig. (1950s on) from (Danish Jersey × Hungarian Brown) × (Danish Jersey × Hungarian Pied); HB; Hung. *Tejelő magyar-barna*; syn. *Hungarian Brown Dairy, New Hungarian Brown*; not *Hungarian Red Dairy*; graded to Hungarofries or Holstein

[Dairy Hungarian Pied] (Hungary); d.m; orig. (1950s on) from Danish Jersey × Hungarian Pied backcrossed to Hungarian Pied; Hung. *Tejelő magyar-tarka*; syn. *Hungarian Spotted Dairy*; not *New Hungarian Red*; graded to Hungarofries or Holstein

Dairy Indo-European (Rio de Janeiro, Brazil); d; in formation at Instituto do Zootecnia from Friesian *et al.* × zebu; Port. *Indo-europeu leiteiro*; ? discontinued

Dairy Shorthorn (Great Britain); d.m; Shorthorn group; BS 1905, HB (Dairy section) 1959; BS also in Australia, New Zealand (Milking Shorthorn 1913); *cf.* Milking Shorthorn (USA)

Dairy Synthetic (Alberta Univ., Canada); m; 30% Holstein, 30% American Brown Swiss, 6% Simmental, 34% beef breeds; syn. *dairy-beef synthetic*

Dairy Zebu of Uberaba (Minas Gerais, Brazil); d; orig. since 1948 by selection of Brazilian Gir (*et al.*) at government farm 'Getulio Vargas'; Port. *Zebu leiteiro de Uberaba*; *cf.* Dairy Gir

Dajjal (Dera Ghazi Khan, W. Punjab, Pakistan); var. of Bhagnari (by crossing larger type with local cattle); not *Dajal, Dajil, Dazzal*

Dales Shorthorn: see Northern Dairy Shorthorn

Damara (S. Angola and N. Namibia); Sanga type; usu. red pied or yellow pied; long horns; syn. *Herero*

Damascus (Syria); d; ? zebu blood, sim. to Cyprus, Egyptian and Lebanese; brown; syn. *Aleppo, Damascene, Halabi, Halep* (Turkey), *Shami* or *Shamia*

Damerghou: see Azaouak

Damietta (N. Delta, Egypt); d; var. of Egyptian; syn. *Domiatta, Domiatti, Domyati, Dumiati, Dumyati*

Danakil (Dancalia, *i.e.* S. Eritrea, E. Tigray and Welo, Ethiopia, and N.E. Djibouti); d; Sanga type; light chestnut, blond or ash-grey; long horns; syn. *Adal, Adali, Afar, Dancalian, Keriyu, Raya*; var: Raya-Azebó

Dancalian: see Danakil

Dangi (W. Ghats, N.W. Maharashtra, India); dr; z; sim. to Deoni and Gir; spotted; BSd; syn. *Ghauti, Kanada, Konkani*; vars: Kalakheri (black-and-white), Sonkheri (red-and-white)

Danish Black Pied (Jutland, Denmark); d; orig. (1949) from Jutland Black Pied + Friesian, chiefly Dutch, some East Friesian and Swedish;

Friesian predominates; HB; Dan. *Sortbroget Dansk Malkekvæg* (= *SDM*); syn. *Black Pied Danish, Danish Black-and-White Milk*

Danish Blue-and-White (Denmark); m; Dan. *Dansk Blåhvidt kvæg*; = Belgian Blue; HB; rare

Danish Jersey (Denmark, esp. W. Fünen); var. of Jersey from imports from Sweden (1896) and Jersey (1902-9); BS 1902, HB 1925

Danish Red (Denmark—islands); d; Baltic Red type; orig. from North Slesvig Red (+ Angeln and Ballum) × local island (1841-63); recog. 1878, HB 1885; Dan. *Rødt Dansk Malkekvæg* (= *RDM*); syn. *Fünen* (Dan. *Fynsk*), *Red Dane, Red Danish*; orig. of British Dane, Bulgarian Red, *et al.*; HB also in USSR, USA (American Red Dane) 1948-68, New Zealand

Danish Red Pied (Denmark); d; orig. from Shorthorn with German Red Pied and Meuse-Rhine-Yssel blood in 1950s; Dan. *Dansk Rødbroget Kvæg* (= *DRK*); syn. *Danish Red and White, Danish Red-and-White Shorthorn*

[Danube] (Burgenland and Lower Austria); former var. of Austrian Simmental; Ger. *Donau*

Danyang: see Shandong

[Darbalara]; strain of Australian Milking Shorthorn; latter now absorbed by Illawarra

Dark Andalusian: see Retinta

Dashtiari (S.E. Baluchestan, Iran); m; z; brown, black, white or pied

Dauara: see Garre; not *Danara, Daura*

Dazzal: see Dajjal

De Lidia: see Fighting bull

[Demonte] (Cuneo, Italy); d.m; red to straw-coloured var. of Piedmont in Stura valley

Dengchuan (N.W. Yunnan, China); ♂ small hump; *cf.* Central Chinese type

Deoni (Bidar, N. Karnataka, India); dr.d; z; sim. to Dangi and Gir; black- or red-and-white; syn. *Dongari, Dongarpatti*

Desan: see Gir

desi (India) = local, indigenous; z; not *deshi*

Devarakota (Tamil Nadu, India); z; local var. sim. to Ongole

Devni (Udgir taluka, Osmanabad, Maharashtra, India); z; local var.

Devon (S.W. England); m.[dr]; sim. to Sussex; cherry red; HB 1851, BS 1884; syn. *Beef Devon, North Devon, Red Devon, Red Ruby*; m.d. var. in E. Devon; orig. of Milking Devon (USA); BS also in USA 1905 (HB 1855), Australia 1929 (HB 1873), S. Africa 1917 (HB 1906), HB also in Brazil 1952, New Zealand 1964; do not confuse with South Devon

[Dewsland]; var. of South Wales Black

Dexter (Ireland); d.m; red or black; short-legged (achondroplastic); orig.
from Kerry in 18th c; BS and HB in Ireland 1887-1919; imported to
England 1886, BS, HB 1900; BS also in USA 1911, S. Africa 1958;
syn. *Dexter-Kerry*; rare. [? etym.]

Dexter-Kerry (Cape Province, S. Africa); d; dun and black; orig. from
Kerry with Ayrshire, Jersey, Shorthorn and Friesian blood

Dhagestan: see Dagestan

Dhanni (Rawalpindi, N. Punjab, Pakistan); dr; z; white with black
markings (usu. spotted or coloursided), black with white markings,
red-and-white, or white; HB 1938; syn. *Awankari, Pahari* or *Pakhari,
Pothwari*; not *Dhani, Dhaniri*

dhee: see yak ♀

dhimjo: see dzo

Diakoré: see Djakoré

Diali (S.W. Niger); m; West African Zebu type; white or pied; variable
(esp. horns); Hausa *Jalli, Shanun Bayaro*, Fulani *Jalliji*, Fr. *Peul
nigérien* (= *Nigerian Fulani*); syn. *Djeli, Jali, Jeli*

Didinga (S. Sudan): see Mongalla

dimdzo, dimjo, dimschu: see dzo

Dinka: see Nilotic

Dishley: see Longhorn

Dishti (N. and E. of Amarah, Iraq); var. of Iraqi; small or no hump;
light tan to cream or golden. [= living in open]

[Dithmarscher]; orig. var. of Red Pied Schleswig-Holstein

Djafoun: see Red Bororo

Djakoré (Senegal); m; Gobra zebu × N'Dama cross; white, grey or
yellow; syn. *race du Sine*; not *Diakoré, Jakoré*; var: Bambey

Djebeli (Syria): see Baladi

Djelani: see Jaulan

Djeli: see Diali

Dnieper (Ukraine, USSR); m; orig. 1961-79 from Chianina (66.7%),
Charolais (8.3%), Russian Simmental (16.7%) and Ukrainian Grey
(8.3%); recog. 1979; Russ. *Pridneprovskiĭ tip*

Doayo (Poli, N.W. Cameroon); var. of West African Savanna Shorthorn;
black, black pied or black spotted, occ. brown or brown spotted; syn.
Kirdi (= *pagan*), *M'Bougi* (sing. *M'Bouyé*), *Namchi, Namji* or *Namshi*;
not *Doai*; rare

Dobrogea Red (E. Romania); d; *brachyceros* type; red, sometimes white
on udder; Rom. *Roşie Dobrogeană* or *de Dobrogea*; syn. *Dobruja Red*;
improved by Red Steppe and Danish Red and with them forms
Romanian Red

[Døle] (Norway); d; vars: Gudbrandsdal (dark brown), Østerdal (black);
recog. 1880, HB 1909, restarted 1922; not *Døla*; graded to Norwegian

Red-and-White since 1950 and combined in Norwegian Red 1963. [=
valley]

Domiatta, Domiatti, Domyati: see Damietta

Domshino, Domshinskaya: see Yaroslavl

Donau: see Danube

Dongari, Dongarpatti: see Deoni

Dongola (N. Sudan); strain of Red Desert sim. to Butana

Dongolé: see Kuri

[Donnersberg] (Palatinate, Germany); orig. in late 18th c. from Bernese
× native; united with Glan in 1890 to form Glan-Donnersberg

Doran (Costa Rica); m; Criollo type said to contain Shorthorn blood;
white with red speckling or patches. [corruption of Durham =
Shorthorn]

Dorna (Suceava dist. esp. Vatra Dornei, N. Romania); d; black (with
Pinzgauer pattern) var. of Transylvanian Pinzgau; orig. in early 20th
c. from Pinzgauer or Romanian Mountain (also some Swiss Brown
blood); syn. *Black Pinzgau*

Dörtyol (S. Turkey); small var. of South Anatolian Red; sim. to Baladi
of Syria

Drakensberger (W. Natal, S. Africa); m.d; sim. to Basuto; black; orig.
from Sanga (inc. Africander) with Friesian blood; specifically (1947)
from Uys + Kemp + Tintern Black; BS 1947; syn. *Black Africander*

dri: see yak ♀

dridzo: see dzo

DRK: see Danish Red Pied

drong, drongdri: see yak, wild

Drontheimer: see Trondheim

Droughtmaster (N. Queensland, Australia); m; red; hd or pd; orig. since
1930s from Brahman ($\frac{3}{8}$ - $\frac{1}{2}$) × Shorthorn; BS 1956

Dschau-bei: see Zaobei

Dscholan: see Jaulan

Duara: see Garre

dulong (N.W. Yunnan, China): see mithun

Dumiati, Dumyati: see Damietta

Dun Galloway (Scotland); colour var. of Galloway; BS (with Belted
Galloway) 1921-52; HB; now with Galloway Society; HB also in USA
(with Galloway)

Durham: see Shorthorn

Durham-Mancelle: see Maine-Anjou

Dutch (Netherlands): see Dutch Black Pied, Groningen Whiteheaded,
Meuse-Rhine-Yssel

Dutch (elsewhere): see Friesian

Dutch Argentine: see Argentine Friesian

Dutch Belted (USA); d; black with white belt; occ. pd; orig. from Lakenvelder imported from Netherlands 1838-48 and 1906; BS 1886; syn. *Dutch Belt*; rare

Dutch Black-and-White, Dutch Lowland: see Dutch Black Pied

Dutch Black Pied (Netherlands); d.m; BS and HB 1874 (NRS = *Nederlands Rundvee Stamboek*) and 1879 (FRS = *Fries Rundvee Stamboek*); Du. *Zwartbont Fries-Hollands*; syn. *Black-and-White Holland, Black Pied Dutch, Dutch Black-and-White, Dutch Friesian, Dutch Lowland, Holland, Netherlands Black Pied, West Friesian*; orig. of Friesian type

Dutch Red-and-White, Dutch Red Pied: see Meuse-Rhine-Yssel

dwarf, *i.e.* height at withers 100 cm or less

Europe: see Albanian Dwarf, Betizuak and Cachena (Spain), Dagestan Mountain (USSR), Dexter, Posavina (Yugoslavia), Rodopi (Bulgaria), Valachian Dwarf (Slovakia), West Macedonian (Greece)

Asia: see Indian Hill, Kedah-Kelantan (Malaysia), Konari (Afghanistan), Nepalese Hill, Punganur (India), Sinhala (Sri Lanka), Tibetan

Africa: see [Binga, Govuvu and Pecanite] (Zimbabwe), Chagga (Tanzania), Kabyle (Algeria), Nuba Mountain (Sudan), Socotra, West African Dwarf Shorthorn

America: see Puerto Rican

Dwarf Humpless, Dwarf Shorthorn (W. Africa): see West African Shorthorn, dwarf vars.

dzo (Tibet); any yak-cattle cross; Tibetan *mdzo*, Ch. *pian niu*, Russ. *haĭnyk* (or *hanik*) from Mongolian *hainag* (= yak); syn. *dzoz, je, zo*

♂ (sterile) is dzobo; Tibetan *mdzo-po*; syn. *dzopkhyo, jhopke, joppa, zebkyo, zhopkyo, zopkio* (Nepal)

♀ is dzomo; Tibetan *mdzo-mo*; syn. chauri (Nepal) *q.v., jommu, jum, zhum, zomo, zum*

yak ♂ × domestic cow, F_1, is *dridzo* (C. Tibet), *urang* (Nepal), *pamjommu* (Assam), *maran-hainag* (= *sun yak*) (Mongolia)

domestic bull × yak ♀, F_1, the commoner cross, is *pandzo* (C. Tibet), *dhimjo, dimdzo, dimjo* or *dimschu* (Nepal), *saran-hainag* (= *moon yak*) (Mongolia)

backcross to yak ♂ is *ah gohr* or *galiba* (China), *ago* (Russ.)

EAST AFRICAN SHORTHORNED ZEBU (Ethiopia to Malawi); m.dr; thoracic musculo-fatty hump; syn. *East African Humped, Shorthorned Zebu*; inc. Abyssinian Zebus, Angoni, Boran, Karamajong, Small East African Zebu, Somali, Toposa and Turkana

East African Zebu: see East African Shorthorned Zebu, Madagascar Zebu, North Sudan Zebu, and Nuba Mountain

East Anatolian Red (N.E. Turkey); d.m; orig. from Caucasian; Turk. *Şarkî* (or *Doğu*) *Anadolu kırmızı*; syn. *Eastern Red*; vars: Cildir, Göle

Eastern Black Pied (Belgium): see Hervé Black Pied

Eastern Nuer (N.E. of S. Sudan); local var. of Nilotic

Eastern Province Zebu (Uganda): see Nkedi

Eastern Red and White, Eastern Red Pied (France): see French Red Pied group

[Eastern Red Pied] (E. Liège, Belgium); d; former name for Red Pied (Meuse-Rhine-Yssel) in Eupen and Malmédy; inc. in Belgian Red Pied; Fr. *Pie rouge de l'Est, Pie rouge Ardennes-Liège*

Eastern Spotted (France): see Pie Rouge de l'Est

East Finnish (E. Finland); d; red-and-white (coloursided) var. of Finnish; BS 1898-1950; Finn. *Itä-Suomalainen Karja* (= *ISK*), Swed. *Ostfinsk*; syn. *Red-and-White Finnish, Red Pied Karelian*; formerly also in Karelian ASSR (HB); rare

East Flemish Red Pied: see Belgian White-and-Red

East Friesian (Ostfriesland, Germany); d.m; orig. var. of German Black Pied; HB 1883; Ger. *Ostfriesen, Ostfriesisches*; syn. *Black Pied East Friesian, East Friesland*; see also Red East Friesian, Red Pied East Friesian

East Friesian Red Pied: see Red Pied East Friesian

Eastland (Norway): see Red Polled Østland

East Macedonian (and Thrace); former var. of Greek Shorthorn

[East Prussian] (Germany); d.m; orig. var. of German Black Pied (until 1945); orig. from East Friesian and Dutch Friesian, imported in mid-19th c; Ger. *Ostpreussen, Ostpreussisch Holländer*; now see Mazury

East Siberian: see Yakut

[East Styrian Spotted] (Austria); former var. of Austrian Simmental; Ger. *Öststeirisches Fleckvieh*

Ecuador Criollo; m; Sp. *Criollo ecuatoriano*; vars: smaller Sierra (inc. Páramo and Hoyas) and larger [Costa] (inc. El Oro and Esmeraldas); being graded to exotic breeds

Egerland, Egerländer: see Cheb

Egyptian (Egypt); dr.(d); *brachyceros* with zebu blood, sim. to Cyprus, Damascus, and Lebanese; yellow-brown to black; vars: Baladi (inc. Menufi) and Damietta (Lower Egypt), Saidi (Upper Egypt), and Maryuti (Western Desert

[Elling] (Germany); orig. from Grey Mountain × native Franconian red; absorbed by Yellow Franconian

English Longhorn: see Longhorn

Enns, Ennstaler: see Bergscheck

[Eo] (N.W. Asturias, Spain); d.m.dr; local var. of North Spanish type;
yellow, sometimes with white markings; long horns; Sp. *Agrupación
Eo*

Epirus; former var. of Greek Shorthorn

Eringer: see Hérens

Estonian Black Pied (N.W. and N. Estonia, USSR); d; inc. in Baltic
Black Pied; orig. in 2nd half of 19th c. from Dutch and East
Friesian × Estonian Native; HB 1885, named 1951; Russ. *Èstonskaya
chernopestraya*; syn. *Estonian Black Spotted*; obs. syn. *Estonian Dutch-
Friesian*

Estonian Brown: see Estonian Red

Estonian Dutch-Friesian: see Estonian Black Pied

Estonian Native (Estonia, USSR); d; North European Polled type; red
or yellow- brown with white flecks; pd; some West Finnish and Jersey
blood (1955-67); HB 1914; Russ. *Mestnaya èstonskaya*; syn. *Local
Estonian*; orig. (with Angeln and Danish Red) of Estonian Red; rare

Estonian Red (S.C. and E. Estonia, USSR); d; Baltic Red type; pale to
dark red; orig. from Angeln and Danish Red × Estonian Native in
early and mid-19th c; HB 1885; Russ. *Krasnaya èstonskaya*; syn.
Estonian Brown, Estonian Red-Brown

Ethiopian Boran (S. Ethiopia); orig. (unimproved) var. of Boran; syn.
Avai or *Somali Boran, Borana, Tanaland Boran* or *Galla* (E. Kenya)

Etschtaler (Austria): see Grey Adige

EUROPEAN BLACK-AND-WHITE; BS 1966 (*European Confederation of Black
and White Breed Societies, Confédération Européenne des Eleveurs de
la Race Pie-Noire, Europäische Vereinigung der Schwarzbuntzüchter*);
inc. FRS, NRS, and HBs of Belgian Black Pied, British Friesian,
Danish Black Pied, French Friesian, German Black Pied, Italian
Friesian and Swedish Friesian; syn. *European Black Pied, European
Friesian*

EUROPEAN BLOND AND YELLOW; BS 1962 (*Europäische Blond- und
Gelbviehzüchtervereinigung, Fédération Européenne des Races Bovines
Blondes et Jaunes*); inc. Austrian Yellow, Blonde d'Aquitaine and
Limousin (France), Gelbvieh (German Yellow), Piedmont (Italy)

EUROPEAN RED; BS 1956 (*Europäische Vereinigung der Rotviehzüchter,
Fédération Européenne des Eleveurs des Races Bovines Rouges*); inc.
Angeln, Belgian Red, Danish Red, Flemish (France), German Red;
see also Baltic Red, Bulgarian Red, Central European Red, Gorbatov
Red, Red Poll, Red Steppe, Romanian Red, Tambov Red

European wild ox: see aurochs

Evolene (Switzerland); off-colour vars of Hérens; red-and-white, black-
and-white, dun or with white dorsal stripe; Fr. *Evolenard*; almost
extinct

Extremadura, Extremadura Red, Extremeña: see Retinta

Faeroes; d; ? Nor. orig.; Dan. *Færøerne*
Falkland: see Fife Horned
Fao: see Jenubi
Faridpur: see Dacca-Faridpur
Fellata (Chad); West African (shorthorned) Zebu type, sim. to Shuwa
    but larger hump and bred by Fulani; not *Filata*. [Kanouri = Fulani]
Fellata (W. Sudan and Gambela, S.W. Ethiopia): see Red Bororo
[Fémeline] (Sâone valley, E. France); dr.d; sim. to Tourache but more
    of lowland, refined, dairy, "female" type; fawn or red; crossed with
    Shorthorn at end of 19th c. and graded to Simmental in early 20th c.
    to form part of Pie Rouge de l'Est; not *Feme*. [Fr. *femelle* = female]
[Fergana] (Uzbekistan, USSR); z; var. of Central Asian Zebu (or Zeboid);
    Russ. *Ferganskiĭ zebu*
Ferrandais (Puy-de-Dôme, France); d.m.[dr]; brick-red and white; declin-
    ing by crossing with Pie Rouge de l'Est and Salers; rare
FFPN: see French Friesian
Fiemme: see Grey Val di Fiemme
[Fife Horned] (E. Scotland); syn. *Falkland*
Fighting bull (Spain and Portugal); bulls for fighting (Sp. *toro de lidia* or
    ganado bravo) are bred in Andalucia, Extremadura, New Castille,
    Salamanca, and Ribatejo (Portugal); usu. black or dark brown; BS,
    HB
Filani: see Fulani
Filata: see Fellata
finchbacked, finched: see coloursided
Finnish (Finland); d; pd; BS 1946; Finn. *Suomalainen Karja* (= *SK*),
    Swe. *Finsk*; syn. *Finncattle*; vars: East Finnish (red-and-white), North
    Finnish (white), West Finnish (red)
Finnish Ayrshire (Finland); d.m; var. of Ayrshire from cattle imported
    1847-1923; BS 1901; Finn. *Suomalainen Ayrshirekarja*, Swe. *Finsk
    Ayrshire*
Fjäll: see Swedish Mountain
Fjord: see Vestland Fjord
Flamande: see Flemish
Flanders, Flandrine: see Flemish
Fleckvieh: see Simmental
Flemish (Belgium): see Belgian Red, Belgian White-and-Red
Flemish (Flanders, N. France); d; mahogany; HB 1886; Fr. *Flamande,
    Flandrine*; former vars: Maroilles, Picardy; being crossed with Danish
    Red and Belgian Red

Flemish Red (Flanders, N. France); d.m; Fr. *Rouge flamande*: syn. *Rouge du Nord*; d. var: Flemish + Danish Red × Flemish; m.d. var: Belgian Red × Flemish crosses

Flemish Red Pied: see Belgian White-and-Red

Florida Scrub (USA); all colours; small; Sp. orig. in 16th c; syn. *Florida Cracker, Florida Native, Pineywoods* (Louisiana); rare

Fogera (L. Tana, Gonder and Gojam, N.W. Ethiopia); dr.m.d; Zebu-Sanga intermediate; often white or white with black spots; short horns, occ. pd; small hump; not *Fogara, Fogerra, Uogherá, Wagara*

Fogha: see Red Bororo

Formentina: see Reggiana

Formosa: see Taiwan Zebu

Fort Cross (Fort William farm, Thunder Bay, Ontario, Canada); m; Charolais × (Lincoln Red × Hereford)

Foula, Foulah, Foulani, Foulawa, Foulbé: see Fulani

Fouta Djallon, Fouta Jallon, Fouta Longhorn, Fouta Malinke: see N'Dama

Franconian: see Yellow Franconian

Franqueiro (N. São Paulo, Brazil); long horns sim. to Junqueiro; orig. from Southern Crioulo in late 19th c; var: [Pedreiro]; nearly extinct. [from town and district of Franca]

Frati (N. Italy); d; Italian Brown × Friesian, 1st cross; *cf*. Preti. [It. *frate* = friar, *i.e.* dark brown]

Freiburg, Freiburger: see Fribourg

French Brown (France); d.m.[dr]; orig. from Swiss Brown imported 1827 on; BS and HB 1911; Fr. *Brune des Alpes* (= *Brown Alpine*)

French Canadian: see Canadian

French Friesian (N.E. and S.W. France); d; orig. from Dutch Black Pied first imported in 18th c; BS 1911, HB 1922; Fr. *Française frisonne pie-noire* (*FFPN*); syn. *Hollandaise pie-noire*

French Red Pied group (E. France); inc. (1946) Abondance, Montbéliard and Pie rouge de l'Est, Fr. *Races pie rouge frànçaises*; syn. *Eastern Red and White, Eastern Red Pied, Pied Eastern*

French Red Pied Lowland: see Pie Rouge des Plaines

French Simmental: see Pie Rouge de l'Est

Friauler: see Friuli

[Fribourg] (W. Switzerland); d.m.dr; black pied; BS and HB; Fr. *Fribourgeois*, Ger. *Freiburger*; since 1966 crossed with Holstein to give Swiss Black Pied; last purebred bull died 1973

FRIESIAN; d.(m); black-and-white; Fr. *Frisonne*, It. *Frisona*, Sp. *Frisia*; syn. *Black Pied (Lowland), Black-and-White, Dutch, Holland*; inc. Dutch Black Pied, East Friesian and their derivatives: American Beef Friesian, Argentine Friesian, Belgian Black Pied, British Friesian, British Holstein, Danish Black Pied, French Friesian, Friesland (S.

Africa), German Black Pied, Holstein (USA), Israeli Friesian, Italian Friesian, Polish Black-and-White Lowland, Russian Black Pied, Swedish Friesian, Turino (Portugal); BS/HB also in Australia, Austria, New Zealand 1911, Brazil 1934, Spain, *et al.*; see also Red and White Friesian; not *Frisian, Fresian*

Friesland (S. Africa); breed of Friesian; HB 1906, BS 1912

Frisia, Frisian, Frisona, Frisonne: see Friesian

[Friuli] (Venetia, Italy); straw-coloured; It. *Friulana*, Ger. *Friauler*; syn. *Red Friuli*; orig. (with Simmental) of Italian Red Pied

Friuli-Simmental: see Italian Red Pied; It. *Simmenthal-friulana*

Froment du Léon (St Brieuc, Brittany, France); d; nearly extinct. *[froment = corn coloured]*

FRS (Friesland, Netherlands) = *Fries Rundvee Stamboek*; var. of Dutch Black Pied with its own BS and HB

Fula (Guinea-Bissau): see N'Gabou

FULANI (W. Africa); z; see Adamawa (Cameroon), Diali (Niger), Fellata (Chad), Gobra (Senegal), Red Bororo, Sudanese Fulani (Mali), White Fulani (Nigeria); Fr. *Peul* (*Peuhl, Peulh, Peulhé*, or *Peul-Peul*); Hausa *Filani, Fulani* or *Fulawa* (sing. *Fula* or *Fulah*); Kanouri (Chad) *Fellata* or *Filata*; syn. *Foulbé* or *Fulbé* (sing. *Poulo* or *Pullo*, also *Poul-Foulo, Poul-Poulo*). [Fulani are a cattle-owning tribe]

Fünen: see Danish Red

Fung: see Kenana

Futa, Futa Jallon: see N'Dama

Fynsk: see Danish Red

Gabaruyé: see Maure

Gabassaé: see Red Bororo

Gabú: see N'Gabou

Gacko (S.E. Hercegovina, Yugoslavia); grey; orig. from Tyrol Grey × Buša; Serbo-cro. *Gatačko goveče*

Gadéhé: see Red Bororo

Gado da Terra (Ribatejo, Portugal); black; sim. to Morucha and Fighting bull; rare. [= native cattle]

Gajamavu: see Gujamavu

Galega (Portugal): see Minhota

galiba (China); back cross of dzo (yak-cattle hybrid) to yak; syn. *ago, ah gohr*

Galician Blond (N.W. Spain); m.(dr.d); North Spanish type; cream to golden-red; HB 1933, BS 1973; Sp. *Rubia gallega*; improved with Simmental (1914 on), Swiss Brown (little) and South Devon (1958); orig. type (in Monteroso and Carballino) almost extinct; = Minhota

(Portugal)

Galla (Ethiopia): see Sanga

Galla (Kenya): see Ethiopian Boran

Galla-Azebó: see Raya-Azebó

Galloway (S.W. Scotland); m; brownish-black; Polled HB (with Aberdeen-Angus) 1862, BS 1877; obs. syn. *Southern Scots Polled*; vars: Belted Galloway, Dun Galloway, Red Galloway, White Galloway (Dun registered by Galloway BS and Red and White by Belted BS); BS also in USA 1882, Canada 1882 (HB 1874), New Zealand 1949, Australia 1952 (HB 1963), Germany 1984, HB also in S. Africa, USSR

Galway (England); see Lord Caernarvon's breed

[Gambia Dwarf]; var. of West African Dwarf Shorthorn; syn. *West African Shorthorn (Gambia strain)*

Gambian N'Dama (Gambia, Senegal and S.W. Mali); larger var. of N'Dama, ? with zebu blood; fawn or white; syn. *N'Dama Grande* (Senegal), *N'Dama of Kaarta* (Mali)

ganado bravo (Spain): see Fighting bull

Gangatiri: see Shahabadi

Gaolao (N.E. Maharashtra and S.C. Madhya Pradesh, India); dr.d; z; grey-white shorthorned type; syn. *Arvi, Gaulgani*

Garbatov: see Gorbatov Red

Garfagnina (Garfagnana, Lucca, Italy); d.m.[dr]; grey; syn. *Grigia appeninica* (= *Grey Apennine*), *Modenese di Monte, Montanara* (= *mountain*), *Nostrana* (= *local*); nearly extinct by crossing with Italian Brown

[Garonnais] (Lot-et-Garonne, France); m.dr; yellow or yellow-brown; HB 1898; syn. *Garonnais de plaine* till 1922 when *Garonnais de coteau* separated as Quercy; Garonnais and Quercy rejoined in 1961 to form Blonde d'Aquitaine

Garre (C. Somalia); z; Somali group; often red, also red pied or black pied; horns small, sometimes pd; syn. *Dauara* (not *Danara, Daura, Duara*), *Gerra, Gherra*; small var: Bimal (*cf.* Gasara)

Gasara (Somalia); z; Somali group; lead-grey or red; small; syn. *Abgal, Aria, razzetta delle dune* (= *little breed of the dunes*); var: Magal (? with Jiddu blood); *cf.* Bimal

Gascon (Gascony, S.W. France); m.[dr]; grey (with or without black points and mucosae); vars: *à muqueuses noires* (= with black mucosae) and *aréolé* (= with pink aureole round anus and vulva); HBs 1894, vars combined in single HB 1955; declining, Gascon aréolé (= *Mirandais*) nearly extinct

Gâtinais, Gâtine, Gâtinelle: see Parthenais

Gaulan: see Jaulan

Gaulgani: see Gaolao

gaur (hill forests of Indian peninsula and S.E. Asia) = *Bos (Bibos) gaurus* Smith; brown to black, pale feet; syn. *Indian bison*; vars: Indian gaur = *B.g. gaurus*, Burmese gaur = *B.g. readei*, seladang (Malaya) = *B.g. hubbacki*; orig. of mithun; not *gore, gour*; rare. [Hindi]

gayal: see mithun

Geest: see Holstein Geest

Gelbvieh (Austria): see Austrian Yellow

Gelbvieh (C. Germany); m.d.[dr]; cream to reddish-yellow; orig. from self-coloured Bernese and Swiss Brown × local red or red spotted in late 18th and early 19th c; BS; syn. *Einfarbig gelbes Hohenvieh* (= *self-coloured Yellow Hill*), *German Yellow*; former vars. (combined *c*. 1920): Glan-Donnersberg (to 1961), Lahn, Limpurg, Yellow Franconian; BS also in GB 1972, USA 1972, Canada 1973

Georgian Mountain (Georgia, USSR); d; local Caucasian on Greater Caucasus; black, black pied or red pied; Russ. *Gruzinskiĭ gornyĭ skot*: not *Georgian Alpine*; var: Khevsurian

German Angus (Germany); m; black to dark brown or red to yellow-grey, sometimes with white marks; usu. pd; orig. (1960s) from Aberdeen-Angus × German Black Pied, German Simmental, *et al.*; HB; Ger. *Deutsch-Angus* (or *Deutsches-Angus-Fleischrind*

German Black Pied (N. Germany); d.m; Friesian type; BS; Ger. *Deutsche Schwarzbunte*; syn. *German Friesian, Schwarzbuntes Niederungsvieh* (= *Black-and-White Lowland* or *Black Pied Lowland*); orig. vars: East Friesian (HB 1883), East Prussian, Jeverland (HB 1878), Oldenburg-Wesermarsch (HB 1880); orig. of Estonian Black Pied, Lithuanian Black Pied, Polish Black-and-White Lowland *et al.*; Holstein blood in 1960s and 1970s

German Black Pied Dairy (E. Germany); d; orig. (1970s) from (British Friesian × Danish Jersey) × German Black Pied; Ger. *Schwarzbuntes Milchrind* (*SMR*)

German Brown (S.W. Bavaria and E. Württemberg, Germany); d.m.[dr]; Brown (Mountain) type; BS; Ger. *Deutsches Braunvieh*; syn. *Allgäu* (Ger. *Allgäuer*); American Brown Swiss blood since 1966; *cf.* Murnau-Werdenfels

German Friesian: see German Black Pied

German Red (C. Germany); d.m.[dr]; Central European Red type; BS 1911; Ger. *Deutsches Rotvieh*; syn. (till 1937) *Middle German Red* (Ger. *Mitteldeutsches Rotvieh*), *Mitteldeutsches Gebirgsvieh* (= *hill cattle*), *Red cattle of Central Germany, Red Hill* or *Red Mountain* (*Rotes Höhenvieh*); former vars: Bavarian Red, Harz, Hesse-Westphalian (inc. Odenwald, Vogelsberg, Waldeck and Westphalian Red), Silesian Red, Vogtland; linked with Angeln since 1942, absorbed Glan-Donnersberg 1961

German Red Pied (N.W. Germany); d.m; sim. to Meuse-Rhine-Yssel (interchange of blood in 19th c); BS 1922; Ger. *Deutsche Rotbunte*; syn. *Rotbuntes Niederungsvieh* (= *Red Pied Lowland* or *Red-and-White Lowland*); orig. vars: Red Pied East Friesian (HB 1878), Red Pied Schleswig-Holstein, Red Pied Westphalian (HB 1892), Rhineland (HB 1875), united 1934

German Shorthorn (W. Schleswig, Germany); m.d; orig. from Shorthorn × German Red Pied in mid-19th c; HB; Ger. *Land Shorthorn*; nearly extinct

German Simmental (S. Germany); d.m.[dr]; orig. in 19th c. from Bernese and Simmental × local; BS; Ger. *Deutsches Fleckvieh*; obs. syn. *Alpenfleckvieh, Grosses Fleckvieh, Höhenfleckvieh, Red Spotted Highland, Scheckvieh*; orig. vars: Messkircher (Baden), Miesbacher (Bavaria), Württemberg Spotted; not *Brindled Highland*; *cf.* Austrian Simmental

German Spotted: see German Simmental

German Yellow: see Gelbvieh

Gerra: see Garre

Gessien: see Gex

[Gex] (N.E. Ain, E. France); orig. from Swiss Simmental; HB fused with Pie rouge de l'Est 1945; Fr. *Gessien*

Ghana Sanga (N. Ghana); Ghana Shorthorn × zebu; syn. *pseudo-Sanga*; inc. N'Dama Sanga (with N'Dama blood), White Sanga (White Fulani × Ghana Shorthorn) and Ndagu (N'Dama × Sokoto Gudali)

Ghana Shorthorn (N. Ghana); var. of West African Savanna Shorthorn with zebu blood; syn. *Ghanaian Shorthorn, Gold Coast Shorthorn, West African Shorthorn* (*WAS*)

Ghauti: see Dangi

Gherra: see Garre

Ghumsur: see Goomsur

Gidda: see Malnad Gidda

Giddu: see Jiddu

Gilan: see Mazandarani

Gir (S. Kathiawar, Gujarat, India); d.dr.m; z; sim. to Dangi and Deoni; mottled red and white; BSd and HB; syn. *Desan, Gujarati* (Sri Lanka), *Kathiawari, Sorthi, Surati* or *Surti*; orig. (with Khillari) of Nimari; orig. of Brazilian Gir

Giriama (S. Kenya); local Small East African Zebu

Girolando (Brazil) = Gir × Friesian (Holandés) cross

[Glamorgan] (Wales); sim. to Gloucester but light red and light brindle with white 'finching'

Glan (Palatinate, Germany); orig. in late 18th c. from Swiss Brown × native; united with Donnersberg in 1890 to form Glan-Donnersberg;

BS revived 1985

Glan-Donnersberg (Rhineland-Palatinate, Germany); orig. in 1890 from Glan + Donnersberg; var. of Gelbvieh (German Yellow) till 1961; since 1950 crossed with Danish Red and inc. in German Red since 1961; Ger. *Glan-Donnersberger*; nearly extinct (but Glan BS reformed 1985)

glang: see Tibetan ♂; ♀ is *glangmu*

Glatz Mountain: see Kłodzka

Gloucester (England); d; sim. to Glamorgan; black-brown with white tail, escutcheon and belly; BS 1919-66 and 1973 on; syn. *Gloucestershire, Old Gloucester(shire)*; nearly extinct

Gobra (Senegal); m.dr; West African (lyrehorned) Zebu type; white, red pied, or yellow-brown; Fr. *Zébu peul sénégalais*; syn. *Senegal Fulani, Senegal Zebu*; not *Cobra*; orig. (with N'Dama) of Djakoré

Goda: see Sheko

Godali: see Adamawa or Sokoto Gudali

Goias: see Curraleiro

Golan: see Jaulan

Gold Coast Shorthorn: see Ghana Shorthorn

Göle (E. Turkey); var. of East Anatolian Red; not *Köle*

Golpayegani (Esfahan, Iran); d.m.(dr); usu. black, also red; not *Golpaegani*

Goodhope Red: see Jamaica Red

Goomsur (Orissa, India); dr; z; local var; not *Ghumsur, Gumsur*

Gorbatov Red (Gorki, USSR); d.m; orig. in 19th c. from Zillertal × local Oka (Russ. *Priokskaya*); HB 1921; Russ. *Krasnaya gorbatovskaya* or *Krasnogorbatovskaya* (= *Red Gorbatov*); not *Garbatov*

gore: see gaur

Goryn (Stolin district, Brest prov, Byelorussia, USSR); d.m; red pied; orig. from local crossed with old-type Simmental and Polish Red; Russ. *Gorynskaya*; rare

gour: see gaur

[Govuvu] (Zimbabwe); dwarf forest cattle of Sanga type; syn. *Kavuvu, Kwavovu*

Grati (E. Java, Indonesia); d; orig. (1925 on) from Friesian × native Javanese and Madura, with some Ayrshire and Jersey blood; Indonesian *Sapi perahan Grati* (= *Grati dairy cattle*)

Graubraunes Höhenvieh: see Brown Mountain

Grauvieh: see Grey Alpine, Tyrol Grey

Greater Caucasus (USSR); smaller, usu. black, var of Caucasian; Russ. *Velikokavkazskaya*; inc. Dagestan Mountain and Georgian Mountain (*q.v.*)

Greek Shorthorn (Greece); dr.m; Iberian type; sim. to Albanian and

Buša (Yugoslavia); grey-blond to dark brown; former vars: Cretan
Lowland, Cretan Mountain, East Macedonian and Thrace, Epirus,
Mainland, West Macedonian, Peloponnesus, Thessaly; being crossed
with Swiss Brown; rare

Greek Steppe (N.E. Greece); dr; Grey Steppe type; vars: Katerini (plains
of N.E.), Sykia (Khalkidiki); rare

Grey (Austria): see Tyrol Grey

[Grey Adige] (Trentino/Alto Adige, Italy); dr.d.m; BSd 1931, HB 1934;
It. *Grigia di Val d'Adige*; syn. *Etschtaler* (Austria), *Ulten* (Ger.), *Ultimo*
(It.); absorbed by Grey Alpine

Grey Alpine (Trentino/Alto Adige, Italy); d.m.[dr]; Grey Mountain type;
HB; It. *Grigia* (or *bigia*) *alpina*; syn. *South Tyrol Grey*; not *Grey Swiss*;
= Tyrol Grey (Austria)

Grey Apennine: see Garfagnina

Grey-Brown (Mountain): see Brown Mountain

Grey Bulgarian: see Iskar

grey Cambodian: see kou-prey

Grey Hungarian: see Hungarian Grey

Grey Iskur: see Iskar

Grey Mountain; Ger. *Graues Gebirgsvieh, Grauvieh*; see Grey Adige and
Grey Alpine (Italy), Tyrol Grey (Austria)

Grey Sindhi: see Thari

GREY STEPPE (S.E. Europe); dr; grey-white, grey, or white; long lyre
horns; *primigenius* type; syn. *Podolian* (Slav *Podolska*), *Steppe*; inc. Iskar
(Bulgaria), Greek Steppe, Hungarian Grey, Istrian, Mursi (Albania),
Podolian (Italy), Romanian Steppe, Turkish Grey Steppe, Ukrainian
Grey, Yugoslav Steppe

Grey Transylvanian: see Transylvanian

Grey Ukrainian: see Ukrainian Grey

Grey Val d'Adige: see Grèy Adige

[Grey Val di Fiemme] (N.E. Italy); d.m.dr; It. *Grigia di Val di Fiemme*;
graded to Italian Brown in 20th c; grade called *sorcino*

GREY-WHITE SHORTHORNED (N.W. and C. India, and Pakistan); dr.(d);
z; inc. Bachaur, Bhagnari, Gaolao, Hariana, Hissar, Krishna Valley,
Mewati, Nagori, Ongole, Rath, Shahabadi

Grigia appeninica: see Garfagnina

Groningen Whiteheaded (N. Netherlands); d.m; black (5% red) with
white head and belly; HB 1906; Du. *Groninger* (or *Gronings*) *Blaarkop*,
Ger. *Groninger*, Fr. *Groningue*; syn. *Zwartblaar* or *Zwartwitkop* (=
black with white head), *Roodblaar* or *Roodwitkop* (= *red with white
head*)

Grossetana; former var. of Maremmana

Gruzian, Gruzinski: see Georgian

[Guademar] (Bahia, Brazil); orig. from Curraleiro with zebu blood (2 Ongole ♂♂ imported in English ship in 1868 or 1882); not *Godemale, Godemar, Guademão, Guadiman*. [? from Goodman - the captain of the ship, or from *godemes* - popular Brazilian for 'Englishmen']

Guadiana Spotted (S.E. Alentejo, Portugal); dr; var. of Mértolenga; red-and-white; orig. from Berrenda; Port. *Malhada do baixo Guadiana*

Guadiana White (Spain): see White Caceres

Guangnan: see Wenshan

Guanling (S. Guizhou, China); dr.m; ♂ small hump; syn. *Guanling Yellow, Guizhou*; *cf.* Central Chinese type

Guarapuéva: see Igarapé

Gudali: see Adamawa or Sokoto Gudali

[Gudbrandsdal] (Norway); var. of Døle; dark brown or other colours

Guelma (E. Algeria and Tunisia); former var. of Brown Atlas; grey; subvars: Chaouia, Cheurfa, Guelma (*s.s.*), Kabyle, and Tunisian

Guernsey (Channel Islands); d; brown-and-white; ? French orig.; BSd 1842, HB 1878; BS in England 1884, USA 1877, Australia, Canada 1905, S. Africa 1930, Brazil 1941, Zimbabwe, Kenya, Ireland

Gujamavu; var. of Hallikar; not *Gajamavu, Gujjamavu, Gujmavu*

Gujarat (Brazil): see Guzerá

Gujarati (Sri Lanka): see Gir

Gujrati (Brazil): see Guzerá

Gumsur: see Goomsur

Guserá: see Guzerá

Gutsul'skaya: see Hutsul

Guzerá (Brazil); m.d; z; grey-white; orig. from Kankrej imported 1875-1964; HB 1936; not *Gujarat, Gujrati, Guserá, Guzerat, Guzerath*; var: Polled Guzerá

Guzerando (Brazil) = Guzerá × Friesian (Holandés) cross

Gyr: see Brazilian Gir

[Hagalvadi]; former var. of Amritmahal now merged in Hallikar

hainag, hainak, hainyk: see dzo

Hainan (Hainan I, Guanxi, China); South China Zebu type; syn. *Hainan High-hump*; rare

Halabi, Halep: see Damascus

Halhïn Gol (N.E. Mongolia); larger var. of Mongolian; Russ. *Khalkhin-gol'skiĭ skot*; not *Khalkhingol*

Hallikar (S. Karnataka, India); dr; z; Mysore type; dark grey; orig. of Amritmahal; var: Gujamavu; not *Halikar*

[Hamitic Longhorn] (Ancient Egypt); ? orig. from African aurochs (*Bos primigenius opisthonomus*); syn. *Ancient Egyptian, Egyptian Longhorn*;

orig. of West African longhorns, and (with zebu) of Sanga
Hana, Haná-Berner: see Moravian Red Pied
Hanagamba: see Red Bororo
Hanam: see Atpadi Mahal
hanik: see dzo
Hanna-Berne: see Moravian Red Pied
Hansi, Hansi-Hissar: see Hissar
Hariana (Haryana, India); dr.d; z; grey-white shorthorned type; BSd and HB; orig. (with Kankrej *et al.*) of Hissar var; not *Haryana*
Hartón (Upper Cauca valley, Colombia); d.m; Criollo type; usu. tan; syn. *Vallecaucana* or *Valle de Cauca*; not *Artón del Valle, Hortón del Valle*
Harz (C. Germany); var. of German Red; inc. Angeln and Danish Red blood; Ger. *Harzer Rotvieh*; purebreds now rare
[Hash Cross] (Wyoming, USA); m; orig. by E. and F. Barnes from Milking Shorthorn × Hereford 1950, with Red Angus bulls since 1956 and Highland since 1959; Beefmaker also used in separate line; combined in Ranger breed 1970. (*H*ighland, *A*ngus, *S*horthorn, *Here*ford]
Hatton (C. Sri Lanka); d; orig. from European imports via Cape of Good Hope by Dutch 1765-1815; syn. *Cape*; not *Hatta*; rare
Hawaiian wild (S.W. Hawaii); feral; orig. from Mexican cattle first imported 1793, with British blood later; rare
Hays Converter (H. Hays' farm, Calgary, Alberta, Canada); m; black with white face, occ. red with white face; orig. 1952 on from Hereford × (Holstein × Hereford) + American Brown Swiss × Hereford; BS
[Hedmark] (S.E. Norway); d; local type of Swedish Red-and-White orig; inc. in Norwegian Red since 1939
[Heilbronn] (Württemberg, Germany); orig. from Bernese × German Red; part orig. of Scheinfeld and Yellow Franconian; syn. *Neckar*
Heilongjiang Dairy: see Pinzhou, Sanhe
Helmete: see Bergscheck
Herebu: see Braford
Hereford (W. England); m; red with white head and underside; hd and pd vars; recog. mid-18th c; HB 1846, BS 1878; syn. *Pampa* (Uruguay); BS also in USA 1881, Australia 1885 (HB 1890), Uruguay (HB 1887), Argentina 1924 (HB 1889), Canada 1890 (HB 1899), New Zealand 1896, S. Africa 1917 (HB 1906), Brazil 1906, Zimbabwe 1958, Chile, Denmark, Ireland, Portugal, Spain, Sweden, USSR (HB), Zambia
Hereford pattern: see white-faced
Hereland (Great Britain); Hereford × Highland, 1st cross
Hérens (C. Valais, Switzerland); d.m.dr; dark red-brown; BSd 1884, BS 1917; Ger. *Eringer*; syn. *Valais*; colour vars: Evolene

Herero: see Damara

[Herrgård] (Sweden); local var. absorbed into Red Pied Swedish. [= estate]

[Hervé Black Pied] (C. Liège, Belgium); d; orig. from Dutch Friesian × local red pied since 1860; HB 1919; Fr. *Pie-noire (du Pays) de Hervé*, Flem. *Zwartbont ras van het Land van Herve*; syn. *Eastern Black Pied* (Fr. *Pie-noire de l'Est de la Belgique*, Flem. *Zwartbont ras van Oost-België*); fused with Polders Black Pied 1966 to form Belgian Black Pied

[Hesse-Westphalian Red] (Germany); var. of German Red inc. Odenwald, Vogelsberg, Waldeck (Hesse) and Westphalian Red; Ger. *Hessisch-Westfälisches Rotvieh*

HIGHLAND (Germany); Ger, *Höhenvieh*; syn. *hill, mountain, upland*; inc. German Brown, German Red, German Simmental, German Yellow (Gelbvieh), Mottled Hill, Murnau-Werdenfels

Highland (N.W. Scotland); m; usu. red-brown, also brindle, dun, or black; long horns and hair; BS 1884, HB 1885; syn. *Kiloe, Kyloe, Scotch Highland, Scottish Highland, West Highland*; BS in USA 1948, Canada 1964, Sweden 1978, Germany; part orig. of Luing

hill (India): see Indian hill

Hinterwald (S. Black Forest, Baden, Germany); d.m.[dr]; small; red or yellow pied, head and legs white; BS 1889; Ger. *Hinterwälder*; rare; see also Vorderwald

Hissar (S. Punjab, India); dr.d; z; var. of Hariana; orig. 1815-98 from Kankrej, Hariana, Gir, Nagori and also Ongole, Tharparkar, and Krishna Valley, selected for type and fast trotting 1899-1912, and backcrossed to Hariana (1912 on) to improve milk yield; syn. *Hansi, Hansi-Hissar, Hissar-Hansi, Hissar-Hariana*

Höhenfleckvieh: see Simmental

Höhenvieh: see Highland (Germany)

Holandesa: see Dutch

Holando-Argentino: see Argentine Friesian

[Holderness] (E. Yorkshire, England); sim. to Teeswater; Dutch orig; syn. *Yorkshire*; orig. (+ Teeswater) of Shorthorn

Holgus (Texas, USA); Holstein × Angus cross

Holland, Hollandaise, Holländisch: see Dutch, esp. Dutch Black Pied

Holmogor, Holmogorskaya: see Kholmogory

Holmonger (Namibia); m.d; light dun; orig. since 1949 from yellow Africander × Brown Swiss by Johan *Holm* at *Ong*anjera Farm

Holstein (Germany): see Red Pied Schleswig-Holstein

Holstein (USA and Canada); d; orig. from Dutch Black Pied imported chiefly 1857-87; USA—Holstein BS 1871, HB 1872, Dutch Friesian BS 1877, HB 1880, combined as Holstein-Friesian 1885, since 1977

name usu. simplified to Holstein; Canada—Holstein-Friesian BS 1884, HB 1892, name changed to Holstein 1984; syn. *American Friesian, Canadian Friesian, Holstein-Friesian*; var: Red and White Holstein; orig. of British Holstein; BS also in Australia

[Holstein Geest]; orig. var. of Red Pied Schleswig-Holstein; Ger. *Holsteinische Geest*

Holstein Marsh, Holstein Red Pied (Germany): see Red Pied Schleswig-Holstein

Horned Lowland (Norway): see Norwegian Red-and-White

Horned Sinú: see Costeño con Cuernos

Hornet slettefe (Norway): see Norwegian Red-and-White

Horosan: see Khurasani

Horro (Horro Gudru, Welega, also Ilubabor and Kefa, Ethiopia); m; Sanga-Zebu intermediate; brown; small to medium hump; syn. *Wallega* or *Wollega* (It. *Uollega*)

Hortón del Valle: see Hartón

[Hottentot] (S. Africa); Sanga type; syn. *Namaqua*; orig. of Africander

Hřbínecký (N. Moravia, Czechoslovakia); var. of Czech Pied; white head (Hereford pattern); syn. *Schönhengst* (Ger.), *Šenhengský* (Cz.)

hsaine: see tsine

Huangpi (E. Hubei, China); inc. in Dabieshan; W.G. *Huang-p'ei* or *Huang-p'o*; not *Hwangpei, Hwangpo*

Huertana; chief var. of Murcian. [= local]

Humbi (S.W. Angola); local Sanga type sim. to Ovambo

humlie: see Buchan Humlie. [homyll, hummell = pd]

[Hungarian Brown] (N. Hungary); small var. of Swiss Brown sim. to Carpathian Brown; orig. (with Jersey) of Dairy Hungarian Brown; graded to Holstein or Hungarofries

Hungarian Grey (Hungary); m.[dr.d]; Grey Steppe type; Maremmana blood in 1930s; Hung. *Magyar szürke* or *Magyar alföldi*; syn. *Grey Hungarian, Hungarian Steppe, White Hungarian*; rare; cf. Transylvanian

Hungarian Pied (Hungary); m.d.[dr]; orig. (1884 on) from Hungarian Grey graded to Simmental; BS and HB 1896; Hung. *Magyartarka*, Ger. *Ungarisches Fleckvieh*; syn. *Hungarian Red and White, Hungarian Red Pied, Hungarian (Red) Spotted, Hungarian Simmental*; former var: Bonyhádi; orig. (with Jersey) of Dairy Hungarian Pied

Hungarian Steppe: see Hungarian Grey

Hungarofries (Hungary); d.m; orig. (1963 on) from Holstein × (Danish Jersey × Hungarian Pied) or Holstein × [(Holstein × Danish Jersey) × (Holstein × Hungarian Pied)]; not *Hungaro-Fries, Hungarofriesian*

[Hutsul] (Bukovina, W. Ukraine, USSR); orig. from Moldavian × Carpathian Brown; Russ. *Gutsul'skaya*; extinct by crossing with Simmental

Hwangpei, Hwangpo: see Huangpi

[Ialomiţa] (Walachia, Romania); former var. of Romanian Steppe; ? orig. from Moldavian × Transylvanian; Rom. *Ialomiţeană*, Ger. *Jalomitzaner*; not *Ialomitza, Jalomita*

Ibagé (Bagé, Rio Grande do Sul, Brazil); m; black; pd; orig. from Nelore ($\frac{3}{8}$) × Aberdeen-Angus ($\frac{5}{8}$) since 1955 at Cinco Cruzes Research Sta.

IBERIAN (E. and S. Mediterranean); shades of brown or red; small; short horns; *brachyceros* type; inc. Albanian, Brown Atlas, Buša (Yugoslavia), Corsican, Greek Shorthorn, Libyan, Rodopi (Bulgaria), Romanian Mountain; *cf.* also Anatolian Black

Iberian (W. Mediterranean) = Spanish + Portuguese

Icelandic (Iceland); d; usu. pd, 14% hd; 40% red or red-and-white, also brindle, brown, black, grey, white or pied; Nor. orig. since 10th c; BS 1903, HB

[Igarapé] (mts and seashores of São Paulo, Brazil); ? Iberian orig.; syn. *Guarapuéva, Nanico* (= dwarf). [= canal or sea-furrow]

IJssel: see Meuse-Rhine-Yssel

Ila: sing. of Baila

Illawarra (NSW, Australia); d; usu. red or roan; inc. Australian Milking Shorthorn; orig. in early 19th c. from Shorthorn, with admixture of dairy breeds; BS 1930; syn. *A.I.S., Australian Illawarra Shorthorn* (till 1984), *South Coast cattle*; BS also in USA

Illyrian; Iberian type, sim. to Greek Shorthorn; used by Adametz to inc. Albanian and Buša (Yugoslavia); syn. *Balkan*

Ilocos; var. of Philippine Native; usu. red, brown or pied; large and small types; Sp. *Ilocano*

Iloilo; var. of Philippine Native; usu. black, also fawn, chestnut or pied

Improved Boran: see Kenya Boran

Improved Criollo (Venezuela): see Rio Limón Dairy Criollo

Improved Friuli: see Italian Pied

Improved Maremmana: see Chianino-Maremmana

Improved Rodopi (Bulgaria); d.m; Jersey × (Bulgarian Brown × Rodopi); Ger. *Veredeltes Rhodopenrind*

Improved Shorthorn, Improved Teeswater: see Shorthorn

Indian bison: see gaur

INDIAN HILL (Himalayas, Baluchistan, *etc.*); z; small; red, black or pied; inc. Kumauni, Las Bela, Lohani, Morang, Nepalese Hill, Purnea, Rojhan, Siri; *cf.* Sinhala (Sri Lanka)

INDIAN ZEBU (India and Pakistan); inc. grey-white shorthorned type, lyrehorned type, Gir type, hill type, Mysore type, Red Sindhi, Sahiwal, and Dhanni; also inc. desi; orig. of Brahman (USA) and Indo-Brazilian

Indo-African Zebu: see Mpwapwa

Indo-Brazilian (Uberaba, Minas Gerais, Brazil); m; z; white to dark grey;

orig. 1910-30 from Gir and Kankrej, with some Ongole, imported from India 1875-1930; HB 1936; Port. *Indubrasil*; syn. *Induberaba*

Indo-Chinese: see Cambodian, Moi, Vietnamese

Indo-Chinese forest ox: see kou-prey

Indo-europeu leiteiro: see Dairy Indo-European

Indonesian: see Bali cattle, Borneo, Javanese, Madura, Merauke

Induberaba, Indú-Brasil: see Indo-Brazilian

Indu-Europeu: see Azebuado

Ingessana (S. Blue Nile, Sudan); z; sim. to Abyssinian Shorthorned Zebu but with Kenana blood

inkone: colour type *i.e.* coloursided; not *nkone*. [Zulu]

Inkuku (Rwanda); common var. of Watusi Ankole as distinct from royal, giant-horned Inyambo; not *Kukku, Kuku*

[Innviertel] (Upper Austria); former var. of Austrian Simmental; Ger. *Innviertler*

INRA 9 (France); m; selected strain of double-muscled Charolais at Station Centrale de Génétique Animale, *I*nstitut *N*ational de *R*echerche *A*gronomique

[Inyambo] (Rwanda); giant-lyrehorned var. of Watusi Ankole owned by king and chiefs as distinct from common Inkuku; not *Nyambo, Nyembo*

Iranian (Iran): see Bami, Dashtiari, Golpayegani, Mazandarani, Nejdi, Sarabi, Sistani; obs. syn. *Persian*

Iraqi (Iraq); m.dr; zebu blood; vars: Dishti, Jenubi, Rustaqi, Sharabi; see also Kurdi

[Irecé] (Bahia, N.E. Brazil); d; var. of Curraleiro; Port. *Crioulo leiteiro de Irecé*

[Iringa Red]; local strain of Small East African Zebu in Tanzania

[Irish Dun] (Ireland); d; pd; sim. to Suffolk Dun; syn. *Polled Irish*

Irish Moiled (N.W. Ireland); d.m; usu. red or roan coloursided, formerly also grey, dun, black or white; pd; BS 1926-57, revived 1982, HB 1926-66, revived 1983; syn. *Irish Polled*; not *Maoile, Maol, Maoline, Moile, Moilie, Moyle, Moyled*; nearly extinct. [from Irish *maol* = polled]

Irish Polled: see Irish Dun, Irish Moiled

ISK: see East Finnish

Iskar (Bulgaria); dr.m.d; Grey Steppe type with some *brachyceros* blood; Bulg. *Isk"rsko govedo*; syn. *Bulgarian Grey* or *Grey Native cattle* (Bulg. *Sivo mestno govedo*, Ger. *Bulgarisches Grauvieh)*, *Bulgarian Steppe, Grey Iskur, Vit*; not *Isker*; formerly Iskar was larger, lowland var. of Bulgarian Grey, with extinction of smaller mountain var. (Stara Planina), Iskar and Bulgarian Grey are now syn.; rare

Israeli Friesian (Israel); d; orig. from local (chiefly Damascus, also Lebanese) graded to Friesian imported from Netherlands 1922-33, Canada 1946, and USA 1949-55; HB, BSd 1951

Istoben (Kirov, USSR); d; usu. black or black pied, occ. red or red pied; orig. from Kholmogory (to 1912), Swiss Brown (1913 on), and East Friesian (1930 on), × local; HB 1935, approved 1943; Russ. *Istobenskaya*

Istrian (Istra, Croatia, Yugoslavia); var. of Grey Steppe type; Serbo-cro. *Istarsko goveče* or *Istar-Kvarner*

Italian Brown (Italy); d.(m); var. of Swiss Brown; HB 1956; It. *Bruna alpina* (= *Brown Alpine*); syn. *North Italian Brown, Svitto, Svizzera*; var: Sardinian Brown; being crossed with American Brown Swiss

Italian Friesian (Italy, esp. Po valley); d.(m); orig. from imports since 1872 esp. from Netherlands, Canada and USA; named 1951, HB 1956; It. *Frisona italiana*; syn. *Pezzata nera* (= *black pied*); not *Carnation*

Italian Red Pied (N.E. Italy); m.d.[dr]; orig. from Simmental × Friuli (1880-1900); BSd 1931, HB 1957; It. *Pezzata rossa italiana*; syn. *Friuli-Simmental, Improved Friuli, Italian Simmental, Red Pied Friuli* (It. *Pezzata rossa friulana*), *Simmenthal Friulana*

Italian Simmental: see Italian Red Pied

Izankayi: see Bolowana

Jakoré: see Djakoré
Jakut, Jakutskaja: see Yakut
Jali, Jalli, Jalliji: see Diali
Jalomita, Jalomitza: see Ialomiţa
Jamaica Black; m; pd; recent orig. from Aberdeen-Angus × zebu ($\frac{1}{4}$-$\frac{3}{8}$); BS and HB 1954
Jamaica Brahman; m; z; orig. from Ongole, Hissar, and Mysore zebus; BS and HB 1949
Jamaica Hope; d; orig. 1920-52 from Jersey (80%) × zebu (15%) (chiefly 1 Sahiwal ♂) with 5% Friesian blood at Hope Stock Farm; BS and HB 1953; syn. *Montgomery-Jersey, Jersey-Zebu*
Jamaica Red; m; pd; recent orig. from Red Poll, Devon, and zebu; BS 1952; syn. *Goodhope Red, Jamaica Red Poll*
Janubi: see Jenubi
Japanese Black (Japan); m; orig. 1868-1910 from Japanese Native crossed with Shorthorn, American Brown Swiss, Simmental, Devon and Ayrshire; recog. 1944; black with brownish hair tips
Japanese Brown (Kumamoto prefecture, Kyushu, and Kochi prefecture, Shikohu, Japan); m; orig. 1868-1910 from Japanese Native crossed with Simmental, Korean and Devon; recog. 1944; Kumamoto strain has more Simmental blood and is light brown, Kochi has more Korean blood and is reddish-brown with black mucosae
Japanese Improved (Japan); m; syn. *Kairyo-Washu, Nipponese Improved*;

orig. from Japanese Native by crossing with European breeds 1868-1910; inc. Japanese Black, Japanese Brown, Japanese Poll, Japanese Shorthorn; recog. 1919

Japanese Native (Japan); m.dr; almost eliminated by crossing with European breeds 1868-1910; existing vars: Kuchinoshima and Mishima; Jap. *Wagyu* (= *Japanese cattle*); orig. of Japanese Improved

Japanese Poll (Yamaguchi prefecture, S.E. Honshu, Japan); m; black; orig. 1868-1910 from Japanese Native crossed with Aberdeen-Angus; recog. 1944; syn. *Japanese Polled*

Japanese Shorthorn (N. Honshiu, and Hokkaido, Japan); m; orig. from Japanese Native crossed with Shorthorn 1868-1910 (some Ayrshire and Devon blood); BS 1957; red, red-and-white, or roan

[Jarlsberg] (Vestfold, Norway); coloursided var. of Red Polled Østland

Jarmelista (Jarmelo, Beira, Portugal); d; local var. of Mirandesa; disappearing

Jaroslav, Jaroslavl: see Yaroslavl

Jathi madu: see Umblachery

jatsa ($\mathcal{S}$ - dr) and jatsun ($\mathcal{Q}$ - d) (Bhutan); F₁ mithun $\mathcal{S}$ × Siri $\mathcal{Q}$; not *jesha* ($\mathcal{S}$), *jatshum, jescham* or *jesham* ($\mathcal{Q}$)

Jaulan (Jebel ed Druz, S.W. Syria); dr.m.d; *brachyceros* type; sim. to Baladi but larger; black with white markings, often white head and black spectacles; 15% pd; syn. *Bisre, Khamissi*; not *Djelani, Dscholan, Gaulan, Golan, Jolan, Julani*

[Javanês] (Paraiba, Brazil); orig. by Brito Bastos, Rio Formoso, from one grey zebu bull named Javanês crossed on local cows in mid-19th c.

Javanese (Indonesia); z; small hump

Javanese Ongole (Java, Indonesia); dr; orig. from Ongole × Javanese; Indonesian *Peranakan Ongole*; syn. *Grade Ongole*; Sumba Ongole is purebred Ongole (imported 1914)

Javanese Zebu (Papua New Guinea); m; z; orig. from cattle imported from Java, Sumatra and Thailand in 19th c.

je: see dzo

Jeju: see Cheju

Jeli: see Diali

Jellicut (Tamil Nadu, India); dr; z; syn. *Kilakad, Kilakattu, Kilkad, Pulikulam*; var: Kappiliyan; not *Jellikut*. [= bull baiting]

Jem-Jem Zebu (high plateau of Sidamo, Ethiopia); Abyssinian Zebu group; usu. black, occ. spotted; syn. *Black Zebu*

Jenubi (S.E. and C. Iraq); d; z; var. of Iraqi; usu. red (golden to bright bay); syn. *Fao, Ma'amir, Zubairi*; orig. of Rustaqi; not *Genubi, Janubi, Jenoubi*. [= southern]

Jerdi (Brazil) = Jersey × Red Sindhi cross

Jersey (Channel Islands); d; fawn, mulberry or grey, often with black skin pigment; BSd 1844, HB 1866; Fr. *Jersiais*; BS in UK 1878, USA 1868, Australia 1900, Canada 1901, France 1903, S. Africa 1920 (HB 1906), Brazil 1938, Kenya, Sweden 1955, Germany, Netherlands (HB 1967), Japan, Argentina, Belgium, Colombia, Costa Rica, India, Ireland, Ecuador, Norway, Uruguay, Zimbabwe; orig. of Danish Jersey, New Zealand Jersey

Jersian (Great Britain); d; name for Jersey × Friesian, F_1

Jersind (Allahabad, India); d; orig. from Jersey ($\frac{3}{8}$-$\frac{5}{8}$) × Red Sindhi at Allahabad Agric. Institute in 1960s

jesha and *jescham* or *jesham*: see jatsa and jatsum

[Jeverländer] (Oldenburg, Germany); d.m; orig. var. of German Black Pied; HB 1878-1938 (joined with East Friesian)

jhopke: see dzo ♂

Jiddu (S.E. Ethiopia and S. Somalia); Sanga-Zebu intermediate; It. *Giddu*; syn. (Somalia) *Macien* (*magien* = spotted), *Sorco, Sucra, Surco, Surco Sanga, Surug* or *Suruq* (= red-and-white); = Tuni (Kenya)

Jie: see Karamajong

Jijjiga Zebu (W. Harer, Ethiopia); d; Abyssinian Zebu group; chestnut, black, white, dark grey, red, *et al.*; short horns, sometimes pd; syn. *Ogaden Zebu, Small Zebu*

Jinnan (S. Shanxi, China); Central Chinese type

Jochberg Hummel (Austria); pd var. of Pinzgauer; Ger. *Jochberger Hummel*. [hummel = pd]

Jolan: see Jaulan

jolang: see Tibetan ♂

jommu: see dzo ♀

joppa: see dzo ♂

Jotko (Bornu, Nigeria); var. of Kuri, ? with zebu blood; syn. *Jotkoram*

Julani: see Jaulan

jum: see dzo ♀

[Junqueiro] (Minas Gerais, Brazil); long horns; sim. to Franqueiro; selected from Southern Crioulo by Junqueiro family in 19th c.

Jurin, Jurinskaja: see Yurin

[Jutland Black Pied] (Denmark); d; Dan. *Sortbroget Jydsk Malkekvæg* (= *SJM*); syn. *Black Pied Jutland, Black Spotted Jutland Milk, Black and White Jutland*; joined (1949) with local Friesian to form Danish Black Pied

Kabota; var. of Borneo Zebu

Kabuli: see Afghan

Kabyle (Algeria); dwarf; former subvar. of Guelma var. of Brown Atlas

Kachcha Siri (E. Nepal); Siri × Nepalese Hill crossbred. [*kachcha* =

inferior]

Kachhi (India): see Cutchi

Kachhi (Pakistan): see Bhagnari

Kaiama: see Keteku

Kairyo-Washu: see Japanese Improved

Kalakheri; black-and-white var. of Dangi

Kalmyk (N. of Caspian Sea, USSR); m; Turano-Mongolian type; red, often white on head, belly, and feet; HB; Russ. *Kalmytskaya*; syn. (*Red*) *Astrakhan* (Russ. *Krasno-astrakhanskaya*); not *Kalmuck*; regional vars in North Caucasus, Lower Volga, Kazakhstan and Siberia

Kamasia (W. Kenya); local Small East African Zebu

Kamba (S.E. Kenya); local Small East African Zebu; syn. *Akamba, Ukamba, Wakamba*

Kamdhino (Bangladesh); z; local var.

Kampeten: see Bergscheck

Kanada: see Dangi

Kandahari (Afghanistan); d.m; var. of Afghan; yellowish-red to black

Kanem (Chad); Kuri × Arab (Shuwa) zebu

Kanganad: see Kangayam

Kangayam (S.E. Coimbatore, Tamil Nadu, India); dr; z; Mysore type; white or grey with red calves; BSd and HB; syn. *Kanganad, Kongu*; var: Umblachery; not *Kangayan, Kangiam, Kangyam*

Kaningan; var. of Borneo Zebu

Kankrej (S.E. of Rann of Cutch, Gujarat, India); dr.d; z; lyrehorned type; grey; BSd and HB; syn. *Bannai, Nagar, Talabda, Vagadia, Wagad* or *Waged* (Cutch); *Vadhiyar, Wadhiar, Wadhir* or *Wadial* (Radhanpur); var: Sanchori (Jodhpur); orig. of Guzerá (Brazil); not *Kankerej, Kankreji, Kankrij*

Kaokoveld (N.W. Namibia); Sanga type; ? large var. of Ovambo; red, black, pied or coloursided; long horns, crescent or lyre

Kappiliyan; var. of Jellicut

Kapsiki (Mokolo, Mandara mts, N. Cameroon); var. of West African Savanna Shorthorn; syn. *Kirdi* (= pagan); rare

Karacabey Brown, Karacabey Montafon: see Turkish Brown

Karachi, Red: see Red Sindhi

Karadi: see Kurdi

Karamajong (Karamoja, N.E. Uganda); East African Zebu sim. to Toposa and Turkana; usu. grey-white, fawn or tan; inc. Jie

Karan Swiss (India); d; light grey to dark brown; orig. from American Brown Swiss × Sahiwal at National Dairy Research Institute, Karnal

Karavaevo: see Kostroma

[Karelian] (USSR); = East Finnish

Kärntner Blondvieh: see Austrian Blond

Kataku: see Keteku

Katerini (N.E. Greece); larger black var. of Greek Steppe; rare

Kathiawari: see Gir

Kaveri: see Alambadi

Kavirondo (W.Kenya); local Small East African Zebu

Kavuvu: see Govuvu

Kazakh (Kirgizia and Kazakhstan, USSR and N.W. Xinjiang, China); m; Turano-Mongolian type; Russ. *Kazakhskaya*; syn. *Kirgiz* (not *Kirghiz*); orig. of Ala-Tau, Aulie-Ata, Kazakh White-headed and Xinjiang Brown; nearly extinct in USSR

Kazakh Whiteheaded (N. Kazakhstan, USSR); m. or m.d; white head, belly and feet; orig. from Hereford (imported 1928-32 from England and Uruguay) × Kazakh; recog. 1950, HB; Russ. *Kazakhskaya belogolovaya*

[Kea] (Greece); orig. from Swiss Brown × Greek Shorthorn; extinct 1980s by crossing with Swiss Brown and Friesian

Kedah-Kelantan (N. and E. Malaysia); dr.m; z; usu. red or reddish-dun; often dwarf in E; orig. from Thai; syn. *Kedah-Thailand, Kelantan, Kelantan-Kedah, KK, Siam-Kedah, Thai-Kedah, Terengganu* or *Trengganu*

Kelantan, Kelantan-Kedah: see Kedah-Kelantan

[Kelheimer] (Upper Palatinate, Bavaria, Germany); dr.m.d; sim. to Westerwald; brown with white markings; not *Kehlheim*; extinct *c.* 1940

[Kemerovo] (Siberia); d.m; orig. 1930-53 from Siberian crossed first with Simmental, Kholmogory or Ukrainian Red, and then with East Friesian or its grades; Russ. *Kemerovskaya*; absorbed by Black Pied

[Kemp] (Natal, S. Africa); m.d; early var. of Drakensberger; sim. to Africander but black; orig. from Friesian × Africander, by R. Kemp (1911-47)

Kempen, Kempisch: see Campine Red Pied

Kenana (Fung, Sudan); d.dr; North Sudan Zebu group; light blue-grey with black points; syn. *Blue Nile, Fung, Rufa'ai*; var: White Nile (with Baggara blood); not *Kenanna, Kennana*

Kenia (Sri Lanka): see Kinniya

Kenkatha (R. Ken, and Bundelkhand, S. Uttar Pradesh and N. Madhya Pradesh, India); dr; z; lyrehorned type sim. to Malvi; rufous, brown or black; syn. *Kenwariya* (not *Kenwaryia*)

Kenran (Japan); Mishima × Holstein-Friesian cross. [= Mishima/Dutch]

Kenwariya: see Kenkatha

Kenya Boran (C. Kenya); m; improved var. of Boran; BS 1951; syn. *Improved Boran*

Kenya Zebu: Small East African Zebu in S. and W. Kenya is called

Giriama, Kamasia, Kamba, Kavirondo, Kikuyu, Masai, Nandi, Samburu, Suk, according to district

Keriyo: see Danakil

Kerry (S.W. Ireland); d; black; recog. 1839, HB 1890, BS 1917; BS also in UK 1882 (HB 1890), USA 1911-21; orig. of Dexter; rare

Keteku (W. Nigeria) = Borgou (Benin) (*q.v.*); syn. *Kaiama*; not *Kataku, Ketaku, Ketari, Kettije*

Khairigarh: see Kherigarh

Khalkhingol: see Halhïn Gol

Khamala (Betul, S. Madhya Pradesh, India); z; local var.

Khamissi: see Jaulan

Khandari: see Red Khandari

Khargaon, Khargoni: see Nimari

Kherigarh (N. Kheri, N.C. Uttar Pradesh, India); dr; z; lyrehorned type, sim. to Ponwar but grey or white; syn. *Kheri*; not *Khairigarh*

Khevsurian; var. of Georgian Mountain; Russ. *Khevsurskaya gruppa*; rare

Khillari (S. Maharashtra, India); dr; z; Mysore type; grey or white; BSd; syn. *Mandeshi, Shikari*; vars: Atpadi Mahal, Mhaswad, Nakali, Thillari; not *Kilhari, Kilkaree, Killari*. [= cattle herdsman]

Kholmogory (Archangel, USSR); d; usu. black pied, also red pied, black or red; local orig. with Friesian blood since 1765; HB 1927; Russ. *Kholmogorskaya*; not *Cholmogor, Holmogor, Kholmogor*; var: Pechora

Khurasani (Turkmenistan, USSR); var. of Central Asian Zebu; usu. red or black, also brown pied or spotted; Russ. *Khorosanskiĭ zebu*

Khurdi: see Kurdi

Khurgoni: see Nimari

Kigezi (S.W. Uganda); var. of Ankole; smaller and with shorter horns; sim. to Bashi

Kikuyu (C. Kenya); local Small East African Zebu

Kilakad, Kilakattu: see Jellicut

Kilara (N. of Chad); colour var. of Shuwa

Kilhari: see Khillari

Kilis (S. Turkey); d; var. of South Anatolian Red; sim. to Damascus

Kilkad: see Jellicut

Kilkaree, Killari: see Khillari

Kiloe: see Highland

Kimberley Shorthorn: see Australian Shorthorn

Kinniya (Mahaweli Ganga, Sri Lanka); z; local var. sim. to Mysore type; grey; not *Kenia*

Kirgiz: see Kazakh

kirko: see Tibetan ♂

Kisantu (S. of Kinshasa, Zaïre); orig. from Angola cattle with European

blood
Kistna Valley: see Krishna Valley
Kivu: see Watusi var. of Ankole
KK: see Kedah-Kelantan
Kleiti (Syria): see Baladi
[Kłodzka] (Silesia, Poland); dr.d; red or brown with white head, back-stripe and belly; orig. from Sudeten; Ger. *Glatzer Gebirgsrind* (= *Glatz Mountain*), Cz. *Kladsko sudetský červený*; syn. *Silesian Whiteback* (Ger. *Schlesisches Rückenscheck*)
Koalib: see Nuba Mountain
Köle: see Göle
Kolubara (N.W. Serbia, Yugoslavia); var. of Yugoslav Steppe with Buša blood; Serbo-cro. *Kolubarac* or *Kolubarsko goveče*; rare
Konari (Jalalabad, Afghanistan); d; var. of Afghan; red or black with white marks, usu. white face and belly; dwarf; not *Kunar*
Kongu: see Kangayam
Konkani: see Dangi
Korean Black: see Cheju
Korean Native (Korea); m.dr; sim. to Mongolian and to Japanese Native; yellow-brown; Jap. *Chosen*; syn. *Korean Brown*; var: Cheju
Kosi (Cameroon): see Bakosi
Kosi (Uttar Pradesh, India): see Mewati
Kostroma (Yaroslavl, USSR); d.m; grey; orig. at Karavaevo state farm 1890-1945 from Swiss Brown × improved local (Babaev and Miskov); recog. 1944, HB; Russ. *Kostromskaya*; syn. *Karavaevo*
kou-prey (N. Kampuchea) = *Bos (Bibos) sauveli* Urbain; grey with white stockings; syn. *Cambodian wild ox* (Fr. *boeuf sauvage cambodgien*), *grey Cambodian ox, Indo-Chinese forest ox*; not *kou-proh*; nearly extinct
Kouri: see Kuri
Krasnodarsk: see Kuban-Black Sea
Kravařský (Silesia, Czechoslovakia); var. of Czech Pied; coloursided; Ger. *Kuhländer*
Kréda: see Red Bororo
Krishnagiri (Tamil Nadu, India); z; local var; not *Krisnagiri*
Krishna Valley (W.C. Andhra Pradesh, India); dr.d; z; grey-white shorthorned type; orig. (1880 on) from Ongole, Gir and Kankrej with Mysore × blood; syn. *Kistna Valley*
[Kuban-Black Sea] (N. Caucasus, USSR); m.d.dr; grey, brown, or yellow; orig. in 19th c. from Swiss Brown and Simmental, × Ukrainian Grey; Russ. *Kubano-Chernomorskaya*; syn. *Krasnodarsk*
Kuburi: see Kuri
Kuchinoshima (Tokara Is, Japan); var. of Japanese Native; BS; feral; nearly extinct

Kuhland, Kuhländer: see Kravařský
Kuku: see Inkuku
Kula: see Bulgarian Simmental
[Kultak] (Turkey); small var. of Turkish Grey Steppe
Kumauni (N. Uttar Pradesh, India); z; hill type; not *Kumaon*
Kunar: see Konari
[Kuramin] (Uzbekistan, USSR); z; var. of Central Asian Zebu (or
    zeboid); Russ. *Kuraminskiĭ zebu*
Kurdi (Kurdistan); m; *brachyceros* type; black, often with light markings;
    not *Karadi, Khurdi*
Kurgan (S.W. Siberia, USSR); d.m; red, red-and-white, or roan; orig.
    (1890 on) from Shorthorn × (Simmental, Dutch, Bestuzhev, Tagil,
    Red Steppe, or Swiss Brown, × local Siberian), recog. 1949, HB; Russ.
    Kurganskaya
Kuri (Lake Chad, West Africa); m.d: light or white, sometimes with
    spots; gigantic bulbous horns; Fr. *Kouri*; syn. *Baharié* (*Bare* or *Borrié*),
    Buduma (*Budduma, Budumu,* or *Boudouma*), *Chad, Dongolé, Kuburi,*
    White Lake Chad; var: Jotko (Nigeria); also vars in Bornu and Kanem
    with zebu blood; not *Koni*
Kwavovu: see Govuvu
Kyoga (C. Uganda); Sanga-Zebu intermediate, very sim. to Nganda
Kyloe: see Highland (Scotland)

Ladakhi (Kashmir); z; local var; not *Ladaki*
Lagoon: see Lagune
Laguiole: see Aubrac
Lagune (coast of Ivory Coast, Togo and Benin); var. of West African
    Dwarf Shorthorn; syn. *Dahomey* (Zaïre), *Lagoon* (Ghana), *Lagunaire,*
    Mayumbe or *Mayombe* (Zaïre), *Race des Lagunes*
[Lahn] (Nassau, Germany); var. of Gelbvieh (German Yellow); orig. in
    early 19th c. from Bernese × Vogelsberg and Westerwald; syn. *Limburg*
Lake Chad: see Kuri
Lakenvelder (Netherlands); black or red (25%) with white belt; HB
    1918-31, BS; orig. of Dutch Belted (USA); rare. [= sheeted field]
Lakhalbhinda, Lakhalbunda: see Red Khandari
Lambadi: see Alambadi
Lambi Bar: see Sahiwal
Lancashire: see Longhorn
Landim: see Nguni
Land Shorthorn (Germany): see German Shorthorn
lang: see Tibetan ♂
Lango: see Nkedi

Lanka: see Sinhala

Las Bela (Baluchistan, Pakistan); z; hill type; prim. var. of Red Sindhi; not *Lasbella*

Lateral-horned Zebu: see Africander

Latuka (S. Sudan): see Mongalla

[Latvian Black Pied] (Latvia, USSR); d; orig. from German Black Pied; Russ. *Latviĭskaya chernopestraya*; syn. *LM*; extinct in 1950s; see Baltic Black Pied

Latvian Brown (Latvia, USSR); d. or d.m; Baltic Red type; brown or dark red; orig. from local crossed with Angeln (mid-19th c. on) and Danish Red (late 19th c. and early 20th c.); HB 1911; Lat. *Latvijas brūnā*, Russ. *Buraya latviĭskaya* or *Krasnoburaya latviĭskaya* (= Latvian Red-Brown—the official name since 1947); syn. *LB, Latvian Red*

Latvian Brown-and-White: see Latvian Red Pied

Latvian Red, Latvian Red-Brown: see Latvian Brown

[Latvian Red Pied] (Livonia, USSR); d; Russ. *Latviĭskaya krasnopestraya*; syn. *Latvian Brown-and-White, LR*

Lavanttal: see Austrian Blond

La Velasquez (Colombia); m; red; pd; orig. from Red Poll × (zebu × Romosinuano) by José Velasquez at Hazienda 'Africa', La Dorada, Caldas

Lavinia (W. São Paulo, Brazil); m.d; orig. (1954 on) by Franco de Mello at Santa Maria farm, Lavinia, from Brown Swiss ($\frac{5}{8}$) × Guzerá ($\frac{3}{8}$); BS

LB: see Latvian Brown

Lebanese (coast of Lebanon, Syria and Hatay); d.m; ? var. of Damascus or Damascus × Baladi intermediate; shades of brown; syn. *Antakli* (from Antakya = Hatay), *Beirut, Beyrouth*

[Lebaniega] (Liébana, W. Santander, Spain); smaller, highland var. of Santander; syn. *Picos de Europa*; absorbed by Tudanca in 1940s

Lebedin (Sumy, N.E. Ukraine, USSR); d.m; orig. 1902-46 from Swiss Brown × local Ukrainian Grey; recog. 1950, HB; Russ. *Lebedinskaya*; syn. *Lebedin-Schwyz*

[Lechtal] (Tyrol, Austria); intermediate between Allgäu (Brown Mountain) and Tyrol Grey; Ger. *Lechtaler*; absorbed in Tyrol Brown

Legítimo: see Southern Crioulo

Leicestershire: see Longhorn

Le Mans: see Mancelle

[Leonese] (N. Spain); dr.d.m; North Spanish type; usu. red to chestnut; Sp. *Mantequera* (= *butter producer*) *leonesa*; displaced by Swiss Brown; extinct in 1970s

Lesser Caucasus (Lesser Caucasus and lowlands of Transcaucasia, USSR); d.m.dr; larger var. of Caucasian; usu. red, also brown or grey; Russ. *Malokavkazskaya*; subvars: [Azerbaijan Red], Mingrelian Red

(q.v.)
Levantina (Spain): see Murcian
lhang: see Tibetan ♂
Liberian Dwarf (S.E. Liberia); var. of West African Dwarf Shorthorn;
   black or pied; syn. *Muturu of Liberia*
Libyan (Libya); m.d.dr; Iberian type, sim. to Brown Atlas; fawn, red or
   black; syn. *Libyan Brown Atlas, Libyan Shorthorn*
L.I.D.: see Local Indian Dairy
Lidia: see Fighting bull
Liébana: see Lebaniega
Light Alpine, Light Mountain (Austria): see Austrian Yellow
Lim (Serbia, Yugoslavia); var. of Buša; red; Serbo-cro. *Polimska buša*
Limburg (Nassau, Germany): see Lahn var. of Gelbvieh (German Yellow)
Limiana (La Limia, S. Orense, Spain); m.dr; Morenas del Noroeste
   group; chestnut with blackish shading
Limón, Limonero: see Rio Limón Criollo
Limousin (C. France); m.[dr]; dark yellow-red; HB 1886; former vars:
   Meymac, Meyssac, Treignac, Vendonnais; BS also in USA and Canada
   1969, GB 1970, New Zealand, Australia, Ireland, S. Africa, Denmark
Limpurger (Württemberg, Germany); var. of Gelbvieh (German Yellow);
   BS 1890; not *Limburg*; nearly extinct
Lincoln Red (E. England); m; now usu. pd; orig. from Shorthorn ×
   local in early 19th c; HB 1822 (as var. of Shorthorn), BS 1894 (inc. in
   Shorthorn HB again 1935-41); syn. *Lincoln(shire) Red Shorthorn* (to
   1960); var: Polled Lincoln Red is absorbing hd var; BS also in Canada
   1969, New Zealand, Australia 1971, S. Africa
Lincolnshire Beef Poll: see Polled Lincoln Red
Lineback: see American Lineback
[Lišna Red] (Český Těšin, N.E. Moravia, Czechoslovakia); d; var. of
   Moravian Red; Cz. *Lišňanský červený*
Lithuanian Black Pied (Lithuania, USSR); d; inc. in Baltic Black Pied;
   orig. from Dutch Black Pied (also Swedish Friesian and East Friesian)
   × local Lithuanian; recog. 1951; Russ. *Chernopestraya litovskaya*
Lithuanian Red (Lithuania, USSR); d; Central European Red type sim.
   to Polish and Byelorussian Red; hd or pd; some Ayrshire blood in N.
   and Swiss Brown blood in S.E., also Danish Red and Angeln blood;
   HB; Russ. *Krasnaya litovskaya*
Llanero (llanos of S.W. Venezuela); m; Criollo type; = Casanareño
   (Colombia)
LM: see Latvian Black Pied
Lobi (S.W. Burkina Faso); var. of West African Savanna Shorthorn
   sim. to Baoulé; dark or pied; syn. *Lobi-Gouin, Méré*
Local Estonian: see Estonian Native

Local Indian Dairy (Malaysia); d; z; white, grey or red; orig. from Kangayam, Red Sindhi, Tharparkar, Hallikar and Ongole imported by Indian settlers since early 20th c; syn. *L.I.D.*

Lohani (N. Baluchistan to Kohat, Pakistan); dr.d; z; hill type, sim. to Rojhan; usu. red with white patches; syn. *Acchai*; not *Lohanni*

Lola: see Sahiwal

Longhorn (N.W. and C. England and Ireland); m; dark red brindle, coloursided; BS, HB 1878; syn. *English Longhorn*; obs. syn. (18th c.) *Dishley, Lancashire, Leicestershire, Warwickshire*; rare

Longhorn (USA): see Texas Longhorn

[Lord Caernarvon's breed] (Hampshire, England); white with black or red spots; pd; syn. *Galway*

[Lorquina] (Lorca, S.W. Murcia. Spain); former var. of Murcian with Spanish Mountain blood; usu. pale, sometimes dark red or chestnut

[Loriï] (Armenia, USSR); d.m; brown with lighter or darker patches; orig. at Loriï State Farm by grading Lesser Caucasus to Swiss Brown 1934-40 and then mating *inter se*; absorbed by Caucasian Brown

Lourdais (Hautes Pyrénées, France); d.m; nearly extinct

Lower Guadiana Spotted: see Guadiana Spotted

Lower Rhine: see Rhineland

LOWLAND (N. Germany); Ger. *Niederungsvieh* or *Tieflandrind*; inc. Angeln, German Black Pied, German Red Pied, German Shorthorn

Lowlands Black Pied: see Dutch Black Pied

Lozi: see Barotse

LR: see Latvian Red Pied

LSK: see West Finnish

Lucanian (Basilicata, Italy); former var. of Apulian Podolian; It. *Lucana*

Lucerna (Lower Cauca valley, Colombia); d.m; cherry red; orig. at Hacienda Lucerna from Holstein-Friesian (40%), and Milking Shorthorn (30%) × Criollo (Hartón) (30%) during 1937-56

Lugware (N.E. Kibali-Ituri, Zaïre, and W. West Nile, Uganda); var. of Small East African Zebu; often black pied, grey or red pied; syn. *Bahu*; not *Lugbara, Lugwaret, Lugwari; cf*. Mongalla

Luing (Argyll, Scotland); m; usu. red-brown, occ. yellow, roan or white; orig. 1949-65 by Cadzow brothers from Beef Shorthorn × Highland; BS and HB 1966; BS also in Canada 1975, USA, New Zealand, Australia

Luso-Holandese: see Turino

Luxi (W. Shandong, China); Central Chinese type

[Lyngdal] (Norway); red; pd; joined with Vestland Red Polled, and then with Vestland Fjord (1947) to form South and West Norwegian

LYREHORNED (W. and N. India, and Pakistan); dr.(d); z; inc. Kankrej, Kenkatha, Kherigarh, Malvi, Ponwar, Tarai, Thari and Tharparkar

lyrehorned zebu (W. Africa); see West African Zebu (Fulani)

Maalsalv: see Målselv
Ma'amir: see Jenubi
Maasai: see Masai
Maas-Rijn-IJssel: see Meuse-Rhine-Yssel
Macedonian Blue (Yugoslavia); var. of Buša; usu. blue roan; Serbo-cro.
   Makedonska buša or *Plava povardarska*; *cf.* East Macedonian, West
   Macedonian (Greece)
Macien: see Jiddu
Madagascar Zebu; m.dr.d; many colours; lyre horns; syn. *Malagasy*,
   Malgache; orig. of Rana and of Renitelo (with Limousin and Africand-
   er)
Madaripur (Bangladesh); z; local var; brown
Madura (Madura, also in Flores and S. Kalimantan, Indonesia); dr.m;
   chestnut with pale underparts; small hump; orig. from zebu and Bali
   cattle; Du. *Madoera*; syn. *Madurese*; not *Madoura*
Magal (Juba, Somalia); z; var. of Gasara (? with Jiddu blood); black;
   syn. *Correi*; not *Mogol*. [= black]
Maghreb: see Brown Atlas
Magien: see Jiddu
Magyar: see Hungarian
Mahabharat Lekh: see Nepalese Hill
Mahadeopuri: see Malvi
Mahadeswarabetta: see Alambadi
Mahonesa: see Minorcan
Maia, Maiana: see Barrosã
Maine: see Mancelle
Maine-Anjou (N.W. France); m.d; sim. to Armorican but larger; red,
   red-and-white, or roan; orig. from Shorthorn × Mancelle *c.* 1830 on,
   recog. 1925; HB 1925; obs. syn. *Durham-Mancelle*; federated with
   Armorican 1962-70 under name Rouge de l'Ouest; BS in USA 1969,
   Canada 1970, UK, New Zealand, Australia
Makalanga, Makaranga: see Mashona
Makaweli (Robinson ranch, Kauai, Hawaii); m; red; orig. from Short-
   horn and Devon
[Malabar] (N.E. Brazil); m; red-brown to black; orig. in 19th c. from
   Curraleiro with Indian Zebu blood
Malagasy: see Madagascar Zebu
Malai-madu: see Alambadi
[Malakan] (N.E. Turkey): orig. from Ukrainian Grey; syn. *Okranya*; not
   Malokan, Molokan. [Molokan was religious sect in Russia, offshoot of

Doukhobors, from Russ. *moloko* = milk]

Malawi Zebu; var. of Angoni; formerly divided into South Malawi Zebu and North Malawi Zebu

Malayan bison, Malayan gaur: see seladang

Malay banteng (N. Malaysia) = *Bos (Bibos) javanicus butleri* (Lydekker); var. of banteng; syn. *sapi utan* (= wild cattle); ? extinct

Malgache: see Madagascar Zebu

Malinke: see N'Dama

Malir: see Red Sindhi

Malnad Gidda (Karnataka, India); d; local var; dark coat; small size

Målselv (Tromsø, N. Norway); red; usu. pd; orig. from Dutch (to 1860) and Ayrshire (1860-1900) × local; combined with Red Trondheim in 1951, now local var. of Norwegian Red

Maltese (Malta); nearly extinct

Malvi (C. Malwa, W. Madhya Pradesh, India); dr; z; grey; lyrehorned type; BSd; syn. *Mahadeopuri, Manthani*; not *Malwa, Malwi*

Mampati (Madhya Pradesh, India); z; local var.

Manapari (Tamil Nadu, India); z; Kangayam × local

[Mancelle] (Maine, France); syn. *Le Mans, Maine*; orig. (with Shorthorn) of Maine-Anjou

Mandalong Special (NSW, Australia); m; light cream to biscuit; pd or hd; orig. at 'Mandalong Park', nr Sydney, in mid-1960s from Charolais, Chianina, Poll Shorthorn, British White and Brahman; now 58% Continental, 25% British and 17% Brahman

Mandé: see Bambara

Mandeshi: see Khillari

Mandingo: see N'Dama

Mango: see Somba

Mangoni, Manguni: see Nkone

Mangwato (E. Botswana); var. of Tswana; syn. *Amabowe, Bamangwato, Ngwato*; orig. of Tuli; not *Mongconto*

Manhartsberg: see Waldviertel

Manjaca (coast of Guinea-Bissau); var. of West African Dwarf Shorthorn; nearly extinct

Manthani: see Malvi

Mantiqueira (S.E. São Paulo, Brazil); d; in formation at Instituto de Zootecnia, Pindamonhangaba, from Friesian ($\frac{5}{8}$) × Gir ($\frac{3}{8}$); white and black (inverse of Friesian); syn. *Tribofe* (= 3 lungs, referring to physical fitness). [name of mts]

Maoile, Maol, Maoline: see Irish Moiled

Maramureş Brown: see Romanian Brown

Marchigiana (Marche, Abruzzi and Molise, E.C. Italy); m.[dr]; white with black points; Podolian orig. improved by Chianina from mid-19th c. to early 20th c. to give improved Marchigiana (*Marchigiana gentile*) of plains as distinct from orig. Podolian (*montanara*) of mountains and the intermediate *brina* (= grey) of hills; Romagnola blood up to 1928, bred pure since 1932, HB 1957; syn. *Del Cubante* (Avellino); BS in Brazil 1972, Canada, USA 1973, GB, Australia

[Marchois] (La Creuse, France); d.m; absorbed by Limousin and Charolais

Maremmana (Maremma, Tuscany and Latium, Italy); m.[dr]; Podolian type; grey; long, open-lyre horns; BSd and HB 1935; former vars: Grossetana, Roman, and Improved (*stabulata*); orig. (with Chianina) of Chianino-Maremmana

Mariahof: see Austrian Blond

Marianas (Oceania); Spanish orig.; syn. *Marianne*

[Marinera] (Balearic Is, Spain); orig. of Minorcan

Marinhoa (N.W. coast of Portugal); dr.m; var. of Mirandesa

[Maroilles]; former var. of Flemish; Fr. *Maroillais, Marollais*

Maronesa (Terra Quente, N.E. Portugal); m.dr.(d); orig. from Barrosã × Mirandesa. [from Mt Marão]

Marwari: see Sanchori

Maryuti (N.W. Egypt); var. of Egyptian with less zebu blood; syn. *Arabian*; not *Marriouti*

Masai (Kenya-Tanzania); local Small East African Zebu; syn. *Maasai*

Mashona (E. Zimbabwe); m; Sanga type; usu. black or red; often pd (*izuma*); BS 1950, HB 1954; Chishona *Ngombe dza Maswina*, Sindebele *Amanjanja*; syn. *Makalanga, Makaranga, Ngombe dza Vakaranga* (= *cattle of the Karanga*), *Shona*

Mashuk, Mashukulumbwe: see Baila; not *Mashakalumbe, Mashukalumbe, Mashukulumbu*

Massa: see Toupouri

Massanais: see Alberes

Maswina: see Mashona

Matabele (S.W. Zimbabwe); mixed Sanga type raided by Ndebele 1822-93 and inc. Barotse, Batawana, Mashona, Nguni, and Tonga blood; orig. of Nkone

Mateba (I. in mouth of R. Zaïre); m; Sanga type; brown; orig. from Angola cattle crossed with European breeds and finally with Africander whose blood predominates

Maure (Mauritania); pa.dr.d; West African (shorthorned) Zebu type; red, black, or pied; syn. *Arab, Gabaruyé, Mauritanian, Moor, Moorish*

Maurine: see Meymac

Mauritanian: see Maure

Mauritius Creole (Indian Ocean); d; usu. white with black points or with coloured flecks; also brown, or brown-and-white; pd; ? Fr. orig. in 18th c.

Mayombe, Mayumbe: see Lagune

Mazandarani (N. Iran); m.d.(dr); z; all colours; syn. *Gilani*; not Mazander-ani

Mazury (Olsztyn, Poland); d.m; var. of Polish Black-and-White Lowland by revival of East Prussian since 1946; Pol. *Mazurska*; syn. *Masurenland, Masurian*

Mbororo: see Red Bororo

M'Bougi, M'Bouyé: see Doayo

Megrel, Megrelian: see Mingrelian Red

Mehwati: see Mewati

Meknès Black Pied (Morocco); d; orig. from breeds imported in 19th c. (Friesian, Breton or Bordelais)

[Menno-Friesian] (USSR); East Prussian Black Pied Lowland cattle taken to Russia by Mennonites in late 18th and early 19th c.

Menorcan, Menorquina: see Minorcan

menscha: see mithun

Menufi (S.E. Delta, Egypt); dr.m; var. of Baladi; not *Menoufi, Minufi*

Merauke (W. Irian, Indonesia); z; small

Méré (Mali): see Bambara (and other crosses)

Méré (S. Burkina Faso and N.E. Ivory Coast); Fulani Zebu × Baoulé Shorthorn cross; often white; name also used for purebred Baoulé or Lobi. [Fulani = small, not zebu]

Mértolenga (Mertola, S.E. Portugal); dr.m; red or red pied; orig. from Alentejana; HB 1977; vars: Bragado do Sorraia and Guadiana Spotted

Messaoria; larger, lowland, var. of Cyprus

Messara: see Cretan Lowland

[Messkircher] (Baden, Germany); orig. var. of German Simmental from Simmentals first imported 1843, BS 1882; syn. *Upper Baden Spotted* (Ger. *Oberbädisches Fleckvieh*)

Metohija Red (Yugoslavia); var. of Buša; usu. red; Serbo-cro. *Crvena metohijska* or *Metohijska buša*

Meuse-Rhine-Yssel (S.E. Netherlands); d.m; HB 1906; Du. *Roodbont* (= *Red Pied*) *Maas-Rijn-IJssel*, Ger. *Rotbunte holländische*, Fr. *Mosane-rhénane-ysseloise*; syn. *Dutch Red-and-White, MRI, MRY, Red Pied Dutch*; var: Brandrood IJsselvee (= dark red MRY); BS in Canada, GB, USA

Mewati (E. Rajasthan, India); dr; z; grey-white shorthorned type; sim. to Hariana with Gir blood; syn. *Kosi* (Uttar Pradesh); not *Mehwati, Mhewati, Mowati*

[Meymac] (C. France); orig. from Limousin × Marchois; syn. *Maurine* [Meyssac]; former var. of Limousin

[Mézenc] (Haute Loire-Ardèche, S. France); dr.m; sim. to Villard-de-Lans; yellow-brown; extinct in late 1960s

Mezzalina; upland var. of Modicana

Mhaswad; var. of Khillari; not *Mhasvad*

Mhewati: see Mewati

Mid-Belgian: see Belgian Blue

Middle German Red: see German Red

Middle-horned (Great Britain); inc. Devon, Hereford, Gloucester, South Devon, Sussex, and Welsh Black

[Miesbacher] (Bavaria, Germany); orig. var. of German Simmental; syn. *Upper Bavarian Spotted* (Ger. *Oberbayrisches Alpenfleckvieh*)

Milking Criollo: see Tropical Dairy Criollo

Milking Devon (Vermont, USA); d.m; orig. var. of Devon; BS 1952, reorg. 1978; rare

Milking Shorthorn (New Zealand): see Dairy Shorthorn

Milking Shorthorn (USA); d.m; var. of Shorthorn developed 1885 on; BS 1912; *cf.* Dairy Shorthorn (Great Britain)

Mineiro: see Southern Crioulo

Mingrelian Red (W. Georgia, USSR); d; derivative of Lesser Caucasus var. of Caucasian; Russ. *Krasnyĭ megrelskiĭ skot*; syn. *Megrel, Megrelian, Mingrelian*

Minhota (N.W. Portugal); dr.m.d; yellow-brown; syn. *Galega*; = Galician Blond (Spain); declining, by crossing with Barrosã, Turino and esp. Gelbvieh

Minorcan (Menorca, Balearic Is, Spain); d.m; blond to red; usu. pd; orig. from Marinera; Sp. *Menorquina*; syn. *Mahonesa* (from Mahón); rare

Minufi: see Menufi

Mirandais: see Gascon aréolé

Mirandesa (C. and N.E. Portugal); dr.m; light to dark chestnut; HB 1977; syn. *Ratinha*; vars: Beiroa and Bragança, also Jarmelista and Marinhoa; orig. of Berciana and Verinesa (Spain). [from Miranda do Douro]

Mishima (I. W. of Honshu, Japan); var. of Japanese Native; BS; nearly extinct

[Miskov] (Kostroma, USSR); m.d; local type improved by Yaroslavl, Kholmogory and Ayrshire; orig. (with Babaev) of Kostroma

mithun (hill forests of Assam, Bhutan and N.W. Burma) = *Bos (Bibos) 'frontalis'* Lambert; = domesticated gaur; syn. *bami* or *menscha* (Bhutan), *dulong* (Yunnan), *gayal* (Hindi and Bengali); not *mithan, mythun*. [Assamese]

Mitteldeutsches Gebirgsvieh or *Rotvieh*: see German Red

Mitzan: see Sheko

[Mkalama Dun]; local strain of Small East African Zebu in Tanzania
Mocaniţa: see Romanian Mountain. [Rom. *mocan* = mountain peasant]
Mocha nacional: see Brazilian Polled
Modenese (Modena, Emilia, Italy); d.m.[dr]; white with dark points; ?
 orig. from Reggiana × Romagnola; BSd and HB 1957; syn. *Carpigiana*
 (from Carpi), *White Po* (It. *Bianca val padana*); rare
Modenese di Monte: see Garfagnina
Modicana (Sicily, Italy); d.m.[dr]; Podolian type; orig. lowland var. of
 Sicilian; dark red; BSd and HB 1952; syn. *Olivastra modicana, Sicilian*;
 vars: Mezzalina (uplands) and Montanara (mts); orig. of Sardo-
 Modicana. [from Modica in S.E. Sicily]
Modicano-Sarda, Modica-Sardinian: see Sardo-Modicana
Mogol: see Magal
Moi (Kampuchea); z. orig.; disappearing
Moile, Moiled, Moilie: see Irish Moiled
[Moldavian] (Romania); dr.d; former var. of Romanian Steppe; white
 to ash-grey; Rom. *Moldovenească*
[Mölltal] (Austria-Italy); former var. of Pinzgauer in S.W. Carinthia (to
 1925) and N.E. Udine as distinct from Pinzgauer and Pustertaler
 Sprinzen in Salzburg and N.E Bolzano; Ger. *Mölltaler*, It. *Pezzata
 rossa norica*; syn. *Mölltal-Pinzgau, Norica-Pinzgau;* not *Mölthal*
Molokan: see Malakan
Monchina (S.W. Viscaya and S.E. Santander, Spain); m; red. [=
 mountain]
Mongalla (S. Sudan); var. of Small East African Zebu; all colours; syn.
 South-eastern Hills Zebu, Southern Sudan Hill Zebu; inc. Bari (? with
 Nilotic blood), Didinga (? with Toposa blood) and Latuka
Mongconto: see Mangwato
Mongolian (Mongolia and N. China); d.m.dr; Turano-Mongolian type;
 usu. brindle or reddish-brown, sometimes black, yellow or pied; vars:
 Halhïn Gol, Ujumqin
Montafon (Vorarlberg, Austria); former var. of Austrian Brown; orig.
 from local graded to Swiss Brown; BS 1923; Ger. *Montafoner*; syn.
 Vorarlberg Brown; not *Montavon*
Montana (borders of Lombardy, Emilia, Liguria and Piedmont, Italy);
 d.m.[dr]; sim. to Pontremolese but smaller; pale straw colour, brown at
 birth; syn. *(Bionda) Tortonese* (from Tortona, Alessandria), *Cabellota*
 (from Cabella, Genoa), *Ottonese* (from Ottone, Piacenza), *Red Mount-
 ain* (It. *Montana rossa* or *Rossa montanina*), *Varzese* (from Varzi,
 Pavia); rare (by crossing with Reggiana and Italian Brown)
Montaña (Spain): see Santander. [= mountain (province)]
Montanara (Italy): see Garfagnina; also mountain vars of Marchigiana
 and Modicana

Montbéliard (Haute Saône-Doubs, France); d.m.[dr]; French Red Pied group; bright red and white; orig. from Bernese brought by Mennonites in 18th c; named 1870; HB and BS 1889; absorbed Tourache c. 1900

Montgomery: see Sahiwal

Montgomery-Jersey: see Jamaica Hope

mooly, moolley: see mulley

Moor, Moorish: see Maure

Morang (Nepal); z; hill type; sim. to Purnea; *cf.* Nepalese Hill

[Moravian Red] (Czechoslovakia); d.m.dr; Central European Red type; Cz. *Moravský červený*; syn. *Moravian Carpathian, Moravian Land*; var: Lišna Red; extinct c. 1960

[Moravian Red Pied]; former var. of Czech Pied; Cz. *Moravský červeno-strakatý*; syn. *Bernese-Hanna, Berno-Hana* (*Bernskohanácký*), *Haná-Berner, Hanna-Berne* (*Hanáckobernský*), *Moravian Red Spotted, Spotted Moravian*

Moravian Sudeten: see Sudeten

Morbihan, Morbihannais: see Breton Black Pied

Morenas del Noroeste (S. Galicia and N.W. Zamora, Spain); dr.m.d; sim. to Black Iberian; black-brown; inc. Alistana-Sanabresa, Caldelana, Limiana, Sayaguesa, Verinesa, Vianesa. [= dark (cattle) of northwest]

Moroccan: see Brown Atlas and Oulmès Blond

Moroccan Blond: see Oulmès Blond

Moroccan Brown: see Brown Atlas

Morucha (Salamanca, Spain); m.dr; black or grey (*cárdena*); ? orig. from Black Iberian; BS 1974; Sp. *Salmantina* (from Salamanca); not *Salmanquina*. [= black]

Moruno-Sinuano: see Romosinuano

[Morvan] (Burgundy, France); replaced by Charolais; Fr. *Morvandelle*

Mottai madu: see Umblachery

Mottled Hill (Germany); dr.m.d; Ger. *Schecken und Blässen,* or *Scheckiges und rückenblessiges Höhenvieh*; names used in Germany c. 1936-45 to inc. Black Forest (Hinterwald and Vorderwald), White-marked (Kelheimer and Westerwald), Whitebacked (Glatz, Pinzgauer, Sudeten and Vosges), and Bergscheck

Mountain Grey: see Grey Mountain

Mountain Spotted: see Bergscheck, Simmental

Mount Mahabharat: see Nepalese Hill

Mowati: see Mewati

Moyle, Moyled: see Irish Moiled

Mozambique Angoni (Angonia, Tete, Mozambique); m; var. of Angoni; usu. black or black with white on head, throat or dewlap, also brown or red; hd or pd

Mpwapwa (Tanzania); d.m; z; usu. light to dark red; orig. from Sahiwal *et al.*; crossing started 1940s, breeding programme 1958; in 1971 was 32% Red Sindhi, 30% Sahiwal, 19% Tanzanian Zebu, 10% Boran and 9% Ayrshire and Shorthorn; then selected towards Sahiwal and is now c. 75% Sahiwal; syn. *Indo-African Zebu*; rare

MRI, MRY: see Meuse-Rhine-Yssel

Mucca pisana: see Pisana

mulley (USA) = polled; ? orig. from Polled Derby; orig. of single standard Polled Shorthorn; not *mooly, moolley, muley*. [from Gaelic *maol* = bald, hornless]

Multani: see Sahiwal

Munich cattle (Munich zoo, Germany); orig. (1926 on) from Corsican, (Scottish) Highland, Hungarian Grey, Friesian, Murnau-Werdenfels and Allgäu (German Brown) by Heinz Heck; so-called 'bred-back aurochs'; *cf.* Berlin cattle

Munshigunj (Bangladesh); z; local var.

[Murboden] (Mur valley, Styria, Austria, and Slovenia, Yugoslavia); d.m.dr; pale yellow-brown with darker points; orig. from Bergscheck × Mürztal in 19th c, recog. 1869; Ger. *Murbodner*, Serbo-cro. *Pomurska*; syn. *Murboden-Mürztal, Svetlolisata* (Slovenia); inc. in Austrian Yellow c. 1960

Murcian (Valencia to Almería, E. Spain); m.dr; dark red; Sp. *Murciana*; syn. *Levantina* (= *eastern*); former vars: Huertana (= Murcian *s.s.*), Almanzoreña, Calasparreña, Lorquina; nearly extinct

Murgese (Murge, Apulia, Italy); former var. of Apulian Podolian

Murle (S.E. Sudan); z; sim. to Toposa but smaller; ? orig. from Abyssinian Shorthorned Zebu

Murnau-Werdenfels (Weilheim-Garmisch-Landsberg, Bavaria, Germany); d.m.[dr]; local breed sim. to German Brown but smaller and more red-yellow in colour; BS and HB; Ger. *Murnau-Werdenfelser*; rare

Murray Grey (Upper Murray R. valley, Victoria, Australia); m; silver-grey to grey-dun; pd; orig. from 12 grey calves (born 1905 on) out of a light roan (nearly white) Shorthorn ♀ by an Aberdeen-Angus ♂; graded to Aberdeen-Angus and selected for grey (dun); BS 1962; absorbed Tasmanian Grey c. 1979; BS also in USA 1969, Canada 1970, GB 1974, New Zealand; *cf.* Australian Grey

Mursi (S. Albania); dr; Grey Steppe type; grey with black points

[Mürztal] (Austria); orig. (with Bergscheck) of Murboden in 19th c; recombined with Murboden 1913

Muturu (Cameroon): see Bakwiri

Muturu (Liberia): see Liberian Dwarf

Muturu (S. Nigeria); var. of West African Shorthorn; black or pied; syn. *Nigerian Dwarf, Nigerian Shorthorn, Pagan*; vars: Savanna Muturu and Forest Muturu (dwarf). [Hausa = humpless]

[Mysol] (Costa Rica); d; local zebu × Criollo cross

MYSORE (S. India); z; rapid draft; usu. grey; vertical horns; basic breed is Hallikar; also inc. Alambadi, Amritmahal, Bargur, Kangayam, and Khillari

mythun: see mithun

Nadjdi: see Nejdi

Nagar: see Kankrej

Nagori (Nagaur, C. Rajasthan, India); dr; z; grey-white shorthorned type; not *Nagauri, Nagoni, Nagore*

nak: see yak ♀

Nakali; var. of Khillari; not *Nakli*. [= imitation]

Nama (S. Namibia); orig. from Hottentot, Ovambo, Damara, Friesian and Africander

Namaqua: see Hottentot

Namchi, Namji, Namshi: see Doayo

Nandi (W. Kenya); local Small East African Zebu; syn. *Nandi Blue*

Nanico: see Igarapé

Nantais; paler var. of Parthenais lacking black mucosae. [from Nantes]

Nanyang (Henan and N. Hubei, China); dr; Central Chinese type; usu. red with white or grey spots; mountain and lowland vars; Russ. *Nan'yan*

naran-hainag: see dzo

Nari: see Bhagnari

Nata: see Niata

Native Black (Turkey): see Anatolian Black

Ndagu (Ghana); N'Dama × Sokoto Gudali crossbreds on exp. stas

N'Dama (Fouta Djallon, Guinea, and neighbouring countries); d.m.dr; West African small humpless (trypanotolerant) type; usu. fawn, red, or brown, occ. pied or black; lyre or crescent horns; syn. *Boenca* or *Boyenca* (Guinea-Bissau), *Fouta Jallon, Fouta Longhorn, Fouta Malinke, Futa, Malinke, Mandingo* (Liberia), *N'Dama Petite* (Senegal); vars: Gambian N'Dama (syn. *N'Dama Grande*), N'Gabou (Guinea-Bissau); not *Dama, Ndama*

N'Dama Sanga (Ghana); N'Dama × zebu × Ghana Shorthorn

Ndawana: see Batawana

Neckar: see Heilbronn

Negra iberica: see Black Iberian

Nejdi (Khuzestan, Iran); d; all colours; hd or pd; humped or not; orig. from Jersey and Sindhi × local; syn. *Arabi*; not *Nadjdi*

Nellore (Asia): see Ongole

Nelore (Brazil); m; z; white; orig. from Ongole imported 1895-1964; HB 1936; not *Nellore*; vars: Polled Nelore, Red Nelore (Port. *Nelore vermelho*)

Nelthropp: see Senepol

Nepalese, Nepali Zebu: see Achham, Morang, Nepalese Hill, Tarai

Nepalese Hill (Churia Ghati and Mahabharat Range, Nepal); z; Indian Hill type; black; syn. *Black Hill Zebu, Nepali Hill Zebu*; *cf.* Morang

Netherlands Black Pied: see Dutch Black Pied

Netherlands Indies: see Indonesian

New Zealand Jersey (New Zealand); var. of Jersey from 19th c. imports; BS 1902, HB 1903

N'Gabou (Guinea-Bissau and Casamance, Senegal); var. of N'Dama; white with black points; syn. *Fula, Gabú*

N'Gami, Ngami: see Batawana

Nganda (Buganda, Uganda); Sanga-Zebu intermediate; usu. yellow-dun or light red, often red-and-white, occ. black or white; ? orig. from Ankole × Nkedi; local syn. *Sese Island*; sim. vars: Kyoga, Nyoro, Serere, Toro

N'Gaoundéré (Cameroon); typical var. of Adamawa; brown, roan, red pied or black pied; syn. *Bamenda* (Nigeria); not *Ngaundere*

Ngoni: see Angoni

Nguni (Zululand, S. Africa, Swaziland, and Mozambique S. of R. Save); d.dr; Sanga type; often coloursided (*inkone*); BS (S. Africa) 1986; syn. *Landim* or *Sul do Save* (Mozambique), *Swazi, Zulu*; var: Bapedi (Transvaal); not *Ngune*

Ngwato: see Mangwato

[Niata] (Uruguay); var. with bulldog snout; not *Nata*

Niederrheiner, Niederrheinisch: see Rhineland

Niederungsvieh: see Lowland

Nigerian Fulani: see Diali

Nigerian Shorthorn: see Muturu

[Nilo] (Rio de Janeiro, Brazil); orig. from African Zebu imported by Emperor Pedro I in 1826 and crossed with local cows

Nilotic (Sudan S. of lat. 10°N); m; Sanga type; usu. off-white or cream, also red, black or pied; syn. *Southern Sudanese, Sudanese Longhorn, Wadai-Dinka*; local tribal vars: Aliab Dinka (S.E.), Aweil Dinka (N.W.), Nuer, Eastern Nuer (N.E.), Abigar (S.W. Ethiopia)

Nimari (Nimar, S.W. Madhya Pradesh, India); dr; z; usu. red with white markings; ? orig. from Gir and Khillari; BSd; syn. *Khargaon, Khargoni, Khurgoni*

Nioka: see Alur

Nipponese Improved: see Japanese Improved

Nizhegorod: see Yurino

Nkedi (E. and N. Uganda); var. of Small East African Zebu; many colours; syn. *Bukedi, Eastern Province Zebu, Lango, Teso*
nkone: see inkone
Nkone (Zimbabwe); m; Sanga type; usu. coloursided, red-and-white, also black-and-white; selected (1946 on) from *inkone* type (? orig. from Nguni) in Matabele cattle; BS 1967; syn. *Mangoni, Manguni* (1961-69); not *Inkone*
Nordland: see Blacksided Trondheim and Nordland
[Norfolk Horned] (England); m; red with white or mottled face; syn. *Old Norfolk, Red Norfolk*; orig. (× Suffolk Polled) of Red Poll
Norfolk Polled: see Red Poll
Noric: see Pinzgauer
Normande (Normandy, France); d.m; red-brown and white, often brindled, usu. red spectacles; orig. from local (*e.g.* Cotentin and Augeron) with some Shorthorn and Jersey blood 1845-60; BS 1883, reorg. 1926; syn. *Norman*; BS also in Colombia, Uruguay, USA 1974
Normanzu (Brazil); Normande × zebu (Gir or Guzerá) cross
Norsk: see Norwegian
North Australian Shorthorn: see Australian Shorthorn
North Bangladesh Grey; z; local var; syn. *North Bengal Grey*
North Devon: see Devon
Northeastern Crioulo: see Curraleiro
Northern Dairy Shorthorn (N. England); d.m; var. of Shorthorn probably descended directly from Teeswater; BS and HB 1944-69 (then combined with Dairy Shorthorn); syn. *Dales Shorthorn*; nearly extinct
Northern Riverain (Sudan): see Kenana, Butana
Northern Scotch Polled: see Aberdeen-Angus
Northern Territory Shorthorn: see Australian Shorthorn
NORTH EUROPEAN POLLED; inc. Aberdeen-Angus, British White, Galloway, and Red Poll (Great Britain); Irish Moiled; Blacksided Trondheim and Nordland, Red Polled Østland, and Vestland Polled (Norway); Icelandic; Swedish Polled; Finnish; Estonian Native, polled Pechora and Vychegda-Vym (USSR)
North Finnish (N. Finland); d; white var. of Finnish; sim. to Swedish Mountain and to Blacksided Trondheim and Nordland (Norway); BS 1905-50; Finn. *Pohjois-Suomolainen Karja* (= *PSK*), Swe. *Nordfinsk*; nearly extinct
North Italian Brown: see Italian Brown
Northland (Norway): see Blacksided Trondheim and Nordland
North Malawi Zebu; former var. of Malawi Zebu ? with Sanga blood; obs. syn. *Nyasaland Angoni*
North Manchurian Dairy: see Pinzhou
[North Slesvig Red] (Germany-Denmark); sim. to Angeln but with

Shorthorn blood; absorbed in Danish Red; Dan. *Nord Slesvig Rød,*
Ger. *Rotes Nordschleswiger*
North Somali (N. Somalia); z; Somali group; usu. chestnut or black,
sometimes white; *cf.* Aden
NORTH SPANISH (N. Spain); dr.m.d; brown to red; inc. Asturian, Galician,
[Leonese], Pyrenean, Tudanca
NORTH SUDAN ZEBU (Sudan, N. of lat. 10N); d.dr.m; medium-sized
thoracic or cervico-thoracic muscular hump; short horns; syn. *Arab,
Sudanese Shorthorned Zebu*; inc. Baggara, Barka, Beja (?), Butana,
Kenana
North Swedish: see Swedish Polled
[North Wales Black]; m; HB 1883-1904; syn. *Anglesey*; orig. (+ South
Wales Black) of Welsh Black
Norwegian Red (Norway); d; red (or red with some white); hd or pd;
orig. 1961 by union of Norwegian Red-and-White (inc. Red Trondheim)
and Red Polled Østland; absorbed Døle 1963, South and West
Norwegian 1968; BS and HB; Nor. *Norsk rødt fe* (= *NRF*); BS also
in USA
[Norwegian Red-and-White] (S.E. Norway); d; red with small white
markings on legs and lower body; orig. from Swedish Red-and-White
× local Ayrshire (first imported 1860s), Red Trondheim and Hedmark;
BS 1923, named 1939; Finnish Ayrshire blood in 1950s; absorbed Red
Trondheim in 1960; Nor. *Norsk rødt og hvitt fe* (= *NRF*); obs. syn.
(1923-39) *Hornet slettefe* (= *Horned lowland cattle*); joined with Red
Polled Østland in 1961 to form Norwegian Red
Norwegian Red Polled: see Red Polled Østland
Nostrana (Lucca, Italy): see Garfagnina
NRF: see Norwegian Red
NRS (Netherlands) = *Nederlands Rundvee Stamboek*; HB which registers
Dutch Black Pied (except in Friesland), Meuse-Rhine-Yssel and
Groningen Whiteheaded
Nsagalla: see Bahima var. of Ankole
Nuba Mountain (S. Kordofan, Sudan); z; dwarf; variable hump; ? orig.
from Baggara × dwarf humpless; syn. *Koalib*
Nuer (N.W. of S. Sudan); local var. of Nilotic
Nuras (Namibia); m; $\frac{1}{2}$ Africander, $\frac{1}{4}$ Simmental, $\frac{1}{4}$ Hereford
Nyambo: see Inyambo
Nyasaland Angoni: see (North) Malawi Zebu
Nyasaland Zebu, Nyasa Zebu: see (South) Malawi Zebu
Nyoro (Bunyoro, N.W. Uganda); enclave of Sanga-Zebu intermediates
sim. to Nganda; not *Banioro, Banyoro, Bunyoro*

Oberbaden, Oberbädisches: see Messkircher

Oberinntaler Grauvieh, Oberinntal Grey: see Tyrol Grey
[Ocampo] (Venezuela); in formation 1940s and 1950s on Ocampo estate from Friesian × (Ongole × local Criollo); graded to American Brown Swiss in 1970s
[Odenwald] (S. Hesse, Germany); subvar. of Hesse-Westphalian var. of German Red; HB 1899; Ger. *Odenwälder*
Ogaden Zebu: see Jijjiga Zebu
[Oka] (Gorki, USSR); orig. of Gorbatov Red; Russ. *Priokskaya*
[Oka Black Pied] (Ryazan, USSR); d; orig. from East Friesian or Kholmogory × Simmental and Swiss Brown grades with Jersey bulls since 1952; Russ. *Priokskaya chernopestraya*; absorbed by Black Pied
Okranya: see Molokan
Oksh: see Baladi
[Oldenburg-Wesermarsch] (Oldenburg, Germany); d.m; orig. var. of German Black Pied, orig. with Shorthorn blood; HB 1880; Ger. *Oldenburger-Wesermarsch*; orig. of Podolian Black Pied (Ukraine); not *Wesermarsh*
Old Gloucestershire: see Gloucester
[Old Marlborough Red] (Devon, England); d
Old Norfolk: see Norfolk Horned
Omby rana: see Rana
[Ondongolo] (Transkei, Cape Province, S. Africa); Sanga type; sacred herd of Chief Tyelinzima in Bomvanaland; *cf.* Bolowana
Ongole (Guntur-Nellore, S. Andhra Pradesh, India); dr.d; z; grey-white shorthorned type; BSd and HB, BS 1983; syn. *Nellore, Sumba Ongole* (Indonesia); orig. of Javanese Ongole, Nelore (Brazil)
Oran (Algeria); former subvar. of Moroccan var. of Brown Atlas
Oristanese, Oristano: see Sardo-Modicana
[Orkney] (Scotland); var. of Shetland
Oropa (Biella, Piedmont, Italy); d.m; larger var. of Aosta with Simmental blood; red pied with white head; It. *Pezzata rossa d'Oropa*
[Ossolana] (N.E. Piedmont, Italy); local var. absorbed by Italian Brown
[Østerdal] (Norway); var. of Døle; black
Østland: see Red Polled Østland
Ottone, Ottonese: see Montana
Oulmès Blond (N.W. Morocco); sim. to (orig. from) Brown Atlas; pale fawn; Fr. *Blonde des plateaux d'Oulmès et des Zaërs*; syn. *Blond Moroccan, Blond Zaërs, Moroccan Blond, Oulmès*
Ovambo (N. Namibia); Sanga type; sim. to Kaokoveld but smaller; usu. dun or black; sing. *Ambo*; *cf.* Humbi (S.W. Angola)
Overo colorado = (German) Red Pied in Chile
Ozierese, Ozieri: see Sardinian Brown
[Pabli] (Upper Pendjari valley, N.W. Benin); var. of West African

Savanna Shorthorn sim. to Somba but usu. red
Pabna (Bangladesh); z; local var.
Padana: see Modenese
Pagan: see Doayo, Kapsiki, Muturu
Pahari, Pakhari: see Dhanni
Pajuna (mts of E. Andalucía, Spain); m.dr; red; syn. *Serrana*. [= rustic, primitive]
Pale Alpine, Pale Highland, Pale Mountain (Austria): see Austrian Yellow
Palmera (La Palma, Canary Is, Spain); m.dr.d; yellow or dirty white; syn. *Palmeña*; nearly extinct
pamjommu: see dzo
Pampa: see Hereford
pandzo: see dzo
Pankota Red (Hungary); m; 80-95% Lincoln Red, 5-20% Hungarian Pied; Hung. *Pankotai vörös értéke*
Pantaneiro (R. Paraguay valley, S.W. Mato Grosso, Brazil); Crioulo type; syn. *Cuiabano* (from R. Cuyabá). [Port. *pantano* = marsh]
Pantelleria (Italy); d; mixed population, chiefly Modicana, also Italian Brown and Simmental blood
Panwar: see Ponwar
Paphos; smaller, hill, var. of Cyprus
Park: see British White, White Park
Parthenais (Deux-Sèvres, W. France); m.(d.)[dr]; fawn; BS 1893; syn. *Choletais, Gâtinais, Gâtine* or *Gâtinelle, Vendée-Parthenay*; vars: Nantais, Vendée Marsh; declining. [from Parthenay]
[Pasiega] (E. Santander, Spain); upland var. of Santander; absorbed or displaced by Swiss Brown in 1940s. [from Pas]
[Pasturina] (Casentino, Arezzo, Tuscany, Italy); local var. from Chianina × Podolian
[Patuá] (N.E. Minas Gerais, Rio de Janeiro, Espírito Santo and S.E. Bahia, Brazil); grey or yellow-red; small; probably some zebu blood
[Pecanite] (Zimbabwe); dwarf; humpless; ? Dexter blood. [grazed under pecan trees]
Pechora (Komi, N. European Russia); d; var. of Kholmogory (recog. 1972); black-and-white or red-and-white; orig. 16th to 20th c. from Zyryanka cattle of Komi and from Mezen; improved by Kholmogory 1930-47; Russ. *Pechorskiĭ tip Kholmogorskogo skota*; *cf.* Vychegda-Vym; pd var. extinct
Pedi: see Bapedi
[Pedreiro] (S. Mato Grosso, Brazil); var. of Franqueiro. [Port. *pedra* = stone]
Pé duro: see Curraleiro

Pee Wee (Alberta Univ., Canada); m; a composite of Charolais, Aberdeen-Angus, Galloway and Hereford selected for low yearling weight
Peking Black-and-White, Peking Black-Pied: see Beijing Black Pied
Peloponnesus; former var. of Greek Shorthorn
Pembroke: see South Wales Black
Perijanero (Perija mts, W. Venezuela); m; Criollo type
Persian: see Iranian
[Perugina] (Perugia, Umbria, Italy); former var. of Chianina
Pešter (W. Serbia and Montenegro, Yugoslavia); local, heavier var. of Buša; grey; Serbo-cro. *Pešterska buša*
Peuhl, Peul, Peulh, Peulhé, Peul-Peul: see Fulani
Pezzata degli altipiani (Italy): see Burlina
[Philamin] (Philippines); m.dr; orig. $\frac{1}{2}$ Hereford $\frac{3}{8}$ Ongole $\frac{1}{8}$ Philippine Native; extinct *c.* 1945
Philippine Native; dr.m; orig. from Chinese and Mexican; small hump in ♂; vars: Batanes Black, Batangas, Ilocos (large and small), Iloilo
pian niu: see dzo; W.G. *p'ien niu*. [= inclined cattle]
[Picardy] (France); former var. (by crossing) of Flemish; Fr. *Picarde*
Picos de Europa: see Lebaniega
Pied Eastern (France): see French Red Pied group
Piedmont (N.W. Italy); m.(d.)[dr]; *brachyceros* type; white or pale grey with black points; HB 1887-91, 1958 on, BS 1934; It. *Piemontese*; vars: Albese, [Demonte]; BS in Brazil 1974
Piedrahita, Piedrahitense: see Avileña
p'ien niu: see *pian niu*
Pie Rouge de l'Est (Belgium): see Campine Red Pied
Pie Rouge de l'Est (E.C. France esp. Côte d'Or); m.d.[dr]; French Red Pied group; orig. in early 20th c. from Simmental × local (Bressane and Fémeline) in Saône valley, HB 1930, absorbed Gex and Alsatian Simmental 1945; obs. syn. *Tachetée de l'Est* (to 1959); syn. *Eastern Spotted, French Simmental, Red Spotted*
Pie Rouge des Plaines (N. Brittany, France); d.m; HB 1970 to combine Armorican, German Red Pied, Meuse-Rhine-Yssel and their crosses; syn. *French Red Pied Lowland*
Pie rouge française de Montagne: see Abondance
Pin-chou, Pinchow: see Pinzhou
Pineywoods: see Florida Scrub
Pinzgauer (Salzburg, Austria; S.E. Bavaria, Germany; and N.E. Italy); d.m.[dr]; red-brown, coloursided with coloured head; BS and HB in each country; syn. *Pinzgau*; pd var: Jochberg Hummel; former vars: Mölltal (S.W. Carinthia, Austria, and N.E Udine, Italy), Pustertaler Sprinzen (N.E. Bolzano, Italy); orig. of Slovakian Pinzgau, Transylvanian Pinzgau, Yugoslav Pinzgau; BS also in Namibia 1955, S. Africa

1963, USA 1973, Brazil 1975, Canada, UK 1976
Pinzhou (N.W. Heilongjiang, China); d; Simmental × local Mongolian crosses; yellow-, red-, or black-pied; W.G. *Pin-chou*; syn. *North Manchurian Dairy, Pinchow*; cf. Sanhe
Pisana (Pisa, Tuscany, Italy); m.d.[dr]; chestnut to black; ? orig. from Swiss Brown × Chianina in mid-19th c; It. *Mucca (nera) pisana* (= *(Black) Pisa milch cow*); rare, by crossing with Italian Brown
Pitangueiras (São Paulo, Brazil); d; pd; red; orig. (1944 on) from Red Poll (⅜) × zebu (chiefly Guzerá and Gir) at farm of Frigorífico Anglo, Pitangueiras; BS 1974
Plava: see Slovenian White
Pleven, Plevna, Plevne: see Turkish Grey Steppe
Po: see Modena
PODOLIAN (C. and S. Italy); m.[dr]; Grey Steppe type; It. *Podolica*; inc. Apulian Podolian, Cinisara, Marchigiana, Maremmana, Modicana, Romagnola
Podolian (S.E. Europe): see Grey Steppe
[Podolian Black Pied] (Kamenets-Podolsk, W. Ukraine, USSR); d; orig. from Oldenburg × local in late 19th c; HB; Russ. *Chernopestraya podol'skaya*; syn. *Ukrainian Oldenburg*; absorbed by Black Pied
Podolic, Podolska (S.E. Europe): see Grey Steppe
Poggese: see Venetian
[Polders Black Pied] (W. Antwerp and N. Flanders, Belgium); d; = Dutch Black Pied in Belgium; Flem. *Zwartbont ras van de Polders*, Fr. *Pie-noire des Polders*; joined with Hervé Black Pied 1966 to form Belgian Black Pied
[Polesian] (Pripet Marshes, USSR); syn. *Polish Grey*
Poli: see Doayo
Polimska: see Lim
Polish Black-and-White Lowland (C., W. and N. Poland); d.m; Friesian type; orig. from German and Dutch imports in 19th and 20th c; Pol. *Nizinna czarno-biała*; syn. *Polish Black Pied, Polish Lowland*; var: Mazury
Polish Grey: see Polesian
[Polish Marsh]; d; all white var. of Polish Whitebacked; Pol. *Żuławka*
Polish Red (S.E. Poland); d.m.(dr); Central European Red type; BS 1894, HB 1916; Pol. *Czerwona polska*, Russ. *Krasnaya pol'skaya*; syn. *Polish Red-Brown*; former vars: upland (*podgórska*) in W. Carpathians, lowland (*dolinowa*) in Białystok, Rawicka (Poznań), and Silesian Red; being crossed with Angeln; purebreds rare; HB also in USSR
Polish Red-and-White Lowland (S.W. Poland); d.m.(dr); orig. from German Red Pied and Meuse-Rhine-Yssel; HB; Pol. *Nizinna czerwono-biała*

Polish Simmental (S.E. Rzeszów, S.E. Poland); d.m.(dr); var. of Simmental; Pol. *Simentalska*

[Polish Whitebacked] (N.E. and C. Poland); d; black or brown, coloursided; Pol. *Białogrzbietka*, Ger. *Rückenscheckig*; var: (with colour reduced to a few spots on side) Polish Marsh; *cf.* Ukrainian Whitebacked

polled: see also Brazilian polled, North European polled

Polled Aberdeenshire: see Buchan Humlie

Polled Angus: see Aberdeen-Angus

Polled Charolais (USA)

[Polled Derby] (England); ? orig. of mulley

Polled Durham: see Polled Shorthorn

Polled Gir (Brazil); pd var. of Brazilian Gir; HB; Port. *Gir mocho*

Polled Guzerá (Brazil); pd var. of Guzerá; Port. *Guzerá mocho*

Polled Hereford (Great Britain): see British Polled Hereford

Polled Hereford (USA and Canada); pd var. of Hereford; (1) Single Standard, orig. *c.* 1893 by grading up Aberdeen-Angus and Red Poll, BS 1900, (2) Double Standard, orig. in 1901 by mutation, HB 1913; syn. Poll Hereford (Australia BS 1920 and Great Britain BS 1955)

Polled Irish: see Irish Dun, Irish Moiled

Polled Jersey (USA); var. of Jersey; BS 1895

Polled Lincoln Red (Lincolnshire, England); started by E. Pentecost *c.* 1940 from red Aberdeen-Angus × Lincoln Red, recog. 1952; obs. syn. *Lincolnshire Beef Poll*; now = Lincoln Red

Polled Nelore (Brazil); pd var. of Nelore with blood of Brazilian Polled; HB 1969; Port. *Nelore mocho*

Polled Norfolk: see Red Poll

Polled Scots: see Aberdeen-Angus, Galloway; joint HB 1862-77

Polled Shorthorn (Ohio, USA); m; var. of Beef Shorthorn; (1) [Single Standard] orig. *c.* 1870 by grading up mulley cows, (2) Double Standard (purebred), orig. by mutation in 1880s; BS 1889-1923, HB 1894; syn. *Polled Durham* (to 1919)

Polled Simmental (USA); m; orig. by grading Angus to Simmental

Polled Sinú: see Romosinuano

Polled Suffolk: see Suffolk Polled

Polled Sussex (England and S. Africa); m; var. of Sussex (1950 on) from red Aberdeen-Angus × Sussex

Polled Welsh Black (Wales); var. of Welsh Black recog. late 1940s

Polled Zebu (Brazil); see Polled Gir, Polled Guzerá, Polled Nelore and Tabapuã; Port. *Zebu mocho*; syn. *Indu mocho*

Poll Friesian (Great Britain); var. of British Friesian; BS 1960, HB 1961

Poll Hereford: see Polled Hereford

Poll Shorthorn (Australia); var. of Beef Shorthorn; first recorded 1874,

HB 1935
Pomurska: see Murboden
Pontremolese (Magra valley in Massa and La Spezia, Ligurian Apennines, Italy); m.d.[dr]; sim. to Montana; yellowish-brown with pale dorsal stripe; BS and HB 1935; syn. *Bettolese* (from Bettola, Piacenza); var: [Bardigiana] (Parma); nearly extinct by crossing with Italian Brown. [from Pontremoli]
Ponwar (Puranpur, N.C. Uttar Pradesh, India); dr; z; lyrehorned type, sim. to Kherigarh but black-and-white; not *Panwar*
Porto Amboim (W. and C. Angola); ? var. of Barotse; beige to brown, black, or pied
Portuguese Friesian: see Turino
Posavina (Sava valley, Yugoslavia); small var. of Yugoslav Steppe; Serbo-cro. *Posavska gulja*; syn. *Sava*; rare
Pothwari: see Dhanni
Poul-Foulo, Poulo, Poul-Poulo: see Fulani
Preti (N. Italy); d; Friesian × Italian Brown 1st cross; *cf.* Frati. [It. *prete* = priest, *i.e.* black]
Préwakwa (Cameroon); m; z; Brahman × Adamawa, F₁; red or red pied; to be bred *inter se* and backcrossed to both breeds to give Wakwa
Pridneprovskiĭ: see Dnieper
Prioka Red, Priokskaya: see Oka
Pritashkentskaya: see Bushuev
PSK: see North Finnish
Puerto Rican (West Indies); Sp. orig; some dwarf
Puglia, Pugliese: see Apulian Podolian
Pulikulam: see Jellicut
Pullo: see Fulani
Pul-Mbor (Cameroon); Red Bororo × Adamawa, 1st cross. [*i.e. Peul* × *Mbor*oro]
Punganur (Chittoor, S. Andhra Pradesh, India); dwarf var. sim. to Mysore type; white or grey to red or brown, occ. black; not *Punganoor*; almost extinct
Purnea (N.E. Bihar, India); dr; z; hill type, sim. to Morang; black or red
[Pustertaler Sprinzen] (N.E. Bolzano, Italy); var. of Pinzgauer with red- or black-pied sides, not plain red; It. *Pusteria*; syn. *Pusstataler, Pustertaler Schecken* (= spotted); replaced by Pinzgauer; extinct 1980s
pyaung, pyun: see Burmese gaur
Pyrenean (France): see Pyrenean Blond, Central Pyrenean
Pyrenean (N. Navarre, Spain); m.(d); North Spanish type; red to cream, paler extremities and underparts; HB 1933; Sp. *Pirenaica*; obs. syn. *Basque*; *cf.* Pyrenean Blond (France); absorbed by Friesian and by

Swiss Brown in Vascongadas
[Pyrenean Blond] (Hautes- and Basses-Pyrénées, France); dr.m.(d);
yellow to yellow-brown with pink mucosae; Fr. *Blonde des Pyrénées à
muqueuses roses*; syn. *Basque*; much crossed with Limousin and
Garonnais and absorbed by Blonde d'Aquitaine in 1960s; purebred
remnants remain as Béarnais; *cf.* Pyrenean (Spain)

Qinchuan (C. Shaanxi, China); dr; Central Chinese type; usu. red, also
yellow; cervical hump; W.G. *Ch'in-ch'uan*, Russ. *Chinchuan', Tsinchuan*
or *Tsin'chun'*; formerly *Chinchwan*
Quasah (Queensland, Australia); m; red; orig. from Sahiwal × selected
Beef Shorthorn; not *Quasar*
Quebec Jersey: see Canadian
[Quercy] (Tarn-et-Garonne, France); m.dr; yellow-brown; orig. from
Garonnais with Limousin blood in late 19th and early 20th c; recog.
1920; syn. *Garonnais du Coteau* (till 1920); reunited with Garonnais
1961 to form Blonde d'Aquitaine
[Quinhentão] (São Paulo, Brazil); red; orig. from one Ongole × Friesian
bull crossed with Franqueiro cows on farms of Martinico Prado about
1870

Rahaji, Rahaza: see Red Bororo
Ramgarhi (E. Mandla, Madhya Pradesh, India); z; local var.
Ramo Grande (Ilha Terceira, Azores, Portugal); red-brown; rare
Rana (C. Madagascar); d.m; often speckled fawn, grey or black pied;
orig. from Bordelais and Garonnais and later Normande and Friesian
imported since 1840 × Madagascar Zebu; syn. *omby rana* (Swahili
ngombe = cattle)
Ranger (W. ranges, USA); m; orig. 1970 by combination of Hash Cross
with Ritchie herd (Wyoming) which used Simmental (1968), Hash
Cross (1967), Beefmaster (1966), Hereford, Brahman and Highland ×
Shorthorn (1950) bulls on Brahman cross cows, and with Watson herd
(California) using American Brown Swiss (1970), Red Angus × Red
Holstein (1969), Beefmaster (1968), Hash Cross (1968) and dairy breed
bulls (1967) on Hereford cows
Rath (Alwar, E. Rajasthan, India); dr.d; z; grey-white shorthorned type;
sim. to Hariana, ? with Red Sindhi and Sahiwal blood; not *Rathi*
Ratinha: see Mirandesa
[Rawicka] (Rawicz, Poznań, Poland); former var. of Polish Red
Raya: see Danakil
Raya-Azebó (E. Tigray, Ethiopia); dr; var. of Danakil; syn. *Galla-Azebó*
RDM: see Danish Red

Red: see European Red
Red (Germany): see German Red
Red Aberdeen-Angus: see Red Angus
Red Afrikaner: see Africander
Red and White Dairy Cattle (USA); BS 1964 to register Red and White
 Holsteins (90%) and other red-and-white dairy cattle (*e.g.* Ayrshire,
 Guernsey, Milking Shorthorn and Danish Red crosses)
Red and White East Flemish: see Belgian White-and-Red
Red-and-White Finnish: see East Finnish
Red and White Friesian; in Great Britain BS and HB 1951 for red var.
 of British Friesian; small section in Dutch Black Pied HB (FRS); in
 Brazil (São Paulo and Minas Gerais) *Holandesa vermelha (e branca)*;
 see also Red and White Holstein (USA)
Red and White Holstein (USA); d; colour var. of Holstein; syn. *Red
 Holstein*
Red and White Hungarian: see Hungarian Pied
Red-and-White Meuse-Rhine-Yssel: see Meuse-Rhine-Yssel
Red Angeln: see Angeln
Red Angus; colour var. of Aberdeen-Angus; BS in USA 1954, Australia
 1960s; syn. *Aberdeen-Angus colorado* (Argentina), *Red Aberdeen-Angus*
Red Astrakhan: see Kalmyk
Red Bavarian: see Bavarian Red
Red Belted Galloway (Great Britain); colour var. of Belted Galloway;
 rare
Red Bessarabian: see Bessarabian Red
Red Bororo (E. Niger, N. Nigeria, W. Chad, and N. Cameroon); m;
 West African (long lyrehorned) Zebu type; mahogany; pl. *Bororodji*;
 Hausa *Abori, Rahaji,* Fulani *Bodadi* (Wodabe tribe); syn. *Brahaza,
 Djafoun* (Cameroon), *Fellata* (Chad and Ethiopia), *Fogha, Gabassaé,
 Gadéhé, Hanagamba, Kréda* (Chad), *Mbororo, Rahaza, Red Fulani, Red
 Longhorn*; not *Boro, Borroro*
Red Brangus (Texas, USA); m; red var. of Brangus; pd; orig. from
 Brahman × American Angus; BS 1956
Red Butana: see Butana
Red Colonist, Red Crimean: see Red Steppe
Red Croatian: see Croatian Red
Red Dane, Red Danish: see Danish Red
Red Desert (N. Sudan); inc. Bambawa, Butana, Dongola and Shendi in
 North Sudan Zebu group
[Red East Friesian] (Germany); d.m; Ger. *Rote Ostfriesen*; syn. *Red-
 Brown East Friesian*; extinct *c.* 1940
Red Finnish: see West Finnish
Red Flemish: see Belgian Red

Red Fulani: see Red Bororo

Red Galloway (Great Britain); colour var. of Galloway; HB (with Belted Galloway) 1982; HB (with Galloway) also in USA; rare

Red German (USSR): see Red Steppe

Red Gorbatov: see Gorbatov Red

Red Hill: see German Red

Red Holstein: see Red and White Holstein

Red Kandhari (E.C. Maharashtra, India); dr.d; z; local var. sim. to Deoni but red; syn. *Lakhalbunda* (Berar); not *Khandari*

Red Karachi: see Red Sindhi

Red Longhorn: see Red Bororo

Red Mountain (Germany): see German Red

Red Mountain (Italy): see Montana

Red Norfolk: see Norfolk Horned

Red North Slesvig: see North Slesvig Red

Red Pied Aosta: see Aosta Red Pied

Red Pied Campine: see Belgian Red Pied

Red Pied Danish: see Danish Red Pied

Red Pied Dutch: see Meuse-Rhine-Yssel

[Red Pied East Friesian] (East Friesland, Germany); d.m; var. of German Red Pied; HB 1878; Ger. *Rotbunte Ostfriesen*; syn. *Red-White East Friesian*

Red Pied Flemish: see Belgian White-and-Red

Red Pied Friuli: see Italian Red Pied

Red Pied Holstein: see Red Pied Schleswig-Holstein

Red Pied Karelian: see East Finnish

RED PIED LOWLAND (N.W. Europe); Ger. *Rotbuntes Niederungsvieh*; inc. Belgian Red Pied, German Red Pied, Meuse-Rhine-Yssel, Pie Rouge des Plaines (France), Polish Red-and-White Lowland

Red Pied Lowland (Germany): see German Red Pied

[Red Pied Schleswig-Holstein] (N.W. Germany); d.m; var. of German Red Pied (? with Shorthorn blood); orig. by union of Breitenburger, Dithmarscher, Holstein Geest, and Wilstermarsch; BS and HB 1875, BSd 1934; Ger. *Rotbunte Schleswig-Holsteiner*; syn. *Holstein Marsh, Holstein Red Pied, Red Pied Holstein*

[Red Pied Swedish] (Sweden); d; orig. in late 19th c. from Ayrshire and Shorthorn × local (Herrgård and Småland); BS and HB 1892-1928; Swe. *Rödbrokig Svensk Boskap* (= *RSB*); joined with Swedish Ayrshire in 1928 to form Swedish Red-and-White

Red Pied Valdostana: see Aosta Red Pied

[Red Pied Westphalian] (Münsterland, W. Germany); d.m; var. of German Red Pied; orig. from Rhineland and Meuse-Rhine-Yssel; HB 1892; Ger. *Rotbuntes Westfälisches* or *Rotbunte Westfalen*

Red Polish: see Polish Red
Red Poll (E. England); d.m; red; pd; orig. in early 19th c. from Suffolk
Polled and Norfolk Horned; recog. 1847, HB 1873, BS 1888; obs. syn.
Norfolk Polled, Norfolk and Suffolk Red Polled (to 1882), *Red Polled*
(to 1908); BS also in Australia, Brazil, Canada, Colombia, New
Zealand, S. Africa 1921 (HB 1906), USA 1883 (HB 1887), Zimbabwe
1934
Red Polled (Norway): see Red Polled Østland
Red Polled (Sweden): see Swedish Red Polled
[Red Polled Østland] (S.E. Norway; d; sim. to Swedish Red Polled;
Swedish Red-and-White (1930s) and Ayrshire (1958) blood; recog.
1892, HB; Nor. *Raukolle, Rødkolle, Rautt* (or *Rødt) kollet Østlandsfe*;
syn. *Eastland, Norwegian Red Polled, Østland, Red Polled, Red Polled
Eastland*; not *Red Poll*; coloursided var: Jarlsberg; combined with
Norwegian Red-and-White 1961 to form Norwegian Red
Red Ruby: see Devon
[Red Sadovo] (Plovdiv, Bulgaria); d; orig. (1883 on) from Angeln ×
Simmental and Friesian, at Sadovo Agric. School; Bulg. *Chervena
sadovska*; Ger. *Rotes Sadowo*; absorbed in Bulgarian Red *c.* 1960
Red Senegal: see Senegal N'Dama (small type)
Red Silesian: see Silesian Red
Red Sindhi (W. Sind, Pakistan); d; z; BSd and HB; syn. *Malir* (Baluchi-
stan), *Red Karachi, Sindhi*; var: Las Bela (Baluchistan); not *Scindhi,
Scindi, Sindi*; BS Brazil (*Sindi*) 1960 from imports 1930 and 1952; part
orig. of Australian Milking Zebu, Brownsind, Jersind; BS/HB Australia
from imports in 1950s
Red Speckled: see Simmental
Red Spotted (France): see Pie Rouge de l'Est
Red Spotted (Highland): see Simmental
Red Spotted Moravian: see Moravian Red Pied
Red Steppe (S. European USSR); d; orig. by Mennonites 1789-1824 from
Red East Friesian and Angeln, × Ukrainian Grey with later some
blood of East Friesian, Swiss Brown *et al.*; HB 1923; Russ. *Krasnaya
stepnaya*; obs. syn. *Red Colonist* (Russ. *Krasnaya kolonistskaya*), *Red
German* (Russ. *Krasnaya nemetskaya*) (to 1941), *Red Ukrainian* (Russ.
Krasnaya ukrainskaya); inc. Bessarabian Red and Crimean Red
Red Tambov: see Tambov Red
[Red Trondheim] (Norway); d.m; orig. 1850-91 from Ayrshire × local;
HB 1951; Målselv var. (smaller and usu. pd) absorbed in 1951; Nor.
Rødt (or *Rautt) trønderfe og målselvfe*; graded to Norwegian Red-and-
White and finally absorbed 1960; not *Drontheimer, Trondhjem*
Red Ukrainian: see Red Steppe
Red West Flemish: see Belgian Red

Red-White: see Red Pied, Red-and-White
Red White-Russian: see Byelorussian Red
reem: see aurochs
Reggiana (Reggio, Emilia, Italy); d.m.[dr]; red to yellow-brown; HB 1935; syn. *Formentina*; rare
Regus (Beckton Stock Farm, Sheridan, Wyoming, USA); m; red; pd; herd of Red Angus developed by grading Hereford to Angus
Rendena (Brenta valley, Padua-Vicenza, Venetia, Italy); d.(m); small local var. sim to Italian Brown; dark chestnut; HB 1982; syn. *Brina di Val di Rendena*; being crossed with Italian Brown
Renitelo (Madagascar); m.dr; red, often with paler underside and mucosae; orig. from Limousin (1930-62) (25%) and Africander (1946-62) (48%), × Madagascar Zebu (27%); crosses bred *inter se* since 1956, breed recog. 1962. [= 3 mothers]
Restagi: see Rustaqi
Retinta (Extremadura and W. Andalucía, Spain); m.(dr); dark red; open lyre horns; orig. by union of Andalusian Red (Sp. *Retinta andaluza*), Extremadura Red (Sp. *Colorada extremeña*) and Andalusian Blond (Sp. *Rubia andaluza*); HB 1933, BS. [= dark red]
Reyna: see Central American Dairy Criollo
Rhaetian Grey (N.E. Graubünden, Switzerland); Ger. *Rätische Grauvieh*; *cf.* Tyrol Grey; nearly extinct
[Rhineland] (W. Germany); d.m; var. of German Red Pied very close to Meuse-Rhine-Yssel; HB 1875; Ger. *Rheinisches, Rheinland*; syn. *Lower Rhine* (Ger. *Niederrheiner* or *Niederrheinisches*)
Rhodope: see Rodopi
Ribatejana (Ribatejo, C. Portugal): see Fighting bull
rigget: see coloursided
Rigi: see Swiss Brown
rimu: see aurochs
Rio Limón Dairy Criollo (Venezuela); var. of Tropical Dairy Criollo; Sp. *Criollo lechero limonero*; syn. *Criollo lechero Venezuelano* (*Venezuelan Dairy Criollo*), *Improved Criollo*; BS
Riopardense (São José do Rio Pardo, São Paulo, Brazil); d; orig. (1953 on) from Holstein ($\frac{5}{8}$) × Guzerá ($\frac{3}{8}$) by Osmany Junqueira Dias at Fazenda Graminha; usu. black, also black pied, or black, blue roan and white
Ristagi: see Rustaqi
Rød Dansk Malkekvæg: see Danish Red
Rødkolle: see Red Polled Østland
Röd Kullig Lantras: see Swedish Red Polled
Rodopi (S.W. Bulgaria); prim. *brachyceros* type; brown-black with white eel-stripe; dwarf; Bulg. *Rodopska k"soroga* (= *shorthorned*), Ger.

Rhodopen; not *Rodopit*; *cf.* West Macedonian; rare
Rødt kollet Østlandsfe: see Red Polled Østland
Rojhan (Dera Ghazi Khan, Punjab, Pakistan); z; hill type, sim. to Lohani; usu. red with white markings
Romagnola (Romagna, Italy); m.[dr]; Podolian type; grey to white; HB 1956; former vars: improved (It. *gentile*) with Chianina and Reggiana blood 1850-80, and mountain (It. *di montagna*) with Maremmana blood; BS in GB 1973, Canada 1974, USA 1974, Australia, New Zealand, Argentina
Roman; former var. of Maremmana; It. *Romana*
Romana Red (Dominican Republic); m; z; orig. in 1930s by Central Romana Corporation, from Mysore and Nelore zebus × red Puerto Rican Criollo
Romanian Brown (S. and E. Romania); d.m; shades of brown; orig. early 20th c. from Grey Steppe graded to Swiss Brown; Rom. *Brună*; syn. *Maramureş Brown*; used to grade Mocaniţa and Grey Steppe in S; not *Grey*
Romanian Mountain (Romania); d; *brachyceros* type; light grey, red-brown or dark grey; Rom. *Rasa (românească) de munte*; syn. *Mocaniţa* (not *Mocanitza*); almost extinct by crossing with Romanian Brown
Romanian Pinzgau: see Transylvanian Pinzgau
Romanian Red (S.E. Romania); d; Rom. *Roşie*; inc. Danish Red, Dobrogea Red and Red Steppe
Romanian Simmental (Romania); m.d; yellow- to red-pied; orig. from Grey Steppe graded to Simmental (imports *c.* 1910-48); Rom. *Bălţată românească* (= *Spotted Romanian*); syn. *Romanian Spotted, Romanian Yellow Spotted*
Romanian Spotted: see Romanian Simmental
Romanian Steppe (Romania); dr.m.d; Grey Steppe type; Rom. *Sură de Stepă*; former vars: Bucşan, Ialomiţa, Moldavian, Transylvanian; disappearing by crossing with Simmental, Swiss Brown and Romanian Red (chiefly Danish Red)
Romosinuano (R. Sinú valley, N. Colombia); m; Criollo type; red-brown; pd; orig. end of 19th c. from Costeño con Cuernos, ? by mutation or with Red Poll or Aberdeen-Angus blood; BS; syn. *Coastal Polled, Moruno-Sinuano*; not *Romo-Sinuano*; HB also in Costa Rica. [= polled Sinú]
Røros: see Blacksided Trondheim and Nordland
Rossa montanina: see Montana
Rotbunt: see Red Pied
Rotfleckvieh: see Simmental
[Rottal] (Bavaria, Germany); absorbed by German Simmental
[Rouge de l'Ouest] (N.W. France); m.d; federation 1962-70 of Armorican

and Maine-Anjou; HB 1966. [= western red]
Rouge du Nord (France): see Flemish Red
Rowzi, Rozi: see Barotse
RSB: see Red Pied Swedish
Rückenblessen, Rückenscheck: see coloursided, whitebacked
Rufa'ai: see Kenana
Ruggelde, Ruggelds, Ruggelings: see Witrik
Russian Black Pied (USSR); d; recog. 1925, national strains united 1959,
    HB 1940; Russ. *Chernopestraya*; syn. *Russian Friesian*; vars: Baltic
    Black Pied (Estonian and Lithuanian), Central Russian Black Pied,
    Siberian Black Pied, Ural Black Pied, *q.v.*
Russian Brown (USSR); orig. from Swiss Brown and German Brown
    first imported early in 19th c; HB; Russ. *Shvitskaya* (= *Schwyz*); orig.
    of Ala-Tau, Carpathian Brown, Caucasian Brown, Kostroma, Lebedin;
    part orig. of Schwyz-Zeboid
Russian Brown-zebu: see Schwyz-Zeboid
Russian Simmental (USSR); orig. from Swiss and German imports in
    early, and Austrian in late, 19th c; HB 1925; vars: Far Eastern,
    Siberian, Steppe, Sychevka (*q.v.*), Ukrainian, Ural (*Priuralski*), Volga
    (*Privolzhski*)
[Russo-Siberian]; d; var. of Siberian
Rustaqi (Hilla, Iraq); improved var. of Iraqi; light tan; orig. from
    Jenubi, ? with Red Sindhi blood; not *Restagi, Ristagi, Rustagi*. [from
    government farm at Rustaq, nr Baghdad]
Rwanda: see Watusi var. of Ankole

Sabre (Lambert ranch, Refugio, Texas); m; red; orig. (1950 on) from
    Sussex ($\frac{7}{8}$) × Brahman ($\frac{1}{8}$)
Sachor: see Sanchori
Sadhe: see Sandhe
Sahabadi: see Shahabadi
Sahford (Australia); Sahiwal × Hereford cross
Sahiwal (S. Punjab, Pakistan); d; z; usu. reddish-dun usu. with white
    markings; syn. *Lambi Bar, Lola, Montgomery, Multani* (Bihar), *Teli*;
    not *Sanewal, Saniwal*; BSd and HB (India), BS in Australia 1969,
    Kenya; part orig. of Australian Friesian Sahiwal, Australian Milking
    Zebu, Jamaica Hope, Quasah
Saidi (Upper Egypt); dr.m; var. of Egyptian with more zebu blood; not
    Saiidi. [= valley, *i.e.* of Nile]
saing: see tsine
St Croix: see Senepol
St Girons et Aure: see Aure et Saint-Girons

saladang: see seladang
Salamanca: see Morucha
Salem: see Alambadi
Salers (Cantal, Auvergne, France); m.d.[dr]; mahogany; recog. 1853; BS 1908; BS also in Canada and USA
Salinera: see Berrenda en colorado
Salmanquina, Salmantina: see Morucha
Samburu (C. Kenya); local Small East African Zebu
Sanabresa: see Alistana-Sanabresa
Sanchori (Jodhpur, Rajasthan, India); dr.d; z; var. of Kankrej; syn. *Marwari*; not *Sachor, Sanchore*
Sandhe: see Brahmin; Nepalese *Sādhe*
Sanewal, Saniwal: see Sahiwal
SANGA (E. and S. Africa); dr; long horns; small cervico-thoracic hump; ? orig. from zebu and Hamitic Longhorn; syn. *Bantu*; inc. Africander, Ankole, Barotse, Barra do Cuanzo, Basuto, Bavenda, Damara, Danakil, Kaokoveld, Mashona, Mateba, Nguni, Nkone, Nilotic, Ovambo, Tonga, Tswana, Tuli. [Galla = ox]
Sanga (Ghana): see Ghana Sanga
SANGA-ZEBU (E. Africa); intermediates between Sanga and East African Shorthorned Zebu; inc. Alur, Aradó, Fogera, Horro, Ngaṇda, Sukuma, Tuni
Sanhe (N.E. Inner Mongolia, China); d.m; usu. red-and-white also black-and-white; orig. from Siberian, Simmental and Friesian, × Mongolian about 1900; W.G. *Sanho*; syn. *Three-river breed*; *cf.* Pinzhou
San Martinero (Meta and Caquita provs, C. Colombia); m.(d); Criollo type sim. to Costeño con Cuernos but better conformation; yellow-red or chestnut; syn. *San Martin, Sanmartiniana*
Sanogai: see Achham
Santa Gabriela (N.E. São Paulo, Brazil); d.m; usu. red, sometimes yellow; pd; orig. (1965 on) from Red Pied Friesian × (red pd zebu × Devon-Guzerá), *i.e.* $\frac{3}{8}$ zebu $\frac{5}{8}$ European, at Estação Experimental de Zootecnia de Sertãozinho (formerly Fazenda Santa Gabriela); discontinued
Santa Gertrudis (Texas, USA); m; red; hd or pd; orig. 1910-40, $\frac{5}{8}$ Shorthorn $\frac{3}{8}$ Brahman; BS 1951; BS also in Brazil 1961, Canada 1967, Mexico, Australia, Zimbabwe, New Zealand, HB also in USSR. [division of King Ranch]
[Santander] (Spain); m.d.dr; North Spanish type; syn. *Montaña*; former vars: Campurriana, Lebaniega, Pasiega; only Tudanca survives
Santander Hairless: see Chino Santandereano
sapi utan: see Malay banteng
Sarabi (Iranian Azerbaijan); d.m.(dr); red; ? zebu blood; syn. *Ardebili*;

not *Saribi*

saran-hainag: see dzo

Sardinian (Sardinia, Italy); m.d.[dr]; orig. type now only in mts; many colours, self or pied, ♂ often black or dark red, ♀ often red or yellow-brown, occ. brindle; It. *Sarda*; orig. (with Italian Brown) of Sardinian Brown and (with Modicana) of Sardo-Modicana; *cf.* Corsican

Sardinian Brown (C. Sardinia); d; var. of Italian Brown by grading Sardinian *c.* 1880 on; It. *Bruno-sarda*; syn. *Ozierese* (from Ozieri), *Sardo-Schwyz, Sardo-Swiss, Svitto-Sarda*

Sardo-Modicana (S. and E. Sardinia); m.d.[dr] yellow-brown to dark red; orig. from Modicana × Sardinian (1860 on); HB 1936; syn. *Modica-Sardinian* or *Modicano-Sarda, Oristanese* (from Oristano)

Sardo-Schwyz, Sardo-Swiss: see Sardinian Brown

Sauerland: see Westphalian Red

Sava: see Posavina

Save: see Nguni

Savinja Grey (Upper Savinja, N. Slovenia, Yugoslavia); d.m; Serbo-Cro. *Sivka iz Gorne Savinje*; orig. from Austrian Blond and Istrian improved by Slovenian Brown and American Brown Swiss

Savoiarda, Savoy: see Tarentaise, Tarina

Sayaguesa (Sayago, S.W. Zamora, Spain); m.dr; Morenas del Noroeste group; black, with brown back-stripe in ♂; syn. *Zamorana*

Scheckvieh: see German Simmental

[Scheinfeld] (Germany); orig. from Heilbronn × native Franconian red in mid-19th c; absorbed by Yellow Franconian

Schiltern: see Waldviertel

Schlesisch: see Silesian

Schönhengst: see Hřbínecký

Schwarzbunt: see Black Pied

Schwarzfleckvieh (Switzerland): see Swiss Black Pied

Schwyz: see Swiss Brown

Schwyz-Zeboid (Tajikistan, USSR); m.d; orig. (1937 on) from Russian Brown × Tajik zeboid; Russ. *Shvitsezebuvidnyĭ skot*; syn. *Russian Brown-zebu, Swiss-zebu*

Scindhi, Scindi: see Red Sindhi

Scotch (or *Scottish*) *Highland*: see Highland

Scotch (or *Scottish*) *Shorthorn*: see Beef Shorthorn

Scotch Polled: see Aberdeen-Angus, Galloway

Scutari: see Shkodra

SDM: see Danish Black Pied

Sechsämter: see Bavarian Red

Sechuana: see Tswana

Seferihisar (Izmir, W. Turkey); d; local var; red; ? orig. from Simmental

× Aleppo (*i.e.* Damascus)

Seistani: see Sistani

Sekgatla: see Southern Tswana

seladang (Malay peninsula) = *Bos (Bibos) gaurus hubbacki* (Lydekker); var. of gaur; syn. *Malayan bison, Malayan gaur*; not *saladang, sladang*; numbers declining rapidly. [Malay]

selembu (Malaysia) = seladang × cattle hybrid

Senegal Fulani: see Gobra

Senegal N'Dama; large type (*N'Dama Grande*): see Gambian N'Dama; small type (*N'Dama Petite* or *Red Senegal*): see N'Dama; orig. (× Red Poll) of Senepol (Leeward Is)

Senepol (St Croix, US Virgin Is); d.m; red; pd; orig. 1918-49 from Red Poll × smaller var. of Senegal N'Dama imported in 1860 to Nelthropp herd, St Croix; BS; syn. *Nelthropp*; not *Nelthrop*

Sengologa (S.C. Botswana); var. of Tswana belonging to Bangologa; rare

Šenhengský: see Hřbínecký

Serenge, Serenli: see Tuni

Serere (Serere peninsula, Uganda); Sanga-Zebu intermediate sim. to Nganda

Serrana (Spain): see Black Iberian, Pajuna

Sertanejo: see Curraleiro

Sese (or *Sesse*) *Island*: see Nganda

Seshaga (S.C. Botswana); var. of Tswana belonging to Bashaga; rare

Setswana: see Tswana

Shahabadi (W. Bihar and E. Uttar Pradesh, India); dr.d; z; grey; sim. to Hariana; syn. *Gangatiri*; not *Sahabadi, Shahbadi*

Shakhansurri (Afghanistan); var. of Afghan; black with little white

Shami, Shamia: see Damascus

Shandong (China); m.dr; Central Chinese type; yellowish-brown, occ. dun or black; W.G. *Shan-tung*, Russ. *Shan'dun*; syn. *Danyang* (W.G. *Tanyang*) (S. Jiangsu), *Syhyang* (N. Jiangsu); ? = Luxi

Sharabi (Tigris valley N. of Mosul, Iraq); black coloursided; small hump in ♂; not *Sarabi*

sheeted: see belted

[Sheeted Somerset] (England); hd or pd; red, belted; syn. *Somerset, Somersetshire Sheeted, White-sheeted Somerset*; extinct *c.* 1890

Sheko (S.W. Kefa, S.W. Ethiopia); d; brown or black-and-white; hd or pd; humpless or tiny hump; syn. *Goda, Mitzan*; rare

Shendi; var. of Butana (or related strain)

Shetland (Scotland); d.m; formerly various colours, now only black-and-white; Shorthorn, Angus and Friesian blood; BS 1910, HB 1912-21 and 1982 on; syn. *Zetland*; var. [Orkney]; nearly extinct

Shikari: see Khillari

Shkodra Red; var. of Albanian; It. *Scutari*

Shoa (W. Africa): see Shuwa

Shona: see Mashona

SHORTHORN (N.E. England); m.d; red, roan, or white, occ. red-and-white or roan-and-white; orig. from Holderness + Teeswater in late 18th c; HB 1822, BS 1875; syn. *Durham, Improved Shorthorn, Improved Teeswater*; inc. Beef Shorthorn, Dairy Shorthorn, Milking Shorthorn (USA), Northern Dairy Shorthorn, Poll and Polled Shorthorn, White-bred Shorthorn; part orig. of Armorican, Belgian breeds, Danish Red Pied, German Shorthorn, Illawarra, Japanese Shorthorn, Lincoln Red, Maine-Anjou, *et al.*; BS also in Canada, S. Africa 1912 (HB 1906), HB also in Brazil 1906

Shorthorned Sahelian Zebu: see West African (shorthorned) Zebu

Shorthorned Zebu: see East African Shorthorned Zebu, Grey-white Shorthorned (India), West African (shorthorned) Zebu

Shuwa (Chad and N.E. Nigeria); pa.m.d; West African (shorthorned) Zebu type, sim. to Azaouak; usu. dark red, also black or pied; Fr. *Choa*, Hausa *Wadara* (Nigeria); syn. *Arab* (Chad), *Tur*; vars: Kilara, Toupouri

Siamese: see Thai

Siam-Kedah: see Kedah-Kelantan

Sibasa: see Bavenda

[Siberian] (USSR); d; Turano-Mongolian type; Russ. *Sibirskiĭ skot*; vars: Altai, Russo-Siberian, West Siberian and Yakut; extinct by 1960 (except Yakut)

Siberian Black Pied (W. Siberia, USSR); d.m; var. of Russian Black Pied; orig. since 1929 from East Friesian × local Siberian; Russ. *Chernopestryĭ skot Sibiri* or *Sibirskaya chernopestraya*

Siberian White (Novosibirsk, USSR); white with black ears; Russ. *Beliy sibirskiy skot*; rare

Siboney (Cuba); d; $\frac{5}{8}$ Holstein-Friesian $\frac{3}{8}$ Cuban Zebu

[Sicilian] (Sicily, Italy); dr.m.d; dark red; orig. Iberian type decimated 1860 and crossed with Chianina, Reggiana, Calabrian *et al.* to produce Mezzalina (upland), Modicana (lowland) and Montanara (mountain) vars; now Sicilian = Modicana (*q.v.*) which has absorbed the other two vars

Siebenburgisch: see Transylvanian

Siegerland, Siegerländer: see Westphalian Red

Sierra Leone: see N'Dama

[Silesian Red]; var. of Polish Red (to 1945 var. of German Red) with Danish Red blood; Pol. *Śląska czerwona*, Ger. *Schlesisches Rotvieh*

Silesian White-Back: see Kłodzka

Simbrah (USA); cross of Simmental ($\frac{1}{2}$-$\frac{3}{4}$) × Brahman ($\frac{1}{2}$-$\frac{1}{4}$) registered by American Simmental Association; syn. (to 1978) *Brahmental*; not *Simbra*

Simford (Israel); m; orig. 1970s from Simmental × Hereford

Simford (NSW, Australia); m; deep honey to red with white face; orig. at 'Waterloo Station' from Simmental × Hereford

Simmalo (California, USA); m; orig. from $\frac{1}{2}$ Simmental, $\frac{1}{4}$ bison, $\frac{1}{4}$ Hereford by Mel Lauriton

SIMMENTAL; Ger. *Fleckvieh* (= *pied cattle*) or *Rotfleckvieh* (= *red pied cattle*); inc. Simmental (Switzerland) and its derivatives: Austrian Simmental, Bulgarian Simmental, Czech Pied, French Red Pied, German Simmental, Hungarian Pied, Italian Red Pied, Polish Simmental, Romanian Simmental, Russian Simmental, Slovakian Pied, Yugoslav Pied; BS also in Southern Africa 1950 (HB Namibia 1921, S. Africa 1951), Brazil 1963, Argentina 1966, USA 1968, Canada 1969, GB 1971, Sweden 1975, Australia, Ireland, New Zealand, Zambia, Zimbabwe, Uruguay, China 1981

Simmental (W. Switzerland); d.m.dr; dun-red or leather-yellow, and white; white face; orig. from Bernese; recog. 1862, BS and HB 1890; Fr. *Tachetée rouge* (or *Pie rouge*) *du Simmental*, Ger. *Simmentaler Fleckvieh*; syn. *Swiss Red Spotted* (= *Schweizer Rotfleckvieh*), *Swiss Simmental Spotted*; Red Holstein blood in 1960s and 70s

Simmental d'Alsace: see Alsatian Simmental

Simmenthal-Friulana: see Italian Red Pied

Sindhi: see Red Sindhi

Sindhi, Grey: see Thari

Sindi: see Red Sindhi

Siné, race du: see Djakoré

[Singida White]; local strain of Small East African Zebu in Tanzania

Sinhala (Sri Lanka); z; sim. to Indian hill type; usu. black or red, sometimes pied; dwarf; syn. *Lanka*

Sinú, Sinuano: see Romosinuano

Sinuano de cuernos: see Costeño con Cuernos

Siri (Bhutan); dr.d; z; hill type; ? Tibetan blood; usu. black- or red-and-white; syn. *Trahbum* (Bhutanese); orig. (× Nepalese Hill) of Kachcha Siri

Sistani (E. Iran); m; z; black or pied; hd or pd or scurs; not *Seistani*

Sitamarhi: see Bachaur

SJB: see Swedish Jersey

SJM: see Jutland Black Pied

[Skåne] (Sweden); orig. from Red Pied Holstein and Dutch, × local; absorbed by Red Pied Swedish; syn. *Scanian*

SKB: see Swedish Polled

sladang: see seladang
Slavonian Podolian: see Yugoslav Steppe
SLB: see Swedish Friesian
Slesvig Marsh: see Ballum
Slovakian Pied (Slovakia, Czechoslovakia); d.m; orig. from Simmental
    × local; Sl. *Slovenský strakatý*; syn. *Slovakian Red and White, Slovakian
    Simmental, Slovakian Spotted, Slovakian Yellow Spotted, Slovakish
    Yellow*
Slovakian Pinzgau (Slovakia, Czechoslovakia); d.m; orig. from Pinzgauer
    × local; Sl. *Slovenský Pincgavský*
[Slovakian Red] (Slovakia, Czechoslovakia); d.m.dr; Central European
    Red type sim. to Polish Red; Sl. *Slovenský červený*; extinct 1965
Slovenian Brown (Slovenia, Yugoslavia); orig. from Austrian Brown
[Slovenian White] (Yugoslavia); = Austrian Blond; Serbo-cro. *Sloven-
    ačko belo goveče*; syn. *Koruško plavo*
[Småland] (Sweden); local; absorbed into Red Pied Swedish
Small East African Zebu; East African Shorthorned Zebu group; inc.
    Lugware (N.E. Congo), Mongalla (S. Sudan), Nkedi (Uganda), and
    Kenya, Tanzania and Zanzibar Zebus; *cf.* Abyssinian and Somali
Small Spotted Hill (Germany): see Black Forest
Small Zebu (Ethiopia): see Jijjiga Zebu
SMR: see German Black Pied Dairy
Socotra (Socotra I, Indian Ocean); dwarf; humpless; short horns
Sofia Brown: see Bulgarian Brown
Sokoto Gudali (N.W. Nigeria); d.dr; West African (shorthorned) Zebu
    type; grey or dun; Fulani *Gudali*; syn. *Bokoloji, Godali, Sokoto*
Somali (Somalia); East African Shorthorned Zebu type; horns short,
    sometimes absent; syn. *Small zebus of Somalia, Somaliland Zebu*; vars:
    Garre, Gasara, North Somali
Somali Boran: see Ethiopian Boran
Somaliland Zebu: see Somali
Somba (Atakora Highlands, N. Togo and Benin); var. of West African
    Savanna Shorthorn; black, black pied or red pied; syn. *Atacora* (Benin),
    Mango (Togo)
Sonkheri; red-and-white var. of Dangi
Son Valley (Madhya Pradesh, India); z; local var.
Sorco: see Jiddu
Sorraia: see Bragado do Sorraia
Sorthi: see Gir
South African Brown Swiss (S. Africa); orig. from American, Swiss and
    German imports since 1907; BS 1926, HB 1954
South Anatolian Red (Turkey); d; Turk. *Cenubî* (or *Güney*) *Anadolu
    Kırmızı*; syn. *Southern Yellow-Red*; vars: Aleppo (= Damascus),

Çukurova, Dörtyol, Kilis

[South and West Norwegian] (S.W. Norway); d; usu. red, also dun; hd or pd; orig. 1947 by joining Lyngdal and Vestland Red Polled with Vestland Fjord; HB 1947; Nor. *Sør og vestlandsfe* (= *South and Westland cattle*); absorbed by Norwegian Red 1968

South China Zebu (Guangdong, Guangxi, Fujian and Yunnan, China); dr; z; usu. light brown, also black, brown or dun; syn. *South China Draft*; inc. Hainan, Xuwen and Yunnan Zebu

South Coast (Australia): see Illawarra

South Devon (S.W. England); d.m; light red; BS and HB 1891; obs. syn. *South Hams*; BS also in S. Africa 1914, USA 1974, Canada 1974, S. America, New Zealand, Australia, Ireland; see also Devon

Southeastern Hills Zebu (Sudan): see Mongalla

Southern (India): see Umblachery

[Southern Crioulo] (Brazil, S. of lat. 18-20°S); m; sim. to Argentine Criollo, Texas Longhorn and Romosinuano; brown, orange or pied; long horns; Port. orig. (? from Alentejana); Port. *Crioulo do Sul;* syn. *Bruxo* or *Legítimo* (Minas Gerais), *Coloniã* (from Coloniã do Sacramento, Uruguay), *Mineiro* (Rio de Janeiro, *i.e.* from Minas Gerais); orig. of Caracú, Franqueiro and Junqueiro; not *Criôlo*. [= native]

Southern Sudanese: see Nilotic

Southern Sudan Hill Zebu: see Mongalla

Southern Tswana (S. Botswana); var. of Tswana with Africander blood; syn. *Dikgomo tsa Borwa* (= cattle of the south); inc. Sekgatla (cattle of the Bakgatla)

Southern Ukrainian (Ukraine, USSR); m; orig. from Charolais ($\frac{1}{2}$), Hereford ($\frac{1}{4}$), Red Steppe ($\frac{1}{4}$); Russ *Yuzhnoukraïnskaya*

South Hams: see South Devon

South Malawi Zebu; former var. of Malawi Zebu; obs. syn. *Nyasa Zebu* or *Nyasaland Zebu*

South Siberian: see Altai

South Tyrol Grey: see Grey Alpine

[South Wales Black]; m.d; HB 1874-1904; syn. *Pembroke*; vars: Castle Martin, Dewsland; orig. (+ North Wales Black) of Welsh Black

Spanish Brown (N. Spain); orig. from Swiss Brown imported since 1850 but esp. 1880-1910; HB; Sp. *Parda alpina* (*PA*); syn. *Parda suiza, Schwyz española*

Spanish Mountain: see Black Iberian, Pajuna; Sp. *Serrana* or *Agrupaciones serranas*

Spanish Pied: see Berrenda

Spotted: see Simmental

Spotted cattle of the lower Guadiana: see Guadiana Spotted

Spotted Moravian: see Moravian Red Pied
Spotted Mountain: see Simmental
Spotted Romanian: see Romanian Simmental
Spotted Valdostana: see Aosta
Spreča (N.E. Bosnia, Yugoslavia); yellow-grey; orig. from Yugoslav
  Steppe with Buša blood; Serbo-cro. *Sprečko goveče*; syn. *Tuzla*; nearly
  extinct
SRB: see Swedish Red-and-White
[Stara Planina] (W. Bulgaria); dr; dark grey; smaller mountain var. of
  Bulgarian Grey with more *brachyceros* blood; Bulg. *Staroplaninska
  k"soroga* (= *shorthorned*)
Steierisch, Steiermärkler: see Styrian
Steppe: see Grey Steppe
Styrian Blond: see Austrian Blond
[Styrian Brown] (Austria); former var. of Austrian Brown; Ger. *Steier-
  isches Braunvieh*
Styrian Spotted: see East Styrian Spotted
Sucra: see Jiddu
Sudanese Fulani (Mali); m; West African (lyrehorned) Zebu type; usu.
  light grey; Fr. *Zébu peul soudanais*; var: Toronké
Sudanese Longhorn: see Nilotic
Sudanese Shorthorned Zebu: see North Sudan Zebu
[Sudeten] (Czechoslovakia); d.m.dr; orig. from Central European Red;
  Cz. *Sudetský*; syn. *Moravian Sudeten*; vars: Sudeten Pied (often
  coloursided), Sudeten Red; orig. of Kłodzka (Glatz Mountain)
[Suffolk Polled] (England); dun or red-brown; syn. *Suffolk Dun*; orig.
  (× Norfolk Horned) of Red Poll
Suiá (Matto Grosso, Brazil) = Marchigiana × Nelore cross at Suiá
  farm of Liquifarm
Suisbu (Argentina); m; American Brown Swiss × zebu. [Pardo *Suizo*
  × *zebu*]
Suk (N.W. Kenya); local Small East African Zebu, ? with Karamajong
  blood
Suksun (Perm, USSR); d; red; orig. in late 19th c. from Danish Red ×
  local, followed by Angeln in early 20th c. with Red Steppe, Estonian
  Red and Latvian Brown blood (1933-38); HB 1941; Russ. *Suksunskaya*
Sukuma (S. of L. Victoria, Tanzania); Sanga-Zebu intermediate; usu.
  red, light dun, red roan or blue roan
Sul do Save: see Nguni
[Šumava] (Bohemia, Czechoslovakia); d.m.dr; sim. to Bergscheck; yellow
  to grey; Cz. *Šumavský*; syn. *Budějovice* (Cz. *Budějovický*, Ger.
  Budweiser); extinct *c.* 1945
Sumba Ongole (Indonesia): see Ongole

Sunandini (Kerala, India); d.dr; shades of fawn, brown or grey-brown; orig. 1966-85 from Swiss Brown ($\frac{5}{8}$) × local zebu; named 1979

Surati: see Gir

Surco, Surco Sanga: see Jiddu

Surti: see Gir

Surug, Suruq: see Jiddu

Sussex (Sussex and Kent, England); m.[dr]; sim. to Devon; red; BS and HB 1879; var: Polled Sussex; BS also in USA 1884, reformed 1966, S. Africa 1920 (HB 1906), New Zealand, Zambia

Svensk: see Swedish

Svetlolisata: see Murboden

Svitto-Sarda: see Sardinian Brown

Swabian Spotted: see Württemberg Spotted

Swazi: see Nguni

Swedish Ayrshire (Sweden); d; orig. from Ayrshire (imported 1847-1905) × local; BS 1899-1928, 1952 on, HB 1901-27, 1954 on (subsection in Swedish Red-and-White HB); Swe. *Svensk Ayrshire Boskap* (= *SAB*); joined with Red Pied Swedish in 1928 to form Swedish Red-and-White

Swedish Friesian (S. Sweden); d.(m); orig. from Dutch imports 1860-1907 and recent; orig. with local and East Friesian blood; HB 1891, BS 1913; Swe. *Svensk Låglands Boskap* (= *SLB*); syn. *Black-and-White Swedish, Swedish Lowland*

Swedish Highland: see Swedish Mountain

Swedish Jersey (S. Sweden); d; var. of Jersey first imported 1890s and reimported from Denmark after 1945; BS 1949, HB 1955; Swe. *Svensk Jersey Boskap* (= *SJB*)

Swedish Lowland: see Swedish Friesian

Swedish Mountain; white var. of Swedish Polled, with red or black points and side spots; sim. to North Finnish and to Blacksided Trondheim and Nordland (Norway); HB 1892, BS 1920-38; Swe. *Fjällras*; syn. *Swedish Highland*; declining

Swedish Polled (N. Sweden); d; BS and HB 1938; Swe. *Svensk Kullig Boskap* (= *SKB*); syn. *North Swedish*; inc. (since 1938) Swedish Mountain (white) and Swedish Red Polled; declining

Swedish Red-and-White (Sweden); d; red with small white markings; orig. 1928 from Red Pied Swedish + Swedish Ayrshire; BS and HB 1928; Swe. *Svensk Röd och Vit Boskap* (= *SRB*); syn. *Swedish Red Spotted*

Swedish Red Pied: see Red Pied Swedish

Swedish Red Polled; var. of Swedish Polled; sim. to Red Polled Østland (Norway) and West Finnish (some recent imports); HB 1913, BS 1913-38; Swe. *Röd Kullig Lantras* or *Röd Kullig Boskap*; nearly extinct

Swiss Black Pied (Fribourg, Switzerland); d; orig. 1960s and 70s from Holstein × Fribourg; Fr. *Tachetée noire*, Ger. *Schwarzfleckvieh*; syn.

108 DICTIONARY OF BREEDS

Swiss Black Spotted
Swiss Brown (E. Switzerland); d.m.dr; grey-brown, very occ. belted or
coloursided; BS 1897, HB 1878, reorg. 1911; Ger. *Schweizerisches
Braunvieh*, Fr. *Brune suisse*, It. *Bruna svizzera*; syn. *Rigi* (obs.), *Schwyz*
(not *Schwitz, Schwiz*); orig. of Brown (Mountain) breeds; American
Brown Swiss blood in 1960s and 70s
Swiss Red Spotted: see Simmental
Swiss Simmental Spotted: see Simmental
Swiss-zebu: see Schwyz-Zeboid
Sychevka (Smolensk, USSR); d.m; var. of Russian Simmental; orig.
(1880 on) from Simmental × local; recog. 1950; HB; Russ. *Sychëvskaya*;
syn. *Sychevka Simmental, Western Simmental*; not *Sychovsk*
Syhyang: see Shandong
Sykia (Khalkidiki, N.E. Greece); smaller grey var. of Greek Steppe; rare

Tabapuã (São Paulo, Brazil); m; z; pd; grey-white; orig. from one pd
Indo-Brazilian ♂ born 1940 and used on Nelore ♀♀ on farm of
Ortemblad family, 'Agua Milagrossa', Tabapuã; BS and HB 1959
Tachetée de l'Est (France): see Pie Rouge de l'Est
Tagama: see Azaouak
Tagil (Sverdlovsk, S. Urals, USSR); d; usu. black pied, also black, red
or red pied; orig. in mid-19th c. from Friesian, Kholmogory, *et al.* ×
local; HB 1931; Russ. *Tagil'skaya*
Taino (Cuba); d; in formation from $\frac{3}{4}$ Criollo $\frac{1}{4}$ Holstein and $\frac{3}{8}$ Criollo $\frac{5}{8}$
Holstein
Taiwan Zebu (China); dr; usu. yellow, red or brown, also black or grey;
orig. from local Chinese Yellow with Red Sindhi and Kankrej blood
since 1910; syn. *Formosa Draft*
Tajik: see Central Asian Zebu
Talabda: see Kankrej
Talysh: see Azerbaijan Zebu
Tamankaduwa (N.E. Sri Lanka); local z. var; usu. white or light; ? orig.
from imported Indian breeds
Tambov Red (Tambov, USSR); m.d; orig. early 19th c. from Zillertal ×
local with some Devon and Simmental blood; recog. 1948, HB; Russ.
Krasnaya tambovskaya or *Krasnotambovskaya* (= *Red Tambov*)
Tanaland Boran: see Ethiopian Boran
Tanganyika Zebu: see Tanzanian Zebu
Tanjore: see Umblachery
Tanyang: see Shandong
Tanzanian Zebu: *i.e.* Small East African Zebu in Tanzania; syn.
Tanganyika Zebu; local strains were once called Iringa Red, Masai

Grey, Mkalama Dun, Singida White but are no longer recognisable; Chagga is dwarf var.

Tapi, Tapti: see Thillari

Tarai (S. Nepal); z; lyrehorned type; Hariana influence; usu. white or grey; not *Terai*

Tarentaise (French Alps); d.m; fawn to yellow; recog. 1859, HB 1880; not *Tarentais, Tarente*; = Tarina (Italy); BS in Canada 1973, USA 1973

Targhi, Targi, Targui: see Tuareg

Tarina (Susa and Chirone valleys, Turin, Italy); d.m; BS and HB 1888, reorg. 1949; Fr. *Tarine*; syn. *Savoy* (It. *Savoiarda*); = Tarentaise (France); nearly extinct

Taro: see Valtarese

Tashkent: see Bushuev

[Tasmanian Grey] (Tasmania, Australia); m; sim. to Murray Grey; orig. from crossbred Aberdeen-Angus × white Shorthorn born at Parknook 1938; [BS]; absorbed by Murray Grey *c.* 1979; see also Australian Grey

Tattabareji: see Yola

[Tatu] (Rio de Janeiro, Brazil); orig. from crosses of Red Sindhi or Sahiwal bulls imported about 1850

Taurache: see Tourache

[Taurindicus] (Tanga, Tanzania); d; herd of crossbred European dairy cattle × East African Zebus started 1946, disbanded 1966

Tawana: see Batawana

Taylor (Patna, Bihar, India); d; red, grey or black; no hump; orig. from 4 Shorthorn and Channel Island bulls, imported by Commissioner Taylor in 1856, × local zebu; not *Taypor*; rare

[Teck] (Württemberg, Germany); absorbed by German Simmental

[Teeswater] (Durham, England); sim. to Holderness; Dutch orig.; syn. (unimproved) Shorthorn; orig. (+ Holderness) of Shorthorn

Telemark (Norway); d; coloursided, usu. red or brindle; lyre horns; recog. 1856, BS 1895, HB 1926; var: Valdres; being crossed with Norwegian Red; rare

Teli: see Sahiwal

Terai: see Tarai

Terengganu: see Kedah-Kelantan

Teso: see Nkedi

Texas Longhorn (USA); all colours and patterns, red commonest base colour; Spanish orig. (? Andalusian) first imported in 1640; BS 1964; syn. *Longhorn*; *cf.* Criollo and Southern Crioulo

Thai (Thailand); dr; z; yellow, red, brown, or black; syn. *Siamese*; orig. of Kedah-Kelantan (Malaysia)

Thai-Kedah: see Kedah-Kelantan

Thailand Fighting (S. Thailand); z; 65-70% red or brown, 30-35% dark or black

Thanh-Hoa (N. Vietnam); var. of Vietnamese

Thari (S.E. Sind, Pakistan); d.dr; z; lyrehorned; grey; syn. *Grey Sindhi*; orig. of Tharparkar (India)

Tharparkar (India); d.dr; z; lyrehorned type; grey; orig. from Thari; BSd and HB; not *Thar Parkar*

Therkuthi madu: see Umblachery

Thessaly; former var. of Greek Shorthorn

Thibar (Tunisia); m.d; 40-50% z; usu. red-brown, also red, fawn or ash-grey; orig. from Brown Atlas crossed with Modicana (1897), Ongole (1907), Charolais (1908-10), Red Sindhi, Tarentaise, and Montbéliard (1917)

Thillari; var. of Khillari; white; syn. *Tapi, Tapti.* [= cattle breeder]

Thrace (Greece): see East Macedonian (and Thrace)

Thracian (Turkey): see Turkish Grey Steppe

Three-river breed (China): see Sanhe

Tibetan (Tibet and Qinghai, China); sim. to Mongolian but dwarf; variable colour inc. brindle and coloursided; ♂ is *lang* (Tibetan *glang*, syn. *cholung, jolang, kirko* or *lhang*); syn. *humpless dwarf cattle of Tibet*

Tieflandrind: see Lowland

Tigray, Tigré: see Aradó

Tinima (Cuba); m; double-muscled strain of Criollo; darker and more hump in bull

Tinos (Greece, pure on Tinos, crossed on Ikaria, Samos, Rhodes); orig. from Near East cattle

[Tintern Black] (Natal, S. Africa); m.d; early var. of Drakensberger; orig. from Africander × local in early 20th c. in Tintern herd

[Tipo Carora] (Lara, Venezuela); d; orig. 1950s from American Brown Swiss × Criollo ($\frac{1}{4}$-$\frac{3}{8}$); BS; syn. *Caroreña*; graded to American Brown Swiss in 1970s

Tiroler Grauvieh: see Tyrol Grey

Tirolese: see Tux-Zillertal

Tonga (S. Zambia); Sanga type; usu. red, black or pied; orig. (by crossing with Barotse) of Baila (earlier Baila and Tonga were syn.)

Toposa (S.E. Sudan); East African Zebu sim. to Karamajong and Turkana; all colours; Murle is similar but smaller

Toro (W. Uganda); Sanga-Zebu intermediate sim. to Nganda but with more Ankole blood

toro de lidia (Spain): see Fighting bull

Toronké Fulani (Mali); m.d; var. of Sudanese Fulani sim. to Gobra; usu. white

Tortona, Tortonese: see Montana

Touareg: see Tuareg

Toubou (E. Niger); Red Bororo × Kuri cross

Toupouri (Chad); var. of Shuwa; syn. *Massa*

[Tourache] (Franche Comté, E. France); dr.d; sim. to Fémeline but coarser, highland more bull-like type; usu. dark red and white; absorbed by Montbéliard in late 19th and early 20th c; syn. *Comtois, Taurache*. [Fr. *taureau* = bull]

Trahbum: see Siri

Transcaucasian: see Caucasian

Transtagana: see Alentejana

[Transylvanian] (Romania); former var. of Romanian Steppe with huge horns; Rom. *Transilvăneană*, Ger. *Siebenburgisch*; syn. *Grey Transylvanian, Transylvanian Steppe*; cf. Hungarian Grey

Transylvanian Pinzgau (N.W. Romania); d.m.dr; red with white back, escutcheon and belly; orig. from Grey Steppe graded to Pinzgauer in early 20th c; Rom. *Pinzgau de Transilvania*; syn. *Romanian Pinzgau*; black var: Dorna

[Treignac]; former var. of Limousin

Trengganu: see Kedah-Kelantan

Tribofe: see Mantiqueira

Trønder, Trondheim, Trondhjem: see Blacksided Trondheim, Red Trondheim

Tropical (Argentina); d; Argentine Friesian × zebu

Tropical Dairy Criollo (Costa Rica, Dominican Republic, Mexico, Nicaragua and Venezuela); d; light dun to deep red often with black points and round eyes; Sp. *Criollo lechero tropical*; syn. *Improved Criollo, Milking Criollo*; vars: Central American Dairy Criollo (Costa Rica), Dominican Criollo, Rio Limón Criollo (Venezuela)

Tropicana (Argentina); d; Guernsey × zebu

tsauri: see chauri

Tsinchuan, Tsin'chun: see Qinchuan

tsine (Burma, N. Thailand, Laos and Kampuchea) = *Bos (Bibos) javanicus birmanicus*; var. of banteng; syn. *Burmese banteng*; not *hsaine, saing, tsaine, tsaing*

TSSHZ-1 (Tajikistan, USSR); d.m; orig. from Russian Brown × Tajik zebu; recog. 1985

Tswana (Botswana); Sanga type, sim. to Barotse and Tuli; usu. red pied or black or black pied; syn. *Bechuana, Sechuana, Setswana*; local vars: Batawana, Mangwato, Sengologa, Seshaga, Southern Tswana

Tuareg: see Azaouak; Fr. *Touareg*; sing. *Targui* (*Targhi* or *Targi*)

tucura (Mato Grosso and Pará, Brazil); popular name for stunted cattle (or horse), often applied to Pantaneiro; syn. *Guabiru* (= rat). [= grasshopper]

Tudanca (S.W. Santander, Spain); m.(dr.d); mountain, and only surviving var. of Santander; ♂ black, ♀ black to grey, brown or hazel; BS; declining by crossing with Swiss Brown

Tuli (S.W. Zimbabwe); Sanga type; yellow, golden-brown or red; hd or pd; selected (1946 on) from Mangwato var. of Tswana; BS 1961

Tuni (E. Kenya); d.m.dr; Sanga-Zebu intermediate; usu. red with diffuse white spots, also red or pied; syn. *Serenli, Serengi*; = Jiddu (Ethiopia and Somalia)

Tunisian: see Brown Atlas and Cape Bon Blond

Tur: see Shuwa

TURANO-MONGOLIAN (Central Asia); inc. Kalmyk, Kazakh, Mongolian, Siberian, Tibetan

Turino (Portugal and Brazil); d.(m); orig. from Dutch Black Pied imported in 18th c; HB; syn. *Frisia, Holandese, Luso-Holandese, Portuguese Friesian*; not *Tourino*. [Port. (old slang) = dandy]

Turkana (N.W. Kenya); East African Zebu sim. to Karamajong and Toposa

Turkestan Zebu: see Central Asian Zebu

Turkish Brown (N.W. Turkey); d.m; orig. from Montafon (and Brown Swiss) × Turkish Grey Steppe (and a few Anatolian Black) initially at Karacabey State farm in 1925; syn. *Çifteler Brown, Karacabey Brown, Karacabey Montafon*

Turkish Grey Steppe (N.W. Turkey); m.d.dr; Grey Steppe type; orig. from Iskar (Bulgaria); Turk. *Boz Step* (= Grey Steppe) or *Plevne*; syn. *Pleven, Plevna, Thracian, Turkish Grey*; former var: Kultak

Turkish native: see Anatolian Black, East Anatolian Red, South Anatolian Red

Turkmen; var. of Central Asian Zebu

[Tux]; var. of Tux-Zillertal; black or reddish-black with white tail and belly; Ger. *Tuxer*

Tux-Zillertal (Tyrol, Austria); syn. *Tirolese, Tyrolean*; Ger. *Tux-Zillertaler*; former vars: Tux (black), Zillertal (red); nearly extinct *c*. 1975

Tuy-Hoa (S.E. Vietnam); var. of Vietnamese

Tuzla: see Spreča

Tyrol, Tyrolean, Tyrolese: see Tyrol Grey, Tux-Zillertal

[Tyrol Brown] (Austria); former var. of Austrian Brown; orig. from Montafon, Lechtal and Swiss Brown; Ger. *Tiroler Braunvieh*

Tyrol Grey (Tyrol, Austria); d.m.[dr]; silver-grey; BS 1924, HB; Ger. *Tiroler Grauvieh*; syn. *Oberinntaler Grauvieh, Tyrolean Grey*; orig. (with Buša) of Gacko (Yugoslavia); = Grey Alpine (Italy) but also inc. Etschtaler (= Grey Adige) and Wipptal

[Tyrol Spotted] (Tyrol, Austria); former var. of Austrian Simmental; Simmental first used 1870, named *Unterinntaler Fleckvieh* 1890, BS

1906, HB 1933, name changed to *Tiroler Fleckvieh* 1938

Uberaba: see Dairy Zebu of Uberaba
Uganda Zebu: see Karamajong, Nkedi
Ujumqin (Inner Mongolia, China): var. of Mongolian
Ukamba: see Kamba
Ukrainian Grey (USSR); m.dr.d; Grey Steppe type; recog. 1910, HB 1935; Russ. *Seraya ukrainskaya* or *Seroukrainskaya* (= *Grey Ukrainian*); syn. *Ukrainian Grey Steppe*; rare
Ukrainian Oldenburg: see Podolian Black Pied
Ukrainian Red: see Red Steppe
[Ukrainian Whitebacked] (N.W. Ukraine, USSR); m; black, red, brown or grey with white, coloursided; *cf.* Polish Whitebacked
Ukrainian Whiteheaded (N.W. Ukraine, USSR); d; red (or black) with white head, feet and belly; orig. end of 18th and early 19th c. from Dutch cattle (Groningen Whiteheaded) brought by Mennonites, × local Ukrainian Grey and/or Polesian; HB 1926; Russ. *Ukrainskaya belogolovaya*; obs. syn. (to *c.* 1945) *Whiteheaded Colonist* (Russ. *Belogolovokolonistskaya*)
Ulten, Ultimo: see Grey Adige
Umblachery (Thanjanvur, Tamil Nadu, India); dr; z; local var. sim. to Kangayam but smaller; grey with white points and back-line; calves red or brown with white markings; steers dehorned and ears clipped; syn. *Jathi madu, Mottai madu, Southern, Tanjore, Therkuthi madu*; not *Umblacheri*; rare
Unterinntal: see Tyrol Spotted
Uogherá: see Fogera
Uollega: see Horro
Upper Baden Spotted: see Messkircher
Upper Bavarian Spotted: see Miesbacher
Upper Swabian Spotted: see Württemberg Spotted
ur: see aurochs
Ural Black Pied (Sverdlovsk, Chelyabinsk and Perm, USSR); d; var. of Russian Black Pied; orig. 1937 on, esp. at Istok State Farm, from East Friesian × Tagil and backcross to Friesian; HB 1951; Russ. *Ural'skaya chernopestraya*
urang: see dzo; not *uryang*
Urinsk: see Yurino
urus: see aurochs
[Uys] (Natal, S. Africa); d.m.dr; early var. of Drakensberger; ? orig. from black Friesian × Africander, ? with Zulu blood, in late 19th c. by D. Uys or from Vaderlander (= Groningen) × local

Vadhiyar: see Kankrej
Vagadia: see Kankrej
Vakaranga: see Mashona
[Valachian Dwarf] (Slovakia, Czechoslovakia); brown pied or red pied;
   Cz. *Valašský*; not *Walachian*
Val d'Adige: see Grey Adige
Val d'Aosta: see Aosta
[Valdarno] (Florence and Pisa, Italy); former var. of Chianina
[Val di Chiana] (Siena, Italy); orig. var. of Chianina
Valdostana: see Aosta
Valdres (Norway); var. of Telemark; nearly extinct
Val d'Ultimo: see Grey Adige
Vale and Vaalbonte (Netherlands); dun or dun-and-white colour var;
   rare
Vallecaucana, Valle de Cauca: see Hartón
[Valtarese]; dark reddish-grey var. of Bardigiana; syn. *Valle del Taro*
Varzese, Varzi: see Montana
Vaynol (England); herd of pure White Park cattle orig. from Argyll
   herd; at Vaynol (N. Wales) 1872-1980, since 1983 owned by Rare
   Breeds Survival Trust at Bemborough farm, Glos.
Vendée Marsh; var. of Parthenais; Fr. *Vendéen maraîchin*
Vendée-Parthenay: see Parthenais
[Vendonnais]; former var. of Limousin
[Venetian] (S. Venetia, Italy); former var. of Apulian Podolian; It.
   Pugliese del basso Veneto; syn. *Poggese*
Venezuela Criollo: see Llanero, Perijanero and Rio Limón Dairy Criollo
Venezuelan Dairy Criollo: see Rio Limón Dairy Criollo
Venezuelan Zebu (Venezuela); z; m; usu. red or pied; orig. from Gir *et
   al.*; Sp. *Cebú venezuelano*; BS
Verinesa (Verin, S. Orense, Spain); Morenas del Noroeste group; orig.
   from Vianesa by grading to Mirandesa
[Vestland Fjord] (Norway); usu. dun, also red or black; usu. hd; orig.
   1866-95 from black hd (Hordaland) and grey pd (Møre and Ramsdal);
   Nor. *Vestlandsk fjordfe*; syn. *Fjord, West Coast Fjord, Westland Horned*;
   combined with Lyngdal and Vestland Red Polled 1947 to form South
   and West Norwegian
[Vestland Red Polled] (Norway); Nor. *Vestlandsk raukolle*; syn. *West
   Coast Red Polled, Westland Polled*; combined with Lyngdal, then with
   Vestland Fjord 1947 to form South and West Norwegian
Vianesa (Viana del Bollo, S.E. Orense, Spain); m.dr.d; Morenas del
   Noroeste group; brown
Victoria (Texas, USA); m; orig. 1946 from Hereford ($\frac{3}{4}$) and Brahman ($\frac{1}{4}$)
Vietnamese (Vietnam); z. orig.; syn. *Annamese*; vars: Baria, Cham-Doc,

Thanh-Hoa, Tuy-Hoa

Villard-de-Lans (Isère, S.E. France); m.d.[dr]; sim. to Mézenc; yellow-brown; recog. 1863; not *Villars de Lans*; federated with Blonde d'Aquitaine (as var.) 1969-76; nearly extinct

Vit: see Iskar

Vladimir: see Yaroslavl

Vogelsberg (Hesse, Germany); subvar. of Hesse-Westphalian var. of German Red; BS 1885; Ger. *Vogelsberger*; nearly extinct

[Vogtland] (Saxony, Germany); var. of German Red; Ger. *Vogtländer* or *Vogtländisches Rotvieh*; displaced by German Simmental

Vollega: see Horro

Volynsk (Ukraine, USSR); m; orig. from Aberdeen-Angus ($\frac{1}{4}$), Limousin ($\frac{1}{4}$), Hereford ($\frac{1}{4}$), Russian Black Pied ($\frac{1}{4}$); Russ. *Volynskaya*

Vorarlberg Brown: see Montafon

Vorderwald (C. Black Forest, Baden, Germany); d.m.[dr]; red pied with white face and legs; HB; Ger. *Vorderwälder*; see also Hinterwald

Vosges (Alsace, N.E. France); d.m.[dr]; black-and-white, coloursided; HB; Fr. *Vosgienne*, Ger. *Vogesen*

[Vychegda-Vym] (Komi, USSR); d; black (28%), black pied (20%), red or red pied (47%); pd; Russ. *Vychegodsko-vymskaya*; absorbed by Kholmogory

Wachagga: see Chagga

Wadai-Dinka: see Nilotic

Wadara: see Shuwa

Wadhiar, Wadial: see Kankrej

Wagad: see Kankrej

Wagara: see Fogera

Wagyu: see Japanese

Wahima: see Bahima

Wakamba: see Kamba

Wakuma: see Bahima

Wakwa: see Préwakwa

Walachian: see Valachian

[Waldeck] (N. Hesse, Germany); subvar. of Hesse-Westphalian var. of German Red; Ger. *Waldecker*

Wäldervieh: see Black Forest

[Waldviertel] (Lower Austria); white or pale yellow; Ger. *Waldviertler Blondvieh;* syn. *Manhartsberg, Schiltern* (Czechoslovakia); not *Waldriert*; crossed with Glan-Donnersberg 1940; inc. in Austrian Yellow *c.* 1960; extinct *c.* 1970

Wallega: see Horro

Warwickshire: see Longhorn

WAS: see Ghana Shorthorn. [= West African Shorthorn]

Watusi (Rwanda, Burundi, and neighbouring areas of N. Kivu, Zaïre, and N.W. Tanzania); var. of Ankole; syn. *Burundi, Kivu, Rwanda*; in Rwanda common strain is called Inkuku; giant-horned Inyambo strain was owned by kings and chiefs; not *Batusi, Batutsi, Watussi*

Watusi (USA); orig. from Ankole used to grade Texas Longhorn; BS 1971; rare

Welsh Black (Wales); m.(d); orig. 1904 from North Wales Black + South Wales Black; HB 1874, BS 1904; Welsh *Gwartheg Duon Cymreig*; var: Polled Welsh Black; for colour vars: see Ancient Cattle of Wales; BS also in Canada 1971, New Zealand 1974, USA 1975

Welsh runt (English Midlands) = Welsh Black bullock

Wenshan (S.E. Yunnan, China); dr.m; yellow; ♂ humped; syn. *Guangnan*; *cf.* Central Chinese type

Werdenfels: see Murnau-Werdenfels

Wesermarsch: see Oldenburg-Wesermarsch

West African Dwarf Shorthorn: see West African Shorthorn (dwarf vars)

West African humpless; syn. *Taurine* (Fr.); see Kuri (Lake Chad), and West African small humpless (N'Dama and West African Shorthorn)

West African longhorns; ? orig. from Hamitic Longhorn; see Kuri, N'Dama

West African Shorthorn (Liberia to Cameroon); West African small humpless (trypanotolerant) type; usu. black, also pied or brown; inc. Savanna Shorthorn vars: Baoulé (Ivory Coast), Lobi (Burkina Faso), Ghana Shorthorn, Somba (Togo and Benin), [Pabli] (Benin), Savanna Muturu (Nigeria), and Bakosi, Doayo, Kapsiki and [Bamiléké] (Cameroon); and Dwarf Shorthorn vars: [Gambia Dwarf], Manjaca (Guinea-Bissau), Liberian Dwarf, Lagune (Ivory Coast, Togo and Benin), Forest Muturu (Nigeria) and Bakwiri (Cameroon)

West African small humpless; inc. N'Dama and West African Shorthorn; trypanotolerant

WEST AFRICAN ZEBU; inc. shorthorned (Azaouak, Fellata, Maure, Shuwa, Sokoto), medium-horned (Adamawa, Diali), lyrehorned (Gobra, Sudanese Fulani, White Fulani), and long lyrehorned (Red Bororo)

West Coast (Norway): see Vestland

Western Simmental (USSR): see Sychevka

[Westerwald] (Rhineland-Nassau, Germany); dr.m.d; sim. to Kelheimer; red-brown with white markings; Ger. *Westerwälder*; syn. *Wittgensteiner Blässvieh*; extinct c. 1940

West Finnish (W. Finland); d; red var. of Finnish; BS 1906-50; Finn. *Länsi-Suomalainen Karja* (= *LSK*), Swe. *Västfinsk*: syn. *Brown Finnish,*

Red Finnish; part orig. of Estonian Native
West Flemish, West Flemish Red: see Belgian Red
West Friesian: see Dutch Black Pied
West Highland (Scotland): see Highland
Westland (Norway): see Vestland
West Macedonian; dwarf var. of Greek Shorthorn; *cf.* Rodopi (Bulgaria)
  and Macedonian Blue (Yugoslavia)
West Nile (N.W. Uganda): see Lugware
[Westphalian Red] (S. Westphalia, Germany); subvar. of Hesse-
  Westphalian var. of German Red; Westerwald blood; Ger. *Westfäl-
  isches Rotvieh*; syn. *Sauerland, Siegerland* (Ger. *Siegerländer*)
Westphalian Red Pied: see Red Pied Westphalian
[West Siberian]; m; var. of Siberian; sim. to Kalmyk
Whitebacked: see coloursided and esp. Polish Whitebacked, Ukrainian
  Whitebacked; Ger. *Rückenblessen, Rückenscheck*; Germany (1936-45):
  see Glatz (Kłodzka), Pinzgauer, Sudeten
White Bororo: see White Fulani
Whitebred Shorthorn (Cumbria, N. England); m; white var. of Shorthorn
  for crossing with Galloway to produce Blue Grey; HB 1961, BS 1962;
  syn. *Cumberland White*; rare
White Cáceres (Extremadura, Spain); m; lyre horns; Sp.*Blanca cacereña*;
  syn. *Blanca guadianese* (= *White Guadiana*); ? white var. of Retinta;
  nearly extinct
white-face, *i.e.* Hereford pattern—white head, belly, feet and tail-tip: see
  Hereford, Kazakh Whiteheaded and Hřbínecký (white more extensive),
  Groningen Whiteheaded, Ukrainian Whiteheaded and Yaroslavl (white
  less extensive)
White Finnish: see North Finnish
White Forest: see White Park
White Fulani (N. Nigeria); dr.d.m; West African (lyrehorned) Zebu type;
  usu. white with black skin and points; Hausa *Bunaji*, Fulani *Yakanaji*,
  Fr. *Foulbé blanc*; syn. *Akou* or *White Bororo* (Cameroon), *White Kano*
White Galloway (Great Britain); colour var. of Galloway; white with
  coloured points; HB (with Belted Galloway) 1982; HB (with Galloway)
  also in USA 1973; rare
White Guadiana: see White Cáceres
Whiteheaded Colonist: see Ukrainian Whiteheaded
Whiteheaded Kazakh: see Kazakh Whiteheaded
White Horned (Great Britain): see White Park
White Hungarian: see Hungarian Grey
White Kano: see White Fulani
White Lake Chad: see Kuri
[White-marked] (Germany); dr.m.d; brown with white markings; Ger.

Blässiges, Braunscheck; syn. *Blazed*; inc. Kelheimer and Westerwald
White Meuse and Schelde: see Belgian Blue
white-middled: see belted
White Nile (Kosti district, Sudan); var. of Kenana with Baggara blood
White Park (Great Britain); white with black points; HB 1974, BS
    1983; 5 ancient and several new herds; ancient are Chillingham
    (Northumberland) (*q.v.*); Cadzow or Hamilton (Lanarkshire)—hetero-
    zygous for colour; Vaynol (N. Wales)(*q.v.*); Chartley (orig. Staffs, then
    Woburn, now Suffolk)—Longhorn blood; Dynevor (S. Wales)—long
    horns; syn. *Park, White Forest, White Horned, Wild White*; ? orig. of
    British White; rare
White Park (USA): see American White Park
White Po: see Modenese
White Polled (Great Britain): see British White
White-Russian Red: see Byelorussian Red
White Sanga (S. Ghana); White Fulani × Ghana Shorthorn
White-sheeted Somerset: see Sheeted Somerset
White Siberian: see Siberian White
White Slovenian: see Slovenian White
White Tortona: see Montana
White Welsh (Wales); var. of Ancient Cattle of Wales with colour of
    White Park; rare
wild: see aurochs, banteng, gaur, kou-prey, yak
Wild White (Great Britain): see White Park
[Wilstermarsch]; orig. var. of Red Pied Schleswig-Holstein; BS 1855;
    Ger. *Elb- und Wilstermarsch*
[Wipptal] (Tyrol, Austria); Ger. *Wipptaler*; absorbed in Tyrol Grey
Witrik (Netherlands); coloursided (red or white) var; syn. *Aalstreep* (=
    eelstripe) (Holland), *Ruggelde, Ruggelds, Ruggelings, Witrug*; rare. [=
    white back]
Wittgenstein, Wittgensteiner Blässvieh: see Westerwald
Wodabe (Cameroon); intermediates between White Fulani and Red
    Bororo
Wokalup (W. Australia); m; cross derived from Charolais, Brahman,
    Friesian and Aberdeen-Angus or Hereford
Wollega: see Horro
[Württemberg Spotted] (Germany); orig. var. of German Simmental; Ger.
    Württemberger Fleckvieh; syn. *Upper Swabian Spotted*; not *Wurtemburg*

Xinjiang Brown (N.W. Xinjiang, China); d.m; brown, also yellow or
    pied; orig. from Swiss Brown × Kazakh
Xuwen (N. of Leizhou peninsula, Guangxi, China); South China Zebu

type; syn. *Xuwen Humped*; not *Xuwin*; rare

Yacumeño (Beni, E. Bolivia); m; selected from nearly extinct Beni Criollo at Espiritu ranch on R. Yacumá; dun or red

yak, domestic (Tibetan plateau, Himalayas, Altai, Mongolia); usu. black or brown, also white, grey, blue roan, or pied; Tibetan *g.yag* (♂), Ch. *mao niu* (= *hairy cattle*); ♀ yak is *dri* (Tibetan *'bri*, syn. *bree, dhee*) or *nak* (Tibetan *gnag*); F₁ × cattle is dzo, *q.v.*

yak, wild (N.C. Tibet) = *Bos (Poëphagus) mutus* Przewalski; dark brown to black with grey dorsal line; Tibetan *'brong* (= *drong*); ♀ is *'brong-'bri* (= *drongdri*); orig. of domestic yak (*Poëphagus 'grunniens'* Linnaeus); rare

Yakanaji: see White Fulani

Yakut (Yakutia, USSR); m.d; formerly var. of Siberian; black, red or spotted with white back-line; Russ. *Yakutskiǐ skot*; syn. *East Siberian*; not *Yakutian*; rare

Yanbian (S.E. Jilin, China); dr.m

yanka (or *yanku*) (♂) and yankum (♀) (Bhutan); backcross of jatsum (mithun × Siri) to Siri ♂

Yaroslavl (USSR); d; usu. black (occ. red) with white head and feet; orig. in late 19th c, Kholmogory blood (*et al.*); HB 1924; Russ. *Yaroslavskaya*; syn. *Domshino* (Russ. *Domshinskaya*), *Vladimir*; not *Jaroslav, Jaroslavl, Yaroslav*

Yellow (Europe): see Austrian Yellow, Gelbvieh (German Yellow)

Yellow and Blond Mountain, Yellow and Pale Highland: see European Blond and Yellow

yellow cattle (China) = common cattle as distinct from buffalo and yak; inc. common yellow (Mongolian, Central Chinese) and humped (South China Zebu); Ch. *Huang niu*; Jap. *Kôgyû*

Yellow Franconian (Bavaria, Germany); only survivng var. of Gelbvieh (German Yellow); orig. in late 19th c. from Simmental, Elling, Scheinfeld, *et al.*; Ger. *Gelbes Frankenvieh*; syn. *Franconian*

Yellow Hill: see Gelbvieh

Yemeni Zebu (N. Yemen); dr; usu. red. also brown, grey or fawn, occ. black

[Yola] (N.E. Nigeria); var. of Adamawa with Muturu blood; red, black, brown or dun, pied or speckled with white; Fulani *Tattabareji* (= *speckled*)

Yorkshire: see Holderness

Yssel: see Meuse-Rhine-Yssel

Yugoslav Pied (N. Yugoslavia); orig. from Simmental × local; HB; Serbo-cro. *Domaće šareno goveče* (= *local pied cattle*); syn. *Croatian*

Simmental (*Hrvatski Simentalac*), *Yugoslav Red and White*
Yugoslav Pinzgau (Slovenia and Croatia, Yugoslavia); d; local graded
to Pinzgauer; Serbo-cro. *Pinzgavac*; rare
Yugoslav Steppe (S.E. Vojvodina, N.E. Yugoslavia); dr; Grey Steppe
type; Serbo-cro. *Podolsko goveče, Podolac* (= *Podolian*) or *Slavonskopo-
dolsko* (= *Slavonian Podolian*); small vars: Kolubara and Spreča (with
Buša blood) and Posavina; nearly extinct; see also Istrian
Yunnan Zebu (S. and S.W. Yunnan, China); South China Zebu type;
syn. *Yunnan High-hump*
Yurino (Mari ASSR, USSR); d.m; red or brown; orig. from Gorbatov
Red and Zillertal (1812-80) and Swiss Brown (1880-1908), × local,
with some Simmental blood; HB 1937, recog. 1943; Russ. *Yurinskaya*,
syn. *Nizhegorod*; not *Urinsk*, *Yurin*; rare

Zaërs: see Oulmès Blond
Zambia Angoni (N.E. Zambia); var. of Angoni
Zamorana: see Sayaguesa
Zanzibar Zebu (Zanzibar and Pemba, Tanzania); var. of Small East
African Zebu; some Indian, Somali and Boran blood
Zaobei (W. Hubei, China); dr.m; Central Chinese type sim. to Nanyang;
yellow, brown or red; W.G. *Chou-pei*, Ger. *Dschau-bei*; syn. *Chowpei*
Zavot (N.E. Turkey); d; orig. from Schwyz and Simmental (in Caucasus);
pl. *Zavotlar*. [Russ. *zavod* = factory]
zebkyo: see dzo ♂
zeboid; intermediates between zebu and humpless cattle, inc. Central
Chinese, Sanga and many new breeds, *e.g.* Brangus, Droughtmaster,
Santa Gertrudis; Russ. *Zebuvidnyĭ*; syn. *Azebuado* (Brazil)
ZEBU = humped cattle; inc. Indian, East African, West African, South
China, S.E. Asian, Brazilian, *et al.*; orig. of Central Chinese, Sanga,
et al.; Sp. *cebú*; syn. *Brahman* (USA). [? from Port. *gebo* = hunchback,
from Latin *gibbus* = hump, or from Tibetan *zeu* or *zeba*]
Zeburano: see Azebuado
Zetland: see Shetland
zhopkyo: see dzo ♂
zhum: see dzo ♀
[Zillertal]; var. of Tux-Zillertal; red or red-brown; Ger. *Zillertaler*; part
orig. of Gorbatov Red, Tambov Red and Yurino
Znamensk (Ukraine, USSR); m; orig. from Aberdeen-Angus (62.5%),
Charolais (25%), Russian Simmental (12.5%); Russ. *Znamenskaya*
zo: see dzo
zomo: see dzo ♀
zopkio: see dzo ♂

Zubairi: see Jenubi
Żuławka: see Polish Marsh
Zulu: see Nguni
zum: see dzo ♀

Addendum

Byelorussian Synthetic (Byelorussia, USSR); m; 25% Maine-Anjou, 25% Limousin, 25% Salers, 12.5% Russian Simmental. 12.5% Russian Brown

Chaqueño (Chaco, Bolivia and Paraguay); m; Criollo type

Chusco (high Andes, Ecuador, Peru and Bolivia); Criollo type; syn. *Serrano*

Crioulo Lageano (Lages, Santa Caterina, Brazil); m.d; not *Lajeano*; rare

Dominican Criollo (Dominican Republic); var. of Tropical Dairy Criollo

Frijolillo (Lower California, Mexico); m; Criollo type. [colour often speckled like native pinto bean (*fréjol*)]

Karan Fries (India); d; orig. since 1971 from Friesian × Tharparkar ($\frac{3}{8}$-$\frac{1}{2}$) at National Dairy Res. Institute, Karnal

GOAT

Abaza (N.E. Turkey); d; pinkish white with coloured marks around mouth and eyes and on legs; ♂ hd, ♀ usu. pd; syn. *Abkhasian* (Russ. *Abkhazskaya*); not *Abchasan*

Abgal (N.E. Somalia); var. of Somali; usu. pd

Abyssinian ibex (Semien, Ethiopia) = *Capra walie* Rüppell (or *C. ibex walie*); syn. *wali*; nearly extinct

Abyssinian Short-eared (Ethiopia); many local vars

Adal (Dancalia, Ethiopia)

Adany (Iran); d

Afghan Native Black: see Vatani

Africander, Afrikaner: see Boer

African Dwarf: see West African Dwarf

agrimi: see Cretan wild goat

Akyab (Jaffna, Sri Lanka); d; local dwarf short-legged var; often cream or fawn; usu. hd; ? Burmese origin; not *Akyat*

Alashan Down (Helan Shan, Inner Mongolia, China); ca; white; syn. *Erlongshan Down*; not *Downy*

Albanian (Albania); d.hr; Balkan type; larger mountain var. (usu. grey, or brown), and smaller plains var. (usu. red), also Capore var. (with corkscrew horns)

Albas Down (Inner Mongolia, China); ca; white; not *Downy*

Alemã: see Toggenburg

Alentejana (S.W. Alentejo, S. Portugal); m; var. of Charnequeira; syn. *Machuna*; not *Alemtejana*; name also used for Serpentina

Aleppo (Turkey): see Damascus

Algarvia (Algarve, S. Portugal); d.(m); usu. white with brown or black spots; ? orig. from Charnequeira

Algerian Red: see Mzabite

ALPINE: inc. French Alpine, Italian Alpine, Oberhasli, Spanish Alpine, Swiss Mountain

Alpine ibex (Italian Alps, reintroduced into Swiss, French, Austrian and Bavarian Alps) = *Capra ibex ibex* Linnaeus; var. of ibex; syn. *alpine wild goat*; rare

Alpine wild: see Alpine ibex

Altai Mountain (Gorno Altai, USSR); ca.m; black with grey undercoat; Russ. *Gornoaltaĭskaya*; local improved by Don (after failure with Angora and Orenburg) since 1938, recog. as breed group 1968, as breed 1982

American Lamancha: see Lamancha

American Pygmy (USA); m.d; often agouti with dorsal and face-stripes; orig. from West African Dwarf; HB 1975; HB also in Canada

Anatolian Black (Turkey); m.d.hr; Syrian type; usu. black, also brown, grey or pied; Turk. *Kıl-Keçi* (= *hair goat*); syn. *Adi Keçi* (= *ordinary goat*), *Kara Keçi* (= *black goat*), *Turkish Native*

Andalusian White (Andalucía, Spain); m; Roman nose; twisted horns; Sp. *Blanca andaluza*; syn. *Cordobesa* (from Córdoba), *Serrana andaluza* (= *Andalusian mountain*); var: Barros; with Castille Mountain = Spanish White

Anglo-Nubian (Great Britain); d; hd or pd; orig. in late 19th c. from Oriental lop-eared (Zaraibi, Chitral, and Jamnapari) × Old English; HB 1890; syn. *Nubian* (USA); HB also in Australia, USA, Canada

Anglo-Nubian-Swiss: see British

Angora (C. Turkey); mo.m; usu. white; Turk. *Ankara* or *Tiftik-Keçi* (= *mohair goat*); syn. *Sybokke* (S. Africa); orig. of Indian Mohair, Soviet Mohair; BS in USA 1900, S. Africa 1921 (HB 1906), Australia 1975, UK 1984, France 1982, Canada; also in Argentina and Lesotho

[Angora-Don] (USSR); ca; orig. from Angora × Don; Russ. *Angoro-Pridonskaya*

Ankara: see Angora

Appenzell (N.E. Switzerland); d; white; long hair; pd or hd; Ger. *Appenzeller*, It. *Appenzellese*; rare

Apulian: see Murge and Garganica; It. *Pugliese*

Aquila (Abruzzo, Italy); d.m; white, brown, grey or black; hd or pd; Toggenburg, Alpine, Maltese and Girgentana blood; It. *di L'Aquila*

Arab (Somalia): see Somali Arab

Arab (Teheran, Iran); d; long twisted horns, black or dark brown; = Syrian?

Arab (W. Africa): see Sahelian

Arabian ibex: see South Arabian ibex

Arapawa (I. in Marlborough Sounds, New Zealand); feral; brown, black or pied; long twisted horns; ? orig. from Old English

[Askanian Mohair] (Ukraine, USSR); mo; *cf.* Soviet Mohair

Asmari (Afghanistan); white, pied or coloured; larger than Vatani

Assam Hill (N.E. India); m; var. of Bengal; usu. white; long hair; syn. *Khasi*

Attaouia (Draa valley, Morocco); local var.

Auckland Island (New Zealand); feral; usu. white or pied; first introduced 1865

Australian feral (Australia); some have ca. or mo.

Auvergne: see Massif Central

Azerbaijan (Armenia and Azerbaijan, USSR); m.d; usu. black dappled with red, also black, red, pied or grey; Russ. *Azerbaĭdzhanskaya*; syn. *Long-haired Caucasian, South Caucasian, Transcaucasian*; rare

Bagot (England); formerly feral at Blithfield Hall, Staffordshire, scattered since 1957; sim. to Valais Blackneck; ? orig. from Swiss imports in 14th c; HB; rare. [name of family]
Baguirmi (Chad); intermediate between Sahelian and West African Dwarf
Bahu: see Congo Dwarf
Baigani; smaller var. of Ganjam
Baladi (Lower Egypt); d.hr; Syrian type; ♂ hd, ♀ hd or pd; var: Sharkawi; syn. *Bedouin, Egyptian*
Baladi (Syria): see Damascus or Mamber
BALKAN (S.E. Europe); inc. Albanian, Bulgarian, Greek, Red Bosnian
Baltistani (N. Kashmir); d.m.hr; black with some white; small
Baluchi: see Khurasani
Banat White (W. Romania); d; orig. from (Dutch) Saanen and German Improved White × local; Rom. *Rasa de Banat* or *Vansaanen*
Banjiao (E. Sichuan, China); m; usu. white
Bantu (N. Transvaal, S. Africa); m; short coat, ears and horns
Barbari (urban areas of Sind and Punjab, Pakistan, and Punjab, Haryana and Uttar Pradesh, India); d.m; often white with red-brown spots; small; short coat, ears and horns; not *Bar-Bari, Barbary, Bari, Barri*; pd var. is Thori-Bari. [? from Berbera in Somalia]
Bari, Barri: see Barbari
Barki (N.W. Egypt); m.d.hr; sim. to Libyan; usu. black, often white spots on head and legs
Barreña (Sierra Morena, Andalucía and S.E. Extremadura, Spain); m.d; var. of Andalusian White with blood of goats from Barros, Extremadura; pied, often chestnut hindquarters and head with light forequarters and legs; usu. hd; not *Barro*
Barrosã: see Bravia
[Bashkir] (N.W. Bashkiria, USSR); d.m; var. of North Russian; Russ. *Bashkirskaya koza preduralya* (*Cis-Ural Bashkir goat*)
Bashkir (Trans-Ural): see Orenburg
Bastarda (Italy): see Benevento
Béarn, Béarnais: see Pyrenean
beden: see Nubian ibex
Bedouin: see Syrian type
Beetal (Punjab, Pakistan and India); d.m; sim. to Jamnapari but smaller and ♂ long twisted horns; usu. red, black or pied; long ears; not *Betal*

Beiari (Azad Kashmir, Pakistan); d.m; white and grey; long ears; orig. from Beetal × Sindhi; syn. *Chamber*

Beiroa (Beira, Portugal); d.m; var. of Charnequeira; smaller, less spiral horns or pd

Beladi: see Sudanese Nubian

Belgian Fawn (Belgium); pd; orig. from Chamois Coloured; HB 1931; Fr. *Chamoisé*, Flem. *Hertegeit*

Belgian White: see Campine

Benadir (Webi Shibeli, S. Somalia); d.m; often red- or black-spotted; lop ears; syn. *deguen* or *digwain* (= *long ears*); vars: Bimal, Garre, Tuni

Benevento (Campania, Italy); d.m; tawny and white; usu. pd; lop ears; ? orig. from local with Maltese, Garganica and Alpine blood; It. *di Benevento*; syn. *Bastarda*; nearly extinct

Bengal (Bengal, Bihar, Orissa and N.E. India, and Bangladesh); m.d; small to dwarf; prolific; usu. black, also brown, white or grey; short coat and ears; bearded; syn. *Black Bengal*; var: Assam Hill

Berari (Nagpur and Wardha, N. Maharashtra, and Nimar, Madhya Pradesh, India); d.m; usu. black

Berber (Maghreb, N. Africa); d.m; in E. sim. to Libyan, in W. variable in colour, and ears, horns and hair shorter

[Berry-Touraine] (France); d; orig. from French Alpine × Poitou; Fr. *Race mantelée de Berry-Touraine*

Betal: see Beetal

bezoar (Caucasus and S. Anatolia through Iran to Baluchistan and Sind, Pakistan) = *Capra aegagrus* Erxleben; scimitar (or sabre) horns with sharp anterior edge; Persian *pazan* (or *pasang*); syn. *Persian wild, wild goat*; vars: Cretan wild, Sind wild; orig. of domestic goat C. *'hircus'* Linnaeus. [Persian *pád-zahr*, Arabic *bazahr* = antidote (stomach concretion)]

Bhotia: see Tibetan

Bhuj (N.E. Brazil); d.m; usu. black with white or spotted long lop ears; Roman nose; orig. from Kutchi; Port. *Bhuj Brasileira*; not *Bhuji, Buhj, Buj, Buji*. [town in N. Gujarat, India]

Bhungri: see Gujarati

Bikanari, Bikaneri: see Nachi

Bimal (S. Somalia); small coastal var. of Benadir; d; white with small dark spots

Binbei Dairy (China); d; in formation

Black Bedouin: see Syrian type

Black Bengal: see Bengal

[Black Forest] (Germany); part orig. (with Chamois Coloured) of German Improved Fawn; Ger. *Schwarzwald*

Blackneck, Blackthroat: see Valais Blackneck

Black Verzasca: see Verzasca
Bligon: see Peranakan Ettawah
Blue goat: see Jining Grey
Boer (S. Africa); m.d; many colours; usu. lop ears; usu. hd; orig. from local goats (inc. Bantu) with European, Angora and Indian blood; BS 1959; syn. *Africander, Afrikaner, South African common goat*
Boran (N. Kenya); cream or fawn with black dorsal stripe; short ears
Bornu white; var. of Nigerian
Bosnian: see Red Bosnian
bouquetin: see ibex
Bravia (Minho and Trás-os-Montes, N. Portugal); m; sim. to Charnequeira; usu. black or brown, also spotted; syn. *Barrosã, Brava, cabra da Serra*. [= wild]
Brienz: see Oberhasli-Brienz
British (Great Britain); d; inc. crossbreds from British, Swiss and Anglo-Nubian pedigree parents; HB 1896; syn. *Anglo-Nubian-Swiss*
British Alpine (Great Britain); d; black with light points and face-stripes; hd or pd; orig. from Swiss Mountain (imported 1903) and British; recog. 1921, HB 1925; HB also in S. Africa 1922, Australia
British feral (mts of Wales, Scotland and N. England); all colours; long coat; wide horns in ♂; diverse orig.
British Saanen (Great Britain); d; white; hd or pd; orig. from Saanen (imported 1903 and 1922) and British; recog. 1921; HB 1925
British Toggenburg (Great Britain); d; brown with light points and face-stripes; pd or hd; orig. from Toggenburg (imported 1890s, 1904, 1922 and 1965) and British; recog. 1921; HB 1925
Brown Bengal: see Bengal
Brown Kano: see Kano brown
Buchi (Azad Kashmir, Pakistan); m.d.hr; black or grey; orig. from Kooti; crossed with Labri to reduce ear length and produce Shurri. [= short ear]
Bukovica (Dalmatia, Yugoslavia); d; white with black saddle
Bulgarian (Bulgaria); Balkan type; Bulg. *mestna koza* (= *local goat*); syn. *Bulgarian Landrace*
Bulgarian White Dairy (Bulgaria); d; orig. at Kostinbrod from Saanen × Bulgarian; Bulg. *B''lgarska byala mlechna*; syn. *Bulgarian White Milk*
Bündner: see Grisons

Cagnanese; twisted-horn var. of Garganica
Calabrian (Italy); local var; fawn or brown; It. *Calabrese*
Cameroons Dwarf: see West African Dwarf

Camosciata delle Alpi (Italian Alps); d; chamois coloured
Campine (N. Belgium); pd; orig. from Saanen × local; HB 1931; syn. *Belgian White*
Campobasso (Molise, Italy); m.d; usu. white, grey or brown; long hair; ? orig. from local with Maltese, Garganica and Alpine blood; It. *di Campobasso*
Canary Island (Spain); d; any colour; sabre or twisted horns; Sp. *Canaria*; syn. *Güera* (Morocco to Mauritania)
Canindé (Ceará and Piauí, N.E. Brazil); colour type selected from SRD—black with pale face-stripes and belly. [town in Ceará]
Canton Dairy (Guangzhou, China); d; in formation
Capore; var. of Albanian with long corkscrew horns; pied. [= like a buck]
Carpathian (S.E. Europe); d.m; many colours in Romania, usu. white in Poland; long hair; twisted horns; Pol. *Karpacka*, Rom. *Carpatină*
Cashgora (Australia, New Zealand and Great Britain); ca.mo; Angora × feral or × Cashmere, 1st cross
cashmere; produced by Central Asian Cashmere goat, by Russian down goat and by Liaoning Cashmere, Chengde Polled, Wuan and Jining Grey (China), Chigu (India), Vatani (Afghanistan), Kurdi (Iraq) and Morghose (Iran); syn. *down* (Russ. *pukh*), *pashmina*
Castelhana: see Serpentina
Castille Mountain (mts of Guadalajara, Castellón and Albacete, Spain); m; white; twisted horns; Sp. *Blanca celtibérica* or *Serrana de Castilla y Levante*; with Andalusian White = Spanish White
Catalan (S.E. Pyrénées Orientales, France); d.m; usu. red, also black or pied; nearly extinct
Caucasian (Turkey): see Mingrelian
Caucasian (USSR): see Azerbaijan, Dagestan, Karachai, Mingrelian
Caucasian ibex, Caucasian tur: see tur and west Caucasian tur
Celtibérico: see Castille Mountain
CENTRAL ASIAN CASHMERE GOAT; ca; usu. white; long hair; twisted horns (occ. heteronymous); erect or horizontal ears; syn. *Cashmere goat, Pashmina goat*; inc. Changthangi (Kashmir), Mongolian, Alashan Down, Albas Down, Hexi Down, Tibetan and Xinjiang (China); BS in Australia
Chad (W. Africa); var. of Sahelian; white; long lop ears; syn. *Arab*
Chamba: see Gaddi
Chamber: see Beiari
chamois (mts of S. and C. Europe, Caucasus and E. Anatolia) = *Rupicapra rupicapra* Linnaeus. [Fr.]
Chamois Coloured (Switzerland); d.m; Swiss Mountain group; brown with black face-stripes, back-stripe, belly and legs; hd or pd; Ger.

Gemsfarbige Gebirgsziege, Fr. *Chamoisé des Alpes* (or *Chamoix alpine*), It. *Camosciata alpina*; vars: Grisons Chamois-coloured, Gruyère, Oberhasli-Brienz; orig. of Belgian Fawn, German Improved Fawn, Camosciata delle Alpi (Italy), Oberhasli (USA)

Chamoisé (Belgium): see Belgian Fawn

Changra: see Tibetan

Changthangi (Ladakh, Kashmir, India); m.ca.pa; white, also black, grey or brown; large twisted horns; syn. *Kashmiri, Pashmina goat*; not *Changthong, Chiangthangi*

Chappar (Sind and Las Bela, Baluchistan, Pakistan); m.ca.hr.d; black, white or pied; syn. *Jabli, Jablu, Kohistani, Takru*; not *Chapar, Chaper, Chapper*

Charkissar (Down): see Uzbek Black

Charnequeira (Portugal); m.d; red (or pied); wide twisted lyre horns or pd; vars: Alentejana, Beiroa; ? orig. of Algarvia. [*charneco* = uncultivated area]

Cheghu, Chegu: see Chigu

Chekiang: see Zhejiang

Chengde Polled (N. Hebei, China); m.ca; syn. *Yanshan Polled*

Chengdu Brown (Sichuan, China); m.d; prolific; brown with dark face- and back-stripes; occ. pd; syn. *Chengdu Grey, Ma, Mah*; not *Chengtu*

Chiangthangi: see Changthangi

Chigu (N.E. Himachal Pradesh and N. of Uttar Pradesh, India); ca.m; usu. white; long twisted horns; syn. *Kangra Valley*; not *Cheghu, Chegu*

[Chitral] (N. Pakistan); part orig. of Anglo-Nubian; ? = Sirli

Chkalov: see Orenburg

Chungwei: see Zhongwei

Congo Dwarf (N.E. Zaïre); brown, black or pied; syn. *Bahu*

Conocchiola; shorthorned var. of Garganica

Córdoba: see Andalusian Mountain

Corsican (Corsica); d; all colours; long hair; Fr. *Corse*

Cosenza (Calabria, Italy); m.d; white, brown or black; ? Maltese and Garganica blood; It. *di Cosenza*

Costeña: see Málaga

Creole (W. Indies); m; often black or brown, also pied; short hair; prick ears; ? orig. from W. African Dwarf; *cf.* Criollo; syn. *West Indian*

Cretan wild goat (Crete, Greece) = *Capra aegagrus cretica* Schinz; ? var. of bezoar; probably descended from early domestic introductions; syn. *agrimi, kri-kri*

[Crimean] (Crimea, USSR); m.d; usu. white, white with black head, grey or pied; Russ. *Krymskaya*

Criollo (Spanish America, esp. Mexico, Argentina, Bolivia, Peru and Venezuela); m.d; Sp. orig. in 16th c; ? orig. of Lamancha. [= native]

Crioulo (N.E. Brazil); short-eared, short-haired, multi-coloured goats of
European (? Portuguese) and W. African (?) orig.; orig. of SRD
Curaçá: see Marota
Cutch-cross (N. Kerala, India); d; former var. of Malabari; usu, brown
with some black or red spots, also black or white; long hair and long
lop ears; Roman nose; ? orig. from Gujarati and Arab
Cutchi: see Kutchi
Cyprus; m.d; erect ears, short hair; hd or pd; syn. *Cyprus free-range*;
orig. of Peratiki; spotted in hills, white var. in mts is rare
Czechoslovakian White Polled (Czechoslovakia); d; pd; orig. from
Saanen; Cz. *Bílá bezrohá krátkosrstá koza* (= *white hornless short-
haired goat*)

Dagestan (USSR); m.d; Russ. *Dagestanskaya*; syn. *East Caucasian*; vars:
long-haired (ca), black, white or grey; short-haired, sim. to Karachai,
usu. red or black; rare
Dagestan White (Dagestan, USSR); ca; orig. from Soviet Mohair ×
local Dagestan; being improved by Altai Mountain; Russ. *Belaya
dagestanskaya*
Daira Deen Panah: see Dera Din Panah
Dalua; larger var. of Ganjam
Damagaran dapple-grey; var. of Nigerian
Damani (Dera Ismail Khan, N.W.F.P., Pakistan); m.d; usu. black with
brown head and legs; syn. *Lama*
Damara (Namibia); m; many colours; medium horns; lop ears
Damascus (Syria and Lebanon); d; Nubian type; usu. red or brown, also
pied or grey; long hair; hd or pd; often tassels; syn. *Aleppo* (Turk.
Halep) (Turkey), *Baladi, Damascene, Shami*
Danish Landrace (Denmark); d; white, grey, brown or black; orig. from
Saanen and Harz × local; nearly extinct
Daqingshan: see Taihang
Da Serra (Guarda, N.E. Portugal); var. of Serrana; black; small
Deccani (W. Andhra Pradesh, India); d; sim. to Osmanabadi; usu. black,
also pied
deghier, deg-ier, deg yer: see Somali
deguen: see Benadir
Dera Din Panah (Punjab, Pakistan); d.hr.m; usu. black, also red-brown;
long ears; not *Daira Deen Panah*
desi (India) = local, indigenous
Desi (Pakistan): see Jattal, Sind Desi
dighi yer: see Somali
digwain: see Benadir

Djelab: see Mamber

Døle (E. Norway); d; former var. of Norwegian; often blue pied or brown; pd; Nor. *Dølageit*; syn. *Gudbrandsdal*. [= valley]

Don (R. Don basin and Lower Volga, USSR); ca.d; usu. black, occ. white; HB 1934; Russ. *Pridonskaya*; white var: Volgograd White; orig. of Altai Mountain

Don-Kirgiz cross (Kirgizia, USSR); ca; orig. from Don × local Kirgiz; Russ. *Pridono-kirgizskye pomes'*

down: see cashmere

Drenthe: see Dutch Toggenburg

Duan (Guangxi, China); m; white, black or pied; not *Tuan*

Dutch Dwarf (Netherlands); orig. from West African Dwarf

Dutch Landrace (Netherlands); usu. white or pied; ♂ twisted horns; long hair; BS 1982; Du. *Nederlandse Landgeit*; syn. *Veluwse* (= from Veluwe); rare

Dutch Pied (Netherlands); d; usu. pied; Saanen and Toggenburg blood; Du. *Zwartbonte Zeeuwse en Zuidhollandse geit* (= *Black Pied Zeeland and South Holland Goat*); rare

Dutch Toggenburg (Drenthe, Netherlands); d; Du. *Nederlandse Toggen-burger*; orig. from Toggenburg × local; HB

Dutch White (Netherlands, except Drenthe); d; pd; orig. from Saanen (imported 1905-11) × local; HB; Du. *Nederlandse witte geit*, Fr. *Blanc néerlandais*; syn. *Dutch White Polled, Improved Dutch, Netherlands White*

dwarf: see Bengal, Congo Dwarf, Hejazi, Lapland Dwarf, Sinai, Southern Sudan, Tarai, West African Dwarf and its derivatives

East Caucasian: see Dagestan

east Caucasian tur: see tur

Egyptian: see Baladi, Saidi, Zaraibi

English (England); grey (or brown) with dark stripe on front of legs and along back, wide sweeping horns in ♂; attempt to reform Old English from feral stock; BS 1978; rare

Epileptic: see Tennessee Fainting

Erlongshan Down: see Alashan Down

Etawah, Ettawa: see Jamnapari

Etna Silver (Sicily, Italy); d; local var; It. *Capra argentata dell'Etna* (= *silvered goat of Mount Etna*); rare

Fainting: see Tennessee Fainting

Fawn German Improved: see German Improved Fawn

feral: see Australian, British, Galapagos, Guadalupe, Juan Fernandez,

New Zealand, San Clemente, Santa Catalina

Fergana: see Uzbek Black

Fiji; m; mixed origin (inc. Anglo-Nubian, Indian and Swiss breeds) in 19th and 20th c; mixed colours

Finnish Landrace (Finland); d; absorbed by Norwegian to form Nordic; usu. white, also grey or pied; hd or pd; long or short hair; Finn. *Suomalainen vuohi*; rare

Fouta Djallon, Fouta Jallon: see West African Dwarf

Franconian; var. of German Improved Fawn; dark brown with black back-stripe, belly and lower leg; Ger. *Frankenziege*

French Alpine (France); d; many colours but chiefly chamois-coloured; hd or pd; orig. from Swiss × local; HB 1930; Fr. *Alpine*; former vars: Sundgau, Tarentaise; also in USA (cou-clair *i.e.* pale neck, shoulder and chest, black belly, rump and feet), Canada

French Saanen (France); d; orig. from local graded to Saanen; HB 1939

Fulani: see Sahelian

Fuqing (Fujian, China); m; black-brown; usu. hd

Fuyang (Anhui, China); m; prolific; white; ? to be combined with Huaipi and Xuhai to form Huanghai breed

Gaddi (Himachal Pradesh and N. of Uttar Pradesh, India); hr.m.pa; sim. to Chigu but larger and live at lower altitudes; usu. white, also black or brown; long ears; syn. *Chamba, Gadderan, Gadhairun, Kangra Valley, White Himalayan*. [*Gaddi* are tribe of nomads]

Gaddi (N. Pakistan); hr.d; usu. black, also white or grey; long ears

Gadhairun: see Gaddi

Galapagos (Is off Ecuador); feral; usu. black, light brown, red or pied; first introduced 1813

Galla: see Somali

Ganjam (S. Orissa, India); m.d; usu. black, occ. brown, white or pied; straight or screw upward horns; vars: Dalua (larger) and Baigani (smaller)

Garganica (Gargano peninsula, Apulia, Italy); m.d; black to dark brown; long hair; twisted horns (Cagnanese) or short horns (Conocchiola); HB

Garre (S. Somalia); d.m; var. of Benadir; brown-and-white; not *Gerra, Gherra*

Gembrong (E. Bali, Indonesia); white; long forelock of ♂ used for lures for fish hooks; nearly extinct

Gemsfarbig: see Chamois Coloured

Georgian: see Mingrelian

German Alpine: see German Improved Fawn

German Improved Fawn (S. Germany); d; red-brown to fawn with black face-stripes, back-stripe, belly and feet (pale var. has pale belly and brown feet); pd; orig. from Chamois Coloured (first imported 1887) × native (Black Forest, Harz, Langensalza, Saxon, *etc.*); HB 1928; Ger. *Bunte* (or *Rehfarbene* or *Rehfarbige*) *deutsche Edelziege*; syn. *Deer-coloured German Improved, German Alpine*; vars: Franconian, Thuringian; not *Pied* (or *Spotted*) *German Improved*

German Improved White (N. Germany); d; pd; orig. from Saanen (first imported 1892) × native (Hessian, *etc.*); HB 1928; Ger. *Weisse deutsche Edelziege*; not *German White Purebred* or *Thoroughbred*

German Toggenburg: see Thuringian

Gerra: see Garre

Gessenay: see Saanen

Gherra: see Garre

Girgentana (Sicily, Italy); d.(m); white with brown spots on head and neck; vertical screw horns; HB; syn. *Agrigentina* (from Agrigento). [Girgenti is old name for Agrigento]

goatex = ibex × domestic goat hybrid

Gohilwadi (S. Kathiawar, Gujarat, India); d.hr; Gujarati type

Golden Guernsey (Channel Is);d; cream to brown; usu. pd; orig. from local improved by Anglo-Nubian and improved British (Swiss) breeds 1920-50; BS 1971; Fr. *Guérnesiais*; syn. (to 1893) *Golden Gessenay*; rare

goral (China, Korea, Himalayas) = *Nemorhaedus goral* (Hardwicke); not *gooral, goural, Naemorhedus*

Gorki (USSR); d; white; sim. to Russian White; orig. from Russian White by 2 crosses of Saanen; Russ. *Gorkovskaya*

goural: see goral

Granada (Andalucía, Spain); d; part orig. of Murcia-Granada; black; HB 1933; Sp. *Granadina*

Graubündner: see Grisons

Gredos ibex (C. Spain) = *Capra pyrenaica victoriae* Cabrera; var. of Spanish ibex; rare

Greek (Greece); d.m; Balkan type; usu. black, brown or pied, also grey, red or white; hd or pd; var: Ulokeros

Grey Bengal: see Bengal

Grey-Black (or *Grey-Black-White*) *Mountain goat*: see Peacock goat

Greyerzer: see Gruyère

Grigioni, Grigionese: see Grisons

Grisons Chamois-coloured (S.E. Switzerland); var. of Chamois Coloured; hd; Ger. *Bündner gemsfarbige Gebirgsziege*, Fr. *Chamoisé des Grisons*, It. *Camosciata dei Grigioni*

Grisons Striped (S.E. Switzerland); Swiss Mountain group; d.m; black with pale face-stripe and legs; hd or pd; Ger. *Bündner Strahlenziege*,

It. *Grigionese strisciata*
Gruyère (Fribourg and W. Berne, Switzerland); var. of Chamois Colour-
ed; pd; Ger. *Greyerzer*; inc. *Schwarzenburg-Guggisberg*
Gruzinskaya: see Mingrelian
Guadalupe Island (Lower California, Mexico); feral; black, grey or
white; ? orig. from Orenburg
Guadarrama (Sierra de Guadarrama, C. Spain) d.m; usu. dark coloured
or pied; long hair; hd or pd; Sp. *Rasa del Guadarrama*; syn. *Del
Moncayo y Guadarrama, Del Centro de España, Guadarrameña*
Guanzhong Dairy (Shaanxi, China); d; white; usu. pd; orig. from
Canadian Saanen × local since 1940s
Guanzhong White (Shaanxi, China); m; hd or pd
Gudbrandsdal: see Døle
Güera: see Canary Island
Guggisberg: see Gruyère
Guinea: see West African
Guizhou White (Guizhou, China); m; usu. white, occ. black or pied
GUJARATI TYPE (W. Gujarat and W. Rajasthan, India); d.hr; long black
hair; twisted horns; long lop ears, usu. white or spotted; Roman nose;
inc. Gohilwadi, Kutchi, Marwari, Mehsana, Zalawaḍi; syn. *Bhungri*
Gürcü: see Mingrelian

Hailun (Heilongjiang, China); d; white, also black, pied, grey, brown or
yellow; orig. from Saanen and Toggenburg × local
Haimen (Zhejiang, China); m; white; prolific; syn. *Shanghai White,
Zhejiang White*
Halep (Turkey): see Damascus
[Harz]; part orig. (with Chamois Coloured) of German Improved Fawn
Hasli: see Oberhasli-Brienz
Hebei Dairy (China); d; in formation
Hejazi (Arabia); m; usu. black; sim. to Mamber but dwarf; long hair
Henan Dairy (China); d; in formation
Hertegeit: see Belgian Fawn
[Hessian] (Germany); orig. (with Saanen) of German Improved White;
Ger. *Hessen*
Hexi Down (N. Gansu, China); ca; usu. white, also black, brown or
pied; not *Downy*
Himalayan wild: see goral, serow, tahr
Huaipi (Henan, China); m; prolific; white; hd or pd; ? to be combined
with Fuyang and Xuhai to form Huanghuai breed
Huanghuai (China); suggested new breed by combining Fuyang, Huaipi
and Xuhai

Huertana: see Murcian
Hungarian Improved (Hungary); d; black, white, red or cream, with white patches; orig. from Swiss dairy breeds (esp. Saanen) × local

ibex = *Capra ibex* Linnaeus; scimitar horns with flat anterior edge; Fr. *bouquetin*, Ger. *Steinbock*, It. *stambecco*; vars: Abyssinian, Alpine, Nubian, Siberian; see also Spanish ibex. [Latin]
Icelandic (Iceland); rare
Improved Dutch: see Dutch White
Improved German: see German Improved
Improved North Russian: see Russian White
Improved Polish: see Polish Improved
Indian long-haired white: see Chigu, Gaddi
Indian Mohair (Maharashtra, India); mo; orig. from Angora ($\frac{7}{8}$) × Sangamneri since 1973
Indo-Chinese (esp. Tongking); m.(d); usu. fawn, sometimes with white or black extremities and back; short hair; erect ears; short horns
Indonesian: see Katjang
Ingessana; local var. of Southern Sudan
Ionica (Taranto, Apulia, Italy); d; white; pd or hd; lop ears; orig. from Maltese × local; HB; not *Jonica*. [from Ionian sea]
Iraqi (Iraq); Syrian type; usu. black, usu. white on ears; lop ears
Irish (Ireland); grey or black; long hair; almost extinct
Israeli Saanen (Israel); d; orig. 1932-50 from local Mamber graded to Saanen
Istrian (Gorizia, N.E. Italy); d.m; white; pd; ? Yugoslav orig; It. *Istriana*; nearly extinct
Italian Alpine (N. Italy); d; sim. to Swiss Mountain; It. *Alpina*

Jabli, Jablu: see Chappar
Jamnapari (Etawah, Uttar Pradesh, India); d.m; sim. to Beetal but larger; often white with tan patches on head and neck; long ears; syn. *Etawah*; not *Jamna Para, Jamunapari, Jumna Pari, Jumnapari, Jumunapari, Yamnapari*; var: Ramdhan
Jämtland; var. of old Swedish Landrace at Thüringer Zoopark, Erfurt, E. Germany; rare
Jarakheil (N. Kashmir, Pakistan); hr.d.m; usu. black with white patches, also brown with white; long ears
Jarmelista (Jarmelo, N.E. Portugal); d; var. of Serrana; black or brown with yellowish streaks; syn. *Jarmelênce*
Jattal (Azad Kashmir, Pakistan); m.hr; black; ? cross of Pothohari × local; syn. *Desi*

Jebel: see Mamber

Jhakrana (Alwar, E. Rajasthan, India); d; black with white spots on ears and muzzle; not *Jakharana*; syn. *Zakhrana*

Jining Grey (S.W. Shandong, China); fur pelt, ca; prolific; mixed black and white hairs; not *Blue goat, Jining Green*

Jonica: see Ionica

Juan Fernandez (Is off Chile); feral; often reddish with black dorsal and shoulder-stripes, also black or pied; first introduced (? from Spain) 1573-80

Jumna Pari, Jumunapari: see Jamnapari

Kabuli: see Vatani

Kafkas (Turkey): see Mingrelian

Kaghani (Hazara, N. Pakistan); m.hr; usu. black, also grey or white

Kail: ? = Kooti

Kajli (Loralai, Baluchistan, and Dera Ghazi Khan, Punjab, Pakistan); m.hr.d; usu. black, also white, brown or grey, with face-stripes; long hair; syn. *Pahari, Pat*, or *Pattu* (Kashmir)

kambing (Indonesia and Malaysia) = goat

Kambing Katjang: see Katjang

Kamori (Sind, Pakistan); d.(m); usu. red-brown, black or white; very long ears. [= fed on *kamo*, a creeper]

Kandahari: see Vatani

Kangra Valley: see Chigu, Gaddi

Kannaiadu (S. Tamil Nadu, India); m; black or black with white spots; ♂ hd, ♀ pd; syn. *Karapuadu, Pullaiadu*

Kano brown; var. of Nigerian; ? orig. from Red Sokoto; syn. *Kyasuwa, Zinder Brown* (Niger)

Karachai (N. Caucasus, USSR); m.d.ca; pied, red, grey, black or white; Russ. *Karachaevskaya*; syn. *North Caucasian*; rare

Karapuadu: see Kannaiadu

Kashmiri: see Changthangi; not *Cashmere, Kashmere*

Katchi: see Kutchi

Kathiawari: see Kutchi

Katjang (Malaysia and Indonesia); m; usu. black or black-and-white, also brown or pied; short hair; erect ears; syn. *Kacang, Kambing Katjang* (= *bean goat*); not *Katjan*; var: Maritja (Indonesia); ? orig. of Philippine

Katsina light-brown; var. of Nigerian

Kazakh (Kazakhstan, USSR); m.d.ca; Russian Central Asian coarse-haired group

[Kazimierz] (E.C. Poland); d; black with amber eyes; Pol. *Kazimierzowska*

Kel: ? = Kooti
Kenya: see Boran, Somali, Small East African
Khandeshi: see Surti
Khari (Siwalik range, Nepal); m.d; sim. to Tarai but larger; black, white or grey; syn. *Nepalese Southern Hill*
Khasi: see Assam Hill
Khurasani (N. Baluchistan, Pakistan); d.m.(hr); usu. black, also white or grey; syn. *Baluchi*; not *Khurassani*
Kigezi (S.W. Uganda); long-haired var. of Small East African; black or grey
Kiko (New Zealand); m; orig. from large dairy ♂ (*e.g.* Anglo-Nubian) × New Zealand base stock backcrossed to dairy ♂ and then selected for twinning, growth rate and constitution
Kilis (S.E. Turkey); d; usu. black; lop ears; orig. from Damascus × Anatolian Black
Kıl-Keçi: see Anatolian Black
Kirdi, Kirdimi: see West African Dwarf
Kirgiz (Kirgizia, USSR); Russian Central Asian coarse-haired group; Russ. *Kirgizskaya*; orig. of Don-Kirgiz cross
Kohai Ghizer (N. Kashmir, Pakistan); d.m.hr; black with white on belly; small
Kohistani: see Chappar
Kooti (Azad Kashmir, Pakistan); d.m.hr; black-and-white; orig. of Buchi
Korean (S. Korea); m; usu. black, also grey or white; sim. to Taiwan Black
Kosi: see West African Dwarf
Kottukachchiya (Sri Lanka); m; usu. black, also pied or brown; usu. hd; short lop ears; short coat; orig. at Kottukachchiya farm from S. Indian imports
kri-kri: see Cretan wild goat
Kuban ibex, Kubanski goat: see west Caucasian tur
Kunyi: see Surti
Kurdi (Kurdistan, Iraq and Iran); ca; white, black or brown; syn. *Kurdish, Marghaz, Markhoz, Morghose,* or *Morghoz* (Iran)
Kutchi (N.W. Gujarat, India); d.m.hr; Gujarati type; syn. *Kathiawari*; not *Cutchi, Katchi*; orig. of Bhuj (Brazil)
Kyasuwa: see Kano brown

Labi; short-eared var. of Lehri
Labri (Azad Kashmir, Pakistan); d.m.hr; usu. black; very long ears
Lama: see Damani
Lamancha (Oregon, USA); d; all colours; earless; orig. in Texas from

short-eared Spanish goats from Mexico; recog. 1958 (HB); syn. *American Lamancha*; not *LaMancha*; HB also in Canada. [foundation inc. one goat from La Mancha, Spain]
Landim: see Small East African
[Langensalza] (Thuringia, Germany); part orig. (with Chamois Coloured) of German Improved Fawn
Lantras: see Swedish Landrace
Laoshan Dairy (Shandong, China); d; white; orig. from Saanen × local since 1919; not *Laushan, Loushan*
Lapland Dwarf (N. Norway); d; usu. white, also yellow or pied; bezoar horns
Latuka-Bari; local var. of Southern Sudan
Laushan Dairy: see Laoshan Dairy
Lehri (Sibi, Baluchistan, Pakistan); m.hr; usu. black, also white; long ears; short-eared var: Labi; not *Leri, Lerri*
Leizhou (Guangdong, China); m; prolific; usu. black, also white or pied
Leri, Lerri: see Lehri
Liaoning Cashmere (Liaoning, China); ca; white; ♂ lateral twisted horns
Libyan (Libya); m.d; sim. to Barki and Baladi (Egypt); black, brown or pied; long hair; ears usu. lop
Lori (S. and C. Iran); d; black or brown
Loushan Dairy: see Laoshan Dairy

Ma, Mah: see Chengdu Brown
Machuna: see Alentejana
Malabari (N. Kerala, India); d.m; white, black, brown or pied; hd or pd; short or long hair; Arab × Indian orig; syn. *Tellicherry* (not *Tellichery*), *West Coast*; formerly divided into Tellicherry (short hair and ears) and Cutch-cross (long hair and ears); not *Malbari*
Málaga (S. Andalucía, Spain); d; red; pd or hd; Sp. *Malagueña*; syn. *Costeña* (= *coastal*); HB 1977; vars: with twisted horns, with sabre horns (*clássica*) or pd (*moderna* or *mejorada*)
Malawian (Malawi); var. of Small East African
Maltese (Malta, now mainly S. Italy and other Mediterranean countries); d; usu. white with black patches on head and neck, also cream or chestnut; usu. pd; lop ears; HB in Italy; rare in Malta
Mamber (Syria, Lebanon, N. Israel, Jordan); m.d.hr; Syrian type; syn. *Black Bedouin, Djelab* or *Jebel, Mambrine* or *Membrine, Northern Mountain* (Israel), *Palestinian, Syrian Black, Syrian Mountain*; var: Samar (Aleppo)
Mambilla; var. of Nigerian
Maradi (S. Niger) = Red Sokoto (Nigeria)

Marghaz: see Kurdi

Maritja (Sulawesi, Indonesia); small var. of Katjang; syn. *Kambing Maritja* (= *pepper goat*)

markhor (N.E. Afghanistan and adjacent mountain areas in S. Uzbekistan, S.W. Tajikistan, W. Pakistan and W. Kashmir) = *Capra falconeri* Wagner; screw horns; not *markhoor, markhore, markhorn*. [Persian = snake eater]

Markhoz: see Kurdi

Marota (N.E. Brazil); colour type selected from SRD; white; syn. *Curaçá*

Marungu (Zaïre); d.m; syn. *Mayema*

Marwari (W. Rajasthan and N. Gujarat, India); d.m.hr; Gujarati type

Massif-Central (France); d; brown or black; long hair; syn. *Auvergne*; crossed with French Alpine in E; rare

Matou (Hubei and Hunan, China); m; white; long or short hair; pd; W.G. *Ma-t'ou*; not *Madu*. [= horse head]

Maure; var. of Sahelian

Mauritian (Mauritius); m; often black; sim. to Katjang; mixed orig.

Mawr (N. Tihama, N. Yemen); almost white with small black spots

Mayema: see Marungu

Mediterranean ibex (mts of S. Spain) = *Capra pyrenaica hispanica* Schimper; var. of Spanish ibex; nearly extinct

Megrel: see Mingrelian

Mehsana (Mahsana, Gujarat, India); d.m.hr; Gujarati type

Membrine: see Mamber

Mengrelian: see Mingrelian

Meridional (Brazil); m; Crioulo type; usu. white. [= southern]

Meriz: see Miriz

Meseta (Castille, León and Extremadura, Spain); m.(d); mixed population; yellow, grey or brown; usu. hd (twisted or sabre); Sp. *Raza de las Mesetas*. Fr. *Race des plateaux*

Mingrelian (W.Georgia, USSR); d; brown, black, white, roan or grey; ♂ hd, ♀ hd or pd; Russ. *Megrel'skaya*; syn. *Georgian* (Russ. *Gruzinskaya*, Turk. *Gürcü*), *Megrel, Mengrelian, Tiflis, (West) Caucasian* (Turk. *Kafkas*); highland and lowland vars

Miriz (N. Iraq); Angora type; black; not *Meriz*

Modi bakri: see Shekhawati

Modugh: see Somali

Mohair: see Angora

Moncayo: see Guadarrama

Mongolian (Mongolia; Inner Mongolia, Gansu and Qinghai, China); ca.d.m; usu. white, also black, blue, grey, brown or pied; syn. *Cashmere goat of Mongolia*

Morghose, Morghoz: see Kurdi

Mountain (Syria and Israel): see Mamber

Moxotó (Pernambuco, N.E. Brazil); colour type selected from SRD; white or cream with black face-stripes, back-stripe and belly; syn. *Black-Back*

Mubende (Buganda, Uganda); leather; var. of Small East African; usu. black, also pied; short hair; sometimes pd

Mudugh: see Somali

Murcia-Granada (S. Spain); d; mahogany or black; usu. pd; formed in 1975 by combining Murcian and Granada; BS; Sp. *Murciana-Granadina*; suggested syn. *Orospeda*; vars: Veguensis or de Vega (= lowland) and Montana (= mountain)

Murcian (Levante, Spain); d; part orig. of Murcia-Granada; mahogany; HB 1933; Sp. *Murciana*

Murge (Apulia, Italy); d; local var. usu. pied; hd or pd; short hair; It. *capra delle Murge* or *Murgese*

Mzabite (S. Algeria); d; Nubian type; syn. *Algerian Red, Touggourt*

Nachi (S.E. Punjab, Pakistan); d.m.hr; usu. black, sometimes pied; syn. *Bikaneri* (not *Bikanari*); ? = Marwari (India)

Nadjdi (Khuzestan, Iran); d.hr; grey or brown; lop ears; tassels; not *Najdi, Nejdi*

Negev (S. Israel); Syrian type, intermediate between Syrian Mountain and Hejazi

Nejdi: see Nadjdi

Nepalese Northern Hill (Pahar and Mahabharat range, Nepal); m.d.(pa); usu. black, white or grey; long hair

Nepalese Southern Hill: see Khari

Nervous: see Tennessee Fainting

Netherlands White: see Dutch White

New Zealand base stock; recaptured feral bred in captivity

New Zealand feral; esp. Arapawa and Auckland I. (*q.v.*)

Nguni (Swaziland and Zululand); m; intermediate between Small East African and lop-eared

Nigerian (Nigeria): Sahelian or intermediates with West African Dwarf; vars: Bornu white, Damagaran dapple-grey, Kano brown, Katsina light-brown, Mambilla, Red Sokoto (*q.v.*)

Nigerian Dwarf (Nigeria): see West African Dwarf

Nigerian Dwarf (USA); smaller than American Pygmy; often black-and-white or brown; orig. from West African Dwarf; HB 1980

Nilotic; main var. of Southern Sudan

Nimari: see Surti

Nongdong Black; var. of Zhiwulin Black

Nonglin (W. Yunnan, China); m; red-brown; ♂ hd, ♀ pd
Nordic (chiefly Norway, also Sweden and Finland); d; various colours; hd or pd; long hair; inc. Norwegian, Swedish Landrace and Finnish Landrace
Nordfjord: see Vestland
Nordland (N. Norway); former var. of Norwegian sim. to Døle; often blue-grey; Nor. *Nord-norsk geit*
North Caucasian: see Karachai
Northern Mountain (Israel): see Mamber
North Gujerat: see Gujarati
[North Russian] (European Russia north of Smolensk to Tatar ASSR); d; usu. white; Russ. *Severorusskaya*; syn. *Tatar*; var: Bashkir; orig. (with Saanen) of Russian White
Norwegian (Norway); has absorbed Swedish and Finnish Landrace to form Nordic; former vars: Døle, Nordland, Rogaland, Telemark, Vestland
Nuba Mountain; local var. of Southern Sudan
Nubian (USA): see Anglo-Nubian
Nubian ibex (Red Sea coast from N. Eritrea *via* Sinai, Israel and Jordan to S.W. and S. Arabia) = *Capra ibex nubiana* Cuvier; var. of ibex; syn. *beden*; vars: Sinai or Syrian ibex, South Arabian ibex
NUBIAN TYPE (N.E. Africa); d; usu. pd; Roman nose, long lop ears, usu. short hair, long legs; inc. Mzabite (Algeria), Shukria (Eritrea), Sudanese Nubian, Zaraibi (Egypt), also Damascus (Syria)

Oberhasli (USA); d; chamois-coloured, occ. black; pd; orig. from Oberhasli-Brienz imported chiefly 1936; obs. syn. *Swiss Alpine*; HB 1978
Oberhasli-Brienz (Bernese Oberland, Switzerland); var. of Chamois Coloured; pd; syn. *Brienz, Hasli, Oberhasli*
Ogaden; var. of Somali
Okinawa (Japan); m; black, brown or pied
[Old English] (England); orig. native type; HB 1920-c.1930; orig. (× oriental lop-eared) of Anglo-Nubian and (× Swiss) of British; *cf.* Irish, Welsh; extinct 1930; being revived as English
Orenburg (Orenburg, Chelyabinsk and S.E. Bashkiria, USSR); ca.d; usu. black, occ. tan, grey or pied; obs. syn. *Chkalov, Trans-Ural Bashkir* (Russ. *Bashkirskaya koza Zauralya*)
Orospeda: suggested name for Murcia-Granada
Osmanabadi (S.E. Maharashtra, India); m.d; sim. to Deccani usu. black, often white or pied; ♂ usu. hd, ♀ hd or pd; long- and short-haired vars; not *Oosmanabad*

Pafúri (W. Mozambique); long ears; sim. to Boer

Pahari: see Kajli

Pak Angora (Pakistan)

Palestinian: see Mamber

Parbatsar (Nagaur, W. Rajasthan, India); d.m; light brown to dark chocolate; lop ears

pasan, pasang: see bezoar

pashmina: see cashmere

Pashmina goat: see Central Asian cashmere goat

Pat: see Kajli

Pateri; var. of Surti; not *Patiri*

Pattu: see Kajli

pazan: see bezoar

Peacock goat (Graubünden, Switzerland); Swiss Mountain group; white forequarters, hind legs and tail, black hindquarters, feet and face-stripe; Ger. *Pfauenziege*; syn. *Grauschwarze Gebirgsziege* (= *Grey-Black Mountain goat*), *Grau-schwarz-weisse Gebirgsziege* (= *Grey-black-white Mountain goat*); rare

Peranakan Etawah (Indonesia); Jamnapari × Katjang cross; syn. *Bligon, P.E.*

Peratiki (Cyprus); d; mixed population of Cyprus free-range, Maltese and Damascus orig; usu. light in colour; short hair; usu. pd; syn. *Cyprus tethered*

Persian wild: see bezoar

Pfauenziege: see Peacock goat

Philippine; m; coarse hair var: cream, beige or light brown; usu. pd; fine hair var: black or brown with or without white belt (which may have coloured spots); usu. hd; ? orig. from Katjang

Piamiri (N. Kashmir, Pakistan); hr.d.m; usu. black; small

Pied German Improved: see German Improved Fawn

Pinzgau (W. Austria); d; Ger. *Pinzgauer gemsfarbige* (= *chamois coloured*); fawn pd and black hd vars

Poitou (W. France); d; black-brown with pale belly and legs; long hair; usu. pd; BS; Fr. *Poitevin*; rare

Polish Improved Fawn (Poznań and Silesia, Poland); *cf.* German Improved Fawn; Pol. *Barwna uszlachetniona*

Polish Improved White (W. Poland); *cf.* German Improved White; Pol. *Biała uszlachetniona*

[Portuguese ibex] = *Capra pyrenaica lusitanica* Schlegel; var. of Spanish ibex; Port. *cabra montez de Portugal, cabra do Gerez*, Sp. *cabra montés portuguesa*, Fr. *bouquetin du Gerez*; extinct 1892

Portuguese Mountain: see Serrana

Potenza (Basilicata, Italy); d.m; brown, grey or black; long hair; lop ears; usu. hd; ? Maltese, Alpine and Garganica blood; It. *di Potenza*; rare

Pothohari (Azad Kashmir/Punjab, Pakistan); d.m; black, grey or white

Pridon, Pridonskaya: see Don

Provençal (Provence, France); variable in colour, horn, coat and ears; rare

Pugliese: see Apulian

Pullaiadu: see Kannaiadu

Pygmy: see American Pygmy, West African Dwarf

Pyrenean (French and Spanish Pyrenees, and Cantabrian mts, Spain); d.m; usu. dark brown or black with paler belly and feet; hd or pd; usu. long hair; Sp. *Pirenaica*, Fr. *Pyrénéen* or *Race des Pyrénées*; syn. *Béarnais* (from Béarn); rare in France

Pyrenean ibex = *Capra pyrenaica pyrenaica* Schinz; var. of Spanish ibex; Fr. *bouquetin des Pyrénées*; nearly extinct

Rahnama (Afghanistan); sim. to Asmari but taller. [= leader]

Raiana: see Serpentina

Raini (Kirman, Iran); hr.d.m; grey, yellow, black or white; medium ears

Ramdhan (Uttar Pradesh, India); strain of Jamnapari orig. from cross with ♀ from Alwar, Rajasthan; syn. *Kandari Ka Khana*

Red Algerian: see Mzabite

Red Bosnian (Yugoslavia); d; Balkan type; red, grey, black, brown or pied; Serbo-Cro. *Crvena bosanska*

Red Skin: see Red Sokoto

Red Sokoto (N.W. Nigeria); Morocco leather, d.m; var. of Nigerian; intermediate between Sahelian and West African Dwarf; syn. *Red Skin*; = Maradi (Niger)

Repartida (N.E. Brazil); colour type selected from SRD; black forequarters, brown hind; syn. *Surrão*. [= divided (*i.e.* in colour)]

Retinta Extremeña (Cáceres, Extremadura, Spain); d.m; dark red; twisted horns; syn. *Retinta Cacereña*

Ribatejana (Ribatejo, C. Portugal); var. of Serrana

Rila Monastery (Bulgaria); d; Bulg. *Rilamonastirska*

Roccaverano (Le Langhe, Piedmont, Italy); d; white, chestnut or pied; long or short hair; usu. pd; rare

[Rock Alpine] (California, USA); d; usu. black pied; orig. from Oberhasli × Toggenburg; recog. 1935; extinct by 1978. [bred by Mary Rock]

Rocky Mountain goat (N. America) = *Oreamnos americanus* (Blainville); actually a goat-like antelope

Rodamit, Rodmit: see Rovmit

Rogaland (Norway); d; former var. of Norwegian

Roman (Italy); m; local var; usu. white; long hair; It. *Romana*

Rove (Provence, France); d.m; usu. red, also black or pied; ♂ wide twisted horns; BS 1979; rare

[Rovmit] (Tajikistan, USSR); d; not *Rodamit, Rodmit*

RUSSIAN CENTRAL ASIAN LOCAL COARSE-HAIRED GOATS (Altai, Kazakhstan, Kirgizia, Tajikistan, Turkmenistan and Uzbekistan, USSR); m.d.ca; usu. black, sometimes grey, occ. tan or pied (non-black commonest in E. Kazakhstan and Altai); Russ. *Mestnye grubosherstnye kozy Srednei̇ Azii*

Russian down goats; ca; usu. black; Russ. *Pukhovye porody*; inc. Altai Mountain, Don, Orenburg and Uzbek Black

Russian White (N. European Russia); d; orig. (1905 on) from Saanen × local North Russian; Russ. *Russkaya belaya*; syn. *Improved North Russian, Russian Dairy, Russian White, Russian White Dairy*; cf. Gorki

Saanen (W. and N.W. Switzerland); d; white; pd; BS, HB; Fr. *Gessenay*; orig. of Banat White (Romania), British Saanen, Bulgarian White, Campine (Belgium), Czechoslovakian White Polled, Dutch White, French Saanen, German Improved White, Guanzhong Dairy and Laoshan Dairy (China), Israeli Friesian, Polish Improved White, Russian White and Gorki (USSR); HB also in S. Africa 1922, USA 1954, GB, Australia, Canada; not *Sannen*

Sable (USA); black var. of Saanen; rare

Sahelian (N. of W. Africa); d.m; syn. *Arab, Fulani, West African Long-legged*; vars: Chad, Maure, Tuareg, Upper Volta; see also Nigerian

Sahely: see Tali

Saidi (Upper Egypt); Syrian type; sim. to Baladi but bigger. [= valley, *i.e.* of Nile]

St Gallen (N.E. Switzerland); Swiss Mountain group; sim. to Grisons Striped; yellow-grey with brown back-stripe and feet or brown with black back-stripe and feet; Ger. *St Galler Stiefelgeiss (= booted goat)*; nearly extinct

Salerno (Campania, Italy); d.m; black with short hair or brown with long hair; ? Maltese, Alpine and Garganica blood; It. *di Salerno*; nearly extinct

Saloia: see Serrana

Salt Range (N.W. Punjab, Pakistan); d.hr; black-and-white or black; lop ears; vertical screw horns

Samar (N.W. Syria); d; var. of Syrian Mountain

San Clemente (I. off California); feral orig; forequarters black, hindquarters tan but no sharp division; rare

[Sandomierz] (S.E. Poland); d; pied, usu. tricolour; Pol. *Sandomierska*

Sangamneri (Poona and Ahmednagar, Maharashtra, India); d.m.hr; white, black, brown or pied

Santa Catalina (I. off California); feral; brown with black markings; Sp. orig.

Sardinian (Italy); d.m; usu. white or black pied, also grey or brown, self or pied; twisted horns, occ. pd; HB; It. *Sarda*

[Saxon]; part orig. (with Chamois Coloured) of German Improved Fawn; var: Wiesental

Schwarzenburg-Guggisberg: see Gruyère

Schwarzhals, Schwarzweisse Sattelziege: see Valais Blackneck

Schwarzwald: see Black Forest

Sciucria: see Shukria

Sempione (Vercelli, Piedmont, Italy); m; white; nearly extinct

serow (S.E. Asia—Sumatra to S. China and Kashmir) = *Capricornis sumatraensis* (Bechstein); Malay *kambing gurum*

Serpentina (Alentejo, Portugal); m.d; white with black back-stripe, belly, feet and tail; syn. *Alentejana, Castelhana, Raiana, Spanish*. [from Serpa]

Serrana (C. and N. Portugal); d.m; black, brown or yellowish; long hair; syn. *Saloia, Serra da Estrela*; vars: Da Serra, Jarmelista, Ribatejana, Transmontana

Serrana (Spain): see Spanish White

Shekhawati (W. Rajasthan, India); d; black; pd; syn. *Modi bakri*

Shaanan White (S. Shaanxi, China); m; white; long hair; smaller hd and larger pd vars; not *Shannan*

Shaanbei Black; var. of Zhiwulin Black

Shami: see Damascus

Shanghai White: see Haimen

Shannan White: see Shaanan White

Shanxi Large Black (S. Shanxi, China); ? to be combined with Taihang Black and Wuan to form Taihangshan breed; syn. *Big Black in Shanxi*

Sharkawi (Lower Egypt); var. of Baladi

Shiba (Nagasaki, Japan); miniature; white; rare

Shukria (W. Eritrea, Ethiopia); d; Nubian type but hd and long hair; sim. to Sudanese Nubian; brown; It. *Sciucria*

Shurri (Azad Kashmir, Pakistan); d.m; white, grey or black; orig. from Buchi × Labri

Siberian ibex (C. Asia—Afghanistan to Mongolia) = *Capra ibex siberica* Pallas; var. of ibex

Sicilian (Sicily, Italy); m; long hair; see also Etna Silver, Girgentana

Silvered goat of Mount Etna: see Etna Silver

Sinai (Israel/Egypt); sim. to Negev but dwarf

Sinai ibex: see Syrian ibex

Sind Desi (C. Sind, Pakistan); d.m; usu. black, also pied or grey; long ears; ? orig. from Kamori × Chappar

Sind wild goat (W. Sind and Baluchistan, Pakistan) = *Capra aegagrus blythi* Hume; var. of bezoar; syn. *Sind ibex*

Sinhal (Nepal mts); m.hr.(d); all colours; Nepali *Sìnghal*; not *Sindhal*. [Sanskrit *sinha* = horn]

Sinkiang: see Xinjiang

Sirli (N. Pakistan); hr.m; lop ears

Sirohi (S. Rajasthan and N. Gujarat, India); d.m; pied, light and dark brown, occ. white; long ears; usu. tassels

Slovakian (Czechoslovakia); *cf.* Carpathian; Sl. *Slovenská*

Small East African (E. Africa from Kenya to Mozambique); m; all colours; short coat and ears; tassels common; syn. *Landim* (Mozambique)

Sokoto Red: see Red Sokoto

Somali (Somalia, Ogaden and N.E. Kenya); m; white, occ. with coloured spots or patches; short hair and ears; ♂ hd, ♀ hd or pd; syn. *Galla, Modugh* or *Mudugh, deghier* or *dighi yer* (= *short ears*); vars: Abgal, Ogaden; see also Benadir

Somali Arab (coast of Somalia); d; usu. brown; short ears; long hair; orig. from Arabia

South African: see Bantu, Boer

South Arabian ibex (S.W. Arabia); var. of Nubian ibex; syn. *Arabian ibex*

South Caucasian: see Azerbaijan

Southern Sudan; all colours; small to dwarf; short hair and ears; ♂ hd, ♀ often pd; vars: Ingessana, Latuka-Bari, Nilotic, Nuba Mountain, Toposa, Yei

Soviet Mohair (Kazakh, Tajik, Turkmen and Uzbek republics, USSR); mo.m; white; orig. (1937 on) from Angora (USA) × Russian Central Asian coarse-haired goats; recog. 1962; Russ. *Sovetskaya sherstnaya*

Spanish (Portugal): see Serpentina

Spanish (Texas, USA); m; orig. from Mexican Criollo

Spanish Angora (USA); dwarf; rare

Spanish ibex = *Capra pyrenaica* Schinz; Sp. *cabra montés* (= *mountain goat*); vars: Gredos, Mediterranean, [Portuguese], Pyrenean; rare

Spanish Mountain: see Spanish White

Spanish White (Spain); inc. Andalusian White and Castille Mountain; Sp. *Blanca española*; syn. *Spanish Mountain* (*Serrana española*)

Spotted German Improved: see German Improved Fawn

Sri Lankan (Sri Lanka); m; local population with Indian blood

SRD (N.E. Brazil); m; derived from Crioulo with some recent oriental lop-eared blood (chiefly Anglo-Nubian and Bhuj); orig. of Canindé, Marota, Moxotó and Repartida. [Sem Raça Definida = without

defined breed]
stambecco, Steinbock: see ibex
Stiefelgeiss: see St Gallen
Stiff-legged: see Tennessee Fainting
Sudanese Desert (N. Sudan); light grey; ears variable; ♂ maned
Sudanese Nubian (Sudan, riverain N. of lat. 12°N); d; Nubian type but
hd and long hair; sim. to Syrian Mountain; black; lop ears; syn. *Beladi*;
Shukria is sim. var. in Eritrea
Sundgau (S. Haut Rhin, Alsace, France); former var. of French Alpine;
black with white stripes on face and white markings on body
Surdud (N.E of Hodeida, N. Yemen); red-and-white
Surrão: see Repartida
Surti (S. Gujarat and N.W. Maharashtra, India); d.m; usu. white; short
hair; ? Arab blood; syn. *Khandeshi, Kunyi, Nimari*; var: Pateri; not
Surati
Swedish Landrace (N. Sweden); d; absorbed by Norwegian to form
Nordic; black, brown or white; hd or pd; hair usu. long; HB; Swed.
Svensk Lantras; var: Jämtland
Swiss Alpine (USA): see Oberhasli
Swiss Improved: see White Swiss Improved
SWISS MOUNTAIN (Switzerland); inc. Chamois Coloured, Grisons Striped,
Pfauenziege, St Gallen, and Verzasca; syn. *Swiss Alpine*
Sybokke (S. Africa): see Angora
Syrian Black, Syrian Mountain: see Mamber
Syrian derivative (Sicily, Italy); d.m; red-brown; long hair; ♂ usu. hd, ♀
usu. pd; semi-lop ears; ? orig. from Damascus; It. *Derivata di Siria*
Syrian ibex (Sinai to Syria); var. of Nubian ibex; syn. *Sinai ibex*
SYRIAN TYPE (Middle East); usu. black; long hair; long lop ears; usu. hd;
inc. Anatolian Black (Turkey), Iraqi, Mamber (Syria), Negev (Israel),
Baladi and Saidi (Egypt)

tahr = *Hemitragus*; inc. Arabian tahr (Oman) = *H. jayakari* (rare),
Himalayan tahr = *H. jemlahicus*, and Nilgiris tahr (S. India) = *H.
hylocrius*; not *tehr, thar*
Taicheng (Taicheng mt, Shanxi/Hebei, China); syn. *Daqingshan*
Taihang Black (S. Shanxi/ Hebei, China); ? to be combined with Shanxi
Large Black and Wuan to form Taihangshan breed
Taihangshan (China); suggested new breed by combining Shanxi Large
Black, Taihang Black and Wuan
Taiwan; m; usu. black in W. and brown in E; occ. pd; horizontal or
erect ears; short hair
Taiz Black (Ta'izz, N. Yemen)

Taiz Red (Ta'izz, N. Yemen); red or brown with white belly and black back-line

Tajik (Tajikistan, USSR); Russian Central Asian coarse-haired group

Tajiki (Afghanistan): see Vatani

Takru: see Chappar

Tali (S.W. Iran); d; dirty white; syn. *Sahely*

Tan: see Zhongwei

Tanzania: see Small East African

Tarai (S. Nepal); m.(d); dwarf; usu. black or fawn; short hair and ears; not *Terai*

Tarentaise; former var. of French Alpine

Tartar, tatar, tatarskaya: see North Russian

Teddy (N.E. Punjab, Pakistan); m; white, brown, black or pied; hd or pd

tehr: see tahr

Telemark (Norway); d; former var. of Norwegian; white; usu. pd

Tellicherry: see Malabari; name formerly restricted to short-haired var.

Tennessee Fainting (USA); hereditary myotonia; black, white or piebald; imported from Asia (possibly India) in early 1880s; BS; syn. *Nervous, Epileptic* or *Stiff-legged goats*; rare

Terai: see Tarai

Teramo (Abruzzo, Italy); d; grey, black or brown; long hair; It. *di Teramo*; being crossed with Garganica; rare

Tessin: see Verzasca

Thai (Thailand); sim. to Katjang; often brown with black dorsal and shoulder-stripes

thar: see tahr

Thori, Thori Bari: see Barbari, pd var.

Thuringian; var. of German Improved Fawn; chocolate-brown with white face-stripes and legs; orig. from Toggenburg; Ger. *Thüringer Wald*; syn. *German Toggenburg*

Tibetan (Qinghai-Tibet plateau, China); ca; usu. white, also pied, black, brown or grey; syn. *Bhotia* or *Changra* (Mustang dist., N. Nepal), *Cashmere goat of Tibet*

Tibetana, Tibetan Dwarf (Italy): see West African Dwarf

Ticino: see Verzasca

Tiflis (Turkey): see Mingrelian

Tiftik-Keçi: see Angora

Toggenburg (N.E. Switzerland); d; brown to mouse-grey with white face-stripes and feet; pd or hd; long or short coat; BS, HB; Ger. *Toggenburger*, Fr. *Toggenbourg*; syn. *Alemã* (= German) (Brazil); orig. of British Toggenburg, Dutch Toggenburg, Thuringian; not *Toggenborg*; HB also in S. Africa 1922, USA, GB, Australia, Canada

Tokara (Japan); m; prim.; brown with black back-stripe; rare
Toposa; local, larger var. of Southern Sudan; black or black-and-white
Touareg: see Tuareg
Touggourt: see Mzabite
Touraine: see Berry-Touraine
Transmontana (Tras-os-Montes, N.E. Portugal); m.(d); var. of Serrana;
   yellowish
Tswana (Botswana); m; all colours; short horns; lop ears
Tuan: see Duan
Tuareg; var. of Sahelian; pd
Tuni (S. Somalia); m; large var. of Benadir; black forequarters; not
   Tunni
tur (E. Caucasus, USSR) = *Capra cylindricornis*; syn. *Caucasian tur,
   east Caucasian tur*; formerly *C. caucasica*; not *Caucasian ibex*
Turkish Native: see Anatolian Black
Turkmen (Turkmenistan, USSR); Russian Central Asian coarse-haired
   group

Uganda: see Small East African, Mubende, Kigezi
Ulokeros; var. of Greek with spiral horns
Upper Volta (Burkina Faso); var. of Sahelian
Uzbek (Uzbekistan, USSR); d.m.ca; Russian Central Asian coarse-
   haired group; orig. (with Angora) of Uzbek Black and of Soviet
   Mohair
Uzbek Black (Uzbekistan, USSR); ca.d; orig. as byproduct of formation
   of Soviet Mohair from Angora × local Uzbek; recog. as breed group
   1961; Russ. *Chernye pukhovye kozy Uzbekistana*; syn. *Fergana*; obs.
   syn. *Charkissar (Down)*

Valais Blackneck (S.W. Switzerland); m.d; black forequarters, white
   hindquarters; long hair; Fr. *Valaisan á col noir*, Ger. *Walliser Schwarz-
   hals, Schwarzweisse Walliser Sattelziege*, It. *Vallesana del collo nero*;
   syn. *Valais Blackthroat, Viège*; ? orig. of Bagot (GB); orig. of Vallesano
   (Italy)
Val di Livo (Como, Lombardy, Italy); d; mixed population; rare
Valgerola (Sondrio, Lombardy, Italy); d.m; hazel, brown, black or pied;
   twisted horns; rare
Vallesano (Novara, Piedmont, Italy); m.d; black forequarters, white
   hindquarters; orig. from Valais Blackneck; rare
Vansaanen: see Banat White
Vatani (Afghanistan); ca; usu. black, also grey, white or brown; long
   hair and short down; long horns and ears; syn. *Afghan Native Black,*

Kabuli, Kandahari, Tajiki
Veluwse: see Dutch Landrace
Verata (Vera, Cáceres, Spain); m.d; chestnut, black or grey; twisted horns
Verzasca (Ticino, Switzerland); d.m; Swiss Mountain group; black; Ger. *Schwarzer Tessiner* (= *Black Ticino*); syn. *Black Verzasca, Ticino*
Vestland (S.W. Norway); d; former var. of Norwegian; usu. dark brown; syn. *Nordfjord, West Coast*
Viège: see Valais Blackneck
Vogan (Togo); West African Dwarf × Sahelian cross
Volgograd White; white var. of Don; rare

wali: see Abyssinian ibex
Walliser Sattelziege or *Schwarzhals*: see Valais Blackneck
[Welsh] (Wales); *cf.* Old English, Irish
West African Dwarf (coast of W. and C. Africa); m; all colours; trypanotolerant; syn. *African Dwarf, Cameroon Dwarf, Chèvre de Casamance* (Senegal), *Djallonké, Dwarf West African, Forest goat, Fouta Djallon, Grassland Dwarf, Guinean, Guinean Dwarf, Kirdi* or *Kirdimi* (Chad), *Kosi, Nigerian Dwarf, Pygmy* (BS in GB), *Tibetana* (Italy); orig. of American Pygmy and Nigerian Dwarf (USA), Dutch Dwarf
West African Long-legged: see Sahelian
West Caucasian: see Mingrelian
west Caucasian tur (W. Caucasus, USSR) = *Capra caucasica*; syn. *Caucasian ibex, Kuban ibex, Kubanski goat, west Caucasian ibex*; formerly *C. ibex severtsovi*; see also tur
West Coast (India): see Malabari
West Coast (Norway): see Vestland
White Bearded Bengal: see Bengal
White German Improved: see German Improved White
White Dagestan: see Dagestan White
White Himalayan (India): see Chigu, Gaddi
[White Swiss Improved] (Zurich, Switzerland); pd; orig. from Appenzell × Saanen; Ger. *Weisse Schweizerziege, Weisse veredelte Landziege*; syn. *Zurich* (Ger. *Zürcher*)
[Wiesental]; var. of Saxon
wild: see bezoar, chamois, goral, ibex, markhor, Rocky Mountain, serow, tahr, tur, west Caucasian tur
Wuan (S. Hebei, China); m.ca; black head, grey body; ? to be combined with Shanxi Large Black and Taihang Black to form Taihangshan breed

Xinjiang (mts of Xinjiang, China); ca.m.d; white, black or brown; W.G.
Sinkiang
Xuhai (Jiangsu, China); m; ? to be combined with Fuyang and Huaipi
to form Huanghuai breed

yaez (Israel); m; orig. from Nubian ibex × domestic goat (Saanen,
Damascus, Mamber, Negev and Sinai). [*ya*el (Hebrew for ibex) + *ez*
(Hebrew for goat)]
Yahyaouia (Draa valley, Morocco); local var.
Yamnapari: see Jamnapari
Yanbian Dairy (Sichuan, China); d; in formation
Yanshan Polled: see Chengde Polled
Yei (W. Equatoria, Sudan); very small var. of Southern Sudan, sim. to
Congo Dwarf
Yemeni (N. Yemen): see Mawr, Surdud, Taiz Black, Taiz Red, Yemen
Mountain
Yemen Mountain (mts of N. Yemen); usu. black; long hair

Zakhrana: see Jhakrana
Zalawadi (Surendranagar and Rajkot, Gujarat, India); d.m.hr; Gujarati
type; erect corkscrew horns; not *Zalawand, Zalawari*
Zambian (Zambia); m; var. of Small East African
Zaraibi (Upper Egypt); d; Nubian type; often light brown with dark
spots, also black with spots; pd or hd; syn. *Egyptian Nubian*; not
Zaraiby, Zareber. [= penned; *cf.* also Zarabi, nr Asyut]
Zhejiang White: see Haimen; formerly *Chekiang*
Zhiwulin Black (N. Shaanxi, China); m.ca; vars: Nongdong Black,
Shaanbei Black
Zhongwei (Ningxia, China); fur, m.ca; usu. white, sometimes black; W.G.
Chung-wei, Russ. *Chzhun'veĭskaya*; syn. *Tan*
Zinder Brown: see Kano brown
Zurich, Zürcher: see White Swiss Improved

Addendum
Sakhar (Brannitsa mts, S.E. Bulgaria); hr; usu. black

HORSE

Abtenauer (Abtenau, Salzburg, Austria); dr; often black; small local var. of Noric; nearly extinct

Abyssinian (Ethiopia); py-l; variable in colour, size and conformation; syn. *Abyssinian-Galla, Galla, Yellow*

Achal-Teké: see Akhal-Teke

Adaev (between Caspian and Aral Seas, USSR); l.r; var. of Kazakh, ? with Turkmen blood; Russ. *Adaevskaya*; not *Adayev*

AITPR (N. Italy); h.dr; orig. in early 20th c. from Ardennes, Boulonnais and Hackney, graded to Breton since 1926; inc. Breton derivatives of Cremonese; HB; AITPR = Agricola Italiana da Tiro Pesante Rapido (*rapid heavy draft*)

Akhal-Teke (Turkmenistan, USSR); l; sim. to Iomud but larger; Russ. *Akhal- tekinskaya*; syn. *Turki, Turkmen, Turkmenian, Turkoman*; not *Achal-Teké, Ahal-Teke, Akhal-Tekin*

Albanian (Albania); py; Balkan Pony type; vars: Albanian Mountain (smaller) and Myzeqeja (plains)

Albanian Mountain; var. of Albanian

Albino: see American Creme and American White

Algerian: see Barb

Altai (USSR); dr.d.m; Siberian pony group; chestnut, bay, black or grey, occ. speckled; Russ. *Altaĭskaya*; syn. *Oirot*

Altér (Portugal); state stud breeding the Lusitanian horse since 1830

American Albino: see American Creme and American White

American Cream Draft (Iowa, USA); h.dr; cream with white mane and tail and pink skin; orig. in early 20th c. from cream-coloured draft mare; HB 1935, BS 1944, recog. 1950; syn. *American Cream* ; rare

American Creme and American White (USA); l. or py; BS 1937 for dilute white (Creme) and dominant white heterozygotes (White—formerly called 'albino'); rare

American Indian: see Indian

American Miniature (USA); HB 1972 for Shetland Ponies 34 inches or less at maturity

American Mustang (USA); HB 1962 for Western horses of feral ancestry, Spanish or non-Spanish orig.

American Quarter Horse or *Quarter Running Horse*: see Quarter Horse

American Saddle Horse (Kentucky, USA); l; bay, brown, chestnut, grey or black; orig. in 19th c. from Thoroughbred, Morgan, Canadian and

American Trotter; BS 1891; syn. *American Saddler, Kentucky Saddle Horse, Five-gaited Horse, Saddlebred*; var: Ysabella; BS also in Canada 1948

American Shetland Pony (USA); vars: Classic (= Shetland Pony, refined) and Modern (with up to 50% Hackney or Welsh blood)

American Spotted: see Appaloosa, Colorado Ranger, Kanata Pony, Morocco Spotted and Pony of the Americas

American Trotter (USA); l; orig. in early 19th c. from Thoroughbred, Hackney, Morgan, *et al.*; BS 1871; syn. *American Trotting Horse, Standardbred* (usu. in USA); orig. (with Orlov Trotter) of Russian Trotter; BS also in Canada

American Walking Pony (Georgia, USA); orig. from Welsh Pony × Tennessee Walking Horse; BS 1968

American White: see American Creme and American White

[Amur] (Siberia); l; orig. from Transbaikal improved by Tomsk; Russ. *Amurskaya*; extinct by crossing with Orlov and Russian Trotters, Don and Budyonny

Anatolian Native (Turkey); py; Turk. *Anadolu Yerli*; vars: Canik, Hinis

Andalusian (Guadalquivir valley, Spain); l; usu. brown, grey or black; orig. from Arab and Barb; HB; Sp. *Andalusa*; syn. *Andalusian-Barb, Andalusian-Lusitanian, Andalusian-Valenzuela, Bético, Guzman, Spanish*; former strains: Cartuja, Córdoba, Extremadura, Marismeño, Ronda, Seville; orig. of Criollo and mustang (America); BS in USA 1963, GB, France, Germany, Australia, Mexico, Costa Rica, Guatemala

Andean; py; var. of Peruvian Criollo; Sp. *Andino*; inc. Morochuca

ANGLO-ARAB; l; Arab × Thoroughbred 1st or later cross, or breed orig. from this cross, *e.g.* Gidran (Hungary), French Anglo-Arab, Hispano-Anglo-Arabe; syn. *Anglo-Arabian*; HB in USA 1930

Anglo-Arabo-Sarda (Sardinia, Italy); l; orig. from Sardinian since 1936 by further crossing with Thoroughbred and later with French Anglo-Arab

Anglo-Don (USSR); l; Thoroughbred × Don, 1st cross

Anglo-Kabarda (N.Caucasus, USSR); l; breed group; bay, black-brown or black; orig. from Thoroughbred × Kabarda; Russ. *Anglo-Kabardinskaya porodnaya -gruppa*

Anglo-Karachai (N. Caucasus, USSR); l; Thoroughbred × Karachai 1st cross; Russ. *Anglo-Karachaevskaya*

[Anglo-Norman] (Normandy, France); l; inc. in French Saddle Horse; orig. in 20th c. from Norman Coach Horse with more Thoroughbred blood; Fr. *Anglo-Normand*; syn. *Norman*; orig. of Charentais, Charolais, Vendée

Anglo-Teke (Turkmenistan, USSR); l; Thoroughbred × Akhal-Teke,

(1st) cross; Russ. *Anglo-tekinskaya*

Annamese, Annamite Pony: see Vietnamese

Appaloosa (Oregon, USA); l; colour type; usu. chubary (white rump usu. with small spots), also white with spots over whole body, or coloured with spots over body or on rump only, or blue roan; BS 1938, HB 1947; syn. *Palouse*; not *Apaloosa, Appolousey*; BS also in Australia, Canada, GB 1976, Mexico, HB in Netherlands; see also Colorado Ranger, Kanata Pony, Pony of the Americas, and Toby. [from Palouse R.]

Appaloosa Pony (USA); sim. to Appaloosa but smaller; BS 1963

[Apulian] (Italy); l; It. *Pugliese*: see also Capitanata, Murgese

Arab; l.ri; original strains inc. Keheilan, Maneghi, Saglawi; syn. *Arabian* (USA); see also Egyptian, Persian Arab, Syrian, Turkish Arab; BS in Australia, Canada 1958, Czechoslovakia, England 1918, Germany 1949, Hungary, India, Netherlands 1935, New Zealand, Pakistan, Poland, South Africa *c.* 1961, USA 1908, HB in France 1833, Spain, USSR

Arab-Barb (W. Africa): see West African Barb

[Aragonese] (Aragon, Spain); l.dr; usu. dapple grey; orig. from Percheron (+ Breton and Ardennes) × local

Ardennes (Belgium); h.dr; lighter (mountain) var. of Belgian; BS 1926; Fr. *Ardennais*; orig. of Baltic Ardennes, Russian Heavy Draft and Swedish Ardennes; HB also in Spain

Ardennes (France): see French Ardennais

Argentine Criollo (Argentina and Uruguay); l; Criollo type, revived 1875-90; syn. *Argentine Landrace, Criollo*

Argentine Dwarf: see Falabella Pony

Ariège: see Mérens

asil (Middle East) = purebred (Arab)

Assateague Pony (I. off Maryland, USA); semi-wild; *cf.* Chincoteague Pony

Astrakhan: see Kalmyk

Asturian pony (mt Suéve, Oviedo, N. Spain); bay; BS; Sp. *Poney asturiano* or *Caballo asturcón*; syn. *Suéve*; at one time combined with Galician as *Galician-Asturian*; nearly extinct

[Augeron] (Auge, Normandy, France); local HB (1913-66) for Percheron (orig. with Norman blood)

[Australian Waler] (NSW, Australia); l; replaced by Australian Stock Horse (BS 1970). [from New South *Wales*]

Austrian Warmblood (Austria); l; based on Oldenburg (heavier— Upper and Lower Austria), English Halfbred and Nonius (lighter— Burgenland and Carinthia); Ger. *Österreichisches Warmblut*

Auxois (Burgundy, France); h.dr; var. of French Ardennais; bay, roan or grey; orig. from French heavy breeds (since 1913 only Ardennes) × local (descended from Morvan crosses); BS 1913; rare

Avar (mountain Dagestan, USSR); pa.ri; smallest var. of Dagestan Pony; Russ. *Avarskaya*

Avelignese: see Hafling

Azerbaijan (USSR); l-py; grey; improved by saddle breeds 1927-29, and 1940s; Russ. *Azerbaidzhanskaya (kazakhskaya)*; orig. of Deliboz; rare

Azores Pony (Ilha Terceira, Azores, Portugal)

Bábolna Arab: see Shagya Arab

Baduck: see Batak

Bagual (Argentina); feral, in process of redomestication; Sp. orig. like mustang (USA) and Criollo; not *Bagnal*

Bahia (Brazil): see Pantaneiro

Bahr-el-Ghazal (Chad); var. of W. African Dongola; syn. *Kréda, Ganaston*

Baikal: see Transbaikal

Baise Pony: see Guangxi Pony

Baixo-Amazona: see Marajoaro

Bakhtiari; var. of Plateau Persian

Baladi: see Egyptian

BALKAN PONY; inc. Albanian, Bosnian Pony, Bulgarian Native, Greek Pony, [Krk Island Pony] and Macedoniam Pony (Yugoslavia)

Balkar; var. of Kabarda

Baloch: see Baluchi

[Baltic Ardennes] (Baltic states, USSR); h; orig. from Ardennes × draft breeds and local; Russ. *Baltiĭskaya-Ardenskaya*; syn. *Latvian Ardennes*; absorbed by Estonian Draft, Latvian and Lithuanian Heavy Draft

[Baltic Trotter] (Baltic states, USSR); l; orig. from trotter × konik; Ger. *Panjepferd im Trabertyp*; absorbed by Latvian, Orlov and Russian Trotters

Baluchi (Baluchistan and Derajat, Pakistan); l; turned-in ears; syn. *Baloch*

Banamba: see Bélédougou

Banat (Timis plateau, Romania); l.dr; orig. from Nonius, Noric, Ardennes, Oldenburg and Lipitsa

Bandiagara (Niger bend, Mali, W. Africa); local var. of Dongola-Barb orig; syn. *Gondo*

Barb (Maghreb, N. Africa); l; orig. of West African Barb and of Spanish Barb (USA); not *Barbary, Berber*

Bardigiana (Bardi, Parma, Italy); py; usu. bay; HB 1977

Barranca: see Pottok

[Barra Pony] (Hebrides, Scotland); var. of Hebridean Pony

Barthais, Barthes Pony: see Landais

Bashkir (USSR); d.m.l; Mongolian type improved by various breeds; Russ. *Bashkirskaya*

Bashkir Curly (Nevada, USA); long, curly winter coat; orig. in 1898 from feral horses, ? of Bashkir orig; BS 1971; not *Curley*; rare

Basque, Basque-Navarre Pony: see Pottok

Basseri (Iran); var. of Plateau Persian

Basuto Pony (Lesotho); orig. from Cape Horse 1825 on; disappearing in 20th c. by crossing with Arab and Thoroughbred; orig. of Nooitgedacht Pony

Batak Pony (Sumatra, Indonesia); South-East Asia pony group; syn. *Deli*; not *Baduck* (Jap.), *Battak*

Beetewk: see Bityug

Bélédougou (Mali); var. of West African Barb; syn. *Banamba*

Belgian (Belgium); h; BS 1886, HB 1890; Fr. *Cheval de gros trait belge* (= *Belgian Heavy Draft Horse*); syn. *Belgian Draft*; obs. syn. (heavy type): *Brabançon* (esp. USSR); lighter mountain var: Ardennes; orig. of Rhenish (Germany), French Ardennais (France) and Soviet Heavy Draft; BS also in USA 1889, Canada 1907

Belgian Saddlebred (Belgium); orig. from Hanoverian, Anglo-Norman *et al.*; syn *Belgian Warmblood*

Belgian Trotter (Belgium)

Belgian Warmblood: see Belgian Saddlebred and Belgian Trotter

Berber: see Barb

[Berrichon] (Berry, C. France); local HB (1923-66) for Percheron

Bessarabian: see Bulgarian Colonist, German Bessarabian

Betic, Bético: see Andalusian. [Latin *Betica* = Andalucía]

Bético-lusitano: see Lusitanian

Bhimthadi: see Deccani

Bhirum Pony (N. Nigeria); dwarf; *cf.* Kirdi; syn. *Pagan*; not *Birom*

Bhotia Pony (Nepal, Bhutan, Sikkim and Darjeeling, India); ri.pa; sim. to Tibetan pony but less broad; often white or bay; Nepali *Bhote ghoda*; syn. *Bhutan Pony, Bhutani, Bhutia Pony*; vars: Chyanta (smaller, ri), Tanghan (larger, ri), Tattu (smallest, pa). [= Tibetan]

Bigourdan: see Tarbes

Billie: see Quarter Horse

Bimanese; var. of Sumbawa Pony

Birom: see Bhirum

[Bityug] (Voronezh, USSR); h; sim. to Voronezh; orig. from heavy trotter × local in 19th c; Russ. *Bityug, Bityugskaya*; not *Beetewk, Bitjug*

Black Forest (Germany); chestnut with light mane; orig. from Rhenish; BS 1896; Ger. *Schwarzwälder Kaltblut*; syn. *Sankt Märgener Fuchs*; rare

[Black Sea] (Krasnodar-Rostov area, USSR); 1; orig. from Nogai ×
saddle horse in 18th c, × mountain, Thoroughbred, Don, Karabakh,
et al. in 19th and 20th c; Russ. *Chernomorskaya*; absorbed by
Budyonny, Don and Ukrainian Saddle Horse

blood horse; Ger. *Vollblut*, Fr. *pur sang*; inc. Arab, Barb, Thoroughbred

Bobo (Burkina Faso, W. Africa); py; ? degenerate Barb; syn. *Bobodi*

Boer (S. Africa); revival of old Boer (Cape Horse) from suitable breeds;
BS 1957; Afrik. *Boerperd*; orig. of Calvinia

Bolivian Pony; dwarf var. of Criollo; syn. *Sunicho*

Bornu (N.E. Nigeria); var. of West African Dongola

Bosnian Pony (Yugoslavia); Balkan Pony type; orig. from Buša Pony in
18th c; prim. Karst type in Hercegovina, brown or dun; improved by
Arab in C. and E. Bosnia, taller, white (28%), brown (30%), black
(18%) or chestnut (13%); Serbo-cro. *Bosanski brdski konj*; syn.
Bosniak, Bosnian Mountain

Boulonnais (Boulogne district, N. France); h.m.dr; usu. grey; HB 1886

Bourbonnais (Allier, C. France); local HB (1923-66) for Percheron (but
BS still extant)

Bovenlander (Netherlands): see Oldenburg. [= upland]

Brabançon, Brabant: see Belgian (excluding Ardennes var.)

[Brandenburg] (Germany); 1; Ger. *Brandenburger Warmblut*; absorbed
by Edles Warmblut 1960s

Brazilian: see Campolino, Crioulo, Mangalarga, and Northeastern

Breton (Brittany, France); h.dr.m; HB 1909; orig. of Hispano-Bretona;
HB also in Spain; vars: 1. Draft; Fr. *Trait breton*; 2. Post-horse; orig.
c. 1850-1914 from Hackney × local; Fr. *Postier breton*; syn. *Breton
Cob, Norfolk Breton*; 3. Small mountain draft; l.dr

Breton Saddle Horse: see Corlais

British Spotted Horse and Pony (England); BS 1946-76; replaced by
British Appaloosa and British Spotted Pony societies

British Spotted Pony (England); coloured spots on white background or
vice versa; BS 1946 (with Spotted Horse), split 1976

bronco (USA); unruly type of Western pony. [Sp. *bronco* = rough,
coarse]

broomtail (USA); feral; remnants of mustang

brumbie (Australia); 1; feral

Buckskin (USA); BS 1971 for buckskin (golden with black dorsal stripe,
mane, tail and on legs) or dun

Budyonny (USSR); 1; usu. chestnut or bay; orig. by S.M. Budënnyĭ 1921-
49 from Don, Thoroughbred, *et al.*; HB 1951; Russ. *Budënnovskaya*;
not *Budjonny*

Bulgarian: see Danube, East Bulgarian, Pleven

[Bulgarian Colonist] (S. Bessarabia); py; sim. to Dobrogea; orig. from

Bulgarian, Moldavian, and Ukrainian; syn. *Bessarabian*

Bulgarian Heavy Draft (Bulgaria); dr; orig. (1950 on) from Ardennes, Soviet Heavy Draft and esp. Russian Heavy Draft, × East Bulgarian, Arab and crossbred draft ♀♀; Bulg. *Tezhkovozna*

Bulgarian Mountain; inc. Karakachan, Rila Mountain, Stara Planina

Bulgarian Native; py; Balkan Pony type; vars: Deli-Orman, Dolny-Iskar, Karakachan, Rila Mountain, Stara Planina; ? extinct

[Burgdorf] (Switzerland); h.dr; orig. from Ardennes × Jura

[Burguetana] (Burguete, Navarre, Spain); l.dr; usu. black or bay; orig. in late 19th c. from Pottok graded to Breton

Burmese Pony: see Shan Pony

Buryat (Buryatia, USSR); Siberian Pony group; Russ. *Buryatskaya*; syn. *Buryat-Mongolian, Transbaikal* (Russ. *Zabaĭkal'skaya*); not *Buriat*; rare

[Buša Pony] (Yugoslavia); orig of Bosnian Pony and Posavina

Byelorussian Harness (Byelorussia, USSR); l.dr.m.d; orig. in late 19th and 20th c. from various draft and coach breeds (esp. Døle) × local; Russ. *Belorusskaya* or *Belorusskaya upryazhnaya*; syn. *White-Russian Carriage, Coach, Draft* or *Harness*

Calabrian (Calabria, Italy); l.ri; orig. from Oriental × local, improved by Salernitana and then by Thoroughbred; It. *Calabrese*; rare

Calvinia (S.Africa); l; orig. from Boer crossed with Thoroughbred, Hackney and Cleveland Bay

Camargue (Rhône delta, S. France); py for herding bulls; white, born grey; recog. 1968; BS; Fr. *Camarguais*; syn. *battle horse, bull horse*; purebreds rare

Cambodian (Kampuchea); South-East Asia pony group, sim. to Thai and Vietnamese; Fr. *Cambodgien*

Campolino (Minas Gerais, Brazil); l.(dr); usu. bay, sorrel or chestnut; orig. from native horse (Crioulo) by C. Campolino in mid-19th c. with blood of Anglo-Norman, Holstein, American Saddle and Mangalarga; BS 1951

Canadian (Quebec, Canada); l.dr; orig. in late 17th and early 18th c. from Arab, Breton, Norman; BS 1895, HB 1885; revived 1909 on; Fr. *Canadien*; obs. syn. *French Canadian*; var: Canadian Pacer; rare

Canadian Hunter (Canada); l.

[Canadian Pacer]; var. of Canadian with blood of Narragansett

[Canary Island Pony] (Spain); Sp. *Jaca canaria*

Canik (N.E. Turkey); local var. of Anatolian Native; not *Çenik, Cenik*

Cantabrian Pony: see North Spanish Pony

Cape Harness (S. Africa); l.dr; orig. from Anglo-Arab, Friesian and Hackney

[Cape Horse] (S. Africa); l; orig. from Oriental imported 1652-1778, Thoroughbred 1782-1860 and Hackney 1860-1891; syn. *Boer* (old), *Hantam, South African*; orig. of Basuto Pony, Boer (new), Namaqua Pony; nearly extinct after 1900

Capitanata (Foggia, Apulia, Italy); l.dr; improved by Maremmana, Murgese and Anglo-Norman; see also Apulian

Carpathian Pony: see Hutsul

[Cartuja]; former strain of Andalusian; Sp. *Cartujana*; not *Carthusian*

Caspian (Gilan and Mazandaran, Iran); py; usu. bay, grey or chestnut, occ. black; BS; BS also in GB 1976, USA, Australia, New Zealand; syn. *Caspian Miniature*; rare

[Castilian] (Spain); l; Sp. *Castellana, de Castilla*

Catalan, Catalonian: see Hispano-Bretona

Cayuse (USA); var. of Indian

Celebes: see Macassar Pony

CELTIC PONY; inc. Connemara, Faroes, Hebridean, Iceland, and Shetland Ponies

Cenik: see Canik

Chapman Horse: see Cleveland Bay

[Charentais] (W. France); l; inc. in French Saddlebred; derivative of Anglo- Norman + Anglo-Arab

[Charolais] (C. France); l; inc. in French Saddlebred; orig. from Anglo-Norman × local; not *Charollais*

Charysh (Siberia, USSR); local var; rare

Cheju (Korea); South-East Asia pony group; syn. *Korean* (Jap. *Chosen*, not *Corean*), *Saishu Island*

Chenarani (N.E. Iran); l; Plateau Persian × Turkoman cross; not *Tcheraran*

Chickasaw (Tennessee and N. Carolina, USA); Indian orig; BS 1959; not *Chicksaw*; rare. [Chickasaw Indians]

Chilean (Chile); l; Criollo type; first imported 1541, HB 1893, revived 1913; Sp. *Chileno*

Chincoteague Pony (I. off Virginia, USA); semi-wild; *cf.* Assateague Pony

Chinese: see Datong Pony, Hequ, Ili, Jinzhou, Mongolian, Sanhe, South China Ponies, Tatung Pony, Tibetan Pony

Chola: medium var. of Peruvian Criollo; syn. *Serrana*

Chosen: see Cheju

Chukorova: see Çukorova

Chummarti (Tibet, and Kumaur dist, Himachal Pradesh, India); l; sim. to Spiti

Chumysh (N.E. Altai, USSR); l.ri.dr; breed group; orig. from Siberian Pony improved by Russian breeds 1770-1850 and by trotters and draft breeds 1850-1917; Russ. *Chumyshskaya porodnaya gruppa*; rare

Chunk Morgan (USA); old heavy strain of Morgan; rare

[Chuvash] (Chuvashia, USSR); py; local horse of forest type improved by trotter, Soviet Heavy Draft and Vladimir Heavy Draft; Russ. *Chuvashskaya*

Chyanta (Nepal); ri; smaller var. of Bhotia Pony; Nepali *Cyāntā* (= dwarf)

cimarron (Spanish America); feral horse; Port. *cimarrão* (Brazil); *cf.* mustang

Cleveland Bay (E. Yorkshire, England); l.dr; BS 1884; syn. *Chapman Horse*; Yorkshire Coach Horse was var. with Thoroughbred blood 1886-1937; BS also in USA 1879; rare

Clydesdale (Scotland); h.dr; sim. to Shire (Shire blood); usu. bay, brown, or black, with white on face and feet; orig. from Great Horse; BS 1877, HB 1878; BS also in Australia, Canada 1886, New Zealand 1911, S. Africa, USA 1879; orig. of Vladimir Heavy Draft (USSR); rare in GB

cob (Great Britain); l.ri; any heavy-weight, short-legged, riding horse (hack); syn. *riding cob*; see also Irish Cob, Norman Cob, Welsh Cob

COLDBLOOD (Germany) = heavy draft; Ger. *Kaltblut*; inc. Black Forest, Rhenish, Schleswig and South German

Cold Deck: see Quarter Horse

Colombian Criollo (Colombia); Criollo type

Colorado Ranger (Colorado, USA); l.ri; colour type; spotted sim. to Appaloosa; BS 1938; syn. *Rangerbred*

Comtois (Doubs, E. France); h-l.m.dr; bay or chestnut; local breed sim. to Freiberg (Switzerland) improved by Ardennes; HB 1919; syn. *Maiche*. [from Franche Comté]

[Conestoga] (USA); l.

Connemara Pony (W. Ireland); usu. grey, black, bay, brown, or dun; orig. from Irish Hobby; BS 1923, HB 1926; BS also in England 1947 (HB 1900), USA 1956, Sweden 1965, Germany, Netherlands, HB also in France

Copper Bottom: see Quarter Horse

[Córdoba]; former strain of Andalusian; Sp. *Cordobesa*

Corean: see Cheju

[Corlais] (Corlay, Brittany, France); l.ri; orig. in 19th c. from Thoroughbred (and Arab) × local; inc. in French Saddlebred; syn. *Breton Saddle Horse*

[Corsican Pony] (Corsica, France); Fr. *Corse*

[Cossack] (Russia); orig. in 18th c. from Nogai × Mongolian and

Kalmyk; syn. *Old Don*; orig. of Don
Costeña; larger var. of Peruvian Criollo; bay, chestnut or roan. [=
coastal]
Cotocoli: see Koto-Koli
cow pony (USA); type of Western pony; orig. from mustang *et al.*
Cracker: see Seminole
Creme and White: see American Creme and American White
[Cremonese] (Cremona, Italy); h.dr; orig. from Belgian with Breton and
Percheron blood; syn. *Padana* (from Po valley); remnants absorbed
by AITPR
CRIOLLO (Spanish America); l. or py; Sp. (Andalusian) orig. from 16th
c. on; sim. to (or =) Crioulo (Brazil); inc. Argentine Criollo, Bolivian
Pony, Chilean, Colombian Criollo, Mexican Pony, Peruvian Criollo,
Venezuelan Criollo. [= native]
Crioulo (Rio Grande do Sul, Brazil); py; var. of (or =) Criollo; BS; not
Criôlo; see also Northeastern. [= native]
Croatian Coldblood: see Yugoslav Draft
Cuban Trotter (Cuba); Sp. *Caballo cubano de paso*
Çukurova (S. Turkey); l; orig. from Anatolian Native, Arab, and
'Circassian'; not *Chukorova, Cukorova, Tschoukourova*
Curraleiro: see Northeastern
[Cushendal] (N. Ireland); py
Cutchi: see Kathiawari
Czech Coldblood (Czechoslovakia); h.dr; Noric and Belgian orig; Cz.
Český chladnokrevník
Czech Trotter (Czechoslovakia); Hungarian, Austrian, German and
Russian orig; Cz. *Český klusák*
Czech Warmblood (Czechoslovakia); based on Hanoverian with some
Trakehner blood; Cz. *Český teplokrevník*

Dąbrowa-Tarnowska (S. Poland); halfbred of Gidran orig; Pol. *Dąbrowo-
tarnowski* or *Tarnowsko-dąbrowski*; combined with Sącz to form
Kraków-Rzeszow
Dagestan Pony (N. Caucasus, USSR); d; Russ. *Dagestanskiĭ poni*; vars:
Avar, Kumyk, Lezgian; rare
Dales Pony (N.E. England); sim. to Fell Pony but larger, owing to draft-
horse blood; usu. black, dark brown, grey, or dark bay; BS 1916 (split
1957), HB 1918; rare
Danish: see Jutland
Danube (Bulgaria); l; orig. (1924 on) from Nonius × Pleven, halfbred
riding and local, with some Russian Trotter blood (1955-65); Bulg.
Dunavska

Darashoori: see Shirazi
Darfur Pony: see Western Sudan Pony
Daror: see Somali Pony
Dartmoor Pony (S.W. England); usu. black, brown, bay or grey; HB 1899, BS 1925; BS also in USA, Netherlands, HB also in France, Germany; rare
Datong Pony (N.E. Qinghai, China); pa; W.G. *Ta-t'ung*
[Davert] (Münster, Westphalia, Germany); py; feral; sim to Dülmen Pony; syn. *Davertnickel*; extinct 1812
Deccani (Bombay, India); py; syn. *Bhimthadi*; nearly extinct
Deli: see Batak
Deliboz (W. Azerbaijan, USSR); l-py; grey or bay; orig. in early 20th c. from Turkish Arab × Karabakh and Azerbaijan in S. Azerbaijan; rare. [name of stud]
Deli-Orman (N. Bulgaria); var. of Bulgarian Native; not *Deliorman*
demi-sang: see halfbred
[Devon Pack Horse] (England); py
[Dhanni] (Punjab, India); l; not *Dhunni*
Djerma (middle Niger, W. Africa); l; dark; orig. from Barb × Dongola
Dobrogea (Romania); py; former var. of Romanian, sim. to Moldavian but smaller; Rom. *Dobrogeană*; not *Dobrudja, Dobruja*
Døle (E. Norway); l.dr; usu. brown or bay, also black, occ. chestnut; orig. from Frederiksborg × local in 18th c; HB 1902; syn. *Døle-Gudbrandsdal, Gudbrandsdal, Østland* (= *Eastland*) (till 1947); orig. of Døle Trotter, North Swedish. [= valley]
Døle Trotter (Norway); orig. from Døle with Trotter blood; HB; syn. *Norwegian Trotter*
Dolny-Iskar; var. of Bulgarian Native
Don (USSR); l; golden chestnut; orig. from Cossack (= Old Don) improved in 19th c. successively with Persian and Karabakh, Arab and Orlov-Rostopchin, and Thoroughbred; HB; Russ. *Donskaya*; syn. *Trans-Don*; orig. (with Thoroughbred) of Anglo-Don; eastern, large and riding vars
Dongola (N. Sudan and W. Eritrea); l; reddish-bay, often with white face-blaze and feet; syn. *Dongalawi, Dongolas, Dongolaw*; orig. of West African Dongola
Dor: see Somali Pony
Dülmen Pony (Münsterland, Westphalia, Germany); py; all colours; single semi-wild herd on Duke of Croy's estate at Meerfelder Bruch; Ger. *Dülmener*; syn. *Münsterland*; sim. vars or herds: Davert, Senne (orig); orig. of Nordkirchen Pony
Dutch Coach: see Gelderland and Groningen
Dutch Draft (Netherlands); h.dr; sim. to Belgian (due to Belgian blood

c. 1880 on); HB 1915, BS; Du. *Nederlandse Trekpaard*; syn. *Holland Heavy, Netherlands Draft*
Dutch Trotter: see Netherlands Trotter
Dzhabe: see Jabe

East Bulgarian; 1.ri.dr; orig. since *c.* 1900 from Thoroughbred and English Halfbred × Anglo-Arab, Arab and Bulgarian Native; Bulg. *Istochno-b''lgarska*
Eastern: see Oriental
East Friesian (Germany); l.[dr]; sim. to Oldenburg; usu. black or bay; [BS]; Ger. *Ostfriesisches Warmblut*; syn. *East Friesland*; nearly extinct; remains, with Oldenburg and Cleveland Bay, is forming Heavy Warmblood (Ger. *Schweres Warmblutpferd*)
Eastland: see Døle
East Prussian: see Trakehner
Edles Warmblut (E. Germany); 1; orig. 1960s from Brandenburg and Mecklenburg with Hanoverian, Thoroughbred and Trakehner blood
Egyptian (Egypt); l; Arab type; syn. *Baladi*
[Einsiedeln]; var. of Swiss Halfblood; orig. from Anglo-Norman; Ger. *Einsiedler*; syn. *Schwyz*
English Cart-horse: see Shire
English Race-horse, English Thoroughbred: see Thoroughbred
Eriskay Pony (Hebrides, Scotland); only surviving var. of Hebridean Pony; orig. Celtic type with no imported blood; born black, turning grey or white; BS 1972; rare
[Erlenbach]; var. of Swiss Halfblood; orig. from Mecklenburg × Danish; syn. *Simmental*
Esperia Pony (Ciociaria, Latium, Italy); l.dr.pa.ri; It. *Pony di Esperia*; rare
[Estonian Draft] (Rakvere, Estonia, USSR); h; orig. from Ardennes (also Clydesdale and Shire) imported 1862-1935 × Estonian Native; Russ. *Ėstonskiĭ tyazhelovoz*
Estonian Native (Estonia, USSR); Northern type; sim. to Žemaitukai; chestnut, bay, light bay, dun or grey; HB; Russ. *Mestnaya ėstonskaya* or *Ėstonskaya loshad'*; syn. *Estonian Klepper, Estonian Pony*; orig. (with Hackney) of Tori, and (with Ardennes) of Estonian Draft; not *Esthonian*; rare
European wild: see tarpan
Exmoor Pony (N.E. Devon and W. Somerset, S.W. England); bay, dun or brown, mealy nose, no white markings; BS 1921, HB 1961; HB also in USA; rare
[Extremadura]; former strain of Andalusian; Sp. *Extremeña*

Faeroes Pony; sim. to Iceland Pony; not *Faroe*

Falabella Pony (Argentina); ? orig. from Shetland Pony; syn. *Argentine Dwarf, Miniature horse, Toy horse*; BS in GB, USA

[Feldmoching] (Bavaria, Germany); py; Ger. *Feldmochinger Moospferd*

Fell Pony (N.W. England); sim. to Dales Pony but smaller; BS 1893, HB 1899

Filipino: see Philippine Pony

Finnish (Finland); dr; Northern type; usu. chestnut, sometimes brown; Finn. *Suomalainen hevonen*, Swe. *Finsk*; syn. *Finnhorse*; heavy (draft) var. (rare), and light (universal) var.

Five-gaited Horse: see American Saddle Horse

Fjord (W. Norway); py; usu. dun with dark mane, tail and back-stripe; HB 1910; syn. *Fjording, Nordbag, Nordfjord, Norwegian Dun, Norwegian Fjord, Norwegian Pony, Vestland* (= *Westland*) (till 1947), *West Norway, West Norwegian*; not *Fiord*; BS also in Canada 1980, GB, Germany, Netherlands, USA 1977, HB also in France

Flanders: see Flemish

[Flemish] (Flanders); h.dr; orig. of Belgian, Dutch, *et al.*; *cf.* Great Horse (Britain); syn. *Flanders*

Fleuve (Senegal, W. Africa); l; orig. from Barb (from Hodh or Kayes) × local pony; Fr. *Cheval du fleuve*; orig. of Fouta. [Fr. = river]

Flores: see Timor

Florida: see Seminole

Fouta (Senegal, W. Africa); l; orig. from Fleuve × M'Bayar; syn. *Foutanké*

Fox Trot: see Missouri Fox Trotting Horse

Franche Montagne: see Freiberg

Frederiksborg (Denmark); l.dr; usu. chestnut; orig. in late 19th c. from stallions from Royal F. Stud (flourished in 17th and 18th c. with Andalusian, Arab and Thoroughbred) × local Zealand mares; Oldenburg and East Friesian blood since 1939; not *Fredericksborg, Fredriksborg*; rare

Freiberg (N.W. Switzerland); l.dr; sim. to Comtois (France); orig. from local, improved in late 19th and early 20th c. by imported coach (esp. Anglo-Norman) and draft horses (esp. Ardennes); Ger. *Freiberger*; syn. *Franche-Montagne, Jura*

French Anglo-Arab (esp. Limousin and S.W. France); inc. Limousin; HB

French Ardennais (Ardennes, N.E. France); h.m.dr; orig. from Belgian; HB 1908-14, 1923 on; vars: Auxois, Northern Ardennais

French Canadian: see Canadian

[French Coach] (USA) = demi-sang (*i.e.* halfbred)

[Frencher] (Canada); Thoroughbred × Canadian, 1st cross

French Riding Pony (France); orig. 1970s from Arab *et al.* × local

ponies; HB; Fr. *Poney Français de Selle*; syn. *French Saddlebred Pony*
French Saddlebred (France); l.ri; orig. 1958 from halfbreds, inc. Anglo-
Norman and its derivatives—Charentais, Charolais, Vendéen—and
also Corlais; HB; Fr. *Cheval de selle français*
French Trotter (Normandy, France); l; orig. in 20th c. from Norman
Coach Horse with Thoroughbred, Hackney, and American Trotter
blood; HB 1906, breed recog. 1922, BS; Fr. *Trotteur français*; syn.
Anglo-Norman Trotter, Norman Trotter
Friesian (Friesland, Netherlands); l.dr.ri; black; HB 1879, BS 1914; Du.
Friese, Friesch or *Inlands Fries* (= *Friesian native*); not *Fresian, Frisian*
Friesian (Germany): see East Friesian
Fulani: see West African Dongola
Furioso, Furioso-Northstar: see Mezőhegyes Halfbred

Gaju: see Gayoe
Galiceño (Mexico); py; orig. from Galician Pony; BS in USA 1958
Galician Pony (N.W. Spain); pa.m; semi-feral; Sp. *Jaca gallega* or *Poney
gallego*; at one time combined with Asturian as *Galician-Asturian* (Sp.
Poney galaico-asturiano or *galaico-asturico*); orig. of Galiceño (Mexico);
cf. Garrano (Portugal)
Galla: see Abyssinian
[Galloway Pony] (S.W. Scotland); sim. to Fell Pony and to Garron
Ganaston: see Bahr-el-Ghazal
Garrano (N.W. Portugal); py; Port. *Garrano Luso-Galeico* (or *Luso-
Galiziano*) (= *Lusitanian-Galician pony*); syn. *Minho pony*; *cf.* Galician
Pony (Spain). [= pony]
Garron (N.W. Scotland); larger, mainland var. of Highland Pony; not
Garran. [Gaelic *gearran* = gelding, work-horse]
Garwolin (Warsaw, Poland); l-h.dr; local var. sim to Sokolka; orig.
*c.*1922-56 from Breton, Ardennes, and Boulonnais, × local; Pol.
Garwoliński
Gayoe Pony (Sumatra, Indonesia); South-East Asia pony group; Du.
Gaju; not *Kaju* (Jap.)
Gelderland (C. Netherlands); l.ri.(dr); usu. chestnut or grey, often white
on legs and face; orig. from Oldenburg and Anglo-Norman × local;
sim. to Groningen, but lighter; HB 1880-90, recently reorg., BS; Du.
Gelderse paard; not *Guelderland, Guelders*; rare
[German Bessarabian] (Bessarabia); l; black; mixed orig; syn. *German
Colonist*
[German Coach] (USA) = warmblood. esp. Hanoverian and Oldenburg
German Riding Horse (Germany); l; union of warmblood breeds since
1975; inc. Hanoverian, Holstein, Westphalian, Zweibrücken; BS; Ger.

Deutsches Reitpferd
German riding pony; pony suitable for riding, of any breed or cross; BS; Ger. *Deutsches Reitpony*

German Trotter (Germany); orig. from American and French Trotters; BS 1896; Ger. *Traber*

Gharkawi: see Western Sudan Pony

Giara Pony (Sardinia, Italy); It. *Cavallino della Giara*; rare

Giawf (N.Yemen)

Gidran (S.E. Europe); l; strain of Anglo-Arab bred at Mezőhegyes, Hungary; syn. *Gidran-Arabian*; rare. [name of foundation Arab stallion]

[Gocan] (Mull, Scotland); small Highland pony of Hebridean type; syn. *Mull*

Gondo: see Bandiagara

[Goonhilly] (Cornwall, England); py

Gotland Pony (Sweden); black, brown or bay; BS 1910, HB 1943; Swe. *Skogsruss*; syn. *Gotlandsruss, Skogsbagge, Skogshäst* (= *forest horse*); BS also in USA 1960; rare

Graditz (Saxony, Germany); Saxony Warmblood stud with some Thoroughbred blood

[Great Horse] (Britain); sim. to Flemish; syn. *Old English Black* (or *War*) *Horse*; orig. of Clydesdale and Shire

Greek Pony (Greece); Balkan Pony type; syn. *Greek Native*; vars: Peneia, Pindos and Skyros Ponies

Groningen (Netherlands); l.ri; usu. black or brown; orig. from local draft graded to Oldenburg (1870 on); sim. to Gelderland but heavier; HB 1880-90, reorg. recently, BS 1982; Du. *Groninger, Groningse paard*; nearly extinct (saved since 1978)

Guangxi Pony (China); inc. Baise and Shishan; dwarf

Gudbrandsdal: see Døle

Guelderland, Guelders: see Gelderland

Guizhou (China); py; syn. *Kweichow*

Gurgul (Carpathians, Slovakia, Czechoslovakia)

Guzman: see Andalusian

hack (Great Britain); l; any horse suitable for riding. [= hackney]

Hackney (England); l.dr; ? orig. from Thoroughbred and local horse of Norse orig; BS 1883, HB 1884; syn. *Norfolk, Norfolk Hackney, Norfolk Roadster, Norfolk Trotter, Yorkshire Hackney, Yorkshire Trotter*; BS also in Australia, Canada 1892, Netherlands, S. Africa 1962 (HB 1967), USA 1891 (horse and pony). [hackney = a horse for ordinary riding or driving]

Hackney Pony (England); orig. from Hackney; HB in Netherlands

Haflinger (Tyrol, Austria-Italy, also S. Germany); py; ri.dr; chestnut with light mane and tail; light Noric and Arab blood; BS/HB Austria, Germany, Italy; It. *Avelignese*; syn. *Hafling (Mountain) Pony*; not *Hafflinger*; BS also in USA, GB, Canada 1982; HB also in France, Netherlands

Hailar: see Sanhe

halfblood: see halfbred

HALFBRED; orig. from blood horse × native or draft; Ger. *Halbblut*, Fr. *demi-sang*; syn. *halfblood, warmblood*

Hanoverian (Hanover, Germany); l; orig. (late 18th and early 19th c.) from Thoroughbred, Trakehner, *et al.* × local; BS 1888; Ger. *Hannoveraner, Hannoversches Warmblut*; syn. *Hanover*; derivatives— Brandenburg, Mecklenburg, Westphalian; BS also in USA 1973; inc. in German Riding Horse 1975

Hantam: see Cape Horse

Hausa (Niger and N. Nigeria); var. of West African Dongola

Heavy Warmblood (Saxony and Thuringia, E. Germany); l. dr; orig. 1960s from Oldenburg and East Friesian and absorbed Saxony Warmblood; Ger. *Schweres Warmblut*

[Hebridean Pony] (Scotland); smaller orig. var. of Highland pony; syn. *Western Isles Pony*; former vars: Barra, Mull, Rhum, Skye, Uist; extinct (by crossing) except for Eriskay Pony

Heilongjiang (China); dr; in formation from Soviet breeds × local; W.G. *Heilungkiang*

Hequ (S.E. Qinghai/S.W. Gansu/N.W. Sichuan, China); dr.ri; W.G. *Khetshui*, Russ. *Khetsyuĭ*

Herati (Afghanistan); l.

Highland Pony (N.W. Scotland); usu. grey, dun, black, or brown, with eel-stripe; BS *c.* 1910, HB 1889; vars (till 1932): Garron (mainland) (over 14 hands) and Hebridean Pony (under 14.3 hands); obs. syn. *Scotch Pony*; HB also in France

Hinis (N.E. Anatolia); local var. of Anatolian Native with short forelegs; Turk. *Hınısın Kolu Kısası* (= *Hinis short arm*)

Hirzai (Baluchistan, Pakistan); l; white or grey; Arab orig; rare

Hispano-Anglo-Arabe (Spain); various crosses of Andalusian, Thoroughbred, Arab and Anglo-Arab and their derivatives; syn. *Tres sangres* (= 3 bloods)

Hispano-Arabe (Spain); l; orig. from Arab × Andalusian

Hispano-Bretona (N.E. Spain); m.(dr); sim. to Breton; orig. from Breton × Andalusian; syn. *Catalan, Catalonian*

Hobby: see Irish Hobby

Hodh (Mali-Mauritania); var. of West African Barb

Hokkaido Pony (Japan); var. of Japanese Native; rare
Holland Heavy: see Dutch Draft
Holstein (Holstein, Germany); l; inc. Holstein Marsh and Schleswig-
Holstein; Yorkshire Coach Horse blood; BS 1886; Ger. *Holsteiner
Warmblut*; HB also in USA 1978; inc. in Germany Riding Horse 1975
Hsiangcheng: see Sikang Pony
Hsi-ning: see Sining
Hucul: see Hutsul
Hungarian (Hungary); l; Mongolian and Oriental orig; improved by
Arab, Spanish, and Thoroughbred; now graded to Hungarian Halfbred;
syn. *Hungarian Native*; orig. of Hungarian Draft
Hungarian (USA); imported from Hungary 1945; BS 1966; rare
Hungarian Draft (W. Hungary); h.dr; orig. from Noric (late 19th c),
Percheron, and Ardennes, × Hungarian; Hung. *Magyar hidegvérü* (=
cold blood); former var: [Pinkafeld]; see also Mur Island
Hungarian Halfbred; inc. Gidran, Kisbér, and Mezőhegyes Halfbred;
used for improvement of Hungarian
Hunter (Great Britain); l; any horse suitable for riding to hounds (fox-
hunting), usu. heavy Thoroughbred or Thoroughbred cross; BS 1885;
BS also in Canada
Hutsul (E. Carpathians); py; konik type; Pol. *Hucuł* or *Huculska*, Cz.
Hucul, Rom. *Huțul*, Ger. *Huzul*; syn. *Carpathian Pony*; not *Hutzul*
Huzul: see Hutsul

[Ialomița] (Walachia, Romania); var. of Transylvanian; not *Jalomitza*
Iceland Pony; 30% chestnut, also bay, black, grey, or dun; orig. from
Scandinavian and North British types introduced in 11th and 12th c;
BS; Ice. *Íslenzki hesturinn*; syn. *Icelandic*; BS also in Germany, GB,
Netherlands, USA 1982, Canada 1982, HB also in France
Ili (N.W. Xinjiang, China); l.ri.dr.(m.d); Mongolian type; usu. chestnut,
brown or black; orig. from Russian breeds × Mongolian; not *Yili,
Yilee*
Indian (USA); orig. from mustang; BS 1961 for Western horses of
Spanish and non-Spanish orig; syn. *American Indian, Indian Pony*; see
also Cayuse, Chickasaw, Seminole
Iomud (Turkmenistan, USSR); l; sim. to Akhal-Teke but smaller; grey
or chestnut, occ. golden chestnut or black; Russ. *Iomudskaya*; not
Iomut, Jomud, Jomut, Yomud, Yomut, Yomuth; rare
Iranian: see Caspian, Chenarani, Plateau Persian, Turkmen
Irish Cob (Ireland); l.
Irish Draught; h.dr; orig. from Irish Hobby and Great Horse; HB; syn.
Irish Cart-horse; BS also in GB; rare

[Irish Hobby]; orig. of Connemara Pony and Irish Draught
Irish Hunter; l; orig. from Irish Thoroughbred × Irish Draught *et al.*
Irish Thoroughbred; strain of Thoroughbred
Isabella; coat colour—yellow to golden with white tail and mane; Sp.
  Isabelo; syn. *Claybank Dun* (USA), *Yellow Dun* (inc. Palomino) (GB);
  see also Ysabella
Íslenzki hesturinn: see Iceland Pony
Italian Trotter (N. Italy); orig. since late 19th c. from American Trotter
Ivanovo Clydesdale: see Vladimir Heavy Draft

Jabe (W. Kazakhstan, USSR); l.m; heavier var. of Kazakh; Russ.
  Dzhabe; former syn. *Western Kazakh*
jaca (Spain) = cob (or pony)
Jaf (Kordestan, Iran); l; var. of Plateau Persian; see also Kurdi
Jakut, Jakutskaja: see Yakut
Jalomiţa: see Ialomiţa
Japanese Native (Japan); South-East Asia pony group; smaller island
  type (Miyako, Taishu, Tokara and Yonaguni) and larger mainland
  type (Hokkaido, Kiso, Misaki, and Noma); BS; rare
Jiangchang (S. Sichuan, China); py. pa.ri
Jilin (China); dr; in formation from Soviet breeds × local; W.G. *Kirin*;
  syn. *Jilin Harness*
Jinzhou (Jin county, Liaoning, China); ri.dr.(d.m)
Jomud, Jomut: see Iomud
Jugoslavian: see Yugoslav
[Jumla Pony] (Uttar Pradesh, India)
Jura: see Freiberg
Jutland (Denmark); h.dr; usu. chestnut; improved by Shire stallion
  imported 1862; BS 1888; Dan. *Jydsk*; syn. *Danish*; orig. (with Suffolk)
  of Schleswig; rare

Kabarda (N. Caucasus, USSR); l; bay or black-brown, occ. black; HB
  1935; Russ. *Kabardinskaya*; mountain var: Balkar; Karachai was
  formerly considered a var.
kadish (Middle East) = impure (Arab)
Kaimanawa 'wild' horse (C. North Island, New Zealand); feral; rare
Kaju: see Gayoe Pony
Kalmyk (Astrakhan and Volgograd, USSR); l; Russ. *Kalmytskaya*; syn.
  Astrakhan; being absorbed by Don and other breeds; nearly extinct
Kaltblut: see coldblood
Kanata Pony (Canada and USA); BS for py of Appaloosa colour
  (spotted); *cf.* Pony of the Americas

Karabagh, Karabah: see Karabakh
Karabair (Uzbekistan and N. Tajikistan, USSR); chestnut, grey or black; Russ. *Karabairskaya*; not *Kara-Bair*
Karabakh (Azerbaijan, USSR); l; chestnut or bay; improved in 18th c. by crossing with Arab and Turkmen; HB 1981; Russ. *Karabakhskaya*; not *Karabagh, Karabah*; rare
Karacabey Halfbred Arab (Turkey); l; Turk. *Karacabey yarımkan arap*
Karachai (N. Caucasus, USSR); l; sim. to (formerly var. of) Kabarda; Russ. *Karachaevskaya*; not *Karachaev, Karachayevsk*
Karakachan; var. of Bulgarian Native; Bulg. *Karakachanska*; not *Karakatschan*. [(Romanian) nomad]
[Karelian] (Karelia, USSR); North Russian Pony group; Russ. *Karel'-skaya*; var: Onega
Kathiawari (Gujarat, India); l; chestnut, bay, brown, grey, dun, piebald or skewbald; turned-in ears; syn. *Cutchi, Kathi, Kutchi*
Kazakh (Azerbaijan, USSR): see Azerbaijan
Kazakh (Kazakhstan, USSR); l.m.d; Mongolian type; former syn. *Kirgiz* or *Kirgiz Mountain*; vars: Adaev, Jabe; orig. of Kushum; not *Kazah, Kazak*
Keheilan; orig. strain of Arab; not *Khiolan, Khiolawi, Koheilan, Kuhailan*. [from Arabic *kohl* = antimony]
Kentucky Saddle Horse: see American Saddle Horse
Kentucky Whip: see Quarter Horse
Khetshui, Khetsyuǐ: see Hequ
Khiolan, Khiolawi: see Keheilan
Kielce (Poland); combined with Lublin to form Lublin-Kielce; Pol. *Kielecki*
Kirdi Pony (S.W. Chad); syn. *Lakka, Logone, Mbai, Pagan, Sara*; cf. Bhirum (Nigeria). [*kirdi* = pagan]
Kirgiz (Kirgizia, USSR); py; Mongolian type; Russ. *Kirgizskaya*; syn. *Kirgiz Mountain*; orig. of New Kirgiz; not *Kirghiz*; rare. [Kirgiz was formerly used as syn. or var. of Kazakh]
Kisbér Halfbred (Hungary); English Halfbred from Kisbér stud which uses Thoroughbred ♂♂; not *Kis-Ber*; rare
Kiso (C. Honshu, Japan); var. of Japanese Native; BS 1948; nearly extinct
Kladruby (Czechoslovakia); l.ri; Spanish-Neapolitan orig; black and grey (white) vars; Cz. *Kladrubský*, Ger. *Kladruber*; not *Kladrub, Kladrup*; nearly extinct. [name of stud, founded 1562]
Klepper: see Estonian Pony. [Ger. = riding horse]
Knabstrup (Denmark); sim. to Frederiksborg but spotted; orig. from one ♀ × spotted ♂ in early 19th c. on Knabstrup farm
Kobczyk: see Kopczyk Podlaski

Koheilan: see Keheilan
Kolyma: see Middle Kolyma
Konik (Poland–USSR); py; inc. Polish Konik, Hutsul (Carpathians), Polesian, and Žemaitukai (Lithuania). [= small horse]
Kopczyk Podlaski (Poland); h; line of Belgian orig. from stallion 'Kopczyk'; not *Kobczyk*; rare
Kordofani: see Western Sudan Pony
Korean: see Cheju, Taejung
Koto-Koli Pony (N. Benin and Togo); syn. *Cotocoli, Togo Pony*
Kraków-Rzeszów (Poland); inc. Sacz (Pol. *Sądecki*) and Dąbrowa-Tarnowska; combined with Lublin-Kielce to form Małopolski; Pol. *Krakowsko-rzeszowski*
Kréda: see Bahr-el-Ghazal
[Krk Island Pony] (Yugoslavia); Balkan Pony type; Serbo-cro. *Krčki konj*, It. *Veglia*
Kuhailan: see Keheilan
Kumingan Pony (W. Java, Indonesia); South-East Asia Pony group
Kumyk (coastal plains of Dagestan, USSR); d.l; largest var. of Dagestan Pony; Russ. *Kumykskaya*
Kurdi (Kurdistan); l-py
Kushum (W. Kazakhstan, USSR); l.ri.dr.m.d; bay or chestnut; orig. (1930-76) from trotter, Thoroughbred, Don and Budyonny × Kazakh; recog. 1976; Russ. *Kushumskaya*; syn. *West Kazakh Saddle-Draft* (Russ. *Zapadno-kazakhstanskaya verkhovo-upryazhnaya*)
Kustanai (N.W. Kazakhstan, USSR); l; usu. bay or chestnut, also reddish-grey or brown; orig. (1887-1951) from Kazakh improved by Don, Orlov-Rostopchin *et al.*; recog. 1951; HB; Russ. *Kustanaĭskaya*; not *Kustanair*; vars: general purpose, saddle and steppe (m)
Kutchi: see Kathiawari
Kuznetsk (Kemerovo and Novosibirsk, W. Siberia); l; breed group; Siberian Pony type improved in late 19th and early 20th c. by trotter, saddle, and draft breeds (Clydesdale and Brabançon) and hence light, basic and heavy types; Russ. *Kuznetskaya porodnaya gruppa*; rare
Kweichow: see Guizhou

La Barranca: see Pottok
Laka, Lakka: see Kirdi
Landais (Landes, S.W. France); py; black, bay or chestnut; HB; syn. *Barthes* (Fr. *Barthais*); rare
[Latgale Trotter] (Latvia, USSR); strain of Baltic Trotter; orig. from Orlov and American Trotters × local; Russ. *Latgal'skiĭ rysak*; absorbed by Latvian

Latvian (Latvia, USSR); dr; bay, dark bay or black, sometimes chestnut; orig. 1952 from native Northern type improved by various breeds at Riga State Stud (1893 on) and by Oldenburg, Groningen and Hanoverian (1921-39); Russ. *Latviĭskaya* or *Latviĭskiĭ upryazhnyĭ*; syn. *Latvian Carriage, Latvian Coach, Latvian Draft*; light and heavy types
Latvian Ardennes: see Baltic Ardennes
[Lebaniega] (Liébana, Santander, N. Spain); py
Lezgian (S. Dagestan, USSR); ri.pa; var. of Dagestan Pony; Russ. *Lezginskaya*
Lidzbark (Olsztyn prov., Poland); h.dr; dun or mousy, occ. bay; developed since 1945 by settlers from Oszmiana; Pol. *Lidzbarski*
Liébana: see Lebaniega
Lijiang (Yunnan, China); py. pa.ri
Limousin (C. France); l; usu. bay or chestnut; var. of French Anglo-Arab; Anglo- Arab orig. in late 19th c; HB 1909-1914; Fr. *Anglo-Arabe du Limousin*
Lipitsa (S.E. Europe); l; usu. grey; orig. from Spanish and Arab at Lipitsa stud near Trieste (founded 1580); Serbo-cro. *Lipica* or *Lipicanac*, Hung. *Lipicai*, Rom. *Lipiţana*, It. *Lipizzana*, Ger. *Lipizzaner*; not *Lipitza*; BS in USA 1968 (Lipizzan), GB (Lipizzaner)
Liptako: see Yagha
Lithuanian: see Žemaitukai
Lithuanian Heavy Draft (Lithuania, USSR); dr; chestnut, also bay; orig. (1879 on) from Žemaitukai with Arab, Ardennes, Brabançon and Shire blood, graded (since 1923-25) to Swedish Ardennes (3 crosses); recog. 1963; Russ. *Litovskaya tyazhelovozaya* or *tyazheloupryazhnaya*
Liukiu: see Miyako, Yonaguni. [= Ryukyu]
Ljutomer Trotter (N.E. Slovenia, Yugoslavia); l; local type; orig. from American Trotter × Anglo-Arab
Llanero: see Venezuelan Criollo
[Lofoten] (Norway); py; sim. to Nordland
Logone: see Kirdi
[Loire] (C. France); local Percheron HB (1933-66)
Lokai (Tajikistan, USSR); l; some Iomud, Akhal-Teke, Karabair and Arab blood; bay, grey, chestnut *et al.*; Russ. *Lokaĭskaya*; orig. of Tajik Riding Horse
[Long Mynd] (Shropshire, England); py
[Losina] (Losa, Burgos, Spain); py
[Lovets] (Astrakhan, USSR); l; basically Kalmyk or Kazakh breed used to draw fish carts; recently crossed with Don or Orlov Trotter; Russ. *Lovetskaya*. [= hunter; *rybolovets* = fisher]
Lower Amazon: see Marajoaro
Łowicz (Warsaw, Poland); h.dr; local improved by Belgian and esp.

Ardennes, *c.* 1936-56; Pol. *Łowicki* or *Łowisko-sochaczowski*
Lublin (Poland); l.dr; orig. from pure and halfbred Arab with some blood of Thoroughbred, Halfbred and Anglo-Arab; Pol. *Lubelski kón szlachetny* (= *Lublin thoroughbred horse*)
Lublin-Kielce (Poland); orig. from Lublin and Kielce; combined with Kraków-Rzeszów to form Małopolski; Pol. *Lubelsko-Kielecki*
Lundy Pony (Lundy I, Great Britain); orig. from Welsh/Arab × New Forest (1928) with later Welsh and Connemara blood; BS 1971; rare
Lusitanian (S. Portugal); l.ri.dr; sim. to Andalusian; Port. *Lusitano*; syn. *Bético-lusitano, National, Peninsular, Portuguese*
Lusitanian-Galician pony: see Garrano
Luso-galiziano: see Garrano
Lyngen: see Nordland

Maaneghi: see Maneghi
Macassar Pony (S. Sulawesi, Indonesia); South-East Asia pony group
Macedonian Pony (S. Yugoslavia); Balkan Pony type, sim. to Bosnian Pony; Serbo-cro. *Makedonski brdski konj*; obs. syn. *Vardarska*
Maiche: see Comtois
[Maine] (N.W. France); local HB (1907-66) for Percheron; syn. *Mayenne* (Fr. *Mayennais*)
Makra (Sind, Pakistan); l; colour type (dun); rare
Malakan (N.E. Turkey); l-h; orig. from native Russian, Orlov, Bityug, *et al.*; not *Molokan*; rare. [*cf.* Malakan cattle]
Mallani: see Marwari
Małopolski (S.E. Poland); l.dr; orig. 1963 by combining Lublin-Kielce (Pol. *Lubelsko-Kielecki*) and Kraków-Rzeszów (Pol. *Krakowsko-rzeszowski*); HB
Maneghi; strain of Arab; not *Maaneghi, Man'aqi, Manegi, Munighi, Muniki*
Mangalarga (Minas Gerais and São Paulo, Brazil); l; orig. in mid-19th c. from Altér (Port.) and Brazilian native (Crioulo); BS 1934; vars: Marchador or Mineiro (Minas Gerais) and Paulisto (São Paulo) (lighter, leggier, more recent)
Manipuri Pony (Manipur and Assam, India); South-East Asia pony type
[Manx] (Isle of Man); py
Marajoaro (Marajo I, Brazil); var. of Northeastern; syn. *Baixo-Amazona* (= *Lower Amazon*)
Marchador (Minas Gerais, Brazil); orig. var. of Mangalarga; BS; syn. *Mineiro*
Maremmana (Maremma, Tuscany, Italy); l.pa.dr.ri; usu. chestnut or bay; Oriental orig; var: Monterufoli Pony; rare

[Marismeña] (marshes of lower R. Guadalquivir, Spain); former strain
of Andalusian; not *Marismenna*. [Sp. *marisma* = marsh]
Marwari (Rajasthan, India); l; sim. to Kathiawari; usu. chestnut or bay,
also grey or brown, occ. pied or cream; syn. *Mallani*
Masuren: see Mazury
Mayennais, Mayenne: see Maine
Mazari (Afghanistan); l.
Mazury (N.E. Poland); orig. from East Prussian (Trakehner); combined
with Poznań to form Wielkopolski; Pol. *Mazurski*; not *Masuren*
Mbai: see Kirdi
M'Bayar (Baol, Senegal); py; bay or chestnut; ? degenerate Barb; orig.
(with Fleuve) of Fouta. [M'Bayar is adj. from Baol]
M'Baye (Chad): see Kirdi Pony
[Mecklenburg] (Germany); l; orig. from local graded to Hanoverian (and
Holstein); Ger. *Mecklenburger Warmblut*; absorbed by Edles Warmblut
1960s
Megrel: see Mingrelian
Mérens Pony (Ariège, S. France); dr.pa.ri; black; BS 1947; Fr. *Race
ariègeoise de Mérens*; rare
Mexican Pony (Mexico); Criollo type
Mezen (N.E. Archangel and Komi, USSR); North Russian Pony group;
Russ. *Mezenskaya*; not *Mezien*; rare
Mezőhegyes Halfbred (Hungary, also in Romania); l.dr; strain of English
Halfbred; orig. from Thoroughbred stallions 'Furioso' (bought 1841)
and 'North Star' (bought 1852); Hung. *Mezőhegyesi félvér*; syn. *Furioso-
Northstar*; rare
Middle Kolyma (Yakutia, USSR); var. of Yakut; Russ. *Srednekolym-
skaya*; syn. *Verkhoyansk*
Midilli: see Mytilene Pony
Mijertinian: see Somali Pony
Mimoso (Brazil): see Pantaneiro
Mineiro: see Marchador
Mingrelian (W. Georgia, USSR); py; Russ. *Mingrel'skaya* or *Megrel'-
skaya*; rare
Minho Pony, Minhota: see Garrano
miniature horse: see American Miniature, Falabella Pony
[Minusinsk] (S. Krasnoyarsk, USSR); l.
Mira Pony (Coimbra, Portugal); Port. *garrano de Mira*
Misaki (cape Toi, S. Kyushu, Japan); var. of Japanese Native; usu.
brown; nearly extinct
Missouri Fox Trotting Horse (Ozark hills, Missouri, USA); usu. sorrel;
BS 1948
Miyako (Ryu-Kyu Is, Japan); var. of Japanese Native; nearly extinct

Moldavian (Romania); l-py; former var. of Romanian; Rom. *Moldovene-scă*

Molokan: see Malakan

Mongolian (Mongolia, and N, N.E. and N.W. China); py.ri.dr.d.m; all colours; syn. *Mongolian Pony*; obs. syn. *China Pony*; var: Ujumqin; orig. of Sanhe

Mongolian tarpan, Mongolian wild: see Przewalski horse

MONGOLIAN TYPE; inc. Bashkir, Ili, Kazakh, Kirgiz, Mongolian, Siberian Pony; sim. to Northern type; syn. *Tartar, Tatar*

Monterufoli Pony (upper Cecine valley, Pisa, Tuscany, Italy); var. of Maremmana; It. *Cavallino di Monterufoli* or *Monterufolina*; nearly extinct

Moospferd: see Feldmoching

Morab (USA); Morgan × Arab cross named 1920s, breed selected since 1955, ♂ may be Morab, Arab or Morgan; BS 1973

Morgan (Vermont, USA); l; sim. to American Trotter; HB 1891, BS 1909; BS also in Canada 1968, GB; var: Chunk Morgan. [from Justin Morgan, a sire of Thoroughbred orig. born in 1793]

Morocco Spotted (midwest, USA); l.ri; colour type; orig. from Hackney, American Saddle Horse, French Coach *et al.*; BS 1935. [reputed orig. from Moroccan Barb]

Morochuca; var. of Peruvian Criollo; mountain py

[Morvan] (Côte d'Or, France); Fr. *Morvandeaux*; orig. of Auxois

Mossi (Burkina Faso); local var. of Dongola-Barb orig.

M'Par (Cayor, Senegal); py; bay or chestnut; ? degenerate Barb; syn. *Cayor*

Mulassière: see Poitou

Mull: see Gocan

Munighi. Muniki: see Maneghi

Münsterland: see Dülmen Pony

Mura (R. Mur, N.W. Yugoslavia); var. of Yugoslav Draft; *cf.* Mur Island (Hungary)

Muraközi: see Mur Island

Murgese (Murge, Apulia, Italy); l.dr.ri; usu. black, also grey; orig. from Oriental × local

Mur Island (Yugoslavia-Hungary); l.dr; sim. to Pinkafeld; Hung. *Muraközi*, Ger. *Murinsulaner*; *cf.* Mura (Yugoslavia); nearly extinct

mustang (USA); feral; chiefly Spanish orig; orig. of cow pony, Indian Pony; remnants = broomtail; for BSs see American Mustang, Indian, Spanish Barb, Spanish Mustang. [Sp. *mesteño*]

Muzakiya, Muzekja: see Myzeqeja

Mytilene Pony (N.W. Anatolia, Turkey); local var; Turk. *Midilli*

Myzeqeja; var. of Albanian; not *Muzakiya, Muzekja, Mysekeja, Myzeqe*

Nagai: see Nogai

[Namaqua Pony] (N.W. Cape Province, S. Africa); sim. to Basuto Pony; orig. from Cape Horse in early 19th c.

[Nanbu] (N.E. Honshiu, Japan); var. of Japanese Native; not *Nambu*

Nanfan: see Tibetan Pony

[Narragansett Pacer] (Rhode Island, USA)

Narym (Tomsk, Siberia, USSR); var. of Siberian Pony; rare

National (Portugal): see Lusitanian

Navarra, Navarre (Spain): see Pottok

Navarre (France): see Tarbes

Nefza Pony (Tunisia)

Netherlands Draft: see Dutch Draft

Netherlands Trotter; orig. from American and French Trotters with some Orlov Trotter blood; BS 1879, HB; Du. *Nederlandse Draver*; syn. *Dutch Trotter*

New Cleveland Bay: see Yorkshire Coach Horse

New Forest Pony (S. Hampshire, England); BS 1891, HB 1910; HB also in France, Germany

Newfoundland Pony (Canada); HB

New Kirgiz (Kirgizia, USSR); l.m.d; chestnut or bay; orig. from Kirgiz improved in 19th and 20th c. (esp. since 1919) by Don and saddle breeds; recog. 1954; Russ. *Novokirgizskaya*; 3 types according to size, and amount of Kirgiz blood

Nigerian: see West African Dongola

[Nivernais] (Nièvre, C. France); local Percheron HB (1880-1966)

[Nogai] (S. Ukraine); orig. of Cossack (= Old Don) and of Black Sea; not *Nagai, Nogay*

Nogali: see Somali Pony

Noma (Shikoku, Japan); var. of Japanese Native; nearly extinct

Nonius (S.E. Europe); l.dr; brown, dark brown, or black; orig. from Anglo-Norman stallion 'Nonius Senior' born 1810 and used at Mezőhegyes, Hungary, from 1816 on light mares; Hung. *Nóniusz*

Nooitgedacht Pony (E. Transvaal. S. Africa); orig. (1952 on) from Basuto Pony with some Boer and Arab blood at Nooitgedacht Research Station nr Ermelo; BS 1969

Noram Trotter (France, Italy and Austria)

Nordbag, Nordfjord: see Fjord

Nordkirchen Pony (Münsterland, Westphalia, Germany); orig. from Dülmen Pony crossed with Polish Konik in 1920s and later with Arab and Welsh Pony; Ger. *Nordkirchner*

Nordland (N. Norway); py; Northern type sim. to Lofoten; syn. *Lyngen* (Nor. *Lyngshest*); rare. [= northland]

Norfolk: see Hackney

Norfolk-Breton: see Breton Post-horse
Norfolk Hackney, Norfolk Roadster, Norfolk Trotter: see Hackney
Noric (Austria); h.dr; usu. brown, bay or chestnut, also black, grey or
    spotted; Ger. *Noriker* or *Norisches Kaltblut*; syn. *Pinzgau*; pure Noric
    in S.E. Bavaria, Germany, called *Pinzgau* (to 1914) or *heavy Noric*
    (1914-34) and var. in S.W. Bavaria with Warmblood influence called
    Oberland (to 1914) or *light Noric* (1914-34); now combined and called
    Oberland (1934-45) or South German Coldblood (Ger. *Süddeutsches
    Kaltblut*) *q.v.*; var: Abtenauer. [Roman Province of Noricum = Austria
    and S. Bavaria]
Norman: see Anglo-Norman
[Norman Coach Horse] (France); orig. 1806-60 from Hackney and
    Thoroughbred × native; Fr. *Carrossier normand*; syn. *Norman, Nor-
    mandy Carriage Horse, Old Norman*; orig. of Anglo-Norman, Norman
    Cob, and French Trotter
Norman Cob (France); l-h.dr.m; HB; orig. in 20th c. from Norman
    Coach Horse; Fr. *Cob (Normand)*
Normand, Normandy: see Anglo-Norman
Norman Trotter: see French Trotter
Northeastern (N.E. Brazil); dark bay (40%), grey (25%), isabella or
    light bay (15%), sorrel (15%); Port. orig. from 16th c. on; BS 1974;
    Port. *Nordestino*; syn. *Curraleiro, Sertanejo (= inland)*; var: Marajoaro;
    saddle (*sela*) and pack (*quartau*) types
NORTHERN (N. Eurasia); sim. to konik type to the west and Mongolian
    type to the east; inc. Estonian Native, Finnish, Lyngen, North Russian
    Pony; syn. *Northern Pony*
Northern Ardennais; var. of French Ardennais; HB 1919; Fr. *Ardennais
    du Nord*; syn. *Trait du Nord*
Northland: see Nordland
North Russian Pony (USSR); Northern type; inc. Karelian, Mezen, Ob,
    Pechora, Tavda, Vyatka
North Spanish Pony (Spain); syn. *Cantabrian Pony* (Sp. *Cantabrica*);
    inc. Asturian, Galician, [Lebaniega], [Losina], and Pottok
North Star: see Mezőhegyes Halfbred
North Swedish (Sweden); l.dr; orig. 1850-1900 from Døle (Norway) ×
    improved local; HB 1903, BS 1924; Swe. *Nordsvensk häst*
North Swedish Trotter; usu. chestnut or brown; separated from North
    Swedish 1964; HB 1971; Swe. *Nordsvensk travare*
Norwegian Dun, Norwegian Fjord, Norwegian Pony: see Fjord
Norwegian Trotter: see Døle Trotter
Novokirgiz: see New Kirgiz
Nowosądecki, Nowy Sącz: see Sącz

Ob (W. Siberia, USSR); North Russian Pony group; Russ. *Priobskaya*; syn. *Ostyak-Vogul*; rare

Oberland (Germany): see South German Coldblood; till 1934 used only for light var. of Noric

[Obva] (W. Siberia, USSR); py; Russ. *Obvinskaya*

Oirot: see Altai

Oldenburg (Germany); l.[dr]; sim. to East Friesian; bay, bay-brown or black; some Thoroughbred blood since late 19th c; BS; Ger. *Oldenburger Warmblut*; syn. *Bovenlander* (Netherlands); orig. of Gelderland and Groningen (Netherlands), Austrian Warmblood, Saxony Warmblood and Silesian (Warmblood); nearly extinct

Old English Black, Old English War Horse: see Great Horse

Old Norman: see Norman Coach Horse

[Onega] (Karelia, USSR); py; var. of Karelian; Russ. *Onezhskaya*

Onezhskaya: see Onega

ORIENTAL; syn. *Eastern*; inc. Akhal-Teke, Arab, Barb, Persian Arab, Syrian, Turkish Arab, *etc.*

Orlov-American Trotter, Orlovo-Amerikanskiĭ rysak: see Russian Trotter

[Orlov-Rostopchin] (USSR); l; orig. in late 19th c. from Orlov Saddle Horse and Rostopchin; Russ. *Orlovo-Rostopchinskaya*; syn. *Russian Saddle Horse* (Russ. *Russkaya krovnaya verkhovaya*); absorbed by Ukrainian Saddle Horse since 1945

[Orlov Saddle Horse] (Russia); Anglo-Arab orig. in late 18th c; orig. (with Rostopchin) of Orlov-Rostopchin; Russ. *Orlovskaya verkhovaya*; syn. *Orlov Riding Horse*

Orlov Trotter (USSR); l; grey, bay, black or chestnut; orig. 1775-1845 by Count Orlov at Khrenov stud from Arab, Thoroughbred and Persian, with Danish Saddle, Dutch Draft, Mecklenburg, and Hackney blood; HB 1927; Russ. *Orlovskiĭ rysak*; syn. (*c.* 1920-49) *Russian Trotter*; not *Orloff*; orig. (with American Trotter) of Russian Trotter

Østland: see Døle

Ostyak-Vogul: see Ob

overo; pied horse with colour on back; recessive gene; syn. *pio bajo*

Padana: see Cremonese

Pagan: see Bhirum, Kirdi

Paint (USA); BS 1962 for pied colour type (overo or tobiano) of Paint, Quarter Horse or Thoroughbred breeding; *cf.* Pinto

Palatinate: see Zweibrücken

Palomino (USA); l; colour type (golden with white mane and tail, *i.e.* golden Isabella); HB 1932, BS 1941; not *Palamino*; BS also in Canada 1952, GB

Palouse: see Appaloosa

Panje: see Polish Konik

Pantaneiro (N. Mato Grosso, Brazil); l; usu. grey (45%), bay (17%), black-and-white (13%) or brown (10%); BS 1972; syn. *Bahiano* (from Bahia), *Mimoseano* (from Mimoso). [Port. *pantanais* = flooded lands]

Parsano: see Persano

Paso (USA); l; BSs (Paso Fino 1973 and Peruvian Paso 1967) for same horse; any colour; gait is a broken pace; orig. from Criollo (Caribbean, Colombian, Peruvian)

Paulisto (São Paulo, Brazil); var. of Mangalarga

Pechora (Komi, USSR); North Russian Pony group; Russ. *Pechorskaya*; rare

Pegu: see Shan Pony

Peneia Pony (Peloponnese, Greece); var. of Greek Pony

Peninsular: see Lusitanian

Percheron (Le Perche, Normandy, France); h.dr.m; grey, white or black; HB 1883, local HBs (till 1966): Augeron, Berrichon, Bourbonnais, Loire, Maine, Nivernais, Saône-et-Loire; BS in Great Britain 1918, USA 1876, Canada 1907, HB in S. Africa 1940, USSR, Spain

[Persano] (Salerno, Italy); l; state stud founded 1763; predominantly Sardinian, Salernitana, Arab and Thoroughbred blood; not *Parsano*

Persian: see Iranian

Persian Arab (Iran); l.

Peruvian Criollo (Peru); vars: Andean (inc. Morochuca), Chola, and Costeña; BS in Canada

Peruvian Paso: see Paso

petiço (Rio Grande do Sul, Santa Caterina, Paraná and S. of São Paulo, Brazil) = small horse or pony

Pfalz, Pfälzisches: see Zweibrücken

Philippine Pony; South-East Asia pony group with foreign blood; usu. bay, brown, grey or roan; Sp. *Filipino*

Pindos Pony; var. of Greek Pony; syn. *Pindhos, Pindus*

[Pinkafeld] (Austria-Hungary); h; sim. to Mur Island; orig. var. of Hungarian Draft; Hung. *Pinkafö*

Pinto (western USA); l. or py; BS 1956 for pied colour of any breed type; inc. overo and tobiano; cf. Paint. [Sp. = painted]

Pinzgau: see Noric

Plantation Walking Horse: see Tennessee Walking Horse

Plateau Persian (Iran); l; inc. Bakhtiari, Basseri, Jaf, Qashqai, Shirazi, Sistani and Persian Arab

Pleven (Bulgaria); l; sim. to East Bulgarian with addition of Anglo-Arab and Gidran ♂♂ in its formation; Bulg. *Plevenska*; syn. *Plevna*

Po: see Cremonese

Podlaski: see Kopczyk Podlaski

Poitou (France); h.dr; ? orig. from Dutch; HB 1885; Fr. *Poitevine mulassière* (= *mule producer*); rare

Polesian (Byelorussia, USSR); py; Konik type; Russ. *Polesskaya*; not *Polesié, Polessian, Polessye*; rare

Polish Konik (Poland); Konik type; Ger. *Panjepferd*; syn. *Polish Pony, Polish Primitive*; rare. [= small horse]

Polo Pony (England); l; Arab or Thoroughbred × pony

Pony of the Americas (USA); BS 1954 for ponies with Appaloosa spotting; *cf.* Kanata Pony; not *Pony of America*

Portuguese: see Lusitanian

Portuguese Galician: see Garrano

Portuguese ponies: see Azores, Garrano, Mira, Sorraia

[Posavina] (R. Sava, N.W. Yugoslavia); l.dr; var. of Yugoslav Draft (based on Buša Pony); bay, black, chestnut, white or wild type; Serbo-cro. *Posavska*; extinct before 1982. [R. Sava valley]

Pottok (Basque country, France and Spain, and Navarre, Spain); py; semi-feral; usu. black or bay; BS France, HB Spain; pronounced *Potiok*; pl. *Pottokak*; syn. *Basque* (Sp. *Vasca*), *Basque-Navarre Pony* (Sp. *Jaca Vasca-Navarra* or *Poney Vasco-Navarro*), *de la Barranca, Navarre Pony* (Sp. *Jaca Navarra*); not *Pottak, Pottock*; rare in France

Poznań (Poland); l.dr.ri; orig. from Trakehner × Polish Konik with Thoroughbred blood; combined with Mazury to form Wielkopolski; Pol. *Poznański*

Printer: see Quarter Horse

Priob: see Ob

Przedświt (Poland); halfbred strain derived from Thoroughbred stallion Przedświt in Hungary (also in Czechoslovakia)

Przewalski horse (Central Asia); = *Equus ferus przewalskii* Poliakov; py; red-brown with light underparts, dark back-stripe, shoulder-stripe and leg bars; erect mane; syn. *Asiatic wild horse, Mongolian wild horse, Mongolian tarpan, taki*; ? orig. of domestic horse (*E. 'caballus'* Linnaeus); not *Prejvalsky's, Prezwalski, Prjevalsky's, Przevalskii's, Przevalsky, Przewalsky's, Przhevalski's, Przrewalskii's*; extinct in wild, rare in captivity; BS in USA

p.s.c, p.s.i.: see Thoroughbred

Puno Pony (Chile); feral; Sp. orig. like Bagual (Argentina) and Criollo

Puro sangre de carrera, Puro sangue inglese: see Thoroughbred

Qashqai; var. of Plateau Persian; not *Quashquai*

Qatgani (Afghanistan); l.

Quarter Horse (Texas, USA); l; orig. in 18th, revived in 20th c, from

Thoroughbred, Criollo, *et al.*; BS 1940; syn. *Billie, Cold Deck, Copper Bottom. Kentucky Whip, Printer, Rondo, Shilo, Steeldust*; not *American Quarter Running Horse*; BS also in Canada 1956, GB. [from quarter-mile races of colonial period]

Quarter Pony (USA); BS 1976

Rajshahi Pony (Bangladesh)

Ranger, Rangerbred: see Colorado Ranger

Rastopchin: see Rostopchin

Rhenish (Germany); h.dr; usu. grey, bay or chestnut; orig. from Belgian; BS 1876; Ger. *Rheinisches Kaltblut* or *Rheinisch-deutsches Kaltblut*; syn. *Rhenish-Belgian, Rhenish-German, Rhenish-Westphalian* (Ger. *Rheinisch-Westfälisches*), *Rhineland Heavy Draft*; strains in Saxony, Silesia and Westphalia; orig. of Black Forest; rare

Rhineland: see Rhenish

Rila Mountain; var. of Bulgarian Native

Rio Grande do Sul: see Crioulo

Rodopi (Bulgaria)

Romanian (Romania); l. or py; Rom. *Rasa românească*; former vars: Dobrogea, Moldavian, Romanian Mountain, Transylvanian; not *Roumanian, Rumanian*

Romanian Light Draft; Rom. *Semigreu Românesca*

Romanian Mountain; py; former var. of Romanian; Rom. *Calul românesc de munte*

Romanian Trotter; orig. from American Trotter Rom. *Trapaș românesc*

[Ronda]; former strain of Andalusian; Sp. *Rondeña*

Rondo: see Quarter Horse

[Rostopchin] (Russia); l; Anglo-Arab orig. in early 19th c; orig. (with Orlov Saddle Horse) of Orlov-Rostopchin; not *Rastopchin*

Rottal (Bavaria, Germany); l.[dr]; usu. bay, also black; orig. from local, improved by Anglo-Norman, Thoroughbred and Cleveland Bay in 19th c. and by Oldenburg in 20th; HB; Ger. *Rottaler Warmblut*; nearly extinct

[Rumelian Pony] (Balkans); generic term for ponies in former European provinces of Turkey

Russ (= *Skogsruss*): see Gotland Pony

Russian Ardennes: see Russian Heavy Draft

Russian Clydesdale: see Vladimir Heavy Draft

Russian Heavy Draft (USSR); h.dr.d; usu. chestnut, also brown or bay; orig. (since mid-19th c.) from Ardennes × local; smaller than Ardennes; Russ. *Russkiĭ tyazhelovoz* or *Russkaya tyazhelovoznaya*; syn. *Russian Ardennes* (till 1952), *Russian Draft*; Ural and Ukrainian vars.

Russian Saddle Horse: see Orlov-Rostopchin
Russian tarpan: see tarpan
Russian Trotter (USSR); l; bay, black or chestnut, occ. grey; orig. 1890-1926 from Orlov and American Trotters; HB 1927, recog. 1949; Russ. *Russkiĭ rysak* or *Russkaya rysistaya*; syn. *Orlov-American Trotter, Russo-American Trotter* (*c.* 1920-49)
Russian Trotter (1920-49): see Orlov Trotter
Russo-American Trotter (1920-49): see Russian Trotter
Ryukyu: see Miyako, Yonaguni
Rzeszów: see Kraków-Rzeszów

Sable Island Pony (Nova Scotia, Canada); feral since at least 1739; ♂♂ of various breeds introduced 1800-1945; bay, brown, black or sorrel; rare
Sächsisch: see Saxon
Sącz (Nowy Sącz, Kraków, Poland); l.dr.ri; inc. in Kraków-Rzeszów; orig. from Hungarian Halfbred in early 20th c; Pol. *Sądecki* or *Nowosądecki*
Saddlebred: see American Saddle Horse
Sądecki: see Sącz
Saglawi; strain of Arab; not *Saklawi, Seglawi, Siglavy*
Sahel (Mali); var. of West African Barb with Arab blood
[St Lawrence] (Canada); h; orig. from French Canadian, Shire, Clydesdale, *et al.*
Saishu Island: see Cheju
Saklawi: see Saglawi
Salernitana (Salerno, Campania, Italy); l; orig. from local with Andalusian and Arab blood and with Thoroughbred from early 1900s; nearly extinct
Samogitian: see Žemaitukai
[Samolaca] (Sondrio, Lombardy, Italy)
Sandalwood Pony (Sumba, Indonesia); South-East Asia pony group; Du. *Sandelhoutpaard*; syn. *Soemba, Sumbanese*; not *Sandelwood*
Sanfratellana (San Fratello, Messina, Sicily, Italy); l; semi-feral; usu. bay; orig. from local with Oriental, Thoroughbred, Maremmana and Nonius blood; rare
Sanhe (N.E. Inner Mongolia, China); l.ri.dr; red-brown, black, brindle, grey or isabella; orig. from Russian breeds × local Mongolian; W.G. *Sanho*, Russ. *San'khe*; obs. syn. *Hailar* (W.G. *Hai-la-erh*), *Sanpeitze*. [from Sanhochan]
Sankt Märgener Fuchse: see Black Forest
Sanpeitze: see Sanhe; W.G. *San-pei-tzŭ;* not *Sanpaitze, Sappapaitze*

[Saône-et-Loire] (C. France); local HB (1927-66) for Percheron and Ardennes

Sara: see Kirdi

[Sardinian] (Sardinia, Italy); l; usu. bay, chestnut, or grey; orig. from Arab and Thoroughbred × local in late 18th and early 19th c. (native had Andalusian blood in 16th c. and various European halfblood introductions in late 17th and early 18th c); It. *Sarda*; syn. *Arabo-Sarda* or *Sardo-Arab*; since 1936 crossed with Thoroughbred to form Anglo-Arabo-Sarda

Sardo-Arab: see Sardinian

Sava: see Posavina

Saxony Coldblood (Germany); strain of Rhenish; Ger. *Sächsisches Kaltblut*; rare

[Saxony Warmblood] (Germany); orig. from Hanoverian and Oldenburg; Ger. *Sächsisches Warmblut*; absorbed by Heavy Warmblood 1960s

Schlesisch: see Silesian

Schleswig (Germany); h.dr; usu. chestnut; orig. from Jutland × Suffolk; BS 1891; Ger. *Schleswiger*; syn. *Schleswig Heavy Draft*; rare

Schleswig-Holstein: see Holstein

Schweike: see Sweyki

Schwyz: see Einsiedeln

Scotch Pony: see Highland Pony

Seglawi: see Saglawi

Seistan: see Sistani

Selle français: see French Saddlebred

Seminole (Florida, USA); Indian pony type; syn. *Cracker*; rare

Senne (Westphalia, Germany); orig. from semi-wild (till 1870) improved by Spanish and Oriental; Ger. *Senner*; nearly extinct

Sertanejo: see Northeastern

[Seville]; former strain of Andalusian; Sp. *Sevillana*

Shagya Arab (Hungary); strain of Arab with Hungarian blood; syn. *Bábolna Arab*; rare

Shan Pony (Burma); South-East Asia pony group; syn. *Burmese Pony*, *Pegu*

Shetland Pony (Scotland); dwarf; BS 1890, HB 1891; syn. *Sheltie*; BS also in Australia, Belgium 1954, Denmark, France 1958, Germany 1942, Netherlands 1937, USA 1888

Shilo: see Quarter Horse

Shirazi (Fars, Iran); l; syn. *Darashoori*

Shire (Midland shires, England); h.dr; sim. to Clydesdale; black, brown, bay or grey; orig. from Great Horse; BS 1878, HB 1882; syn. *English Cart-horse*; BS also in USA 1885

Shirvan (Azerbaijan, USSR); l.

Shishan Pony: see Guangxi Pony

Siamese Pony: see Thai Pony

Siberian Pony (USSR); Mongolian type; inc. Altai, Buryat, Narym, Tuva, Yakut; orig. of Kuznetsk

Sicilian (Sicily, Italy); l; often bay; orig. from Oriental × native; see also Sanfratellana; rare

Siebenburgisch: see Transylvanian

Siglavy: see Saglawi

Sikang Pony (E. Tibet and W. Sichuan, China); pa; often white or grey; ? orig. from Sining (or Tibetan) × South China Pony; syn. *Hsiangcheng, Hsi-k'ang*; not *Sikong*; not now recog.

Silesian (S.W. Poland); l.dr; orig. from Oldenburg, East Friesian and Hanoverian; Pol. *Śląski*, Ger. *Schlesisches Warmblut* (= *Silesian Warmblood*)

[Silesian Coldblood]; strain of Rhenish (1858 on); Ger. *Schlesisches Kaltblut*

Simmental: see Erlenbach

Sining (E. Qinghai and S.W. Gansu, China); ri.pa.py; usu. black, also chestnut, grey or dun; orig. from Mongolian × Tibetan Pony; W.G. *Hsi-ning*; not now recog.

Sistani; var. of Plateau Persian; not *Seistan*

Skogsbagge, Skogshäst, Skogsruss: see Gotland Pony

Skyros Pony (Greece); var. of Greek pony; white, dun, chestnut or bay

Slovakian Mountain (Czechoslovakia); Sl. *Slovenský horský*; orig. from Czech Coldblood × Hutsul

Smudisch: see Žemaitukai

Soemba: see Sandalwood Pony

Sokółka (Białystok, Poland); l-h.dr; usu. chestnut; orig. (1922 on) from Ardennes, Belgian and Breton Post-horse × local; Pol. *Sokólski*

Somali Pony (Somalia); usu. chestnut or grey; inc. Dor, Mijertinian or Daror, Nogali; rare

Songhaï (Niger bend, Mali); l. to py; var. of West African Dongola with Barb blood; syn. *Sonraï*

Sorraia (R. Sorraia, Spain and Portugal); py; usu. dun with dorsal stripe and zebra stripes on legs; Sp. *Sorraiana*

South African: see Cape Horse

South China ponies (mts of S.W. China); pa.dr; South-East Asia pony group; inc. Guangxi, Guizhou, Jiangchang, Lijiang

SOUTH-EAST ASIA PONY; ? orig from Mongolian and Arab; inc. Batak and Gayoe (Sumatra), Cambodian, Cheju and Taejung (Korea), Japanese, Kumingan (Java), Macassar (Sulawesi), Manipuri (Assam), Philippine, Sandalwood (Sumba), Shan (Burma), Thai, South China, Sumbawa, Timor, Vietnamese

Southern Barbarian: see Tibetan Pony

South German Coldblood (S. Bavaria and Württemberg, Germany); h-l.dr; usu. bay or chestnut; orig. from Noric with some Warmblood infusion; HB; Ger. *Süddeutsches Kaltblut*; syn. (1934-45) *Oberland* (Ger. *Oberländer Kaltblut*)

Soviet Heavy Draft (C. European USSR, esp. Mordovia and Pochinok); h.dr.d; usu. chestnut, brown or bay; orig. from local mares graded to Brabançon since late 19th c; recog. 1952; Russ. *Sovetskiĭ tyazhelovoz* or *Sovetskaya tyazhelovozskaya*; syn. *Soviet Draft*

Spanish: see Andalusian

Spanish Barb (Oshoto, Wyoming, USA); any colour except tobiano; BS 1972 for horse of Barb ancestry (mustang, Criollo and African Barb)

Spanish Mustang (western USA); BS 1957 for mustangs of pure Spanish ancestry

Spanish ponies (Spain): see Canary Island Pony, North Spanish Pony

Spanish Trotter (Balearic Is, Spain); HB; Sp. *Trotador español*

Spiti Pony (Kangra valley, N.E. Punjab, India); usu. grey or dun, occ. bay or black

Spotted: see Appaloosa, British Spotted, British Spotted Pony, Colorado Ranger, Knabstrup, Morocco Spotted, Kanata Pony, Pony of the Americas

Standardbred (USA); official name for American Trotter

Stara Planina; var. of Bulgarian Native

Steeldust: see Quarter Horse

[Strelets] (S.E. Ukraine, USSR); l; Arab and Thoroughbred orig. in late 19th c. at Strelets state stud; orig. of Tersk

Suffolk (E. England); h.dr; chestnut; BS 1877, HB 1880; syn. *Suffolk Punch*; BS also in USA 1911; rare

Sulawesi: see Macassar Pony

Sulebawa (Nigeria); var. of West African Barb; ? orig. from Niger

Sumba Pony: see Sandalwood

Sumbawa Pony (Indonesia); South-East Asia pony group; Du. *Soembawa*; var: Bimanese

Sunicho: see Bolivian Pony

Swedish Ardennes (Sweden); h.dr; orig. from Ardennes (imported since 1873) × local; BS and HB 1901; Swe. *Svensk Ardenner*

Swedish Halfbred; ri; orig. based on East Prussian (Trakehner), Hanoverian and Thoroughbred; syn. *Swedish Warmblood*

[Sweyki] (East Prussia); Ger. *Schweike*; orig. (with Thoroughbred and Trakehner) of East Prussian; cf. Konik

[Swiss Halfblood] (Switzerland); orig. from Anglo-Norman, Holstein, Württemberg, Hackney, *et al.* × local; vars: Einsiedeln, Erlenbach

Syrian (Syria); l; Arab type

Sztum (N. Poland); h.dr; orig. end of 19th and early 20th c. from Belgian and Rhenish × local; Pol. *Sztumski*

Taejung (Korea); South-East Asia Pony group
Taishu Pony (Tsushima I, Japan); var. of Japanese Native; nearly extinct
Tajik Riding Horse (Tajikistan, USSR); l; breed group; orig. 1953-83 from Arab, Thoroughbred *et al.* × Lokai; Russ. *Tadzhikskaya verkhovaya*
Takara: see Tokara
taki: see Przewalski horse
Tanghan (Nepal and Bhutan); ri; larger var. of Bhotia Pony; Nepali *Tāṅan* or *Tāgan*; not *Tangan, Tangum, Tangun.* [Tanghastan—old name for mts of Bhutan]
Tarai Pony (S. Nepal); usu. bay, occ. white with dark skin; not *Terai*
[Tarbes] (Pyrenees, France); l; usu. dark brown or bay; orig. from Arab and Thoroughbred × Andalusian; Fr. *Tarbésan, Tarbeux*; syn. *Bigourdan* (from Bigorre), *Navarre*; not *Tarbenian*; disappeared by crossing with Anglo-Arab and Breton
[tarpan] (E. Europe) = *Equus ferus gmelini* Boddaert; mouse-grey with black back-stripe; syn. *European wild horse, Russian tarpan*; extinct *c.* 1813 in Poland, 1876 in Ukraine, 1918 in captivity; orig. of domestic horse, *E. 'caballus'*. [Kirgiz]
'tarpan', bred-back; Poland—orig. from Polish Konik in 1920s; Germany—orig. from Iceland Pony, Gotland Pony and Przewalski horse at Munich zoo in 1930s; BS in USA 1971
tarpan, Mongolian: see Przewalski horse
Tartar, Tatar: see Mongolian type
Tattu (Nepal); pa; smallest var. of Bhotia Pony; Nepali *Tāttu*
Tatung, Ta-t'ung: see Datong Pony
Tavda (W. Siberia); North Russian pony group; Russ. *Tavdinskaya*; not *Tawda*; rare
T.B., T.B.E.: see Thoroughbred
Tcherarani: see Chenarani
Tennessee Walking Horse (USA); l; orig. in late 19th and early 20th c. from Morgan, American Saddle Horse, American Trotter, and Thoroughbred; BS 1938; syn. *Plantation Walking Horse, Tennessee Walker*
Terai: see Tarai
Tersk (N. Caucasus, USSR); l; silver-grey, bay or chestnut; orig. at Tersk stud in 19th c. from Strelets × Arab, Don, and Kabarda, and at Stavropol stud 1920-40s; recog. 1949; Russ. *Terskaya*; not *Terky*
Thai Pony (Thailand); South-East Asia pony group; syn. *Siamese Pony*

Thorcheron Hunter (USA); Thoroughbred × Percheron; BS 1974

Thoroughbred (England); l.ri; orig. from Oriental (chiefly Arab) × local British ♀♀ in 17th and early 18th c; HB 1791, BS 1917; syn. *English Racehorse, English Thoroughbred, T.B., T.B.E.*; Ger. *Englisches Vollblut*, Fr. *Pur-sang anglais*, It. *Puro sangue inglese* or *p.s.i.*, Sp. *Puro sangre de carrera* or *p.s.c.*, Russ. *(Angliĭskaya) chistokrovnaya verkhovaya*; BS also in Argentina, Australia, Canada, Czechoslovakia, Greece, Ireland, Italy, Japan, Netherlands 1879, New Zealand, Poland, Sweden, USA 1894 (HB 1868), HB also in France 1833, Germany 1847, S. Africa 1906, Spain, USSR

Tibetan Pony (Tibetan plateau, China); ri.pa; often yellow-dun with dark dorsal stripe; sim. to Bhotia Pony but more slender; syn. *Nanfan* (= *Southern Native*); not *Thibetan*

Tieling Harness (Liaoning, China); dr; in formation from Soviet breeds × local; syn. *Tieling*

Timor Pony (Indonesia); South-East Asia pony group; syn. *Flores*

[Tiree] (Scotland); var. of Hebridean Pony

tobiano; pied horse with black on belly and white back; dominant gene; syn. *pio alto.* [Don Rafael Tobias bred such horses in Brazil *c.* 1846]

Toby (USA); BS for 'real' Appaloosa, not merely a colour type

Togara: see Tokara

Togo Pony: see Koto-Koli

Tokara Pony; small (island) var. of Japanese Native; usu. dark brown with darker mane and tail; imported from Kikai Island in Oshima group about 1900; not *Takara, Togara*; almost extinct

Tolfetana (Tolfa, Latium, Italy); l; often black or dark bay, also chestnut or grey; rare

[Tomsk] (Tomsk and Tobolsk, Siberia, USSR); orig. from local improved by trotter or W. European draft breeds; Russ. *Tomskaya*

Tori (Estonia, USSR); l.dr; chestnut or bay; orig. at Tori stud from Hackney × Estonian 1896-1926 with Breton Post-horse blood to 1970 and some Hanoverian and Trakehner blood in 1970s; Russ. *Toriĭskaya*; not *Toric*

Torodi (W. Niger); py; ? degenerate Barb

Toy horse: see Falabella Pony

TPR: see AITPR

Trait du Nord: see Northern Ardennais

Trakehner (Germany and USSR); l; chestnut, bay or grey; orig. from Trakehnen stud (E. Prussia) (chiefly Thoroughbred and Arab) founded 1732; HB 1878; used to grade up Sweyki 1787-1914; removed to W. Germany and USSR 1945; Russ. *Trakenenskaya*; obs. syn. *Ostpreussisches Warmblut Trakehner Abstammung* (= *E. Prussian warmblood of Trakehnen descent*); orig. of Mazury; BS in USA 1974, Canada, GB

Transbaikal: see Buryat
Trans-Don: see Don
Transylvanian; l; former var. of Romanian; ? orig. from Bessarabian ×
 Hungarian; Rom. *Transilvăneană*, Ger. *Siebenburgisch*; subvar: [Ialom-
 iţa]
Transylvanian Lowland (Romania); l.dr; orig. (1961 on) from Ardennes
 × Mezőhegyes Halfbred; Rom. *Tip de cal semigreu pentru Transilvania*
 TROTTER; inc. American, Baltic, Belgian, Cuban, Czech, Døle, French,
 German, Italian, Ljutomer, Netherlands, North Swedish, Orlov,
 Romanian, Russian, Spanish
Tsushima: see Taishu
Turki: see Akhal-Teke, Iomud
Turkish Arab (Turkey); l; orig. from Arab and Anatolian Native
Turkmen, Turkmenian, Turkoman: see Akhal-Teke, Iomud
Tushin (E. Georgia, USSR); l-py; Russ. *Tushinskaya*; rare
Tuva (Siberia, USSR); py; Siberian pony group; orig. of Upper Yenisei;
 Russ. *Tuvinskaya*; rare, by crossing with Don and Budyonny
[Tuva Coach] (Tuva, USSR); l; orig. from Tuva improved by Kuznetsk
 and Chumysh (1870 on) and also by heavy Orlov Trotter and Don;
 Russ. *Tuvinskaya upryazhnaya*

Ujumqin (E. Inner Mongolia, China); l.ri.dr; improved var. of Mongo-
 lian; syn. *Wuchumutsin* (W.G. *Wu-chu-mu-ch'in*); not *Wuchuminsin*
Ukrainian Saddle Horse (Ukraine, USSR); l.ri; bay, chestnut or brown;
 orig. since 1945 from Hungarian Halfbred × Trakehner, Hanoverian
 and Thoroughbred; Russ. *Ukrainskaya verkhovaya porodnaya gruppa*
 (= *Ukrainian Riding breed group*); has absorbed Orlov-Rostopchin
 (Russian Saddle Horse)
Unmol (N.W. Punjab, Pakistan); l; usu. bay or grey; nearly extinct. [=
 priceless]
Upper Yenisei (Tuva, USSR); l; orig. 1893-1917 from local Tuva and
 Mongolian ♀♀ improved by Russian Trotter and draft breeds; Russ.
 Verkhne-eniseĭskaya; rare
Uzunyayla (E.C. Turkey); l; orig. from 'Circassian'; not *Uzuniala*; syn.
 Çerkes atlar (= *Circassian horse*)
Vardarska: see Macedonian

[Vardy] (Northumbria, England); dr; sim. to Cleveland Bay but heavier;
 orig. from Shire × Cleveland Bay; syn. *Bakewell, Northumberland
 Chapman*; extinct by 1910. [bred by George Vardy in the 19th c.]
Vasca, Vasca-Navarra: see Pottok
Veglia: see Krk

[Vendéen] (Vendée, W. France); l; orig from Anglo-Norman and Tho-roughbred × local; inc. in French Saddlebred

Venezuelan Criollo; py; syn. *Llanero* (= *prairie horse*)

Verkhoyansk: see Middle Kolyma

Vestland Pony: see Fjord

Vietnamese Pony (Vietnam); South-East Asia pony group; syn. *Anna-mese, Annamite*

Vladimir Heavy Draft (Vladimir and Ivanovo, USSR); h; bay, also brown or black; orig. (1886 on) from Clydesdale, earlier with Percheron, Danish, Suffolk, and Dutch blood, and later (1919-24) some Shire blood; recog. 1946; Russ. *Vladimirskaya tyazhelovoznaya* or *Vladimir-skiǐ tyazhelovoz*; syn. *Ivanovo Clydesdale, Russian Clydesdale, Vladimir Clydesdale, Vladimir Draught*

Vollblut: see blood horse

[Voronezh Coach] (USSR); h-l.dr; orig. in 20th c. from Clydesdale × heavy trotter; Russ. *Voronezhskaya upryazhnaya*; syn. *Voronezh Draft*

Vyatka (Udmurt, USSR); North Russian Pony group; often roan with black back-stripe, shoulder marks and zebra stripes on legs; Russ. *Vyatskaya*; not *Viatka*; rare

Waler: see Australian Waler

WARMBLOOD (Germany); = halfbred; Ger. *Warmblut*; inc. East Friesian, Hanoverian, Holstein, Mecklenburg, Oldenburg, Rottal, Saxony, Trakehner, Westphalian, Württemberg, Zweibrücken; elsewhere term may include also Thoroughbred and Arab

Waziri (N.W. Pakistan, and Afghanistan); l.

Welara Pony (USA); BS

Welsh Cob (Wales); l.ri.dr; orig. from Welsh Mountain Pony with blood of English riding and coach breeds

Welsh Pony (Wales); ri; BS 1902, HB 1903; inc. Welsh Mountain Pony and its derivatives: Riding Pony (with Arab or Thoroughbred blood) and Cob-Pony (with Welsh Cob blood); BS also in USA 1906, S. Africa 1957, Belgium, Canada 1979, Denmark, Netherlands, New Zealand, France (all 1960s)

West African Barb (W. of West Africa); l; usu. grey; orig. from Barb; syn. *Arab-Barb*; vars: Bélédougou, Djerma (× Dongola), Hodh, Sahel, Southern, Sulebawa (Nigeria)

West African Dongola (E. of West Africa); l; dark with white stockings; orig. from Dongola (Sudan); syn. *Fulani*; vars: Bahr-el-Ghazal (Chad), Hausa and Bornu (Nigeria); orig. (with Barb) of Bandiagara, Djerma, Mossi, Songhaï and Yagha (all in Niger bend)

West African ponies: see Bhirum, Bobo, Kirdi, Koto-Koli, M'Bayar,

M'Par, Torodi
Western Isles Pony: see Hebridean Pony
Western Kazakh: see Kushum
Western pony (USA); inc. bronco. cow pony, Indian Pony, mustang; for BSs see American Mustang, Indian, Spanish Barb, Spanish Mustang
Western Sudan Pony (S. Darfur and S.W. Kordofan, Sudan); l-py; usu. light bay, chestnut or grey, with white markings; syn. *Darfur Pony, Gharkawi* (= *western*), *Kordofani*
West Kazakh, West Kazakh Saddle-Draft: see Kushum
Westland, West Norway, West Norwegian: see Fjord
Westphalian Coldblood (Germany); strain of Rhenish; Ger. *Westfälisches Kaltblut*; rare
Westphalian Pony: see Dülmen Pony
Westphalian Warmblood (Germany); l; orig. from local graded to Hanoverian; BS 1904; Ger. *Westfälisches Warmblut*; inc. in German Riding Horse 1975
White: see American Creme and American White
White-Russian: see Byelorussian
Wielkopolski (W.C. Poland); l.dr; orig. 1964 by combining Mazury and Poznań; HB; syn. *Mazursko-Poznański*
Wuchuminsin, Wu-chu-mu-ch'in, Wuchumutsin: see Ujumqin
Württemberg (Germany); l.dr.ri; usu. brown, bay, chestnut, or black, with white markings; BS 1895; Ger. *Württemberger Warmblut*; inc. in German Riding Horse 1975

Yabu (Iran and Afghanistan); mixed type; not *Yaboo*. [= pack-horse]
Yagha (N. Burkina Faso, W. Africa); local var. of Dongola-Barb orig; syn. *Liptako*
Yakut (USSR); m.d.ri; Siberian Pony group; bay, grey-brown or grey with back-stripe, often shoulder bar, and zebra stripes on legs; Russ. *Yakutskaya*; vars: northern, Middle Kolyma or Verkhoyansk; small southern; and large southern (with blood of improver breeds)
Yellow (Ethiopia): see Abyssinian
Yenisei: see Upper Yenisei
Yerli: see Anatolian Native
Yilee, Yili: see Ili
Yomud, Yomut, Yomuth: see Iomud
Yonaguni (Ryukyu Is, Japan); var. of Japanese Native; nearly extinct
[Yorkshire Coach Horse] (England); var. of Cleveland Bay from Thoroughbred cross in early 19th c; BS 1886-1937, then reabsorbed; syn. *New Cleveland Bay*
Yorkshire Hackney, Yorkshire Trotter: see Hackney

Ysabella (Indiana, USA); colour type of American Saddle Horse; golden, white or chestnut with flaxen, silver or white mane and tail

Yugoslav Draft (N.W. Yugoslavia); h.dr; usu. chestnut or brown; orig. from Belgian and Pinzgau (but lighter); Serbo-cro. *Domać Hladnokrvan* (= *local coldblood*); syn. *Croatian Coldblood, Jugoslav, Yugoslavian Draft*; vars: Mura (heavier) and Posavina (lighter)

Yugoslav Mountain Pony: see Bosnian Pony, Macedonian Pony; Serbo-cro. *Domaći brdski konj*

Zabaikal: see Buryat

Zaniskari Pony (Leh, Ladakh, Kashmir); not *Zanskari, Zaskari*

[Zeeland] (Netherlands); Du. *Zeeuwse Paard*; extinct by crossing with Belgian to form Dutch Draft

Žemaitukai (Lithuania, USSR); py-l.dr; konik group; sim to Estonian Native; grey, black or bay; improved since 1963 by North Swedish; Russ. *Zhemaichu, Zhmud* or *Zhmudka*, Pol. *Żmudzki*, Ger. *Smudisch*; syn. *Lithuanian Landrace, Samogitian*; not *Zemaituka, Zemaitukas*

Zhmud, Zhmudka, Žmudka, Żmudzin, Żmudzki: see Žemaitukai

Zobnatica Halfbred (Yugoslavia); l; orig. from Trakehner, Mezőhegyes Halfbred, and Hanoverian at Zobnatica stud since 1946; Serbo-cro. *Engleski polukrvnji zobnatičkog tipa*

Zweibrücken (Palatinate, Germany); l; orig. from Arab, Thoroughbred, Anglo-Norman and Hanoverian; Ger. *Zweibrückner*; syn. *Pfälzisches Warmblut* (= *Palatinate Warmblood*); inc. in German Riding Horse 1975

PIG

[Abruzzese] (Abruzzi, Italy); black; semi-lop ears
Ahyb: see Hungahyb
Aksaï Black Pied (Alma Ata, S.E. Kazakhstan, USSR); m.ld; breed
group; orig. (1952 on) at Aksaï Exp. farm from Large White ×
local with some Berkshire blood; Russ. *Aksaïskaya chernopestraya
porodnaya gruppa*
[Alabuzin] (Kalinin, USSR); ld; breed group; white, sometimes spotted;
orig. (late 19th and early 20th c.) from Large White (also Middle
White and Large Black) × local lop-eared; Russ. *Alabuzinskaya
porodnaya gruppa*; extinct by 1984
Álava: see Vitoria
Albanian (Albanian); usu. white, also pied or coloured; var: Shkodra
Alentejana (Alentejo, Portugal); Iberian type; sim. to Extremadura Red
(Spain); red, golden or black; BSd; syn. *Portuguese, Red Portuguese,
Transtagana*; not *Alemtejana*
Alföldi: see Ancient Alföldi
[Amélioré de l'Est] (Alsace, France): see German (Improved) Landrace;
disappeared 1960s by crossing with French Landrace and by spread
of Large White. [= improved eastern]
American Berkshire (USA); m.[ld]; var. of Berkshire from imports 1820-
50; BS 1875
American Essex (USA); m; black; orig. from Black Essex; BS 1887;
nearly extinct 1967, revived as exp. breed at Texas A. and M. Univ.,
College Station with name *Greer-Radeleff Miniature* (1967-77); syn.
Guinea-Essex
American Landrace (USA); m; orig. from Danish Landrace imported
1934, and 38 Norwegian Landrace ♂♂ imported 1954; BS 1950
American Yorkshire (USA); orig. from Large White imported 1890-1900;
BS 1893
[Ancient Alföldi] (C. Hungary); ld; sim. to Mangalitsa and absorbed by
it in early 19th c.
Andalusian Black: see Black Iberian
[Andalusian Blond] (W. Andalucía, Spain); Iberian type; whitish to
golden; Sp. *Andaluza rubia (campiñesa)*
Andalusian Red: see Extremadura Red
Andalusian Spotted (Jabugo, Huelva, Spain); var. of Iberian; whitish
with irregular black speckles, esp. on head and rump; ? orig. end 19th

c. from Large White × Black Iberian *et al*.; Sp. *Andaluza manchada*; syn. *Jabugo Spotted* (Sp. *Manchada de Jabugo*); nearly extinct

Angeln Saddleback (Schleswig, Germany); black head and rump; orig. from local pied Land pig with Wessex Saddleback blood; HB 1928; Ger. *Angler Sattelschwein*; syn. *Angeln*; orig. of German Red Pied; + Swabian-Hall = German Saddleback; rare

Ankamali (Kerala, Karnataka, Tamil Nadu and Maharashtra, India); black with white patches or rusty grey

Annamese, Annamite: see Vietnamese

[Apulian] (Apulia and Lucania, Italy); white, often with black markings, esp. on face and rump; It. *Pugliese*; syn. *Apulo-Lucanian* (It. *Appulo-luccana*), *Mascherina* (= *masked*); former vars in: N.E. Lucania and Capitanata (Foggia), Murge, S.E. Lucania, Gargano; extinct *c*. 1980

Ashanti Dwarf (Ghana); var. of West African; black, brown and/or white

ASIAN; inc. Chinese, Indian, Indonesian, Thai, Philippine and Vietnamese breeds; orig. from Asian wild; syn. *Asiatic*

Asian wild = Asian subspp. of *Sus scrofa*; orig. of Asian domestic breeds; syn. *Asiatic wild*

[Asturian] (N. Spain); m; black; local var. sim. to Vitoria; orig. from Celtic × Iberian; extinct by crossing with Large White

Austrian Yorkshire: see Edelschwein

Axford: see Oxford Sandy-and-Black

Baasen: see Bazna

Baé: see Tatú

[Bagun] (N. Croatia, Yugoslavia); ld; whitish-yellow; curly coat; short ears; Ger. *Baguner*; *cf*. Bakony (Hungary); disappeared by crossing with Middle White; extinct before 1982

Bahia, Baia, Baié: see Tatú

[Bakony] (Transdanubia, W. Hungary); prim. 18th c. var; absorbed into Mangalitsa in early 19th c.

Bakosi (Cameroon); var. of West African

Baldinger Spotted (Donaueschingen, Württemberg, Germany); white with black spots; Ger. *Baldinger Tigerschwein*; nearly extinct

Balearic: see Majorcan

Balinese (Bali, Indonesia); ld; black or black with white on belly and legs; erect ears; orig. from South China × local (which remains in mts in E.)

Băltăreţ (Danube marshes, Romania); marsh var. of Romanian Native; syn. *Marsh Stocli*. [*bălta* = marsh]

Bamei (Shaanxi, Gansu, Ningxia and Qinghai, China); North China type; prolific

Banat White (W. and S. Banat, W. Romania); m; orig. in early 20th c. from Middle White and Edelschwein × Mangalitsa with possibly some blood of Small White, Berkshire, Large White and German (Improved) Landrace; Rom. *Porcul Alb de Banat*

Banheco (Guyana)

Bantu (S. Africa); usu. brown, also black, or white with black spots; orig. from early European and Asian imports

Basilicata: see Lucanian

Basna, Basner: see Bazna

Basque Black Pied (S.W. France); m.ld; Iberian type, sim. to Limousin; black pied, esp. black head and rump; BSd 1921; Fr. *Pie noir du pays basque*; syn. *Béarn* (Fr. *Béarnais*); nearly extinct

Basque-Navarre: see Vitoria

[Bastianella] (Faenza, Emilia, Italy); strain of inbred Large White (imported 1875) used for crossing with Romagnola; sim. to San Lazzaro

Baston: see Lincolnshire Curly Coat

[Bavarian Landrace] (Germany); fore end white, hind end red; Ger. *Halbrotes bayerisches Landschwein*

Ba Xuyen (Vietnam)

[Bayeux] (Normandy, France); m; black spots; orig. from Berkshire × Normand in 19th c; HB; disappeared in 1960s by crossing with Piétrain

Bazna (C. Transylvania, Romania); p; black with white belt; orig. since 1872 from Berkshire × Mangalitsa; Rom. *Porcul de Banat*, Ger. *Basner*; not *Baasen, Basna*

[Baztán] (Navarre, Spain); white or white with a few blue spots; local Celtic cross

Béarn, Béarnais: see Basque Black Pied

Beijing Black (China); m; black, occ. white markings; orig. 1962 from Berkshire and Large White × local; recog. 1982; syn. *Peking Black*

Beïra, Beiroa: see Bisaro

Belgian Landrace (N. Belgium); m; orig. from local improved first by English breeds, then graded to German (Improved) Landrace (1930-45) with Dutch Landrace blood 1945 on; HB 1930; Fr. *Landrace belge*, Flem. *Belgisch Landvarken*; syn. *Belgian Improved Landrace* (Flem. *Veredeld Landvarken*), *Improved Belgian* (1956-73) (Fr. *Indigène amélioré*); var: BN; also in Germany

Belgian Yorkshire (Belgium); var. of Large White from imports esp. since 1928; HB 1928; Fr. *Grand Yorkshire belge*, Flem. *Belgisch Groot Yorkshire*; syn. *Belgian Large White*; rare

Belted: see Saddleback

[Beltsville No. 1] (Maryland, USA); m; black with white spots; moderate lop ears; inbred orig. 1934-51, 75% Danish Landrace, 25% Poland China; HB 1951

[Beltsville No. 2] (Maryland, USA); red with white underline, occ. black spots; short erect ears; inbred orig. 1940-52, 58% Danish Large White, 32% Duroc, 5% Danish Landrace and 5% Hampshire; HB 1952

Bentheim Black Pied (S. Oldenburg, Germany); spotted; lop ears; Piétrain blood since 1960; Ger. *Schwarz-Weisses Bentheimer* or *Buntes Schwein*; syn. *Wettringer*; nearly extinct

Berkjala (Philippines); ld; black; short ears; orig. (1915 on) $\frac{5}{8}$ Berkshire, $\frac{3}{8}$ Jalajala; nearly extinct 1941-46

Berkshire (England); m; black with white points; orig. from Chinese (Cantonese) (and Siamese) × local Old English before 1830 and Neapolitan (Casertana) in 1830; HB 1884; vars: American Berkshire, Canadian Berkshire; orig. of Bayeux, Dermantsi Spotted, German Berkshire, Kentucky Red Berkshire, Murcian; also in China, USSR; nearly extinct in GB

BHZP (W. Germany); commercial hybrid cross of 4 lines orig. from German Landrace (MM), Large White (MF), Hampshire (FM) and Piétrain (FF) imported 1969 and kept closed. [= Bundes Hybrid Zucht Programm]

[Bigourdain] (Bigorre, Hautes-Pyrénées, S.W. France); syn. *Bigourdan*

Bikovačka, Bikovo: see Subotica White

Bilsdale: see Yorkshire Blue and White

Birish: see Peton

Bisaro (N. Portugal); Celtic type (with Large White blood); black, white or pied; syn. *Beïra, Beiroa*; not *Bizaro, Bizarra*

Bispectacled White: see Rongchang

Black Andalusian: see Black Iberian

Black Edelschwein: see German Berkshire

Black Emilian: see Parmense

[Black Essex] (England); var. of Small Black; orig. of American Essex; syn. *Old Essex*

Black Hairless (Extremadura and W. Andalucía, Spain); ld; var. of Black Iberian without bristles and skin folds; slate black; Sp. *Negra lampiña*; syn. *Guadiana* (Sp. *Pelón guadianés = bald Guadiana*) in Badajoz; nearly extinct

Black hairless (Latin America): see Pelón

Black Hamprace: see Montana No. 1

Black Iberian (Extremadura and W. Andalucía, Spain); ld.m; var. of Iberian sim. to Extremadura Red; Sp. *Negra iberica*; syn. *Andalusian Black, Extremadura Black*; subvars: Black Hairless (Sp. *Negra lampiña*) *q.v.* and [Black hairy] (Sp. *Negra entrepelada*)

[Black Mangalitsa] (Syrmia, Yugoslavia); ld; var. of Mangalitsa; black-brown with yellow belly; syn. *Lasasta* (= *weasel*), *swallow-bellied, Syrmian* (Serbo-cro. *Sremica*); extinct before 1982

Black Parma: see Parmense

Black Slavonian (E. Slavonia, Yugoslavia); m.ld; black; semi-lop ears; orig. (by Count Pfeifer) from Berkshire and Poland China × Black Mangalitsa, 1860 on; Serbo-cro. *Crna slavonska*, Ger. *Schwarzes slavonisches*; syn. *Pfeifer*; not *Black Slavonic*; rare

[Black Suffolk] (England); var. of Small Black; *cf.* Black Essex

Black Umbrian: see Maremmana

Blanc de l'Ouest: see West French White

Bohemian Blue Spotted: see Přeštice

Bologna, Bolognese: see Romagnola

[Borghigiana] (Borgo, Emilia, Italy); syn. *Fidenza* (It. *Fidentina*)

[Boulonnais] (Pas de Calais, France); Celtic type; Flemish orig. with Craonnnais and Large White blood; inc. in West French White 1955

[Bourdeaux] (Drôme, France); Celtic type; black; not *Bordeaux*

Brahma (USA)

Breitov (Yaroslavl, USSR); m.ld; lop ears; orig. 1908-34 from Danish Landrace (1908 on), Middle White (1913 on) and Large White (1924-26) × local lop-eared; recog. 1948; HB; Russ. *Breĭtovskaya*

[Bresse] (Ain, France); Iberian type; black pied; absorbed by Large White; Fr. *Bressane* or *Bresanne*

[Breton] (Brittany, France); Celtic type; crossed with Craonnais and Large White and absorbed by West French White 1955

Brinati: see Fumati

British Landrace (Great Britain); orig. from Swedish Landrace imported 1953-55; BS 1953

British Lop (S.W. England); m; sim. to old Welsh (joint HB 1926-28); also sim. to Large Black, but white; BS and HB 1921; Landrace blood since 1953; syn. *Cornish White, Cornish White Lop-eared, Devon Lop, Devon Lop-eared, Devonshire White, Lop White, National Long White Lop-eared, White Large Black, White Lop*; nearly extinct

British Saddleback (England); formed 1967 by union of Essex and Wessex Saddleback; HB; nearly extinct

[Bronze] (Germany); orig. (1925 on) from European wild boar × Bavarian Landrace and German Pasture, improved by Berkshire

BSI (Vietnam); orig. from Berkshire × Í

Bug: see Nadbużańska

Bulgarian Native; prim.; nearly extinct—a few remain in Botevgrad area; see also East Balkan

Bulgarian White (Bulgaria); m; orig. from Bulgarian Native graded up by Large White (first imported early 20th c.) and by Edelschwein;

Bulg. *B''lgarska byala,* Ger. *Bulgarisches weisses*; obs. syn. *Bulgarian Improved White*

Byelorussian Black Pied (Minsk, Byelorussia, USSR); m.ld; orig. from Large White, Large Black, Berkshire and Middle White × local in late 19th c. and in 1920s; recog. as breed group 1957, as breed 1976; Russ. *Belorusskaya chernopestraya*; syn. *White-Russian Pied* (or *Spotted*)

Byelorussian commercial hybrid (Byelorussia, USSR); m; syn. *White Russian Meat type*

Calabrian (Calabria, Italy); black; It. *Calabrese*; former vars: Catanzarese, Cosentina, Lagonegrese, Reggitana; nearly extinct

Camborough (England); minimal disease Large White × British Landrace cross at Pig Improvement Co, Fyfield Wick, Berks, developed with advice from *Cam*bridge and Edin*burgh*

Campiñesa: see Andalusian Blond

Canadian Berkshire; m; var. of Berkshire; nearly extinct

Canadian Yorkshire (Canada); var. of Large White

Canary Black (Canary Is, Spain); m; orig. from Large Black and Berkshire × Spanish and African breeds; Sp. *Cerdo negro canaria*; nearly extinct

Canastra (Brazil); ld; Iberian type; black; ? orig. from Alentejana; var: Furão. [? etym.]

Canastrão (Minas Gerais and Rio de Janeiro, Brazil); Celtic type; often curly coated; ? orig. from Bisaro. [? etym.]

Canastra-Pereira (Brazil); orig. from Canastra × Pereira

Canastrinho (Brazil)

Cantonese (Zhujiang delta, Guangdong, China); ld.m; Central China type; black-and-white; Ch. *Dahuabai* (= *large spotted white*); W.G. *Ta-hua-pai*; Ger. *Kanton*; syn. *Chinese* (GB), *Guangdong Large White Spot, Large Black White, Macao* (Portugal and Brazil), *Pearl River Delta*; see also Hong Kong

Cappuccia d'Anghiari, Cappuccio: see Chianina

Captain Cooker (New Zealand); feral; introduced by Captain Cook in 1769

Carioca: see Piau

Caruncho (Brazil); ld; white or sandy with black spots; syn. *Carunchinho*. [? etym.]

Casco de mula: see Mulefoot

Casentinese, Casentino: see Chianina

Casertana (Caserta, Campania, Italy); p; black or grey; usu. tassels; Thai or Indo-Chinese blood; syn. *Napolitana (= Neapolitan), Pelatella (=*

plucked, i.e. hairless); nearly extinct

Castagnona: see Romagnola

Catalan: see Vich

Catalina (Santa Catalina I, California, USA); feral

[Catanzarese] (Catanzaro); former var. of Calabrian

Cavallino (N.W. Lucania, Italy); m; usu. black with abundant, white-tipped bristles; nearly extinct

[Cazères] (Haute Garonne, S.W. France); sim. to Miélan; white with a few blue spots; orig. (1860 on) from Large White or Lauraguais, × Gascony, F_1 or later; Fr. *de Cazères* or *Cazèrien*; extinct 1970

Celta, Céltica (Spain): see Galician

CELTIC (N.W. Europe); m; usu. white, also spotted or saddleback; long lop ears; inc. lop-eared native pigs (Landraces) of N. Europe (except German Pasture); used esp. to distinguish Bisaro (N. Portugal), Baztán, Galician, Lermeño, Vich, and Vitoria (N. Spain), West French White (N. France), from Iberian types in Mediterranean areas

CENTRAL CHINA TYPE; black or pied; small lop or semi-lop ears; see Cantonese, Daweizi, Fuzhou Black, Ganzhongnan Spotted, Hang, Huazhong Two-End-Black, Jinhua, Leping, Longyou Black, Minbei Spotted, Nanyang Black, Ningxiang, Putian, Qingping, Shenxian Spotted, Tongcheng, Wanzhe Spotted, Wuyi Black, Xiangxi Black, Yujiang

Cerdo coscate: see Mexican Wattled

Charbin, Charbiner: see Harbin

[Charolais] (France); black pied

Chato de Murcia, Chato murciano: see Murcian

Chato de Vitoria: see Vitoria

[Chausy] (Byelorussia, USSR); m; breed group; Russ. *Chausskaya porodnaya gruppa*; extinct by 1984

Chayuan; var. of South Central Jiangxi Spotted

Chenghua (lowland Sichuan, China); ld.m; S.W. China type; black; Ger. *Tshen-Hua*; not *Chenhwa*

Cheng-hwai: see Huai

[Cheshire] (New York, USA); m; orig. in 1850s from pigs from Cheshire and Yorkshire; BS 1884; extinct by 1979

Chester White (Chester county, S.E. Pennsylvania, USA); m.[ld]; orig. in early 19th c. from English imports in late 18th and early 19th c; named *Chester County White* in 1848; BS 1884; orig. of O.I.C. (Ohio Improved Chester)

[Chianina] (upper Chiana and Tiber valleys, Tuscany-Umbria, Italy); sim. to Siena Belted, but grey with white head and feet; syn. *Cappuccia d'Anghiari, Cappuccio* (= *hooded*), *Casentino* (It. *Casentinese*); extinct by 1976

Chien-li: see Jianli

Chilin Black: see Jilin Black

CHINESE (China); usu. black or pied; wrinkled face (and often body); straight tail; syn. *Chinese Mask*; see Central China, Hong Kong, Lower Changjiang Basin, North China, Plateau, South China, South-West China, Taiwan

Chinese (Great Britain, Portugal and Brazil); in the past 'Chinese' = Cantonese

Chinese (Malaysia): see South China and South China Black

Chinese new breeds: see Beijing Black, Fannong Spotted, Ganzhou White, Hanzhong White, Harbin White, Laoshan, Lutai White, Nanjing Black, New Huai, North-East China Spotted, Sanjiang White, Shanghai White, Shanxi Black, Xinjin, Yili White, Yimeng Black

Ching Ching: see Xinjin

Ching-Huai: see Jinhua

Chin-hua: see Jinhua

Choctaw (USA)

Chunan Spotted; var. of Wanzhe Spotted

Chung-li: see Taoyuan

Cinta Italiana, Cinta Senese, Cinto: see Siena Belted

Co (Vietnam); local breed in midlands

Coleshill: see Middle White

Colorada (Spain): see Extremadura Red

Cornish: see Large Black

Cornish White (Lop-eared): see British Lop

Cornwall: see Large Black

[Corrèze] (C. France); local population of Craonnais × Limousin orig, now crossed with Large White; Fr. *Corrèzien*

Corsican (Corsica, France); usu. black with sparse white spots, also grey, roan, fawn or white; small and prim.; Fr. *Corse*; purebreds rare

[Cosentina] (Cosenza, Italy); former var. of Calabrian; syn. *Orielese*

Cotswold (England); m; orig. 1961-69 from Large White, Landrace, Welsh and Wessex Saddleback by Cotswold Pig Development Co; used as ♀ line for crossing with Large White strain to produce Cotswold hybrid ♀♀; HB

[Craonnais] (Craon, Mayenne, France); m; Celtic type; inc. in West French White 1955; HB; not *Crâon*

Creole (Belize); variable in type and colour

Criollo (Spanish America); Celtic type; Sp. orig; see also Cuino, Honduras Switch-tail, Mexican Wattled, Pelón, Sampedreño, Venezuelan Black, Zungo. [= native]

Cuino (highlands of Mexico); ld; black, spotted or yellow; ? Ch. orig. in 16th c; syn. *Mexican Dwarf*; nearly extinct

Cuino de Pachuca (Mexico); Berkshire × Cuino
[Cumberland] (England); m; lop ears; recog. 1811; BS 1917; last boar
licensed 1955/56, last sow 1960
Cuprem (Nebraska, USA); m; hybrid developed by A. Mulford, Kenesaw
Czech Improved White (Bohemia and Moravia, Czechoslovakia); inc.
Moravian Large Yorkshire; orig. from Large White (late 19th c),
Edelschwein and German (Improved) Landrace (1925 on) and local;
Cz. *České bílé ušlechtilé prase*, Ger. *Tschechisches weisses Edelschwein*;
not *White Thoroughbred*; orig. of Slovakian White
Czech Miniature (Vet. Res. Inst., Brno, Czechoslovakia); orig. from
Göttingen, Minnesota and Landrace; Cz. *Bílé miniaturní prase* (=
White miniature pig)
Czechoslovakian Black Pied (or *Spotted*): see Slovakian Black Pied

Dahe (Yunnan, China); var. of Wujin; black or brown; W.G. *Ta-ho*
Dahuabai: see Cantonese
Damin (China); var. of Min
Danish Black Pied (Denmark); m; often tassels; ? orig. from unimproved
Landrace with blood of coloured English breeds (*e.g.* Berkshire); Dan.
Sortbroget; syn. *Danish Black Spotted, Danish White and Black*; rare
Danish Landrace (Denmark); m; recog. 1896; Large White blood introdu-
ced at end of 19th c. (up to 1895) but selected against; Dan. *Dansk
Landrace*; orig. of Swedish Landrace and other Landraces (esp. Dutch,
French and Norwegian)
Danois: see French Landrace
[Dauphiné] (S.E. France); black pied; Fr. *Dauphinois*; not *Dauphin*
Daweizi (Hunan, China); ld.m; Central China type, sim. to Ningxiang;
black, usu. with white feet; large and medium-sized vars; W.G. *Ta-
wei-tzu*, Ger. *Da-We-Ze* or *Daweze*; not *Dawetze*
DBI (Vietnam); orig. from Large White × Í. [= Dai Bach Í]
Delta: see Annamese
Dengchang: see Tunchang
Dermantsi Pied (Lukovit, N. Bulgaria); ld; black with white points or
white with black spots; orig. (1895 on) from Berkshire (and Mangalitsa
since 1940) × native; Bulg. *P"stra dermanska*; syn. *Dermantsi Black
Spotted* (Bulg. *Dermanska chernosharena*, Ger. *Schwarzbuntes Derman-
zi*)
Deshi (Uttar Pradesh, Bihar, Madya Pradesh and Punjab, India); rusty
grey to brown or black; syn. *Desi*. [= local or village]
Devon: see Large Black (N.) or British Lop (S.)
Diani (Batangas, Philippines); black, sometimes spotted; orig. from
Berkshire and Poland China × Philippine Native

Dian-nan Small-ear: see South Yunnan Short-eared

Ding (Dingxian, Hebei, China); var. of Huang-Huai-Hai Black; ? some
    Poland China blood since 1929-30; horizontal or lop ears; W.G. *Ting*
    or *Tinghsien*, Russ. *Dinsyan*

Din-Hsiang-Chi: see Tingshuanhsi

Djen-li: see Jianli

Djing-Hua: see Jinhua

DM-1: see Don

[Dnieper] (Cherkassy, Ukraine, USSR); ld; black spotted; breed group;
    sim. to Krolevets, Mirgorod and Podolian; orig. from Mirgorod,
    Berkshire (1911) and Large White (1937-38), × local short-eared;
    Russ. *Dneprovskaya* or *Pridneprovskaya porodnaya gruppa*; extinct by
    1984

Dnepropetrovsk Hybrid (Ukraine, USSR); crossbred Russian Large
    White × Berkshire × Landrace

[Dobrinka] (Lipetsk, USSR); breed group; orig. 1932 on from Large
    White × local; Russ. *Dobrinskaya porodnaya gruppa*

Dobrogea Black (Romania); m; 5% pied; orig. 1949-67 from Large
    Black × Russian Large White; Rom. *Porcul negru de Dobrogea*

Dome: see Ghori

[Don] (Kamenski, Rostov, USSR); breed group; orig. from Cornwall
    (*sic*), Large Black and long-eared white × local Large White; Russ.
    Pridonskaya; extinct by 1984

Don type (N. Caucasus, USSR); m; cross from Piétrain × North
    Caucasus; recog. 1978; Russ. *Donskoĭ tip*; syn. *DM-1, Don meat type,
    Don hybrid*

Dongbeihua: see North-East China Spotted

Dongchuan (N. Jiangsu, China); Lower Changjiang Basin type

Dongyang (Zhejiang, China); var. of Jinhua; W.G. *Tung-yang*, Russ.
    Dunsyan

[Dorset Gold Tip] (Dorset, England); m; red with black markings and
    gold tip to bristles; semi-lop ears; ? orig. from Tamworth × Berkshire,
    with Gloucester Old Spot blood; last boar licensed 1955/56

Dsien-li: see Jianli

Dunsyan: see Dongyang

Duroc (USA); m.[ld]; red; orig. 1822-77 from old Duroc of New York
    + Jersey Red of New Jersey combined in 1860; BS 1883; syn. (1877-
    1934) *Duroc-Jersey*. [from racehorse named after General Duroc]

Dutch Landrace (E. Netherlands); m; orig. from German (Improved)
    Landrace ($\frac{3}{8}$) (imported since 1902) and Danish Landrace ($\frac{5}{8}$) (imported
    1929-33) × local; HB 1933 (dates from 1913-18); Du. *Nederlands
    (veredeld) Landvarken* (= *Netherlands (improved) landpig*), Fr. *Indi-
    gène néerlandaise*, Ger. *Niederländisches Landschwein*; syn. *Netherlands*

Landrace, P.R.N.
Dutch Large White: see Dutch Yorkshire
Dutch Yorkshire (W. Netherlands); p; orig. from Edelschwein and Large
White imported since *c.* 1870; HB since 1913-18; Du. *Nederlands Groot-*
Yorkshire Varken, Ger. *Niederländisches Edelschwein*; syn. *Dutch Large*
White, Edelwarken, Netherlands Large White
Džumalia (Macedonia, Yugoslavia); sim. to Resava; spotted; Serbo-cro.
Džumaliska

East Balkan (E. Bulgaria); prim.; usu. black, occ. pied; prick ears; orig.
from Asian × European wild pig; Bulg. *Istochnobalkanska*; syn.
Kamchiya (Bulg. *Kamchiska*)
Edelschwein (Germany); m; orig. from German Land pig graded up by
Large White and Middle White imported 1880 on; recog. 1904; Ger.
Deutsches weisses Edelschwein (= *German white thoroughbred pig*); syn.
German Large White, German Short-eared, German White Prick-
eared (= *Deutsches weisses Stehohrschwein*), *German Yorkshire, White*
Edelschwein; orig. of Latvian White, Russian Short-eared White, White
Prick-eared (Poland); not *German Pedigree, German Purebred*; see also
Swiss Edelschwein
EKB1: see Estonian Large White
Enshi Black (S.W. Hubei, China)
Erhualian (Lower Changjiang basin, China); var. of Taihu
[Essex] (England); m; white belt, feet and tail; orig. from Old English;
BS 1918-67; combined with Wessex in 1967 to form British Saddleback;
syn. *Essex Half- black, Sheeted Essex, White-shouldered Essex*; see also
American Essex
Estonian Bacon (Estonia, USSR); m; orig. from local crossed with
Danish, Finnish and German (Improved) Landrace and Large White;
recog. 1961; Russ. *Éstonskaya bekonnaya*; syn. *Estonian Lop-eared*
(Russ. *Éstonskaya visloukhaya*)
Estonian Large White (Estonia, USSR); m; regional type of Russian
Large White; Russ. *Éstonskaya krupnaya belaya*; syn. *EKB1*
Estremadura, Estremeña: see Extremadura
European wild = European subspp. of *Sus scrofa*; orig. of European
domestic breeds
Extremadura Black: see Black Iberian
Extremadura Red (Extremadura and Andalucía, Spain); m; chief var. of
Iberian, sim. to Alentejana (Portugal) and to Black Iberian; Sp.
Extremeña retinta or *colorada*; syn. *Andalusian Red, Red Iberian*; orig.
var: Oliventina (Badajoz) improved by Alentejana

[Faentina] (Faenza, Italy); former var. of Romagnola with reddish coat
Fannong Spotted (Henan, China); m; black and white; Yorkshire and
    Berkshire blood. [Huangfannong farm in Sihua county]
Fastback (England); m; cross developed 1963-73 by British Oil and Cake
    Mills from (British Saddleback), Landrace and Large White
[Fa Yuen] (Hong Kong); var. of Cantonese; black spots on back; W.G.
    Hua-hsien
Fengjing (S. Shanghai, China); var of Taihu; long- and short-snouted
    types; Ger. *Fong Djing*; syn. *Fungcheng, Rice-bran pig*; not *Fengjin, Fen
    Jin, Fenjing*
feral: see Catalina, Kangaroo Island, Ossabaw Island, Pineywoods,
    Razor Back
Fidentina, Fidenza: see Borghigiana
Finnish Landrace (Finland); native lop-eared; may have blue spots; orig.
    from short-eared East Finnish and lop-eared West Finnish with
    some Swedish Landrace blood in 1940s; BS 1908; Finn. *Suomalainen
    maatiaisrotu*, Swe. *Finsk lantras*
[Flemish] (French Flanders); Celtic type; inc. in West French White
    1955; HB 1937-55; Fr. *Flamand, Flandrin*
Fong Djing: see Fengjing
Fonte Bôa Pied (Portugal); Port. *Fonte Bôa malhada*
Forest Mountain (Armenia, USSR); m.ld; breed group; orig. in 1950s
    from Mangalitsa × (Large White × local); grey; long-haired in winter;
    Russ. *Lesogornaya porodnaya gruppa*; obs. syn. *New Lesogor* (Russ.
    Novaya lesogornaya); rare
[Forlivese] (Forli, Italy); former var. of Romagnola
Formosa: see Taiwan
Freixianda (Alvaiázere dist., Coimbra, Portugal); local var; red with
    black spots; not *Freixiandra*
French Landrace (N.W. France); m; orig. from Danish Landrace (first
    imported 1930) with Swedish and Dutch Landrace; BS 1952; Fr.
    Landrace Français; obs. syn. *Porc français de type danois* (*French
    Danish*)
French Large White; var. of Large White first imported at end of 19th
    c; BS 1923, HB 1926; syn. *Large White Yorkshire*
[Friuli Black] (Venetia, Italy); m; It. *Friulana nera, Nera del Friuli*; syn.
    San Daniele (It. *Sandanielese*); nearly extinct 1951 by crossing with
    Edelschwein (1908-40), Large White, *et al.*; extinct *c.* 1980
Fujian Small Pig (Fujian, China); black or black-and-white; inc. Huai,
    North Fujian Black-and-White, Putian Black; W.G. *Fukien*
[Fumati] (Emilia, Italy); Bastianella or San Lazzaro (inbred Large White)
    × Romagnola, F$_1$; light copper-coloured; syn. *Brinati*. [= smoky]
Fungcheng: see Fengjing

Furão (Brazil); degenerate var. of Canastra; syn. *Vara*
Fuzhou Black (Fujian, China); m.ld; Central China type

[Galician] (N.W. Spain); m; Celtic type; small reddish or black spots on head and rump; Sp. *Gallega*; syn. *Celta, Céltica, Santiaguesa* (from Santiago)
Gallega: see Galician
Ganzhongnan Spotted (C. Jiangxi, China); Central China type; black-and-white
Ganzhou White (Jiangxi, China); orig. from Large White × local Ganzhou before 1949
[Gargano]; var. of Apulian
[Garlasco] (Lomellina, Pavia, Italy); grey with white head; nearly extinct by 1949
Gascony (Haute Garonne and Gers, S.W. France); m.ld; Iberian type; black; Fr. *Gascon*; orig. (with Large White) of Miélan and Cazères; nearly extinct, by crossing with Large White
Gempshir: see Hampshire
Georgian (USSR); see [Imeretian], Kakhetian, [Kartolinian]; Russ. *Gruzinskaya*
[German Berkshire] (Germany); orig. from German Land pig, graded to Berkshire; syn. *Black Edelschwein*
[German Cornwall] (Germany); var. of Large Black
German Edelschwein: see Edelschwein
[German Land pig]; orig. of German Landrace; Ger. *Deutsches Land-schwein*
German Landrace (Germany); m; orig. from Large White or Edelschwein × German Land pig; recog. 1904; Dutch Landrace blood (esp. in Schleswig-Holstein) since 1953; Ger. *Deutsche Landrasse*; syn. (to 1969) *German Improved Landrace* (Ger. *Deutsches veredeltes Landschwein*); obs. syn. *Améliorée de l'Est* (France), *German Long-eared, German White Lop-eared* (Ger. *Deutsches weisses Schlappohrschwein*), *V.D.L.*; former local vars: Hoya, Meissen; orig. of Belgian Landrace, Dutch Landrace (with Danish), Russian Long-eared White, Swiss Improved Landrace
German Large White: see Edelschwein
German Long-eared: see German Landrace
[German Pasture]; ld; black head and rump; rough hair; prick ears; BS 1899; Limousin and Hampshire blood; Ger. *Deutsches Weideschwein*; syn. *Hanover-Brunswick* (Ger. *Hannover-Braunschweig*), *Hildesheim*; Güstin Pasture was sim. but smooth-haired; not *German Grazing, Hanover-Bismarck*

[German Red Pied] (Schleswig-Holstein, Germany); red with white belt; orig. about 1900 from red sports of Angeln Saddleback with Tamworth blood; BS 1954; Ger. *Rotbuntes Schwein*

German Saddleback: see Angeln Saddleback and Swabian-Hall; Ger. *Deutsches Sattelschwein*

German Short-eared: see Edelschwein

German Yorkshire: see Edelschwein

Ghori (N.E. India; also Bhutan and Bangladesh); syn. *Dome* or *Pygmy* (Assam and Bangladesh)

Glamorgan: see Welsh

Gloucester Old Spot (England); m; HB 1914; syn. *Gloucester, Gloucestershire Old Spots*; rare

Gołab, Gołębska: see Puławy; not *Golamb*

Göttingen Miniature (Göttingen Univ., Germany); orig. (1960 on) from Minnesota Miniature × Vietnamese; Ger. *Göttinger Miniaturschwein* or *Minischwein*; coloured var. is black, brown, white or pied; white var. has dominant white from German Landrace

Grand Yorkshire: see Large White

Greer-Radeleff Miniature: see American Essex

Guadiana: see Black Hairless

Guanchao; var. of South Central Jiangxi Spotted

Guangdong Small Ear; var. of Liang Guang Small Spotted

Guanling (C.S. Guizhou); S.W. China type; black; not *Guanglin*

Guinea-Essex: see American Essex

Guinea hog (Alabama, USA); feral; syn. *Gulf pig*; orig. of Minnesota Miniature

Gulf pig (USA): see Guinea hog, Pineywoods

Gurktal (Slovenia, Yugoslavia); ld; sim. to Turopolje

[Güstin Pasture] (Rügen, Pomerania, Germany); local var. sim. to German Pasture but smooth-haired; Ger. *Güstiner Weideschwein*; not *Güsting*

Hailum (S. Thailand); black with white marks; ? orig. from Hainan; syn. *Hainan*; not *Hailam*

Hainan (Hainan I, China); ld; South China type; small to dwarf; black head and back, white snout, blaze, flanks, belly and legs; smooth skin; long head; prick ears; vars: Lingao, Tunchang, Wenchang

Hainan (Thailand): see Hailum

Half-red Bavarian Landrace: see Bavarian Landrace

Hall, Hällische: see Swabian-Hall

Hampen (England) = Hampshire × Landrace cross

Hamprace: see Montana No. 1

Hampshire (Kentucky, USA); m.[ld]; black with white belt; orig. in 19th c. ultimately from Old English (? from Hampshire); BS 1893; Russ. *Gempshir*; syn. *Belted, Mackay, Norfolk Thin Rind, Ring Middle, Ring Necked, Saddleback, Woburn*; also in GB *et al.*

Hanford Miniature (Washington State, USA); orig. since 1958 at Pacific North West Laboratory from Palouse and Pineywoods

Hang (Jiangxi, China); Central China type; black head, back and rump

Hanjiang Black (S. Shaanxi, China); North China type

Hannover-Braunschweig, Hanover-Brunswick: see German Pasture

Hanzhong White (S.W. Shaanxi, China); contains Russian Large White, Yorkshire and Berkshire blood

Harbin White (Heilongjiang, China); m.ld; white; erect ears; usu. kinky tail; orig. from Large White × local (Min), using imports from Russia (1896) and Canada (1926); Ch. *Haerbinbai*; Russ. *Kharbinskaya belaya*, Ger. *Weisse Charbiner*; not *Kharbin*

Heihua (China); = black spotted: see North-East China Spotted

Hereford (Missouri, USA); [ld].m; red with white head, legs, belly and tail (colour and pattern of Hereford cattle); ? orig. 1902-20 from Chester White, Duroc, Poland China, and Hampshire; BS 1934; syn. *White-faced*

Hetao Lop-ear (Inner Mongolia, China); Ch. *Hetao Daer*

Hezuo (S.W. Gansu, China); Plateau type; black; small to dwarf

Hildesheim: see German Pasture

Honduras Switch-tail (C. mts of Honduras); long tail with hairy switch

Hong Kong; former vars of Cantonese in Hong Kong: Fa Yuen, Kwanchow Wan, Wai Chow

Hongqiao (Zhejiang, China); Lower Changjiang Basin type

Hormel: see Minnesota Miniature

[Hoya] (Bremen); former local var. of German Improved Landrace; Ger. *Hoyaer*

Hsin-chin: see Xinjin

Huai (N. Jiangsu and Anhui, China); var. of Huang-Huai-Hai Black; large lop ears; syn. *Jiangsu Huai*; not *Cheng-hwai, Hwai, Wuai*; orig. (with Large White) of New Huai

Huai (S.E. Fujian, China); South China type; black; inc. in Fujian Small Pig

Huang-Huai-Hai Black (N. Jiangsu, N. Anhui, Shandong, Shanxi, Hebei, Henan and Inner Mongolia, China); m; North China type; vars. inc. Ding, Huai, Shenxian

Huazhong Two-end Black (Lower Changjiang basin, China); Central China type; black head and tail; Ch. *Huazhongliangtouwu*; vars inc. Jianli, Satzeling and Tongcheng

Huchuan Mountain; S.W. China type; black

Hungahyb (Hungary); 4-line hybrid derived from Hungarian White, Dutch Landrace, Hampshire and Piétrain or Belgian Landrace; syn. *Ahyb*

Hungarian Curly Coat: see Mangalitsa

Hungarian White (Hungary); m; orig. from Large White with some blood of Middle White, Edelschwein, and German (Improved) Landrace; HB 1923; Hung. *Fehér hússertés*, Ger. *Ungarisches weisses Fleischschwein* (= *Hungarian white meat pig*); syn. *Hungarian Yorkshire*

Hwai: see Huai

Hypor (Netherlands); m; hybrid orig. from Dutch Landrace, Saddleback, Hampshire, German Landrace and Large White

Í (N. Vietnam); black

Iban (Sarawak); prim.; grey with white feet; small ears; long snout; straight tail; syn. *Kayan*

IBERIAN (S. Europe); ld; usu. coloured (red, black or pied); medium semi-erect ears; long snout; inc. native breeds of Mediterranean countries; used esp. to distinguish Alentejana (S. Portugal), Iberian (S. Spain), and Limousin, Gascony and Basque (C. and S. France), from Celtic types in N. of these countries; syn. *Mediterranean*

Iberian (S. Spain); inc. Extremadura Red (dominant), Andalusian Spotted and Black Iberian; Sp. *Ibérica*

[Ievlev] (Tula, USSR); ld; usu. black spotted, also black, white or white-spotted; lop ears; breed group; orig. from Large White, Large Black, 'Middle Black', and 'Black Spotted', × local; Russ. *Ievlevskaya porodnaya gruppa*; Ger. *Jewlewsker*; extinct by 1984

Ilocos; var. of Philippine Native; usu. black with white spots; Sp. *Ilocano*

[Imeretian] (Georgia, USSR); local with Polish White Lop-eared blood; Russ. *Imeretinskaya*; not *Imeritian*

Improved Belgian: see Belgian Landrace

Improved Eastern (Alsace, France): see Amélioré de l'Est

Improved Landrace: see Belgian, Dutch, German, Swiss; Ger. *Veredeltes Landschwein*

Improved Ningan: see Ning-an

Indo-Chinese: see Vietnamese

Indonesian: see Balinese, Javanese, Nias, Sumatran, Sumba

Iron Age pig (England); attempt to breed back from wild × Tamworth

Italian Belted: see Siena Belted

Ivanovo (Ukraine, USSR); breed group

Jabugo, Jabugo Spotted: see Andalusian Spotted

Jalajala; var. of Philippine Native; orig. (with Berkshire) of Berkjala

Javanese (Indonesia); orig. from European breeds × native
[Jersey Red] (New Jersey, USA); part orig. of Duroc
Jewlewsker: see Ievlev
Jiangsu Huai: see Huai (Jiangsu)
Jiangquhai (N. Jiangsu, China); Lower Changjiang Basin type; not
   Jangquhai, Jiangchuhai
Jianli (S. Hubei, China); var. of Huazhong Two-end Black; W.G. *Chien-
   li*, Ger. *Djen-li* or *Dsien-li*; syn. *Kienli*
Jiaoxi (China); var. of Taihu
Jiaxing Black (N.E. Zhejiang, China); var. of Taihu; not *Jiashing, Jia
   Xin, Kia Sing, Tia Sing*
Jilin Black (Jilin, N.E. China); m; var. of Xinjin; Russ. *Tszilin chernaya*;
   not *Chilin* or *Kirin Black*
Jinhua (Upper Fuchun R, Zhejiang, China); ld; Central China type;
   black-and-white, usu. black head and rump; W.G. *Chin-hua, Russ.
   Tsinkhua*, Ger. *Ching-Huai, Djing-Hua* or *Khinghua*; syn. *Black-at-
   both-ends* or *Two-end-black pig*; not *Kinhwa, Tsinghwa*; vars: Dongyang,
   Yongkang
Jungchang, Jungtschang: see Rongchang
Jungkang, Junkan: see Yongkang

Ka Done: see Raad
Kahyb (Hungary); rotational cross of 5 lines inc. Large White, Landrace
   and some Duroc, Hampshire and Lacombe; not *Kakhib*. [Kaposvar
   hybrid]
Kakhetian (E. Georgia, USSR); ld.m; prim.; breed group; Russ. *Kakhetin-
   skaya*; rare
[Kalikin] (Ryazan, USSR); ld; grey pied; orig. from Large White and
   Berkshire × local lop-eared; Russ. *Kalikinskaya*; extinct by 1984
[Kama] (Solikamsk, Perm, USSR); breed group; orig. from Large White
   and Breitov × local short-eared; Russ. *Prikamskaya porodnaya gruppa*;
   not *Kamsk*
Kaman (Batangas, Philippines); red; orig. from Duroc × Philippine
   Native
Kamchiya, Kamčija, Kamčik, Kamčiska: see East Balkan
Kangaroo Island (S. Australia); feral; small to dwarf; black spotted;
   ? orig. from British breeds released in 1801
Kanton: see Cantonese
[Kartolinian] (Georgia, USSR); local with Large White blood; Russ.
   Kartolinskaya
Kayan: see Iban
Kazakh hybrid: see Semirechensk

Keelung: see Ting-Shuang-Hsi

Kele (Guizhou mts, Yunnan, China); ld; South-West China type; black

Kelomive: see Kemerovo

Kemerovo (S. Siberia, USSR); ld; black or black-pied; orig. from Berkshire × local Siberian, with Large White blood; recog. 1961; HB; Russ. *Kemerovskaya*; syn. *Kelomive, Kemiroff* (China)

Kemerovo type: see KM-1

Kemiroff: see Kemerovo

[Kentucky Red Berkshire] (USA); [ld]; orig. from Berkshire in early 19th c; BS 1923; syn. *Red Berkshire*

Keopra: see Raad

Kharbin: see Harbin

Kharkov (Ukraine, USSR); m; orig. from Russian Large White, Landrace and Welsh; syn. *Kharkov hybrid*

Khinghua: see Jinhua

Kiangsu Hwai: see Huai (Jiangsu)

Kia Sing: see Jiaxing Black

Kienli: see Jianli

Kinhwa: see Jinhua

Kirin Black: see Jilin Black

Kirin Min: see Min

KM-1 (Siberia); m; orig. 1968-78 (new type recog.) from (Landrace × Kemerovo) × [Landrace × (Landrace × Kemerovo)] *i.e.* $\frac{5}{8}$ Landrace $\frac{3}{8}$ Kemerovo, selected for thin back fat and efficient food conversion; syn. *Kemerovo meat type* (Russ. *Kemerovskiĭ myasnyĭ typ*)

Korean Improved (Korea); orig. from Berkshire × North China

Korean Native (Korea); prim.; black

Korhogo (N. Ivory Coast); orig. (1930 on) from Berkshire and Large White × local West African

Koronadal (General Santos, Cotabato, Philippines); ash-red with dark spots; orig. from Berkjala, Poland China and Duroc

Krasnodar: see Kuban, Lesogor

[Krolevets] (N. Ukraine, USSR); ld; breed group; black pied or black; sim. to Dnieper, Mirgorod, and Podolian; orig. from English breeds × local Polesian; Russ. *Krolevetskaya porodnaya gruppa*; syn. *Polesian Lard* (Russ. *Polesskaya salnaya*); extinct by 1984

[Krškopolje Saddleback] (Slovenia, Yugoslavia); black-and-white; lop ears; Serbo-cro. *Krškopoljska Černo-pasasta* or *K. prasica*; local type with blood of German (Improved) Landrace and possibly also Berkshire and Large Black; extinct before 1982

Kula (N.W. Bulgaria); ld; var. of Mangalitsa from local crossed with Šumadija and Mangalitsa; black, red-brown or dirty white; Bulg. *Kulska*; syn. *Kula-Mangalitsa*

Kunekune (North I, New Zealand); ld; all colours; tassels; ? orig; syn. *Maori*; rare. [= fat]

Kwai (N. Thailand); black, sometimes white on shoulder and legs. [= buffalo]

[Kwangchow Wan] (Hong Kong); var. of Cantonese; black back, white belly; W.G. *Kuang-chou Wan*

Lacombe (Alberta, Canada); m; lop ears; orig. 1947-58 from Danish Landrace (55%), Chester White (22%) and Berkshire (23%); BS 1959, HB 1961

[Lagonegrese] (Lagonegro, S.W. Lucania, Italy); former var. of Calabrian

Lampiña negra (Spain): see Black Hairless

LANDRACE; inc. improved native white lop-eared (Celtic) breeds of N.W. Europe (Danish Landrace, Finnish Landrace, German Landrace, Norwegian Landrace, Swedish Landrace), and their derivatives (American Landrace, Belgian Landrace, British Landrace, Dutch Landrace, French Landrace, Polish White Lop-eared, South African Landrace, Swiss Improved Landrace). [= local, native, indigenous breed]

Landrace: see Danish Landrace

Landrase: see Norwegian Landrace

Landschwein: see German Land pig

Lang Hong (Vietnam)

Lantang (Guangdong, China); ld.m; South China type; head and back black, belly and feet white; not *Lantan*

Lantian Spotted: see Wannan Spotted

Lantras: see Swedish Landrace

Laoshan (Shandong, China); m.ld; orig. from Berkshire and Middle White × local black

Large Black (England); m; sim. to British Lop but black; HB 1899; syn. *Cornwall, Devon, Lop-eared Black*; formerly vars in (1) Cornwall and Devon, (2) Suffolk and Essex (orig. from Small Black); orig. of German Cornwall; nearly extinct in GB; HB also in USSR

Large Black White: see Cantonese

[Large Polish Long-eared] (Poland, except S.E.); prim.; black, red, or pied; Pol. *Wielka polska długoucha*; syn. *local long-eared, native long-eared*; orig. of Złotniki

Large White (England); m; prick ears; orig. from local Yorkshire with Chinese (Cantonese) blood in late 18th c; recog. 1868, HB 1884; syn. *Grand Yorkshire, Large English, Large White English, Large White Yorkshire, Large York, Yorkshire*; orig. of American Yorkshire, Belgian Yorkshire, Bulgarian Improved White, Canadian Yorkshire, Dutch

Yorkshire, Edelschwein, Estonian White, French Large White, Hungarian White, Latvian White, Lithuanian White, Polish Large White, Russian Large White, Swedish Large White, Swiss Edelschwein, Ukrainian White Steppe; also in China *et al.*

Large White Lop-eared: see British Lop

[Large White Ulster] (N. Ireland); m.ld; lop ears; HB 1908-33; syn. *Ulster, Ulster White*; last boar licensed 1956; extinct *c.* 1960

Lasasta: see Black Mangalitsa

Latvian White (Latvia, USSR); m; orig. from Berkshire and (Russian) Short-eared White × long-eared and short-eared Latvian in late 19th c. with Large White and Edelschwein blood in 20th c; recog. 1967; Russ. *Latviĭskaya belaya*

Lee-Sung (Taiwan); miniature; orig. since 1974 by selection of Taiwan Short-eared; syn. *Taiwan Miniature*

Leping (Jiangxi, China); m; Central China type; black with white forehead, belly and feet; not *Lepin*

[Lermeña] (Burgos, Spain); local Celtic type, sim. to Vitoria

[Lesogor] (Krasnodar, N. Caucasus, USSR); breed group of European short-eared type; Russ. *Lesogornaya porodnaya gruppa.* [= forest-mountain]

Levant type (Castellón to Almería, E. Spain); local graded to Large White, Berkshire (= Murcian), and Vitoria; Sp. *Agrupación levantina*; extinct except Murcian

Liang Guang Small Spotted (Guanxi and Guangdong, China); South China type; black-and-white; Ch. *Liang Guang Xiaohua*; vars inc. Guangdong Small Ear, Luchuan

Liangshan (mts of Sichuan, China)

Limousin (Haute Vienne, C. France); ld; Iberian type; white with black head and rump and often small spots on body; syn. *St Yrieix*; var: Périgord; nearly extinct by crossing with Craonnais and Large White

[Lincoln Red] (New Zealand); m; orig. 1940-59 from Large White × Tamworth, at Canterbury Agric. College, Lincoln; programme given up in 1959

[Lincolnshire Curly Coat] (England); m.ld; lop ears; syn. *Baston, Lincoln, Lincoln Curly Coat, Lincoln Curly Coated White, Lincolnshire Curly-Coated*; BS 1906-60; last boar licensed 1963/64

Lingao (Hainan I, China); var. of Hainan

Lithuanian White (Lithuania, USSR); m. or m.ld; orig. from Large White, Edelschwein and German Landrace × local Lithuanian; recog. 1967; Lith. *Lietuvos baltųjų*, Russ. *Litovskaya belaya*

Liujia (China)

Livny (Orel, USSR); ld; white or black-pied, occ. red-pied or black; semi-lop ears; orig. in early 20th c. from Middle and Large Whites,

and Berkshire, × local lop-eared; recog. 1949; HB; Russ. *Livenskaya*;
not *Liven, Livensky*
[Loches] (Touraine, France); *cf.* Montmorillon; absorbed by Large White
Long-eared White (USSR): see Russian Long-eared White
Longlin (N.E. Guanxi, China); South China type; black
Long White Lop-eared: see British Lop
Longyou Black (Jiangxi, China); Central China type; not *Longyu*
Lop-eared Black: see Large Black
lop-eared white (United Kingdom): see British Lop, [Cumberland],
[Large White Ulster], Welsh
Lop White: see British Lop
LOWER CHANGJIANG BASIN TYPE (China); black; lop ears; see Dongchuan,
Hongqiao, Jiangquhai, Taihu, Wei, Yangxin
[Lucanian]; vars of Apulian; syn. *Basilicata*
Luchuan (S.E. Guanxi, China); ld; South China type; var. of Liang
Guang Small Spotted; black-and-white (usu. black head and back),
occ. black or white; W.G. *Lu-ch'uan*, Russ. *Luchuan'chzhu*, Ger.
Lutschuan; not *Luchwan*
Lung Kong: see Wai Chow
Lung-Tan-Po: see Taoyuan
Lutai White (Lutai farm, Hebei, China); m; Russian Large White ×
Large White

Macao (Portugal and Brazil): see Cantonese (and its derivatives, *e.g.*
Tatú)
Macchiaiola: see Maremmana
Mackay: see Hampshire
Madonie-Sicilian (Madonie mts, Sicily, Italy); mixed type with blood of
Casertana, Large White, Large Black, *et al.*; It. *Siciliana delle Madonie*;
rare
Mai Schan, Maishan: see Meishan
[Majorcan] (Balearic Is, Spain); ld; Iberian type; slate-grey or black;
tassels; Sp. *Mallorquina* or *Agrupación balear*; syn. *Balearic*; not
Mallorcan
Mallorcan, Mallorquina: see Majorcan
Managra (Manitoba, Canada); m; lop ears; orig. (1956 on) from Swedish
Landrace (45%), Wessex Saddleback (20%), Welsh (12%), Berkshire,
Minnesota No.1, Tamworth and Yorkshire
Manchada de Jabugo: see Andalusian Spotted
Mangalitsa (N.E. Yugoslavia, Hungary and Romania); ld; curly hair;
lop ears; orig. from Šumadija (Serbia) in late 18th c; imported to
Hungary in 1833 and used to improve local (Ancient Alföldi, Bakony,

Szalonta, *etc.*); HB (Hungary) 1927; Serbo-cro. *Mangulica* (♀) or *Mangulac*, Ger. *Mangaliza*, Hung. *Mangalica*, Rom. *Mangaliţa*; syn. *Hungarian Curly Coat, Wollschwein*; vars: yellowish-white (chief), black or swallow-bellied (Syrmia), red (bristles) (Crişana, Romania), and Kula (Bulgaria); orig. of Bikovo; not *Mangalitza, Mangalizza, Mangolitsa, Mangulitza, Mongolitsa, Mongulitsa*. [Serbo-cro. = easily fattened, ? from Rom. *mancare* = eating]

Mangouste (Seychelles); ld; black; Asian orig.

Manor Hybrid (England); Large White × Landrace cross, bred by Northern Pig Development Co, Manor Farm, Belford, Yorks

[Manx Purr] (Isle of Man); feral; spotted sandy-grey; long hair; extinct end 18th c.

Maori: see Kunekune

[Maremmana] (Maremma, Tuscany, Italy); semi-wild; black; syn. *Macchiaiola* (=*forest pig*), *Nera umbra* (= *black Umbrian*), *Roman*; extinct by 1949

[Marseilles] (France); Iberian type with English blood (1850 on); absorbed by Large White; Fr. *Marseillais*

[Maryland No.1] (Maryland, USA); m; black with white spots; erect or semi-erect ears; inbred orig. 1941-51 by Maryland Agric. Exp. Sta. from Danish Landrace × Berkshire backcrossed first to Berkshire and then to Danish Landrace and then bred *inter se*; $\frac{5}{8}$ Danish Landrace, $\frac{3}{8}$ Berkshire; HB 1951

Mascherina: see Apulian

Mashen (N. Shanxi, China); m.ld; North China type

Mask, Masked: see Chinese

Mediterranean: see Iberian

Mega (France); Belgian Landrace × Hampshire cross

[Meinung] (Taiwan); ld; sim. to Taoyuan but smaller; W.G. *Mi-nung*, Jap. *Mino*; extinct by 1979

Meishan (N. Shanghai, China); var. of Taihu; white feet; Ger. *Mai Schan*; not *Maishan*

[Meissen] (Saxony); early local var. of German Improved Landrace; BS 1888; Ger. *Meissener* or *Meissner*

Meixin (China) = Meishan × Xinjin cross

Meo (Vietnam); local breed in mts

[Meshchovsk] (Kaluga, USSR); breed group; orig. from Large White × local; Russ. *Meshchovskaya porodnaya gruppa*; extinct by 1984

Mexican Dwarf: see Cuino

Mexican Wattled (Mexico); red, black or spotted; Sp. *Cerdo coscate*

Mi (China); var. of Taihu

[Miami] (S.W. Ohio, USA); orig. from Big China, Byfield, and Russian strains and local pigs of Miami valley in early 19th c; part orig. of

Poland China; syn. *Warren County*

Middlesex: see Small White

Middle White (England); m; orig. from Large White × Small White; recog. 1852, HB 1884; syn. *Coleshill, Middle White Yorkshire, Middle Yorkshire, Windsor*; also in China; nearly extinct in GB [Miélan] (Gers, S.W. France); sim. to Cazères; sometimes small grey spots on rump; orig. from Large White × Gascony *c.* 1880; var: Piégut

Miloš, Milosch, Miloševa: see Šumadija. [from Prince Miloš Obrenović]

Min (Liaoning, Jilin and Heilongjiang, N.E. China); m.ld; North China type; black; large lop ears; hy; prolific; not *Ming, Kirin Min*; var: Damin

Minbei Spotted (Fujian, China); Central China type; black-and-white

Ming: see Min

Miniature: see American Essex, Czech, Göttingen, Hanford, Lee Sung, Minisib, Minnesota, Munich, Ohmini, Pitman-Moore, Sinclair, Vita Vet Lab, Yucatan; syn. *mini-pig*

Minisib (USSR); miniature; orig. from Vietnamese (43-56%), Swedish Landrace (24-32%) and wild (20-25%)

Minnesota Miniature (Minnesota, USA); spotted; small pig for medical research selected (1949 on) at Hormel Institute, St Paul, from cross of 3 feral strains—Guinea (Alabama), Pineywoods (Louisiana) and Catalina I (California)—and Ras-n-lansa (Guam); syn. *Hormel Miniature*; orig. of Göttingen Miniature and Czech Miniature; extinct in USA

Minnesota No.1 (USA); m; red; orig. 1936-46 from Tamworth (52%) and Danish Landrace (48%) at Minnesota Agric. Exp. Sta.; HB 1946; rare

[Minnesota No.2] (USA); m; black spotted; orig. 1941-8 from Canadian Yorkshire (40%) and Poland China (60%); HB 1948

[Minnesota No.3] (USA); orig. from Gloucester Old Spot (31%), Poland China (21%), Welsh (13%), Large White (12%), Beltsville No.2 (6%), Minnesota No.1 (6%), Minnesota No.2 (5%) and San Pierre (5%)

[Minnesota No.4] (USA); exp. population at Minnesota Agric. Exp. Sta. from Minnesota Nos 1, 2 and 3; experiment ended early 1970s

Mino, Mi-nung, Mi-nung-chung: see Meinung

Mirgorod (C. Ukraine, USSR); ld; usu. black pied, occ. black, black-and-tan or tan; sim. to Dnieper, Krolevets and Podolian; orig. since 1882 from Large White, Middle White, and Berkshire (with some Large Black and Tamworth) × local short-eared Ukrainian, recog. 1940; Russ. *Mirgorodskaya*; syn. *Mirgorod Spotted* (Russ. *Mirgorodskaya ryakaya*)

[Modena Red] (Emilia, Italy); It. *Rossa modenese*; extinct 1873

Modenese (Modena, Emilia, Italy); black-and-white; orig. (1873 on)

from Large White × local Iberian type; nearly extinct

[Moldavian Black] (Moldavia, USSR); ld; breed group; orig. (1948 on) from Berkshire *et al.* × local black, F$_1$ bred *inter se*; Russ. *Chernaya moldavskaya porodnaya gruppa*; extinct by 1984

Mong Cai (Vietnam)

Mongolitsa, Mongulitsa: see Mangalitsa

Montagnola: see Siena Belted

Montana No.1 (USA); m; black; inbred orig. 1936-48 from Danish Landrace (55%) and black (unbelted) Hampshire (45%) crossed reciprocally and backcrossed to both breeds at Miles City, Montana; named *Black Hamprace* 1947, renamed and HB 1948; rare

[Montmorillon] (Vienne, France); orig. in late 19th c. from Large White × Craonnais; Fr. *Montmorillonnais*; syn. *Poitou*; absorbed by Large White

Moor: see Romagnola

Mora, Mora romagnola: see Romagnola

Morava (Serbia, Yugoslavia); m.ld; black; lop ears; orig. from Berkshire × Mangalitsa or Šumadija; Serbo-cro. *Moravka* or *Moravska svinja*; being improved by Large Black; *cf.* Resava

Moravian Improved White, Moravian Large Yorkshire: see Czechoslovakian Improved White

Muang Khong (Vietnam); local breed in mts

Mulefoot (Ohio, USA); sim. to Poland China but solid-hoofed; BS 1908; also in Colombia; Sp. *Casco de mula*; nearly extinct

Mundi (Minas Gerais, Brazil); in formation in one closed herd at State School of Agriculture

Munich Miniature (Munich, Germany); white skin, red or black hair, or spotted; orig. from Hanford Miniature crossed with Columbian Portions pig; syn. *Troll*

Murcian (E. Spain); m; var. of Levant type; local graded to Berkshire; Sp. *Chato de Murcia* or *Chato murciano* (= *short-nosed Murcian*); nearly extinct

[Murgese] (Murge); var. of Apulian

Murom (Vladimir, USSR); m.ld; orig. in 1930s from Large White and Lithuanian White × local long-eared; recog. 1957; HB; Russ. *Muromskaya*

Nadbużańska (R. Bug, Poland); prim.; nearly extinct

Nai-Djang: see Neijiang

Nanjing Black (Jiangsu, China); orig. (1972 on) from Shanzhu, Jinhua, Berkshire, Large White, and Landrace

Nanyang Black (Hunan, China); Central China type

Napolitana: see Casertana
National Long White Lop-eared: see British Lop
Neapolitan: see Casertana
Negra entrepelada (Spain): see Black Iberian
Negra lampiña (Spain): see Black Hairless. [*lampiño* = beardless]
Neijiang (Sichuan, China); ld.m; South-West China type; black; W.G.
   Nei-chiang, Russ. *Neĭ-tszyan*, Ger. *Nai-Djang*; not *Neikiang*
Nepalese Dwarf (hills of Nepal); prim.; black; *cf.* Ghori
Netherlands (Improved) Landrace: see Dutch Landrace
Netherlands Indies: see Indonesian
New Guinea Native (Papua New Guinea); black, black spotted, white,
   red or grey; newborn often striped; straight tail
New Huai (N. Jiangsu, China); m.ld; black; lop ears; orig. 1959 from
   Large White (50%) × Huai (50%); Ch. *Xin Huai*; not *Sin Hwai*
New Lesogor: see Forest Mountain
Nias (Indonesia)
Nigerian Native; var. of West African; syn. *Nigerian indigenous*
Nilo (Brazil); ld; Iberian type; black; hairless; BSd; syn. *Nilo-Canastra*. [?
   etym.]
Ning-an (S.E. Heilongjiang, China); var. of Xinjin; syn. *Improved Ningan*
Ningxiang (Hunan, China); ld; Central China type; white belly and black
   (or black-and-white) back; W.G. *Ning-hsiang*, Russ. *Ninsya* or *Ninsyan*,
   Ger. *Ning-Chang*; not *Ning hsing, Ningsiang*
Nitra Hybrid (Slovakia, Czechoslovakia); orig. from Czech Improved
   White, Slovakian Black Pied, Landrace, Hampshire, Slovakian White
   and Large White
Norfolk Thin Rind: see Hampshire
Normand (Cherbourg peninsula, Normandy, France); m; Celtic type;
   much crossed with Craonnais and Large White, and absorbed by West
   French White 1955; BS 1937; nearly extinct
North Caucasus (N. Caucasus, USSR); m.ld; black pied; orig. from local
   Kuban with 2 crosses of Large White (1929-38), 2 of Berkshire (1938-
   41) and 1 of White Short-eared (1946); recog. 1955; HB; Russ.
   Severokavkazskaya; syn. *North(ern) Caucasian, Novocherkassk*; var:
   Don
NORTH CHINA TYPE; black; lop ears; see Bamei, Hanjiang Black, Huang-
   Huai-Hai Black, Min, Yimeng Black
North-East China Spotted (N.E. China); m; orig. from Berkshire ×
   Min; Ch. *Dongbeihua*
North East Min: see Min
North Fujian Black-and-White (China); var. of Fujian Small Pig
North Siberian (N. Omsk and Novosibirsk, USSR); ld; orig. since 1933
   from Large White × Siberian, recog. 1942; HB; Russ. *Sibirskaya*

severnaya
Norwegian Landrace (Norway); m; orig. from Large and Middle Whites
(1880-90) and Danish Landrace (1900), × local; Swedish Landrace
blood since 1945; Nor. *Norsk Landrase*
Novocherkassk: see North Caucasus
Novosibirsk: see Siberian
Novosibirsk Spotted: see Siberian Spotted

Ohio Improved Chester: see O.I.C.
Ohmini (Japan); miniature; black, occ. black pied; orig. from Chinese
miniatures (imported 1942-48) and Minnesota Miniature (imported
1952) at Institute of Japan Livestock Development
[O.I.C.] (Ohio, USA); [ld]; orig. 1865-97 from Chester White; BS 1897;
syn. *Ohio Improved Chester*
[Old English]; orig. of Essex, Hampshire, and Wessex Saddleback
Old Glamorgan: see Welsh
Old Oxford: see Oxford Sandy-and-Black
[Old Swedish Spotted] (Sweden); syn. *Black-White-Red Spotted*; extinct
1978
Oliventina (Badajoz, Spain); orig. var of Extremadura Red improved by
(or orig. from) Alentejana; syn. *Raya* (= frontier, *i.e.* of Spain and
Portugal). [from Olivenza]
[Omsk Grey] (Omsk, USSR); m; breed group; orig. 1949-63 from
Kemerovo, Siberian Spotted and Large White × local (Tara); Russ.
Omskaya seraya porodnaya gruppa; extinct by 1984
Orielese: see Cosentina
Ossabaw Island (Georgia, USA); ? spotted; obese; feral; HB for those
maintained elsewhere
Oxford Sandy-and-Black (Oxfordshire, England); m; red with sandy
hairs and black blotches; semi-lop ears; syn. *Axford, Old Oxford,
Oxford Forest, Plum Pudding pig, Sandy Oxford*; nearly extinct after
last boar licensed 1963/64; revived BS 1985

[Palouse] (Washington, USA); m; orig. 1945-56 from 5 Danish Landrace
♂♂ (65%) × 25 Chester White ♀♀ (35%) at Washington Agric. Exp.
Sta.; HB 1956
[Parmense] (Parma, Emilia, Italy); dark grey; syn. *Black Emilian* (It.
Emiliana negra), *Black Parma, Parmigiana, Reggio* (It. *Reggiana*);
extinct by 1976
Pasture: see German Pasture
Pearl River Delta: see Cantonese
Peking Black: see Beijing Black

Pelatella: see Casertana

Pelón (Mexico to Colombia); ld; Iberian type; black; syn. *Black hairless of the tropics*, *Birish* (Yucatan, Mexico), *Pelón de cartago* (Costa Rica), *Pelón Tabasqueno* (Tabasco, Mexico). [= hairless]

Penbuk (N. Korea); orig. from North China × local Korean

Pereira (São Paulo, Brazil); ld; Iberian type; grey (or black) sometimes with red spots; orig. by D. Pereira Lima from Canastra, ? with Duroc blood

Périgord (France); var. of Limousin, larger; crossed with Craonnais and Large White; Fr. *Périgourdin*; almost extinct

[Perugina] (Perugia, Umbria, Italy); sim. to Chianina; grey with white spots

Petren: see Piétrain

Pfeifer, Pfeiffer: see Black Slavonian

Philippine Native; black or black with white belly; vars inc. Ilocos, Jalajala; orig. of Berkjala, Diani, Kaman, Koronadel

Piau (Paranaíba R. basin, S.W. Brazil); m.ld; Iberian type; white (or grey or sandy) with black spots; orig. from Canastra and/or Canastrão; BSd; syn. *Carioca* (Rio de Janeiro); not *Piauí*. [? etym.]

[Piégut] (Bussière-Badil, Dordogne, France); local var. of Miélan since early 20th c.

Piétrain (Brabant, Belgium); m; dirty white with black or reddish spots, often red hairs; semi-lop ears; ? orig. (*c.* 1919-20) from Bayeux (? and Tamworth) × local; HB 1950, BS 1952, general recog. 1955; Russ. *P'etren*; not *Petren*; HB also in France 1958, Germany, GB, Luxembourg, Netherlands, Spain, Italy, Brazil

Pilsen: see Přeštice

Pineywoods (Louisiana, USA); feral; syn. *Gulf pig, Swamp hog*; not *Piney Woods*

Pirapitinga (Minas Gerais, Brazil); ld; ? var. of Tatú; black or violet; Chinese orig; not *Pirapetinga*

[Pitman-Moore Miniature] (Iowa, USA); selected from Vita Vet Lab Minipig 1967-73 at College of Medicine, Univ. of Iowa

PLATEAU TYPE (China): see Hezuo, Hu, Tibetan

Plaung: see Raad

Plum Pudding pig: see Oxford Sandy-and-Black

Plzeň: see Přeštice

[Podolian] (W. Ukraine, USSR); ld; black pied; breed group; sim. to Dnieper, Krolevets and Mirgorod; orig. from Berkshire, Middle White, and Large White × local; Russ. *Podol'skaya porodnaya gruppa*; syn. *Podolian Black Pied* (Russ. *Podol'skaya chernopestraya*); extinct by 1984

Poitou: see Montmorillon

Poland China (Ohio, USA); m.[ld]; black with white points; orig. 1835-72 from Berkshire, Miami, *et al.*; HB 1878, united BS 1946; part orig. of Spotted; not *Poland-China.* [a settler from Poland and 'Big Chinas'— one of strains forming Miami]

[Polesian] (Pripet Marshes, USSR); formerly var. of Small Polish Prick-eared; Russ. *Polesskaya*; syn. *Sarny*; orig of Krolevets

Polesian Lard: see Krolevets

Polish Landrace (Poland); m; orig. from Polish Marsh improved since mid-19th c. by English and German breeds, since 1908 by German (Improved) Landrace and (one var. only) since 1954 by Swedish Landrace; BSd; syn. *Polish White Lop-eared* (Pol. *Biała zwisłoucha*, Ger. *Schlappohriges Landschwein*)

Polish Large White (Poland); m. or m.ld; orig. since late 19th c. from Large White and Edelschwein × Polish Native, re-formed (new imports) 1947, recog. and HB 1956; BSd; Pol. *Wielka biała (polska)*; vars: (combined 1956) Pomeranian Large White, White Prick-eared, English Large White

[Polish Marsh] (N. Poland); prim.; lop ears; Pol. *Żuławska*; orig. of Polish Landrace

[Polish Native]: see Large Polish Long-eared, Polish Marsh, Small Polish Prick-eared

Polish White Lop-eared: see Polish Landrace

Poltava (Ukraine, USSR); m; orig. since 1966 from Russian Large White, Mirgorod, Landrace, Piétrain and Welsh at Poltava Pig Breeding Research Institute; Russ. *Poltavskaya*; syn. *Poltava commercial hybrid*

[Pomeranian Large White] (N.W. Poland); m.ld; former var. of Polish Large White; orig. in 20th c. from Large White × White Prick-eared, recog. 1936, graded to Edelschwein 1940-45; Pol. *Wielka biała pomorska*; syn. *Pomorze*

Pomorze: see Pomeranian

Porc français de type danois: see French Landrace

Portuguese: see Alentejana, Bisaro

Přeštice (Plzeň, Bohemia, Czechoslovakia); m.ld; black pied; local Saddleback improved (1957) by Wessex; Cz. *Přeštické*; obs. syn. *Bohemian Blue Spotted, Pilsen, Plzeň, Saaz*

Prikamskaya: see Kama

Prisheksninsk (Vologda, USSR); m.ld; var. of Large White with local blood; Russ. *Prisheksninskaya*

P.R.N.: see Dutch Landrace

Puang: see Raad

Pugliese: see Apulian

Puławy (Lublin, Poland); ld; black-and-white or black-and-red-and-white; orig. since 1926 from local pied pigs (orig. from Berkshire ×

Small Polish Prick-eared in early 20th c); BSd; Pol. *Puławska*; syn. (1926-43) *Gołębska* (from Gołąb)
Putian (Fujian, China); Central China type; black; inc. in Fujian Small Pig; syn. *Fujian Black*
Pygmy: see Ghori

Qingping (C. Hubei, China); Central China type; black

Raad (N. Thailand); black; syn. *Plaung* or *Puang* (N.E.), *Ka Done* or *Keopra* (S.); not *Rad*
Rad: see Raad
Ras-n-lansa (Guam, Mariana Is); dwarf
Raya (Spain): see Olivenza
Razor Back (Arkansas, USA); feral
Red Andalusian : see Extremadura Red
Red Berkshire: see Kentucky Red Berkshire
[Red Hamprace]; red line (red with black spots) occurring during formation of Montana No.1 (Black Hamprace)
Red Iberian: see Alentejana, Extremadura Red
Red Portuguese: see Alentejana
Red Wattle (USA); tassels; HB; syn. *Red Waddle*; not *Wattler*
Reggiana, Reggio (Emilia): see Parmense
[Reggitana] (Reggio, Calabria); former var. of Calabrian
Reichenau: see Rychnov
Rena (France); Large White × British Landrace cross
Resava (Serbia, Yugoslavia); m.ld; black spotted; lop ears; ? orig. from Berkshire × Mangalitsa and Šumadija; Serbo-cro. *Resavka* or *Resavska svinja*; syn. *Vezičevka* (from Vezičevo); *cf.* Morava
Retinta (Spain): see Extremadura Red
Rice-bran pig: see Fengjing
[Riminese] (Rimini, Italy); former var. of Romagnola with star on forehead
Ring Middle, Ring Necked: see Hampshire
[Romagnola] (Emilia, Italy); p; dark brown or copper coloured; It. *Mora* or *Mora romagnola*; syn. *Bologna* (It. *Bolognese*), *Castagnona* (= *chestnut*), *Moor*; former vars: Faentina, Forlivese, Riminese; F_1 by Bastianella or San Lazzaro (inbred Large White) = Fumati (smoky) or Brinati; extinct by 1976
Roman: see Maremmana
Romanian Large White (Romania); Rom. *Marele alba*
Romanian Meat Pig (Bărăgon Steppe, S. Romania); m; orig. at Ruşeţu Exp. Sta. since 1950 from Russian Large White × local Stocli sows

backcrossed to Large White; Rom. *Porcul românesc de carne*, Ger.
Rumänisches weisses Fleischschwein
Romanian Native (Danube valley, S. Romania); prim.; grey; prick ears;
vars: Stocli (mountains), Băltăreț (marshes) and [Transylvanian];
disappearing
Rongchang (uplands of Sichuan, China); ld.m; bristles; S.W. China type;
white with black spectacles, occ. with black spots elsewhere or all white;
W.G. *Jung-ch'ang*, Russ. *Zhunchan* or *Zhungan*, Ger. *Jungtschang*; syn.
Bispectacled White, Jungchang White; not *Young-tschang, Yungchang*
[Rossosh Black Pied] (Voronezh, USSR); ld; breed group; orig. from
Berkshire 1943 × (Large White × local) with Berkshire × Mirgorod
blood in 1949; Russ. *Rossoshanskaya chernopestraya porodnaya gruppa*;
extinct by 1984
Rostov (USSR); m; breed group; orig. since 1973 from Russian Large
White, Russian Short-eared White, Piétrain and Welsh; syn. *Rostov
Meat*
Rubia, Rubia campiñesa (Spain): see Andalusian Blond
Ruijin; var. of South Central Jiangxi Spotted
Russian Large White (European Russia); m; orig. from Large White
imported since 1880 and esp. since 1922; HB 1932; Russ. *Krupnaya
belaya*; syn. *Soviet Large White*; var: UKB-1; also in China
Russian Long-eared White (USSR); m; = German (Improved) Landrace
imported to Kuibyshev in 1931; Russ. *Dlinnoukhaya belaya*
Russian Short-eared White (USSR); = German Edelschwein imported
to Krasnodar (N. Caucasus) 1927 on; Russ. *Korotkoukhaya belaya*
[Rychnov] (Czechoslovakia); orig. 1865 from Large and Middle Whites
and Poland China, × local; Cz. *Rychnovské*, Ger. *Reichenau*; extinct
1933 by crossing with Edelschwein

Saaz: see Přeštice
Saddleback: see Angeln, Basque, Bazna, British, German Pasture,
Hampshire, Jinhua, Limousin, Přeštice, Siena, Swabian-Hall; syn.
Belted, Sheeted
St Yrieix: see Limousin; not *St Yriex*
Sakhalin White (E. Siberia, USSR); ld; orig. from Large White (imported
1932) × local; Russ. *Belaya sakhalinskaya*
Samoan (S. Pacific)
Sampedreño (Colombia); Criollo type
San Daniele, Sandanielese: see Friuli Black
Sandy Oxford: see Oxford Sandy-and-Black
Sanjiang White (Heilongjiang, China); m; lop ears; orig. from Landrace

× (Landrace × Min) 1973-83 (recog.). [= 3 rivers]
[San Lazzaro] (Faenza, Italy); strain of inbred Large White (imported 1875) used for crossing with Romagnola; sim. to Bastianella
[San Pierre] (Indiana, USA); black-and-white; orig. 1953 from Chester White and Berkshire
Santiago, Santiaguesa: see Galician
Sardinian (Italy); local with Craonnais, Large White, Berkshire and Casertana blood; black, grey, fulvous, or pied; long bristles; It. *Sarda*
Sarny: see Polesian
Satzeling (Hunan, China); var. of Huazhong Two-end Black; small lop ears; Ger. *Sa-ze-ling*
Schischka: see Šiška
Schumadija: see Šumadija
Schwäbisch-Hällisches: see Swabian-Hall
Schwerfurt Meat pig (E. Germany); m; hybrid orig.; Ger. *Schwerfurter Fleischschwein*
Scutari: see Shkodra
Semirechensk (S.E. Kazakhstan, USSR); m.ld; white, occ. black-pied, dark brown or tan; hy; short ears; orig. 1947-66 from Asiatic wild ($\frac{1}{16}$ - $\frac{1}{8}$) × Large White ($\frac{3}{4}$ - $\frac{7}{8}$) and Kemerovo ($\frac{1}{16}$ - $\frac{1}{8}$); recog. 1978; Russ. *Semirechenskaya*; syn. (till 1978) *Kazakh hybrid breed group* (Russ. *Kazakhskaya gibridnaya porodnaya gruppa*)
Serbian: see Šumadija
Shahutou; var. of Taihu
Shanghai White (Shanghai, China); m; semi-erect ears; orig. from Large White × Fengjing and Meishan
Shanxi Black (Shanxi, China); m.ld; orig. from Yorkshire, Berkshire, Russian Large White, Neijiang and Mashen
Shanzhu (Jiangsu, China); black; lop ears; not *Shantu*; orig. of Nanjing Black
Sheeted: see Saddleback
Shengxian Spotted (Zhejiang, China); Central China type; black with white feet
Shenxian (Hebei, China); var. of Huang-Huai-Hai Black
Shiang: see Xiang
Shishka: see Šiška
Shkodra; var. of Albanian; often black spots; It. *Scutari*; not *Skutari*
Short-eared White (USSR): see Russian Short-eared White
Shumadija, Shumadinka: see Šumadija
Siamese (Thailand): see Hailum, Kwai, Raad
[Siberian] (Omsk and Novosibirsk, USSR); prim.; coloured; syn. *local Siberian, local Novosibirsk, Tara* (Russ. *Tarskaya*); orig. of Kemerovo, North Siberian, Omsk Grey, Siberian Black Pied

Siberian Black Pied (N. Omsk and Novosibirsk, USSR); breed group; orig. from coloured culls in breeding North Siberian; Russ. *Sibirskaya chernopestraya*; syn. *Novosibirsk Spotted, Siberian Spotted*; part orig. of Omsk Grey

Sicilian: see Madonie-Sicilian

Siena Belted (Tuscany, Italy); black with white belt; It. *Cinta senese*; syn. *Cinta, Cinta italiana, Montagnola*; F_1 ($\times$ Large White) = Siena Grey; rare

Siena Grey (Tuscany, Italy); p.ld; Large White $\times$ Siena Belted, 1st cross; white with grey spots; It. *Grigia senese*

Sinchin: see Xinjin

Sinclair Miniature (USA); orig. from Minnesota and Pitman-Moore Miniatures at Sinclair Farm, Missouri, by Mike Tumbelson

Sin Hwai: see New Huai

Sintrão: see Torrejano

[Šiška] (S. Yugoslavia); m; prim.; grey; prick-eared; orig. of Šumadija, Turopolje; Ger. *Schischka*; not *Shishka, Siska*; extinct before 1982

Sitsin, Sitsiner, Sitszin: see Xinjin

Skutari: see Shkodra

Slavonian: see Black Slavonian

Slovakian Black Pied (Nitra, Czechoslovakia); ld; orig. (1952 on) from Mangalitsa, Berkshire, Large Black, Czech Improved White, Piétrain *et al.*; Sl. *Slovenské čiernostrakaté*; syn. *Czechoslovakian Black Pied, Slovakian Black Spotted*

Slovakian White (Slovakia, Czechoslovakia); orig. 1962-79 (recog. 1980) from Czech Improved White (37.5%) and Landrace (62.5%); Sl. *Slovenské biele mäsové* (= *Slovakian white meat*); syn. *Slovakian Improved Landschwein*

Slovenian White (Slovenia, Yugoslavia); m; Serbo-cro. *Slovenačka bela*

Slovhyb-1 (Slovakia, Czechoslovakia); orig. from Czech Improved White, Landrace and Slovakian White

[Slutsk Black Pied] (W. Byelorussia, USSR); ld; breed group; orig. from imported $\times$ native before 1919; Russ. *Chernopestraya slutskaya porodnaya gruppa*, Ger. *Slusker*; extinct by 1984

[Small Black] (E. England); vars: Black Essex and Black Suffolk; orig. of Suffolk-and-Essex var. of Large Black, and of American Essex; Neapolitan blood 1830; ? Chinese blood

Small Kansu: see Hezuo

[Small Polish Prick-eared] (S.E. Poland); prim.; black, red, pied or white; Pol. *Mała polska ostroucha*; syn. *local short-eared, native prick-eared*; formerly inc. Polesian; orig. (with Berkshire) of Puławy

[Small White] (England); Chinese (Cantonese) blood 1780 on; HB 1884; syn. *Middlesex, Small Yorkshire*

South African Landrace (S.Africa); m; orig. from Danish, Dutch and Swedish Landraces; HB 1959

South Central Jiangxi Spotted (S. Jiangxi, China); m; black-and-white; vars: Chayuan, Guanchao, Ruijin

South China (W. Malaysia); m; head and back black, belly and legs white

South China Black (W. Malaysia); m; black; syn. *Cantonese*

SOUTH CHINA TYPE: see Hainan, Huai, Lantang, Liang Guang Small Spotted, Longlin, South Yunnan Short-eared, Wuzhishan, Xiang, Yuedong Black

SOUTH-WEST CHINA TYPE; semi-lop ears; see Chenghua, Guanling, Kele, Huchuan Mountain, Neijiang, Rongchang, Wujin, Yanan

South Yunnan Short-eared (Yunnan, China); South China type; black; syn. *Dian-nan Small-ear, Southern Yunnan Small-eared*

Soviet Large White: see Russian Large White

Spotted (Indiana, USA); ld; black with white spots; orig. from local spotted (with Miami blood), Poland China, Gloucester Old Spot (1 ♂ and 1 ♀ imported 1914); BS 1914; syn. *Spot, Spotted Poland China* (to 1961)

Spotted Andalusian, Spotted Jabugo: see Andalusian Spotted

Srem, Sremica: see Black Mangalitsa

Sri Lanka Native (Sri Lanka); prim.; usu. black, also dark grey, tan, tan-and-grey, tan-and-black

Staffordshire: see Tamworth

Stocli; mountain var. of Romanian Native; syn. *Mountain Stocli*; not *Stokli*

Strei (Hunedoara, Transylvania, Romania); ld.m; black; orig. (1877 on) from Large Black and Mangalitsa × local. [R. Strei]

Subai (China)

Subotica White (N. Vojvodina, Yugoslavia); m; white; curly coat; orig. from Large White × Mangalitsa; Serbo-cro. *Domaća mesnata* (= *local meat*); syn. *Bikovačka* (from Bikovo)

Suffolk (England): see Black Suffolk

[Suffolk] (USA); m; orig. from Small White; extinct by 1979

[Šumadija] (N. Serbia, Yugoslavia); ld; orig. from Šiška; Serbo-cro. *Šumadinka* or *Šumadinska svinja*, Ger. *Schumadija*; syn. *Miloš* (Serbo-cro. *Miloševa*, Ger. *Milosch*); orig. of Mangalitsa; not *Shumadinka, Shumadija, Sumadia*; extinct before 1982

Sumatran (Indonesia); wild type

Sumba (Indonesia)

Swabian-Hall (Württemberg, Germany); white with black head and rump; lop ears; orig. from local Land pig with Berkshire and Essex blood in late 19th c. and Wessex in 1927; BSd 1925; BS till 1970, revived

1985; Ger. *Schwäbisch-Hällisches*; not *Swabian-Halle*; + Angeln = German Saddleback; nearly extinct

Swedish Landrace (Sweden); m; orig. from local (0.2%) graded to Danish Landrace (98.5%) imported chiefly 1914-15 and 1935-39, with some German blood (1.3%); BS 1907, HB 1911; Swe. *Svensk Lantras* or *Förädlad Lantras* (= *improved Landrace*); orig. of British Landrace

Swedish Large White; var. of Large White from British and German imports; Swe. *Stora vita Engelska* or *Svensk Yorkshire*

Swedish Spotted: see Old Swedish Spotted

Swiss Edelschwein (W. Switzerland); m; orig. from Large and Middle Whites; Ger. *Schweizerisches Edelschwein*, Fr. *Grand porc blanc*; syn. *Swiss Large White, Swiss Yorkshire*

Swiss Improved Landrace (C. and E. Switzerland); m; orig. from Large White (imported 1880-90) and German (Improved) Landrace (imported 1910-53), × native, improved by Dutch Landrace and Danish Landrace (1981); Ger. *Schweizerisches veredeltes Landschwein*, Fr. *Porc amélioré du pays*

Swiss Yorkshire: see Swiss Edelschwein

Syrmia: see Black Mangalitsa

[Szalonta] (N.E. Hungary); prim. 18th c. var; red; absorbed into Mangalitsa in early 19th c.

Ta-ho: see Dahe

Ta-hua-pai: see Cantonese

[Taichung] (C.Taiwan); ld; black; orig. 1960s at Taichung Dist. Agric. Improvement Sta., Peitou, from Taoyuan × Tingshuanghsi; extinct by 1979

Taihu (Taihu (= great lake) area of Jiangsu and Zhejiang, China); m; Lower Changjiang basin type; prolific; black; wrinkled face; long lop ears; vars: Erhualian, Fengjing, Jiaoxi, Jiaxing Black, Meishan, Mi, Shahutou; not *Taiwu*

Taiwan Miniature: see Lee-Sung

Taiwan Native: see Meinung, Taichung, Taoyuan, Tingshuanghsi; syn. *Formosa*

[Taiwan Small Black] (S.W. Taiwan); prim.; black; long straight face, very small ears; ? orig. from local Taiwan wild with South China blood; syn. *aboriginal, small short-eared, small long-snout*; ? extinct

[Taiwan Small Red] (Wushe, Taiwan); prim.; red; slightly dished wrinkled face, short ears, straight tail, stiff mane in ♂; ? orig. from South China with blood of local Taiwan wild

Taiwu: see Taihu

Tamworth (England); m; golden red; recog. 1850-60; BS and HB 1906;

syn. *Staffordshire*: nearly extinct in GB; BS also USA (rare), Australia

Tanyang: see Danyang

Taoyuan (N.W. Taiwan); ld; black or dark grey; lop ears; wrinkled skin; straight tail; orig. from S. China; W.G. *T'ao-yüan*, Jap. *Toyen*; syn. *Lung-tan-po, Chung-li*; not *Tauyuen*; nearly extinct

Tara, Tarskaya: see Siberian

Tatú (S. Brazil); ld; sim. to Pirapitinga; usu. black and hairless; Chinese orig; syn. *Bahia* (not *Baé, Baia, Baié*) (N.E.), *Macao, Tatuzinho*. [= armadillo (from shape of head)]

Tauyuen: see Taoyuan

Ta-wei-tzu: see Daweizi

Tetra-S (Hungary); 3-line hybrid derived from Duroc, Dutch Landrace and Large White or Belgian Landrace

Thai, Thailand: see Hailum, Kwai, Raad

Thin Rind: see Hampshire

Thuoc Nhieu (Vietnam)

Tia Sing: see Jiaxing Black

Tibetan (Qinghai-Tibet plateau, China); Plateau type; dwarf; black, occ. brown; hy; Ch. *Zangzhu* (= *Tibetan pig*)

Ting, Tinger, Tinghsien: see Ding

[Tingshuanghsi] (N.E. Taiwan); ld; sim. to Taoyuan but larger frame; not *Din-Hsiang-Chi*; extinct by 1979

Tongcheng (S.E. Hubei, China); var. of Huazhong Two-end Black; W.G. *T'ung-ch'eng*, Ger. *Tung-tschen*

Torrejano (C. Portugal); black and white; crossbred orig. from Bisaro; syn. *Sintrão*; disappearing. [from Torres Vedras]

Toyen: see Taoyuan

Transtagana: see Alentejana

[Transylvanian]; var. of Romanian Native

Troll: see Munich Miniature

Tshen-Hua: see Chenghua

Tsinghwa: see Jinhua

Tsivilsk (Chuvash ASSR, USSR); m.ld; breed group; orig. *c.* 1956 from local Large White × local Chuvash; Russ. *Tsivilskaya porodnaya gruppa*; Ger. *Zivilsker*

Tszilin: see Jilin

Tszinkhua: see Jinhua

Tunchang (Hainan I, China); ld; black back, white body; var. of Hainan; syn. *Denchang*

Tungcheng, T'ung-ch'eng, Tung-tschen: see Tongcheng

Tungyang: see Dongyang

Turopolje (Croatia, Yugoslavia); ld; white with black spots; orig. from Šiška with Berkshire blood at end of 19th c; Serbo-cro. *Turopoljska*;

syn. *Zagreb*; rare

UKB-1 (Ukraine, USSR); strain of Russian Large White recog. 1984; syn. *Ukrainian Large White - 1*

[Ukrainian] (USSR); local population of European short-eared type; spotted; orig. (with English breeds) of Dnieper, Mirgorod, Podolian, Ukrainian Spotted Steppe and Ukrainian White Steppe

Ukrainian Large White - 1: see UKB-1

Ukrainian Spotted Steppe (S. Ukraine, USSR); ld.m; sim. to Ukrainian White Steppe but spotted and with bristles; orig. from Ukrainian White Steppe × local spotted with some Berkshire blood; recog. 1961; Russ. *Ukrainskaya stepnaya ryabaya*

Ukrainian White Steppe (S. Ukraine, USSR); m.ld; orig. since 1925 (recog. 1934) from Ukrainian with 2 or 3 crosses of Large White; Russ. *Ukrainskaya stepnaya belaya*; syn. *White Ukrainian*

Ulster, Ulster White: see Large White Ulster

Unhudo de Goias (Goias, Brazil); large hoof

Urzhum (Kirov, USSR); m; orig. (crossing since 1893, breed development since 1945, recog. 1957) from Large White × local lop-eared; HB; Russ. *Urzhumskaya*

[Valtellina] (N. Lombardy, Italy); m; black

Vara: see Furão

V.D.L.; see German (Improved) Landrace

Venezuelan Black (llanos of S. Venezuela and Colombia); semi-feral

Vezičevka, Vezičevo: see Resava

[Vich] (Catalonia, Spain); Celtic type, sim. to Vitoria; syn. *Catalan*

[Victoria] (Indiana, USA); ld; orig. 1850-86 from Poland China, Berkshire, Chester White, and Suffolk; BS 1886; extinct by 1979. [from sow named Queen Victoria]

Vietnamese (Vietnam); see Ba Xuyen, Co, Í, Lang Hong, Meo, Mong Cai, Muang Khong, Thuoc Nhieu; syn. *Annamese* (Fr. *Annamite*), *Delta*

[Vita Vet Lab Minipig] (Marion, Indiana, USA); light grey; orig. from Florida swamp pigs, 1948 on

[Vitoria] (Álava, N. Spain); m; hairless; orig. from local Celtic type improved by Large White *et al.*; Sp. *Vitoriana* or *Chato de Vitoria*; syn. *Álava, Basque-Navarre, Chato* (= *short-nosed*) *vitoriano*

Waddle: see Red Wattle

[Wai Chow] (Hong Kong); var. of Cantonese; black; W.G. *Wei-chou*;

syn. *Lung Kong*
Wannan Spotted; var. of Wanzhe Spotted; syn. *Lantian Spotted*
Wanshan: see Wenchang
Wanzhe Spotted (Anhui/Zhejiang, China); m; Central China type; black-and-white; vars: Chunan Spotted, Wannan Spotted
Warren County: see Miami
Wattle, Wattler: see Red Wattle
Wei (S.E. Anhui, China); Lower Changjiang Basin type
Wei-chou: see Wai Chow
Welsh (Wales); m; lop ears; BS and HB 1918; crossed with Swedish Landrace since 1953; syn. (before Landrace cross) *Old Glamorgan*
Wenchang (Hainan I, China); var. of Hainan; Ger. *Wenschan*; not *Wanshan*
Wenzhan White (China)
[Wessex Saddleback] (England); m; black with white belt; orig. from Old English; HB and BS 1918-1967; combined with Essex 1967 to form British Saddleback; syn. *Belted, Sheeted Wessex*
West African (S. of lat. 10°-14° N); prim.; Iberian type; black, white or pied; inc. Ashanti Dwarf (Ghana), Bakosi (Cameroon), Nigerian Native; ? Port. orig.
West French White (N.W. France); m; Celtic type; formed 1955 by joining Boulonnais, Breton, Craonnais, Flemish, Normand; HB 1958; Fr. *Blanc de l'Ouest*: syn. *Western White*; nearly extinct—only Normand remains
Westrain (England); m; orig. by Walls from *Wes*sex × Pié*train*
Wettringer: see Bentheim Black Pied
White: see Large, Middle, Small
White Edelschwein: see Edelschwein
White-faced: see Hereford
White Large Black: see British Lop
White Long-eared (USSR): see Russian Long-eared White
White Lop: see British Lop
[White Prick-eared] (W. Poland); m.ld; former var. of Polish Large White; orig. since late 19th c. from Edelschwein × Polish Native; named 1918; Pol. *Biała ostroucha*; syn. *Polish White Short-eared*; combined with Large White in 1956 to form Polish Large White
White-Russian Black Pied or *Spotted*: see Byelorussian Black Pied
White Russian Meat type: see Byelorussian commercial hybrid
White Short-eared (USSR): see Russian Short-eared White
White Ukrainian: see Ukrainian White Steppe
wild (Europe and Asia) = *Sus scrofa* Linnaeus; divided into about 20 subspp.
Windsor: see Middle White

Woburn: see Hampshire
Wujin (border of Yunnan, Guizhou and Sichuan, China); S.W. China type; small; usu. black, occ. brown; not *Wugin, Wujing*; var: Dahe
Wuyi Black (Jiangxi/Fujian, China); Central China type. [Wuyi mts]
Wuzhishan (Hainan and C. mts of Guangdong); South China type; black with white belly and feet

Xiang (S. Guizhou and N. Guangxi, China); South China type; black, usu. with white belly and feet; not *Shiang*
Xiangxi Black (Hunan, China); Central China type
Xiaoer (China); = small-eared
Xiaohua (China); = small spotted: see Liang Guang Small Spotted
Xinhuai: see New Huai; not *Xinhui*
Xinjin (N.E. China); m; black with white points; orig. in 1920s from Berkshire × local (Min); W.G. *Hsin-chin*, Ger. *Ching Ching*; syn. *Sitsin, Sitsiner, Sitszin*; not *Sinchin*; vars: Jilin Black (Jilin), Ning-an (Heilongjiang), Xinjin (Liaoning)

Yanan (Sichuan, China); ld.m; South-West China type; black
Yangxin (S.E. Hubei, China); Lower Changjiang Basin type
Yili White (N.W. Xinjiang, China); m; orig. from Russian Large White × local white crossbreds
Yimeng Black (Shandong, China); m.ld; North China type. [Ling*yi* and *Meng*yang counties]
Yongkang (Zhejiang, China); var. of Jinhua; W.G. *Yung-k'ang*, Russ. *Yunkan*, Ger. *Jungkang*
York, Yorkshire: see Large White, Middle White, Small White
[Yorkshire Blue and White] (N. England); local var; ? orig. from Large White × Large Black; syn. *Bilsdale Blue*; last boar licensed 1963/64
Young-tshang: see Rongchang
Yucatan Miniature (Colorado, USA); local Yucatan selected for small size at Colorado State Univ. since 1972; grey; hairless
Yuedong Black (E. Guangdong, China); South China type
Yugoslav Meat White
Yujiang (*Yu*shan, Jiangxi and *Jiang*shan, Zhejiang, China); Central China type; syn. *Yushan Black*
Yungchang: see Rongchang
Yungkang: see Yongkang
Yunnan Small-eared: see South Yunnan Short-eared
Yushan Black: see Yujiang

Zang, Zangzhu: see Tibetan

Zhunchan, Zhungan: see Rongchang

Złotniki (Poznań, Poland); p.(ld); orig. (1946-62) by selection from Large Polish Long-eared with some Large White blood; Pol. *Złotnicka*; pied (black spotted) and white vars; rare

Żuławska: see Polish Marsh

Zungo (Colombia); ld; grey; hairless; Criollo type; syn. *Zungo costeño*

Addendum

BN; var. of Belgian Landrace selected for resistance to stress; syn. *Landrace Belge Halothane Négatif*

SHEEP

Abda: see Doukkala

Abidi: see Ibeidi

ABRO Damline (Scotland); m; pd; line to replace Border Leicester as sire of lowland ewes, developed at Animal Breeding Research Organisation, Edinburgh since 1967 from Finnish Landrace (47%), East Friesian (24%), Border Leicester (17%), Dorset Horn (12%), selected for 8-week litter weight

Abyssinian: see Ethiopian

Acchelé Guzai: see Akele Guzai

Adali (Dancalia, N.E. Ethiopia); m; blond (white to light brown), occ. pied or dark brown; hy; pd; syn. *Afar*

Adikarasial: see Kilakarsal

Adromalicha: see Sfakia

Afar: see Adali

Afghan: see Afghan Arabi (N), Baluchi (extreme S), Gadik (N.E), Ghiljai (S.E), Hazaragie (C), Kandahari (S. and W), Karakul (extreme N), Turki (N.E.)

Afghan Arabi (N. Afghanistan); cw.m; usu. black or grey with white face-blaze, also white; long ears; pd; fr; vars in Herat (usu. white with black nose—probably Kandahari blood) and in Kataghan and Bamyan (usu. brown—probably crosses with Turki)

Africana (S. America): see Red African

Africander (S. Africa); African Long-fat-tailed type; various colours; hy; pd or hd; lft; orig. from Hottentot; Afrik. *Afrikaner*; syn. *Cape Fat-tailed*; vars: Damara, Namaqua, Ronderib; not *Africaner, Afrikander*

AFRICAN LONG-FAT-TAILED (E. and S. Africa); hy; tail usu. long and fat—broad with hanging tip, twisted, cylindrical, strap-shaped, funnel-shaped or carrot-shaped; inc. Africander, Madagascar, Malawi, Mondombes, Nguni, Sabi, Tanzania Long-tailed, Tswana

AFRICAN LONG-LEGGED; hy; ♂ hd, ♀ pd; lop ears; thin tail; inc. Angola Long-legged, Baluba, Sahelian, Sudan Desert, Zaïre Long-legged; orig. from Ancient Egyptian

Afridi: see Tirahi

Afrino (S. Africa); m.fw; orig. 1969-76 (named) at Carnarvon Exp. Sta., Cape prov., from South African Mutton Merino × (Ronderib Africander × South African Merino)

Afshari (Iranian Kurdistan); m; ? var. of Red Karaman

Agnis (Indiana, USA); mahogany red with white poll and tail tip
Agra: see White Karaman
agrinon: see Cyprus mouflon
Agul; var. of Lezgian
Ainsi (S. of N. Yemen); m.cw; brown (*bunni*), black, and white vars; pd;
   ft; syn. *Ansi*
Ait Barka (S.E. of Marrakech, Morocco); black var. of Berber
Ait Haddidou (Morocco); var. of Berber; white, often with black marks
   on head
Ait Mohad (Morocco); large var. of Berber; white; pd
Akele Guzai (Eritrea); cw. var. of Abyssinian; usu. black; It. *Acchelé
   Guzai*; syn. *Shimenzana* (It. *Scimenzana*)
Akhangaran Mutton-Wool (Uzbekistan, USSR); m.w; orig. from Caucas-
   ian and Lincoln × Jaidara; Russ. *Akhangaranskaya myaso-sherstnaya*
Ak-Karaman: see White Karaman
Aknoul (Morocco); small earless var. of Berber; black
Akrah: see White Karaman
Aktyubinsk Semicoarsewool (N.E. Kazakhstan, USSR); m.mw; orig.
   from Sary-Ja × Kazakh Fat-rumped; Russ. *Aktyubinskaya polugrubo-
   sherstnaya*
Alai (S. Kirgizia, USSR); m.w; occ. coloured spots on head and legs; ♂
   pd or small horns, ♀ pd; fr; orig. 1934-81 from Kirgiz Fat-rumped
   with Précoce blood 1938-40 and 1945, and Sary-Ja blood since 1953;
   Russ. *Alaiskaya* or *Alaiskaya kurdyuchnaya* (= *Alai Fat-rumped*)
Alaskan white: see Dall's sheep
Ala-Tau argali: see arkhar
Albanian Vlach: see Arvanitovlach
Albanian Zackel; inc. Common Albanian, Mati, Pied Polish, Shkodra
Alcarreña (La Alcarria, Guadalajara and Cuenca, New Castille, Spain);
   m.mw; Entrefino type; sometimes light brown marks on head and
   legs, occ. all black; pd; syn. *Manchega pequeña* (*i.e. small var. of
   Manchega*)
Alfort: see Dishley Merino
Algarve Churro (S. Faro, Portugal); m.cw; white with black spots on
   face and feet, or black (10%); hd; Port. *Churra algarvia*; orig. from
   Andalusian Churro imported *c.* 1870-90
Algerian: see Algerian Arab, Raimbi and Beni Guil
Algerian Arab (Algeria); m.cw; ♂ hd, ♀ pd; syn. *Ouled Jellal*; orig. of
   Tadmit
Alpagota (Alpago, Belluno, Venetia, Italy); mw.m.d; Lop-eared Alpine
   group but small ears; black or chestnut spots on face; HB; syn. *Pagota*
Alpine: see French Alpine, Lop-eared Alpine, Savoy, Swiss White
   Mountain, Thônes-Marthod

Alpine Lop-eared: see Lop-eared Alpine

Alpine Piedmont: see Biellese

Altai (S.W. Siberia, USSR); fw.m; orig. 1934-49 at Rubtsovsk state farm (now Ovtsevod breeding centre) from American Rambouillet (1928-36), Caucasian and Australian Merino (1936 on), × Siberian Merino; recog. as breed group in 1940 and named *Siberian Rambouillet* (Russ. *Sibirskiĭ Rambulye*) or *Soviet Rambouillet of Siberian type* (Russ. *Sovetskiĭ Rambulye sibirskogo tipa*); recog. as breed 1948; HB; Russ. *Altaĭskaya* or *Altaĭskaya poroda tonkorunnykh ovets* (= *Altai breed of finewooled sheep*); syn. *Altai Merino*; not *Altay, Altayan*

Altai, Altaĭskaya: see also Telengit

Altai Mountain (USSR); mw; breed group; orig. from Tsigai 1945 × [Merino × (Merino × local coarsewooled) 1940]; Russ. *Gorno-altaĭskaya porodnaya gruppa*

Altamurana (Altamura, Bari, Apulia, Italy); d.cw.(m); Moscia type; occ. dark spots on face; ♂ usu. pd, ♀ pd; BSd 1958, HB; syn. *delle Murge*

Altay Fat-rumped (N. Xinjiang, China); var. of Kazakh Fat-rumped

Amalé: see Sudan Desert

Amasya Herik: see Herik

American bighorn: see bighorn

American Four-horned: see Jacob, Navajo-Churro

AMERICAN HAIR SHEEP (Tropical America); m; usu. tan or white, also pied; hy, ♂ usu. with mane and throat ruff (except Brazil); pd; orig. from West African Dwarf (? from C. Africa *e.g.* Angola); inc. Bahama Native, Barbados Blackbelly, Morada Nova, Pelibüey, Red African, Santa Inês, Virgin Island White

American Merino (USA); fw; orig. from Spanish Merino imported 1793-1811; BS 1906; vars: A type or Vermont, B type, and C type or Delaine

American Rambouillet (USA); fw.m; ♂ hd or pd, ♀ pd; orig. from Rambouillet imported 1840-60 from France and 1882-*c*.1900 from Germany; BS 1889; HB also in Canada; var: Polled Rambouillet

American Tunis (USA); m; red face and legs; pd; [ft]; orig. from Tunisian Barbary imported in 1799; BS 1896; rare

ammon: see argali

Amran Black (N. and N.W. of San'a, N. Yemen); m.cw; pd; ft

Amran Grey (N.W. and W. of San'a, N. Yemen); m.cw; light to dark grey; pd; ft

Anatolian fat-tailed breeds: see Awassi, Dağliç, Herik, Red Karaman, White Karaman

Anatolian Merino: see Central Anatolian Merino

Anatolian red (S. Anatolia, Turkey) = *Ovis orientalis anatolica* Val.; var. of red sheep; syn. *Anatolian wild, Cilician*

[Ancient Egyptian] (N.E. Africa); hy; ♂ hd; lop ears; thin tail; orig. of African Long-legged; syn. *Hamitic Long-tailed, Ovis longipes palaeoaegypticus*

[Ancon] (Massachusetts, USA); achondroplastic mutant occurring in 1791, extinct about 1876; syn. *Otter*; similar mutant occurred in Norway in 1919. [Gr. = elbow]

Andalusian Churro (coast of Huelva and Cadiz, Andalucía); largest var. of Spanish Churro; syn. *Atlántica, Lebrijana* (from Lebrija), *Marismeña* (from marshes (*marismas*) of Guadalquivir delta); = Algarve Churro (Portugal)

Andalusian Merino (W. Andalucía, Spain); m.mw-fw; var. of Merino, larger and with coarser wool; subvar: Grazalema; Sp. *Merina andaluza entrefina*; syn. *Campiñesa, Córdoba de la Campaña*

Andi (Dagestan, USSR); Caucasian Fat-tailed type; hd; black (sometimes with white patches on head and tail tip) or white (often with coloured markings on head, legs and tail); Russ. *Andiĭskaya*

Andorra, Andorran: see Spanish Churro

Angara Merino (Irkutsk, USSR); var. of Krasnoyarsk; recog. 1974; orig. from Altai (1955) × (Précoce × Buryat); Russ. *Priangarskiĭ Merinos*

[Anglesey] (N.W. Wales); extinct 1929

[Anglo-Merino] (England); Negretti and Paular strains of Spanish Merino × various English breeds (esp. Southdown and Ryeland) at beginning of 18th c; syn. *English Merino*

Anglo-Merino (Poland): see Polish Anglo-Merino

Angola Long-legged (Malanje and Moxico, Angola); m; African Long-legged group; white, occ. pied; hy; ♂ hd, ♀ pd

Angola Maned (Huambo, C. Angola); m; white, black or pied; hy with mane and throat ruff in ♂; pd or hd; syn. *Coquo*; *cf.* West African Dwarf

Anogia: see Psiloris

Ansi: see Ainsi

Ansotana (Ansó valley, N.W. Huesca, Aragon, Spain); var. of Aragonese with longer wool and semi-open fleece; syn. *Calva*, syn. (with Roncalesa) *Entrefina pirenaica* (= *Pyrenean Semifinewool*)

Aohan Finewool (S. Inner Mongolia, China); fw.m; ♂ hd, ♀ pd; orig. from Russian Merinos × Mongolian in early 1950s with Australian blood in 1970s

Aouasse: see Awassi

aoudad (N.Africa) = *Ammotragus lervia* (Pallas); actually a maned, beardless goat; Fr. *mouflon à manchettes*, Ger. *Mähnerschaf*, It. *muflone berbero*, Sp. *árrui*; syn. *arui, barbary wild sheep, bearded argali*; not *audad, udad*; type sp. in Maghreb, subspp. in Sudan, Egypt (rare), Libya (rare), S. Sahara

APENNINE GROUP (Apennines from Tuscany/Emilia to Abruzzo, Italy); m.d.mw; mixed type orig. from Merino × local with Bergamasca and Sopravissana blood; usu. white, sometimes black; hd or pd; It. *Appenninica*; inc. Apennine, Cornella White, Garfagnina White, Locale, Massese, Nostrana, Pagliarola, Pomarancina, Vissana, Zucca Modenese

Apennine (Apennines, Italy); m.(d.mw); Apennine group; pd; semi-lop ears; HB; It. *Appenninica*; local vars, formerly recog. inc. Cornigliese, Tarina and Varzese (Emilia), Casentinese, Chianina and Senese (Tuscany), Casciana and Perugian Lowland (Umbria), Barisciano and Chietina (Abruzzo)

Appennino-Modenese: see Pavullese

[Appenzell]; part orig. of Swiss White Mountain; Ger. *Appenzeller*

Apulian Merino: see Gentile di Puglia

Aquila, Aquilana: see Barisciano

ara-ara (Niger); call for sheep, not a breed name; syn. *are-are*

Arab (Egypt): see Barki

Arab (Somalia): see Somali Arab

Arab (Turkey): see Awassi

Arab (W. Africa): see Maure

Arabi (Afghanistan): see Afghan Arabi

Arabi (S.W. Iran, S. Iraq, N.E. Arabia); m.cw; Near East Fat-tailed type; black, also pied or white with black head; ♂ hd, ♀ pd; orig. of Wooled Persian (S. Africa); not *Arbi* (fem. *Arbiyah*); *cf.* Shafali (Syria)

Arabi (USSR); black var. of Karakul

Arabian Long-tailed: see Najdi

Aragats (Armenia, USSR); var. of Armenian Semicoarsewool; orig. at Aragats state farm from Balbas × [Rambouillet or Lincoln × (Rambouillet or Lincoln × Balbas)]; Russ. *Aragatsskaya*; obs. syn. *Armenian Semifinewooled Fat-tailed breed group* (Russ. *Armyanskaya polutonkorunnaya zhirnokhvostaya porodnaya gruppa*)

Araghi (Iran): see Baluchi

Aragonese (Aragon and W. Catalonia, Spain); m.mw; Entrefino type; pd; BS; Sp. *Rasa aragonesa*; vars: Ansotana, Monegrina, Roncalesa, Turolense. [Sp. *rasa* = smooth (fleece)]

Aral, Aralsk: see South Kazakh Merino

Aranesa (Arán valley, N.W. Lérida, Catalonia, Spain); = Tarasconnais

Arapawa Island (Marlborough Sounds, New Zealand); fw; feral; usu. black with white blaze, occ. white; hd; orig. from Australian Merino in 1860s; syn. *Arapawa Merino*; rare

Arbi, Arbiyah: see Arabi

Archa: see Harcha

Ardèche, Ardèchois: see Blanc du Massif Central

Ardes (S. Puy-de-Dôme, C. France); d.m.cw; Central Plateau type; pd; orig. from Lacaune × local; not *Ardres*; nearly extinct

are-are: see ara-ara

argali (C. Asia—Himalayas to Mongolia) = *Ovis ammon* Linnaeus; shades of brown; large horns of ammon type; st; syn. *O. polii* Blyth, *ammon*; many vars (subspp.) inc. arkhar, Marco Polo's sheep (*q.v.*). [Mongolian = wild sheep]

Argentine Cormo (Patagonia, Argentina); mw; orig. by John Blake on Condor estate, Rio Gallegas, from Cormo, Peppin Merino ($\frac{3}{16}$) and Corriedale; sim. to Cormo (Australia)

Argentine Merino; fw.m; orig. from Criollo improved by Spanish and Saxony Merinos 1813-74, graded to Rambouillet 1875-90

Argos (Greece); d.m.cw; lft; orig. from Chios or Anatolian fat-tailed × Greek Zackel; syn. *Karamaniko*; rare

arhar: see arkhar

Ariano, Improved: see Improved Ariano

Ariège, Ariègeois: see Tarasconnais

arkal (Ust-Urt, between Caspian and Aral Sea, Russian Turkestan) = *Ovis vignei arkal* Eversmann; var. of urial; syn. *O. orientalis arkal, Transcaspian urial*; not *arkar*

arkhar (Ala-Tau, E. Kirgizia) = *Ovis ammon karelini* Severtzov; var. of argali; syn. *Ala-Tau argali, Issyk Kul argali, Karelin's argali, Tien Shan argali*; orig. (with Merino) of Kazakh Arkhar-Merino; not *arhar, arkar*

Arkhar-Merino: see Kazakh Arkhar-Merino

Arles Merino (Provence, S. France); fw.m.(d); ♂ usu. hd, occ. pd (*motti*), ♀ usu. pd, occ. hd (*banetto*); orig. from local graded to Spanish Merino in late 18th and early 19th c. and improved by Châtillonais var. of Précoce since 1921; HB 1946, BS; Fr. *Mérinos d'Arles*; syn. *Provence Merino, Var Merino*; former vars: Camargue (grey) and Crau (reddish)

Armenian red (Armenia, USSR) = *Ovis orientalis armeniana* Nasonov; var. of red sheep

Armenian Semicoarsewool (Armenia, USSR); mw.m.d; ft; orig. from Rambouillet and Lincoln × Balbas; Russ. *Armyanskaya polugrubo-sherstnaya*; vars. Aragats and Martunin (*q.v.*)

Armenian Semifinewooled Fat-tailed: see Aragats

Arrit (Keren, Eritrea); d.m; usu. white, also blond, red or pied; hy-cw; pd, ♂ occ. hd; fat at base of tail

arrui: see aoudad

Artésien: see Artois

[Artois] (N. France); var. of Flemish Marsh; orig. (with Leicester) of Boulonnais; Fr. *Artésien*

arui: see aoudad

Arusi-Bale; var. of Abyssinian with woolly undercoat; brown, grey, roan or dun; ♂ hd, ♀ pd or hd

Arvanitovlach; mountain var. of Greek Zackel, usu. white with black round eyes; Gr. *Arvanitovlakhiko* (= *Albanian Vlach*)

Asali; var. of Najdi

Ascanian: see Askanian

Ashfal: see Shafali

Ashgur (N. Sudan); commonest var. of Sudan Desert; sandy to red; syn. *Shugor*. [Arabic = fawn]

Ashkhabad; superior var. of Sary-Ja; Russ. *Ashkhabadskaya*

Askanian (S. Ukraine, USSR); fw.m; orig. 1925-34 from Merinos at Askania Nova improved by American Rambouillet; Russ. *Askaniĭskaya* or *Askaniĭskaya poroda tonkorunnykh ovets* (= *Askanian breed of finewool sheep*); obs. syn. *Soviet Rambouillet of Askanian type* (to 1934), *Askanian Rambouillet* (Russ. *Askaniĭskiĭ Rambulye*); not *Ascanian*; HB, also in Bulgaria

Askanian Corriedale (Askania Nova, USSR); m.mw; orig. from English Longwool × Askanian

Assaf (Israel); d; orig. from East Friesian × Israeli Improved Awassi since 1955, 32.5-62.5% East Friesian; HB

Astrakhan: see Karakul; not *Astarakan, Astrakan*

Atlantic Coast (Morocco); Fr. *Race côtière atlantique*; inc. Beni Ahsen, Doukkala, Zemmour

audad: see aoudad

Aure-Campan (S.E. Hautes-Pyrénées, France); m.mw; Central Pyrenean group; pale brownish-grey (*bis*), occ. black; ♂ usu. hd, ♀ usu. pd; HB 1975; Fr. *Race d'Aure et de Campan*, or *Aurois*; syn. *Lannemezan*; former var: Campan (smaller and always pd)

Aurina: see Pusterese

Ausemy, Ausimi: see Ossimi

Australian Merino (Australia and New Zealand); fw; ♂ hd (or pd), ♀ pd (or hd); orig. 1797-1804 from Spanish Merino (Negretti strain) via England and Cape Colony, to give Camden Park Fine Merino (1797 - c.1856), improved in turn by Saxony Merino, Rambouillet, American Rambouillet, American Merino (so-called 'Vermont'); Anglo-Merino and English Longwool blood (1840-70) in strong and medium strains; bred *inter se* since 1907; HB 1923, BS 1959; strains: Fine (Tasmanian), Medium Peppin, Medium Non-Peppin, and Strong (South Australian); vars: Booroola Merino, Fonthill Merino, Poll Merino, Trangie Fertility Merino

Australian Zenith: see Zenith

[Austrian Negretti] (Austria); fw; orig. from Negretti strain of Spanish

Merino × local breeds
Auvergnat, Auvergne: see Central Plateau type
[Avar] (Dagestan, USSR); cw.m; Caucasian Fat-tailed type; white, with
black or red on head and feet; ♂ usu. hd, ♀ hd or pd; Russ. *Avarskaya*;
var: Tlyarota (with Lezgian and Tushin blood)
Avikalin (Rajasthan, India); cw; strain developed at Central Sheep and
Wool Res. Inst., *Avika*nagar, from Rambouillet × Malpura in 1970s
Avivastra (Rajasthan, India); fw; strain developed at Central Sheep and
Wool Res. Inst., *Avi*kanagar from Rambouillet × Chokla; not
Avivastar
Avranchin (S. Manche, N. France); m.lw; sim. to Cotentin but smaller;
brownish face and feet; pd; orig. from Leicester Longwool (+
Southdown and Romney) × local (1830-1900); BS 1928; syn. *Race
du littoral sud de la Manche*. [= Avranches district]
Awassi (Syria, Israel, Lebanon, Jordan, C. and W. Iraq, and S.E.
Turkey); m.d.cw; Near East Fat-tailed type; white with brown head
and legs, sometimes black, white, grey or spotted face, occ. all brown
or black; ♂ hd, ♀ usu. pd; Turk. *Ivesi*; syn. *Arab* (Turkey); *Baladi,
Deiri, Shami* (Syria); *Gezirieh* (Iraq); *Syrian*; vars: Israeli Improved
Awassi, Ne'imi and Shafali (Iraq); orig. of Pak Awassi; not *Aouasse,
Awas, Awasi, Awass, El Awas, Iwessi, Ousi, Oussi, Ussy*
Awsemy: see Ossimi
Azerbaijan Mountain Merino (Kedabek, Azerbaijan, USSR); fw; orig.
from Kedabek Merino × Bozakh; crossed with Askanian 1935;
recog. 1947; Russ. *Azerbaĭdzhanskiĭ gornyĭ Merinos*; not *Azerbaidjan,
Azerbaidzhan*
Azerbaijan Mutton-Wool (Azerbaijan, USSR); breed group; Russ.
Azerbaĭdzhanskaya myaso-sherstnaya porodnaya gruppa
Azov Tsigai (Ukraine, USSR); m.mw; var. of Tsigai; orig. from Romney
× Tsigai, F₁ bred *inter se*; recog. 1963; Russ. *Priazovskaya tsigaiskaya*
Azrou: see Timhadite

Badana (Bragança, N.E. Portugal); m.cw; often brown face and feet; ♂
usu. hd, ♀ pd; syn. *Marialveira* (from Marialva)
Badger Faced Welsh Mountain (Wales); colour var. of Welsh Mountain;
white with black belly and face-stripes; BS 1976; Welsh *Torddu* (=
blackbelly); syn. *Defaid Idloes, Welsh Badger-faced*
Badia, Badiota: see Pusterese
Baghdale (Punjab, Pakistan); fw; brown round eyes; ♂ occ. hd, ♀ pd;
orig. at Kala*bagh* farm, Mianwali, from Hissar*dale* (25%), Damani
(25%) and Rambouillet (50%); not *Bhagdale*
Bagnes: see Roux-de-Bagnes

Bagnolese (Bagnoli Irpino, Avellino, Campania, Italy); m.mw; light chestnut forequarters; pd; sim. to Comisana (by crossing); rare

Bagri (Bagar tract, around Delhi, India); m.cw; local var. of Bikaneri group; usu. brown or black head; not *Bagir*

Bahama Native (Bahamas); m; American Hair sheep group but with European influence; usu. white with coloured spots; ♂ hd, ♀ pd; syn. *Long Island*

Bahawalpuri: see Buchi

Bahu (Kibali-Ituri, N.E. Zaïre); brown or pied; dwarf; hd; syn. *Congo Dwarf*

Bains: see Velay Black

Bakarwal: see Bhakarwal

Bakewell Leicester: see Leicester Longwool

Bakhtiari (Iran); var. of Bakhtiari-Luri; not *Bakhtyari*

Bakhtiari-Luri (Lorestan, Iran); m.d.cw; white, occ. coloured marks on head and legs, occ. all black or brown; pd; lft; vars: Bakhtiari, Luri

Bakkarwal: see Bhakarwal

Bakur (USSR); rare

Baladi (Egypt): see Fellahi

Baladi (Syria): see Awassi

Balami, Balandji, Balani: see Bornu

Balangir (Bolangir, N.W. Orissa, India); cw; white, light brown or pied; ♂ hd, ♀ pd

Balbas (S.E. Armenia and Nakhichevan, USSR); Caucasian Fat-tailed type; black or brown spots on face and feet; ♂ occ. hd, ♀ pd; Russ. *Balbas* or *Balbasskaya*

Baldebukov: see German Merino

Balearic: see Ibiza, Majorcan, Minorcan, Red Majorcan

Balemi: see Bornu

Balestra: see Pavullese

Bali-Bali: see Uda

Baljuša (Metohija, Yugoslavia); Pramenka type; black face

Balkar: see Karachai

Balkhi (extreme N.W. of Pakistan); m.cw; usu. black or grey; hd (short); fr; not *Balkai*; ? = Hissar (Tajikistan)

Balonndi: see Bornu

Baltistani (N. Kashmir, Pakistan); m.cw.d; often brown or tan or pied; pd; st.

Baluba (Katanga, Zaïre); African Long-legged group; hy, maned; lop ears; st.

Baluchi (S.W. Pakistan, E. Iran and S. Afghanistan); cw.d.m; black marks on head and legs; ♂ hd (Pakistan) or pd (Iran and Afghanistan), ♀ pd; ft; syn. *Baluchi dumba, Mengali, Taraki, Shinwari* (Baluchistan),

Araghi, Farahani, Kermani, Khorasani or *Khurasani, Naeini* or *Neini, Yazdi* (Iran); not *Balouchi, Baloutche, Beluj*

Balwen (Powys, Wales); syn. *Defaid Bal*; rare

[Bampton Nott] (Devon, England); orig. (+ Southam Nott and × Leicester Longwool) of Devon Longwoolled. [nott = pd]

Bandur: see Mandya

banetto = hd ♀ Arles Merino

Bangladeshi (Bangladesh); cw; dwarf; prolific; syn. *Bengal, Bera, Bhera* or *Wera* (= sheep)

Bannur: see Mandya; not *Baunur*

Banpala: see Bonpala

Bantu (S. Africa): see Damara, Nguni, Tswana

Bapedi (Sekhukhuneland, N.E. Transvaal, S. Africa); var. of Nguni, ? with Namaqua blood; syn. *Pedi, Transvaal Kaffir*

Baraka (S.W. Keren, Eritrea); sim to Sudan Desert but smaller and with long hair, ? with Arrit blood; ♂ hd or pd, ♀ pd; It. *Barca*; syn. *Begghié Korboraca, Shukria* (It. *Sciucria*)

Barasi, Barazi (N. Syria): see White Karaman

Barbado (Texas, USA); m. hunted; tan, tan with pale or black belly, or pied; hy-cw; ♂ hd, ♀ pd; orig. from Barbados Blackbelly in early 20th c. with blood of American Rambouillet, mouflon *et al.*; rare

Barbados Blackbelly (Barbados); m; prolific; American Hair sheep group; tan with black belly (badger face); pd; mane in ♂; orig. of Barbado (USA)

BARBARY (N. Africa); cw.m; Near East Fat-tailed type; usu. white, also pied, black or brown; ♂ hd, ♀ pd; Fr. *Barbarin*, It. *Barbaresca*; inc. Barki, Libyan Barbary, Tunisian Barbary; orig. of Barbary Halfbred and Ghimi (Libya), Campanian Barbary and Sicilian Barbary (Italy)

Barbary Halfbred (Libya); m.cw; ♂ usu. pd, ♀ pd; ft; orig. from White Karaman × Libyan Barbary

barbary wild sheep: see aoudad

Barca: see Baraka

Barcelonnette: see French Alpine

Bardoka (Metohija, S.W. Serbia, Yugoslavia); d.m.cw; Pramenka type; ♂ usu. pd, ♀ pd; syn. *Beloglava metohiska* (= *Metohija Whitehead*); not *Barloka*. [Alb. *bardhë* = white]

Barègeois (Barèges, S. Hautes-Pyrénées, France); smaller var. of Lourdais; HB 1975

Bargad (Mongolia); var. of Mongolian

Barisciano (Aquila, Abruzzo, Italy); local var. of Apennine; syn. *Aquilana*

Barki (N.W. Egypt); cw.m.d; Barbary type; usu. brown or black head; ♂ hd, ♀ pd; ft; syn. *Arab, Barqi* (correct), *Bedouin, Dernawi* (from Derna), *Maryuti*. [Barka = Cyrenaica]

Barnstaple: see Devon Closewool

Barqi: see Barki

Barros Merino (Tierra de Barros, Badajoz, Spain); var. of non-migratory Spanish Merino; Sp. *Merino de Barros*

Baruwal (Nepal mts and S. Sikkim); m.cw; white, usu. with black head, also black or pied; Nepali *Baduvāl* or *Baduwāl*; syn. *Bonpala* (= raised in forest); not *Barawal, Barawul, Barwal, Bharwal*

Barwal: see Baruwal

Basco-Béarnais (S.E. Basses-Pyrénées, S.W. France); d.m.cw; Pyrenean dairy group; ♂ hd, ♀ hd or pd; orig. 1965 from Basque + Béarnais; HB 1975; = Vasca Carranzana (Spain)

Basilicata: see Improved Lucanian

Basque (E. Pays Basque, S.W. France): orig. (and now var.) of Basco-Béarnais; Fr. *Basquais*; Basque *Muthur churria* (= *white face*)

Basque (Spain): see Lacho, Vasca Carranzana

Bastarda arianese: see Campanian Barbary

Bastarda maremmana, Bastarda spagnola: see Maremmana

Baumshire: see Scottish Halfbred

Bavarian Forest (Bavaria, Germany); m.w; occ. brown; pd; orig. from Zaupel; Ger. *(Bayer) Waldschaf*; nearly extinct

Bayad (Mongolia); var, of Mongolian; syn. *Bait*

Bazakh: see Bozakh

Bazougers: see Bleu du Maine

bearded argali: see aoudad

Béarnais (Béarn, S.W. France); orig. (and now var.) of Basco-Béarnais; usu. red spots on face

Bedouin (Arabia): see Najdi

Bedouin (Egypt): see Barki

Begghié Korboraca: see Baraka

Beira Baixa (Castelo Branco, E. Portugal); var. of Portuguese Merino derived from migratory Spanish Merino; Port. *Merina da Beira Baixa*

Beja (N.E. Sudan); var. of Sudan Desert

Bekrit: see Timhadite

Bela Klementina: see White Klementina

[Belaslatina] (N.W. Bulgaria); local improved var. of Bulgarian Native; Bulg. *Beloslatinska*; not *Bjela Slatinska*

Belclare Improver (Ireland); m.lw; prolific; pd; orig. 1976-79 at Agric. Institute Res. Centre, Belclare, Co. Galway, from prolific Llŷn × (Fingalway × High Fertility) with additional Finnish Landrace and Galway blood; named 1981, BS 1985

Belgian Milk Sheep (Belgium); d; prolific; Fr. *Mouton laitier belge* (or *indigène*); HB; ? = Flemish (Netherlands)

Bellani: see Bornu

Bellary (E.C. Karnataka, India); m.cw; sim. to Deccani; black, grey, white with black face, or pied; ♂ hd or pd, ♀ pd; st; not *Bellari*
Belle-Ile: see Landes de Bretagne
[Bell Multinippled] (Nova Scotia, Canada); selected from local sheep by Graham Bell in 1890 and bred till 1922; orig. of Multinipple
Bellunese (Mansué, Treviso, Venetia, Italy); m.mw.d; Lop-eared Alpine group; black spots on face and legs; ? orig. from Alpagota and Lamon; nearly extinct. [from Belluno]
Beloglava Metohiska: see Bardoka
Belogradchik: see Replyan
Beluj: see Baluchi
Bembur: see Vembur
Beneventana, Benevento: see Campanian Barbary
Bengal: see Bangladeshi
Beni Ahsen (N.W. Morocco); mw.m; Atlantic Coast type; white with coloured face; ♂ usu. hd, ♀ pd; BSd; not *Beni Hassen, Bnihsen*; declining by crossing
Beni Guil (plateaux of E. Morocco and W. Algeria); m.cw; white with tan head and legs; hd (90%) or pd (= Fartass); Fr. *Race des plateaux de l'Est*; syn. *Petit oranais, Hamra* or *Hamyan* (Algeria); vars: Harcha, Tousint; orig. (with Berber) of Zoulay; not *Beni Ghil, Béni-Guill*
Beni Hassen: see Beni Ahsen
Beni Meskine; var. of Tadla; smaller and with coarser wool
Bentheimer (Bentheim, Osnabrück, Germany); m.cw; black round eyes and on ears; pd; orig. from Drenthe var. of Dutch Heath × German Heath; syn. *Bentheimer Landschaf*; rare
Bera: see Bangladeshi
Berari (N. Maharashtra, India); cw; ? pd; local var; syn. *Black Colonial*
Berber (mts of Morocco); m.cw; usu. white, also black or white with black head; hd; syn. *Chleuh, Kabyle*; vars: Ait Barka, Ait Haddidou, Ait Mohad, Aknoul (dwarf, earless), Marmoucha, Tounfite; orig. (with Tadla) of South Moroccan and Zaïan, (with Tousint) of Zoulay; not *Barbary*
Berbera Blackhead: see Somali
Berca: see Roussin de la Hague
Bergamasca (Bergamo, Lombardy, Italy); m.cw; basic breed of Lop-eared Alpine group; HB 1942; Ger. *Bergamasker*; syn. *Gigante di Bergamo, Bergamacia* (Brazil); orig. of other Lop-eared Alpine breeds and of Fabrianese, Pavullese, Perugian Lowland and Zakynthos
Bergerá: see Ripollesa
Bergschaf (Austria): see Tyrol Mountain
Bergschaf (Germany): see German Mountain
Bergueda: see Ripollesa

[Berkshire Knot] (England); orig. (+ Wiltshire Horn and × Southdown) of Hampshire Down; syn. *Old Berkshire*. [knot = pd]

[Berne]; black var. of Jura

Berrichon (Berry, C. France); m.sw; pd; former vars: Boischaut, Brenne, Champagne, Crevant; modern breeds: Berrichon du Cher and Berrichon de l'Indre; not *Berri*

Berrichon de l'Indre (Berry, C. France); m.sw; pd; orig. from Champagne and Crevant vars of Berrichon; HB 1895, BS 1946

Berrichon du Cher (Berry, C. France); m.mw; pd; orig. from Merino (18th c), Southdown, Leicester Longwool, and Dishley Merino (19th c) × Champagne and Boischaut vars of Berrichon; BS 1936

Beskaragai Merino (Semipalatinsk, N.E. Kazakhstan, USSR); fw; orig. from Mazaev and Novocaucasian Merinos × Kazakh Fat-rumped (early 20th c.) crossed with Rambouillet (1932), Askanian (1934 on) and Altai (1947); Russ. *Beskaragaĭskiĭ Merinos*; combined with Sulukol Merino to form North Kazakh Merino

Beulah Speckled Face (N. Breconshire, Wales); sw.m; grey-mottled face; BS; syn. *Eppynt Hill and Beulah Speckled Face*

Bezuidenhout Africander (Orange Free State, S. Africa); m.cw; pd; ft; orig. by W.F. Bezuidenhout (1918 on) from white wooled ♂ (? Africander) × [Wooled Persian (Arabi) × Blackhead Persian]; syn. *Wooled Africander*

Bhadarwah: see Gaddi; not *Bhadiwar*

Bhagdale: see Baghdale

Bhakarwal (S.W. Kashmir, India); cw.m; white with colour on face, occ. coloured; long lop ears; ♂ hd, ♀ pd; not *Bakarwal, Bakkarwal, Bhakarwala, Bharkarwad.* [= class of nomads]

bharal (China and Himalayas) = *Pseudois nayaur* Hodgson; actually a beardless goat; syn. *blue sheep, napo*; not *bhurrel, burhal, burrhel*

Bharwal: see Baruwal

Bhote, Bhotee, Bhotia: see Tibetan

bhurrel: see bharal

Bhyanglung: see Tibetan; Tibetan *byang-lug*

Biangi (Tibet and Himachal Pradesh, India); cw.pa; syn. *Kangra Valley*; not *Biangir, Birangi*

Bibrik (N.E. Baluchistan, Pakistan); m.cw.d; black or brown on face; hd; ft; syn. *Bugti, Marri*; var: Khetrani; not *Bibrick*

Biellese (Piedmont, Italy); m.cw; Lop-eared Alpine group; BSd 1959; syn. *Biellese-Bergamasca* (obs), *Ivrea* (Aosta); inc. true Biellese of Vercelli and type from rest of Piedmont which is *Piemontese alpina* (= *Alpine Piedmont*) or *nostrale* (= *local*) graded to Biellese; var: Tacòla. [from Biella]

Biérois: see Landes de Bretagne

Bierzo White (Léon, Spain); m.cw; pd; Sp. *Blanca del Bierzo*; syn. *Churra berciana* or *Churra del Bierzo*; rare

bighorn (Rocky Mountains, N. America) = *Ovis canadensis* Shaw; syn. *American bighorn, Canadian bighorn, Rocky Mountain*; many local vars; see also snow sheep (Asiatic bighorn) and Dall's sheep

BIKANERI (Rajasthan, India); cw.m; name formerly used to inc. all or some of Rajasthan breeds *i.e.* Bagri, Buchi (Pakistan), Chokla, Jaisalmeri, Magra, Malpura, Marwari, Nali, Pugal; not *Bikaneer, Bikanier, Bikanir, Vicanere*

Bikaneri, Bikaneri Chokla: see Magra

Bilbilitana Red (S.W. Zaragoza, Aragon, Spain); mw.m; black fading to red-brown, often white face-blaze; ♂ usu. hd, ♀ pd; Sp. *Roya bilbilitana*. [from ancient Bilbitis]

Birangi: see Biangi

Birka (Vojvodina, Syrmia, and Slavonia, N.W. Yugoslavia); mw; black, yellow or spotted head and legs; name used for Merino × Tsigai or Merino × Pramenka cross; syn. *Sremska* (= *Syrmian*). [Hung. = sheep]

Bîrsa (Romania); fw.m.(d); orig. since 1953 from Ile de France × (Palas Merino × Tsigai)

Biscay: see Lacho

[Bityug] (Voronezh, USSR); var. of Russian Long-tailed; Russ. *Bityug-skaya*

Bizet (N. Haute Loire and S.E. Puy-de-Dôme, C. France); m.mw; Central Plateau type; grey-brown with black on sides of face and on legs; ♂ usu. hd, ♀ usu. pd; lt; BS 1905, HB 1946; syn. *Chilhac, des Bizets*. [? from *bise* = beige]

Bjela Slatinska: see Belaslatina

Black Bains: see Velay Black

Black Belly: see Barbados Blackbelly

Black Blaze: see Dutch Black Blaze

Black-Brown Mountain (Switzerland): see Swiss Black-Brown Mountain

Black Colonial: see Berari

Black Crioulo (S. Brazil); var. of Crioulo; Sp. *Criollo negro*

Blackface (E. England): see Suffolk

Blackface (Scotland): see Scottish Blackface

BLACKFACED MOUNTAIN (N. England and Scotland); cw; black or mottled face and legs; hd; inc. Dales-Bred, Derbyshire Gritstone, Lonk, Rough Fell, Scottish Blackface, Swaledale; syn. *Blackface Hill, Blackfaced Heath*

Blackface Mutton (Germany): see German Blackheaded Mutton

Blackface Norfolk Horned: see Norfolk Horn

Blackheaded (France): see French Blackheaded

Blackheaded Mutton (Germany): see German Blackheaded Mutton
Blackheaded Mutton (Switzerland): see Swiss Brownheaded Mutton
Blackheaded Pleven: see Pleven Blackhead
Blackheaded Somali: see Somali
Blackhead Persian (S. Africa); m; hy; pd; fr; orig. from Somali imported
1868; HB 1906, BS 1958; Afrik. *Swartkoppersie*; part orig. of Bezuiden-
hout Africander, Brazilian Somali, Dorper, Van Rooy, and Wiltiper;
not *Black Head*, or *Black-headed, Persian*; name also used for Somali
in E. Africa
Black Leicester Longwool (Great Britain); var. of Leicester Longwool
with Black Welsh Mountain blood; rare
Black Maure (W. Africa); m.hr; black, long-haired var. of Maure; syn.
Nar; = Zaghawa (Sudan)
Black Merino (Italy): see Carapellese
Black Merino (Portugal); fw.d.m; brown to black; usu. recessive; domin-
ant var. is Pialdo; Port. *Merino preto*; *cf.* black var. of Spanish Merino
Black Merino (Tunisia): see Thibar
Black Milk sheep (Germany); var. selected from East Friesian; Ger.
Schwarzes Milchschaf
Black Ningsia: see Ningsia Black
Blacknosed Swiss: see Valais Blacknose
black sheep: see Stone's sheep
Black Velay: see Velay Black
Black Welsh Mountain (Great Britain); sw.m; ornamental dominant
black derivative of Welsh Mountain; ♂ hd, ♀ pd; orig. in mid 19th c;
HB and BS 1922
Blanc de Lozère: see Blanc du Massif Central
Blanc du Massif Central (Lozère, Ardèche, Gard and Hérault, S. France);
m.mw.(d); pd; orig. from Caussenard by crossing with Lacaune in
early 20th c, named 1965; BS; syn. *Blanc de Lozère, Lozèrien, Race
des Montagnes de la Lozère* (= *Lozère Mountain*)
[Bleiburger]; former var. of Carinthian
Bleu du Maine (Mayenne, N.W. France); m.lw; dark grey head and legs;
pd; orig. from Leicester Longwool (and Wensleydale) imported 1855–
80 × local (Choletais); BS 1938, HB 1948; syn. *Bazougers, Bluefaced
Maine, Blue-headed Maine, Maine-Anjou, Maine à tête* (or *face*) *bleue,
Mayenne Blue*; *cf.* Rouge de l'Ouest, Whitefaced Maine (absorbed);
BS also in GB
Blinkhaar; only recog. var. of Ronderib Africander. [= smooth hair]
BLM (NSW, Australia); mw.m; pd; orig. (1955 on) at Condobolin
Research Station from *Border Leicester* × *Merino* selected for fertility;
syn. *Border Merino*
Bluefaced Leicester (N. England); English Longwool type; orig. from

Border Leicester with blue face (*i.e.* white hairs on black skin) and finer fleece; selected 1914-39; BS and HB 1963; syn. *Hexham Leicester*
Bluefaced Maine, Blue-headed Maine: see Bleu du Maine
blue sheep: see bharal
Blue Texel; var. of Texel; BS; Du. *Blauwe Texelaar*; rare
Bnihsen: see Beni Ahsen
Bochnia (Kraków, Poland); Polish Longwool group; orig. from East Friesian × local; Pol. *Owca bocheńska*
Bohemian: see Šumava
Böhmerwald: see Šumava
[Boischaut]; former var. of Berrichon; syn. *Bourges*; not *Bois Chaud*
Bokara, Bokhara: see Bukhara
[Bokino] (Tambov, USSR); var. of Russian Long-tailed
Bolangir: see Balangir
Bonga (Kaffa, Ethiopia)
Bonpala (S. Sikkim, India); cw.m; white, black or intermediate; hd; not *Banpala, Bonapala*; = Baruwal (Nepal). [= jungle bred]
Booroola Merino (Australia); fw; strain of medium non-Peppin Australian Merino carrying gene for prolificacy, selected (on ♀♀ only) by Seears brothers at Booroola, Cooma, NSW since *c.*1945 and by CSIRO (on ♂♂ and ♀♀) since 1958; ♂ hd, ♀ usu. pd; syn. *High-Fertility Merino*; BS in New Zealand
BORDALEIRO (Portugal); d.m.mw; white, black or pied; ? orig. from Merino × Churro; inc. Campaniça, Entre Douro e Minho, Saloia, Serra da Estrêla; *cf.* Entrefino (Spain). [? from Port. *bordo* = curly (wool) or from Sp. *burdo* = coarse]
Bordaleiro Churro: see Portuguese Churro
Borde: see Red Majorcan
Border Cheviot: see Cheviot
Borderdale (New Zealand); m.mw; orig. 1930s from Border Leicester × Corriedale; HB
Border Leicester (border of Scotland and England); lw.m; English Longwool type; pd; orig. from Leicester Longwool with Cheviot blood, in late 18th and early 19th c, recog. 1869; BS 1897, HB 1898; orig. of Bluefaced Leicester; BS also in USA 1888, HB also in Canada and New Zealand
Border-Merino (New Zealand); Border Leicester × Merino F_1
Border-Romney (New Zealand); Border Leicester × New Zealand Romney F_1
Boreray (St Kilda, Scotland); cw.m; var. of Scottish Blackface; white or light tan with black, tan or pied head and legs; hd; orig. from Scottish Blackface (introduced 1870) × Hebridean type of Tanface (Old Scottish Shortwool); feral since 1930; syn. *Boreray Blackface, Hebridean*

Blackface; rare

[Borgotarese] (Borgotaro, Parma, Italy); Apennine group; extinct 1979-
83

Borino (Australia); orig. from Border Leicester × Merino

Bornu (N.E. Nigeria, N. Cameroon, and Chad); white var. of Fulani; ♂
hd, ♀ pd; syn. *Balami, Balandji, Balani, Balemi, Balonndi, Bellani,
Fellata* (Chad), *Weiladjo, White Bororo*

Bororo: see Uda

Bosach: see Bozakh

Bosnian Mountain (C. and W. Bosnia and Hercegovina, Yugoslavia);
d.m.cw; Pramenka type; white, often with spots on face and legs, occ.
coloured; ♂ usu. hd, ♀ pd; Serbo-cro. *Bosansko-Hercegovačka*; vars:
Kupres, Privor, Vlašić

Boukhara: see Bukhara

Boulonnais (N. France); m.lw; orig. in 19th c. from Leicester Longwool,
Dishley Merino *et al.*, × Artois; BS; rare. [= Boulogne district]

Bourbonnais: see Velay Black

Bourges: see Boischaut

Boutsiko (Ioánnina, Epirus, Greece); var. of Vlakhiko

Bovec (Upper Isonzo valley, Yugoslavia); d.cw; white (70%) or black;
usu. pd; It. *Plezzana* (from Plezzo), Ger. *Flitsch*; also in Kanaltal (*q.v.*);
rare

bowni: see bunni

Bozakh (Armenia and Azerbaijan, USSR); Caucasian Fat-tailed type;
dirty-white (36%), yellow-white (23%), tan (13%), grey (10%), light
red (9%); usu. pd; Russ. *Bozakh* or *Bozakhskaya*; not *Bazakh, Bosach*;
rare

Bragança Galician (Terra Fria, N.E. Portugal); m.cw; Portuguese Churro
type; white with coloured spots on face, occ. black; ♂ hd, ♀ pd; Port.
Galega bragançana

Brazi: see White Karaman

Brazilian Somali (N.E. Brazil); m; white with black head; hy; pd; small
fr; orig. from Blackhead Persian (imported from W. Indies in 1939)
× local; HB; Port. *Somali Brasileiro*; syn. *Rabo gordo* (= *fat rump*)

Brazilian Woolless (N.E. Brazil); m; mixed population; white, pied or
coloured; hy (some cw); ♂ hd or pd, ♀ pd; orig. from West African (?
× Crioulo); Port. *Deslanado* (*vermelho* or *branco*), or *Pelo de Boi* (=
ox-haired); syn. *Deslanado do Nordeste*; selected breeds are Morada
Nova and Santa Inês (with Bergamasca)

Brecknock Hill Cheviot (Breconshire, Wales); var. of Cheviot from 1850s
with Welsh Mountain blood; BS; syn. *Brecon Cheviot, Sennybridge
Cheviot*

[Brenne]; former var. of Berrichon

Brentegana (Affi and Caprino, Verona, Italy); m.cw; Lop-eared Alpine group; ? orig. from Lamon; syn. *Brentegana veronese*; rare. [? from Brenta]

Breton Dwarf: see Ushant

Brézi: see White Karaman

Breznik (S.W. Bulgaria); m.cw.d; local improved var. of Bulgarian Native; Bulg. *Breznishka*; syn. *Sofia-Breznik*; inc. Sofia White and Radomir

Brianzola (Brianza, Como, Italy); m.(mw); Lop-eared Alpine group; nearly extinct

Brière, Brièron; see Landes de Bretagne

Brigasca/Brigasque (La Brigue, border of S.E. France and N.W. Italy); d.m.cw; sim. to Frabosana; dark spots on head and legs (Italy); usu. hd; semi-lop ears; Roman nose; It. *Brigasca*, Fr. *Brigasque*; rare

British Friesland (Great Britain); BS for East Friesian

British Longwool: see English Longwool

British Milksheep (England); m.(d).lw; prolific; orig. from Friesian (East and West) (70%), Bluefaced Leicester (10%), Polled Dorset (10%), Llŷn (5%) and "Prolific" (5%) by G.L.H. Alderson during 1970s; BS

British Oldenburg (England); m.lw; name given to German Whiteheaded Mutton imported in 1964 and 1969; BS

Brogne (Breonio, Verona, Italy); m.mw; Lop-eared Alpine group but nearly straight profile; occ. brown spots on head; ? orig. from Bergamasca and Lamon; nearly extinct

Broomfield Corriedale (New Zealand); strain selected for resistance to foot rot

Brownheaded Mutton (Switzerland): see Swiss Brownheaded Mutton

Brown Mountain (German Alps); smaller brown var. selected from German Mountain; Ger. *Braunes Bergschaf*

[Bschlabser] (Tyrol, Austria); local var. sim. to Steinschaf but woolly face

Buchi (Bahawalpur, Pakistan); cw; Bikaneri group; usu. tan spots on head and legs; hd (short); st; syn. *Bahawalpuri*; not *Buchni*. [*bucha* = stubby ear]

Budiani; var. of Tushin with shorter denser wool

Bugti: see Bibrik

Bukhara: see Karakul; not *Bokara, Bokhara, Boukhara*

Bulandshari: see Muzaffarnagri

Bulgarian Dairy (Bulgaria); d; in formation (1972) from Stara Zagora, Pleven Blackhead and East Friesian; Bulg. *B"lgarska mlechna*

Bulgarian Merinos: see Danube, North-East Bulgarian, Karnobat Fine-wool, and Thrace Finewools

Bulgarian Native; cw.d.m; Zackel type; coloured in E, usu. white or white with coloured face in W; ♂ hd, ♀ hd or pd; lt; local prim. vars inc. Central Stara Planina, Central Rodopi, Dobruja, Duben, Koprivshten, Kotel Native, Kyustendil, Panagyurishte, Replyan, Sakar, Stranja, Teteven, Western Stara Planina; local improved vars inc. Belaslatina and Breznik; for improved breeds see Svishtov and Pleven Blackhead; for breeds improved by Tsigai see Karnobat, Rila Monastery, Shumen, White Klementina, and White South Bulgarian (Stara Zagora and Plovdiv-Purvomai); see also Karakachan

Bundelkhandi: see Jalauni

Bündner Oberland (Graubünden, Switzerland); cw; white or coloured; prim. type with small horns, descended from Peat sheep, last found in Lugnez, Luzein, Nalps, Tavetsch, Vrin, *etc*; sim. to Steinschaf; Ger. *Bündner Oberländer*; syn. *Graubünden, Grisons*; nearly extinct

Bundoran Comeback (Victoria, Australia); mw; orig. since 1971 on 'Bundoran', Glenthompson, from Australian Merino strains, Polwarth and Zenith

Bungaree Merino (South Australia); strain of South Australian Merino (strong wool) with English Longwool blood

bunni: see Ainsi, brown var; not *bowni*. [Arabic = brown]

Burgundy Merino: see Châtillonais

burhal, burrhel: see bharal

Burmese (Burma); m.cw; lop ears

Burri: see Dhamari

Buryat (Buryat SSR and Chita prov., Siberia, USSR); m.cw; sim. to Mongolian and Siberian; white with black or red on head; ♂ hd, ♀ pd; sft; Russ. *Buryatskaya*; syn. *Buryat-Mongolian*; orig. (with Merino) of Chita and Transbaikal Finewool; not *Buriat-Mongol*

Buti (India): see Patanwadi

Buti (Pakistan): see Thalli

[Butjadingen] (Oldenburg, Germany); Marsh type; orig. of German Whiteheaded Mutton; Ger. *Butjadinger*

Cabreña: see Segureña

[Cadorina] (Cadore, N. Belluno, Venetia, Italy); cw.m; Lop-eared Alpine group; extinct 1970s by crossing with Lamon *et al.*

[Cadzow Improver] (W. Lothian, Scotland); m.sw; ♂ hd, ♀ pd; orig. 1960s from Dorset Horn and Finnish Landrace; ♂ line for crossing on hill ewes

Cagi: see Kagi

Cagliari: see Sardinian, lowland var.

Cago: see Kagi

Caithness: see Keerie

Caithness, Caithness Cheviot: see North Country Cheviot
Cakiel: see Zackel
Calabrese, Calabrian: see Sciara
Calhoor; var. of Sanjabi
California Red (USA); cw; apricot tan with red mane in ♂; pd; orig. 1971 by Glen Spurlock from Barbado × American Tunis recrossed to Tunis by Aimé and Paulette Soulier
California Variegated Mutant (USA); mw; badger-face (white, grey, black or brown with black belly); orig. in 1970 by Glen Eidman, Willows, California, from Romeldale; HB
Calikui, Calokui: *see* Kallakui
Calva: see Ansotana
Camarès: see Lacaune
[Camargue Merino]; former grey var. of Arles Merino; Fr. *Mérinos de la Camargue*
Cambar: see Kombar
[Cambrai]; var. of Flemish Marsh
Cambridge (England); m.sw; dark face; prolific; orig. 1966-76 by J.B. Owen from prolific ewes (*c.* 65% Clun Forest, 15% other British breeds—chiefly Llanwenog, Llŷn and Kerry Hill, but also Bluefaced Leicester, Border Leicester, Radnor and Ryeland—with addition of 20% Finnish Landrace) selected for high litter size; BS. [work started at Cambridge University]
Camden Park (NSW, Australia); early strain (1797-*c.*1856) of Australian Merino; orig. 1797-1804 from Spanish Merino (mainly Negretti) through *a*) Gordon flock, Cape Colony, and *b*) Royal flocks at Windsor and Kew, England, crossed with African and Asian cw. and hy breeds and some English lw. and sw. and backcrossed to Spanish Merino; one flock only
Cameroon Dwarf: see West African Dwarf
[Campan]; former var. of Aure-Campan; pd; smaller
Campanian Barbary (Campania, Italy); d.m.(cw-mw); often dark spots on face and legs; ♂ hd or pd, ♀ pd; sft; orig. from Tunisian Barbary × local thin-tailed breed; HB; It. *Barbaresca della Campania*; syn. *bastarda arianese* (= *Ariano crossbred*), *beneventana* (= from Benevento), *casalinga* or *casareccia* (= *household*), *coda chiatta* (= *flat tail*), *laticauda* (= *broad tail*), *nostrana* (= *local*), *turchessa* (= *Turkish*)
Campaniça (Campo Branco, S. Beja, S. Portugal); m.mw.d; Bordaleiro type; white, usu. with small brown spots on head and legs; ♂ hd, ♀ pd
Campera: see Castilian Churro
Campidano: see Sardinian, lowland var.
[Campine] (N. Belgium); Fr. *Campinois*; extinct *c.* 1950
Campiñesa: see Andalusian Merino

Camura: see Red African
Canadian bighorn: see bighorn
Canadian Corriedale (Alberta, Canada); mw; orig. 1919-34 from Corriedale × (Lincoln × Rambouillet); HB; rare
Canaltaler: see Kanaltaler
Canary Island (Spain); d.cw; usu. parti-coloured; ♂ usu. hd, ♀ usu. pd; ears often vestigial; Sp. *Canaria*
Çandır (Turkey) = Dağliç × White Karaman cross (W. Anatolia) or Red Karaman × Tuj cross (N.E. Turkey); syn. *Kesbır, Kesme, Mazik*; not *Candyr, Zandir*. [= crossbred]
[Cannock Chase] (England); orig. (with Southdown *et al.*) of Shropshire
Cantabrian Churro: see Spanish Churro
Cape Fat-tailed: see Africander
Caralpina: see Ripollesa
Caraman: see Red Karaman, White Karaman
Caramanitico: see Rhodes
[Carapellese] (Carapelle, Foggia, Apulia, Italy); mw.d.m; black; pd; syn. *Gentile moretta, Gentile a vello nero* (= *improved black*), *Merinos a vello nero* (= *black Merino*), *Moretta*; not *Carapella*
Cardy Welsh Mountain (Cardiganshire, Wales); strain of Welsh Mountain with whiter face and finer fleece; syn. *Cardigan*
Carinthian (Austria); cw.m.(d); Lop-eared Alpine group; sim. to Tyrol Mountain (which has been displacing it since 1938) but poorer wool and smaller ears; yellowish-white with black ear tips and spectacles; pd; orig. from Paduan and Bergamasca × local (Steinschaf *et al.*) since early 18th c; Ger. *Kärtner* or *Kärtner Brillenschaf* (= *spectacled sheep*); former (pre-1918) vars: Seeländer (principal, also used as syn), Bleiburger, Gurktaler, Kanaltaler, Petzen, Spiegel (Tyrol), Steiner; orig. of Pusterese (Italy), Solčava (Yugoslavia), Tyrol Mountain; not *German Mountain*; extinct in Austria, a few in S.E. Bavaria
Carinthian Mountain: see Tyrol Mountain
Carnabat: see Karnobat
[Carnica] (Friuli, Italy); extinct 1976-79
Carpathian Mountain (S.W. Ukraine, USSR); m.cw.d; var. of Voloshian; Zackel type; ♂ usu. hd, ♀ usu. pd; Russ. *Gornokarpatskie ovtsi*; lt; inc. Ruthenian Zackel or Racka in Transcarpathian Ukraine, Zackel in Galicia and Turkana in N. Bucovina; orig. (with Tsigai) of Ukrainian Mountain
Carpetmaster (New Zealand); cw; orig. from one cw. Border Leicester-Romney ♂ carrying gene N^J × cw. Perendales; nearly extinct
Carranzana: see Vasca Carranzana
Carsolina: see Dalmatian-Karst
Cartera (S.E. Teruel, Aragon, Spain); m.w; pd; syn. *Cartera paloma*

Casalinga, Casareccia: see Campanian Barbary

Casciana (Cascia, Umbria, Italy); local var. of Apennine

Casentinese (Casentino, Arezzo, Tuscany, Italy); Apennine type with much Sopravissana blood

Cassubian: see Pomeranian

Castilian (Old Castille, Spain); d.m.(mw) (Valladolid and Zamora) or m.(cw) (Salamanca); Entrefino type; white; pd; BS; Sp. *Castellana*; vars: Black (with white spot on head and tail tip), Bilbilitana Red, and [Tudelana]

Castilian Churro (Tierra de Campos, Palencia, Spain); m; orig. and principal var. of Spanish Churro; Sp. *Churra castellana*; syn. *Churra campera*

Castillonais (Castillon, S.W. Ariège, France); m.cw-mw; Central Pyrenean group; white with red head and legs; ♂ hd, ♀ usu. pd; syn. *Pyrénéen central à extrémités rousses* (= *with red extremities*), *St Gironnais* (from St Girons); rare (by crossing with Tarasconnais)

Castlemilk Moorit (Scotland); w; pale red-brown (blond); hd; st; orig. by Buchanan-Jardine on Castlemilk estate, Dumfries, from Soay × Shetland with Manx Loaghtan and possibly mouflon blood in early 20th c; HB 1974, BS 1983; syn. *Castlemilk Shetland, Moorit Shetland* (to 1977); nearly extinct

Catalan (E. Pyrenees, France); m.mw; mixed type with blood of Lacaune, Berrichon, Ile-de-France, and Roussillon Red; white with black or red marks on face

Caucasian (N. Caucasus, USSR); fw.m; orig. 1921-36 in N. Caucasus from Novocaucasian Merino improved by American Rambouillet and by Askanian; Russ. *Kavkazskaya* or *Kavkazskaya tonkorunnaya* (= *Caucasian finewool*); obs. syn. *Soviet Rambouillet of Caucasian type, Caucasian Rambouillet* (Russ. *Kavkazskiĭ Rambulye*), *Caucasian Merino*; HB, also in Bulgaria

CAUCASIAN FAT-TAILED (Caucasus, USSR); m.d.cw; sim. to Karaman (Turkey); inc. Andi, Balbas, Bozakh, Gunib, Imeretian, Karabakh, Karachai, Kyasma, Lak, Lezgian, Mazekh, Shirvan, Tushin

Caucasian Mountain; breed group

[Cauchois] (Caux, N. Normandy, France); m.lw; orig. from Oxford Down, Cotswold *et al.* × local; extinct in 1950s

Caussenard (Causses, S. France); cw; ♂ hd or pd, ♀ usu. pd; inc. Caussenard du Lot, Caussenard des Garrigues; formerly also Caussenard de la Lozère and Larzac and Ségala

[Caussenard de la Lozère] (W. Lozère, S. France); d.m; Roquefort breed; now absorbed by Blanc du Massif Central; ♂ often hd, ♀ pd; syn. *Lozère Causses*

Caussenard des Garrigues (Gard and E. Hérault, S. France); m; face sometimes red; ♂ usu. hd, ♀ usu. pd; syn. *Caussenard du Gard et de l'Hérault*

Caussenard du Lot (Lot, S. France); m.cw; black spectacles and ears; pd; BS; syn. *Gascon à lunettes, Quercy, Quercynois, Race des Causses du Lot*

Central Anatolian Merino (Turkey); fw.m; var. of Turkish Merino; orig. since 1952 at Konya state farm from German Mutton Merino (80%) × White Karaman; syn. *Anatolian Merino, Konya Merino*

CENTRAL PLATEAU (N. Massif Central, France); Fr. *Races du Plateau central* or *Races du Massif Central Nord*; syn. *Auvergnat, Auvergne*; inc. [Ardes], Bizet, Limousin, Rava, Velay Black

Central Pyrenean (C. and E. Pyrenees, France); m.mw; orig. from Merino × local Pyrenean; BS; Fr. *Pyrénéen central* or *Races des Pyrénées centrales*; inc. Aure-Campan, Barégeois, Castillonais, Lourdais, Tarasconnais; formerly only Castillonais and Tarasconnais

Central Rodopi (S. Bulgaria); m.cw.d; local unimproved var. of Bulgarian Native; occ. speckled face; ♂ hd, ♀ usu. pd; Bulg. *Srednorodopska* or *Rilo-Rodopska*; syn. *Rhodope*; rare

Central Stara Planina (C. Bulgaria); m.cw.d; black spots on head and legs; ♂ hd, ♀ pd; Bulg. *Srednostaraplaninska* (or *Srednoplaninska*); rare

Česká selská: see Šumava

Çeşme: see Sakiz

Cévennes, Cévenol: see Raïole

CFS: see Polish Mountain

Chacra (Syria): see Red Karaman

Chaffal: see Shafali

Chagra, Chakra (Syria): see Red Karaman

Chakri: see Magra

Chalkidiki (Khalkidhiki peninsula, Macedonia, Greece); d.m.mw-cw; Ruda type; white (with black or speckled face), also black or grey; ♂ hd, ♀ pd; rare

Chamar (Mongolia); superior var. of Mongolian; ♂ hd, ♀ hd or pd; ft; Russ. *Chamarskaya*

Chamarita (S.E. La Rioja and N.E. Soria, Castille, Spain); m.mw; white; occ. black; usu. pd; syn. *Sampedrana* (from San Pedro Maurique). [= small]

[Champagne]; former var. of Berrichon

[Champagne Merino] (Aube, France); former var. of Précoce; HB 1925-29; Fr. *Mérinos champenois*, or *de la Champagne*

Changthangi (Ladakh, N.E. Kashmir, India); pa.cw; various colours; not *Chanthan*

Chanothar: see Sonadi

Chanthan: see Changthangi

Chapan (Kirgizia, USSR); cw; sim. to Darvaz and Hetian; sft

Chapper: see Chokla

Charmoise (W.C. France); m.sw; pd; orig. at La Charmoise farm, Loir-et-Cher, 1844-52, from Romney × (Berrichon-Merino-Solognot-Touraine); BS 1896, reorg. 1926, HB 1927; not *Charmois*

Charollais (Nièvre, France); m.mw; pd; orig. from Leicester Longwool × local, 1825 on; named 1963, HB 1963, recog. 1974, BS; BS also in GB 1977

Charotar, Charotari, Charothar, Charothri: see Patanwadi

[Châtillonais] (Côte d'Or, France); former var. of Précoce; HB 1924-29; Fr. *Mérinos précoce du Châtillonais*; syn. *Burgundy Merino* (Fr. *Mérinos bourguignon*, or *de la Bourgogne*)

Chechen, Chechenskaya: see Karachai

Cher Berrichon: see Berrichon du Cher

Cherkassy (Ukraine, USSR); var. of Russian Long-tailed (? with English or Merino blood); Russ. *Cherkasskaya*; not *Cherkassian, Cherkassky, Cherkasy, Circassian*

Cherna Chervena: see Karnobat

Chersolina: see Cres

Chevaldshay (Orkney, Scotland); m; North Country Cheviot × North Ronaldsay, 1st cross

Chevali: see Shafali

Cheviot (border of England and Scotland); m.mw; ♂ usu. pd, ♀ pd; orig. at end of 18th c, ? with Leicester Longwool blood, named 1791; BS 1891, HB 1893; Nor. *Sjeviot*; syn. *Border Cheviot, South Country Cheviot*; strain: West Country Cheviot; vars: Brecknock Hill Cheviot, North Country Cheviot; orig. of Dala and Rygja (Norway); BS also in USA 1891, New Zealand 1949 (HB 1895), HB also in Australia, Canada

Cheviot-Corriedale (New Zealand); Cheviot × Corriedale F$_1$

[Chevlin] (New Zealand); m.lw; orig. (1950s) by P.G. Buckleton from Lincoln × Cheviot; extinct 1960s

Chhanotar: see Chanothar

Chianina (Val di Chiana, Tuscany, Italy); local var. of Apennine with much Sopravissana blood

Chietina (Chieti, Abruzzo, Italy); local var. of Apennine

Chilhac: see Bizet

Chilludo: see Criollo

China (or Chinese) Fat-tailed: see Mongolian and its derivatives: Choubei, Han, Hu, Lanzhou Large-tail, Luan, Ningsia Black, Quanglin Large-tail, Shouyang, Taiku, Tan, Tong

Chinese Finewool (Xinjiang and Inner Mongolia, China); fw.m; orig. from Australian Merino × Xinjiang and Mongolian

Chinese Karakul (W. Xinjiang, China); black; ♂ hd, ♀ pd; orig. since 1960s by grading Kuche and Kazakh to Karakul, also from Karakul × Mongolian in Inner Mongolia

Chinese Merinos: see Aohan Finewool, Chinese Finewool, Gansu Alpine Finewool, Inner Mongolian Finewool, North-East China Finewool, Shanxi Finewool, Xinjiang Finewool

Chios (Khíos, Greece); d.m.cw-mw; prolific; white with black or brown spots on face, belly and legs, sometimes black face; ♂ hd, ♀ usu. pd; lft; prolific; orig. of Sakiz (Turkey)

Chiraz: see Grey Shirazi

Chisqueta: see Pallaresa

Chita (Buryat-Mongolia, USSR); mw; breed group; orig. at Voroshilov state farm from Buryat × finewool; Russ. *Chitinskaya porodnaya gruppa*

Chiva: see Zel

Chleuh: see Berber

Chokla (Churu and Sikar districts of Rajasthan, India); cw.m sim. to Magra but smaller and finer wool; dark brown face; pd; syn. *Chapper, Shekhawati* (not *Sherawati*)

[Choletais] (Maine, France); orig. (with Leicester Longwool) of Bluefaced Maine

Cholistani (Bahawalpur, Pakistan); m.cw; black head, neck and lop ears

Chotanagpuri (Bihar, India); cw; light grey or brown; pd; st; not *Chottanagpuri*

Cho-ten-jan: see Hetian

Choubei (N. Hubei, China); cw.m; usu. white, sometimes black head; ♂ usu. hd, ♀ usu. pd; large ft; W.G. *Chou-pei*, Ger. *Dschau-bei*; not now recog.

Choufalié: see Shafali

chubuku: see snow sheep

Chuisk Semifinewool (Kazakhstan, USSR); w; orig. from Kazakh Meat-wool, Stavropol, Précoce and fat-rumped; Russ. *Chuĭskaya polutonkorunnaya*; syn. *Chuisk meat-wool breed group*

Chundi: see Thalli

[Chuntuk] (Ukraine and Crimea, USSR); m.cw; sim. to Kalmyk; brown; pd; fr.

Churra alcarreña, Churra entrefina: see Ojalada

Churra algarvia: see Algarve Churro

Churra berciana, Churra del Bierzo: see Bierzo White

Churra da Terra Quente (Trás-os-Montes, N.E. Portugal); m.cw.d; Portuguese Churro type; hd; syn. *Tarrincha* or *Terrincha*; not *Badana*

Churra de Colmenar: see Colmenareña

Churra do Campo (N.E. Castelo Branco, Beira Baixa, Portugal); m.cw.d;

Portuguese Churro type; ♂ hd, ♀ pd
Churra gallega: see Galician
Churra soriana, Churra turolense: see Ojalada
Churro: see Portuguese Churro, Spanish Churro. [= coarse-wooled]
Chushka (W. Ukraine and Moldavia, USSR); fur, d; sim. to Reshetilovka
     and Sokolki; black or white; ♂ hd, 50% ♀ hd (small); lt; orig. from
     Russian Long-tailed; syn. *Tsushka*
Ciavenasca (N.W. Sondrio, Lombardy, Italy); m; pd; rare
Cigaja: see Tsigai
Cikta (Hungary); cw; ♂ hd, ♀ pd; orig. from Zaupel; nearly extinct
Çıldır: see Tuj
Cilician: see Anatolian red
[Cinta] (Bergamo-Brescia, Italy); extinct 1976-79
Circassian: see Cherkassy
Ciuta (Val Masino, Sondrio, Lombardy, Italy); m; sim. to Ciavenasca;
     hd; nearly extinct
[Cladore] (Connemara, Ireland); Northern Short-tailed type but longer
     tail; occ. coloured; pd; syn. *Cladagh, Cottagh*; only crossbreds
     remain. [= shore]
Closewool: see Devon Closewool
Clun Forest (S.W. Shropshire, England); sw.m; dark brown face and
     legs; pd; ? orig. from Hill Radnor and Shropshire, with Kerry Hill
     blood c.1865; BS and HB 1925; syn. *Clun*; BS also in France 1970,
     USA 1973, HB also in Canada
Coastal Zackel (Croatia, Yugoslavia): see Istrian Milk
[Cobb 101] (Suffolk, England); m.sw; ♂ hd, ♀ pd; orig. 1960s from
     Finnish Landrace *et al.*; ♂ line for crossing on hill ewes
Coburger (Coburg, N. Bavaria, Germany); m.w; red head and legs, born
     red; pd; syn. *Coburger Fuchsschaf, Eifel, Fuchskopf* (= *Red Head*); not
     Foxhead, Koburg; recog. 1966 when nearly extinct, still rare
Coda chiatta: see Campanian Barbary
Coete, Cohete: see Red Majorcan
Coimbatore (W.C. Tamil Nadu, India); cw.m; usu. white with black or
     brown head and neck; ♂ hd or pd, ♀ pd; st; syn. *Coimbatore White,
     Kuruba, Kurumba* or *Kurumbai* (Karnataka), *Kurumbai Adu*
Colbred (Gloucestershire, England); m.mw; pd; orig. (1957 on) by Oscar
     Colburn from East Friesian, Clun Forest, Border Leicester and Dorset
     Horn; BS 1962
Colmenareña (Colmenar Viejo, Madrid, Spain); d.m.mw; white with
     black points; pd or hd; syn. *Oveja de Colmenar, Churra de Colmenar*
Colombian Criollo (Colombia); var. of Criollo; usu. white; ♂ hd or pd,
     ♀ pd or scurs
Colombian Woolless: see Red African

Columbia (Idaho, USA); mw.m; pd; sim. to Panama; orig. (1912 on) from Lincoln × American Rambouillet; BS 1942; HB also in Canada. [? etym.]

Columbia-Southdale (Middlebury, Vermont, and Beltsville, Maryland, USA); m.mw; pd; orig. since 1943 from Columbia × Southdale

Comeback (Australia) = Merino × (English Longwool × Merino); BS 1976; eligible for Polwarth HB after 5 generations of *inter se* breeding

Comisana (S.E. Sicily); d.cw.m; reddish-brown face; pd; semi-lop ears; orig. from Maltese × Sicilian in late 19th and early 20th c; HB and BSd 1942; syn. *Lentinese* (from Lentini) *Red Head* (It. *Testa rossa* or *Faccia rossa*). [from Comiso]

Common Albanian (S. Albania); d.cw.m; small, plains type of Albanian Zackel; usu. red or black spots on face and legs; ♂ hd, ♀ usu. pd; Ger. *Kommunal*; vars: Lushnja, South Albanian

Common Long-tailed, Common Russian: see Russian Long-tailed

Commun des Alpes: see French Alpine

Congo Dwarf: see Bahu

Congo Long-legged: see Zaïre Long-legged

Constantinois: see Tunisian Barbary

Coopworth (S. Island, New Zealand); m.mw; orig. 1956-68 from Border Leicester × New Zealand Romney by I.E. *Coop* at Lincoln College; BS 1968; BS also in Australia, USA 1985

Copper-Red (E. Bulgaria); inc. Karnobat and Shumen; Bulg. *Mednochervena*; syn. *Karnobatoshumenska*

Coquo: see Angola Maned

[Corbières] (S. Aude, S. France); mw; absorbed by Lacaune in 1950s

Córdoba de la Campaña: see Andalusian Merino

Corino (Patagonia, Argentina); mw; orig. since 1970 at 'Monte Dinero', Rio Gallegos, Santa Cruz, from Mer*ino* × Cor*riedale*

Cormo (Tasmania, Australia); mw.m; orig. since 1960 at 'Dungrove' from Polwarth × (Corriedale × Tasmanian Merino); BS; BS also in USA 1976; see also Argentine Cormo. [Cor*riedale-M*erino)

Cornella White (Bologna, Italy); d.m.(mw); Apennine group; hd; It. *Cornella bianca*

[Cornetta] (Modena, Italy); extinct 1976-79

Cornigliese (Corniglio, Emilia, Italy); local var. of Apennine; orig. from Vissana with Merino and Bergamasca blood

Corriedale (New Zealand); mw.m; orig. 1880-1910 from Lincoln (or Leicester Longwool) × Merino; BS 1910, HB 1924; sim. orig. in Australia (BS); orig. of Canadian Corriedale; BS also in USA 1915, S. Africa 1953; see also Askanian Corriedale, Kazakh Corriedale, Poznań Corriedale, Soviet Corriedale; selected strain: Broomfield Corriedale

Corsican (Corsica, France); d.m.cw; usu. white with black marks on head and feet, 30% are black, grey, or red; ♂ hd, ♀ pd or hd; Fr. *Corse*

Corsican mouflon: see mouflon

Corteno (Brescia, Lombardy, Italy); m.(mw); Lop-eared Alpine group; It. *di Corteno*

Cotentin (N. Manche, France); m.lw; pd; sim. to Avranchin but larger; orig. from Leicester Longwool × local (Roussin de la Hague) 1830-1900; BS 1925; syn. *Race du littoral nord de la Manche*

Cotswold (England); lw.m; English Longwool type; Leicester Longwool blood; pd; recog. 1862, BS 1892; orig. (× Hampshire) of Oxford Down and (× Marsh) of German Whiteheaded Mutton; BS also in USA 1878, HB also in Canada; rare in England

Cottagh: see Cladore

Crag, Cragg: see Limestone

Crau Merino; formerly reddish var. of Arles Merino, now syn; Fr. *Mérinos de la Crau*

Creole: see Criollo

Cres: see Island Pramenka; It. *Chersolina*

Cretan Zackel: see Greek Zackel and specifically its Sfakia, Sitia and Psiloris vars

[Crevant]; former var. of Berrichon; not *Crevat*

Crickley Barrow (Gloucestershire, England); m.sw; white with black face and legs; orig. by Oscar Colburn in 1970s from Clun Forest and New Zealand Southdown

Criollo (Spanish America—esp. highlands of Bolivia, Colombia, Ecuador, Guatemala, Mexico, Peru and Venezuela); m.cw; white, black or pied; orig. fron Spanish Churro (and Spanish Merino?) 1548-1812; syn. *Creole* (West Indies), *Chilludo* (= *hairy*) or *Pampa* (Argentina); vars: Colombian, Lucero and Tarhumara (Mexico), Uruguayan, Venezuelan; *cf.* Gulf Coast Native, Navajo-Churro (USA). [= native]

Crioulo (Brazil); cw.m; head and legs sometimes red or black; ♂ hd, ♀ pd or hd (short); orig. from Portuguese Churro; syn. *Curraleiro* (mid Saõ Francisco valley); var: Black Crioulo

Croatian (Zackel) (Yugoslavia): see Dalmatian-Karst, Island Pramenka, Istrian Milk, and Lika

Cross (Scotland): see Greyface

Cruzado, Cruzo: see Entrefino

Cuban Hairy: see Pelibüey

Cuorgné: see Savoy

Cuška: see Chushka

Cutchi (India): see Patanwadi

Cutchi (Pakistan): see Kachhi

Cyprus Fat-tailed; d.cw.m; Near East Fat-tailed type, sim. to Awassi;

usu. white with black (or brown) on face esp. eyes and nose, occ. black,
brown, or white; ♂ usu. hd, ♀ usu. pd
Cyprus mouflon (Troödos mts, Cyprus) = *Ovis orientalis ophion* Blyth;
var. of red sheep; Gr. *agrinon*; syn. *Cyprian mouflon, Cyprian red,
Cyprian wild, Cyprus urial, O. musimon* var. *orientalis*; rare
Czech: see Šumava
Czech Merino (Czechoslovakia); fw.m; orig. from German Mutton
Merino, Caucasian, and Stavropol
Czurkan: see Ţurcana

Dagestan Mountain (USSR); m.mw; orig. 1926-50 from Württemberg
Merino (now Merinolandschaf) × Gunib, backcrossed once or twice
to Württemberg and then mated *inter se*; Russ. *Dagestanskaya gornaya*
Dağliç (W. Anatolia, Turkey); cw.m.d; black spots on head and legs; ♂
usu. hd, ♀ pd; sft; Turk. *Dağlıç*; ? orig. of Chios and Kamakuyruk;
not *Daglich, Daglic*
Dahman: see D'man
Dakshini (Orissa, India); cw; local var.
Dala (Voss and Hordaland, Norway); w; pd; sim. to Cheviot; orig. 1860-
1920 from Cheviot, Leicester Longwool, and Old Norwegian; HB; syn.
Voss; not *Dalas*. [= valley]
Dale-o'-Goyt: see Derbyshire Gritstone
Dales-Bred (Upper Wharfdale, C. Pennines, England); cw; Blackfaced
Mountain type; hd; orig. from Swaledale with Scottish Blackface
blood; BS 1930, HB 1931
Dall's sheep (Alaska and N.W. Canada) = *Ovis dalli*; white; syn. *Alaskan
white, Dall sheep*; var: Stone's or black sheep = *O.d. stonei*
Dalmatian-Karst (Yugoslavia); m.cw.d; small Pramenka type; usu. white
with white, black or spotted head, also black or red-brown; ♂ hd, ♀ usu.
pd; Serbo-cro. *Dalmatinska-Hercegovačka*; syn. *Hum* (Hercegovina),
Karst (Serbo-cro. *Krš*, It. *Carsolina*); orig. (with Merino) of Dubrovnik
Damani (Dera Ismail Khan, Pakistan); d.m.cw; tan or black head or
markings on head and legs; pd; st; often tassels; syn. *Lama*; not
Dhamani
Damara (N. of Namibia); var. of Africander; pied, white, black or
brown; hy-cw; usu. pd; lft; not *Blinkhaar*
Damari: see Harnai
Damline: see ABRO Damline
[Danadara]; possible orig. of Karakul; not *Danadar, Donadar*
[Danish Heath] (Denmark); usu. pd, st. and white-faced; orig. from
Heidschnucke × Northern Short-tailed; Dan. *Hedefår*; orig. of Danish
Landrace

Danish Landrace (Jutland, Denmark); pd; orig. from Danish Heath crossed with Merino in 18th c. and with Leicester Longwool and Oxford Down since 1900; Dan. *Dansk Landfår*; syn. *Klitfår* (= *dune sheep*)

Danube Finewool (N. Bulgaria); fw.m.d; orig. 1950-67 from German Mutton Merino and Caucasian or Askanian × Svishtov and Pleven Blackhead; HB; Bulg. *Dunavska t''nkorunna*

Danube Merino (S. Romania); fw.d.m; 68% white, rest pied or coloured; orig. from Spancă (F_1, Merino × Tsigai) selected F_2, F_3 or backcross to Merino; Rom. *Merinos dunărea*

Dargintsi (Dagestan, USSR); cw.m; Caucasian Fat-tailed type; black or white; ♂ usu. hd, ♀ hd or pd; Russ. *Darginskaya*; syn. *Gad*; not *Dargin, Darginci*

Darkhat (Mongolia); var. of Mongolian

Dartmoor (Devon, England); m.lw; English Longwool type; black or grey spots on nose; pd; orig. (1820-1909) by selection from original Dartmoor, with Longwool blood; BS 1909, HB 1911; syn. *Greyface Dartmoor, Improved Dartmoor*; rare

Darvaz (Tajikistan, USSR); cw.m; sim. to Chapan and Hotan; black, white, brown or pied; ♂ usu. hd, ♀ pd; sft; Russ. *Darvazskaya*; rare

Darvaz Mountain Mutton-Wool (E. Tajikistan, USSR); m.mw-fw; breed group; orig. from Darvaz improved by Württemberg Merino (1941-44 and 1948) and by Caucasian (since 1948); Russ. *Gornodarvazskaya myasosherstnaya porodnaya gruppa*; syn. *Gornodarvazskaya tonkorunnaya* (= *finewool*)

Dazdawi: see Herki

Debouillet (New Mexico, USA); fw; orig. 1920-43 from Delaine Merino × Rambouillet; named 1947, BS 1954

Deccani (C. Maharashtra, N.E. Karnataka and W. Andhra Pradesh, India); m.cw; sim. to Bellary; black or pied, occ. white or brown; ♂ usu. hd, ♀ pd; st.

defaid (Welsh) = sheep

Defaid Idloes: see Badger Faced Welsh Mountain

Degeres Mutton-Wool (Kazakhstan, USSR); m; fr. or sft; orig. from Shropshire (and Précoce) × Kazakh Fat-rumped, 1931-80; Russ. *Degeresskaya myasosherstnaya*; not *Degres*

Deiry (Syria): see Awassi. [from Deir ez Zor]

Delaimi: see Shafali

Delaine Merino; fw.(m); var. of American Merino (C type); BS 1882. [*delaine* (Fr.) wool is combing wool]

Delimi: see Shafali

Del Sasso: see Steinschaf

Demane: see D'man

Demonte, Demontina: see Sambucana
Derbyshire Gritstone (Peak District, England); mw.m; Blackfaced Mountain type, sim. to Lonk but pd; ? orig. from Leicester Longwool × Lonk; BS 1892, HB 1893; syn. *Dale-o'-Goyt*
Derna, Dernawi (Egypt): see Barki
Desert Sudanese: see Sudan Desert
deshi, desi (Gujarat, India): see Patanwadi
desi (India) = local, indigenous; not *deshi*
Deslanado (Brazil): see Brazilian Woolless
Deutsches veredeltes Landschaf: see Merinolandschaf
[Deux] (Brittany, France). [= two, from prolificacy]
Devon: see Dartmoor, Devon Closewool, Devon and Cornwall Longwool, Exmoor Horn, Whiteface Dartmoor
Devon and Cornwall Longwool (Devon and Cornwall, England); lw.m; English Longwool type; pd; orig. by combining Devon Longwoolled and South Devon (1977)
Devon Closewool (N. Devon, England); sw.m; pd; orig. in early 20th c. from Devon Longwoolled × Exmoor Horn; BS, HB 1923; syn. *Barnstaple*
[Devon Longwoolled] (N. Devon, England); lw.m; English Longwool type, sim. to South Devon, but smaller; pd; orig. from Leicester Longwool × Southam Nott and Bampton Nott; recog. 1870s; BS 1898-1977, HB 1900; syn. *Devon Longwool*; combined with South Devon to form Devon and Cornwall Longwool 1977
Dhamani: see Damani
Dhamari (Dhamar, N. Yemen); m.(d); white, usu. with fawn back and legs; hy; pd; semi-lop ears; ft; syn. *Burri, Jahrani*
Dhamda (E. Madhya Pradesh, India); m.cw; usu. black; not *Dhamada*
Dhormundi: see Godavari
Dilem, Dillène: see Shafali
Dinka: see Nilotic
Dishley, Dishley Leicester: see Leicester Longwool
[Dishley Merino] (France); m.mw; orig. 1833-1900 from Leicester Longwool × Merino, renamed Ile-de-France 1922; syn. *Alfort, Grignon*
Djallonké: see West African Dwarf
DLS (Quebec, Canada); m.mw; orig. at Lennoxville Research Station from (Australian Dorset × Leicester Longwool) × (Australian Dorset × Suffolk) bred *inter se* since 1968
D'man (oases of S. Morocco and S. Algeria); cw.m; black, brown, white or pied; pd; lop ears; prolific; syn. *Tafilalet* (Algeria); not *Dahman, Demane*
Dobruja (N.E. Bulgaria); cw; Bulgarian Native sim. to Replyan; spectacles
Dobruja Finewool: see North-East Bulgarian Finewool

Döhne Merino (E. Cape Province, S. Africa); fw.m; pd; orig. *c.*1940 at Döhne Research Station from German (Mutton) Merino × South African Merino; BS

Donadar: see Danadara

Dongola, Donggala, Donggola (Indonesia): see Indonesian Fat-tailed

Dongola (N. Sudan); cw; white or black; pd; syn. *North Riverain* (or *Riverine*) *Wooled*

Donji Vakuf (Yugoslavia); subvar. of Privor var. of Bosnian Mountain; Serbo-cro. *Donjevakufska*

Dormer (Australia); mw.m; orig. from Merino × (Poll Dorset × Merino)

Dormer (S. Africa); m.w; orig. (1941 on) from Dorset Horn × German Mutton Merino at Elsenburg, W. Cape Province; BS; syn. *Dorman*. [*Dor*set *Mer*ino]

Dorper (S. Africa); m; white with black head, often black feet; hy-cw; usu. pd; orig. *c.*1942-50, chiefly at Grootfontein, from Dorset Horn × Blackhead Persian (50:50); BS 1950; var: White Dorper; not *Dorpers*. [*Dor*set *Per*sian]

Dorset: see Dorset Horn

Dorset Down (S. England); sw.m; Down type; brown face and legs; pd; orig. from Southdown × Hampshire Down in early 19th c; BS 1906; obs. syn. *Improved Hampshire Down, West Country Down*; HB also in New Zealand, France, Australia

Dorset Horn (S. England); sw.m; hd; ? orig. from Portland (and Merino); recog. 1862, BS 1891, HB; syn. Dorset (USA); var: Pink-nosed Somerset; orig. of Dormer and Dorper (S. Africa), Poll Dorset (Australia), Polled Dorset Horn (England); BS also in USA 1890, HB in Australia, Canada, S. Africa, New Zealand

Dorsian, Dorsie: see White Dorper. [*Dor*set *Per*sian]

Doukkala (S.W. Morocco); cw.m; Atlantic Coast type; usu. white, head usu. black or brown; ♂ hd, ♀ pd; Fr. *Doukkalide*; syn. *Doukkala-Abda*

Doulemi: see Shafali

Douro e Minho: see Entre Douro e Minho

DOWN (S. England); coloured face; sw. (5-15cm); pd; inc. Dorset Down, Hampshire Down, Oxford Down, Shropshire, Southdown, Suffolk (all with Southdown blood). [Downs are chalk hills of S. England]

Down-Cotswold: see Oxford Down

Drama Native (Volax, E. Macedonia, Greece); m.d.cw; var. of Greek Zackel; black, white or grey; hd or pd; rare

Drasciani, Drashiani: see Sudan Desert

Drenthe Heath (Netherlands); smaller var. of Dutch Heath; white, usu. with red or grey on face and legs (lamb spotted), black, brown or pied; ♂ hd, ♀ hd (small); BS; Du. *Drentse Heideschaap*; rare

Drysdale (New Zealand); cw; ♂ hd, ♀ pd; orig. 1929-67 by selection of monogenic variants (N^d or *nrnr*) in New Zealand Romney by F.W. *Dry* of Massey Agric. College; BS; syn. *Ennendale, N-type Romney*; BS also in Australia

Dschau-bei: see Choubei

Dub; subvar. of Vlašić var. of Bosnian Mountain; Serbo-cro. *Dubska* or *Dupska*

Dubasi (Khartoum to Shendi, Sudan); var. of Sudan Desert; pied; syn. *Northern Riverain*; not *Dubassi*

Duben (Bulgaria); m.cw.d; white or coloured; lt; Bulg. *D"benska*; rare

Dubrovnik (Dalmatia, Yugoslavia); d.m.mw; sim. to Pag Island; white (90%), black or brown; ♂ usu. pd, ♀ pd; ? orig. from Merino × Pramenka in late 18th and early 19th c. or relic of ancient finewool; Serbo-cro. *Dubrovačka* or *Dubrovačka ruda*, It. *Ragusa*; syn. *Ragusa-Šipan* (It. *Giupanna*); rare

Dugli: see Red Karaman

Dulaimi: see Shafali

Dumari: see Harnai

dumba (Iran, Afghanistan, and Pakistan) = fat-tailed; see Iran fat-tailed, Afghan, Pakistan fat-tailed

Dumbi (E. and N. Sind, Pakistan); m.d.cw; black spots on face and ears; ft; ♂ usu. hd, ♀ pd

Dun, Dunface: see Tanface

Durmitor, Durmitorska: see Piva

Dutch Black Blaze (Netherlands); w; black-brown with white face-blaze, feet and tail tip; pd; ? orig. from Texel and Friesian with black colour gene from Drenthe and Schoonebeker; BS 1979; Du. *Zwartbles schaap*; syn. *Six point white*; rare

Dutch Heath (Netherlands); cw; prim.; hd or pd; Du. *Heideschaap*; vars: Drenthe, Kempen, Mergelland, Schoonebeker and Veluwe

Duzbai; var. of Karakul; not *Dusbay*

dwarf: see Bangladeshi, Bahu (Zaïre), Southern Sudan, Ushant (Breton Dwarf), and West African Dwarf

[Dymykh] (Azerbaijan, USSR); cw.m.d; Caucasian Fat-tailed type, ? Mazekh × Karabakh; not *Dymyh, Dymyk*

Dzhaidara: see Jaidara

Dzharo: see Jaro

East African Blackheaded (W. Uganda and Sukumaland, N.W. Tanzania); East African Fat-tailed type; pied—usu. white with black or brown head; hy; usu. pd; sft.

EAST AFRICAN FAT-TAILED; hy; broad, usu. S-shaped ft; inc. East African

Blackheaded, Ethiopian and Masai; see also African Long-fat-tailed
East Friesian (Germany); d; Marsh type; pd; rat tail (woolless); BS 1892;
Ger. *Ostfriesisches Milchschaf*; syn. *East Friesland Milch, Milch sheep*;
var: Black Milksheep; orig. (with Merino) of Pomeranian (Poland);
BS also in GB (as British Friesland); *cf.* Friesian (Netherlands)
East Java(nese) Fat-tailed: see Indonesian Fat-tailed
East Mongolian Semifinewool (Mongolia); w.m; orig. 1962-82 from Altai,
Transbaikal Finewool and Tsigai, × local coarsewool (Mongolian)
East Prussian: see Skudde
East Swiss: see Wildhaus
Ebeidi: see Ibeidi
Edilbaev (N. Kazakhstan, USSR); m.cw.d; black, red or brown; pd; fr;
orig. from Kazakh Fat-rumped with Kalmyk blood; Russ.
Édil'baevskaya; not *Edelbaev*
Egyptian (Egypt); Near East Fat-tailed type: see Barki, Fellahi, Ossimi,
Rahmani; sft-lft: see Ibeidi, Saidi
Eifel: see Coburger
El Awas: see Awassi
Él'dari, Él'darsk, Él'darskaya: see Georgian Finewool Fat-tailed
Electoral Merino: see Saxony Merino
[Electoral-Negretti] (Germany); fw; orig. from Saxony Merino and
Austrian Negretti; Ger. *Deutsches Edelschaf*
Elektoralschaf: see Saxony Merino
El Hammam: see Timhadite
Elliotdale (Tasmania, Australia); cw.m; pd; orig. 1963-77 at Elliot
Research Station from a Drysdale × (Border Leicester × Merino) ♂
× hairy Romney ♀♀; homozygous for mutant carpet wool gene; BS
Embrun, Embrunais: see French Alpine
Engadine Red (Switzerland); Lop-eared Alpine type; white, black or
red-brown; ? orig. from Bergamasca × Steinschaf; Ger. *Engadiner
Fuchsschaf* or *Engadiner Landschaf*; syn. *Paterschaf*; nearly extinct
English Halfbred (England); Border Leicester × Clun Forest, 1st cross;
BS
English Leicester: see Leicester Longwool
ENGLISH LONGWOOL; lw. (15-40 cm); white face; pd; inc. Bluefaced
Leicester, Border Leicester, Cotswold, Dartmoor, Devon and Cornwall
Longwool, Leicester Longwool, Lincoln Longwool, Romney, Tees-
water, Wensleydale, Whiteface Dartmoor; most have Leicester Long-
wool blood; syn. *British Longwool*
English Merino: see Anglo-Merino
Ennendale: see Drysdale
Entre Douro e Minho (N.W. Portugal); mw.m; Bordaleiro type; usu.
white, 8% black; hd; Port. *Bordaleiro de Entre Douro e Minho*

Entrefina pirenaica: see Ansotana and Roncalesa
ENTREFINO (Spain); m.mw; usu. white; pd; ? orig. from Churro and
Merino; syn. *Cruzado* or *Cruzo* (= *crossbred*); inc. Alcarreña,
Aragonese, Castilian, Galician, Manchega, Segureña, Talaverana; *cf.*
Bordaleiro (Portugal). [= medium fine]
Entrefino-fino: see Mestizo Entrefino-fino and Talaverana
Entre Minho e Douro: see Entre Douro e Minho
[Entre-Sambre-et-Meuse] (Belgium); m.cw; extinct *c.* 1950
Epirus (Greece); mountain var. of Greek Zackel; white with red, brown
or black spots on head and legs; Gr. *Ipiros*
Eppynt: see Beulah Speckled Face
Erdelyi Racka: see Ţurcana
[Erek] (Turkmenistan, USSR); cw; white, brown, or black; st; Russ.
Èrek; syn. *Geoclan*
Erik (Amasiya, Armenia, USSR); d.cw; Caucasian Fat-tailed type; sim.
to Tushin but larger and coarser fleece; Russ. *Èrik*; *cf.* Tuj (= *Herik*)
Erzurum: see Red Karaman; not *Erzerum*
[Escurial]; former strain of Spanish Merino; Sp. *Escorial*; not *Eskurial*
Est à laine Mérinos: see Race de l'Est à laine Mérinos
Estonian Darkheaded (C. and N. Estonia, USSR); m.sw; pd; orig. (1940
on) from local graded to Shropshire; Russ. *Temnogolovaya èstonskaya*;
syn. *Rakvereskaya* (from Rakvere)
Estonian Whiteheaded (S. Estonia, USSR); m.sw; pd; orig. from Cheviot
× local coarsewooled; HB; Russ. *Belogolovaya èstonskaya*; rare
Estrêla: see Serra da Estrêla
Ethiopian (Ethiopia); m.d; East African Fat-tailed type; usu. brown; hy
with mane; hd or pd; ft; syn. *Abyssinian* (It. *Pecora abissina*), *Begghié
abesce*; vars with woolly undercoat: Akele-Guzai, Arusi-Bale, Rashaidi,
Tucur; recog. breeds: Adali, Menz (cw), Horro
European mouflon: see mouflon
Evdilon (Ikaria, Greece); d.m.cw; white, often with small spots on head
and legs; ♂ hd or pd, ♀ usu. pd; lft; ? orig. from Anatolian fat-tailed
× local thin-tailed; Gr. *Evdhilos*
Exmoor Horn (N. Devon amd W. Somerset, England); mw.m; hd; BS
1906, HB 1907; syn. *Porlock*; orig. (with Devon Longwoolled) of
Devon Closewool

Fabrianese (Fabriano, Ancona, Italy); m.d.(cw); pd; Roman nose; orig.
from local Apennine graded to Bergamasca; HB
Faccia rossa: see Comisana
Faeroes; Northern Short-tailed type; orig. from Icelandic × Old Norwegian; not *Faroe*

Fagas: see Pomeranian
Farahani (Arak, W.C. Iran): see Baluchi
Farahi: see Kandahari
Fardasca: see Ojalada
Farleton Knott: see Limestone
Fartass; pd var. of Beni Guil; not *Fartas*
Fasanese (Fasano, Brindisi, Italy); var. of Leccese with Pramenka blood
fat-rumped (Africa, Aden): see Somali
FAT-RUMPED (USSR); cw; inc. (1) [Chuntuk] (Ukraine), [Kalmyk] and
  [Karanogai] (N. Caucasus); (2) Degeres, Edilbaev, Kargalin and
  Kazakh (Kazakhstan), Kirgiz and Alai (Kirgizia), Turkmen and
  Sary-Ja (Turkmenistan), Hissar and Tajik (Tajikistan), and Jaidara
  (Uzbekistan); Russ. *kurdyuk* or *kuiryuk*
[Fat-rumped Merino] (Kirgizia, USSR); fw; fr; orig. from 3 crosses of
  Précoce on Kirgiz Fat-rumped; Russ. *Kurdyuchnyĭ Merinos*; syn.
  Kurdyukos
FAT-TAILED Europe: see Red Majorcan (Spain); Campanian Barbary and
  Sicilian Barbary (Italy); Argos, Chios, Evdilon, Mytilene, Rhodes
  (Greece); Malich and Voloshian (Ukraine)
  Asia: see Near East Fat-tailed; Habsi, Hejazi, Najdi, Yemeni (Arabia);
  Anatolian fat-tailed, Caucasian Fat-tailed, Iran fat-tailed, Afghan,
  Pakistan fat-tailed; Chinese fat-tailed; Darvaz and Karakul (Russian
  Turkestan); Buryat, Kulunda, Siberian, Telengit (Siberia); Indone-
  sian Fat-tailed
  Africa: see Barbary, Egyptian, East African Fat-tailed, African Long-
  fat-tailed
Fellahi (Nile delta, Egypt); cw.m; usu. brown; ♂ hd, ♀ usu. pd; ft; syn.
  Baladi; being replaced by Ossimi and Rahmani. [*fellah* = peasant]
Fellata: see Bornu
feral: see Arapawa Island, Hog Island, Hokonui, Pitt Island, Santa Cruz,
  Soay
Fésüs: see Hungarian Combing Wool Merino
Finarda (Po valley, N. Italy); m.(mw); Lop-eared Alpine group; orig.
  from Bergamasca × Biellese
finewool: see Merino, esp. Tasmanian Merino
Fingalway (Ireland); m; orig. from Finnish Landrace × Galway in 1970s
Finn-Dorset (GB and Ireland); Finnish Landrace × Dorset Horn
Finnish Landrace (Finland); w.m; prolific; Northern Short-tailed type;
  usu. white, occ. black, brown or grey; usu. pd; BS 1918; Finn.
  Suomalainen (maatiais) lammas, Swe. *Finsk lantras*; syn. *Finnish
  Native, Finnsheep, Improved Finnish Native*; BS also in USA 1971, HB
  also in Canada, France 1966
Flamand: see Flemish Marsh

Flanders, Flandrin: see Flemish

Flemish (Belgium and S. Holland, Netherlands); d; prolific; Marsh type; Flem. *Vlaamse*, Fr. *Flamand*; syn. *Flemish Landrace*; nearly extinct [Flemish Marsh] (French Flanders); d.m.lw; Marsh type; st; Fr. *Flamand, Flandrin*; vars: Artois, Cambrai, Picardy, St Quentin

Flevoland (Netherlands); orig. from Finnish Landrace × Ile de France

Flitsch: see Bovec

Florida Native; var. of Gulf Coast Native

Florina (N.W. Macedonia, Greece); cross of mountain and lowland Zackels; sometimes black spots around eyes and nose and usu. on ears; syn. *Pelagonia* (Albania)

Fodata: see Vicentina

Fonte Bõa Merino (Portugal); strain of Portuguese Merino; orig. 1902-26 from Rambouillet × Spanish Merino at F.B. Zootechnical Station

Fonthill Merino (Australia); m.fw; orig. from American Rambouillet × Australian Merino

Fornese, Forno: see Massese

Foulbé: see Fulani

Four-horned: see Hebridean, Jacob, Manx Loaghtan; also Icelandic, Karachai, Libyan Barbary, Multihorned Merino, Navajo-Churro, Uruguayan Criollo

Fouta, Fouta Djallon, Fouta Jallon: see West African Dwarf

Fouta Toro: see Toronké

Foxhead: see Coburger

Foza: see Vicentina

Frabosana (Ligurian Alps, Italy); m.d.(cw); sim. to Langhe; usu. a few coloured spots, sometimes all brown; hd; Roman nose; syn. *Roaschina* or *Roascia* (Imperia). [from Frabosa]

[Franconie] (E. France); black spectacles

French Alpine (Hautes-Alpes, France); m.mw; pd; orig. from local with Préalpes du Sud blood; HB 1952; Fr. *Commun des Alpes, Race des Alpes* or *Alpine*; syn. *Barcelonnette* (E. Basses-Alpes), *Embrun* (Fr. *Embrunais*), *Gap* (Fr. *Gapois*), *Trièves* (S.E. Isère); *cf.* also Lop-eared Alpine; nearly extinct (being absorbed by Préalpes du Sud)

[French Blackheaded] (France, esp. Moselle); m.sw; black head and legs; pd; orig. from Suffolk, Hampshire Down, Oxford Down, Southdown and (since 1945) German Blackheaded Mutton; BS and HB 1959; Fr. *Moutons à tête noire*; Suffolk, Hampshire and Dorset Down are now bred separately (society is UPRA, Suffolk-Hampshire-Dorset)

French Merino: see Arles Merino, Précoce, Rambouillet; formerly also [Mérinos de Mauchamp], [Mérinos du Naz] and [Roussillon Merino]

French Southdown (C. and W. France); taller and heavier var. of

Southdown from imports 1855-1962; HB 1947, BS

French Texel (N.E. France); more compact and less fat var. of Texel from imports 1933 on; BS 1935

Friesian (Netherlands); d; prolific; Marsh type, sim. to East Friesian; pd; rat tail; Du. *Friese melkschaap*; BS 1950; syn. *West Friesian*; rare

Friesland: see East Friesian and Friesian

Friserra (Portugal); d; orig. since 1962 from East Friesian × Serra da Estrêla

[Friulana] (Udine, Venetia, Italy); m.mw-cw.d; Lop-eared Alpine group; occ. dark spots on face; syn. *Furlana*; orig. from Lamon and now absorbed by it; extinct *c.* 1971. [from Friuli]

[Frutigen] (Switzerland); part orig. of Swiss Black-Brown Mountain; Ger. *Frutigschaf*

FSL (Roquefort, S. France); d; orig. 1967 on, $\frac{3}{8}$ East Friesian, $\frac{3}{8}$ Sardinian, $\frac{1}{4}$ Lacaune *i.e.* EF(EF × L) × S(S × L)

Fuchskopf, Fuchsschaf: see Coburger

Fulani (Senegal to Cameroon); m; Sahel type; white, pied, or coloured; ♂ hd, ♀ hd or pd; Fr. *Peul* (*Peuhl, Peulh,* or *Peul-Peul*); syn. *Foulbé, Fulbé*; vars: Bornu, Samburu, Toronké, Uda, Woila, Yankasa

Furlana: see Friulana

Gacka: see Lika

gad (N. Baluchistan, Pakistan) = *Ovis vignei cycloceros*; var. of (Afghan) urial in Kalat formerly called Blanford's urial (*O.v. blanfordi*); not *ghad*

Gad (USSR): see Dargintsi

Gaddi (S. Jammu and Kashmir, C. Himachal Pradesh and N. of Uttar Pradesh, India); cw.pa.m; occ. coloured face or body; ♂ hd, ♀ usu. pd; syn. *Bhadarwah, Kangra Valley*; not *Guddi*

Gadertaler: see Pusterese

Gadik (N.E. Afghanistan); cw.m; ears short or long; ♂ hd, ♀ hd or pd; ft; vars: Wakhan Gadik (usu. white) and Panjsher Gadik (usu. black or brown); not *Gadic*

Gala (Apsheron peninsula, Azerbaijan. USSR); var. of Shirvan

Galega: see Galician (Portugal)

Galician (Galicia, Spain); m.(mw); prolific; Entrefino type; ♂ usu. pd, ♀ pd; Sp. *Gallega*; formerly called *Churra gallega* (= *Galician Churro*); syn. *Mariñana*

Galician (Portugal): see Bragança Galician, Miranda Galician

Gallega: see Galician (Spain)

Galloway Blackface (S.W. Scotland); strain of Scottish Blackface with finer wool; syn. *Newton Stewart*

Galway (Clare, Galway, Roscommon and parts of adjacent counties, W. Ireland); m.lw; pd; Border (?) Leicester blood; split off from Roscommon in 1926 and then absorbed it; BS 1922, HB 1931

Gamde, Gamdi: see Taiz Red

Gammelnorsk: see Old Norwegian

Ganadi: see Taiz Red

Ganjam (S. Orissa, India); m; South India hair type; brown or red; ♂ hd, ♀ pd

Gansu Alpine Finewool (Qilan mts, C. Gansu, China); fw; orig. from Caucasian, Salsk and Stavropol × (Xinjiang Finewool × Mongolian and Tibetan) in mid-20th c; syn. *North-West China Merino* or *Northwestern Chinese Merino*

Gap, Gapois: see French Alpine

Garessina (Tanaro, Inferno, and Negrone valleys, Ligurian Alps, Cuneo, Italy); m.d.(mw); pd; sim. to Sambucana but smaller and finer wool; syn. *Muma*; rare. [from Garessio]

Garfagnina White (Garfagnana, N.W. Tuscany, Italy); d.m.(w); Apennine group, sim. to Massese but white and larger; ♂ hd, ♀ usu. hd; It. *Garfagnina bianca*; former var: Pavullese (with Bergamasca blood); nearly extinct

Garha, Gargha (N. Syria): see White Karaman

Garrigues Causses: see Caussenard des Garrigues

Gasc: see Sudan Desert

[Gascon] (Gascony, S.W. France); local var. sim. to Landais and Lauraguais

Gascon à lunettes: see Caussenard du Lot

Gash: see Sudan Desert

Gatačka: see Lika

[Gedek] (Azerbaijan-Dagestan, USSR); var. of Tabasaran; Russ. *Gëdek*

Gegica: see Gekika

[Gekika] (Greece); Ruda type; not *Gegica*; ? = Luma of Albania. [*Gekides* are Albanian nomads]

[Gentile di Calabria] (toe of Italy); former var. of Gentile di Puglia with mw; orig. from Calabrian improved by Gentile di Puglia; syn. *Improved Calabrian*

[Gentile di Lucania] (S. Italy); former var. of Gentile di Puglia with mw; orig. from Gentile di Puglia × local; syn. *Basilicata, Improved Lucanian*

Gentile di Puglia (S. Italy); fw-(mw).m.(d); ♂ hd, ♀ pd; orig. 15th c. on but chiefly 18th, from Spanish Merino × local, also Saxony and Rambouillet blood in 19th c; HB 1942; syn. *Apulian Merino* (It. *Merino di Puglia*), *Improved Apulian, Italian Merino* (It. *Merino d'Italia*), *Merina Gentile*; former vars with less Merino blood: Gentile di Calabria, Gentile di Lucania, Improved Ariano

Gentile moretta, Gentile a vello nero: see Carapellese
Geoclan: see Erek
Georgian (Turkey): see Tuj
Georgian Fat-tailed Finewool (Georgia, USSR); m.fw; ft; orig. 1936-58 at El'dari state farm from Tushin crossed with Soviet Merino and (since 1940) with Caucasian; Russ. *Gruzinskaya zhirnokhvostaya tonkorunnaya*; syn. *El'darskaya tonkorunnaya* (= *Eldari finewool*); rare
Georgian Semifinewool Fat-tailed (E. Georgia, USSR); m.mw; ♂ hd, ♀ pd; ft; orig. 1931-49 chiefly at Udabno farm from Rambouillet or Précoce × Tushin with 1 or 2 backcrosses to Merino ♂, 1 to Tushin ♀, and then *inter se* mating; Russ. *Gruzinskaya polutonkorunnaya zhirnokhvostaya*; syn. *Georgian*; rare
Georgian Thin-tailed Finewool (E. Georgia, USSR); orig. 1950 on, at Samgorsk state farm; Russ. *Tonkorunnaya toshchekhvostaya ovtsa gruzii*
German Blackheaded Mutton (N. and W. Germany); m.sw; pd; orig. 1870-1914 from Hampshire Down + Oxford Down (+ Shropshire + Suffolk); HB; Ger. *Deutsches schwarzköpfiges Fleischschaf*, Pol. *Czarnoglowka*; syn. *German Hampshire, Improved Blackface Mutton, Teutoburg* (Westphalia); orig. of Latvian Darkheaded, Lithuanian Blackheaded, and Polish Blackheaded
German Hampshire: see German Blackheaded Mutton
German Heath: see Heidschnucke
German Improved Land: see Merinolandschaf
German Karakul (E. Germany); native graded to Karakul ($\frac{31}{32}$); Ger. *Karakul Landschaf*; syn. *Land Karakul*; rare
German Merino; formerly inc. Electoral-Negretti and Saxony; Russ. *Baldebukov*; now see German Mutton Merino
German Mountain (S. Bavaria, Germany); cw.m; pd; local mountain breeds (Carinthian, Goggel, Steinschaf, Zaupel *et al.*) graded to Bergamasca and Tyrol Mountain since 1938; Ger. *Deutsches Bergschaf*; ? = Tyrol Mountain; var: Brown Mountain (*Braunes Bergschaf*)
German Mutton Merino (Germany); m.fw; pd; orig. *c.*1904 from Précoce imported *c.*1870; HB; Ger. *Merinofleischschaf*; syn. *German Merino, German Précoce, Merino Meat, Merino Mutton*; BS in S. Africa 1947, HB also in Bulgaria, Spain
German Précoce: see German Mutton Merino
German Whiteheaded Land: see Merinolandschaf
German Whiteheaded Mutton (N.W. Germany); m.w; pd; orig. in mid-19th c. from Cotswold × Marsh (Butjadingen); recog. 1924; recent Texel blood; HB; Ger. *Deutsches weissköpfiges Fleischschaf*; syn. *Oldenburg White Head, Whiteheaded German, Whiteheaded Oldenburg*; orig. of British Oldenburg

Gesel: see Red Karaman
Gessenay: see Saanen
Gezel: see Red Karaman
Gezira (Sudan): see Watish
Gezirieh, Gezrawieh (Iraq): see Awassi
Ghachgai, Ghashgai: see Qashqai
Gharpala: see Kagi
Ghezel: see Red Karaman
Ghiljai (S.E. Afghanistan); cw.m; white with black or brown spots on
  face and legs, or brown or black; lop ears; ♂ hd or pd, ♀ pd; ft; sim.
  to Kandahari but larger and fleece of higher carpet-wool quality
Ghimi (Fezzan, Libya); cw-mw.m; ft; ? orig. from Algerian Arab ×
  Libyan Barbary
Ghizel: see Red Karaman
Gıcık (Turkey): see Herik or other small breeds; also wrongly used for
  Dağliç
Gissar: see Hissar
Giupanna: see Šipan
Glamorgan: see South Wales Mountain
Glossa: see Skopelos
Gmelin's sheep: see red sheep
Gobi-Altai (Mongolia); var. of Mongolian
Godavari (N.W. Andhra Pradesh, and Chanda, N.E. Maharashtra,
  India); m; South India hair type; white or reddish-brown; ? pd; syn.
  Dhormundi; not *Godawari*
[Goggel] (Bavaria, Germany); cw; pd; local term for mountain sheep
  sim. to Steinschaf; probably a cross
Goitred: see Zunu
Gojal (Hunza valley, N. Kashmir, Pakistan); d.m.cw; white and tan with
  black patches and coloured head and legs; ♂ usu. hd, ♀ pd; sft
Gökçeada (Turkey); d.m.cw; Island Zackel type; black spots around
  eyes, nose and ears; ♂ hd, ♀ pd or scurs; syn. *Imroz*
Gorki (USSR); m.sw; brown face; pd; orig. 1936-48 from Hampshire
  Down × local Northern Short-tailed; recog. 1950; HB; Russ. *Gor'kov-
  skaya*; not *Gorky*
Gorno Altai: see Altai Mountain
Gornodarvazskaya: see Darvaz Mountain
Gorodets: see Vyatka
Gotland (Sweden); cw.m; var. of Swedish Landrace; usu. grey, also
  white, yellow, black or pied; hd; Swe. *Gutefår*; syn. *Goth*; orig. of
  Swedish Fur Sheep
Goundoun (Niger); var. of Macina. [corruption of Goundam, a town
  in Macina]

[Grabs] (Switzerland); orig. from Oxford Down × Wildhaus; Ger. *Grabser*; orig. of Swiss Brownheaded Mutton

Grammos (N.E. Greece); mountain var. of Greek Zackel; usu. white with red spot on head; Gr. *Gramoutsiano*

Granada, Granadina: see Montesina

Graubünden: see Bündner Oberland

Grazalema (Cadiz, Spain); d; subvar. of Andalusian Merino selected for milk

Greek island breeds: see Chios, Evdilon, Kymi, Mytilene, Rhodes, Skopelos, Zakynthos; see also Island Zackel

Greek Zackel (Greece); d.m.cw; usu. white with black or red spots on head and legs, occ. coloured; ♂ hd, ♀ usu. pd; obs. syn. *Cretan Zackel, Macedonian, Parnassian*; inc. Island, Florina, Karagouniko and Katsika (lowland), Vlakhiko (mountain)

Greyface: see Scottish Greyface

Greyface Dartmoor: see Dartmoor

Greyface Oldenbred (England); m; British Oldenburg × Scottish Blackface or Swaledale, 1st cross; see also Welsh Oldenbred

Grey Shirazi (Fars, Iran); m.cw.fur; sim. to Karakul but grey; ♂ hd, ♀ pd; ft; Fr. *Chiraz*; var: Zandi

Grignon: see Dishley Merino

Grisons: see Bündner Oberland

Gritstone: see Derbyshire Gritstone

Grivette (Dauphiné, France); sim. to Rava; white, spots at birth; pd; BS

Gromark (NSW, Australia); m.mw; orig. 1965-77 from Border Leicester × Corriedale selected for live weight, twinning and wool; BS

[Groningen] (Netherlands); d; Marsh type, sim. to Friesian; Du. *Groningse melkschaap*

Grozny (Dagestan, USSR); fw; orig. 1929-51 from Australian Merino × Mazaev and Novocaucasian Merinos at stud farm Chervlennye Buruny; HB; Russ. *Groznenskaya*; not *Grozn*

[Guadalupe]; former strain of Spanish Merino; not *Gouadaloupe*

Guddi: see Gaddi

Guerha: see White Karaman

Guinea: see West African

Guinea Long-legged: see Sahel type

Guirra (coast of Valencia, S. Castellón, and N. Alicante, Spain); m.(mw.d); born dark brown paling to red with age; pd; Roman nose; syn. *Rocha, Rotxa* or *Roya* (= red), *Roja levantina* (= *Levant Red*), *Sudad* or *Sudat* (Alicante); rare

Guissar: see Hissar

Gujarati, Gujerati, Gujrati: see Patanwadi

Gulf Coast Native (USA); cw-mw; white, or tan to dark brown; local orig. from Spanish (? Churro) introductions; vars: Florida Native, Louisiana Native; *cf.* Criollo; nearly extinct

Guligas; pink-roan var. of Karakul

Gulijan, Gulijanska: see Svrljig

Gunib (Dagestan, USSR); cw.m; Caucasian Fat-tailed type, sim. to Lak; black; ♂ hd, 25% ♀ pd; Russ. *Gunibskaya*; orig. (with Württemberg Merino) of Dagestan Mountain

Gurez (Kashmir North, Jammu and Kashmir, India); cw-mw.d; usu. white and pd; st.

[Gurktaler] (Carinthia, Austria); former local var. of Carinthian; ? with English Longwool blood

Gyzyl-Gojun: see Mazekh

Habsi (Asir mts, Saudi Arabia); m; hy; ft; sim. to Hejazi but smaller; syn. *Habashi, Habasi* (fem. *Habasiyah*), *Hagari, Hibsi.* [= Abyssinian]

Hadjazi: see Hejazi

Hagari: see Habsi

HAIR SHEEP, *i.e.* with fleece sim. to wild sheep.
  Asia: see Hejazi, South India hair
  Africa: see African Long-legged, African Long-fat-tailed, East African Fat-tailed, Somali and Blackhead Persian, West African Dwarf
  America: see American Hair sheep

Hakasskaya: see Khakass

Halfbred: see English Halfbred, Kent Halfbred, New Zealand Halfbred, Romney Halfbred, Scottish Halfbred, Welsh Half-bred, Yorkshire Half-bred

Halhas: see Khalkhas

Hallenjoo (Dera Ghazi Khan, Pakistan); larger var. of Khijloo; grey with black patches

Hamalé: see Sudan Desert

Hamdani (Arbil, Iraq); cw.m.d; lowland var. of Kurdi type; black head; pd; lop ears; not *Hamadani, Hamadi, Hamdanya*

Hamitic Long-tailed: see Ancient Egyptian

Hammam (Morocco): see Timhadite

Hampshire Down (England); sw.m; Down type; black-brown face and legs; pd; orig. in early 19th c. from Southdown × Wiltshire Horn and Berkshire Knot; recog. 1859; BS 1889, HB 1890; orig. of Dorset Down, (× Cotswold) of Oxford Down, (+ Oxford Down) of German Blackheaded Mutton and Polish Blackheaded, and (× Northern Short-tailed) of Gorki (USSR); syn. *Hampshire* (USA); BS also in USA 1889, Australia, HB also in Canada, New Zealand, S. Africa, France 1957

Hamra (Algeria): see Beni-Guil

Hamra (Syria): see Red Karaman. [Arabic = red]

Hamyan: see Beni Guil

Han (parts of Henan, Shanxi, Hebei, Shandong and Jiangsu, China); mw-cw; prolific; large ft. (pd) and small ft. (hd) vars; orig. from Mongolian; syn. *Han-yang* (= *Han sheep*), Shandong (esp. wool); not *Hangyang, Hanjan, Hanyan*

Hangay (W.C. Mongolia); fw; orig. from Mongolian graded to Altai; not *Hangai*

Hangyang, Hanjan, Hanyan: see Han

Harcha; main var. of Beni Guil; not *Archa*

Hareki, Hargi, Harki: see Herki

Harnai (N.E. Baluchistan, Pakistan); cw.m.d; coloured spots on head; hd (short); ft; syn. *Damari, Dumari*; not *Hasnai*

Harri: see Hejazi

Harrick: see Herki

Hasa, Hasah: see Kazakh

Hashtnagri (C. of N.W.F.P., Pakistan); m.cw; black face; pd; ft; not *Hastnagri*

Hasnai: see Harnai

Hassan (S.C. Karnataka, India); cw.m; white with black or light brown markings; ♂ hd or pd, ♀ pd; syn. *Kolar*; not *Hassen*

Hastnagri: see Hashtnagri

Hausa: see Yankasa

Hawaiian Black Buck (Hawaii); black; hy; hd

Hazaragie (Hazarajat, C. Afghanistan); cw.m; usu. reddish-brown, occ. black or white with brown belly; pd; ft; not *Hazara*

HEATH (N.W. Europe); cw; black face; usu. hd; st; see [Danish Heath], Dutch Heath, Heidschnucke, Skudde, Wrzosówka; orig. of Danish Landrace

Hebridean (Scotland); Northern Short-tailed type; black or dark brown; usu. 4-horned; HB, BS 1987; syn. (till 1977) *St Kilda*

Hedjazi: see Hejazi

Hei (Chinese) = black

Heidschnucke (Lüneburg heath, Hanover, Germany); cw; grey with black face, lambs born black; hd; st; BS; syn. *German Heath*; not *Heidschmucke, Heidschnukke, Heidsnucke*; selected vars: White Horned (*Weisse gehörnte Heidschnucke*) (S. Oldenburg, rare), and White Polled (*Weisse hornlöse Heidschnucke* or *Moorschnucke*) (Lower Saxony, nearly extinct); rat tail

Hejari; var. of Najdi

Hejazi (W. Saudi Arabia); m; usu. white; hy; ♂ pd or scurs, ♀ pd; often earless; often tassels; sft; syn. *Harri, Khazi, Mecca*; not *Hadjazi, Hedjazi*

Hemşin (N.E. Turkey); cw.m; brown, black or white; ♂ hd, ♀ usu. pd; lt. fat at base

Herati: see Kandahari

Hercegovina: see Bosnian Mountain, Dalmatian-Karst; Serbo-cro. *Hercegovačka*

Herdwick (Lake District, N.W. England); cw.m; lamb black face and legs and blue-roan fleece, adult white; ♂ hd, ♀ pd; ? orig; association 1844, BS 1916, HB 1920. [? = let out in herds, or = sheep pasture]

Hereford: see Ryeland

Herero: see Mondombes

Herik (N. Anatolia, Turkey); cw.m.d; sim. to Dağliç; usu. white with dark spots on head; ♂ hd, ♀ usu. pd; sft; syn. *Amasya Herik, Heregi, Gıcık*; name also used for Tuj

Herki (Iranian, Turkish and Syrian Kurdistan); cw.m.d; black face; usu. pd; ft; ? = Iraq Kurdi or another var. of Kurdi type; syn. *Dazdawi, Mosuli* (not *Mossul, Mousouli*); not *Hareki, Hargi, Harki, Harrick, Herrik, Hirik, Hirrick, Hirrik, Hurluck*. [Herki tribe near Mosul]

Herrik (Kurdistan): see Herki

Hetian (W. Xinjiang, China); cw.m; sim. to Tibegolian; white with black or pied head; ♂ hd, ♀ hd or pd; sft; W.G. *Ho-t'ien*; not *Cho-ten-jan, Hotan, Khotan, Kotan*; var: Kargilik, with Kokyar (sim. to Darvaz) and Saku-Bash (sim. to Chapan) subvars

Hexham Leicester: see Bluefaced Leicester

Hibsi: see Habsi

High Fertility (Ireland); prolific; population derived from ♂♂ and ♀♀ screened from commercial flocks 1963-65

Highland: see Scottish Blackface

Hill Radnor (Black Mountains, S.E. Wales); m.sw; sim. to South Wales Mountain; tan or grey face and legs; ♂ usu. hd, ♀ pd; orig. from Welsh Tanface; BS 1926, HB 1955; syn. *Radnor, Radnor Forest*; ? orig. (with Shropshire) of Clun Forest

Hirik, Hirrick, Hirrik: see Herki

Hissar (Tajikistan, USSR); m.cw; brown; pd; fr; Russ. *Gissarskaya*; syn. *Uzbek*; not *Gissar, Guissar*

Hissardale (E. Punjab, India); fw; ♂ hd or pd, ♀ pd; orig. (? 1920s) from Australian Merino ($\frac{7}{8}$) × Bikaneri at Government livestock farm, Hissar; not *Hissar Dale*; rare

Hog Island (USA); feral

Hokonui (Southland, New Zealand); fw; feral; white or coloured; hd or pd; ? orig. from Tasmanian Merino *c*.1858; syn. *Hokonui Merino*

Holstein: see Wilstermarsch

Horned Cragg: see Limestone

Horro (W. Ethiopia); m; tan, occ. cream, brown, black or pied; pd; hy; ft.(triangular)

Hortobágy Racka: see Racka

Hotan, Ho-t'ien: see Hetian

[Hottentot] (S. Africa); hy; ft; ? orig. from Near East Fat-tailed and Ancient Egyptian (long-tailed); vars: Namaqua (white, lft), Cape (many colours, sft); orig. of Africander

Houda: see Uda

Hu (S. Jiangsu, China); cw.pelt; prolific; white; pd; sft; orig. from Mongolian; syn. *Huchow, Hu-yang* (= *Lake sheep*), *Ongti, Shanghai, Wu, Wuxi* (not *Wushing, Wusih*); not *Hujan, Huyan*

Hum: see Dalmatian-Karst

Hungarian Merino (Hungary); fw.d.m; orig. from Racka (+ Bergamasca and Württemberg Merino) graded to Rambouillet, also Précoce, German Mutton Merino and Russian Merino blood; Hung. *Magyar Fésüs Merinó* (= *Hungarian Combing Wool Merino*); inc. Hungarian Mutton Merino (*Magyar Húsmerinó*); orig. of Transylvanian Merino (Romania)

Hungarian Zackel: see Racka

Hurluck: see Herki

Huyan, Hu-yang: see Hu

Hyfer (NSW, Australia); m; prime lamb dam line; orig. 1980s from Booroola Merino ($\frac{1}{2}$), Trangie Fertility Merino ($\frac{1}{4}$) and Dorset (? Horn) ($\frac{1}{4}$); selected for high fertility

Ibeidi (El Minya, Upper Egypt); white, usu. with brown head, occ black; ♂ hd, ♀ usu. pd; sft; not *Abidi, Ebeidi*. [= from Beni 'Ibeid]

IBERIAN (mountain areas, Spain); m.mw; white with coloured marks on face and legs; ♂ occ. hd, ♀ pd; inc. Montesina, Ojalada, Pallaresa; Sp. *Iberica*; syn. *Serrana* (= *mountain*)

Ibicenca: see Ibiza

Ibiza (Balearic Is, Spain); m.cw; pd; Sp. *Ibicenca*; declining

Icelandic (Iceland); w.d.m; Northern Short-tailed type; usu. white with light brown head and legs, sometimes black, grey, brown or pied; usu. hd (sometimes 4 or more); orig. from Old Norwegian; var: Kleifa (pd)

Ideal: see Polwarth

Ikzhaomen (Inner Mongolia, China); var. of Mongolian; Russ. *Ikzhaoménskaya*; not *Ikzhaomeng*

Ile-de-France (N. France); m.mw; pd; orig. as Dishley Merino from Leicester Longwool × Merino, 1833-1900; BS 1922; BS also in GB 1982, HB also in Spain

Imeretian (Abkhasia and Ajaria, Georgia, USSR); Caucasian Fat-tailed type; ♂ hd; lt-ft; Russ. *Imeretinskaya*; syn. *Imeritian*; rare

Imperial (Imperial Calcasieu parish, Louisiana, USA); m.mw; face and legs white to tan; ♂ usu. hd, ♀ pd; orig. from British breeds in late 18th c. with blood of American Tunis

Improved Apulian: see Gentile di Puglia
[Improved Ariano] (Campania, Italy); former var. of Gentile di Puglia
with mw; orig. from Gentile di Puglia × local; syn. *Spanish Ariano* (It.
Spagnola arianese), *Quadrella*
Improved Awassi: see Israeli Improved Awassi
Improved Black (Italy): see Carapellese
Improved Blackface Mutton (Germany): see German Blackheaded Mutton
Improved Blackheaded Mutton-Wool (Switzerland): see Swiss Brownheaded Mutton
Improved Calabrian: see Gentile di Calabria
Improved Dartmoor: see Dartmoor
Improved German Country, Farm, or Land: see Merinolandschaf
Improved Gorodets: see Vyatka
Improved Hampshire Down: see Dorset Down
Improved Haslingden: see Lonk
Improved Leicester: see Leicester Longwool
Improved Lucanian: see Gentile di Lucania
[Improved Mongolian] (N.E. China); orig. from American Rambouillet
× Mongolian in 1920s and 1930s; superseded by North-East China
Finewool
Improved Šumava (Bohemia, Czechoslovakia); m.w; orig. from Šumava
by selection and limited use of Texel, Tsigai and Merinolandschaf; Cz.
Zušlechtěná šumavska; now called Šumava (*Šumavska*)
Improved Valachian (Moravia, Czechoslovakia); m.cw; orig. from Valachian improved by Texel, Cheviot and East Friesian; Cz. *Zušlechtěná valašská*
Improved Valachian (Slovakia, Czechoslovakia); m.mw; orig. from Valachian improved by Texel, Lincoln and Leicester Longwool; Sl. *Zošlachtená valašská*
Improved Whiteheaded Land: see Merinolandschaf
Improved Whiteheaded Mountain: see Swiss White Mountain
Imroz: see Gökçeada
Indian fat-tailed: see Pakistan fat-tailed
Indonesian: see Indonesian Fat-tailed, Javanese Thin-tailed, Priangan
Indonesian Fat-tailed (E. Java, Madura, Lombok and S, Sulawesi);
m.(cw); pd; sft. or lft; ? orig. from fat-tailed breed of S.W.Asia (*e.g.*
Baluchi from Iran) in 18th c; Indonesian *domba ebor gomuk*; syn.
Donggala (not *Dongala, Donggola*) (Sulawesi), *East Java(nese) Fat-tailed, Madurese*
Indre Berrichon: see Berrichon de l'Indre
[Infantado]; former strain of Spanish Merino
Ingessana (S. Sudan); Sudan Desert × Nilotic intermediate

Ingush: see Karachai

Inner Mongolian Finewool (China); orig. from Caucasian × Mongolian

INRA 401 (France); m; prolific strain orig. 1969 on at Bourges Exp. Sta. of Institut National de la Recherche Agronomique (INRA) from Romanov × Berrichon du Cher

[Iomud] (Turkmenistan, USSR); var. of Turkmen Fat-rumped; not *Iomut*

Ipiros: see Epirus

Iran fat-tailed breeds; see Afshari, Arabi, Bakhtiari-Luri, Baluchi, Farahani, Grey Shirazi, Herki, Kallakui, Karakul, Kurdi, Makui, Mehraban, Moghani, Sangesari, Sanjabi, Shal, Turki; syn. *dumba, Persian fat-tailed*

Iran Thin-tailed: see Zel

Iraqi: see Awassi, Arabi, Kurdi; not *Iraki*

Iraq Kurdi (N.E. Iraq); m.cw.d; Kurdi type; black head and legs; pd; ft; not *Karadi, Karradi, Kordi, Kuradi*

Irish Longwool: see Galway, Roscommon

Irish Shortwool: see Wicklow Cheviot

Island Blackface (Hebrides, Scotland); strain of Scottish Blackface with finer wool

Island Pramenka (Yugoslavia); cw-mw.m.d; Pramenka type with some Merino blood; usu, white with white or speckled head and legs, occ. black or brown; ♂ hd, ♀ usu. pd; Serbo-cro. *Otočka Pramenka*; syn. *Island Zackel*; inc. (with increasing Merino blood): Brač, Hvar and Kornat; Krk and Rab; Cres, Dugi Otok, Lošinj and Olib; Silba and Zlarin; culminating in Pag Island (*q.v.*)

Island Zackel (Greece): see Lemnos, Levkimmi, Psiloris, Sfakia, Sitia

Israeli Improved Awassi (Israel); var. of Awassi with Herki (Kurdi) blood (1953-57), selected for milk; HB 1943; orig. (with East Friesian) of Assaf

Issyk Kul argali: see arkhar

Istrian Milk (E. Istra and Croatian coast, Yugoslavia); d.m.cw; Pramenka type; Serbo-cro. *Istarska mlječna*; syn. *Primorska* (= *coastal*

Italian Merino: see Gentile di Puglia

İvessi (Turkey): see Awassi

Ivrea: see Biellese

Iwessi: see Awassi

Jacob (Great Britain); w.m; dark brown patches; usu. 4-horned; ? orig. from Hebridean; BS 1969; syn. *Jacob's sheep, Spanish Piebald, Spotted*;

BS also in USA 1985

Jaffna (Sri Lanka); m; often white with tan or black patches, also white, tan or black; hy; ♂ hd or pd, ♀ usu. pd; orig. from South India hair type

Jahrani: see Dhamari

Jaidara (Uzbekistan, USSR); cw.m; white, tan or brown; ♂ hd or pd, ♀ pd; fr; Russ. *Dzhaĭdara*

Jaisalmeri (Jaisalmer, W. Rajasthan, India); cw; brown or black face; pd; long lop ears; not *Jaiselmeri*

Jalauni (S.W. Uttar Pradesh, India); cw.m.d; face may have coloured markings; pd; long lop ears; not *Jaluan*; syn. *Bundelkhandi* or *Jubbulpuri* (N. Madya Pradesh)

Jaluan: see Jalauni

Jangli: see Magra

[Jaro] (Azerbaijan, USSR); d.cw.m; Caucasian Fat-tailed type; Russ. *Dzharo*

Javanese: see Indonesian Fat-tailed, Javanese Thin-tailed, Priangan

Javanese Thin-tailed (W. and C. Java, Indonesia); m.(cw); usu. white, often black around eyes and nose; ♂ hd, ♀ usu. pd

Jędrzychowice Merino (Osowa Sień State Breeding Centre, Poland); fw; orig. 1954-64 from Polish Merino × (Polish Merino × Caucasian); Pol. *Merynos wełnisty typu jędrzychowickiego*

Jezero-Piva, Jezero-pivska: see Piva

Jezerska, Jezersko-Solčava: see Solčava

Jhalawani; var. of Rakhshani

Jhelum Valley: see Kashmir Valley

Jomoor: see Samhoor

Joria: see Patanwadi

Jubbulpuri: see Jalauni

Jumli (Jumla, N.W. Nepal); m.cw; sim. to Baruwal but smaller; finer wool than Kagi; syn. (?) *Kiu* (or *Kew*)

Junin (C. Peru); m.mw; white or black face; pd; orig. since 1940s at SAIS Tupac Amaru from Columbia, Corriedale, Panama, Romney and Warhill

[Jura]; part orig. of Swiss Black-Brown Mountain; former vars: Berne (black), Solothurn (brown)

Kababish: see Sudan Desert

Kabarda: see Karachai; Russ. *Karbardinskaya*

Kabarliavi; dense-wool var. of Karnobat

Kabyle: see Berber

Kachhi (Thar, Sind, Pakistan); d.cw.m; black or tan face; pd; ears often vestigial; st; syn. *Cutchi, Kutchi*

Kaghani (N. of N.W.F.P., Pakistan); m.cw; tan, grey or black; lop ears; ♂ usu. hd, ♀ usu. pd; st.

Kagi (Pahar of Nepal); m.(cw-hy); small to dwarf; dirty white, often with light brown patches, occ. black; ♂ hd, ♀ usu. pd; often earless; st; syn. *Gharpala* (= *household-raised*); not *Cagi, Cago, Kage*

Kail (Neelam valley, Azad Kashmir, Pakistan); m.cw; white, white with black or brown head, or black or brown around the eyes; ♂ hd, ♀ usu. pd; lop ears

Kajli (Sargodha, Gujrat and Mianwali, Pakistan); m.cw; black nose, eyes and eartips; long lop ears; Roman nose; ♂ hd or pd , ♀ pd; *Kalakou, Kala-Kouh, Kalaku, Kalakuh*: see Kallakui

Kali (Kotli, Azad Kashmir, Pakistan); m.cw; black; ♂ usu. hd, ♀ usu. pd

Kalinin (USSR); var. of Russian Longwool; orig. (1935 on) from Lincoln × Northern Short-tailed; Russ. *Kalininskaya*

Kallakui (Varamin to Qom, N.C. Iran); cw.m.d; sim. to Baluchi; black marks on face and legs; ♂ usu. hd, ♀ pd; not *Calikui, Calokui, Kalakou, Kala-Kouh, Kalaku, Kalakuh, Kellakui*

[Kalmyk] (Astrakhan, USSR); cw.m; sim. to Chuntuk; fr; Russ. *Kalmytskaya*; not *Kalmuck*

Kamakuyruk (N.W. Anatolia, Turkey); Kivircik × Dağliç F_1, and breed derived from it; lt. fat at base; syn. *Pirlak*; not *Kamakyuruk, Kamakuruk.* [= knife-blade tail]

Kambar; golden-brown var. of Karakul; not *Cambar, Kombar*

Kameng: see Tibetan

Kamieniec (Olszytyn province, Poland); m.lw; Polish Longwool group; orig. 1954-64 on Susz State Sheep Improvement Centre, from Romney × Pomeranian with Texel or Leine blood; Pol. *Kamieniecka*

[Kanaltaler]; d; former var. of Carinthian; black ear tips and spectacles; syn. *Canaltaler, Uggowitz*

Kandahari (S. and C.W. Afghanistan); cw; sim. to Ghiljai but smaller; white with black spots on face and legs, or black or brown or mixed; ears long or very short; ♂ hd, ♀ pd; sft; syn. *Farahi, Herati*

Kangal (Sivas and Malatya, Turkey); local var. of White Karaman

Kangani: see Kenguri

Kangra Valley: see Biangi and Gaddi

Karabakh (Azerbaijan, USSR); Caucasian Fat-tailed type; usu. reddish or greyish (dirty white or light brown), occ. black or red; ♂ hd or pd, ♀ pd; Russ. *Karabakh* or *Karabakhskaya*; var: Karadolakh; not *Karabagh*

[Karacabey-Kivircik] (N.W. Anatolia, Turkey); Kivircik × German Mutton Merino crosses at Karacabey stud farm; syn. *Kirma* (= *halfbred*); orig. of Karacabey Merino

Karacabey Merino (N.W. Anatolia, Turkey); mw.m.d; var. of Turkish Merino; orig. from Kivircik graded up (since 1928) with German Mutton Merino (95%) (via Karacabey-Kivircik)

Karachai (N. Caucasus, USSR); Caucasian Fat-tailed type; black (80%),

also grey, tan or white; 2-4 horns; lft; Russ. *Karachaevskaya*; syn. *Balkar, Chechen, Ingush, Kabarda, Ossetian*; not *Karachaev, Karatchayev*
Karachai Mountain Mutton-Wool; orig. from North Caucasus Mutton-Wool × (Karachai × Cherkassy)
Karadi, Karradi: see Kurdi
Karadolakh; var. of Karabakh; Russ. *Karadolakhskaya*
Karagouniko (Thessaly, Greece); d.m.cw; lowland breed of Greek Zackel; usu. black or white, also brown, pied or spotted; not *Karagunica*. [*Karagounides* are farmers in the plain of Thessaly]
Karakachan (Balkans, esp. Macedonia); d.m.cw; Zackel type; usu. black or brown, occ. white (*Bela vlaška*); ♂ hd, ♀ usu. pd; syn. *Karavlaška* or *Crna vlaška* (= *black Vlach*), *Kucovlaška* (Yugoslavia); *Macedonian Nomad, Romanian Nomad* (Bulgaria); *Karakatsan* or *Sarakatzan* (Greece); not *Karakachenski, Karakatschenski*. [Karakachan (= black shepherd) and Kutsovlach (= lame Vlach) are nomadic tribes speaking respectively Greek and Romanian]
Karakaş (Diyarbakir, Turkey); local var. of White Karaman
Karakul (Uzbekistan, USSR); fur, d; ♂ hd, ♀ pd; ft; Russ. *Karakul'* or *Karakul'skaya*; syn. *Astrakhan, Bukhara*; vars: Arabi (black), Duzbai, Guligas (pink-roan), Kambar (brown), Shirazi (grey), Sur (agouti); occ. white or pied; HB; orig. of Chinese Karakul, German Karakul, Large Karakul, Malich, Multifoetal Karakul, Pak Karakul; BS in Namibia 1919, S. Africa 1937, USA 1929, HB also in Spain
Karakul-Landschaf: see German Karakul
Karaman, Karamane: see Red Karaman, White Karaman
Karamaniko (Crete): see Dağliç
Karamaniko (Greece): see Argos, or other ft. breeds
Karamaniko Katsika: see Katsika
Karandhai: see Vembur
[Karanogai] (Manych steppe, N. Caucasus, USSR); cw; m; sim. to Kalmyk; fr; Russ. *Karanogaĭskaya*; syn. *Manych* (Russ. *Manychskaya*), *Nogai*
Karavlaška: see Karakachan
Karayaka (N. Anatolia, Turkey); cw.m.d; usu. white with black eyes (*karagöz*) or black head and legs (*çakrak*), occ. black or brown; ♂ usu. hd, ♀ usu. pd; lt.
Karelin's argali: see arkhar
Kargalin Fat-rumped (Aktyubinsk, Kazakhstan, USSR); m.cw; fr; breed group; orig. since 1931 from Degeres and Sary-Ja × (Edilbaev × Fat-rumped); Russ. *Kargalinskie kurdyuchnye ovtsi* or *Kargalinskaya porodnaya gruppa*
Kargilik (W. Xinjiang, China); var. of Hetian; subvars: Kokyar and Saku-Bash; Russ. *Kargalyk*. [former name of Yecheng]

Karha: see White Karaman

Karman: see Red Karaman, White Karaman

Karnabat: see Karnobat

Karnah (Kashmir North, India); sw; ♂ hd, ♀ pd; st.

Karnobat (S.E. Bulgaria); d.w; sim. to Kivircik; yellow-grey to copper-red to black; ♂ hd, ♀ pd; ? orig. from black Tsigai; Rom. *Carnabat*; syn. *Cherna Chervena* (= *black-red*); vars: Kabarliavi (= dense wool), Rudavi (= soft wool); not *Karnabat*; rare

Kalinin (USSR); var. of Russian Longwool; orig. (1935 on) from Lincoln × Northern Short-tailed; Russ. *Kalininskaya*

Kallakui (Varamin to Qom, N.C. Iran); cw.m.d; sim. to Baluchi; black marks on face and legs; ♂ usu. hd, ♀ pd; not *Calikui, Calokui, Kalakou, Kala-Kouh, Kalaku, Kalakuh, Kellakui*

Karnobat Finewool (S.E. Bulgaria); fw.m.d; orig. 1950-67 from Stavropol × Karnobat; Bulg. *Karnobatska t''nkorunna*; syn. *South-East Bulgaria Finewool* (Bulg. *T''nkorunna Yugo-istochna B''lgarska*)

Karnobatoshumenskaya: see Copper-Red

Karnówka (Poland); white var. of Swiniarka; orig. from Karnów in Lower Silesia

Kärnter: see Carinthian

Kars: see Tuj

Karst: see Dalmatian-Karst

Karuvai: see Kilakarsal

Kashmir Merino (Kashmir, India); w.m; orig. from Delaine Merino (1951-52) × (Tasmanian Merino × local Gaddi, Bhakarwal and Poonchi, 1947 on), then Rambouillet and Soviet Merino ♂♂ used; 50-75% Merino blood

Kashmir Valley (S.W. Kashmir, India); cw; mixed population; usu. coloured; usu. pd; syn. *Valley*

Kasubian: see Pomeranian

Katafigion (S.E. Macedonia, Greece); d.m.mw-cw; Ruda type; ♂ hd, ♀ pd; not *Katafiyion, Katafygion, Kataphygion*; nearly extinct

Katahdin (Maine, USA); m; prolific; white; hy; usu. pd; orig. from Suffolk and Wiltshire Horn × Virgin Island White by M.Piel, Abbot Village; BS 1980

Kathiawari: see Patanwadi

Katseno: see Krapsa

Katsika (Ioánnina basin, Epirus, Greece); lowland breed of Greek Zackel; white with black around eyes and on ears; syn. *Karamaniko Katsika*

Kazakh Arkhar-Merino (S.E. Kazakhstan, USSR); m.fw; ♂ hd, ♀ usu. pd; orig. 1934-49 from arkhar × Merino followed by 2 Merino top crosses; HB; Russ. *Kazakhskiǐ arkharomerinos*

Kazakh Corriedale (S. Kazakhstan, USSR); orig. from Border Leicester,

Romney or Lincoln, × Kazakh Finewool; Russ. *Kazakhskaya Korridel'* Kazakh Fat-rumped (Kazakhstan, USSR, and E. Xinjiang, China); cw.m; reddish-brown; ♂ hd, ♀ pd; Russ. *Kazakhskaya kurdyuchnaya*; vars: Altay (China), Temir; orig. (with Kalmyk) of Edilbaev, (with Shropshire) of Degeres, (with Degeres and Sary-Ja) of Kargalin; not *Kazak, Hasa, Hasah*

Kazakh Finewool (Alma-Ata, Kazakhstan, USSR); m.fw; pd; orig. 1931-45 (recog. 1946) from Kazakh Fat-rumped crossed first with Précoce and then with American Rambouillet; HB; Russ. *Kazakhskaya tonkorunnaya*

Kazakh Semifinewool (S. Kazakhstan, USSR); m.mw; breed group; orig. since 1945 from Lincoln and North Caucasus Mutton-Wool × (Précoce × Kazakh Fat-rumped) improved by Hampshire *et al.*; Russ. *Kazakhskaya polutonkorunnaya porodnaya gruppa*

Kazanluk Semifinewool (Bulgaria); m.mw; orig. from Romney and (German Mutton Merino and Caucasian × Stara Zagora) ♂♂ (1964) × (German Mutton Merino × Panagyurishte) ♀♀; Bulg. *Mestna polut"nkorunna Kazanl"shki raĭon*

Kazil: see Red Karaman

[Kedabek Merino]; local Merino in Kedabek, Azerbaijan; orig. in late 19th c. from Mazaev, Novocaucasian and other Merinos; orig. (with Bozakh) of Azerbaijan Mountain Merino

Keelakaraisal, Kelakarisal: see Kilakarsal

[Keerie] (Caithness, Scotland); Northern Short-tailed type; black; syn. *Rocky*; not *Kerry*. [Gaelic *caora* = sheep, *cf. keero* (Orkney) = feral sheep]

Keezha Karauvai, Keezhak(k)araisal: see Kilakarsal

Kelantan (E. of Malay peninsula); m.cw-hy; usu. white, occ. shades of grey or brown, badger-face, black or pied; ♂ hd, ♀ usu. pd (or scurs); often earless; syn. *Malaysian, Pahang, Thai*

Kellakui: see Kallakui

Kempen Heath (S. Limburg, Netherlands); var. of Dutch Heath; light brown spotted face; pd; BS 1967; Du. *Kempische* (or *Kempense*) *Heideschaap*; rare

Kendal Rough: see Rough Fell

Kenguri (Raichur district, E.C. Karnataka, India); m; South India hair type; usu. red, also white, black or pied; ♂ hd, ♀ pd; st; syn. *Kangani, Keng, Kenga, Teng-Seemai, Tenguri* or *Tonguri, Yalag*

[Kent Halfbred] (Kent, England); sw; pd; Southdown × Romney, 1st cross

Kent, Kent or Romney Marsh: see Romney

Kentmere: see Rough Fell

Kermani (S.E. Iran): see Baluchi

Kerry (S.W. Ireland): see Scottish Blackface
Kerry Hill (Montgomeryshire, Wales); sw.m; black spots on face and legs; pd; recog. 1809, Clun Forest blood 1840-55; BS 1893, HB 1899
Kesbır: see Çandır; not *Kesber*
Kesik: see Tuj
Kesme: see Çandır
Keustendil: see Kyustendil
Kew: ? see Jumli
Khakass (Khakass Autonomous Region, USSR); smaller var. of Krasnoyarsk; Russ. *Khakasskaya*; not *Hakasskaya*
Khalkidhiki: see Chalkidiki
Khamseh (E. Farsistan, Iran); cw; local var; often dark spots on face and legs; ♀ sometimes pd; ft.
Khazi: see Hejazi
Khetrani; var. of Bibrik
Khijloo (Dera Ghazi Khan, Pakistan); cw.m; black marks on face and feet, or tan face and feet; sft; var: Hallenjoo (larger, grey with black patches)
Khios: see Chios
Khorasan Kurdi (N. Khorasan, Iran); m.d.cw; brown; pd; ft.
Khorassan, Khorosani (Iran): see Baluchi
Khotan: see Hetian
Khurasani (Iran): see Baluchi
Kilakarsal (Ramnad, Madurai and Thanjavur, Tamil Nadu, India); m; South India hair type; tan, usu. with black belly; ♂ hd, ♀ pd; usu. tassels; st; syn. *Adikarasial, Karuvai, Keezha Karauvai, Keezhak(k)araisal, Ramnad Karuvi, Ramnad Red*; not *Keelakaraisal, Kelakarisal*
Kimi: see Kymi
Kipsigis (W. Kenya); var. of Masai; syn. *Lumbwa*; not *Kipsikis*
Kirdi, Kirdimi: see West African Dwarf
Kirgiz Fat-rumped (Kirgizia, USSR); cw.m; brown or black; hd (E.) or pd (W.); Russ. *Kirgizskaya kurdyuchnaya*; orig. (with Précoce) of Alai and Fat-rumped Merino; not *Kirghiz*
Kirgiz Finewool (Kirgizia, USSR); fw.m; usu. white; orig. 1932-56 at Juan Tyube state farm (*et al.*) by interbreeding of Württemberg Merino or Précoce, × [Rambouillet × (Novocaucasian or Siberina Merino × Kirgiz Fat-rumped)]; recog. 1956; HB; Russ. *Kirgizskaya tonkorunnaya*
Kirma: see Karacabey-Kivircik. [= halfbred]
Kirmani (Turkey): see Red Karaman, White Karaman
Kisil-Karaman: see Red Karaman
Kiu: ? see Jumli
Kivircik (N.W. Turkey and N.E. Greece); m.d.cw-mw; sim. to Karnobat (Bulgaria) and to Tsigai; white, with white or spotted face, also black

or brown var; ♂ hd, ♀ usu. pd; Turk. *Kıvırcık*; syn. (Greece) *Thrace, Western Thrace* (Gr. *Dhítiki Thráki*); orig. of Karacabey Merino; crosses × Dağliç: see Kamakuyruk and Pirlak; not *Kivirçik, Kivird-jik*. [= curly]

Kizil, Kizil-Karaman: see Red Karaman; not *Kisil-Karaman, Kzyl Kara-man*. [Turk. *kızıl* = red-brown]

Kleifa; pd var. of Icelandic, ? with Cheviot and/or Border Leicester blood

Klementina: see White Klementina

Klitfår: see Danish Landrace

Koburg: see Coburger

Kohai Ghizer (Gilgit to Chatorkhand, N. Kashmir, Pakistan); cw.m; white or tan with brown or black head and legs; pd; sft.

Kokyar (W. Xinjiang, China); subvar. of Kargilik var. of Hetian; sim. to Darvaz

Kolar: see Hassan

Kombar: see Kambar

Kommunal (Albania): see Common Albanian

Konya Merino: see Central Anatolian Merino

Kooka (Sind, Pakistan); cw.m; head usu. black; ♂ hd, ♀ pd; long lop ears; st; not *Kuka*

Koprivshten (Bulgaria); Bulg. *Koprivshtenska*; rare

Kordi: see Kurdi

Kosovo (S. Serbia, Yugoslavia); m.cw; Pramenka type; black face and ⸹ legs; ♂ usu. pd, ♀ pd; Serbo-cro. *Kosovska*

Kotan: see Hetian

Kotel Native (E.C. Bulgaria); m.cw.d; ♂ hd, ♀ pd; Bulg. *Aborigenna kotlenska*; rare

Kouchari: see Kushari

Krapsa (Epirus, Greece); var. of Greek Zackel; syn. *Katseno*

Krasnoyarsk Finewool (S.C. Siberia, USSR); fw; ♂ hd or pd, ♀ pd; orig. 1926 on by improving local Mazaev and Novocaucasian Merinos with Précoce, American Rambouillet and Askanian; recog. 1963; HB; Russ. *Krasnoyarskaya tonkorunnaya*; larger var. at Uchum stud farm, smaller (Khakass) at Moscow and Askizskiĭ state farms and Put k Kommunizma collective farm; also Angara var.

Krivovir (E. Serbia, Yugoslavia); m.cw.d; local Pramenka var; white with brownish-yellow head and legs; occ. brown; ♂ hd, ♀ pd; Serbo-cro. *Krivovirska*; declining as Svrljig spreads. [from Krivi Vir]

Krk: see Island Pramenka; It. *Veglia*

Krš: see Dalmatian-Karst

Krukówka; black var. of Świniarka; not *Krukowska*. [Pol. *kruk* = raven]

Kucharskaya: see Kuche

[Kuche] (W. Xinjiang, China); pelt, m.cw; black (62%), pied (27%), white (7%) or brown (4%); ♂ hd or pd, ♀ usu. pd; st. to sft; ? orig. from Karakul × Mongolian and Kazakh Fat-rumped in late 19th c; W.G. *K'u-ch'e*, Russ. *Kucharskaya* or *Kuchèrskaya*, Pol. *Kucze*; not *Kucha, Kuchar*; graded to Karakul since 1960s to form Chinese Karakul

Kuchugury (Nizhnedevitsk, Voronezh, USSR); m.cw; *c.* 70% black with white patch on head, 30% white; usu. pd; lft; orig. from Voloshian × Russian Long-tailed in late 19th c; Russ. *Kuchugurovskaya*; syn. *Voronezhskaya voloshskaya*

Kucze: see Kuche

Kuibyshev (USSR); m.lw; pd; orig. 1938-48 from Romney × Cherkassy backcrossed to Romney, or from Romney × Vagas (Voloshian); HB

kuirjuk, kuiryuk: see fat-rumped

Kuka: see Kooka

Kulunda (Altai, Siberia, USSR); cw.pelt; black; usu. sft; hd or pd; ? orig. from Siberian, Mongolian, and Kazakh Fat-rumped; Russ. *Kulundinskaya*

Kumukh: see Lak

[Kumyk] (N. Dagestan, USSR); m.cw; Caucasian Fat-tailed type; brown; ♂ hd; Russ. *Kumykskaya*

Kupres (Yugoslavia); var. of Bosnian Mountain; usu. speckled face and legs; usu. pd; Serbo-cro. *Kupreška*

Kuradi: see Kurdi

Kurassi (Qena and Aswan, Upper Egypt); cw.m; usu. black or brown, also fawn, pied or white; pd; lt; *cf.* Dongola

KURDI (Kurdistan); cw; black head; pd; ft; inc. Herki; Iraq Kurdi and Hamdani (Iraq); Khorosan Kurdi, Sangesari and Sanjabi (Iran); not *Karadi, Karradi, Kordi, Kuradi*

kurdyuk: see fat-rumped

Kurdyukos: see Fat-rumped Merino

Kuruba, Kurumba, Kurumbai Adu: see Coimbatore

kushari (Syria) = nomadic sheep; not *kouchari, kuschari*

[Kusman]; var. of Tabasaran

Kustendil: see Kyustendil

Kutchi (India): see Patanwadi

Kutchi (Pakistan): see Kachhi

Kutsovlach, Kutsovlashka, Kutzovlakh: see Karakachan

Kyasma (Amassi, Armenia, USSR); Caucasian Fat-tailed type; orig. from Mazekh × Erik; Russ. *Kyas'ma*; *cf.* Turk. *Kesme* = crossbred

Kymi (Euboea, Greece); d.m.mw; orig. from Skopelos; not *Kimi, Kyme*

[Kyustendil] (S.W. Bulgaria); local unimproved var. of Bulgarian Native; Bulg. *Kyustendilska*; not *Keustendil, Kustendil*

Kzyl-Karaman: see Red Karaman

Lacaune (Tarn, S. France); d.(m.mw); chief Roquefort breed; pd; HB 1945, BS; syn. *Camarès* (Aveyron), *Mazamet*; has absorbed Corbières (Aude), Larzac (Aveyron), Lauraguais (Haute Garonne), Ruthenois, Ségala (Aveyron); orig. of Ardes (Puy-de-Dôme), Blanc du Massif Central (Lozère)

Lacho (Vascongadas and Navarre, Spain); d.cw.m; sim. to Churro but long wool and black (brown or grey) face and feet; ♂ hd, ♀ hd or pd; HB; syn. *Basque, Biscay*; = Manech (France). [? from Basque *latsca* or *latxa* = coarse]

Laguna (Philippines); sw; pd; orig. from Shropshire cross × local cw.hd

Lak (S. Dagestan, USSR); Caucasian Fat-tailed type, sim. to Gunib but smaller; Russ. *Lakskaya*; syn. *Kumukh*

Lake sheep (China): see Hu

Lakka: see West African Dwarf

Lama: see Damani

La Mancha: see Manchega

Lamkanni (Bahawalpur, Pakistan); smaller var. of Lohi with grey ears and no tassels; syn. *Lamochar*

Lamochar: see Lamkanni

Lamon (Belluno, Venetia, Italy); m.(cw.d); Lop-eared Alpine group; dark spots on face and legs; BSd 1942

Lampuchhre (Nepal); sim. to Kagi but larger and longer tail

Lanark Blackface; strain of Scottish Blackface with coarser wool

Landais (Landes, S.W. France); m.cw; coloured spots on head and legs; ♂ usu. hd, ♀ pd; orig. from Pyrenean; nearly extinct by crossing with Berrichon *et al.*

Landes de Bretagne (Loire-Atlantique and Morbihan, Brittany, France); white or spotted; ♂ hd, ♀ pd; syn. *Belle-Ile, Briéron*; not *Biérois*

Landim (Mozambique); var. of Nguni; pd

Land Karakul: see German Karakul

Land Merino (Germany): see Merinolandschaf

Langhe (E. Cuneo, Piedmont, Italy); d.m.cw; sim. to Frabosana; pd; semi-lop ears; HB and BSd 1959; It. *delle Langhe* or *della Langa*

Lannemezan: see Aure-Campan

Lantras: see Swedish Landrace

Lanzhou Large-tail (Gansu, China); m.w; pd; ft; orig. 1862-75 from Tong × Mongolian

Lara-Polisi: see Pied Polisi

Large Karakul (Ukraine, USSR); m.fur; orig. at Askania Nova (1932 on) from Karakul × Hissar; Russ. *Krupnoplodnyĭ Karakul'* (= *Large Progeny Karakul*)

[Larzac] (S.E. Aveyron, S. France); d.m; var. of Caussenard; original Roquefort breed; now absorbed by Lacaune

Lasta: see Tucur

Lati (Salt Range, N.W. Punjab, Pakistan); m.cw; tan or spotted head; ft; syn. *Salt Range*; not *Latti*

Laticauda: see Campanian Barbary

Latuka-Bari: see Mongalla

Latvian Darkheaded (Latvia, USSR); m.sw; pd; orig. 1920-40 from Shropshire, Oxford Down and German Blackheaded Mutton, × local Northern Short-tailed, bred *inter se* since 1937; HB; Latvian *Latvijas tumšgalvas aitu*, Russ. *Latviĭskaya temnogolovaya*; syn. *Latvian Blackfaced, Latvian Blackheaded*

Laughton: see Manx Loaghtan

[Lauraguais] (Haute Garonne, France); m.d.sw; pd; syn. *Toulousain, Toulouse*; not *Lauragais*; absorbed by Lacaune in 1940s

Layda: see Marwari

Lebrija, Lebrijana: see Andalusian Churro

Leccese (Lecce, S. Apulia, Italy); d.cw.m; Moscia type; white with black face and legs, occ. black; ♂ usu. hd, ♀ pd; HB 1937; syn. *Moscia leccese*; Fasanese var. has Pramenka blood; not *Lecca*

Lefkimi: see Levkimmi

Legagora: see Menz

Leicester Longwool (England); lw.m; English Longwool type; pd; orig. 1755-90 from Old Leicester; BS and HB 1893; syn. *Bakewell Leicester, Dishley L, Improved L, New L, Leicester*; var. Black Leicester Longwool; contributed to formation of most English Longwool breeds; BS also in Australia, HB also in Canada, New Zealand; nearly extinct in England

Leine (S. Hanover, Germany); w.m; pd; improved by Leicester Longwool, Cotswold and Berrichon in 19th c. and by Texel *et al.* in 20th; BSd 1906; obs. syn. (to 1886) *rheinisch, flämisch*

Lemnos (Greece); d; island var. of Greek Zackel; Gr. *Limnos*

Lentinese, Lentini: see Comisana

Leonese Merino (mt de Luna, León, Spain); var. of Spanish Merino with less fine wool; syn. *Merino entrefino* or *Merino trasterminante*

Lesbos: see Mytilene

Lessarkani: see Thalli

Lesvos: see Mytilene

Leszno (Poznań, Poland); Polish Longwool group; orig. 1920-39 from Berrichon and Polish Strongwooled Merino *et al.* × local (white Świniarka); Pol. *Owca leszczyńska*

Letelle Merino (Orange Free State, S. Africa); m.fw; orig. 1922-38 by J.P. van der Walt of Zastron from Rambouillet; named 1945, BS 1951; not *Lettelle*. [name of former Kaffir chieftain]

Levant (France): see Préalpes du Sud

Levézou: see Ségala

Levkimmi (S. Corfu, Greece); m.d.cw; var. of Greek Zackel; black eyes, ears and nose; ♂ hd, ♀ usu. pd; not *Lefkimi*; rare

Lezgian (S.W. Dagestan and N.W. Azerbaijan, USSR); Caucasian Fattailed type; white or greyish with coloured or spotted head and feet (75%), also black, red, grey or pied; usu. hd; lft; Russ. *Lezginskaya*; var: Agul

Libyan Barbary (Libya); m.cw.d; white with brown or black (occ. pied) face and legs, sometimes pied or coloured; ♂ hd (occ. 4), ♀ usu. pd; ft; orig. of Barbary Halfbred, Ghimi; *cf.* Barki (Egypt); syn. *Libyan Fattailed*

Lika (Croatia, Yugoslavia); d.m.cw; Pramenka type; white with coloured or pied head and legs, sometimes brown or black; Serbo-cro. *Lička*; syn. *Gacka* (Serbo-cro. *Gatačka*)

[Limestone] (Lancashire-Cumbria, England); sim. to Whiteface Woodland; syn. *Cragg, Farleton Knott, Horned Cragg, Limestone Cragg, Silverdale, Warton Crag*; extinct about 1900

Limousin (Corrèze, C. France); m.mw.(d); Central Plateau type; pd; BS 1906, reorg. 1938, HB 1944; var: Marchois

Linchuan (Shanxi, China); w.m; orig. from Corriedale and Romney × local finewool

Lincoln Longwool (E. England); lw.m; English Longwool type; pd; orig. from Leicester Longwool × Old Lincoln; BS and HB 1892; syn. *Lincoln*; orig. of Kalinin, Liski, Tyan Shan (USSR); BS also in USA 1891, HB also in New Zealand 1912, Canada; rare in GB

Linton: see Scottish Blackface

Lipe (Morava valley, N. Serbia, Yugoslavia); d.m.cw; local Pramenka var; black head and legs; ♂ hd, ♀ usu. pd; Serbo-cro. *Lipska*; declining by spread of Merino and crossing with Tsigai

Liski (Voronezh, USSR); var. of Russian Longwool; some dark spots on face and legs; orig. (1936 on) from Lincoln × Mikhnov backcrossed to Lincoln ♂; recog. 1978; Russ. *Liskinskaya*; syn. *Liskinskaya myasosherstnaya lyustrovaya poroda* (= *mutton-wool lustre breed*); not *Luskin*; subvar: Nizhnedevitsk

Lithuanian Blackheaded (N. Lithuania, USSR); m.sw; orig. 1923-34 from German Blackheaded Mutton and Shropshire × local Northern Short-tailed; HB 1934; Russ. *Litovskaya chernogolovaya*, Lith. *Lietuvos juvdgalviŲ*

Livo (Como, Italy); m.cw-mw; Lop-eared Alpine group but straight profile; rare

Llanwenog (Cardigan, Wales); m.sw; sim. to Clun Forest but smaller; black head and legs; pd; orig. end of 19th c. from Shropshire and local blackfaced sheep; BS

Llŷn (N.W. Wales); m.mw; black nose; pd; ? orig. in late 18th c. from Welsh Mountain with Roscommon and Leicester Longwool blood; BS 1968; not *Lleyn*

Loaghtan, Loaghton, Loaghtyn: see Manx Loaghtan

Locale (La Spezia/Massa Carrara, Italy); m.d.cw; Apennine group; pd

Lockerbie Cheviot: see West Country Cheviot

Loghton: see Manx Loaghtan

Lohi (S. Punjab, Pakistan); cw.m; head dark brown, tan (or black); long lop ears usu. with tassel; pd; st; syn. *Parkanni* (= *tassel*); var: Lamkanni (Bahawalpur)

Lohia (Tarai, Nepal); m.cw; occ. dark spots on body, sometimes coloured head; ♂ usu. hd, ♀ pd; ? orig. from Lohi

Lojeña (Sierra de Loja, S.W. Granada, Spain); m.mw; black, white, red, pied or roan; usu. pd; syn. *Rabada* (or *Rabuda*) *de la Sierra de Loja*

Long Island: see Bahama Native

[Longmynd] (England); black face; hd; orig. (with others) of Shropshire; extinct 1936

Longwool: see English Longwool, Polish Longwool, Russian Longwool

Lonk (C. and S. Pennines, England); cw.m; Blackfaced Mountain type, sim. to Derbyshire Gritstone but hd; BS, HB; syn. *Improved Haslingden*. [? = coarse herbage or by corruption of Lancashire or from *Wlonk*, Old English for proud or haughty]

LOP-EARED ALPINE (Alps); m.(cw-mw); Roman nose; pendent ears; pd; basic breed is Bergamasca; sim. breeds or derivatives are: Alpagota, Bellunese, Biellese, Brentegana, Brianzola, Brogne, [Cadorina], Corteno, Finarda, [Friulana], Lamon, Livo, [Paduan], Pusterese, Saltasassi, Varesina, Vicentina (Italy); Carinthian, Tyrol Mountain (Austria); German Mountain (Germany); Solčava (Yugoslavia); *cf.* also French Alpine, Swiss White Mountain; It. *Razze alpine da carne* (= *Alpine meat breeds*); syn. *Sudanica* (= *Sudanese*, from incorrect association)

Lori, Lorri, Lory: see Luri

Lot Causses: see Caussenard du Lot

Louda: see Uda

Louisiana Native; var. of Gulf Coast Native

Lourdais (Lourdes, S.W. Hautes-Pyrénées, France); m.mw; Central Pyrenean group; white, occ. brown or pied; ♂ hd, ♀ usu. hd; orig. from Béarnais with Merino blood; HB 1975; var: Barègeois

Louri: see Luri

Lowicz (Lodz, Poland); lw.m; Polish Lowland group; pd; orig. 1924-39 from Romney × local (white Swiniarka with Merino blood); Pol. *Owca łowicka*

Lowland: see Marsh

Lozère Causses, Lozère Mountain: see Blanc du Massif Central

Luan (S.E. Shanxi, China); cw; local var. of Mongolian orig. sim. to
Han but with lft; white; ♂ hd, ♀ pd. [former name of town of
Changchih]
Lucanian: see Gentile di Lucania
Lucero (S. Mexico mts); var. of Criollo; black with white spot on head
Lughdoan: see Manx Loaghtan
Lugnez: see Bündner Oberland
Luma (N.E. Albania); d.m.cw-mw; Ruda type; ♂ hd, ♀ pd; ? syn. *Gekika*
(Greece); ? = *ruda* var. of Šar Planina (Yugoslavia)
Lumbwa: see Kipsigis
Luo (W. Kenya); var. of Masai
Luri (Iran); var. of Bakhtiari-Luri; not *Lori, Lorri, Lory, Louri, Lury*
Lushnja; var. of Common Albanian; not *Lushnia*
Luzein: see Bündner Oberland

Macedonian: see Greek Zackel, Karakachan, Ovče Polje and Šar Planina
(Yugoslavia)
Macheri: see Mecheri
machkaroa: see Manech, Red or Speckled-face var. [Basque *maxharo* =
speckled]
Macina (C. delta of Niger, Mali); cw; white, pied or black; ♂ hd, ♀ hd
(small) or pd; lt; var: Goundoun (Niger); not *Massina*
Macou: see Makui
Madagascar; m; African Long-fat-tailed type; white or light brown, often
pied with red, brown or black, often white with black head; hy; ♂ hd
or pd, ♀ pd; long, fat, sickle-shaped tail; syn. *Malagasy, Malgache*
Madras Red (N.E. Tamil Nadu, India); m; South India hair type; sim.
to Nellore but smaller and red or brown; ♂ hd, ♀ pd; st.
Madurese: see Indonesian Fat-tailed; Du. *Madoera*
Maellana (Maella, Zaragoza, Aragon, Spain); m.(mw); pd; reduced fleece
cover; not var. of Aragonese
Maghreb thin-tailed breeds: see Algerian Arab, Atlantic Coast
(Morocco), Beni Guil, Berber, D'man, Raimbi, Tadla, Timhadite
Magra (E. and S. Bikaner, Rajasthan, India); cw.m; light brown around
eyes; pd; syn. *Bikaneri* (obs.), *Bikaneri Chokla, Chakri, Jangli, Mogra*
(Jodhpur)
Magyar: see Hungarian
Mähnerschaf: see aoudad
[Maine à tête blanche] (N.W. France); m.lw; sim. to Cotentin; pd; orig.
from Leicester Longwool (imported 1855-90) × local and improved
by Cotentin; syn. *Maine à face blanche, Mayenne White, Whitefaced
Maine, Whiteheaded Maine*; disappeared in 1950s by spread of Bleu

du Maine

Maine à tête (or *face*) *bleue*: see Bleu du Maine

Maine, Maine-Anjou: see Bleu du Maine, Rouge de l'Ouest

Maiylambadi: see Mecheri

Majorcan (Majorca, Balearic Is, Spain); m.mw; occ. spots on head and legs; ♂ hd or pd, ♀ pd; larger lowland and smaller mountain vars; Sp. *Mallorquina*; see also Red Majorcan

Makui (Maku, N.W. Azerbaijan, Iran); cw.m; sim. to White Karaman; black spots on face and feet; ♂ usu. pd, ♀ pd or scurs; ft; Fr. *Macou*

Malagasy, Malgache: see Madagascar

Malawi; African Long-fat-tailed type sim. to Sabi (Zimbabwe); obs. syn. *Nyasa*

Malaysian: see Kelantan

Malich (Crimea, USSR); fur, d; black, white, or grey; ♂ hd, ♀ pd; ft; orig. from Karakul; Russ. *Malich*; not *Maleech, Malych*

Mallorquina: see Majorcan

Malpura (E. Rajasthan, India); cw.m; sim. to Sonadi; light brown face; pd; short ears

Maltese (Malta); d.m.cw; coloured markings on face; usu. pd; orig. of Comisana (Sicily); rare

Manche: see Avranchin, Cotentin

Manchega (La Mancha, New Castille, Spain); d.m.mw; Entrefino type; usu. white, also black var; pd; HB 1969, BS; milk and meat vars; orig. of Segureña and Talaverana

Manchega pequeña: see Alcarreña

Mandya (S. Karnataka, India); m.hr; South India hair type; pale red-brown patches on anterior; pd; st; syn. *Bandur, Bannur*; not *Manday, Mandaya, Mandi*

Manech (S.W. Basque country, France); d.m.cw; Pyrenean dairy group; coloured face and legs; ♂ hd, ♀ Black-face hd, Red-face pd; vars: Black-face (Basque *muthur belza*), and Red-face (Basque *muthur gorria*) or Speckled-face (Basque *machkaroa*); not *Manesch*; = Lacho (Spain). [Basque = John; men of Soule call those of Basse Navarre and Labourd 'Manechac']

Manx Loaghtan (Isle of Man); Northern Short-tailed type, sim. to Hebridean; brown, formerly also white or black; 2-6 horns, 4 preferred; HB, BS 1976; syn. Loghtan (GB); not *Laughtan, Loaghtyn, Loghton, Lughdoan*; BS also in GB 1988; rare. [Manx *lugh dhoan* = mouse-brown]

Manych, Manychskaya: see Karanogai

Manze: see Menz

Marathwada (S. Maharashtra, India); m; South India hair type, sim. to Nellore; black, red, or pied; ♂ hd, ♀ pd; not *Marhatwada*

[Marchois]; small var. of Limousin (? with blood of Berrichon de l'Indre); extinct in 1930s

Marco Polo's sheep (Pamirs, C. Asia) = *Ovis ammon polii* Blyth; var. of argali; syn. *great Tibetan sheep, nayan* (Nepal), *Pamir argali*

Mareb White (Mareb, N. Yemen); m; white, occ. black face; hy; pd; ft.

[Maremmana] (Maremma, Latium and Tuscany, Italy); former var. of Sopravissana; syn. *Spanish Mongrel* (It. *Bastarda spagnola*), *Bastarda maremmana*

Marhatwada: see Marathwada

Marialva, Marialveira: see Badana

Mariñana: see Galician

Marismeña: see Andalusian Churro

Maritsa Finewool: see Thrace Finewool

Marmoucha (Morocco); vars of Berber; small white and larger black-headed; ♂ hd, ♀ pd

Marquesado (N. Granada, Spain); var. of Segureña; larger size, and less fleece cover; syn. *Marquesa, Marqueseña*

Marrane (N.E. Genoa, Italy); m.cw; straw coloured or light brown; pd; nearly extinct

Marri: see Bibrik

MARSH (N.W. Europe); pd; st. or rat tail; inc. Flemish, [Flemish Marsh], Friesian, [Groningen], Texel, and Zeeland Milk (Netherlands), [Butjadingen], East Friesian and [Wilstermarsch] (Germany), Pomeranian (Poland); orig. (with Cotswold) of German Whiteheaded Mutton; Ger. *Marschschaf*, Du. *Polderschaap*; syn. *Lowland* (Ger. *Niederungsschaf*)

Marthod: see Thônes-Marthod

Martunin (Armenia, USSR); var. of Armenian Semicoarsewool; orig. from Aragats × (Aragats × Balbas); Russ. *Martuninskaya*

Marwari (Jodhpur, Rajasthan, India); cw.m; black face; pd; small ears; syn. *Layda, Marwadi* (N. Gujarat). [Marwar is old name for Jodhpur]

Maryuti: see Barki

Masai (Tanzania and Kenya, also Uganda); m; East African Fat-tailed type; red-brown, occ. pied; hy; ♂ hd or pd, ♀ usu. pd; sft-fr; inc. sheep of Kipsigis, Luo, Nandi and Samburu (all in Kenya); syn. *Red Masai, Tanganyika Short-tailed*

Masekh: see Mazekh

Masham (N. England); Teeswater (or Wensleydale) × Swaledale (or Dales-Bred), 1st cross; ♂ hd, ♀ pd; syn. *Massam* (wool), *Yorkshire cross* (Scotland); see also Scottish Masham, Welsh Masham. [town in N. Yorkshire]

Mashona: see Sabi

Massese (Massa, Tuscany, Italy); d.m.cw; Apennine group, sim. to

Garfagnina but smaller and grey or brown with darker head; hd; Roman nose; syn. *Fornese* (from Forno)

Massina: see Macina

Matesina (Dragoni, Caserta, Campania, Italy); m.mw; dirty white or light hazel; ♂ hd, ♀ pd; orig. from Gentile di Puglia; rare

Mati (C. Albania); cw.d; var. of Albanian Zackel; red head and legs and red hairs in fleece; syn. *Red Head*

Maure (N. of W. Africa); Sahel type, sim. to Tuareg; ♂ hd, ♀ pd; syn. *Arab, Mauritanian, Moor, Moorish*; vars: Black Maure (long-haired) and Touabire (white or pied, short-haired)

Mauritanian: see Maure; not *Mauretanian*

Mayenne Blue: see Bleu du Maine

Mayenne White: see Maine à tête blanche

[Mayo Mountain] (Ireland); absorbed by crossing with Scottish Blackface

[Mazaev Merino] (S. Russia); fw; orig. in mid-19th c. by P.D. Mazaev in S.E. Ukraine by improvement of Russian Infantado; Russ. *Mazaevskiĭ Merinos*; orig. of Novocaucasian and other Russian Merinos

Mazamet: see Lacaune

Mazandarani: see Zel; not *Mazenderani*

Mazekh (Armenia, USSR); m.d.cw; Caucasian Fat-tailed type, sim. to Balbas; red-brown (72%), black (14%), red (9%) or grey (5%); ♂ hd, ♀ pd; Russ. *Mazekh* or *Mazekhskaya*; syn. *Gyzyl-Gojun* (= *red sheep*) (Azerbaijan); not *Masekh, Mazech*; ? = Red Karaman (Turkey); *cf.* Çandır (= *Mazik*)

Mazik: see Çandır

Meatlinc (Lincolnshire, England); m. (terminal meat sire); orig. (1964-76) from Berrichon du Cher, Ile-de-France and Charollais, × Suffolk and Dorset Down, by H. Fell of Worlaby, Brigg

Meatmaster (South Africa)

Meat Merino (Germany): see German Mutton Merino

Mecca: see Hejazi

Mecheri (Salem, W. Tamil Nadu, India); m; South India hair type; light brown, sometimes white patches; pd; st; syn. *Maiylambadi, Mylambadi, Thuvaramchambali* (Coimbatore); not *Macheri, Mechheri*

Mednochervena: see Copper-Red

Mehraban (Hamadan, W. Iran); m.d.cw; light brown, cream or grey; dark face and neck; ft; not *Mehreban*; Shal is sim.

Meidob (N.W. Darfur, Sudan); ? Zaghawa × Sudan Desert cross

[Mele] (Neuenkirchen, Germany); mw.m; pd; orig. *c.*1908 from Leicester Longwool × Merino; absorbed by German Mutton Merino 1934. [*Merino-Leicester*]

Mengali, Menghi, Mengli: see Baluchi

[Mennonite] (Saratov, USSR); m.sw; orig. from East Friesian

Menorquina: see Minorcan

Menz (N. Shoa, Ethiopia); m.cw; brown or black, usu. white spots on head and legs; ♂ hd, ♀ pd; ft; syn. *Legagora*; not *Manze, Mens*

Maraisi: see Ossimi

Mergelland (S. Limburg, Netherlands); var. of Dutch Heath sim. to Kempen; BS; rare

Merilin (Uruguay); mw.m; orig. since 1910 by J.M. Elorga from Rambouillet (¾) and Lincoln (¼) (? + Polwarth). [*Merino-Lin*coln]

MERINO; fw; ♂ usu. hd, ♀ usu. pd; orig. from Spanish Merino; see American, Argentine, Australian, Bulgarian, Chinese, Czech, French, Gentile di Puglia (Italy), German, Hungarian, Polish, Portuguese, Romanian, Russian, Sopravissana (Italy), South African, Turkish, Vojvodina

Mérino de l'Est (France): see Race de l'Est à laine Mérinos

Merinofleischschaf: see German Mutton Merino

Merinolandschaf (Germany); mw.m; pd; orig. in S. Germany from Merino (imported late 18th and 19th c.) × Württemberg Land; HB; recog. 1887-1906 first as *Württemberger* (or *Württemberg Bastard* or *Württemberg Improved Land* or *Württemberg Merino*), then as *Deutsches veredeltes Landschaf* (*German Improved Land*) (also *German Whiteheaded Land, Improved German Farm, Improved Whiteheaded Land*), and named finally 1950; syn. *Land Merino*; orig. of Dagestan Mountain, Race de l'Est à laine Mérinos, and Swiss White Mountain; BS in S. Africa 1957, Spain

Merino Longwool (Erfurt, E. Germany); lw.m; orig. (1971 on) from Merinolandschaf (50%), Lincoln (25%) and North Caucasus Mutton-Wool (25%); Ger. *Merinolangwollschaf*

Merino Meat, Merino Mutton: see German Mutton Merino

[Mérinos de Mauchamp]; former var. of French Merino with silky wool

Merinos de vest (Romania):·see Transylvanian Merino

[Mérinos du Naz]; former var. of French Merino with very fine wool

Merino, Württemberg: see Merinolandschaf

Mestizo Entrefino-fino (C.W. Spain); m.mw; pd; orig. from Merino × Manchega or Castilian; vars: Ciudad Rodrigo (Salamanca), Villuercas (Cáceres), and Campo de Calatrava (Ciudad Real); *cf.* Talaverana

Metaxomalicha: see Sitia

Metelini: see Mytilene

Metohija Whitehead: see Bardoka

meusse = pd Précoce ♂

Michni (Peshawar, Pakistan); m.cw; tan or black ears, muzzle and round eyes; lft.

Middle Atlas: see Timhadite

Mihnov, Mihnovskaya: see Mikhnov

Mikhnov (Voronezh, USSR); orig. from Russian Long-tailed; Russ. *Mikhnovskaya*; not *Mihnov*; rare—crossed with Romney to form Ostrogozhsk and with Lincoln to form Liski

Milch (Germany): see East Friesian

Minho e Douro: see Entre Douro e Minho

[Minnesota 100] (USA); mw.m; orig. 1941–44 at Minnesota Agric. Exp. Sta.; ½ Rambouillet, ¼ Border Leicester, ¼ Cheviot

[Minnesota 102] (USA); w.m; orig. since 1944 at Minnesota Agric. Exp. Sta. from Border Leicester × Shropshire with some Columbia and Targhee blood 1949

Minnesota 103: see North Star Minnesota 103

[Minnesota 105]; orig. 1949–54 from Columbia, Hampshire and Southdown

[Minnesota 107]; inbred Shropshire flock closed since 1937

Minorcan (Menorca, Balearic Is, Spain); d.(cw); pd; BS; Sp. *Menorquina*

[Minusinsk]; var. of Siberian

Minxian Black Fur (S. Gansu, China); fur; black; ♂ hd, ♀ pd

Miranda Galician (Terra Fria, N.E. Portugal); m.cw; Portuguese Churro type; white with spots on face and legs, or black (30%); hd; Port. *Galega mirandesa*

Modenese: see Pavullese, Zucca Modenese

Modern Romney: see New Zealand Romney

Moghani (Moghan steppe, N.W. Iran); m.cw; occ. pale colour marks on head and feet; ♂ usu. pd, ♀ pd; ft; not *Mogani, Mugan*

Mogra: see Magra

Mondegueira (W. Guarda, Beira Alta, Portugal); m.d.cw; Portuguese Churro type; usu. small brown spots on head and legs; hd. [from Mondego]

Mondombes (Moçambes, S.W. Angola); African Long-fat-tailed type; usu. black- or brown-pied; hy; ♂ hd, ♀ usu. pd; syn. *Herero, Mucubais*

Monegrina (Los Monegros, Ebro valley, border of Huesca and Zaragoza, Aragon, Spain); var. of Aragonese, small and fleece reduced

Mongalla (Latuka-Bari, Sudan); var. of Southern Sudanese

Mongolian (Mongolia, and N. China esp. Inner Mongolia); cw.m.d(Mongolia); usu. white with black or brown head, also pied or self-coloured; ♂ hd, ♀ pd; ft; syn. *China Fat-tailed, Mongolian Fat-tailed*; vars: Ikzhaomen and Ujumqin (Inner Mongolia), Bargad, Bait or Bayad, Chamar, Darkhat, Gobi-Altai, Uzemchin (Mongolia); orig. of Choubei, Han, Hu, Lanzhou Large-tail, Luan, Quanglin Large-tail, Shouyang, Taiku, Tan, Tong, and (with Karakul) of Kuche and Ningsia Black (China)

Mongo-tibetan: see Tibegolian

Monselesana, Monselice: see Noventana

Monsetina: see Pallaresa

Montadale (Missouri, USA); mw.m; orig. (1933 on) from Cheviot (40%) × Columbia (60%); BS 1945; not *Montedale*; HB also in Canada

Montagnes de la Lozère: see Blanc du Massif Central

Monta Khia (USA)

Montañesa: see Ripollesa

Montenegro: see Piva, Vasojević and Zeta Yellow vars of Pramenka

Montesina (mountains of Jaén and Granada, Andalucía, Spain); m.mw; Iberian type, sim. to Ojalada; black ear tips, muzzle, round eyes and on lower legs; ♂ usu. pd, ♀ pd; syn. *Granadina, Mora, Ojinegra, Sevillana*; not var. of Manchega. [= mountain]

Moor, Moorish (W. Africa): see Maure

Moor (Turkey): see Red Karaman (= *Mor-Karaman*)

moorit = brown: see Castlemilk, Manx, Shetland

Moorschnucke: see Heidschnucke, White Polled var.

Mora (Spain): see Montesina

Morada Nova (N.E. Brazil); m; American Hair sheep group; red (with white tail tip) and white vars; pd; orig. by selection from Brazilian Woolless; HB, BSd. [town in Ceará]

Moraitiko (Thessaly, Greece); mountain var. of Greek Zackel; black or white with black spots on head, belly and legs; ? orig. from Karakachan × Karagouniko

Moretta (Italy): see Carapellese

[Morfe Common] (England); sim. to Ryeland; coloured face; hd; part orig. of Shropshire

Mor-Karaman: see Red Karaman; not *Moor, Morekaraman*. [Turk. *mor* = maroon]

Morlam (Beltsville, Maryland, USA); m.w; usu. pd, some hd; orig. (1961 on) from Rambouillet × Dorset Horn, Merino, Targhee, Columbia-Southdale, Hampshire and Suffolk, selected for frequent lambing

Moroccan: see Beni Ahsen, Beni Guil, Berber, D'man, Doukkala, South Moroccan, Tadla, Timhadite, Zemmour

[Morvandelle] (Morvan, France)

MOSCIA (S. Italy); d.cw.m; ? Zackel type; inc. Altamurana, Leccese and Sciara. [= straight wool]

Mossul, Mosul, Mosuli: see Herrik

motti = pd ♂ Arles Merino

mouflon (Corsica and Sardinia) = *Ovis musimon* (Pallas); ? early feral; red-brown with dark back-stripe, pale saddle patch and underparts; ♂ hd, ♀ hd or pd; st; It. *muflone*; syn. *Corsican mouflon, European mouflon, musimon, musmon, Sardinian mouflon*; not *moufflon, muflon*; nearly extinct but sucessfully introduced into C. Europe (Germany, Austria, Czechoslovakia, Romania)

mouflon à manchettes: see aoudad
mouflon, oriental: see red sheep
Moulouya: see Tousint and Zoulay vars of Beni Guil
Mountain Corriedale (USSR): see Soviet Mutton-Wool
Mountain Merino: see Azerbaijan, Russian, Spanish
Mountain Tsigai (mts of N. and S. Bulgaria); cw.m; orig. 1950-67 from
    Tsigai × (Tsigai or German Mutton Merino × Replyan); Bulg.
    Planinski tsigaĭ, ? = Improved North Bulgarian
Mountain Zackel (Greece): see Vlakhiko
Mourerous (upper Vésubie and Var valleys, French Alps); m.mw; white
    to yellowish with red to fawn head and legs; ♂ hd, ♀ pd; BS 1983; syn.
    Péone, Rouge de Guillaume; rare
Moussouli: see Herki
Moyen Atlas: see *Middle Atlas* (Timhadite)
Mucubais: see Mondombes
muflon, muflone: see mouflon
muflone berbero: see aoudad
Mug: see Wensleydale
Mugan: see Moghani
Muggs, Mugs: see Wensleydale
Mule: see North of England Mule, Welsh Mule
Multifoetal Karakul (Ukraine); fur; black, also grey var; orig. at Askania
    Nova (1935-52) from Karakul × (Karakul × Romanov), to increase
    twinning rate; Russ. *Mnogoplodnyĭ Karakul'*
Multihorned: see Four-horned
Multihorned Merino (Orange Free State, S. Africa); ? orig.
Multinipple (USA); orig. 1923-41 from Bell Multinippled × (Southdown
    × Rambouillet), + Suffolk × above
Muma: see Garessina
Munjal (Punjab, India); cw; mixed population of Lohi and Nali
Murge: see Altamurana
Murle (S.E. Sudan); var. of Toposa with more Southern Sudanese blood;
    black-pied or brown-pied; ♂ usu. hd, ♀ usu. pd; sft.
musimon, musmon: see mouflon
Muthur belza, Muthur gorria: see Manech
Muthur churria: see Basque (France)
Mutton Merino (Germany): see German, South African, Walrich
Muzaffarnagri (Muzaffarnagar, Uttar Pradesh, India); cw.m.(d); occ.
    colour on face; pd; lt; syn. *Bulandshari*; not *Muzaffarnagari, Muzzafar-
    nagri*
Mylambadi: see Mecheri
Mytilene (W. Lésvos, Greece); d.m.cw; sim. to Kamakuyruk; usu. white
    with spots on nose and legs; sometimes coloured or pied; ♂ hd, ♀ usu.

pd; lft; ? orig. from Turkish breeds × local thin-tailed; Gr. *Mitilini*;
syn. *Lesbos* or *Lesvos*; not *Metelini*

Na'ami, (fem. *Na'amiyah*), *Naimi*: see Ne'imi
Naeini (Iran): see Baluchi
Najdi (C. Saudi Arabia); hr; usu. black with white head; ♂ pd or scurs,
♀ pd; lft; fem. *Najdiyah*; syn. *Arabian Long-tailed, Bedouin*; not *Nejdi,
Nedjed, Nidjy*; vars: Asali, Hejari
Nali (N. Rajasthan and S. Haryana, India); cw.m; light brown face; pd;
long ears
Nalps: see Bündner Oberland
Namaqua Africander (N.W. of Cape Prov., S. Africa, and S. of Namibia);
m; var. of Africander; white, usu. with black or brown head; hy-cw;
♂ hd, ♀ usu. pd; lft; orig. from Namaqua var. of Hottentot; Afrik.
Namakwa Afrikaner; syn. *Nama* (Namibia); disappearing by grading
to Karakul
Nami: see Ne'imi
Nandi (W. Kenya); var. of Masai
napo: see bharal
Nar: see Black Maure
Navajo-Churro (Arizona—New Mexico—Utah, USA); cw; usu. white
with colour on face and legs, also coloured; ♂ usu. hd (occ. 4 or 0), ♀
usu. pd; orig. from Spanish Churro; BS 1986; syn. *Navajo*; not *Navaho*;
cf. Criollo; old type Navajo rare due to crossing
Navargade: see Telingana
nayan: see Marco Polo's sheep
Neahami: see Ne'imi
NEAR EAST FAT-TAILED (N.E. Africa and S.W. Asia); cw.d.m; white,
white with coloured face, black, brown or pied; ♂ usu. hd, ♀ usu. pd;
usu. large S-shaped, bilobed, fat tail; inc. Barbary (Tunisia to Egypt),
Barki, Fellahi, Ossimi, Rahmani (Egypt), Cyprus Fat-tailed, Awassi
(Syria, Israel and Iraq), Arabi (Iraq), Kurdi (Kurdistan); syn. *Semitic
Fat-tailed*
Nedjed: see Najdi
[Negretti]; former strain of Spanish Merino; Sp. *Negrete*; not *Negreo*
Ne'imi (N.W. Iraq); superior var. of Awassi; black or red face, occ. red
fleece; not *Na'ami, Na'amiyah, Naimi, Nami, Neahami, N'eimi, Niami,
Nu'amieh, Nuamiyah*
Neini (Iran): see Baluchi
Nejdi: see Najdi
Nellore (S.E. Andhra Pradesh, India); m; South India hair type; white
(Palla), white with black spots on face (Jodipi) or red-brown (Dora);

♂ hd, ♀ pd; tassels; st.

Nelson: see South Wales Mountain

Nepalese, Nepali: see Baruwal, Jumli, Kagi, Tibetan (*Bhyanglung*)

New Caucasian: see Novocaucasian

Newfoundland (Canada); m.mw; sometimes dark face, or all black; occ. hd; mixed orig. during 19th and 20th c. from North Country Cheviot and Dorset Horn with some Scottish Blackface, Border Leicester, Hampshire, Oxford Down and Suffolk blood

New Kent: see Romney

New Leicester: see Leicester Longwool

New Norfolk Horn: see Norfolk Horn

New South Wales Merino = Australian Merino in NSW

Newton Stewart: see Galloway Blackface

New Zealand Halfbred (South Island, N.Z.); Longwool (Lincoln, Leicester or Romney) × Merino, F_1 or F_2

New Zealand Merino = Australian Merino in New Zealand; HB

New Zealand Romney (New Zealand); orig. from Romney 1900-10; BS 1904, HB 1905; syn. *Modern Romney, New Zealand Romney Marsh, Romney*; orig. of Drysdale (N-type Romney) and Tukidale

Nguni (S.E. Africa); African Long-fat-tailed type; black, brown or pied; hy; ♂ usu. hd, ♀ usu. pd; inc. Bapedi (Transvaal), Landim (Mozambique), Swazi and Zulu

Niami: see Ne'imi

Nidjy: see Najdi

Niederungsschaf: see Marsh

Nigerian Dwarf: see West African Dwarf

Nilgiri (W. Madras, India); m.sw; pd; orig. in early 19th c. from Cheviot, Southdown and Tasmanian Merino × local hy (Coimbatore) in Nilgiri hills; not *Nilagiri*

Nilotic; var. of South Sudanese; syn. *Dinka, Nuer, Shilluk*

Ningxia Black (Ningxia, China); cw.pelt; sim. to Kuche; black or dark brown; ♂ hd, ♀ pd; ft; orig. from Karakul × Mongolian; W.G. *Ninghsia hei*; not *Ningsia*; not now recog.

Nizhnedevitsk; subvar. of Liski var. of Russian Longwool; Russ. *Nizhnedevitskaya*

Nobile di Badia: see Pusterese

Nogai: see Karanogai

Noir de Bains, Noir du Velay: see Velay Black

[Nolinsk] (Kirov, USSR); var. of Russian Northern Short-tailed; Russ. *Nolinskaya*

Nord de la Manche: see Cotentin

Norfolk Horn (Norfolk, Suffolk and Cambridge, England); m; black
face and legs; hd; syn. *Blackface Norfolk Horned, Norfolk Horned, Old
Norfolk, Old Norfolk Horned*; orig. (× Southdown) of Suffolk; nearly
extinct 1973; revived as *New Norfolk Horn* by grading up Suffolk,
Wiltshire Horn and Swaledale (to $\frac{15}{16}$); HB 1978; name reverted to
Norfolk Horn 1984; still nearly extinct
North (England): see Scottish Halfbred
North Bulgarian Improved (Tsigai type); ? = Mountain Tsigai
North Bulgarian Semifinewool (Bulgaria); mw.m; orig. from German
Mutton Merino, Caucasian, Merinolandschaf, Romney, Lincoln and
North Caucasus
North Caucasus Merino; var. of Soviet Merino
North Caucasus Mutton-Wool (Vorontsovo-Aleksandrovskoe district of
Stavropol territory, USSR); m.mw; usu. pd; orig. 1944-60 from Lincoln
and Romney × Stavropol at Stalin state farm (but Romney blood
culled since 1952); Russ. *Severokavkazskaya myaso-sherstnaya*
North Caucasus Semifinewool (Karachaevo-Cherkessk autonomous
prov. and Kabardino-Balkar ASSR, USSR); m.mw; orig. 1949-57
from Romney (or Soviet Corriedale) × (Précoce × Ossetian); Russ.
Severokavkazskaya gornaya porodnaya gruppa polutonkorunnykh ovets
(= *North Caucasus mountain breed group of semifinewool sheep*)
North Country: see Scottish Halfbred
North Country Cheviot (N. Scotland); var. of Cheviot (1792 on, esp.
1805-20); BS 1912, HB 1946; syn. *Caithness*, or *Sutherland Cheviot*;
orig. of Wicklow Cheviot; BS also in USA 1962, HB in Canada
North-East Bulgarian Finewool (N.E. Bulgaria); fw.m.d; orig. 1950-67
from German Mutton Merino, Askanian and some Caucasian, ×
local, and inc. Shumen Finewool; HB; syn. *Dobruja Finewool* (Bulg.
Dobruzhanska t''nkorunna)
North-East China Finewool (N.E. China); fw; orig. from Soviet Merino
and Stavropol × Mongolian; syn. *Northeast(ern) Chinese Merino*
Northeast China Semifinewool (N.E. China); mw.m; pd; orig. from
Corriedale × Mongolian
Northern Longwool: see Teeswater
Northern Riverain (Sudan): see Dubasi
NORTHERN SHORT-TAILED (N. Europe); sim. to Heath; often black, grey
or brown; syn. *Scandinavian Short-tail*; inc. Faeroes, Finnish, Gotland,
Hebridean, Icelandic, Manx Loaghtan, North Ronaldsay, Old Norwe-
gian, Romanov, Russian, Shetland, Soay, Spælsau
North Halfbred: see Scottish Halfbred
North Holland (Netherlands); m; prolific; orig. from Finnish Landrace
× Texel

North Kazakh Merino (N. Kazakhstan, USSR); fw.m; orig. from Beskara-gai Merino combined with Sulukol Merino; recog. 1976; Russ. *Severo-kavkazskiĭ merinos*

North Nigerian Fulani: see Uda

North of England Mule (England); Bluefaced Leicester × Swaledale or Scottish Blackface, 1st cross; BS 1980

North, or *Northern, Sudanese*: see Sudan Desert

North Ossetian Semifinewool (N. Caucasus, USSR)

North Riverain (or *Riverine*) *Wooled* (Sudan): see Dongola

North Ronaldsay (Orkney, Scotland); Northern Short-tailed type; white or grey, occ. black or brown; HB; pronounced *Ronaldshay*; orig. flock on North Ronaldsay; flock on Linga Holm 1975; rare

[North Star Minnesota 103] (USA); mw.m; orig. since 1889 by W.W. Bell of Beaver Creek from Rambouillet, Oxford Down and Lincoln; to Minnesota Agric. Exp. Sta. 1947

North-West China Merino: see Gansu Alpine Finewool

Norwegian: see Dala, Norwegian Fur Sheep, Old Norwegian, Rygja, Spælsau, Steigar

Norwegian Fur sheep (Norway); fur; orig. from Gotland × Old Norwegian, named 1968; HB; Nor. *Norsk Pels-Sau*

Nostrale (Piedmont, Italy): see Biellese

Nostrale (Sicily, Italy): see Pinzirita

Nostrana (Campania, Italy): see Campanian Barbary

Nostrana (Passo della Cisa, Parma/Massa Carrara, Italy); m.cw-mw; Apennine group; usu. pd; ? orig. from Garfagnina; rare

No-tail (S. Dakota, USA); w.m; pd; orig. from two Kazakh Fat-rumped ♂♂ (imported in 1913) and European breeds, Rambouillet blood 1926, Southdown 1935, Columbia 1940s

[Noventana]; var. of Paduan, larger and with finer wool; syn. *Monselesana* (from Monselice). [from Noventa]

[Novocaucasian Merino] (N. Caucasus, Russia); fw; orig. in late 19th c. from Mazaev Merino improved by German Merino and Rambouillet; Russ. *Novokavkazskiĭ Merinos*; syn. *New Caucasian, New Caucasian Mazaev*; orig. of most Russian Merinos

N-type Romney: see Drysdale

Nu'amieh, Nuamiyah: see Ne'imi

Nuba Maned (Nuba mts, Sudan); var. of South Sudanese; all colours but black; ♂ hd, ♀ pd

Nuer: see Nilotic

Nungua Blackhead (Ghana); m; hy; orig. from Blackhead Persian × West African Dwarf

Nyasa: see Malawi

[Oberhasli-Brienz]; part orig. of Swiss White Mountain

Occidental (Spain): see Andalusian Churro

October breed group (Orenburg, USSR); fw; orig. from Grozny or Stavropol (1947-53) × (Précoce × coarsewooled) (1928-46); Russ. *Oktyabrskaya porodnaya gruppa*; joined with Orenburg Finewool to form South Ural

Ödemiş (Küçük Menderes valley, W. Turkey); m.d.cw; black or brown face; ♂ usu. pd, ♀ pd; ft.

Oetztaler: see Ötztaler

Ofche (or *Oftshe*) *Hulmski*: see Panagyurishte

Ogaden: see Somali

Ogiç (Albania) = unshorn Shkodra ♂; usu. black head; horns trained in upward spiral

Ojalada (mts of Guadalajara, Soria, Teruel, Zaragoza, Castellón, and Tarragona, Spain); m.mw; Iberian type, sim. to Montesina; white with black around eyes, on ear tips, muzzle and feet; ♂ usu. pd, ♀ pd; syn. *Churra alcarreña, Churra entrefina, Churra soriana, Churra turolense, Fardasca* (Teruel), *Ojinegra* (= *black-eyed*), *Serrana, Serranet* (Tarragona). [= button-holed]

Ojinegra: see Montesina, Ojalada

Old Berkshire: see Berkshire Knot

Oldenbred (England); m; British Oldenburg × Scottish Blackface or Swaledale 1st cross (= Greyface Oldenbred) or British Oldenburg × Welsh Mountain, 1st cross (= Welsh Oldenbred)

Oldenburg: see British Oldenburg

Oldenburg White Head: see German Whiteheaded Mutton

Old Norfolk, Old Norfolk Horned: see Norfolk Horn

Old Norwegian (Sunnhordland, W. Norway); Northern Short-tailed type; many colours; hd or pd; Nor. *Gammelnorsk*; syn. *Utegangarsau, Vildsau* (= *wild sheep*); orig. of Icelandic, Faeroes and Spælsau; rare

Old Scottish Shortwool: see Tanface

Old Southdown: see Sussex

Old Wiltshire Horned: see Wiltshire Horn

Olkusz (Kraków, Poland); local var. of Polish Longwool group; prolific; Pol. *Olkuska*; not *Olkcucyska*; rare

Omani (Oman); m.cw; white, black, brown or pied; ♂ hd or pd, ♀ pd

Omsk Semifinewool (Siberia, USSR); m.mw; breed group; orig. from Lincoln × local; Russ. *Omskaya myaso-sherstnaya* (= *meat-wool*) *polutonkorunnaya porodnaya gruppa*

Ongti: see Hu

oorial: see urial

Oparino (N.W. Kirov, USSR); m.sw; usu. white with coloured spots on head, neck and legs, 5-10% black or brown; ♂ hd, ♀ usu. pd; orig.

from English mutton breeds × local Russian Long-tailed; Russ.
Oparinskaya; not *Oparina*
Orecchiuta: see Sicilian Barbary
Orenburg Finewool (Orenburg, USSR); orig. from Caucasian and
Grozny (1952 on) × (Précoce *et al.* × local coarsewooled) at Karl
Marx state farm; recog. as breed group 1962; Russ. *Orenburgskaya
tonkorunnaya porodnaya gruppa*; with October breed group now forms
South Ural
Orhon (N. Mongolia); mw.m; orig. 1943-61 from Altai × [Tsigai ×
(Précoce × Mongolian)]; Russ. *Orkhonskaya*
oriental mouflon: see red sheep
Orkhon, Orkhonskaya: see Orhon
Orkney: see North Ronaldsay
Osemi: see Ossimi
Ossetian: see Karachai; Russ. *Osetinskaya*
Ossimi (Lower Egypt); cw.m; white with brown head, often brown neck,
and occ. brown spots; ♂ hd, ♀ pd; ft; syn. *Meraisi*; not *Ausemy, Ausimi,
Awsemy, Osemi, Ousimi*. [from Ausim]
Ostrogozhsk (N.W. Voronezh, USSR); lw.m; breed group; orig. before
1963 from Romney × Mikhnov bred *inter se* or backcrossed to
Romney; Russ. *Ostrogozhskaya porodnaya gruppa*
Otter: see Ancon
[Ötztaler] (Tyrol, Austria); local var. sim. to Tyrol Mountain; syn.
Oetztaler
Ouda: see Uda
Ouessant: see Ushant
Ouled Jellal: see Algerian Arab; Fr. *Ouled Djellal*
Ousemi: see Ossimi
Ousi, Oussi: see Awassi
Ovče Polje (E. Macedonia, Yugoslavia); m.cw.d; Pramenka type; white,
head and legs partly or wholly black or brown, occ. black, brown or
grey; ♂ hd, ♀ usu. pd; Serbo-cro. *Ovčepoljska*. [= sheep plain]
Oxford Down (England); sw.m; Down type; dark brown face and legs;
pd; orig. about 1830 from Cotswold × Hampshire Down (and
Southdown); recog. 1851; BS 1888, HB 1889; obs. syn. *Down-Cotswold,
Oxfordshire Down*; orig. (+ Hampshire Down) of German Blackheaded
Mutton and (+ Grabs) of Swiss Brownheaded Mutton; syn. Oxford
(USA); BS also in USA 1882; HB also in Canada

Padova, Padovana: see Paduan
[Paduan] (Venetia, Italy); d.m.mw; Lop-eared Alpine group; pd; It.
Padovana; var: Noventana; orig. of Carinthian and Solčava; crossed

with Lamon, extinct 1970s

Pag Island (Croatia, Yugoslavia); d.m.mw; sim. to Dubrovnik; white, occ. black; ♂ usu. hd, ♀ usu. pd; st; ? orig. from Merino × Pramenka in early 19th c; Serbo- cro. *Paška*, It. *Pago-Selve*; syn. *Silba*; not *Pashka, Pog*

Pagliarola (Abruzzo and Molise, Italy); m.(cw-mw); Apennine group; yellowish-white, also reddish-black; pd. [= straw-eater]

Pagota: see Alpagota

Pahang: see Kelantan

Pahari (Muzaffarabad, Azad Kashmir, Pakistan); m.cw.d; white with tan, brown or black head, or pied; usu. pd; sometimes sft.

Pak Awassi (Punjab, Pakistan); d.cw.m; orig. from Awassi × Kachhi

Pakistan fat-tailed breeds; see Baluchi, Bibrik, Harnai, Rakhshani (Baluchistan), Hashtnagri, Khijloo, Michni, Tirahi, Waziri (N.W.F.P.), Latti (Punjab), Dumbi (Sind), Gojal and Kohai Ghizer (Kashmir)

Pak Karakul (Punjab, Pakistan); fur; orig. since 1965 at Rakh Kairewala farm, Muzaffargarh, from Karakul × Kachhi

Palas Merino (Constanţa region, S.E. Romania); fw.m; ♂ usu. hd, ♀ usu. pd; orig. 1920-50 at Palas Animal Breeding Station, Constanţa, from Tsigai, Ţurcana and Stogoşă, graded to Rambouillet 1926-34 and to German Mutton Merino 1928-42, with further Rambouillet and Stavropol blood; Rom. *Merinos de Palas*

Pallaresa (Pallars, Lérida, Catalonia, Spain); mw; Iberian type; white, usu. with black or red points; ♂ occ. hd, ♀ pd; syn. *Chisqueta, Sisqueta* or *Tisqueta* (from Catalan *Txisquet*), *Monsetina* (from Montseny); not *Catalan*

Paloma: see Segureña; name also used, confusingly, for Alcarreña and Ansotana

[Pamir] (Tajikistan, USSR); cw.m; sim. to Kirgiz Fat-rumped; Russ. *Pamirskaya*

Pamir argali: see Marco Polo's sheep

Pamir Finewool (Tajikistan, USSR); orig. from Merino × Darvaz

Pampa: see Criollo

Pampara; var. of Tushin with longer wool of lower density

Panagyurishte (Sredna Gora, Bulgaria); m.cw.d; local unimproved var. of Bulgarian Native; white or coloured; ♂ hd or pd, ♀ pd; Bulg. *Panagyurska*, Ger. *Talschaf*; syn. *Ofche Hulmski, Sredna Gora*; not *Panagiurište, Panaguirishte*; rare

Panama (Idaho, USA); mw.m; pd; sim. to Columbia; orig. (1912 on) from Rambouillet × Lincoln; [HB 1951]; rare. [exhibited at Panama-Pacific Exposition, San Francisco, 1915]

Panjsher Gadik (Afghanistan); var. of Gadik; usu. black or brown

Parai: see Tirahi

Parasi: see White Karaman
Pardina: see Ripollesa
Parkanni: see Lohi
Parkent Mutton-Wool (Uzbekistan, USSR); m.w; Russ. *Parkentskaya myaso-sherstnaya*
Parnassian: see Greek Zackel
Pashka, Paška: see Pag Island
Patanwadi (Mahsana, Kutch and Saurashtra, N. Gujarat, India); cw.d.m; brown face and legs; pd; st; occ. tassels; syn. *Buti* (= *tasselled*), *Charotari* (not *Charothar, Charothri*), *Cutchi or Kutchi, desi* or *deshi, Gujarati* (not *Gujerati, Gujrati*), *Joria* (wool type), *Kathiawari, Vadhiyari*; not *Pattanwadi*. [from Patan]
Paterschaf: see Engadine Red
Pattanwadi: see Patanwadi
[Paular]; former strain of Spanish Merino
[Pavullese] (Pavullo, Modena, Emilia, Italy); m.w.d; var. of Garfagnina White with Bergamasca blood; syn. *Appennino-Modenese, Balestra* (= *crossbow, i.e.* horn shape), *Modenese*; extinct 1976-79
[Peat] (Switzerland); remains found in neolithic lake dwellings; orig. of Bündner Oberland and Steinschaf; syn. *Turbary*; Ger. *Torfschaf*
Pechora (Komi, USSR); lw.m; breed group; orig. 1937-50 from Romney × local Russian Northern Short-tailed backcrossed twice to Romney and then bred *inter se*; Russ. *Pechorskaya porodnaya gruppa* or *Pechorskaya polutonkorunnaya* (= *semifinewooled*); rare
Pecora della Roccia, or *delle Rocce*, or *del Sasso*: see Steinschaf
Pedi: see Bapedi
Pelibüey (Cuba and Mexico—chiefly Gulf coast); m; American Hair sheep group; usu. tan, red, white or pied; pd; ♂ usu. mane and throat ruff; syn. *Carnero de pelo de buey, Cuban Hairy, Cubano Rojo* (= *red Cuban*), *Peligüey, Tabasco* (Mexico). [= ox-haired]
Pelo de Boi: see Brazilian Woolless
Pelona: see Red African
[Pembroke Hill] (Wales); local var. of Welsh Mountain, with browner face and hd ♀; extinct in 1930s; syn. *Prescelly Mountain* (not *Precelly*)
Penistone: see Whitefaced Woodland
Péone: see Mourerous
Peppin (Australia); medium-wool strain of Australian Merino developed 1840-70 at Messrs Peppin's stud, Wanganella, NSW, (and elsewhere); English Longwool blood; syn. *Wanganella*
[Perales]; former strain of Spanish Merino
Perendale (New Zealand); m.mw; pd; orig. 1938-60 (chiefly since 1947) from Cheviot × New Zealand Romney; BS 1960, HB 1961; BS also in Australia. [Prof. G. *Peren* of Massey Agric. College]

Permer (Nigeria); m; usu. pied, esp. white with black head; hy-w; orig. in Göttingen, Germany, from Blackhead Persian × German Merino and transported to Ibadan. [*Persian-Merino*]

Persian (S. Africa): see Blackhead Persian

Persian fat-tailed: see Iran fat-tailed

Persian Red (S. Africa): see Wooled Persian

Persian Thin-tailed: see Zel

Perthshire Blackface; strain of Scottish Blackface with coarser wool

Perugian Lowland (Italy); Apennine type with much Bergamasca blood

Pešter, Pešterska: see Sjenica

Petit Oranais: see Beni Guil. [mutton exported from *Oran*, Algeria, to France]

Petrokhan Tsigai (Bulgaria); orig. from Mutton Merino and Tsigai × Sofia White

Pettadale (Shetland, Scotland); m.w; pd; orig. (1959 on) from Romney ($\frac{1}{4}$) × Shetland ($\frac{3}{4}$) on Kergood estate

[Petzen]; former var. of Carinthian

Peuhl, Peul, Peulh, Peul-Peul: see Fulani

Pialdo (Alentejo, Portugal); black; name coined for dominant black Merino. [*Pigmented Alentejo dominant*]

[Picardy]; var. of Flemish Marsh; Fr. *Picard*

Piebald: see Jacob

Pied (W. Africa): see Uda

Piedmont, Piedmont Alpine: see Biellese

Pied Polisi (C. Albania); d.cw.m; var. of Albanian Zackel; black or dark red spectacles; ♂ hd, ♀ usu. pd (80-90%); Alb. *Lara Polisi*

Piemontese alpina: see Biellese

[Pink-nosed Somerset]; var. of Dorset Horn; syn. *Somerset Horn*

Pinzirita (Sicily, Italy); d.m.cw; black or brown marks on face and legs; ♂ hd, ♀ pd; HB; syn. *Siciliana locale, Comune siciliana*, or *nostrale*; not *Pinzonita, Piperina, Piperita*; orig. (with Barbary) of Sicilian Barbary, (with Maltese) of Comisana. [= speckled]

Pirenaica: see Ripollesa

Pirlak: see Kamakuyruk

Pirot (S.E. Serbia, Yugoslavia); m.cw; local Pramenka; often spotted or coloured head; ♂ hd, ♀ usu. pd; Serbo-cro. *Pirotska*; being absorbed by Svrljig

Pitt Island (Chatham Is, New Zealand); fw; feral; usu. coloured; hd; orig. from Saxony Merino from Hutt Valley in 1840s; rare

Piva (N. Montenegro, Yugoslavia); m.cw.d; Pramenka type; usu. white with spotted head and legs, occ. black or grey; Serbo-cro. *Pivska*; syn. *Durmitor* (Serbo-cro. *Durmitorska*), *Jezero-Piva* (Serbo-cro. *Jezero-pivska*)

Pleven Blackhead (N. Bulgaria); d.cw; Bulgarian Native improved by
Tsigai; born black; ♂ hd, ♀ pd; Bulg. *Chernoglava plevenska*, Ger.
Plewener; not *Plevin, Plevna*; rare
Plezzo, Plezzana: see Bovec
Plovdiv Merino: see Thrace Finewool
[Plovdiv-Purvomai] (Maritsa valley, Bulgaria); lw.d.m; var. of White
   South Bulgarian; orig. from Tsigai × local Bulgarian with Merino
   blood; Bulg. *Plovdivsko-P"rvomaĭska*; syn. *Plovdiv, Purvomai*; orig.
   (with Merino) of Thrace Finewool
Podhale; var. of Polish Zackel
Polish Anglo-Merino (Poland); Polish Lowland group; orig. from
   Romney, Lincoln, Leicester Longwool or Leine, × Polish Merino
Polish Blackheaded = German Blackheaded Mutton in N.E. Poland;
   Pol. *Czarnogłowka*
Polish Heath: see Wrzosówka
Polish Highland, Polish Hill, Polish Improved Mountain: see Polish
   Mountain
POLISH LONGWOOL (Poland); orig. from East Friesian, Leine, Texel and
   esp. Romney × local (*e.g.* Świniarka); Pol. *Długowełnista owca polska*;
   inc. Bochnia, Kamieniec, Leszno, Olkusz, Pomeranian, Silesian
POLISH LOWLAND (Poland); orig. from English Longwool × (Polish
   Merino × local); inc. Łowicz, Polish Anglo-Merino, Poznań, Żelazna;
   Pol. *Polska nizinna*; syn. *Polnische Landschafe*
Polish Merino (Poland); fw.m; orig. chiefly from Précoce in late 19th
   and 20th c, named 1946, improved by Caucasian Merino 1952-57; Pol.
   Merynos polska; syn. *Merynos cienkorunny* (= *finewool*), *Merynos
   wełnisto-mięsny* (= *wool-mutton*); vars: Jędrzychowice Merino, Polish
   Strongwooled Merino
Polish Mountain (S. Poland); m.d.cw; usu. white, occ. black, grey or
   pied; pd; orig. from Polish Zackel improved by Transylvanian Zackel
   (imported 1911-13 and 1935-37) and East Friesian (imported 1925-27
   and after 1946); Pol. *Polska owca górska*; syn. *Cakiel-Fryz-Siedmio-
   grodzka* (= *Zackel-Friesian-Transylvanian*), *CFS, Improved Hill, Polish
   Highland, Polish Hill, Polish Improved Mountain*
Polish Strongwooled Merino (Poland); m.mw; var. of Polish Merino
   with Berrichon du Cher and Ile-de-France blood; Pol. *Merynos polski
   pogrubiony*
Polish Zackel (S. Poland); cw.d.pelt; white, also black or brown; hd or
   pd; Pol. *Cakiel*; vars in Podhale (Pol. *Podhalánska*), Tatra and East
   Carpathians; orig. of Polish Mountain
Polisi: see Pied Polisi
Polje: see Ovče Polje
Poll Dorset (S.E. Australia); pd; orig. (1937 on) from Dorset Horn and

Ryeland or Corriedale; BS 1954; syn. Polled Dorset Horn (England)
Polled Rambouillet (USA); pd var. of American Rambouillet
Poll Merino (Australia); pd var. of Australian Merino; HB also in NZ
Poltava Fur-Milch (Ukraine); inc. Reshetilovka and Sokolki; sim. to
     Chushka
Polwarth (Colac, W. Victoria, Australia); mw.m; orig. *c*.1880 from
     Merino × (English Longwool × Merino); *i.e.* Comeback with at least
     5 generations of *inter se* breeding; syn. *Ideal* (S. America); hd and pd
     vars; BS
Polypay (Idaho, USA); m.w; orig. 1969 on from (Targhee × Dorset) ×
     (Rambouillet × Finnish) at US Sheep Exp. Sta., Dubois; bred for 2
     lambs twice a year; BS 1979
Pomarancina (Pomarance, Pisa, Italy); m.d.cw; Apennine group; usu.pd;
     rare
Pomeranian (Pomorze, Poland); d.lw.m; orig. Marsh type, now Polish
     Longwool group; white (earlier also brown or black); pd; orig. from
     Friesian in 18th c, East Friesian and Wilstermarsch blood 1929-39,
     later Texel blood; Pol. *Owca pomorska*; obs. syn. *Fagas* (or *Vagas*),
     Kasubian (or *Casubian*)
Pomeranian Coarsewool (N.E. Germany); cw; grey with black head,
     born black; pd; Ger. *Pommerisches rauwolliges Landschaf*; rare
Poogal: see Pugal
Poonchi (Punch, S.W. Kashmir, Pakistan); cw.m; sometimes black or
     brown head and legs, or pied; ♂ hd, ♀ pd; st.
Porakani: see Thalli
Porlock: see Exmoor Horn
Portland (Dorset, England); tan face, red fleece in lamb; hd; HB 1975;
     orig. (with Merino) of Dorset Horn; nearly extinct
PORTUGUESE CHURRO (N.E. Portugal); white or coloured; ♂ hd, ♀ hd or
     pd; inc. Algarve Churro, Bragança Galician, Churra da Terra Quente,
     Churra do Campo, Miranda Galician, Mondegueira; syn. *Bordaleiro
     Churro*
Portuguese Merino (C. Portugal); fw.d.m; orig. from Bordaleiro crossed
     with Spanish Merino (since 15th c), Rambouillet (since 1903) and,
     predominantly, Précoce (since 1929); vars: Beira Baixa, Black, Fonte
     Bôa
Poznań (Poland); Polish Lowland group; orig. 1948 on, *c.* $\frac{9}{16}$ Romney,
     $\frac{1}{4}$ Merino, $\frac{1}{8}$ Leszno, $\frac{1}{16}$ Swiniarka; Pol. *Poznańska*
Poznań Corriedale (Poland); orig. (1962 on) from Poznań × [Poznań
     × (Romney × Polish Merino)]; Pol. *Koridel poznański*
PRAMENKA (Yugoslavia); m.cw.d; Zackel type; usu. white, also black,
     and white with black on head and legs; ♂ usu. hd, ♀ usu. pd; syn.
     Yugoslavian Zackel; inc. Bosnian Mountain; Dalmatian-Karst, Island,

Istrian Milk, and Lika (Croatia); Karakachan, Ovče Polje and Šar
Planina (Macedonia); Piva and Zeta Yellow (Montenegro); Baljuša,
Bardoka, Kosovo, Krivovir, Lipe, Pirot, Sjenica, Stogoš, and Svrljig
(Serbia); orig. (with Merino) of Dubrovnik and Pag Island (Dalmatia).
[Serbo-cro. *pramen* = staple or lock, hence *pramenka* = with open
fleece]

Préalpes du Sud (Drôme, S.W. Hautes-Alpes and N.E. Vaucluse, S.E.
France); m.sw; pd; named 1947, HB 1948, BS; syn. *Levant, Quint,
Sahune, St Nazaire, Savournon, Valdrôme*

Preanger: see Priangan

Precelly: see Pembroke Hill

Précoce (France); fw.m; ♂ hd or pd (= Meusse), ♀ pd; orig. from Spanish
Merino imported 1799-1811, selected for early maturity; HB 1929 by
fusion of those of Champagne, Châtillonais, and Soissonais Merinos;
Fr. *Mérinos précoce*; orig. of German Mutton Merino, Polish Merino,
Portuguese Merino; HB also in Portugal, Spain; declining. [= early
maturing]

Prescelly Mountain: see Pembroke Hill

Priangan (W. Java, Indonesia); ram fighting, m.(cw); usu. black or pied,
occ. grey or tan; ♂ hd, ♀ pd; often earless; st (fat at base); ? orig. from
Africander (? and Merino) × Javanese Thin-tailed in 19th c; syn.
Garut; not *Preanger, Prianger*

Priangarskiĭ Merinos: see Angara Merino

Priaral'skaya: see South Kazakh Merino

Priazov: see Azov Tsigai

Prijevorska: see Privor

Primorska (Croatia, Yugoslavia): see Istrian Milk

Privor (Yugoslavia); var. of Bosnian Mountain; usu. white muzzle and
black face; ♂ usu. hd, ♀ usu. pd; Serbo-cro. *Privorska*; syn. *Prijevorska*;
subvar: Donji Vakuf

"Prolific" (N. England); m; orig. from Bluefaced Leicester, Poll Dorset
and Llŷn by G.L.H. Alderson, Haltwhistle, Northumberland

Prong Horn: see Zackel

Provence Merino: see Arles Merino

Psiloris (C. Crete, Greece); d.m.cw; var. of Greek Zackel; white with
black spots on face; ♂ hd, ♀ usu. pd; Gr. *Psiloritiana*; syn. *Anogia*

puchia: see Pakistan fat-tailed

Pugal (W. Bikaner, Rajasthan, India); cw.m; black face; pd; not *Poogal*

Puglia, Pugliese: see Apulian

Purvomai: see Plovdiv-Purvomai

Pusterese (Val Pusteria, Bolzano, Italy); m.cw; Lop-eared Alpine group;
orig. from Bergamasca × Steinschaf since 1750, with Lamon blood;
syn. *Gadertaler* (Ger.) or *Nobile di Badia* (It.) (Val Badia), *Pustera*

gigante, Tedesca di Pusteria or *Val di Pusteria, Sextner, Tauferer* (Valle
Aurina); nearly extinct
Pyrenean (France); see Pyrenean dairy breeds (Manech and Basco-
Béarnais), Central Pyrenean (Aure-Campan, Barégeois, Castillonais,
Lourdais and Tarasconnais)
Pyrenean dairy breeds (W. Pyrenees, France); BS; Fr. *Races ovines
laitières des Pyrénées*; inc. Basco-Béarnais and Manech
Pyrenean Semifinewool: see Ansotana and Roncalesa
Pyrénéen central, Pyrénées centrales: see Central Pyrenean
Pyrny (W. Ukraine, USSR); var. of Voloshian; ♂ hd, ♀ hd (short) or
pd; shorter tail; not *Pyrnai*

Qashqai (Fars, Iran); cw.m; local var; coloured spots on head and legs;
♀ pd; ft; Fr. *Ghachgai*; not *Ghashgai*
Qinghai Black Tibetan (Qinghai, China); cw.m; black; pd; orig. from
Tibetan
Qinghai Semifinewool (Qinghai, China); lw.m; ♂ hd, ♀ pd; orig. from
Tsigai × (Xinjiang Finewool × Tibetan) + Romney × above
Qezel, Qizil: see Red Karaman
Quadrella: see Improved Ariano
Quanglin Large-tail (Shanxi, China); m.cw; ♂ hd, ♀ pd; sft; orig. from
Mongolian
Quercy, Quercynois: see Caussenard du Lot
Quint: see Préalpes du Sud

Rabada (or *Rabuda*) *de la sierra de Loja*: see Lojeña
Rabo Largo (Bahia, N.E. Brazil); m.cw-hy; white, pied, or white with
coloured head; hd; lft; ? orig. from hy ft. breed from S. Africa ×
Crioulo; HB. [= broad tail]
Race de l'Est à laine Mérinos (Alsace-Lorraine, France); fw.m; orig. from
Württemberg Merino (now Merinolandschaf) imported since 1870,
named 1950; BS 1947; syn. *Mérino de l'Est*. [= breed in the east with
Merino wool]
Racka (Hungary); d.m.cw; Zackel type; white (with light brown or occ.
grey face and legs) or black; vertical corkscrew horns; Rom. *Raţca*;
syn. *Hortobágy Racka, Hungarian Zackel*; not *Rasko, Ratzka*; rare. [=
Zackel]
Rackulja (Yugoslavia): see Stogoš
Radmani (South Yemen); hy; white; pd; ft; often earless; syn. *Sha'ra* (=
hairy)
Radnor, Radnor Forest: see Hill Radnor
Radomir (S.W. Bulgaria); var. of Breznik; mottled head and feet

Ragusa, Ragusa-Šipan: see Dubrovnik

Rahmani (Beheira, Lower Egypt); cw.m; brown, fading with age; often earless; ♂ hd, ♀ usu. pd; ft. [from Rahmaniya]

Raimbi (Algeria); sim. to Algerian Arab but red-brown; not *Rembi, Rumbi*. [Arabic]

Raïole (Cévennes, C. France); m.cw; Causses type, ? with Barbary blood; sometimes brown or grey; ♂ hd; HB 1980; BS; syn. *Cévenol* (from Cévennes); not *Rayole*

Rajasthani: see Chokla, Jaisalmeri, Magra, Malpura, Marwari, Nali, Pugal, Sonadi

Rakhshani (W. Baluchistan, Pakistan); m.cw.d; black or brown head or muzzle; ♂ hd, ♀ pd; long lop ears; ft; vars: Jhalawani, Sarawani; not *Rakshini*

Rakvere, Rakvereskaya: see Estonian Darkheaded

Rambouillet (France); fw.m; ♂ hd, ♀ pd; orig. from many strains of Spanish Merino, imported 1786 and 1799-1803 and bred only at Bergerie Nationale de Rambouillet near Paris; Fr. *Mérinos de Rambouillet*; orig. of American Rambouillet

Ramliç (Turkey); m.fw; orig. since 1969 at Istanbul Univ. from American Rambouillet (65%) × Dağliç (35%)

Ramnad Karuvi, Ramnad Red: see Kilakarsal

Ramnad White (Ramanathapuram, Tamil Nadu, India); m; South India hair type; usu. white, occ. pied; ♂ hd, ♀ pd; st.

Rampur Bushair (Himachal Pradesh, and N. of Uttar Pradesh, India); cw.pa; white often with tan face, occ. pied or brown; ♂ hd, ♀ usu. pd; long lop ears; st; not *Rampur Bushahr, Rampur Bushier*

Rasa, Rasa aragonese: see Aragonese

Rashaidi (N.E. Eritrea); cw; ? var. of Abyssinian or orig. from Yemen; brown. white, red or pied; pd; It. *Rasciaida*

Rasko: see Racka

Raso: see Aragonese

Raţca, Ratzka: see Racka

Rava (W. Puy-de-Dôme, C. France); m.cw; Central Plateau type; white with black spots on extremities, or black; pd; HB 1973, not *Ravas, Ravat*

Raymond Merino (Dhule, Maharashtra, India); fw; orig. 1973 on; inc. Australian Merino × Polwarth, Merino × Chokla, Merino-Polwarth × Chokla, and Merino-Chokla × Deccani

Rayole: see Raïole

Razlog (S.W. Bulgaria); mw; orig. 1955-67 from Romney and Lincoln × Merino

Red African (N. and C. Colombia and W. Venezuela); m. American Hair sheep group; yellow-red to dark red; pd; ♂ sometimes maned; Sp. *Roja*

africana; syn. *Africana, Camura, Colombian Woolless, Pelona, West African*

Red Head (Albania): see Mati

Red Head (France): see Rouge de l'Ouest

Red Head (Germany): see Coburger

Red Head (Sicily): see Comisana

Redheaded Maine: see Rouge de l'Ouest

Red Karaman (N.E. Turkey); cw.m.d; red or brown; ♂ usu. pd, ♀ pd; Turk. *Kızıl-Karaman* or *Mor-Karaman*; syn. *Dugli, Erzurum, Hamra* (= *red*) or *Shagra* (Fr. *Chacra, Chagra* or *Chakra*) (Syria), *Gesel, Gezel, Ghezel, Kazil, Khezel, Khizel, Kizil, Qezel* or *Qizil* (Iran), *Turkish Brown*; var: Hemşin; see also White Karaman

Red Majorcan (S. Majorca, Balearic Is, Spain); m.(d.mw); white with red head and feet, lambs born red; ♂ hd or pd, ♀ usu. pd; sft; ? orig. from Barbary; Sp. *Roja mallorquina de cola ancha* (= *with broad tail*); syn. *Borde* (= *crossbred*), *Coete* or *Cohete* (from *coe* = tail), *Pigmentada mallorquina*; rare

Red Masai: see Masai

red sheep (Middle East) = *Ovis orientalis* Gmelin, *orientalis, gmelini* and *ophion* sections; intermediate between urial and mouflon; reddish with paler underparts; ♂ hd, ♀ pd; st; Russ. *krasnyĭ samukh*; syn. *oriental mouflon*; type sp. is Elburz red; vars inc. Cyprus mouflon, Anatolian red, Armenian red and subspp. in various parts of Iran; ? part origin of domestic sheep

Red Woolless (Brazil): see Brazilian Woolless

Rehamna-Sraghna; var. of South Moroccan; not *Rehamma-Srarhna* or *Sghrana*

Rembi: see Raimbi

Replyan (N.E. Bulgaria); m.w.d; local unimproved var. of Bulgarian Native; mottled head and feet; ♂ usu. hd, ♀ pd; Bulg. *Replyanska*, Ger. *Repljaner*; syn. *Belogradchik*; orig. (with Tsigai) of Mountain Tsigai; rare

[Reshetilovka] (Ukraine, USSR); black; ♂ hd, ♀ 20-25% pd; orig. from Russian Long-tailed; Russ. *Reshetilovskaya*

[Rhiw Hill] (S. Caernarvon, Wales); local var. sim. to Welsh Mountain but black or mottled face and pd; not *Rhuy*

Rhodes (Dodecanese, Greece); d.m.cw; usu. white with black spots on face and legs; ♂ hd, ♀ pd; sft; ? orig. from thin-tailed × fat-tailed cross; Gr. *Ródhos*, It. *Rodi*; syn. *Caramanitica*

Rhodesian: see Sabi

Rhodope: see Central Rodopi

Rhön (C. Germany); w.m; black head; pd; recog. 1844; BS 1921

Rhuy: see Rhiw Hill

[Rila Monastery] (Bulgaria); d.w; ♂ hd, ♀ pd; local Bulgarian Native improved by Tsigai; Bulg. *Rilomonastirska* or from *Rilskiĭ Monastir*, Ger. *Rilokloster*; syn. *Rila*

Rilo-Rodopska: see Central Rodopi

Ripollesa (Gerona, Catalonia, Spain); m.(mw); white with pigmented face and legs; ♂ hd, ♀ usu. hd; lt; syn. *Bergerá, Bergueda, Caralpina* (from Caralp), *Montañesa, Pardina, Pirenaica, Sardana, Solsonenca, Vicatana* or *Vigatana* (from Vich); ? orig. from Merino × Tarasconnais

Roaschia, Roaschina: see Frabosana

Rocce, Roccia: see Steinschaf

Rocha: see Guirra

Rocky: see Keerie

Rocky Mountain: see bighorn

Ródhos: see Rhodes

Rodopi: see Central Rodopi

Rogaland: see Rygja

Romanian Merino: see Danube Merino, Palas Merino, Transylvanian Merino

Romanian Nomad: see Karakachan

Romanian Zackel: see Ţurcana

Romanov (Yaroslavl, USSR); pelt, cw; prolific; grey with black head and legs and usu. white face-stripe and feet; hd or pd; orig. from Russian Northern Short-tailed in late 17th c; HB; Russ. *Romanovskaya*; BS in France

Romashkov, Romashkovski: see Volgograd

Romeldale (California, USA); mw.m; orig. (1915 on) by A.T. Spencer from New Zealand Romney × American Rambouillet; one flock (J.K. Sexton, Willows, Calif. 95963) closed since 1919

Romnelet (Alberta, Canada); mw.m; orig. 1935-47 from Romney × Rambouillet

Romney (Kent, S. England); lw.m; English Longwool type; pd; orig. from Old Romney Marsh; BS 1895, HB; syn. *Kent, Kent or Romney Marsh, New Kent, Romney Marsh*; var: New Zealand Romney; part orig. of Kuibyshev, Ostrogozhsk, Pechora (USSR); BS also in USA 1911, Australia, HB also in Canada

Romney-Corriedale (New Zealand); New Zealand Romney × Corriedale F₁

Romney Halfbred (England); North Country Cheviot × Romney, 1st cross

[Romsdown] (Tasmania, Australia); orig. from Southdown × Romney

Romshire (Victoria, Australia); m; Wiltshire Horn × Romney, F₁

Ronaldsay, Ronaldshay: see North Ronaldsay

Roncalesa (Roncal and Salazar valleys, N.E. Navarre, Spain); var. of

314 DICTIONARY OF BREEDS

Aragonese with longer wool and semi-open fleece; syn. *Churra navarra, Entrefina pirenaica* (with Ansotana), *Salazenca* (in Salazar valley)
Ronderib Africander (N.C. Cape Prov., S. Africa); m; var. of Africander; white; hy-cw; ♂ usu. hd, ♀ hd or pd; sft; orig. from Cape var. of Hottentot; BS 1937- ? ; Afrik. *Ronderib Afrikaner*; former vars: Blinkhaar (shiny coat) (recog. by BS) and Steekhaar (kempy coat) (not recog.); rare, being displaced by Dorper and Merino. [= round rib, *i.e.* oval in cross section, not flat like Merino]
Ronderib Merino (S. Africa)
ROQUEFORT BREEDS (S. France); *i.e.* milk used for Roquefort cheese; inc. Larzac (original type), Lacaune, and Caussenard de la Lozère; Basco-Béarnais, Manech and Corsican also used˙
[Roscommon] (W. Ireland); lw.m; pd; syn. *Irish Longwool, Roscommon Longwool*; Leicester Longwool blood; absorbed by Galway; BS 1895-1926; extinct *c.*1977
Rosset (Grisanche, Rhêmes and Savaranche valleys, Aosta, Italy); m.cw; sim. to Savoiarda; red-brown spots around eyes and on legs; ♂ usu. pd, ♀ pd; rare
Rouge de Guillaume: see Mourerous
Rouge de l'Ouest (Maine-et-Loire, N.W. France); sim. to Bleu du Maine (same orig.) but with wine-red face; HB 1968; syn. *Tête rouge du Maine* (= *Redheaded Maine*)
Rouge de Roussillon: see Roussillon Red
Rough Fell (N.W. England); cw; Blackfaced Mountain type; hd; BS 1926, HB 1927; syn. *Kendal Rough, Kentmere, Rough*; very local
Roumloukion (C. Macedonia, Greece); m.d.cw; Ruda type; usu. white, occ. with speckled or black head, or all black or brown, or pied; ♂ hd, ♀ pd
[Roussillon Merino] (E. Pyrenees, France); orig. from Spanish Merino in late 18th c; extinct *c.*1940 by crossing with Central Pyrenean
Roussillon Red (coast of Pyrénées-Orientales, France); m.mw; white with red or pied head and legs and red kemp under neck; pd; orig. from local with Merino and Barbary blood; Fr. *Rouge du Roussillon*; syn. *Rouge du Littoral*; nearly extinct
Roussin de la Hague (N. Manche, France); pd; HB 1983; syn. *Berca, Rouge de la Hague*; orig. (with Leicester Longwool) of Cotentin
Roux-de-Bagnes (Val de Bagnes, Valais, Switzerland); red-brown; usu. pd; part orig. of Swiss Black-Brown Mountain; syn. *Bagnes, Bagner-schaf, Roux-du-Pays*; nearly extinct
Roya, Roya bilbilitana: see Bilbilitana
Rubia de El Molar, Rubia de Somosierra, Rubia Serrana: see Somosierra Blond
RUDA (Balkans); type with more uniform and slightly less coarse wool

than Zackel, ? due to Tsigai blood; inc. Luma (Albania); Chalkidiki, Katafigion, Roumloukion, Serrai (Greece); Kivircik (Thrace); *ruda* vars of Ovče Polje, Šar Planina, Sjenica, Svrljig (Yugoslavia); ? Karnobat, Rila Monastery, Shumen, White Klementina and White South Bulgarian (Bulgaria). [Alb. = wavy]

Ruda (Montenegro): see Dubrovnik

Rudavi; soft-wool var. of Karnobat; *cf.* Ruda

Rumbi: see Raimbi

Ruşeţu 1 (Romania); mw.m; orig. from (Romney × Tsigai) × (Corriedale × Tsigai) at Ruşeţu Exp. Sta.

[Russian Long-tailed] (S. European Russia); m.cw; black or white; ♂ hd, ♀ pd; Russ. *Prostaya derevenskaya dlinno-toshchekhvostaya* (= *Common village long-thin-tailed*); syn. *Common Russian, Common Long-tailed*; vars: Bityug, Bokino, Cherkassy; orig. of Chushka, Kuchugury, Mikhnov, Reshetilovka and Sokolki

Russian Longwool (Voronezh and Kalinin, USSR); m.lw; pd; orig. from Lincoln × local coarsewools; recog. 1978; vars: Kalinin and Liski (inc. Nizhnedevitsk); Russ. *Russkaya dlinnosherstnaya*

Russian Merinos (USSR); see Altai, Askanian, Azerbaijan Mountain, Caucasian, Fat-rumped, Georgian, Grozny, Kazakh, Kirgiz, Krasnoyarsk, Mountain, North Kazakh, Salsk, South Kazakh, South Ural, Soviet, Stavropol, Transbaikal, Volgograd, Vyatka

Russian Mountain Merino (N.Caucasus, USSR); fw; orig. from mouflon × Merino backcrossed to Merino ♀♀; Russ. *Gornyĭ merinos*

[Russian Northern Short-tailed] (N. European USSR); pelt, cw; black, grey, white, pied; ♂ usu. hd, ♀ usu. pd; Russ. *Severnaya korotkokhvostaya*; var: Nolinsk; orig. of Romanov

Russian Perseair (S. Africa): see Wooled Persian

Ruthenian Zackel: see Carpathian Mountain

[Ruthenois] (S. France); absorbed by Lacaune

Rya (C. Sweden); m.cw; var. of Swedish Landrace; Swe. *Ryafår*; syn. *Swedish Carpet Wool sheep*. [= carpet]

Ryeland (England); sw.m; pd; recog. 18th c; BS 1909, HB; syn. *Hereford*; HB also in New Zealand 1925, Australia. [= sandy rye-growing land in S. Hereford]

Rygja (Rogaland, Norway); sw; face and legs sometimes coloured; pd; orig. (1850 on) from Cheviot × Old Norwegian with Leicester Longwool or Oxford Down blood, named 1924; HB. [= from Rogaland]

[Saanen]; part orig. of Swiss Black-Brown Mountain; sim. to Simmental; Fr. *Gessenay*; syn. *Saanerland*

Sabi (Zimbabwe); African Long-fat-tailed type; often brown, black or pied; hy; ♂ often hd, ♀ usu. pd; inc. Mashona; obs. syn. *Rhodesian*
Sahabadi: see Shahabadi

SAHEL TYPE (N. of W. Africa); m; white or pied; ♂ hd (long twisted), ♀ usu. pd; lop ears; hy; tassels common; syn. *Guinea Long-legged, Sahelian, West African Long-legged*; inc. Fulani, Maure and Tuareg

Sahune: see Préalpes du Sud

Saidi (Asyut, Upper Egypt); cw.m; black or brown; pd; lft; syn. *Sohagi*; var: Sanabawi. [= valley, *i.e.* of Nile]

St Gallen: see Wildhaus

St Gironnais, St Girons: see Castillonais

St Jean de Maurienne: see Thônes-Marthod

St Kilda: see Hebridean

St Nazaire: see Preálpes du Sud

[St Quentin]; var. of Flemish Marsh

Sakar (Bulgaria); m.cw.d; occ. colour around eyes; ♂ hd; lt; Bulg. *Sakarska*; rare

Sakiz (Izmir, Turkey); d.cw.m; white with black spots around mouth and eyes and on ears and legs; ♂ hd, ♀ usu. pd; lt. with fat at base; orig. from Chios; Turk. *Sakız*; syn. *Çeşme*; not *Sakis, Sakkes*

Saku-Bash (Xinjiang, China); subvar. of Kargilik var. of Hetian; sim. to Chapan

Salamali: see White Karaman; not *Salamli*

Salazenca: see Roncalesa; not *Salacenca*

Saloia (Lisbon, Portugal); d.mw.m; Bordaleiro type; usu. white with pale brown head and legs, occ. brown; ♂ hd, ♀ usu. pd

Salsk (Rostov, N. Caucasus, USSR); fw; orig. 1932-49 from American Rambouillet × Novocaucasian Merino; HB; Russ. *Sal'skaya* or *Sal'skaya poroda tonkorunnykh ovets* (= Salsk breed of finewool sheep); not *Salsky*

Saltasassi (N. Novara, Piedmont, Italy); m.(cw); Lop-eared Alpine group

Salt range: see Lati

Salz (Ebro valley, Spain); d.m; pd; in formation from Romanov × Aragonese

Salzburg Steinschaf: see Steinschaf

Sambre-et-Meuse: see Entre-Sambre-et-Meuse

Sambucana (Sambuco to Demonte, S.W. Cuneo, Italy); mw.m; sim. to Garessina but larger; ♂ usu. pd, ♀ pd; syn. *Demontina*; rare

Samburu (Mali); var. of Fulani; maroon; long horizontal horns; Fr. *Sambourou*

Samburu (N. Kenya); var. of Masai varying in type and colour

Samhoor (Iran); var. of Sanjabi; syn. *Jomoor*

Samur: see Tabasaran

Sana'a White (N.E. and N. of San'a, N. Yemen); m.cw; pd; ft

Sanabawi (Sanbo, Upper Egypt); var. of Saidi with smaller tail; red with red, black or white head; sometimes hd

Sangamneri (Ahmedhagar, Maharashtra, India); strain of Deccani

Sangesari (N. and E. of Tehran, Iran); m.cw; Kurdi type; brown, also black; small; pd; ft; not *Sangsar, Sangsari*

Sanjabi (Kermanshah, Iranian Kurdistan); cw.m; Kurdi type; brown face, feet and, sometimes, tail; pd; lft; not *Sandjabi, Sinjabi*; vars: Calhoor, Samhoor

Santa Cruz (Santa Cruz I, California, USA); feral for *c.* 70 years; ? orig. from Merino, Rambouillet and/or Churro

Santa Inês (Bahia, N.E. Brazil); m; American Hair sheep group; white, red, black or pied; hy; pd; lop ears; ? orig. from Bergamasca × Brazilian Woolless since late 1940s; BSd; syn. *Pelo de Boi de Bahia* (= *Bahia ox-haired*)

Saracatsanica: see Karakachan

Saradgy, Saradzhinskaya, Saraja: see Sary-Ja

Sarakatzan: see Karakachan

Sarawani; var. of Rakhshani

Sarda: see Sardinian

Sardana: see Ripollesa

Sardarsamand (Rajasthan, India); orig. (1935 on) from Australian Merino × Marwari

Sardi (C. Plateau, Moroco); m.cw; black around eyes and on nose; hd

Sardinian (Sardinia, Italy); d.(m.cw); ♂ occ. hd, ♀ pd; HB 1927; It. *Sarda*; former vars: large lowland, white, pd, with Merino and Barbary blood, syn. *Cagliari, Campidano*; small mountain, occ. black, ♂ hd, ♀ often hd; orig. of Tunisian milk sheep

Sardinian mouflon: see mouflon

Šar Planina (W. Macedonia, Yugoslavia); m.cw.d; Pramenka type; ♂ hd, ♀ pd; Serbo-cro. *Šarplaninska*; syn. *Šar Mountain*; not *Schar Planina*; *cf.* Luma (Albania)

Sary-Ja (S.E. Turkmenistan, USSR); cw.m; grey; pd; fr; improved by Degeres since 1950; HB; Russ. *Saradzhinskaya*; not *Saradgy, Saraja*; var: Ashkhabad; part orig. of Alai, Kargalin and Tajik

Sasso: see Steinschaf

Savoiarda (W. Turin, Piedmont, Italy); d.m.cw; black spots on face and legs; ♂ hd, ♀ hd or pd; semi-lop ears; syn. *Cuorgné*; *cf.* Thônes-Marthod; being crossed with Biellese; nearly extinct. [from Savoy]

Savournon: see Préalpes du Sud

Savoyard: see Thônes-Marthod

[Saxony Merino] (Germany); fw; orig. from Escurial (with some Negretti and Infantado) strain of Spanish Merino imported 1765-1815; Ger.

Sächsisches Elektoralschaf; syn. *Electoral Merino*; part orig. of Australian Merino

Sayaguesa (Sayago, Zamora, Spain); m.cw; small var. of Spanish Churro

Scandinavian Short-tail: see Northern Short-tailed

Schnalser: see Tyrol Mountain

Schoonebeker (Schoonebeek, S.E. Drenthe, Netherlands); var. of Dutch Heath; usu. white with red or grey on face and legs, also black, brown or pied; pd; orig. from Drenthe and Veluwe; BS; not *Schoonebecker*; rare

[Schwyz]; part orig. of Swiss White Mountain; syn. *Uri* (Ger. *Urner Landschaf*)

Sciara (Calabria, Italy); d.(m.cw); Moscia type; usu. pd; syn. *Calabrese (Calabrian)* or *Moscia calabrese*; var: [Urbascia] (dark brown)

Scimenzana: see Akele Guzai

Scotch: see Scottish

Scotch Horn: see Scottish Blackface

Scottish Blackface (Scotland and N. England); cw.m; Blackfaced Mountain type; black or pied face; hd; BS *c*.1890; syn. *Blackface, Blackfaced Highland, Kerry* (Ireland), *Linton, Scottish Mountain, Scotch Blackface, Scotch Horn*; strains inc. Galloway and Island (finer wool), Lanark and Perthshire (coarser wool); var. Boreray; BS also in USA 1907

Scottish Greyface (S. Scotland and N. England); cw.m; Border Leicester × Scottish Blackface (or Swaledale), 1st cross; BS; syn. *Cross*

Scottish Halfbred (Scotland—England); Border Leicester × Cheviot, 1st cross; pd; BS; syn. *Baumshire, North, North Country, North Halfbred, Scotch Halfbred*

Scottish Masham (Scotland); Teeswater (or Wensleydale) × Scottish Blackface, 1st cross

Scottish Soft-wool: see Tanface

Screw Horn: see Zackel

Scutari: see Shkodra

Seeboden, Seebodner: see Solčava

[Seeländer] (Austria, pre-1918); local var. (or syn.) of Carinthian

Seeland, Seeland-Sulzbach (Yugoslavia); see Solčava

[Ségala] (Causses de Rodez, Aveyron, S. France); d; Caussenard type; Roquefort breed; now absorbed by Lacaune; syn. *Ségala-Levézou*

Segezia Triple Cross (Foggia, Apulia, Italy); m.d.mw; pd; recent orig. from Merinolandschaf × (Ile-de-France × Gentile di Puglia); It. *Trimeticcia de Segezia*

Segureña (Segura mts and R. valley, S.E. Spain); m.mw; Entrefino type; white, occ. blond spots on face and legs (*rubisca*) or all brown (*mora*); pd; orig. from Manchega; BS, HB 1982; syn. *Cabreña* (Almería and Castellón) or *Paloma* (Granada)—both always white; var: Marquesado

Semitic Fat-tailed: see Near East Fat-tailed

Senales: see Tyrol Mountain

Senese (Siena, Tuscany, Italy); var. of Apennine; syn. *Senese delle Crete*

Sennybridge Cheviot: see Brecknock Hill Cheviot

Serbian (Zackel): see Baljuša, Bardoka, Kosovo, Krivovir, Lipe, Pirot, Sjenica, Stogoš, and Svrljig

Serena Merino (Badajoz, Spain); var. of non-migratory Spanish Merino; Sp. *Merino de la Serena*; not *Serrena*

Serra da Estrêla (N.C. Portugal); d.mw.m; Bordaleiro type; white usu. with brown spots on head and legs, or black

Serrai (N.E. Macedonia, Greece); d.m.cw; Ruda type; usu. white with black marks on head and legs; ♂ hd, ♀ usu. pd; not *Seres, Seris, Serres*

Serrana: see Iberian (esp. Ojalada), Spanish Mountain Merino

Serranet: see Ojalada

Serrena: see Serena Merino

Setswana: see Tswana

Sevillana: see Montesina

Sextner: see Pusterese

Sfakia (W. Crete, Greece); d.m.cw; var. of Greek Zackel; usu. white with black spectacles; ♂ hd or pd, ♀ usu. pd; Gr. *Sfakiana*; syn. *Adromalicha*; not *Sphakia*

Sghrana: see Rehamna-Sraghna

sha: see shapo

Shafali (Iraq and Syria); arable var. of Awassi; red or black; Fr. *Chaffal, Chevali* or *Choufalié*; syn. *Delaimi, Delimi, Dilem, Dillène, Douleimi, Dulaimi*; not *Ashfal, Shaffal, Shevali*; cf. Arabi (Iraq)

Shaffal: see Shafali

shagra (Syria): see redfaced Awassi or Red Karaman

Shahabadi (Bihar, India); cw; white or grey, sometimes black spots (*e.g.* on face); pd; syn. *'plain type sheep'*; not *Sahabadi, Shahbadi*

Shal (Qazvin, Iran); m.cw.d; sim. to Mehraban; black, grey or brown; not *Chall, Shahl, Shall*

Shami (Syria): see Awassi. [= from Damascus]

Shandong: see Han

Shanghai: see Hu

Shantung: see Han

Shanxi Finewool (China); fw; orig. from Merino × Mongolian since 1920s; syn. *Shanxi Merino*; W.G. *Shansi*

shapo (Ladakh and Astor, Kashmir) = *Ovis vignei vignei* Blyth; var. of urial; syn. *O. orientalis vignei, Astor urial, Ladakh urial, urin*; ♂ is *sha*, ♀ is *sham*; not *shapu*. [Tibetan *sha-pho* = wild sheep]

Shekhawati, Sherawati: see Chokla

Shetland (Scotland); mw.m; Northern Short-tailed type; vars: improved—usu. white, mw, ♂ hd, ♀ pd; moorit—brown, hy-w, hd; occ.
black, grey, or piebald; BS 1927, reformed 1985; orig. (with English
Longwool) of Pettadale and (with Soay) of Castlemilk Moorit; declining
by crossing

Shevali: see Shafali

Shilluk: see Nilotic

Shimenzana: see Akeke Guzai

Shinwari: see Baluchi

Shirazi (Iran): see Grey Shirazi

Shirazi (USSR); grey (lethal when homozygous) var. of Karakul; not
Shiraz

Shirvan (E. and C. Azerbaijan, USSR); Caucasian Fat-tailed type,
sim. to Karabakh; off-white (73%), brown, black or pied; Russ.
Shirvanskaya; var: Gala; rare

Shkodra (N.W. Albania); cw.d.m; var. of Albanian Zackel; yellowish
face and legs; ♂ hd, ♀ pd; It. *Scutari*; not *Skutari*; = Zeta Yellow of
Yugoslavia

Shoa: see Menz

short-tailed: Europe: see Heath (some), Marsh and Northern Short-
tailed
Asia: see Erek (Turkmenistan), Tibetan, Nepalese and many Pakistan
breeds *e.g.* Baltistani, Bhadarwah, Buchi, Damani, Kachhi, Kaghani,
Kooka, Lohi, Poonchi, Thalli, and Indian breeds *e.g.* Bellary,
Chotanagpuri, Coimbatore, Deccani, Gurez, Karnah, Patanwadi,
Rampur Bushair, and most S. Indian Hair breeds

Shouyang (Shanxi, China); cw; local var. of Mongolian orig, sim. to
Taiku but smaller and with heavier ft; ♂ hd, ♀ pd; not *Showyang*

Shropshire (England); sw.m; Down type; black-brown face and legs; pd;
orig. early 19th c. from Southdown × heath sheep of Cannock Chase,
Longmynd, Morfe Common, *et al.*; named 1848, BS 1882, HB 1883;
orig. of Estonian Darkheaded; BS also in USA 1884 (HB 1889), HB
also in Australia, New Zealand, Canada

Shugor: see Ashgur

Shukria: see Baraka

Shumen (N.E. Bulgaria); m.w.d; coloured; ♂ hd, ♀ pd; ? orig. from
Tsigai; Bulg. *Mednochervena Shumenska* (= *copper-red Shumen*), Ger.
Schumener; not *Schumen, Shuman*; rare

Shumen Finewool: see North-East Bulgarian Finewool

[Siberian] (S. Siberia, USSR); cw; black; sft; Russ. *Sibirskaya*; local vars:
Minusinsk, Tuva, *et al.*; see also Buryat, Kulunda, Telengit

Siberian Merino (S.W. Siberia); var. of Soviet Merino; orig. in early 20th
c. from Mazaev and Novocaucasian Merinos × local coarsewooled

(Siberian and Kulunda) and Kazakh Fat-rumped; Russ. *Sibirskiĭ
Merinos*; syn. *Siberian Soviet Merino*
Siberian Rambouillet: see Altai
Sicilian, Siciliana locale: see Pinzirita
Sicilian Barbary (C. Sicily, Italy); cw-mw.m.d; usu. dark spots on face
    and legs; pd; lop ears; fat at base of tail; orig. from Tunisian Barbary
    × Pinzirita; BSd 1942, HB; It. *Barbaresca della Sicilia* or *Barbaresca
    siciliana*; syn. *Orecchiuta* (= *long-eared*), *Siciliana migliorata* (=
    improved Sicilian)
Sicilo-Sarde: see Tunisian milk sheep
Sidi Tabet cross (Tunisia); mw; black; orig. from Portuguese Black
    Merino × Thibar
Siena, Sienese: see Senese
Sikkim: see Bonpala
Silba: see Pag Island
Silesian (Lower Silesia, Poland); d.cw; Polish Longwool group, sim. to
    Bochnia; pd; orig. 1932-54 from East Friesian × local; Pol. *Owca
    śląska*
Silverdale: see Limestone
[Simmental]; part orig. of Swiss Black-Brown Mountain; sim. to Saanen
Sinkiang: see Xinjiang

Šipan: see Dubrovnik
Sipli (Bahawalpur, Pakistan); cw.m; white with brown or white face and
    ears; pd
Sisqueta: see Pallaresa
Sitia (E. Crete, Greece); m.d.cw; var. of Greek Zackel; white with black
    spots on head, belly and legs, often coloured or pied; ♂ hd, ♀ pd or
    hd; syn. *Metaxomalicha*; rare (by crossing with Sfakia and Psiloris)
Six point white: see Dutch Black Blaze
Sjenica (S.W. Serbia, Yugoslavia); m.d.cw; Pramenka type; usu. black
    around mouth, ears, and eyes; ♂ usu. hd, ♀ usu. pd; Serbo-cro.
    Sjenička, Peštersko-sjenička or *Sjeničko-pešterska*; syn. *Pešter*; var:
    Vasojević (Montenegro); not *Sjenichka*; being improved by Corriedale
    and Précoce
Sjeviot (Norway): see Cheviot
Skopelos (N. Sporades, Greece); d.m.mw; usu. white with black or
    brown spots on face and legs; ♂ usu. hd, ♀ usu. pd; ? orig. from Ayios
    Evstratios or from Chalkidiki; syn. *Glossa*; orig. of Kymi; not *Scopelos*
Skudde (orig. E. Prussia, now Germany); cw; Heath type; grey-white,
    occ. brown or black; ♂ hd, ♀ scurs or pd; rare
Skutari: see Shkodra

Skye Farm Romney (Hawkes Bay, New Zealand); m.lw; pd; orig. late
1960s from New Zealand Romney × (South Suffolk × Coopworth)
Śląska: see Silesian
Slovakian Merino (Czechoslovakia); fw.m; orig. from (Romney × North
Caucasus Mutton-Wool) × Czech Merino
snow sheep (N. and E. Siberia, USSR) = *Ovis nivicola*; grey-brown with
dark brown stripe across muzzle and white underparts, rump and
posterior face of legs; syn. *Asiatic bighorn, chubuku* (Yakutsk)
Soay (St Kilda, Scotland); w-hy; Northern Short-tailed type; dark brown
with pale belly or light brown; ♂ hd, ♀ hd or pd; feral on St Kilda;
also HB flocks in GB (mainland)
Socotra (Socotra I, Indian Ocean); earless
Sofia-Breznik: see Breznik
Sofia White (S.W. Bulgaria); var. of Breznik; black head and feet
Sohagi: see Saidi
[Soissonais] (Aisne, France); former var. of Précoce; HB 1925-29; Fr.
Mérinos précoce du Soissonais
Sokolki (Ukraine, USSR); fur, d; grey (lethal when homozygous) or occ.
black; ♂ hd, ♀ 20-25% hd; orig. from Russian Long-tailed; Russ.
Sokol'skaya; not *Sokol, Sokolka, Sokolov, Sokolsky*
Solčava (N. Slovenia, Yugoslavia); m.cw-mw.(d); Lop-eared Alpine
group; orig. in late 18th and early 19th c. from Bergamasca and
Paduan × local giving Seeland and Sulzbach vars of Carinthian;
Serbo-cro. *Solčavsko-Jezerska* or *Jezersko-Solčavska*, Ger. *Sulzbach-
Seeland* or *Seeland-Sulzbach*; syn. *Seeboden* (Ger. *Seebodner*); not
Solcava, Soltschava
Solognot (E. Loir-et-Cher, C. France); m.sw; sim. to Berrichon; greyish
with red-brown head and legs; pd; HB 1948, BS. [from Sologne]
[Solothurn]; brown var. of Jura
Solsonenca: see Ripollesa
Somali (Somalia; also E. Ethiopia and N. Kenya); m; white with black
head; hy; pd; fr; syn. *Berbera Blackhead, Blackheaded Somali* (It.
Pecora somala a testa nera), *Ogaden*; var: Toposa; orig. of Blackhead
Persian (S. Africa)
Somali Arab (coast of Somalia); cw-hy; white; pd; ft; ? orig. from
Radmani (Aden)
Somali Brasileiro: see Brazilian Somali
Somerset, Somerset Horn: see Pink-nosed Somerset
Somosierra Blond (N.E. Madrid, Spain); d.m.(cw); white with pale
brown face and legs; usu. hd; Sp. *Rubia di Somosierra*; syn. *Churra de
El Molar, Rubia de El molar, Rubia serrana*
Sonadi (S. Rajasthan and N. Gujarat, India); cw.d.m; sim. to Malpura
but smaller; light brown face, neck and legs; pd; very long ears; syn.

Chanothar (not *Chhanotar*)

Sopravissana (C. Apennines, esp. Latium and Umbria, Italy); fw-mw.d.m; ♂ hd, ♀ pd; orig. from Vissana crossed with Spanish Merino and Rambouillet in 18th and early 19th c. and improved by American and Australian Merinos in 20th c; HB 1942; syn. *Upper Visso*; former var: [Maremmana]

Souss (Morocco)

South African Merino (S. Africa); fw; orig. (1789 on) from Spanish, Saxony, Rambouillet and American Merinos but chiefly from Australian Merino; see also Döhne Merino, Letelle Merino, Multihorned Merino, Mutton Merino; HB 1906

South African Mutton Merino (S. Africa); fw.m; German Mutton Merino imported since 1932; BS 1947; Afrik. *Suid-Afrikaanse Vleismerino*; see also Walrich Mutton Merino

South Albanian; var. of Common Albanian

[Southam Nott] (Devon, England); orig. (+ Bampton Nott and × Leicester Longwool) of Devon Longwoolled; not *Southern Notts.* [nott = pd]

South Australian Merino; strongwool strain of Australian Merino; English Longwool blood 1840-70; inc. Bungaree Merino

[South Bulgarian Finewool] (S.C Bulgaria); orig. 1943-67 from Merino × Stara Zagora; syn. *Stara Zagora Finewool*; now inc. in Thrace Finewool

South Bulgarian Semifinewool; mw.m; orig. from Romney or North Caucasus × (German Mutton Merino and Caucasian × local)

South Country Cheviot: see Cheviot

[Southdale] (Middlebury, Vermont); m.w; pd; orig. 1930-43 from Southdown × Corriedale; crossed with Columbia to form Columbia-Southdale

[South Devon] (S. Devon and Cornwall, England); lw.m; English Longwool type, sim. to Devon Longwoolled but larger; pd; BS and HB 1904; syn. *South Dum*; combined with Devon Longwoolled to form Devon and Cornwall Longwool 1977

South Dorset Down (New Zealand); m.sw; orig. from Dorset Down × Southdown; BS

Southdown (Sussex, England); sw.m; Down type; grey-brown face and legs; pd; orig. from Sussex by selection 1780-1829; BS and HB 1892; basis of Down breeds; var: French Southdown; BS also in USA 1882, Australia, New Zealand 1923 (HB 1893), HB also in Canada

Southdown Norfolk: see Suffolk

South Dum: see South Devon

South-East Bulgaria Finewool: see Karnobat Finewool

Southern (W. Africa): see West African Dwarf

Southern Goat (Algeria): see Tuareg

Southern Karaman (S. Anatolia, Turkey); black var. of White Karaman

South Hampshire (New Zealand); orig. from Southdown × Hampshire; HB

SOUTH INDIA HAIR; m; inc. Ganjam, Godavari, Kenguri, Kilakarsal, Madras Red, Mandya, Marathwada, Mecheri, Nellore, Ramnad White, Tiruchy Black, Vembur; orig. of Jaffna (Sri Lanka)

South Kazakh Merino (Jambul to Kazalinsk, S. Kazakhstan, USSR); fw.m; orig. 1944-64 from Caucasian, Stavropol and Grozny 1942 × (Novocaucasian and Soviet Merino 1932 × Kazakh Fat-rumped); recog. 1966; HB; Russ. *Yuzhnokazakhskiĭ Merinos*; syn. *Aral* (Russ. *Priaral'skaya*)

South Madras (red): see Kilakarsal, Madras Red and Mecheri

South Moroccan (Morocco); hd; orig. from Tadla × Berber; vars: Rehamna-Sraghna and Zemrane

South Sudanese (Sudan S. of lat. 11° N); white usu. with black or tan patches; hy, ♂ usu. with ruff; hd or pd; syn. *Southern Sudan, Sudanese Maned*; vars: Mongalla, Nilotic, Nuba Maned

South Suffolk (Canterbury, New Zealand); m.sw; black face; orig. (1938 on) from Suffolk × Southdown crossed both ways and F₁ bred *inter se*; HB; syn. *South Suffolk Halfbred*

South Ural (Orenburg, USSR); fw.m; ♂ hd, ♀ pd; formed by combining Orenburg Finewool and October breed groups; recog. 1968; Russ. *Yuzhnoural'skaya*

South Wales Mountain (S.Wales); larger var. of Welsh Mountain with tan face, bare belly, and kempy (often red) fleece; BS late 1940s, HB; syn. *Glamorgan, Nelson*

South-West Longwool (England): see Dartmoor, Devon and Cornwall Longwool, and Whiteface Dartmoor

[Soviet Corriedale] (USSR); mw.m; orig. 1926-36 from Lincoln × Rambouillet; Russ. *Sovetskiĭ Korridel'*

Soviet Merino (USSR); fw.m; orig. in 20th c. (esp. 1925-46) from Mazaev and Novocaucasian Merinos improved by American Rambouillet, Askanian and Caucasian and other improved Merino breeds; named 1938; Russ. *Sovetskiĭ Merinos*; vars: North Caucasus, Siberian

Soviet Mutton-Wool (N. Caucasus, USSR); m.lw; pd; orig. from Karachai × finewool mated since 1950 to North Caucasus Mutton-Wool, Lincoln (and Liski) ♂♂; Russ. *Sovetskaya myaso-sherstnaya*; syn. (till 1985) *Mountain Corriedale* (Russ. *Gornyĭ Korridel'*)

Soviet Rambouillet: see Altai, Askanian, Caucasian

Spælsau (W. Norway); w.m; Northern Short-tailed type; usu. white, sometimes coloured; hd or pd; orig. from Old Norwegian with Icelandic and Faeroes blood; syn. *Old Norwegian Short Tail Landrace*;

HB. [= bobtail sheep]

Spagnola arianese: see Improved Ariano

Spancă (S. Romania); mw.d.m; F_1, Merino × Tsigai; selected F_2, F_3 and backcrosses called Danube Merino; not *Spanga*. [? = Spanish]

Spanish Ariano: see Improved Ariano

Spanish Churro (Duero valley, N.W. Spain); d.(m.cw); black eyes, ears, nose and feet; ♂ usu. hd, ♀ usu. pd; sim. to Lacho; BS; vars: Andalusian, Castilian, Sayaguesa, Tensina; orig. of Algarve Churro. [Sp. *churro* = rustic, coarsewooled]

Spanish Merino (Spain, esp. Extremadura, W. Andalucía and parts of Castille); fw.(m); white, also black var; ♂ occ. pd, ♀ usu. pd; BS 1982; former strains: Escurial, Guadalupe, Infantado, Negretti, Paular, Perales; migratory (*trashumante*) and non-migratory (*estante*) types; vars: Andalusian, Barros, Leonese, Serena, Serrana (Spanish Mountain Merino); orig. of Merino type; orig. (with Churro) of Entrefino

Spanish Mongrel (Italy): see Maremmana

Spanish Mountain: see Iberian

Spanish Mountain Merino (mts of Castille, C. Spain); var. of migratory Merino which has become non-migratory in its summer range; Sp. *Merino de montaña* or *Merina serrana*

Spanish Piebald: see Jacob

Speckled-face, Specklefaced Mountain (Wales): see Beulah Speckled Face, Welsh Hill Speckled Face

Sphakia: see Sfakia

Spiegel (S. Tyrol, Austria); former var. of Carinthian; black spectacles (*Nasenspiegel*); orig. (with Bergamasca) of Tyrol Mountain and of Pusterese (Italy); nearly extinct

Spotted: see Jacob

Sraghna, Srarhna: see Rehamna-Sraghna; not *Sghrana, Srarna*

Sredna Gora: see Panagyurishte

Sredna Gora Semifinewool (Bulgaria)

Srednoropodska: see Central Rodopi

Srem, Sremska: see Birka

Stara Zagora; var. of White South Bulgarian; Bulg. *Starozagorska*; rare

Stara Zagora Finewool: see Thrace Finewool

Stavropol (N. Caucasus, USSR); fw; orig. on Sovetskoe Runo state farm from Novocaucasian and Mazaev Merinos 1923, improved by American Rambouillet 1928, and Australian Merino 1936; recog. 1950; HB; Russ. *Stavropol'skaya* or *Stavropol'skaya poroda tonkorun-nykh ovets* (= *Stavropol breed of finewool sheep*); syn. *Stavropol Merino*

Steekhaar; kempy var. of Ronderib Africander. [= rough hair]

Steigar (Steigen, N. Norway); w.m; orig. 1940s from North Country Cheviot × local, recog. 1954; HB

[Steiner] (Steiner alps, Austria); former var. of Carinthian

Steinschaf (Tyrol, Austria); m.cw; small, prim. sim. to Bündner Oberland and to [Zaupel]; white, black, or grey with black head and legs; ♂ usu. hd, ♀ usu. pd; BS 1974; syn. *Pecora della Roccia* or *del Sasso* (Val Venosta, Italy), *Tiroler Steinschaf*; orig. (with Bergamasca) of Carinthian and Tyrol Mountain (Austria), Pusterese (Italy) and German Mountain (Germany); rare

Steppe Screwhorn: see Stogoš

Steppe Voloshian (N. Caucasus and S.W. Siberia, USSR); typical var. of Voloshian; ♂ usu. hd; lft.

Stepska vitaroga (Yugoslavia): see Stogoš

Stogoš (S. Banat, Yugoslavia); m.cw.d; Pramenka type; white, usu. with brown or yellow face and legs, occ. brown or black; ♂ vertical screw horns, ♀ pd; syn. *Rackulja, Stepska vitaroga* (= *Steppe screwhorn*), *Vlaška vitaroga* (= *Vlach screwhorn*)

Stogoşă (Romania); F₁, Tsigai × Ţurcana; syn. *Stogoman*; not *Stogoš, Stogosa, Stogosch, Stogoso*. [Rom. *stog* = with fleece in shape of hay cocks]

Stone's sheep (N.W. British Columbia, Canada) = *Ovis dalli stonei*; var. of Dall's sheep; black with white nose, rump and posterior face of legs; syn. *Stone sheep*

Stranja (S.E. Bulgaria); cw.m; Bulgarian Native; tan, black or speckled face, ears and legs; born black; ♂ hd, ♀ pd; Bulg. *Strandzhanska*; rare

Sudad: see Guirra

Sudan Desert (Sudan N. of lat. 12° N.); d.m; African Long-legged group; hy; usu. pd; lop ears; long fleshy tail; syn. *Amalé (It. Hamalé), Desert Sudanese, Drashiani, (It. Drasciani), Gash* (It. *Gasc*), *Kababish, North Sudanese*; vars: Ashgur, Beja, Dubasi, Watish; *cf.* Baraka (Eritrea)

Sudanese: see Dongola, South Sudanese, Sudan Desert, Zaghawa; It. *Sudanica*

Sudanese Maned: see South Sudanese

Sudanica: see Lop-eared Alpine, Sudanese

Sud de la Manche: see Avranchin

Suffolk (England); sw.m; Down type; black face and legs; pd; orig. from Southdown × Norfolk Horn in early 19th c; recog. 1810, named 1859, BS 1886, HB 1887; syn. *Blackface, Southdown Norfolk*; BS also in USA 1892, Australia, South Africa 1959 (HB 1906), HB also in Canada, France 1957, New Zealand

Suffolk Whiteface: see White Suffolk

Sulukol Merino (Kustanai, N.W. Kazakhstan, USSR); fw; orig. on Sulukol state farm from finewool × Kazakh Fat-rumped, selected since 1958 towards type with ⅝ Askanian blood; Russ. *Sulukol'skiĭ Merinos*; combined with Beskaragai Merino to form North Kazakh

Merino
Sulzbach, Sulzbach-Seeland: see Solčava

Šumava (Bohemia, Czechoslovakia); cw; Zackel type; sim. to Valachian but heavier and less coarse wool; white, usu. with colour on head and legs, also black or pied; ♂ hd, ♀ pd; Cz. *Šumavska*; syn. *Bohemian Land* (Cz. *Česká selská*, Ger. *Böhmerwald*); not *Shumava*; orig. of Improved Šumava; nearly extinct (name now used for Improved Šumava)

Sunnhordland: see Old Norwegian ('wild'); not *Sundhordland*

Sur; agouti (or golden) var. of Karakul

Surkhandarin (Kazakhstan, USSR); Karakul breed type; Russ. *Surkhandarinskiĭ porodnyi typ*

[Sussex] (England); syn. *Old Southdown*; orig. of Southdown

Sutherland Cheviot: see North Country Cheviot

[Svanka] (Svanetski mts, Georgia, USSR); cw; dark; ft; prolific

Svensk Lantras: see Swedish Landrace

Svishtov (N. Bulgaria); cw; Bulgarian Native, improved; pd; Bulg. *Svishtovska*, Ger. *Swistower*; not *Svistov*; rare

Svrljig (E. Serbia, Yugoslavia); m.d.cw; Pramenka type; black on head and legs, occ. all black; ♂ usu. hd, ♀ pd; Serbo-cro. *Svrljiška*; syn. *Gulijanska* (from Gulijan); being improved by Corriedale

Swaddle: see Swaledale

Swaledale (Pennines, England); cw.m; Blackfaced Mountain type; black face with grey-white muzzle; hd; BS, HB 1919; syn. *Swaddle*; orig. of Dales-Bred

Swazi: see Nguni

Swedish Fur Sheep (Sweden); pelt; var. of Swedish Landrace; grey; pd; orig. from Gotland selected for curl and colour; Swe. *Palsfår*

Swedish Landrace; m.w; orig. from Northern Short-tailed; Swe. *Svensk lantras*; syn. *Swedish Native*; inc. white Landrace breeds (Finewool and Rya) and fur breeds (Gotland and Swedish Fur)

Swifter (Netherlands); m; prolific; orig. 1971 at Swifter farm, University of Wageningen, from Texel × Flemish; not *Swift*

[Świniarka] (Poland); w.d; prim.; ♂ hd, ♀ pd; st; vars: Karnówka (white), Krukówka (black); orig. (with Romney) of Łowicz; not *Swinarka*. [Pol. *świnia* = pig]

Swiss Black-Brown Mountain (W. Switzerland); sw.m; pd; orig. 1938 by union of Frutigen, Jura, Roux-de-Bagnes, Saanen, and Simmental; Ger. *Schwarzbraunes Bergschaf* or *Gebirgsschaf*, Fr. *Brun noir du pays*, or *des alpes*, or *des montagnes*

Swiss Brownheaded Mutton (N. Switzerland); m.sw; pd; orig. 1938 from

Grabs + Oxford Down; Ger. *Braunköpfiges Fleischschaf*, Fr. *Mouton à viande à tête brune*; syn. *Improved Blackheaded Mutton-Wool* (Ger. *Veredeltes schwarzköpfiges Fleischwollschaf*), *Swiss Blackheaded Mutton*

Swiss White Alpine (Switzerland); m.sw; orig. (1936 on) from Swiss White Mountain with 50-75% Ile-de-France blood; Fr. *Blanc des Alpes*, Ger. *Weisses Alpenschaf*; syn. *West Swiss White* (Fr. *Blanc de la Suisse Occidentale*), *White Improved* (Ger. *Weisses Edelschaf*, Fr. *Blanc des Alpes amelioré*)

[Swiss White Mountain] (E. Switzerland); m.sw; Lop-eared Alpine type; pd; orig. 1929-38 from Württemberg Merino (Merinolandschaf) × native (Appenzell, Bündner Oberland, Oberhasli-Brienz, Schwyz, and Wildhaus); Fr. *Blanc des Montagnes*, Ger. *Weisses Gebirgs-* (or *Berg*) *Schaf*; syn. *Improved Whiteheaded Mountain* (Ger. *Veredeltes weissköpfiges Gebirgsschaf*); orig. (with Ile-de-France) of Swiss White Alpine and absorbed by it

Swistower: see Svishtov

Syrian: see Awassi

Syrmia: see Birka

[Tabasaran] (Dagestan, USSR); m.d.cw; Caucasian Fat-tailed type; brown or red (64%), or black (36%); often earless; ♂ hd or scurs, ♀ pd; Russ. *Tabasaranskaya*; syn. *Samur*; vars: Gedek, Kusman

Tabasco: see Pelibüey

Tacòla (N. Vercelli, Piedmont, Italy); m; var. of Biellese, smaller and with reduced ears; nearly extinct

Tadla (Morocco—plateaux of west); m.cw; white with coloured legs; hd; Fr. *Race des Plateaux de l'Ouest*; var: Beni Meskine; orig. (with Berber) of South Moroccan and Zaian

Tadmit (Algeria and W. Tunisia); m.mw; ♂ hd, ♀ pd; orig. from Algerian Arab, ? with Merino blood, *c*.1925; syn. *Queue fine de l'Ouest* (= *thin-tailed of the west*) (Tunisia)

Tafilalet: see D'man

Taiku (Shanxi, Hebei and Shaanxi, China); cw; sim. to Mongolian but smaller and with white face and sft; ♂ hd, ♀ pd; W.G. *T'ai-ku*

Taiz Red (Ta'izz, N. Yemen); m; brown or red; hy; pd; ft; syn. *Ganadi* (from Al Ganad) (not *Gainde, Gamdi*)

Tajik (Tajikistan, USSR); w.m; ♂ hd, ♀ pd; fr; orig. (1947-63) from Sary-Ja (and Lincoln) × Hissar, recog. 1963; Russ. *Tadzhikskaya*; syn. *Tajik Semicoarsewooled*

Talaverana (W. Toledo, Spain); m.mw.(d); Entrefino type; sim. to Mestizo Entrefino-fino; pd; orig. from Merino and Manchega beginning

in late 19th c. with some Merinolandschaf blood since 1960. [from
Talavera de la Reina]

Talschaf (Bulgaria): see Panagyurishte

Talybont Welsh (S.E. Breconshire, Wales); larger strain of Welsh
Mountain with tan face and longer kemp-free fleece

Tan (N. Ningxia and neighbouring areas, China); cw.m.pelt; white, usu.
with black or brown head and legs; ♂ hd, ♀ pd or scurs; sft; orig. from
Mongolian; syn. *Tan-yang* (= *Tan sheep*); not *Tang, Tanjan, Tanyan*

[Tanface] (Scotland and N. England); displaced by Blackfaced Mountain
(late 18th c. in N. Scotland); syn. *Dun, Dunface, Old Scottish Shortwool,
Scottish Soft-wool*; *cf.* Welsh Tanface

Tang: see Tan

Tanzania Long-tailed (Tanzania); m; African Long-fat-tailed type; various colours; hy; ♂ often hd, ♀ usu. pd; often earless; lft, sft, or lt;
sometimes tassels; syn. *Tanganyika Long-tailed, Ugogo*

Tanganyika Short-tailed: see Masai

Tanyan, Tan-yang: see Tan

Taraki: see Baluchi

Tarasconnais (C. and E. Pyrenees, France); m.mw; Central Pyrenean
group; white, coloured spots on head and legs now rare, occ. red,
brown or black; ♂ hd, ♀ hd or pd; BS 1975; syn. *Ariègeois* (from
Ariège), *Pyrénéen central à extremités tachetées*, or *charbonées* (= *with
spotted extremities*); = Aranesa (Spain). [from Tarascon]

Targhee (Idaho, USA); mw.m; pd; orig. (1926 on) from Rambouillet ×
(Lincoln × Rambouillet) + Rambouillet × [Corriedale × (Lincoln
× Rambouillet)]; BS 1951; not *Targee*. [Targhee National Forest]

Targhi, Targi, Targui: see Tuareg

Tarhumara (Mexico); var. of Criollo

Tarina (Taro, Emilia, Italy); local var. of Apennine

Tarrincha: see Churra da Terra Quente

Tarset (Mexico); m; Pelibüey (Tabasco) × Dorset

Tasmanian Merino; finewool strain of Australian Merino; orig. from
Saxony Merino imported 1830; syn. *fine-wool, Saxon*

Tatra; var. of Polish Zackel; hd

Tauferer: see Pusterese

Tauter (Tautra I, Trondheim fjord, Norway); sw; pd; orig. from British
breeds (? Ryeland) imported 1770-88, ? Merino blood; nearly extinct

Tavetsch: see Bündner Oberland

Tedesca di Pusteria: see Pusterese

Teeswater (Teesdale, Durham, England); English Longwool type sim.
to Lincoln; white or grey face; BS and HB 1949; syn. *Northern
Longwool*; orig. of Wensleydale

[Tekin] (Turkmenistan, USSR); var. of Turkmen Fat-rumped

Telangana: see Telingana

Telengit (Altai, Siberia, USSR); m.cw; sim. to Mongolian; usu. white with black or red head and neck, also black-pied or red; sft; Russ. *Telengitskaya*; syn. *Altai, Altaĭskaya*

Telingana (Hyderabad, Andhra Pradesh, India); cw.m; local var; usu. black; syn. *Navargade*; not *Telangana*

Temir; var. of Kazakh Fat-rumped; Russ. *Temirskaya*

Teng-Seemai, Tenguri: see Kenguri

Tensina (Tena, Huesca, Spain); m; var. of Spanish Churro

Terrincha: see Churra da Terra Quente

Testa rossa: see Comisana

Tête noire: see French Blackheaded

Tête rouge du Maine: see Rouge de l'Ouest

Teteven (Bulgaria); Bulg. *Tetevenska*; rare

Teutoburg: see German Blackheaded Mutton

Texel (Netherlands); m.lw; Marsh type; pd; orig. in late 19th and early 20th c. from Leicester Longwool, Lincoln, *et al.* × local (Old Texel); HB 1909; Du. *Texelaar, Texelse*; syn. *Improved Texel* (Du. *Verbeterde Texelse*); vars: Blue Texel, French Texel; orig. (with Flemish) of Swifter; BS in Ireland 1976, UK; HB also in W. Germany

Thai: see Kelantan

Thalli (Thal Desert, Punjab, Pakistan); cw.d.m; black, brown or pied head; pd; long or short ears; st; syn. *Buti, Chundi, Lessarkani, Porakani, Tilari*; not Thali, Thall

Thibar (Tunisia); mw; black, occ. with white spot on head or tail; orig. (1911 on) from Arles Merino × Tadmit; HB 1945; Fr. *Noir de Thibar*; syn. *Black Merino*; orig. of Sidi Tabet cross

Thônes-Marthod (Arly and Arc valleys, Savoy, France); m.cw; black spectacles, nose tip, ears and feet; hd; Fr. *Race de Thônes et de Marthod*; syn. *Mauriennais, St Jean de Maurienne* (Italy), *Savoyard*; cf. Savoiarda (Italy); rare

Thrace: see Kivircik

Thrace Finewool (Maritsa valley, S. Bulgaria); fw.m.d; orig. 1943-67 from Caucasian, Rambouillet and German Mutton Merino × South Bulgarian and Plovdiv-Purvomai, and inc. South Bulgarian Finewool; Bulg. *Trakiĭska t''nkorunna;* syn. *Maritsa Finewool* (Bulg. *Marishka t''nkorunna*), *Plovdiv Merino*

Thribble Cross (California, USA); mw; orig. (1903 on) from Delaine Merino × (Cotswold × American Merino). [= 3-way cross]

Thuvaramchambali: see Mecheri

Tian Shan argali: see arkhar

Tibegolian (E. Qinghai, S.W. Gansu and S. Ningxia, China); cw; sim. to Hetian; sometimes black head; hd; st. or sft; orig. from Mongolian

× Tibetan; syn. *Mongo-tibetan*; not now recog.

Tibetan (Qinghai-Tibet plateau, China, also N. Nepal, and N. Sikkim and Kameng, Arunachal Pradesh, India); m.cw.(pa); usu. black or brown head and legs; hd; st; syn. (Nepal) *Bhote, Bhotia* or *Bhyanglung*; vars (Tibet): mountain, plateau or grassland (largest), Yarlang Zangbo or valley (smallest) and Sanjiang; orig. of Qinghai Black Tibetan

Tien Shan: see Tyan Shan

Tiflis-Herik: see Tuj

Ṭigae, Ṭigai, Ṭigaia, Ṭigaie: see Tsigai

Tihama (coast of N. Yemen); m; white; hy; pd; ft.

Tilari: see Thalli

Timhadite (Middle Atlas, Morocco); m.cw; not *Timadhit, Timadit, Timahdit*; syn. *Azrov, Bekrit, El Hammam*

Tirahi (Kohat, Bannu and Peshawar, Pakistan); m.d.cw; light tan, brown or black; ft; syn. *Afridi, Parai*

Tiroler, Tirolese: see Tyrol Mountain

Tiruchy Black (Tiruchirapalli, Tamil Nadu, India); m.hr; South India Hair type; ♂ hd, ♀ pd; st; syn. *Tiruchy Karungurumbai*; not *Tiruch, Trichi, Trichy*

Tisqueta: see Pallaresa

Tjan Shan: see Tyan Shan

[Tlyarota] (Dagestan, USSR); var. of Avar; Russ. *Tlyarotinskaya*

Tom-Tom (Bahrain); prolific

Tong (N. Shaanxi, China); m.cw-mw; white; pd; tassels; large ft; orig. from Mongolian; W.G. *T'ung*; syn. *Tongyang* (= *Tong sheep*), *Tungchow*; not *Tung, Tunyang*; orig. (with Mongolian) of Lanzhou Large-tail

Tonguri: see Kenguri

Toposa (S.E. Sudan); var. of Somali with some Nilotic blood; white or white with black or brown on head; ♂ usu. hd, ♀ sometimes hd; fr; see also Murle

Torddu: see Badger Faced Welsh Mountain

Torfschaf: see Peat

Torki: see Turki

Toronké (Senegal and Mali); var. of Fulani; white or spotted; syn. *Fouta Toro, Large Peul*

Touabire (W. Africa); m; usu. white (also pied), short-haired var. of Maure; syn. *Tuabir, White Arab, White Maure*

Touareg: see Tuareg

Toulousain, Toulouse: see Lauraguais

Tounfite (Morocco); var. of Berber; white, occ. with black marks on head and body; hd

Tousint; var. of Beni Guil in Moulouya valley; not *Tounsint, Tousimet*

Trangie Fertility (NSW, Australia); strain of Australian Merino by selection of Peppin flock for multiple births with some Booroola blood in 1965; ♂ usu. hd, ♀ hd or pd

Transbaikal Finewool (Tsitsin, Siberia, USSR); fw.m; orig. 1927-56 from local coarsewool (Buryat) graded to Précoce, Novocaucasian and Siberian Merinos (1927-30) and later to Altai and Grozny; HB; Russ. *Zabaĭkal'skaya tonkorunnaya*

Transcaspian urial: see arkal

Transdon (USSR); var. of Voloshian; usu. pd; lft; Russ. *Krupnaya zadonskaya* (= *large Transdon*)

Transvaal Kaffir: see Bapedi

Transylvanian Merino (N.W. Romania); fw; orig. from Hungarian Combing Wool Merino; Rom. *Merinos transilvănean*; syn. *Merinos de vest* (= *western Merino*)

Transylvanian Zackel: see Turcana

Travnik, Travnicka: see Vlašić

Trichi, Trichy: see Tiruchy

Trièves: see French Alpine

[Trun] (C. Calvados, N. France); m.w; red head and legs; ? orig. from Cauchois × Solognot; Fr. *Trunier* or *Trunois*; extinct in 1960s

Tsigai (S.E. Europe); mw-cw.d.m; dirty-white and black vars; white var. may have white face (Rom. *Ţigaie bela*), red face (*Ţigaie ruginie*) or black face (*Ţigaie bucălae*); ♂ hd, ♀ pd; Rom. *Ţigaie*, Pol., Hung., and Serbo-cro. *Cigaja*, Russ. *Tsigaiskaya*, Ger. *Zigaja*, Fr. *Tzigaïa*; orig. of Ruda type; orig. (with Replyan) of Mountain Tsigai (Bulgaria); not *Tsigaia, Tsigay*; vars in USSR: Azov, Crimean and Transvolga

Tsushka: see Chushka

Tswana (Botswana and S.W. Zimbabwe); African Long-fat-tailed type; often white or black-and-white; syn. *Setswana*

Tuabir: see Touabire

Tuareg (Sahara); m; Sahel type, sim. to Maure; white, pied, or fawn; ♂ hd, ♀ pd; Fr. *Touareg*; sing. *Targ(u)i*; syn. *Southern Goat* (Algeria) (pd)

Tucur (Lasta, Amhara, Ethiopia); cw-hy; var. of Abyssinian with woolly undercoat; white, brown or pied

[Tudelana] (Navarre, Spain); var. of Castilian

Tuj (Çildir, N.E. Turkey); m.cw.d; sometimes dark marks round eyes and on feet; ♂ hd, ♀ pd; sft. or fr; orig. from Tushin (Georgia); syn. *Çıldır, Georgian* (Turk. *Gürcü*), *Kars, Kesik, Tiflis-Herik* (Turk. *Herigi*), *Tunç*

Tukidale (Hawkes Bay, New Zealand); cw.m; hairy strain of New Zealand Romney with dominant gene N^t; ♂ hd, ♀ pd; orig. 1966 on property of M. Coop, Tuki Tuki; *cf.* Drysdale; BS in Australia

Tunç: see Tuj
Tung, T'ung, Tungchow, Tungyang: see Tong
Tunis: see American Tunis
Tunisian Barbary (Tunisia); m.cw; white with black or red-brown head, occ. black or white; ♂ hd, ♀ usu. pd; ft; HB and BSd 1947; Fr. *Barbarin*; syn. (Algeria) *Constantinois, Moutons de l'Oued Souf, Tunisien*; orig. of Campanian Barbary, Sicilian Barbary
Tunisian milk sheep (Tunisia); d.m.cw; white, black, brown or grey; ♂ hd, ♀ usu. pd; orig. from Sardinian (chiefly) and Sicilian breeds; syn. *Sardinian, Sicilo-Sarde*
Tunjan, Tunyan, Tunyang: see Tong
Turbary: see Peat
Ţurcana (Romania); d.cw; Zackel type; black, grey, or white; Hung. *Erdelyi Racka*; syn. *Romanian Zackel, Transylvanian Zackel*; not *Czurkan, Turkana, Tzourcana, Zurkana*; grey var. (*brumării*) used for crossing with Karakul in N.E. [= Zackel]
Turchessa: see Campanian Barbary
Turkana: see Ţurcana
Turki (Gorgan, N.E. Iran); m.cw; black around eyes; pd; ft; not *Torki, Turkey, Turky*
Turki (N.E. Afghanistan); hy.m; usu. brown (yellowish to black); ♂ usu. pd, ♀ pd; fr; tassels common; very large
Turkish Brown: see Red Karaman
Turkish Merino (Turkey); vars: Central Anatolian Merino and Karacabey Merino (*q.v.*)
[Turkmen Fat-rumped] (Turkmenistan, USSR); cw; usu. grey; Russ. *Turkmenskaya kurdyuchnaya*; vars: Iomud, Tekin
Turolense (Teruel, Aragon, Spain); small var. of Aragonese with less wool
Tushin (Georgia, USSR); Caucasian Fat-tailed type; hd; lft. or sft; Russ. *Tushinskaya*; not *Tushetian, Tushino*; vars: Budiani and Pampara; orig. (with finewool) of Georgian Finewool and Georgian Semifinewool; orig. of Tuj (Turkey)
[Tuva]; var. of Siberian; white with black head, or pied
Twisted Horn: see Zackel
Txisquet: see Pallaresa
Tyan Shan (Kirgizia, USSR); lw.m; orig. 1938-50 from Précoce, Novocaucasian Merino, and Württemberg Merino × Kirgiz Fat-rumped, crossed with Lincoln since 1950; recog. 1966; Russ. *Tyanshanskaya*; syn. *Tien Shan*
Tyrol Mountain (Tyrol, Austria, and Bolzano, Italy); cw.m; Lop-eared Alpine group, sim. to Carinthian but better wool, white face, and longer ears; occ. pied or black; ♂ hd, ♀ pd; orig. from Bergamasca ×

Spiegel var. of Carinthian; Ger. *Tiroler Bergschaf*, It. *Tirolese della Montagna* or *delle Rocce*; syn. *Bergschaf, Carinthian Mountain* (Carinthia), *Tiroler, Val Senales* (It.) or *Schnalser* (Ger.), *Val d'Ultimo* (It.) or *Ultnerschaf* (Ger.); cf. German Mountain (Germany)

Tzigae, Tzigai, Tzigaia, Tzigaya: see Tsigai

Tzourcana, Tzurckana, Tzurkana: see Ţurcana

Uchum; larger var. of Krasnoyarsk Finewool; Russ. *Uchumskaya*

Uda (N. Nigeria, Niger, Chad, and N. Cameroon); var. of Fulani; front half black (or brown), back half white; ♂ hd, ♀ pd; syn. *Bali-Bali* (Niger), *Bororo* (Chad), *Houda, Louda, North Nigerian Fulani, Ouda, Pied*

udad: see aoudad

Uggowitz: see Kanaltaler

Ugogo: see Tanzania Long-tailed

Ujumqin (Inner Mongolia, China); larger var. of Mongolian

Ukrainian Mountain (W. Ukraine, USSR); cw.m; breed group; orig. 1950 from Tsigai × local Carpathian Mountain; Russ. *Ukrainskaya gornaya porodnaya gruppa*

Ultimo: see Tyrol Mountain

Ultnerschaf: see Tyrol Mountain

Upper Visso: see Sopravissana

[Urbascia] (Calabria, Italy); dark brown or black var. of Calabrian (now Sciara)

Uri: see Schwyz

urial (C. Asia—vars in Kashmir, Afghanistan, Punjab, N. Baluchistan and S. Russian Central Asia) = *Ovis vignei* Blyth; intermediate between argali and red sheep (sometimes used to inc. latter); shades of red-brown with pale underparts; ♂ and ♀ hd; st. (up to 10cm); syn. *Ovis orientalis* Gmelin, *vignei* section; vars inc. arkal, gad, shapo, *q.v.*; orig. of domestic sheep, *Ovis 'aries'* Linnaeus; not *oorial*

urin: see shapo

Urner Landschaf: see Schwyz

Uruguayan Criollo (Uruguay); cw; white; hd (4 in ♂); selected by A.G. Gallinal, San Pedro, Cerro Colorado; rare

Ushant (Brittany, France); m.cw; brown, black or white; dwarf; ♂ hd; BS 1977; Fr. *Ouessant*; syn. *Breton Dwarf*; now on mainland only (Pays de Loire); rare

Ussy: see Awassi

Utegangarsau: see Old Norwegian

Uzbek (Tajikistan): see Hissar

Uzbek Mutton-Wool (Uzbekistan, USSR); m.w; black spots on head;

pd; orig. since 1955 from Lincoln × (Caucasian and Lincoln × Jaidara)
Uzemchin (Mongolia); var. of Mongolian

Vadhiyari: see Patanwadi
Vagas (Poland): see Pomeranian
Vagas, Vagaskaya (USSR): see Voloshian
Valachian (E. Moravia and Slovakia, Czechoslovakia); d.m.cw; Zackel type; white or black; ♂ hd, ♀ usu. pd; Cz. *Valašská*; syn. *Wallachian*; orig. of Improved Valachian; nearly extinct
Valachian, Valahian, Valahskaya, Valakhian (USSR): see Voloshian
Valais Blacknose (Switzerland); cw.m; hd; Fr. *Valais nez noir*, Ger. *Walliser Schwarznasenschaf*; syn. *Blacknosed Swiss, Visp, Visperschaf*
Val Badia: see Pusterese
Valdichiana: see Chianina
Val di Pusteria: see Pusterese
Valdrôme: see Préalpes du Sud
Val d'Ultimo: see Tyrol Mountain
Valle Aurina: see Pusterese
Valle del Belice (Sicily, Italy); d; orig. from Pinzirita, Comisana and Sardinian
Valley: see Kashmir Valley
Val Senales: see Tyrol Mountain
Vandor (S. Africa); orig. by C.J. van Vuuren of Zingfontein, near Philipstown, from Dorset Horn × Van Rooy. [*Van* Rooy—*Dor*set]
Van Rooy (Orange Free State, S. Africa); m; all white; hy; pd; small fr; orig. in 20th c. by J. van Rooy from Blackhead Persian × (Rambouillet × Ronderib Africander); BS 1948; Afrik. *Van Rooy-Persie*; syn. *Van Rooy White Persian*
Varesina (Varese, Lombardy, Italy); m.cw; Lop-eared Alpine group; sim. to or var. of Bergamasca; pd; disappearing by crossing with Bergamasca and Biellese
Var Merino: see Arles Merino
Varzese (Varzi, Emilia, Italy); local var. of Apennine
Vasca Carranzana (Basque provinces, Spain); d.m.cw; head and legs shades of reddish-yellow, fleece white; ♂ hd or pd, ♀ pd; Basque *Selay ardiga* (= *meadow sheep*); syn. *Carranzana* (from Carranza), *Vasca* (= *Basque*); = Basco-Béarnais of France
Vasojević (Lim valley, N.E. Montenegro, Yugoslavia); now var. of Sjenica (by grading); Serbo-cro. *Vasojevička*
Veglia: see Krk
Velay Black (Haute-Loire, C. France); m.mw; Central Plateau type;

black with white spot on forehead and white tail tip; pd; lt; BS 1931;
Fr. *Noir du Velay*; syn. *Bourbonnais, Noir de Bains*
Veluwe Heath; var. of Dutch Heath; ♂ scurred or pd, ♀ pd; lt; Du.
Veluwse Heideschaap; rare
Vembur (Tirunelveli, S. Tamil Nadu, India); m; South India Hair type;
white with red or fawn spots; ♂ hd, ♀ pd; st; syn. *Karandhai*; not
Bembur
Vendéen (Vendée, W. France); m.w; grey head and legs; BS 1967; BS
also GB
Venezuelan Criollo (W. Venezuela mts); var. of Criollo; sometimes
coloured or spotted face; ♂ hd or pd, ♀ pd
Veredeltes: see Improved
Vermont Merino; var. of American Merino (A type); HB 1879; nearly
extinct
Versilia: see Massese
Viat: see Vyatka
Vicanere: see Bikaneri
Vicatana: see Ripollesa
Vicentina (Vicenza, Venetia, Italy); var. of Lamon with finer wool; syn.
di Foza or *Fodata*; nearly extinct
Victoria Merino = Australian Merino in Victoria
Vigatana: see Ripollese
Virgin Island White (British and U.S. Virgin Is); m; prolific; American
Hair sheep group; occ. tan or pied; pd; mane in ♂; syn. *St Croix, White
Virgin Islander*; orig. of Katahdin
Visp, Visperschaf: see Valais Blacknose
Vissana (Visso, C. Apennines, Italy); m.d.cw; Apennine group; occ.
black or pied; ♂ usu. pd, ♀ pd; orig. (with Merino) of Sopravissana;
rare
Vlakhiko; mountain vars of Greek Zackel; inc. Arvanitovlach, Boutsiko,
Drama Native, Epirus, Grammos, Karakachan, Krapsa, Moraitiko;
syn. *Vlach, Vlahiko*
Vlashka: see Karakachan
Vlašić (Yugoslavia); var. of Bosnian Mountain; Serbo-cro. *Vlašićka*; syn.
Travnik (Serbo-cro. *Travnicka*); subvar: Dub
Vlaška vitoroga: see Stogoš
Vogan (Togo); m; red- or black-pied or brown-and-black; hy; orig. from
West African Dwarf × Sahelian
Vojvodina Merino (N.E. Yugoslavia); fw.m; ♂ usu. hd, ♀ pd; orig. from
Hungarian and other Merinos in 19th c; Serbo-cro. *Vojvodanski
Merino*; syn. *Domaći tip merina, Yugoslav Merino*
Volgograd (N.E. Volgograd, USSR); m.fw; ♂ usu. pd, ♀ pd; orig.
(1932-78) from Novocaucasian Merino and Précoce × Kazakh and

Astrakhan Fat-rumped, transferred to Romashkovski state farm in 1945 and mated to Caucasian and Grozny ♂♂; recog. as breed group 1963, as breed 1978; Russ. *Volgogradskaya*; syn. *Romashkovski* (Russ. *Romashkovskaya*)

[Volokolamsk] (Moscow, USSR); m.sw; crossbred group (1936 on) from (Hampshire Down × Tsigai) × Northern Short-tailed

Voloshian (Ukraine to Urals and Caucasus, USSR); m.cw; ? orig. from Zackel with ft. blood; white or black; ♂ hd or pd, ♀ pd; lt-lft; Russ. *Valakhskaya* or *Voloshskaya*; syn. *Vagas*(?), *Valachian*, *Valahian*, *Valakhian*, *Volosh, Walachian, Wallachian Zackel, Woloschian*; vars: Carpathian Mountain, Pyrny, Steppe (Caucasus and Siberia), Transdon; orig. of Kuchugury; rare

Voronezh, Voronezhskaya: see Kuchugury

Vrin: see Bündner Oberland

Vyatka (Nolinsk, Kirov, and Gorodets, Gorki, USSR); m.fw; orig. 1936-56 from 2 or 3 crosses of Rambouillet or Précoce on Northern Short-tailed (Nolinsk); Russ. *Vyatskaya, V. myasosherstnaya* (= *mutton-wool*) or *V. tonkorunnaya* (= *finewool*); inc. Improved Gorodets (Russ. *Uluchshennaya gorodetskaya*); not *Viat*

Wakhan Gadik (Afghanistan); var. of Gadik; usu. white

Walachian (Czechoslovakia): see Valachian

Walachian (USSR): see Voloshian

Walcheren Milk, Walcherse melkschaap: see Zeeland Milk

Waldschaf: see Bavarian Forest

Wallachian (Czechoslovakia): see Valachian

Wallachian (USSR): see Voloshian

Walliser Schwarznasen: see Valais Blacknose

Walrich Mutton Merino (S. Africa); fw.m; orig. by *Wal*ter A. Higgs of *Rich*mond, Zastron since 1930 from pd Précoce × South African Merino; BS 1960, recog. 1965; Afrik. *Walrich Vleis Merino*

Wanganella: see Peppin

Waralé (Senegal); hy,m; orig. (1975 on) from Touabire × Fulani at Agric. Res. Institute, Dahra

Warhill (USA); orig. from Merino, Columbia, Corriedale, Panama, and Rambouillet

Waridale (NSW, Australia); fw.m; orig. at New England Univ., Armidale, in 1970s from medium-wool Merino × Border Leicester and Poll Dorset; now 25% B.L., 25% P.D., 50% Merino

Warton Crag: see Limestone

Watish (Gezira, Sudan); var. of Sudan Desert; white

Waziri (Waziristan, N.W. Pakistan); cw.m; black, brown or spotted head, occ. also body; ♂ usu. pd, ♀ pd; lop ears; ft.

Weiladjo: see Bornu

Welsh Half-bred (Wales); m.w; Border Leicester × Welsh Mountain, 1st cross; BS 1955

Welsh Hill Speckled Face (mid Wales); derivative of Welsh Mountain with larger size, finer fleece and speckled face; ♂ hd or pd, ♀ pd; BS

Welsh Masham (Wales); Teeswater (or Wensleydale) × Welsh Mountain (or Speckle-Faced), 1st cross

Welsh Mountain; w.m; white or light tan face; ♂ hd, ♀ pd; orig. from Welsh Tanface; BS 1905, HB 1906; inc. Pedigree (improved) and Hill Flock sections; colour var: Badger Faced Welsh Mountain; local strains: Cardy and Talybont; derived breeds: Black Welsh Mountain, South Wales Mountain, Welsh Hill Speckled Face; see also Beulah Speckled Face; part orig. of Llŷn

Welsh Mule (Wales); Bluefaced Leicester × Welsh Mountain, Welsh Hill Speckled Face, Beulah Speckled Face or Brecknock Hill Cheviot, 1st cross; developed 1970s, BS 1979

Welsh Oldenbred (England); m; British Oldenburg × Welsh Mountain, 1st cross; see also Greyface Oldenbred

[Welsh Tanface] (Wales); orig. of Welsh Mountain; *cf.* Tanface (Scotland)

Wensleydale (N. Yorkshire, England); lw.m; English Longwool type; blue face and legs; pd; orig. *c.*1839-60 from Leicester Longwool ram 'Bluecap' × Teeswater; named 1876, BS and HB 1890; syn. *Mugs, Wensleydale Blueface, Wensleydale Longwool, Yorkshire-Leicester* (Scotland); HB also in Canada; rare

Wera: see Bangladeshi

West African: see Macina (wooled), Sahel type and West African Dwarf (hairy); syn. *Guinea*

West African Dwarf (coast of W. and C. Africa); m; from Senegal to Nigeria, white usu. with black patches, occ. black; in W. of C. Africa, Cameroon to Angola, black, pied, tan with black belly and tricolour also common; ♂ hd, ♀ usu. pd; hy, ♂ throat ruff and mane; trypanotolerant; syn. *Cameroons Dwarf, Djallonké, Fouta Djallon* or *Futa Jallon, Guinean, Kirdi, Kirdimi* or *Lakka* (Chad), *Nigerian Dwarf, Pagan, Southern, West African Maned*; inc. Dwarf Forest type in S. and larger Savanna type in N. of W. Africa

West African Long-legged: see Sahel type

West African Maned: see West African Dwarf

West Country Cheviot (S.W. Scotland); strain of Cheviot; ♂ often hd; syn. *Lockerbie Cheviot*

West Country Down: see Dorset Down

Western (USA): see Whiteface Western

Western, Western Horn (England): see Wiltshire Horn

Western Thrace: see Kivircik

West Friesian: see Friesian

West Indian: see Bahama Native, Barbados Blackbelly, Virgin Island White

West Kazakhstan Mutton-Wool (W. Kazakhstan, USSR); m.mw; orig. since 1948 from (Stavropol × Lincoln) × (Tsigai × Précoce × local cw.); bred *inter se* since 1952; Russ. *Zapadnokazakhstanskaya myasosherstnaya*

West Pyrenean (France): see Pyrenean Dairy

West Stara Planina (Bulgaria); m.w.d; usu. white often with black spots on face and legs; Bulg. *Zapadnostaraplaninska*; rare

West Swiss White: see Swiss White Alpine

White Arab (W. Africa): see Touabire

White Bororo: see Bornu

White Dorper (Transvaal, S. Africa); m; all white var. of Dorper; hy; usu. pd; orig. (1946 on) from Dorset Horn × Blackhead Persian at Pretoria; BS 1960; syn. *Dorsian, Dorsie*

Whiteface Dartmoor (Devon, England); m.lw; English Longwool type; occ. speckled face; ♂ hd or pd, ♀ pd; orig. *c.*1900 from Leicester Longwool × original Dartmoor; revived by BS 1950, HB 1951; syn. *Widecombe Dartmoor, White Face D, White-Faced D.*

Whitefaced Maine: see Maine à tête blanche

Whitefaced Woodland (S. Pennines, England); cw; ♂ hd, ♀ pd; sim. to Limestone; BS 1986; syn. *Penistone, Woodland Whiteface, Woodlands Horned*; not *Whiteface Woodlands*; rare

Whiteface Western (USA); whitefaced ewes of wool breeds from western states, usu. grade Rambouillet, or various mixtures of Rambouillet with Merino, Columbia, Panama or Corriesdale; syn. *Western, Whiteface*

White Fulani: see Bornu, Yankasa

Whiteheaded German, Whiteheaded Mutton, Whiteheaded Oldenburg: see German Whiteheaded Mutton

Whiteheaded Maine: see Maine à tête blanche

White Karaman (C. Anatolia, Turkey); m.d.cw; black on nose and occ. round eyes; ♂ usu. pd, ♀ pd; Turk. *Ak-Karaman*; syn. (Syria) *Barazi* (*Barasi, Brazi, Brézi* or *Parasi*), *Garha* (*Agrah, Akrah, Gargha, Guerha* or *Karha*) or *Salamali*; not *Caraman, Karamane, Karman, Kirmani*; vars: Kangal, Karakaş and Southern; Makui (Iran) is sim.; see also Red Karaman

White Klementina (Bulgaria); w.d; orig. from White Karnobat 1910 and Romanian Tsigai 1916 with some Merino blood, at state farm Klementina (now G. Dimitrov) near Plovdiv; Bulg. *Byala* (or *Bela*) *Klementinska*

White Maure: see Touabire

White Mountain: see German Mountain

White Persian: see Van Rooy

White South Bulgarian (Bulgaria); w.d.m; local Bulgarian Native improved by Tsigai; ♂ hd; lop ears; vars inc. Plovdiv-Purvomai and Stara Zagora; Bulg. *Byala yuzhnob"lgarska*

White Suffolk (NSW, Australia); m.w; orig. (1977 on) from Poll Dorset × Suffolk and Border Leicester × Suffolk, F_2 selected for white face; BS; syn. *Suffolk Whiteface, White-faced Suffolk*

White Swiss: see Swiss White

White Wooled Mountain (Orange Free State, S. Africa); m.cw; ♂ usu. hd, ♀ usu. pd; orig. by A.D. Wentworth, Trompsburg, from German Mutton Merino × (Dorset Horn × Blackhead Persian, 1942)

White Woolless (Brazil): see Brazilian Woolless

Wicklow Cheviot (Ireland); strain of North Country Cheviot by grading of Wicklow Mountain; BS and HB 1943; syn. *Irish Shortwool, Wicklow*

Widecombe Dartmoor: see Whiteface Dartmoor

Wielkopolska (Poland); m.w; orig. from Poznań × Poznań Corriedale

wild: see aoudad, argali, bharal, bighorn, Dall's, mouflon, red, snow, urial

[Wildhaus] (Switzerland); syn. *East Swiss, St Gallen*; orig. (with Oxford Down) of Grabs and (with Württemberg Merino) of Swiss White Mountain

Willamette (Oregon, USA); m.mw; usu. pd; orig. (1952 on) in Willamette valley by Oregon State Univ. from Cheviot × Columbia and Dorset Horn × Columbia crossed reciprocally and selected for weight and score

[Wilstermarsch] (Holstein, Germany); d.m.w; Marsh type; pd; st; syn. *Wilster-Dithmarscher*

Wiltiper (Hartley-Gatooma, Zimbabwe); m; usu. black, also white or brown; hy; hd or pd; orig. (1946 on) from Wiltshire Horn × Blackhead Persian. [*Wilt*shire *Per*sian]

Wiltshire Horn (England, now chiefly Anglesey and Northants); m; hd; woolless, *i.e.* very short shedding fleece; BS and HB 1923; obs. syn. *Old Wiltshire Horned, Western, Western Horn*; orig. (+ Berkshire Knott and × Southdown) of Hampshire Down; not *Wiltshire Horned*; BS also in Australia, USA

Woila (Cameroon); var. of Fulani

Woloschian: see Voloshian

Woodlands Horned, Woodland Whiteface: see Whitefaced Woodland

Wooled Africander: see Bezuidenhout Africander

Wooled Persian (S. Africa); m.cw; usu. brown; pd; ft; orig. from Arabi imported from Iran by Moss and Wardrop *c*.1915; syn. *Russian Perseair, Persian Red*

Woolless (Brazil): see Brazilian Woolless
Woozie: see Hu
Wrzosówka (Białystok, Poland); cw.pelt; grey with black head; ♂ hd, ♀
  pd; st; syn. *Polish Heath*; not *Wrzozowka*; being improved by Romanov;
  cf. Heidschnucke; rare
Wu: see Hu
*Württemberg, Württemberg Bastard, Württemberger, Württemberg
  Improved Land, Württemberg Merino*: see Merinolandschaf; not *Wurt-
  emburg*
Wushing, Wusih, Wuxi: see Hu; not *Woozie*

Xinjiang Finewool (W. Xinjiang, China); fw.m; orig. since 1935 from
  Kazakh Fat-rumped and Mongolian ♀♀ with Novocaucasian Merino
  and Précoce ('plickus') ♂♂; W.G. *Hsin-Chiang*, Russ. *Sin'tszyanskaya*;
  syn. *Sinkiang Fine-wool, Sinkiang Merino*; not *Sintsiang*

Yalag: see Kenguri
Yankasa (N.C. Nigeria); var. of Fulani; white with black eyes and nose;
  ♂ maned; syn. *Hausa, White Fulani, Y'ankasa*. [Hausa = local]
Yazdi (Iran): see Baluchi
Yemeni (N. Yemen); m; pd; often earless; ft; see Dhamari, Mareb White,
  Taiz Red and Tihama (hy), and Ainsi, Amran Black, Amran Grey,
  Sana'a White and Yemen White (cw)
Yemen White (E. and N.E. of N. Yemen); m.cw; pd; ft.
Yorkshire Cross: see Masham
[Yorkshire Halfbred] (Yorkshire Wolds, England); Suffolk × Leicester
  Longwool, 1st cross
Yorkshire-Leicester: see Wensleydale
Yugoslav Merino: see Vojvodina Merino
Yugoslav Zackel: see Pramenka

Zabaĭkal'skaya: see Transbaikal
ZACKEL (S.E. Europe); cw.d.m; usu. white, also black, brown or pied; ♂
  hd (long spiral), ♀ hd or pd; usu. lt; inc. Albanian, Bulgarian,
  Greek, Karakachan (Macedonia), Moscia (Italy), Polish, Pramenka
  (Yugoslavia), Racka (Hungary), Šumava and Valachian (Czechoslo-
  vakia), Ţurcana (Romania), Voloshian (USSR); Pol. *Cakiel*; syn. *Prong
  Horn, Screw Horn, Twisted Horn*; not *Zakel*. [Ger. *Zacke* = prong,
  referring to straight horns of Racka]
Zadonskaya: see Transdon
Zaghawa (N.W. Darfur, Sudan); black; hy; ♂ hd, ♀ pd; = Black Maure

(Chad)

Zaïan (Khenifra, Morocco); var. of Tadla with Berber blood

Zaïre Long-legged (Kibali-Ituri, N.E. Zare); African Long-legged group; white or brown pied; hy; ♂ hd, ♀ pd; lop ears; st; syn. *Congo Long-legged*; see also Baluba

Zakynthos (Ionian Sea, Greece); m.d.(cw); white, occ. black spots on head; ♂ hd or pd, ♀ pd; ? orig. from Bergamasca; It. *Zante*; rare

Zandi (Qom, Iran); black var. of Grey Shirazi

Zandir: see Çandır

Zante: see Zakynthos

[Zaupel] (S. and C. Germany); cw; sim. to Steinschaf; orig. of Deutsches Landschaf (and hence Württemberg Merino) and of German Mountain

Zeeland Milk (Walcheren, Zeeland, Netherlands); d; prolific; Marsh type; rat tail; Du. *Zeeuwse Melkschaap*; syn. *Walcherse Melkschaap* (*Walcheren Milk sheep*); rare

Zel (Mazandaran, N. Iran); d.cw.m; white, sometimes with colour on head and legs, sometimes all black or brown, or pied; ♂ hd, ♀ pd; syn. *Chiva, Iran Thin-tailed, Mazandarani, Persian Thin-tailed*

Żelazna (Poland); Polish Lowland group; orig. from Polish Merino × (Leicester Longwool × Łowicz); Pol. *Żeleżnieńska*. [Żelazna Exp. Farm]

Zembrane: see Zemrane

Zemmour (N.W. Morocco); m.cw; Atlantic Coast type; white with pale brown face; ♂ hd, ♀ pd

Zemrane; var. of South Moroccan with more Berber blood than Rehamna-Sraghna; not *Zembrane*

Zenith (Victoria, Australia); mw; pd; orig. 1947 by L.L. Bassett of Donald from Merino (predominant) and Lincoln; BS 1955; rare

Zenu: see Zunu

Zeta Yellow (S. Montenegro, Yugoslavia); d.m.cw; Pramenka type; brownish-yellow head and legs; Serbo-cro. *Zetska Žuja*; *cf.* Shkodra (Albania)

Zigai, Zigaia, Zigaja, Zigaya: see Tsigai

Zimbabwe: see Sabi

[Zillertal (Tyrol, Austria); local var.

Zlatusha (N. and S.W. Bulgaria); mw; orig. 1965-67 from German Mutton Merino and Merinolandschaf × Sofia White

Zoulay (Upper Moulouya valley, Morocco); orig. from Tousint × Berber; syn. *Berber à laine Zoulai, Mouton de montagne à laine Zoulai*

Zucca Modenese (Emilia, Italy); d.m.cw; Apennine group; pd; Roman nose; nearly extinct

Zulu: see Nguni

Zunu (Angola); hy; lt; syn. *Goitred, Zenu*

Zurkana: see Ţurcana

Addendum

[Minnesota 101] (USA); orig. from Oxford Down, Shropshire and Hampshire; absorbed by North Star Minnesota 103 in 1953

[Minnesota 104] (USA); inbred Hampshire flock; absorbed by North Star Minnesota 103 in 1953

[Minnesota 106] (USA); Columbia flock

Roux du Valais (Upper Valais, Switzerland); red-brown; hd; Ger. *Walliser Landschaf*; nearly extinct

SELECTED BIBLIOGRAPHY OF RECENT PUBLICATIONS ON LIVESTOCK BREEDS

General

Buffalo

MASON, I. L. 1974. Species, types and breeds. In: *The husbandry and health of the domestic buffalo, ed. W. R. Cockrill*, pp.1–47. *Rome: Food and Agriculture Organization of the United Nations.*

Cattle

FELIUS, M. 1985. Genus *Bos*. Cattle breeds of the world. *Rahway, NJ: MSD-AGVET Division of Merck and Co.* 235 pp.

ROUSE, J. E. 1970. World cattle. 2 vols. *Norman: University of Oklahoma Press.* 1046 pp.

Goat

MASON, I. L. 1981. Breeds. In: *Goat production, ed C. Gall*, pp. 57–110. *London: Academic Press.*

Horse

GLYN, R. – Editor. 1971. The world's finest horses and ponies. *London: Harrap.* 128 pp.

HOPE, C. E. G. and JACKSON, G. N. – Editors. 1973. The encyclopaedia of the horse. *London: Ebury Press and Pelham Books.*

GOODALL, D. M. 1973. Horses of the world. 3rd ed. *Newton Abbot, UK: David and Charles.*

SCHWARK, H. J. 1987. Pferdezucht. 3rd. ed. Berlin: VEB Deutscher Landwirtschaftsverlag. 447 pp.

Sheep

EPSTEIN, H. 1970. Fettschwanz– und Fettsteissschafe. *Wittenberg Lutherstadt: Ziemsen Verlag.* 168 pp.

FITZHUGH, H. A. and BRADFORD, G. E. – Editors. 1983. Hair sheep of western Africa and the Americas. *Boulder, Colorado: Westview Press.* 317 pp.

MASON, I. L. 1980. Prolific tropical sheep. *FAO Animal Production and Health Paper* No. 17. 128 pp.

Africa

EPSTEIN, H. 1971. The origin of the domestic animals of Africa. *Leipzig: Edition Leipzig. New York: Africana Publishing Corporation.* Vol. I–573 pp. Vol. II–719 pp.

FAO/ILCA/UNEP. 1980. Trypanotolerant livestock in West and Central Africa. *Addis Ababa: International Livestock Centre for Africa. Rome: Food and Agriculture Organization of the United Nations.* Vol. I–146 pp. Vol. II–303 pp. (Also published in French).

OAU/STRC/IBAR. 1985. Animal genetic resources in Africa. High potential and endangered livestock. *Nairobi: Organisation of African Unity.* 155 pp.

Ethiopia

ALBERRO, M. and HAILE–MARIAM, S. 1982. The indigenous cattle of Ethiopia. *World Animal Review* No. 41: 2-10, No. 42: 27-34.

GALAL, E. S. E. 1983. Sheep germ plasm in Ethiopia. *Animal Genetic Resources Information* No. 1/83: 4-12.

Mozambique

ALBERRO, M. 1983. The indigenous cattle of Mozambique. *World Animal Review* No. 48: 12-17.

America

BECKER, R. B. 1973. Dairy cattle breeds. Origin and development. *Gainesville: University of Florida Press.*

HENSON, E. 1986. North American livestock census. *Pittsboro, NC: American Minor Breeds Conservancy.* 34 pp.

MULLER-HAYE, B. and GELMAN, J. – Editors. 1981. Recursos genéticos animals en América Latina. *FAO Animal Health and Production Paper* No. 22. 168 pp.

ROUSE, J. E. 1973. World cattle. Vol. III. Cattle of North America. *Norman: University of Oklahoma Press.* 650 pp.

ROUSE, J. E. 1977. The Criollo. Spanish cattle in the Americas. *Norman: University of Oklahoma Press.* 303 pp.

WILKINS, J. V. 1984. Criollo cattle of the Americas. *Animal Genetic Resources Information* No. 1/84: 1-19.

Asia

SABRAO. 1980. Proceedings of SABRAO Workshop on Animal Genetic Resources in Asia and Oceania. *Tsukuba, Japan: Tropical Agriculture Research Center.* 555 pp.

YALÇIN, B. C. 1979. The sheep breeds of Afghanistan, Iran and Turkey. *Rome: Food and Agriculture Organization of the United Nations.* 115 pp.

China

JIANG YING, AN MING and WANG SHIQUAN. 1987. Goat production in China. *Proceedings of the IVth International Conference on Goats, March 1987, Brasilia. Vol. 1. Plenary Sessions, Symposia,* pp. 747–772.

ZHANG ZHONGGE – Chief editor. 1986. [Pig breeds in China.] *Shanghai: Shanghai Scientific and Technical Publishers*. 86 pp. [In Chinese.]

ZHENG PILIU [Cheng Peilieu.] 1984. Livestock breeds of China. *FAO Animal Production and Health Paper* No. 46. 217 pp.

India

ACHARYA, R. M. 1982. Sheep and goat breeds of India. *FAO Animal Production and Health Paper* No. 30. 190 pp.

CSIR. 1970. The wealth of India. A dictionary of Indian raw materials and industrial products. Raw materials. Vol. VI. Supplement: Livestock (including poultry). *New Delhi: Council for Scientific and Industrial Research.*

ICAR. 1978. Characteristics of cattle and buffalo breeds in India. 3rd ed. *New Delhi: Indian Council of Agricultural Research.*

Nepal

EPSTEIN, H. 1977. Domestic animals of Nepal. *New York: Holmes and Meier.* 131 pp.

Pakistan

HASNAIN, H. U. 1985. Sheep and goats in Pakistan. *FAO Animal Production and Health Paper* No. 56. 135 pp.

Turkey

YALÇIN, B. C. 1986. Sheep and goats in Turkey. *FAO Animal Production and Health Paper* No. 60. 168 pp.

Australia

AMLC. 1984. Handbook of Australian livestock. *Sydney: Australian Meat and Live-stock Corporation.* 113 pp.

Europe

BROOKE, C. H. and RYDER, M. L. 1978. Declining breeds of Mediterranean sheep. *Rome: Food and Agriculture Organization of the United Nations.* 68 pp.

FAO. 1977. Mediterranean sheep and cattle in crossbreeding. Report of the first FAO Expert Consultation on Breed Evaluation and Crossbreeding, Rome, April 1977. *FAO Animal Production and Health Paper* No. 6. 37 pp.

MAIJALA, K., CHEREKAEV, A. V., DEVILLARD, J. M., REKLEWSKI, Z., ROGNONI, G., SIMON, D. L. and STEANE, D. E. 1984. Conservation of animal genetic resources in Europe. Final Report of an EAAP Working Party. *Livestock Production Science* **11**: 3–22.

SAMBRAUS, H. H. 1986. Atlas der Nutztierrassen. 180 Rassen in Wort und Bild. *Stuttgart: Eugen Ulmer.* 256 pp.

Belgium
Races bovines belges. [? 1974.] [92 pp.] [No date, editor, publisher.]

Bulgaria
ALEKSIEVA, S. 1978. [Some aspects of the problem of preserving native sheep varieties in Bulgaria.] *Zhivotnov'dni Nauki* **15**(4): 50–57. [In Bulgarian]
KRASTANOV, H. 1973. Trends in cattle use in Bulgaria. *Sofia: Centre for Scientific, Technical and Economic Information in Agriculture.* 55 pp.
NAIDENOV, S. 1974. Animaux de reproduction. *Sofia: Edition de la Chambre de Commerce de Bulgarie.* 66 pp.

France
BULLETIN DE L'ÉLEVAGE FRANÇAIS. 1980. L'Élevage français. *Bulletin de l'Élevage Français. Numéro Special* Printemps 1980. 75 pp.
BULLETIN DE L'ÉLEVAGE FRANÇAIS. 1984. Horse breeding in France. *Bulletin de l'Élevage Français* No. 17: 3–35.
ETHNOZOOTECHNIE. [? 1984.] Races domestiques in péril. *Ethnozootechnie* No. 33. 90 pp.
LAUVERGNE, J. J. 1987. Les ressources génétiques ovines et caprines en France. Situation en 1986. *Paris: Bureau des Ressources Génétiques.* 105 pp.
QUITTET, E. and BLANC, H. 1974. Races chevalines en France. 2nd ed. *Paris: La Maison Rustique.* 72 pp.
QUITTET, E. and ZERT, P. 1971. Races porcines en France. *Paris: La Maison Rustique.*

Greece
ZERVAS, N. and BOYAZOGLU, J. G. [? 1977] L'élevage en Grèce. Présent et avenir. *Ethnozootechnie* No. 18. 73 pp.

Italy
CATALANO, A. L. 1984. Valutazione morfo-funzionale del cavallo. Igiene ed etnologia. (Zootecnica 1). *Noceto, Italy: Goliardica Editrice.*
CNR. [n.d.] Atlante etnografico delle populazioni bovine allevate in Italia (1983). *Rome: Consiglio Nazionale delle Ricerche.* 127 pp.
CNR. [n.d.] Atlante etnografico delle populazioni ovine e caprine allevate in Italia (1983). *Rome: Consiglio Nazionale delle Ricerche.* 176 pp.
PILLA, A. M., D'ENRICO, P., D'AMBROSIO, A. and MARIANI, M. 1972. Indagine nazionale su alcuni aspetti degli allevamenti e delle produzioni ovine. No. 1. Razze: consistenza, distribuzione. *Rome: Ministero dell'Agricoltura e delle Foreste. Associazione Nazionale della Pastorizia.* 64 pp.
PILLA, A. M., D'ENRICO, P., D'AMBROSIO, A. and MARIANI, M. 1973. Indagine nazionale su alcuni aspetti degli allevamenti e delle produzioni

caprine. *Rome: Ministero dell'Agricoltura e delle Foreste. Associazione Nazionale della Pastorizia.* 57 pp.

Netherlands

BOTTEMA, S. and CLASEN, A. T. 1979. Het schap in Nederland. *Zutphen: Thieme.* 174 pp.

CLASEN, A. T. – Editor. 1980. Zeldzame huisdierrassen. *Zutphen: Thieme.* 215 pp.

Portugal

RODRIGUES, A. – Editor. 1981. Bovinos em Portugal. *[Lisbon]: Direcção Geral dos Serviços Veterinários.* 327 pp.

SOBRAL, M., ANTERO, C., DOMINGOS BORREGO, J. and NABAIS DOMINGOS, A. 1987. Animal genetic resources. Indigenous breeds. Sheep and goats. *Lisbon: Direcção-Geral da Pecuaria.* 207 pp.

Spain

ESTEBAN MUÑOZ, C. and TEJON TEJON, D. 1980. Catalogo de razas autoctonas españolas. l. Especies ovina y caprina. *Madrid: Ministerio de Agricultura y Pescas.* 207 pp.

SANCHEZ BELDA, A. 1981. Catalogo de razas autoctonas españolas. II. Especie bovina. *Madrid: Ministerio de Agricultura y Pesca.* 219 pp.

SANCHEZ BELDA, A. 1983. La cría caballar en España. Avances en Alimentación y Mejora Animal, **24**(12): 449–467.

SANCHEZ BELDA, A. and SANCHEZ TRUJILLANO, M. C. 1987. Razas ovinas españolas. 2nd ed. *Madrid: Publicaciones de Extension Agraria.* 887 pp.

United Kingdom

MLC. 1976. British beef cattle. *Milton Keynes: Meat and Livestock Commission.* 48 pp.

NCBA. 1980. British cattle. *National Cattle Breeders' Association.* 132 pp.

NSA. [? 1983.] British sheep. 6th ed. *National Sheep Association.* 211 pp.

USSR

DMITRIEV, N. G. and ERNST, L. K. – Editors. 1988. Animal genetic resources of the USSR. *Rome: Food and Agriculture Organization of the United Nations.* (Also published in Russian).